D1616008

# NAHUM

## VOLUME 24F

THE ANCHOR YALE BIBLE is a project of international and interfaith scope in which Protestant, Catholic, and Jewish scholars from many countries contribute individual volumes. The project is not sponsored by any ecclesiastical organization and is not intended to reflect any particular theological doctrine.

THE ANCHOR YALE BIBLE is committed to producing commentaries in the tradition established half a century ago by the founders of the series, William Foxwell Albright and David Noel Freedman. It aims to present the best contemporary scholarship in a way that is accessible not only to scholars but also to the educated nonspecialist. Its approach is grounded in exact translation of the ancient languages and an appreciation of the historical and cultural context in which the biblical books were written, supplemented by insights from modern methods, such as sociological and literary criticism.

*John J. Collins*
GENERAL EDITOR

THE ANCHOR YALE BIBLE

# NAHUM

A New Translation
with Introduction and Commentary

DUANE L. CHRISTENSEN

THE ANCHOR YALE BIBLE

Yale University Press

New Haven and London

Designed by Princeton Editorial Associates, Inc., Scottsdale, Arizona.
Set in Electra with Aldus display by Princeton Editorial Associates, Inc.,
Scottsdale, Arizona.

Printed in the United States of America by Vail-Ballou Press,
Binghamton, New York

Library of Congress Cataloging-in-Publication Data

Bible. O.T. Nahum. English. Christensen. 2009.
  Nahum : a new translation with introduction and commentary /
Duane L. Christensen.
    p.   cm. — (The Anchor Yale Bible ; v. 24F)
  Includes bibliographical references and indexes.
  ISBN 978-0-300-14479-6 (alk. paper)
  1. Bible. O.T. Nahum—Commentaries.   I. Christensen, Duane L.,
1938–  II. Title.
BS1623.C47   2009
224′.94077—dc22                                         2009000086

A catalogue record for this book is available from the British Library.

This paper meets the requirements of ANSI/NISO Z39.48-1992
(Permanence of Paper).

10 9 8 7 6 5 4 3 2 1

To David Noel Freedman,
whose חָזוֹן (vision), like that of Nahum,
enabled him to maintain his pace
well ahead of the rest of us

# CONTENTS

# ACKNOWLEDGMENTS

Some years ago, Casper Labuschagne and I worked together in an attempt to determine the principles at work in the numerical composition of the Book of the Twelve Prophets. A summary of our conclusions was posted on the www.bibal.net website dated April 16, 2002: "Word-Count in the Book of the Twelve—Progress Report." Very few changes have been made in the seven years since those tentative conclusions were posted, and none at all so far as the books of Nahum and Jonah are concerned. At the same time, a great deal has been added to our knowledge of the numerical and musical composition of the biblical text in matters of detail.

I owe a special debt to James Hoard, who introduced me to the concept of mora-counting more than twenty-five years ago, and to Thomas Lambdin, who two years later called my attention to the work of the Polish linguist Jerzy Kurylowicz and the concept of counting syntactic accentual-stress (SAS) units in the analysis of Hebrew poetry. The recent combination of these two methodologies with word count, as practiced by Casper Labuschagne, produced my own methodological synthesis, which I call logoprosodic analysis—on which the substance of this commentary is based.

I am especially indebted to Ernest G. McClain, whose seminal work on harmonics in antiquity in relation to crucial passages in world literature—the *Rig Veda*, Sumerian and Babylonian literary texts, texts from ancient Egypt, the Bible, and Plato—took a great deal of effort on my part to understand because I am not a musician. The section headed "Archaeomusicology and the Study of Nahum" was written jointly with Professor McClain. It is my belief that his work constitutes an intellectual breakthrough of great significance for biblical studies. Only a small part of this material is integrated into the body of this commentary, and much remains to be done on this subject. I had the privilege of presenting a paper titled "Archaeomusicology and the Study of Jonah and Nahum" at the International Conference of Near Eastern Archaeomusicology (ICONEA) held at the British Museum (December 4–6, 2008), where this research on the Hebrew text of Jonah and Nahum was presented along with the work of leading cuneiform scholars who are exploring the world of archaeomusicology and matrix arithmetic in relation to ancient texts dealing with cosmology, mythology, and theology (see http://www.iconea .org/index.html).

Assistance from members of the BIBAL Forum, a Yahoo discussion group, has been invaluable throughout the entire process of writing this commentary. Members of this group who have participated in this intellectual journey include Richard Abbott, Petur Auglysingastofa, Loren Bliese, John Bremer, John Burnett, Bryan Carr, David Crookes, Pete Dello, John Holthouse, Michael Hudson, Jill Mattson, Chatur Mayank, James McMillan, Dan Olson, Aron Pinker, Christopher Rupert, Howard Schatz, Gunnar Tomasson, Rudy Voigt, John Wheeler, and Aldo Yannon. I learned much from each of these colleagues, whose expertise spans a number of academic disciplines, including ancient metrology, art, astronomy, biblical studies, classical studies, cosmology, cuneiform studies, economics, musicology, and philosophy.

Perhaps my deepest debt is to the late David Noel Freedman, editor of this series, for his patience, his many comments and suggestions, and his encouragement from the very outset to continue my exploration of unfamiliar methods in the study of the Hebrew text of Nahum. The publication of this volume brings one aspect of his life goal—to have a commentary published in the Anchor Yale Bible series on every single book in the Bible—close to completion.

I take this opportunity to acknowledge the contribution of my students here at the Ecole Biblique et Archéologique Française de Jérusalem: Stephanie Anthionioz, Paolo Benedetti, Thien Dang, Antonio Dinh Minh Tien, Michael Langlois, Gilson Meurer, and Barbara Strzalkowska. They struggled with me in the process of discovering the Nahum matrix and its relation to the Nineveh matrix in the book of Jonah. Throughout my career as a biblical scholar, I have learned the most from and with my students.

DUANE L. CHRISTENSEN
Jerusalem—April 26, 2008

# Principal Abbreviations

Abbreviations not listed here are the same as those in *The Anchor Yale Bible Dictionary*. The Dead Sea Scrolls and related manuscript sources are referred to using the now standard sigla, as listed by Emmanuel Tov in "A List of the Texts from the Judean Desert," pp. 669–717 in *The Dead Sea Scrolls after Fifty Years: A Comprehensive Assessment*, ed. Peter W. Flint and James C. Vanderkam, vol. 2 (Leiden: Brill, 1999).

| | |
|---|---|
| AASOR | Annual of the American Schools of Oriental Research |
| *ABR* | *Australian Biblical Review* |
| *AfO* | *Archiv für Orientforschung* |
| *AHW* | *Akkadisches Handwörterbuch*. By W. von Soden. Wiesbaden: Harrassowitz, 1965–81. |
| *AJSL* | *American Journal of Semitic Languages and Literature* |
| Akk. | Akkadian |
| AnBib | Analecta biblica |
| *ANEP* | *The Ancient Near East in Pictures*. Ed. J. B. Pritchard. Princeton, N.J.: Princeton University Press, 1954. |
| *ANET* | *Ancient Near Eastern Texts*, 2nd ed. Ed. J. B. Pritchard. Princeton, N.J.: Princeton University Press, 1955; 3rd printing, 1966. |
| *ANET Sup* | *The Ancient Near East: Supplementary Texts and Pictures Relating to the Old Testament*. Ed. J. B. Pritchard. Princeton, N.J.: Princeton University Press, 1969. |
| AnOr | Analecta Orientalia |
| *Ant.* | *Antiquities of the Jews*. By Josephus. |
| AOAT | Alter Orient und Altes Testament |

| ARAB | *Ancient Records of Assyria and Babylon.* By D. D. Luckenbill. 2 vols. Chicago: University of Chicago Press, 1928. |
| ATD | Das Alte Testament Deutsch |
| ATR | *Anglican Theological Review* |
| AUSS | *Andrews University Seminary Studies* |
| ASV | American Standard Version |
| AYB | The Anchor Yale Bible (Commentary) |
| AYBD | *Anchor Yale Bible Dictionary.* Ed. D. N. Freedman. 6 vols. New York: Doubleday, 1992. |
| BA | *Biblical Archaeologist* |
| BASOR | *Bulletin of the American Schools of Oriental Research* |
| BBB | Bonner Biblische Beiträge |
| BCE | before the common era (= B.C.) |
| BDB | Brown, F., S. R. Driver, and C. A. Briggs. *Hebrew and English Lexicon of the Old Testament.* Oxford: Oxford University Press, 1907, 1962. |
| BETL | Bibliotheca ephemeridum theologicarum lovaniensium |
| BH$^2$ | *Biblia Hebraica*, 2nd ed. Ed. R. Kittel. Leipzig: J. C. Hinrichs, 1905. |
| BH$^3$ | *Biblia Hebraica*, 3rd ed. Ed. R. Kittel. Stuttgart: Württemburg Bibelanstalt, 1937. |
| BHQ | *Biblia Hebraica Quinta*, 5th ed., Fascicle 18: General Introduction and *Megilloth*. Ed. J. de Waard, P. B. Dirksen, Y. A. P. Goldman, R. Schäfer, and M. Sæbø. Stuttgart: Deutsche Bibelgesellschaft, 2004–8. |
| BHS | *Biblia Hebraica Stuttgartensia* |
| Bib | *Biblica* |
| BibIS | Biblical Interpretation Series |
| BibOr | Biblica et Orientalia |
| BibSem | The Biblical Seminar |
| BiTr | *Bible Translator* |
| BIOSCS | *Bulletin of the International Organization for Septuagint and Cognate Studies* |
| BM | British Museum |
| BN | *Biblische Notizen* |
| BO | *Bibliotheca Orientalis* |
| BSC | Bible Student Commentary |
| BZ | *Biblische Zeitschrift* |
| BZAW | Beiheft zur Zeitschrift für die Alttestamentliche Wissenschaft |
| c. | century |
| ca. | circa |
| CAD | *The Assyrian Dictionary of the Oriental Institute of the University of Chicago* |

| | |
|---|---|
| *CAH* | *Cambridge Ancient History* |
| CBC | Cambridge Bible Commentary |
| *CBQ* | *Catholic Biblical Quarterly* |
| CBQMS | Catholic Biblical Quarterly Monograph Series |
| CE | common era (= A.D.) |
| ConBOT | Coniectanea biblica, Old Testament |
| *CRAIBL* | *Comptes rendus de l'Académie des Inscriptions et Belles-Lettres* |
| *CRBS* | *Currents in Research: Biblical Studies* |
| CTA | *Corpus des tablettes en cuneiforms alphabétiques découvertes à Ras Shamra-Ugarit 1929–1939.* By A. Herdner. Paris: Imprimerie Nationale / Geuthner, 1963. |
| *CTM* | *Concordia Theological Monthly* |
| d. | died |
| DCH | *The Dictionary of Classical Hebrew.* Ed. David J. A. Clines. Sheffield, England: Sheffield Academic Press, 1993–present. |
| DDD | *Dictionary of Deities and Demons.* Ed. K. van der Toorn, B. Becking, and P. W. van der Horst. Leiden: Brill, 1995. |
| $DDD^2$ | *Dictionary of Deities and Demons*, 2nd ed. Ed. K. van der Toorn et al. Leiden: Brill, 1999. |
| DJD | Discoveries in the Judaean Desert |
| DOTT | *Documents from Old Testament Times.* Ed. D. Winton Thomas. New York: Harper Torchbooks, 1961. |
| EA | *Die El-Amarna Tafeln.* Ed. J. A. Knudtzon. Leipzig: J. C. Hinrichs, 1915. |
| EBib | Etudes bibliques |
| EDBT | *Evangelical Dictionary of Biblical Theology.* Ed. W. A. Elwell. Grand Rapids, Mich.: Baker, 1996. |
| Eng. | English |
| *ErIs* | *Eretz Israel* |
| *EstBib* | *Estudios biblicos* |
| *ExpTim* | *Expository Times* |
| *EvQ* | *Evangelical Quarterly* |
| *EvT* | *Evangelische Theologie* |
| f. | feminine |
| FAT | Forschungen zum Alten Testament |
| FCB | Feminist Companion to the Bible |
| fl. | flourished |
| *FO* | *Folia Orientalia* |
| FOTL | Forms of Old Testament Literature |
| FRLANT | Forschungen zur Religion und Literatur des Alten und Neuen Testaments |
| FS | Festschrift |
| GHB | *Grammaire de l'hébreu biblique.* By P. Joüon. Rome: Institut Biblique Pontifical, 1947. |

| GKC | *Gesenius' Hebrew Grammar*, 2nd Eng. ed. Ed. E. Kautzsch and A. E. Cowley. Oxford: Clarendon Press, 1910, 1956. |
|---|---|
| GTJ | *Grace Theological Journal* |
| HALOT | *Hebräisches und Aramäisches Lexicon zum Alten Testament*, 3rd ed. By W. Baumgartner. Leiden: Brill, 1967–90. |
| HAT | Handbuch zum Alten Testament |
| HBS | Herder's Biblical Studies |
| Heb. | Hebrew |
| HSAT | Die Heilige Schrift des Alten Testaments |
| HSM | Harvard Semitic Monographs |
| HTR | *Harvard Theological Review* |
| HUCA | *Hebrew Union College Annual* |
| IBHS | *An Introduction to Biblical Hebrew Syntax*. By Bruce K. Waltke and Michael P. O'Connor. Winona Lake, Ind.: Eisenbrauns, 1990. |
| IBS | *Irish Biblical Studies* |
| ICC | International Critical Commentary |
| IDB | *Interpreter's Dictionary of the Bible*. Ed. G. A. Buttrick. 4 vols. Nashville, Tenn.: Abingdon, 1972. |
| IDBSup | *Supplementary Volume to IDB*. Ed. K. Crim. Nashville: Abingdon, 1976. |
| IEJ | *Israel Exploration Journal* |
| IJM | *International Journal of Musicology* |
| inf. abs. | infinitive absolute |
| inf. const. | infinitive construct |
| Int | *Interpretation* |
| JANES | *Journal of the Ancient Near Eastern Society of Columbia University* |
| JAOS | *Journal of the American Oriental Society* |
| JBL | *Journal of Biblical Literature* |
| JBQ | *Jewish Bible Quarterly* |
| JCS | *Journal of Cuneiform Studies* |
| JETS | *Journal of the Evangelical Theological Society* |
| JHS | *Journal of Hebrew Scriptures* |
| JJS | *Journal of Jewish Studies* |
| JNES | *Journal of Near Eastern Studies* |
| JNSL | *Journal of Northwest Semitic Languages* |
| JPOS | *Journal of the Palestine Oriental Society* |
| JPS | Jewish Publication Society |
| JQR | *Jewish Quarterly Review* |
| JR | *Journal of Religion* |
| JSOT | *Journal for the Study of the Old Testament* |
| JSOTSup | Journal for the Study of the Old Testament–Supplement Series |

| JSPSup | Journal for the Study of the Pseudepigrapha–Supplement Series |
| JSS | *Journal of Semitic Studies* |
| JThC | *Journal of Theology and the Church* |
| JTS | *Journal of Theological Studies* |
| JTT | *Journal of Translation and Textlinguistics* |
| KAANT | Kleine Arbeiten zum Alten und Neuen Testament |
| KAI | *Kanaanäische und aramäische Inschriften.* By H. Donner and W. Röllig. Wiesbaden: Harrassowitz, 1962–64. |
| KAT | Kommentar zum Alten Testament |
| KEHAT | Kurzgefasstes exegetisches Handbuch zum Alten Testament |
| KHAT | Kurzer Hand-Commentar zum Alten Testament |
| KJV | King James Version |
| KTU | *Die keilalphabetischen Texte aus Ugarit*, vol. 1. Ed. M. Dietrich et al. Kevelaer, Germany: Butzon und Bercker; Neukirchen-Vluyn, Germany: Neukirchener, 1976. |
| KVHS | Korte Verklaring der Heilige Schrift |
| L | *Codex Leningradensis* |
| LXX | Septuagint |
| m. | masculine |
| MEE | *Testi amministrativi della biblioteca L. 2769.* Materiali epigrafici di Ebla 2. Naples: Istituto Universitario Orientale, 1980–. |
| MGWJ | Monatsschrift für Geschichte und Wissenschaft des Judentums |
| MT | Masoretic Text |
| MUSJ | *Mélanges de l'université Saint-Joseph* |
| NASB | New American Standard Bible |
| NEB | Neue Echter Bibel |
| NedTTs | *Nederlands theologiasch tijdschrift* |
| NET Bible | *The NET (New English Translation) Bible,* 1st Beta ed. Richardson, Tex.: Biblical Studies Press, 2001. www.netbible.com. |
| NICOT | New International Commentary on the Old Testament |
| niph. | Niphal |
| NIV | New International Version |
| NRSV | New Revised Standard Version |
| OBO | Orbis Biblicus et Orientalis |
| OIP | Oriental Institute Publications |
| Or | *Orientalia* (Rome) |
| OT | Old Testament |
| OTE | *Old Testament Essays* |
| OTG | Old Testament Guides |
| OTL | Old Testament Library |

| | |
|---|---|
| OTS | *Oudtestamentische Studiën* |
| OTWSA | *Die Ou-Testamentiese Werkgemeenskap in Suid-Afrika* |
| pers. | person |
| pl. | plural |
| POS | Pretoria Oriental Studies |
| POT | De Prediking van het Oude Testament |
| PSBA | *Proceedings of the Society of Biblical Archaeology* |
| RA | *Revue d'Assyriologie et d'Archéologie Orientale* |
| RB | *Revue biblique* |
| REJ | *Revue des études juives* |
| RevQ | *Revue de Qumran* |
| RHPR | *Revue d'Histoire et de Philosophie Religieuses* |
| RHR | *Revue de l'histoire des religions* |
| RLA | *Reallexikon der Assyriologie* |
| RSV | Revised Standard Version |
| RThPh | *Revue de Théologie et de Philosophie* |
| RV | Revised Version, standard English translation of the Bible |
| SAA | State Archives of Assyria. Helsinki: The Neo-Assyrian Text Corpus Project, 1997–. |
| SAS | Syntactic accentual-stress |
| SAT | *Die Schriften des Alten Testaments.* By Hermann Gunkel und Hugo Gressmann. Göttingen: Vandenhoeck und Ruprecht, 1922. |
| SBBS | The Soncino Books of the Bible |
| SBJ | Sainte Bible, Jerusalem |
| SBL | Society of Biblical Literature |
| SBLDS | Society of Biblical Literature Dissertation Series |
| SBLMS | Society of Biblical Literature Monograph Series |
| SBLSP | Society of Biblical Literature Seminar Papers |
| SBPC | La Sainte Bible, Paris (Pirot et Clamer) |
| SBS | Stuttgarter Bibelstudien |
| Sem | *Semitica* |
| sg. | singular |
| SJOT | *Scandinavian Journal of the Old Testament* |
| SOTS | The Society for Old Testament Study |
| Syr. | Syriac |
| TBC | Torch Bible Commentaries |
| TBei | *Theologische Beiträge* |
| TBT | *The Bible Today* |
| TDOT | *Theological Dictionary of the Old Testament.* Ed. G. J. Botterweck, Helmer Ringgren, and H.-J. Fabry. Trans. D. Green et al. 15 vols. Grand Rapids, Mich.: Eerdmans, 1974–2006. |
| Tg | Targum |

| | |
|---|---|
| *ThLZ* | *Theologische Literaturzeitung* |
| *ThR* | *Theologische Rundschau*, Tübingen |
| *TLOT* | *Theological Lexicon of the Old Testament*. Ed. E. Jenni and C. Westermann. 3 vols. English trans., Peabody, Mass.: Hendrickson, 1997. |
| *TRE* | *Theologische Realenzyklopäde* |
| TSAT | Text und Sprache in Alten Testament, St. Ottilien. |
| *TUAT* | *Texte aus der Umwelt des Alten Testaments*. Ed. O. Kaiser. Gütersloh, Germany: Gütersloher, 2004. |
| *TynB* | *Tyndale Bulletin* |
| *UF* | *Ugarit-Forschungen* |
| UP | University Press |
| *UT* | *Ugaritic Textbook*. By C. H. Gordon. Rome: Pontifical Biblical Institute, 1965. |
| Vg | Vulgate |
| *VT* | *Vetus Testamentum* |
| VTSup | Supplements to Vetus Testamentum |
| WA | Martin Luther, *Werke. Kritische Gesamtausgabe* ("Weimarer Ausgabe") |
| WBC | Word Biblical Commentary |
| WMANT | Wissenschaftliche Monographien zum Alten und Neuen Testament |
| WO | *Die Welt des Orients* |
| *WTJ* | *Westminster Theological Journal* |
| ZA | *Zeitschrift für Assyriologie und verwandte Gebiete* |
| ZABR | *Zeitschrift für altorientalische und biblische Rechtgeschichte* |
| ZAW | *Zeitschrift für die alttestamentliche Wissenschaft* |
| ZLH | *Lexicon Hebraicum et Aramaicum Veteris Testamenti*. By F. Zorrell. Rome: Pontificium Institutum Biblicum, 1947–1984. |
| ZDMG | *Zeitschrift der deutschen morgenländischen Wissenschaft* |
| ZKT | *Zeitschrift für katholische Theologie* |
| ZPEB | *Zondervan Pictoral Encyclopedia of the Bible*. Ed. M. Tenney et al., 5 vols. Grand Rapids, Mich.: Zondervan, 1975. |
| ZWTh | *Zeitschrift für wissenschaftliche Theologie* |

# Nahum: A Translation and Logoprosodic Analysis

When not specified, all translations of the biblical text are my own. Below and elsewhere in the text, the Hebrew letters in the left margin indicate that the line begins with that letter in the Hebrew text to form an acrostic pattern. When the letter appears in brackets, as in [ו], the letter is not the first letter in that verset. The * in the middle of v 3 indicates that the word Yhwh is to be read at that point in the sentence acrostic (see the discussion following that point). The Hebrew letters in the right margin indicate that the line ends with that letter to form a telestich that spells out the divine name יהוה (Yhwh). Boldface letters are used for emphasis, particularly to highlight repeated words.

The method of logoprosodic analysis is discussed later in the section headed "Logoprosodic Analysis and the Book of Nahum," where Nahum 1:3 is used as a point of illustration in matters of detail. The boldfacing of the numbers **17, 23, 26,** and **32** (and sometimes multiples of these four numbers) in the columns of numbers in the right margin calls attention to the fact that these numbers are in fact "compositional numbers" in that they were apparently used to mark the boundaries of prosodic units and subunits in terms of running totals (within the verses so indicated). This was probably done with some sort of counting device, such as an abacus.

The numbers placed in square brackets flush right after the heading of each successive strophe, such as [9.4] in the heading for the strophe in Nahum 1:1–2, indicate the distribution of the sum of the disjunctive accent marks in that particular strophe of the Hebrew text. The exact position of each of these disjunctive accent marks is indicated with either a single slash / (for any of the regular disjunctive accents) or a double slash // (for the two strongest disjunctive accents *ʾatnaḥ* and *silluq*). The distribution of these disjunctive

accents is carefully contrived in an inverse concentric pattern so that the opening strophe of Nahum 1:1–2, which scans [9.4] in syntactic accentual-stress
(SAS) units, is balanced by another strophe in Nahum 1:9–10 at the end of
Canto 1 that scans [4.9]. The seven strophes in Canto 1 thus scan in an inverse
menorah pattern in terms of the distribution of SAS units, as follows:

[9.4].[5.5].[4.4].[4.4].[4.4].[5.5].[4.9]

The square box that appears around the slash mark in Nahum 1:5 marks the
structural center of Canto 1 in terms of word count. If there is an even number of words in a given canto, as in Canto 3, this box appears around the two
middle words, as in Nahum 2:5[4]. The square brackets here around the
number 4 indicate that the verse appears as number 4 in the LXX tradition, on
which most English translations are based, rather than verse 5 in the Hebrew
text of the MT. If the structural center falls at the end of a line so that the two
successive Hebrew words cannot be placed within the square box, as in
Nahum 1:5 and 1:12, the box is placed around the SAS marker at the end of
the line (between the two Hebrew words in question), that is, around the single slash / in Nahum 1:5 and around the double slash // in 1:12. If there is an
odd number of words in a given canto, as in Canto 4, the middle word of the
Hebrew text has a box around it, as in Nahum 2:13[12].

# I. THE PSALM OF NAHUM: YHWH'S VENGEANCE (1:1–10)

|  |  | Morae | SAS units | Word count** |  |  |
|---|---|---|---|---|---|---|
| **A.** | **YHWH Takes Vengeance against His Enemies (1:1–2)** |  |  |  |  | [9.4] |
| 1:1 | The exposition / of Nineveh // | 8  2 | 2 | 2 | 0 |  |
|  | Mic 7:17–Nah 1:1a | | | 52 | 28 | 24 |
|  | The scroll of the vision / of Nahum / the Elkoshite //  ˀ  _16  3_ | 4 | 0 | 4 |  |  |
|  | Mic 7:16–Nah 1:1 | | | 67 | 33 | **34** |
| 1:2 א | A zealous and avenging God (ˀEl) / is YHWH / | _14  2_ | 4 | 4 | 0 |  |
|  | Mic 7:17–Nah 1:2a | | | 60 | **32** | 28 |
|  | Avenging is YHWH / and a lord (Baˁal) of wrath //  ה  _16  2_ | 4 | 4 | 0 |  |  |
|  | Mic 7:18–Nah 1:2b | | | 51 | 29 | 22 |
| ב | Avenging is YHWH / against his foes / | _13  2_ | 3 | 0 | 3 |  |
|  | 1:1–1:2c | | | 17 | 10 | 7 |
|  | And he rages / against his enemies //  ו  _13  2_ | 3 | 0 | 3 |  |  |
|  | Mic 7:17–Nah 1:2 | | | 70 | 36 | **34** |

| | | SAS Morae | units | Word count** | | |
|---|---|---|---|---|---|---|

**B.  YHWH Is Slow to Anger but Great in Power (1:3)**                                              [5.5]

| 1:3 ˄ YHWH / he is slow to anger / ᵃbut great in powerᵃ / | | 16 | 3 | 5 | 5 | 0 |
|---|---|---|---|---|---|---|
| and the guilty / he does not acquit // | ה | _9 | 2_ | 3 | 3 | 0 |
| *1:1b–3b* | | | | 26 | 16 | 10 |
| * YHWH / | | _4 | 1_ | 1 | 0 | 1 |
| *1:2–3c* | | | | 23 | 16 | 7 |
| In the whirlwind and in the storm / is his way / | | 15 | 2 | 3 | 0 | 3 |
| and clouds / are the dust of his feet // | | 10 | 2 | 3 | 0 | 3 |
| *1:1–3* | | | | 35 | 18 | 17 |

**C.  YHWH Acts with Cosmic Consequences (1:4)**                                              [4.4]

| 1:4 ב He blasts the Sea / and he dries it up / | | 14 | 2 | 3 | 3 | 0 |
|---|---|---|---|---|---|---|
| and all the Rivers / he desiccates // | | _12 | 2_ | 3 | 3 | 0 |
| *1:1–4b* | | | | 41 | 24 | 17 |
| א Theyᵇ wither away (that is) Bashan / and Carmel / | | 12 | 2 | 3 | 0 | 3 |
| and the green of Lebanon / withers // | | 13 | 2 | 3 | 0 | 3 |
| *1:1–4* | | | | 47 | 24 | 23 |

**D.  The Earth and Its Inhabitants Reel before YHWH (1:5)**                                  [4.4]

| 1:5 ה Mountains / quake before him / | | 14 | 2 | 3 | 3 | 0 |
|---|---|---|---|---|---|---|
| and the hills / melt away // | | _14 | 2_ | 2 | 2 | 0 |
| *1:4–5a* | | | | 17 | 11 | 6 |
| ו And the earth reels / before him /\| | | 14 | 2 | 3 | 0 | 3 |
| and the world / and all who dwell in it // | | _14 | 2_ | 4 | 0 | 4 |
| *1:2–5* | | | | 53 | 27 | 26 |

**E.  YHWH Acts with Cosmic Consequences (1:6)**                                              [4.4]

| 1:6 [ז]In the presence of his fury / who can stand? / | | 12 | 2 | 4 | 4 | 0 |
|---|---|---|---|---|---|---|
| and who can rise up / in the heat of his anger? // | | _15 | 2_ | 4 | 4 | 0 |
| *1:4–6a* | | | | 32 | 19 | 13 |
| ח His wrath / is poured out like fire / | | 13 | 2 | 3 | 0 | 3 |
| and the rocks / are broken asunder by him // | | _14 | 2_ | 3 | 0 | 3 |
| *1:5–6* | | | | 26 | 13 | 13 |

**F.  YHWH Is Good and a Refuge in the Day of Distress (1:7–8)**                              [5.5]

| 1:7 ט Good is YHWH / | | 6 | 1 | 2 | 2 | 0 |
|---|---|---|---|---|---|---|
| indeed a stronghold / in the day of distress // | | _12 | 2_ | 3 | 3 | 0 |
| *1:3–7b* | | | | 58 | 32 | 26 |

| | Morae | SAS units | Word count** | | |
|---|---|---|---|---|---|
| [י] And he knows / those who take refuge in him // | _12 | 2_ | 3 | 0 | 3 |
| 1:5–7 | | | 34 | 18 | 16 |
| 1:8 And in the sweeping torrent / | 7 | 1 | 2 | 2 | 0 |
| [כ] a full end (*kālāh*) / he will make of her place // | 12 | 2 | 3 | 3 | 0 |
| And his enemies / he pursues into darkness // | 12 | 2 | 3 | 0 | 3 |
| 1:3–8 | | | 69 | 37 | 32 |

**G. Yhwh Is Bringing Complete Destruction — A Full End (1:9–10)** [4.9]

| | Morae | SAS units | Word count** | | |
|---|---|---|---|---|---|
| 1:9 [מ] Whatever you (f. pl.) devise / against Yhwh / | _11 | 2_ | 4 | 4 | 0 |
| 1:6–9a | | | 34 | 22 | 12 |
| **A full end** (*kālāh*) / he himself is making // | 9 | 2_ | 3 | 3 | 0 |
| 1:7–9a | | | 23 | 17 | 6 |
| ל Distress / will not arise a second time // | _14 | 2 | 4 | 0 | 4 |
| 1:7–9 | | | 27 | 17 | 10 |
| 1:10 For / while like thorns matted together / | _12 | 2_ | 4 | 4 | 0 |
| 1:1–10a | | | 104 | 58 | 46 |
| And *in* a drunken state / soaked with "drink" // | _11 | 2_ | 2 | 2 | 0 |
| 1:1b–10b | | | 104 | 58 | 46 |
| א Devoured they will be / like dry stubble / **completely** // | 14 | 3 | 4 | 0 | 4 |
| 1:7–10 | | | 37 | 23 | 14 |
| 1:1–10 | | | 110 | 60 | 50 |

## II. THE DEFEAT OF BELIAL (1:11–14)

**A. The Counselor (of) Belial Has Departed Despite Assyria's Numbers (1:11–12b)** [5.4]

| | Morae | SAS units | Word count** | | |
|---|---|---|---|---|---|
| 1:11 From you (f. sg.) he has departed / | 7 | 1 | 2 | 2 | 0 |
| a plotter (m. sg.) of evil / against Yhwh // | _13 | 2_ | 4 | 4 | 0 |
| 1:2–11b | | | 10 | 64 | 46 |
| (He is) the counselor (of) / Belial //   ס | _10 | 2_ | 2 | 0 | 2 |
| 1:1–11 | | | 18 | 66 | 52 |
| 1:12 Thus / says Yhwh / | 9 | 2 | 3 | 3 | 0 |
| "Are they not strong / and ever so numerous? /   אשור | _12 | 2 | 4 | 4 | 0 |
| 1:9–12b | | | 36 | 26 | 10 |

| | Morae | SAS units | Word count** | |
|---|---|---|---|---|

**B.  Yʜᴡʜ Addresses Judah: "I Will Remove the Rod of Assyria" (1:12c–13)**     [5.5]

| | Morae | SAS units | Word count** | |
|---|---|---|---|---|
| But even so they shall be sheared / <sup>c</sup>and they will pass on<sup>c</sup> // | 16 2 | 3 | 3 | 0 |
| though I afflicted you (f. sg.) / I will afflict you / no more //̲ | _14 3_ | 4 | 0 | 4 |
| 1:8–12 | | 51 | 34 | 17 |

**1:13** And now / I will break his rod<sup>d</sup> / from upon you (f. sg.) //     19 3     4     4     0

and your (f. sg.) bonds / I will snap apart //     13 2     2     0     2

1:10–13     36   26   10

**C.  Yʜᴡʜ Addresses Assyria: "I Will Prepare Your Grave" (1:14)**     [4.5]

**1:14** And Yʜᴡʜ / has commanded concerning you (m. sg.) /     13 2     3     3     0

"Seed from your (m. sg.) name will not be sown / again //     _11 2_     4     4     0

1:8–14b     64   45   19

From the house of your (m. sg.) gods /     _9 1_     2     0     2

1:4–14c     112   69   43

I will cut off the graven image /<sup>e</sup> and the cast idol /     12 2     3     0     3

I will prepare your grave / for you are worthless" //     פ     13 2     4     0     4

1:11–14     44   27   17

## III. Tʜᴇ Sᴀᴄᴋ ᴏғ Nɪɴᴇᴠᴇʜ
## (2:1–11 [1:15–2:10])

**A.  Celebrate Your Festivals, O Judah, for Belial Is Utterly Cut Off (2:1 [1:15])**     [5.4]

**2:1 [1:15]** Here now on the mountains / are the feet of a sentinel /     16 2     5     5     0

announcing peace /     _8 1_     2     2     0

1:11–2:1b     51   34   17

Celebrate, O Judah / your (f. sg.) festivals /     _12 2_     3     3     0

1:14–2:1c     26   17   9

Fulfill your vows (f. sg.) //     _10 1_     2     2     0

1:13–2:1d     34   23   11

For never again / will Belial <sup>f</sup>invade you (f. sg.) <sup>f</sup> /     19 2     7     0     7

he is utterly cut off //     6 1     2     0     2

1:11–2:1     65   39   26

| | Morae | SAS units | Word count** | | |
|---|---|---|---|---|---|
| **B.  YHWH Has Come against Nineveh to Restore Israel (2:2–3 [1–2])** | | | [7.7] | | |
| 2:2 [1]A scatterer has come up / against you (f. sg.) / | 13 2 | 4 | 4 | 0 | |
| guard the ramparts // | 9 1 | 2 | 2 | 0 | |
| 1:9–2:2b | | 92 | 58 | 34 | |
| Watch the road / gird the loins / | 11 2 | 4 | 0 | 4 | |
| marshal strength / exceedingly // | 9 2 | 3 | 0 | 3 | |
| 2:1–2 | | 34 | 18 | 16 | |
| 2:3 [2]For YHWH is restoring / the pride of Jacob / | 15 2 | 6 | 6 | 0 | |
| indeed the pride of Israel // | 8 1 | 2 | 2 | 0 | |
| 2:1–3b | | 42 | 26 | 16 | |
| For devastators / have devastated them / | 12 2 | 3 | 0 | 3 | |
| and their vine-branches / they destroyed // | 13 2 | 2 | 0 | 2 | |
| 2:2–3 | | 26 | 14 | 12 | |
| **C.  The Warriors and Chariots Are Prepared for Battle (2:4 [3])** | | | [4.4] | | |
| 2:4 [3]The shields of his warriors / are reddened / | 16 2 | 3 | 3 | 0 | |
| (his) men of valor / are clad in scarlet / | 11 2 | 3 | 3 | 0 | |
| 2:2–4d | | 32 | 20 | 12 | |
| Flashing as with fire are the ᵍchariot coveringsᵍ / | 8 1 | 3 | 3 | 0 | |
| on the day of its preparation // | 8 1 | 2 | 2 | 0 | |
| 1:13–2:4e | | 80 | 48 | 32 | |
| Indeed the juniper arrows / are poisoned // | 12 2 | 2 | 0 | 2 | |
| 2:3–4 | | 26 | 19 | 7 | |
| **D.  There Is Mayhem in Nineveh, and the Palace Melts Away (2:5–7 [4–6])** | | | [(4.6).(6.4)] | | |
| 2:5 [4]In the streets / the chariots run amok / | 15 2 | 3 | 3 | 0 | |
| they rush to and fro / in the squares // | 10 2 | 2 | 2 | 0 | |
| 2:1–5b | | 65 | 42 | 23 | |
| Their (f. pl.) appearance / is like torches / | 10 2 | 2 | 0 | 2 | |
| 2:2–6b | | 46 | 30 | 16 | |
| Like lightning / they dart about // | 13 2 | 2 | 0 | 2 | |
| 2:1–5 | | 69 | 42 | 27 | |
| 2:6 [5]His powerful ones / are brought to remembranceʰ / | 11 2 | 2 | 2 | 0 | |
| 2:2–6a | | 50 | 32 | 18 | |
| They (m. pl.) stumble forward / as they go // | 13 2 | 2 | 2 | 0 | |

| | Morae | SAS units | Word count** | | |
|---|---|---|---|---|---|
| they hasten / to her wall / | 11 | 2 | 2 | 0 | 2 |
| 2:2–6c | | | 54 | 34 | 20 |
| But the mantlet / is (already) set up // | 9 | 2 | 2 | 0 | 2 |
| 2:5–6 | | | 17 | 9 | 8 |
| 2:7 [6]The gates of the rivers / are opened // | 15 | 2 | 3 | 3 | 0 |
| and the palace / melts away // | 10 | 2 | 2 | 0 | 2 |
| 2:4–7 | | | 48 | 31 | 17 |

**E. Nineveh Is Destroyed, and Her People Are Carried Away into Exile (2:8 [7])**    [4.4]

| | Morae | SAS units | Word count** | | |
|---|---|---|---|---|---|
| 2:8 [7]And it is determined / she is stripped /[i] (and) taken away // | 14 | 3 | 3 | 3 | 0 |
| *along with* her maidens / | 8 | 1 | 1 | 0 | 1 |
| 2:3–8c | | | 52 | 34 | 18 |
| *They are* moaning / like the sound of doves / | 12 | 2 | 3 | 0 | 3 |
| beating / on their breasts // | 12 | 2 | 3 | 0 | 3 |
| 2:6–8 | | | 23 | 10 | 13 |

**F. Nineveh Drains Away, and the City Is Plundered (2:9–10 [8–9])**    [7.7]

| | Morae | SAS units | Word count** | | |
|---|---|---|---|---|---|
| 2:9 [8]And Nineveh /[j] is like a pool of water / | 12 | 2 | 3 | 3 | 0 |
| <her waters fall>[k] // | 10 | 1 | 2 | 2 | 0 |
| 2:5–9b | | | 37 | 20 | 17 |
| They are /[l] draining away / | 9 | 2 | 2 | 0 | 2 |
| "Stop! Stop!" (they cry) / but no one turns back // | 13 | 2 | 4 | 0 | 4 |
| 2:7–9 | | | 26 | 11 | 15 |
| 2:10 [9]Plunder silver / plunder gold // | 14 | 2 | 4 | 4 | 0 |
| 2:5–10a | | | 47 | 24 | 23 |
| Indeed there is no end / to the treasure / | 12 | 2 | 3 | 0 | 3 |
| 2:5–10b | | | 50 | 24 | 26 |
| Wealth / from all / its precious vessels // | 13 | 3 | 4 | 0 | 4 |
| 2:8–10 | | | 32 | 12 | 20 |

**G/A. The Destruction Is Total: They Are Gathered as Kindling (2:11 [10])**    [4.5]

| | Morae | SAS units | Word count** | | |
|---|---|---|---|---|---|
| 2:11 [10]Destruction /[m] and desolation / and disintegration // | 19 | 3 | 3 | 3 | 0 |
| and hearts grow faint / | 7 | 1 | 2 | 0 | 2 |
| 2:5–11b | | | 59 | 27 | 32 |

| | Morae | | SAS units | | Word count** |
|---|---|---|---|---|---|
| And knees give way / | 7 | 1 | 2 | 0 | 2 |
| 2:9–11c | 29 | | 12 | | 17 |
| And anguish / is in all loins / and (on) all their faces / | 19 | 3 | 5 | 0 | 5 |
| they are gathered as fuel (for burning) // | 8 | 1 | 2 | 0 | 2 |
| 2:1–11 | 128 | | 64 | | 64 |

## IV. DIRGE ON THE LIONS' DEN
## (2:11–14 [10–13])

**B. Nineveh Is Described Metaphorically as the Lions' Den (2:12 [11])**    [4.4]

| | Morae | | SAS units | | Word count |
|---|---|---|---|---|---|
| 2:12 [11]Where / is the den of the lions / | 11 | 2 | 3 | 3 | 0 |
| and the cave^n / for the young lions? // | 15 | 2 | 3 | 3 | 0 |
| 2:8–12b | 52 | | 21 | | 31 |
| Where the lion went /° the lioness was there / | 14 | 2 | 5 | 0 | 5 |
| the lions' cub / and none to frighten (them) away // | 12 | 2 | 4 | 0 | 4 |
| 2:9–12 | 51 | | 18 | | 33 |

**C. The Lions' Prey Is Consumed in the Lions' Den (2:13 [12])**    [4.4]

| | Morae | | SAS units | | Word count |
|---|---|---|---|---|---|
| 2:13 [12]The lion is tearing / sufficient for ^Phis cubs^P / | 14 | 2 | 4 | 4 | 0 |
| and strangled prey / for his lionesses // | 12 | 2 | 2 | 2 | 0 |
| 2:10–13b | 46 | | 19 | | 27 |
| And he fills with torn flesh (m. sg.) /^q his lairs / | 11 | 2 | 3 | 0 | 3 |
| and his dens / with torn flesh (f. sg.) // | 14 | 2 | 2 | 0 | 2 |
| 2:12–13 | 26 | | 12 | | 14 |

**D. Fire and Sword Will Consume Her Chariots and the Young Lions (2:14 [13])**    [4.5]

| | Morae | | SAS units | | Word count |
|---|---|---|---|---|---|
| 2:14 [13]"Behold, I am against you" / utterance ^r of YHWH of hosts / | 18 | 2 | 5 | 5 | 0 |
| "And I will burn in smoke / her chariots / | 13 | 2 | 3 | 3 | 0 |
| 2:12–14c | 34 | | 20 | | 14 |
| And your young lions / the sword will devour // | 13 | 2 | 3 | 3 | 0 |
| 2:13–14d | 22 | | 17 | | 5 |
| And I will cut (you) off from the land of ^s your prey / | 12 | 1 | 3 | 0 | 3 |
| and will be heard no more / the sound of your (military) heralds" //  ɔ | 18 | 2 | 5 | 0 | 5 |
| 2:11–14 | 59 | | 26 | | 33 |

# V. First Taunt: Nineveh's Shame Will Be Seen by the Nations (3:1–7)

|  | Morae | SAS units | Word count** |  |
|---|---|---|---|---|
| **A.** **"Woe to the City of Bloodshed"—All of It Filled with Deceit and Pillage (3:1)** |  |  | **[3.4]** |  |
| 3:1 Woe / to the city of bloodshed // | 8 2 | 3 | 3 | 0 |
| all of it / | ˙3 1 | 1 | 0 | 1 |
| *2:12–3:1a* | **49** | **26** | **23** |  |
| With deceit *and* pillage / filled / | 9 2 | 4 | 0 | 4 |
| *2:12–3:1c* | **52** | **26** | **26** |  |
| Never without / prey // | 9 2 | 3 | 0 | 3 |
| *2:12–3:1* | **55** | **26** | **29** |  |
| **B.** **The Sounds of Battle Are Heard (3:2)** |  |  | **[3.3]** |  |
| 3:2 The sound of a whip / and the sound / of a rattling wheel // | 13 3 | 5 | 5 | 0 |
| *2:14–3:2a* | **34** | **19** | **15** |  |
| And a horse galloping / | 7 1 | 2 | 0 | 2 |
| *3:1–2b* | **17** | **8** | **9** |  |
| And a chariot / jolting // | 13 2 | 2 | 0 | 2 |
| *2:11–3:2* | **78** | **34** | **44** |  |
| **C.** **The Carnage Is Enormous—There Is No End to the Corpses (3:3)** |  |  | **[4.5]** |  |
| 3:3 Horsemen charging / and flash of sword / | 12 2 | 4 | 4 | 0 |
| and glint of spear / and a multitude of slain / | 14 2 | 4 | 4 | 0 |
| *3:2–3b* | **17** | **13** | **4** |  |
| And a mass of corpses // | 7 1 | 2 | 2 | 0 |
| *2:10–3:3c* | **99** | **48** | **51** |  |
| And there is no end / to the bodies / | 12 2 | 3 | 0 | 3 |
| ᵗand they stumbleᵗ / over their bodies // | 13 2 | 2 | 0 | 2 |
| *3:1–3* | **34** | **18** | **16** |  |
| **D.** **The End Has Come Because of Nineveh's Harlotry (3:4)** |  |  | **[4.4]** |  |
| 3:4 Because of the numerous / harlotries of the harlot / | 13 2 | 3 | 3 | 0 |
| the pleasing charm / of the mistress of sorceries // | 13 2 | 4 | 4 | 0 |
| *3:3–4b* | **22** | **17** | **5** |  |

| | Morae | SAS units | Word count** | | |
|---|---|---|---|---|---|
| The one who acquires[u] nations / for her harlotry / | 15 | 2 | 3 | 0 | 3 |
| and clans / for her sorceries // | 13 | 2 | 2 | 0 | 2 |
| 3:1–4 | | | **46** | **25** | **21** |

**E. YHWH Speaks: "I Will Expose Your Shame to the Nations!" (3:5)** [5.4]

| | Morae | SAS units | | | |
|---|---|---|---|---|---|
| 3:5 "Behold, I am against you" (f. sg.) / | 7 | 1 | 2 | 2 | 0 |
| utterance / of YHWH of hosts / | 11 | 2 | 3 | 3 | 0 |
| 3:4–5b | | | **17** | **12** | **5** |
| "And I will lift your (f. sg.) skirt / over your (f. sg.) face // | 16 | 2 | 4 | 4 | 0 |
| 3:1–5c | | | **55** | **34** | **21** |
| And I will show nations / your (f. sg.) nakedness / | 13 | 2 | 3 | 0 | 3 |
| 3:3–5d | | | **39** | **26** | **13** |
| And kingdoms / your (f. sg.) shame" // | 12 | 2 | 2 | 0 | 2 |
| 3:4–5 | | | **26** | **16** | **10** |

**F. As YHWH's Spectacle of Contempt: "I Will Pelt You with Filth!" (3:6–7a)** [3.3]

| | Morae | SAS units | | | |
|---|---|---|---|---|---|
| 3:6 "I will pelt you (f. sg.) / with filth / | 13 | 2 | 3 | 3 | 0 |
| and I will make you (f. sg.) contemptible // | 5 | 1 | 1 | 1 | 0 |
| 3:1–6b | | | **64** | **38** | **26** |
| And I will make of you (f. sg.)[v] a spectacle // | 9 | 1 | 2 | 0 | 2 |
| 3:4–6 | | | **32** | **20** | **12** |
| 3:7 And everyone who sees you (f. sg.) / will flee from you" / | 16 | 2 | 5 | 5 | 0 |
| 3:3–7a | | | **52** | **35** | **17** |

**G. Observers Say: "Nineveh Is in Ruins! Who Will Grieve for Her?" (3:7b–d)** [4.3]

| | Morae | SAS units | | | |
|---|---|---|---|---|---|
| And he will say / "Nineveh is devastated / | 14 | 2 | 3 | 3 | 0 |
| 3:3–7b | | | **55** | **38** | **17** |
| Who / will grieve for her? // | 8 | 2 | 3 | 3 | 0 |
| 3:6–7c | | | **17** | **15** | **2** |
| Where / can I seek comforters / for you (m. sg.)?" // | 15 | 3 | 4 | 0 | 4 |
| 3:1–7 | | | **81** | **49** | **32** |

## VI. Second Taunt: Like Thebes, Nineveh Will Be Sacked (3:8–13)

|  |  | *Morae* | SAS *units* | *Word count*** |  |  |
|---|---|---|---|---|---|---|
| **A.** | **Are You Better Than Thebes in Egypt? (3:8)** | | | [4.5] | | |
| 3:8 | Are you (f. sg.) better / than *No-Amon* (Thebes) / | 13 2 | | 3 | 3 | 0 |
| | the one who dwells / on the Nile? / | _12 2_ | | 2 | 2 | 0 |
| | | 3:4–8b | | 52 | 36 | 16 |
| | Water / is round about her // | 8 2 | | 3 | 3 | 0 |
| | whose rampart is the sea / | 6 1 | | 3 | 0 | 3 |
| | having from the sea / her wall // | 10 2 | | 2 | 0 | 2 |
| | | 3:6–8 | | 34 | 23 | 11 |
| **B.** | **Thebes Had a Strong Ally in Cush, Who "Was Her Strength" (3:9)** | | | [3.3] | | |
| 3:9 | Cush was her strength / and Egypt / and that without limit // | _18 3_ | | 5 | 5 | 0 |
| | | 3:3–9a | | 80 | 54 | 26 |
| | Put and Libya / they were / among your (f. sg.) allies // | 17 3 | | 4 | 0 | 4 |
| | | 3:2–9 | | 93 | 59 | 34 |
| **C.** | **She Went into Exile with Her Infants Dashed to Pieces (3:10a–d)** | | | [3.3] | | |
| 3:10 | So it was with her / | 3 1 | | 2 | 2 | 0 |
| | into exile / she went in captivity / | _15 2_ | | 3 | 3 | 0 |
| | | 3:2–10b | | 98 | 64 | 34 |
| | Her infants also / were dashed to pieces / | 12 2 | | 3 | 3 | 0 |
| | at the head of all the streets // | 8 1 | | 3 | 3 | 0 |
| | | 3:2–10d | | 104 | 70 | 34 |
| **D.** | **Her Nobles and Dignitaries Were Bound in Fetters (3:10ef)** | | | [2.2] | | |
| | And for <all>w her nobles / lots were cast / | _15 2_ | | 5 | 0 | 5 |
| | | 3:4–10e | | 85 | 55 | 30 |
| | And all her grandees / were bound in fetters // | 16 2 | | 4 | 0 | 4 |
| | | 3:4–10 | | 89 | 55 | 34 |
| **E.** | **May You Be Inebriated and Seek Refuge from Your Enemy (3:11)** | | | [3.3] | | |
| 3:11 | May you (f. sg.) also become drunk / | 6 1 | | 3 | 3 | 0 |

|  | Morae | SAS units | Word count** | | |
|---|---|---|---|---|---|
| may you (f. sg.) / pass out (in a drink-induced stupor) // | 9 2 | 2 | 2 | 2 | 0 |
| 3:9–11a | 34 | 21 | 13 | | |
| May you (f. sg.) also / seek refuge / from your enemy // | 16 3 | 5 | 0 | 5 | |
| 3:8–11 | 52 | 29 | 23 | | |

**F. Your Fortresses Will Fall Like First-Ripe Figs (3:12)** [3.3]

| 3:12 | Morae | SAS units | Word count | | |
|---|---|---|---|---|---|
| All your (f. sg.) fortresses / | 6 1 | 2 | 2 | 0 | |
| are like fig trees / with first-ripe figs // | 11 2 | 3 | 3 | 0 | |
| 3:9–12a | 44 | 26 | 18 | | |
| When shaken / they fall / into the mouth of the eater // | 19 3 | 6 | 0 | 6 | |
| 3:8–12 | 63 | 34 | 29 | | |

**G. Your People and Gates Are Wide Open to Be Violated and Devoured (3:13)** [5.4]

| 3:13 | Morae | SAS units | Word count | | |
|---|---|---|---|---|---|
| Behold /ˣ your (f. sg.) people are women / in your midst / | 14 3 | 4 | 4 | 0 | |
| to your (f. sg.) enemies / | 6 1 | 1 | 1 | 0 | |
| 3:11–13b | 26 | 15 | 11 | | |
| They are wide open / | 9 1 | 2 | 2 | 0 | |
| 3:11–13c | 28 | 17 | 11 | | |
| (Namely) the gates /ᴺ of your (f. sg.) land // | 7 2 | 2 | 2 | 0 | |
| fire devours / your (f. sg.) gate-bars // | 13 2 | 3 | 0 | 3 | |
| 3:1–13 | 156 | 92 | 64 | | |
| 3:8–13 | 75 | 43 | 32 | | |

# VII. THE LOCUST DIRGE:
## AN IMAGE OF IMMINENT RUIN (3:14–19)

**A. Prepare for the Siege — Strengthen Your Defenses (3:14)** [4.4]

| 3:14 | Morae | SAS units | Word count | | |
|---|---|---|---|---|---|
| Water for the siege / draw for yourselves / | 12 2 | 4 | 4 | 0 | |
| strengthen / your defenses // | 10 2 | 2 | 2 | 0 | |
| 3:11–14b | 40 | 26 | 14 | | |
| Go into the mud / and tread the clay / | 15 2 | 4 | 0 | 4 | |
| make strong /ᵉ the brick-mold // | 9 2 | 2 | 0 | 2 | |
| 3:11–14 | 46 | 26 | 20 | | |

|  | Morae | SAS units | Word count** |
|---|---|---|---|

**B. Fire and Sword Will Devour You Like the Locust (3:15a–c)** [2.2]

| | Morae | SAS units | Word count** |
|---|---|---|---|
| 3:15 There ᵃᵃ the fire will devour you / | _9 1_ | 3 | 3 0 |
| 3:12–15a | | 38 | 23 15 |
| The sword will cut you off / | _7 1_ | 2 | 2 0 |
| 3:14–15b | | 17 | 11 6 |
| It will devour you / like the young locust // | 9 2 | 2 | 2 0 |
| 3:11–15c | | 52 | 32 20 |

**C. Your Merchants Have Multiplied Like Locusts That Fly Away (3:15d–16)** [4.4]

| | Morae | SAS units | Word count** |
|---|---|---|---|
| Become heavier (m. sg.) like the young locust / | 7 1 | 2 | 0 2 |
| become heavier (f. sg.) like the winged-locust // | _9 1_ | 2 | 0 2 |
| 3:14–15 | | 23 | 13 10 |
| 3:16 You have increased / your merchants / | _8 2_ | 2 | 2 0 |
| 3:14–16a | | 58 | 34 24 |
| (They are) more than the stars / of the heavens // | 12 2 | 2 | 2 0 |
| a young locust sheds its outer skin / and flies away // | 10 2 | 3 | 0 3 |
| 3:14–16b | | 30 | 17 13 |

**D. Your Palace Officials Are Like Locusts That Fly Away in the Heat (3:17)** [4.2.4]

| | Morae | SAS units | Word count** |
|---|---|---|---|
| 3:17 Your magicians / are like winged locusts / | 10 2 | 2 | 2 0 |
| your astrologers / are like swarming locusts // | _12 2_ | 3 | 3 0 |
| 3:15–17b | | 23 | 16 7 |
| They settle in the walls / on a cold day / | _18 2_ | 4 | 0 4 |
| 3:14–17c | | 39 | 22 17 |
| The sun shines forth / and they fly away / | 11 2 | 3 | 0 3 |
| and their place is not known / where are they? // | 13 2 | 4 | 0 4 |
| 3:16–17 | | 23 | 9 14 |

**E. Your Shepherds Are Asleep and Your People Scattered (3:18)** [4.4]

| | Morae | SAS units | Word count** |
|---|---|---|---|
| 3:18 ꜀ Your shepherds are asleep / O king of Assyria / | _14 2_ | 4 | 4 0 |
| 3:14–18b | | 50 | 26 24 |
| ꜀ Your nobles / slumber // | _10 2_ | 2 | 2 0 |
| 3:14–18b | | 52 | 28 24 |
| ꜀ Your people are scattered / upon the mountains / | _16 2_ | 4 | 0 4 |
| 3:17–18c | | 26 | 11 15 |

|  | Morae | SAS units | Word count** | | |
|---|---|---|---|---|---|
| ו And there is none /bb to gather them // | 7 | 2 | 2 | 0 | 2 |
| 3:17–18 | | | 28 | 11 | 17 |
| **F. There Is No Healing to Your Wound (3:19ab)** | | | | | [2.2] |
| 3:19 There is no assuaging /cc your hurt / | 10 | 2_ | 3 | 3 | 0 |
| | | | 31 | 14 | 17 |
| It is grievous / your wound // | 8 | 2 | 2 | 2 | 0 |
| 3:18–19a | | | 17 | 11 | 6 |
| **G. Your Demise Brings Joy, for Who Has Not Experienced Your Evil? (3:19c–f)** | | | | | [4.4] |
| All / who hear the news of you / | 10 | 2 | 3 | 0 | 3 |
| clap their hands / over you / | 11 | 2_ | 3 | 0 | 3 |
| 3:18–19d | | | 23 | 11 | 12 |
| For / upon whom / | 5 | 2 | 3 | 0 | 3 |
| has not come your evil / unceasingly? // | 16 | 2 | 4 | 0 | 4 |
| 3:14–19 | | | 76 | 33 | 43 |
| 1:1–3:19 | | | 559 | 299 | 260 |

## NOTES

** Column 3 is the sum of columns 4 and 5 in word count. Column 4 is the words in that line before *ʾaṭnaḥ,* column 5 the words after *ʾaṭnaḥ.*

a–a The marginal *qərēʾ,* reading *ûḡəḏol-kōaḥ* ("and great in power"—7 morae), is read in place of *wəḡāḏôl kōaḥ* (8 morae) in 1:3a, which reduces the letter count by one.

b The verb *ʾūmlal* ("wither, languish") in 1:4b is emended to read *ʾūmləlû* so as to agree with the plural subject.

c Reading the plural form *wəʿāḇārû* ("and they will pass on") with Tg in place of *wəʿāḇār* ("and he will pass on") in BHS in 1:12a, with either the loss of *waw* by haplography or the "sharing of a consonant" (Watson 1969: 532). It is also possible to read the 3rd pers. m. sg. *ʿāḇār* ("one passes on; they pass on") in 1:12 as an indefinite personal subject; see GKC §144d.

d Reading *maṭṭēhû* ("his rod") with LXX, Vg, Syriac, Tg, and some Heb. Mss in place of *mōṭēhû* ("his yoke") in BHS in 1:13a.

e Reading the sequence of *ʾazlâ* plus *dargâ* here in 1:14b as disjunctive.

f–f The marginal *qərēʾ,* reading *laʿăḇor-bāḵ* ("to invade you"), is read in 2:1b, which reduces the letter count by one.

g–g Reading *pilăḏôt reḵeḇ* ("chariot coverings") in place of *pəlāḏôt hārekeḇ* ("the coverings of the chariots") in 2:4a in BHS to improve the balance in terms of mora count.

[h] Reading the Niphal 3rd pers. m. pl. form *yizzākərû* ("they are brought to remembrance") in place of *yizkōr* ("he will remember") in 2:6a. LXX has 3rd pers. pl. μνησθήσονται ("they bethink themselves"); so also Syriac ("they are obedient to their officers").

[i] Reading the *mûnaḥ* in 2:8a on the word *gullətāh* ("she is stripped") as disjunctive.

[j] Reading the *mêrəkâ* in 2:9a on the word *wənînəwēh* ("and Nineveh"), followed by *gaʿyâ* (= *meteḡ*), as disjunctive.

[k] Reading the *mûnaḥ* in 2:9b on the word *wəhēmmāh* ("and they") as disjunctive.

[l] Reading *mêmêhā hāwʾû hēmmāh nāsîm* ("her waters fall / they flee") in 2:9b in place of *mîmê hîʾ wəhēmmāh nāsîm* ("from of old she is / and they flee") in MT.

[m] Reading the *mêrəkâ* in 2:11a on the word *bûqāh* ("destruction") as disjunctive.

[n] The word *ûmirʿeh* ("and the feeding place, pasture") in 2:12a is emended to read *ûməʿārāh* ("and the cave") along with many scholars, which improves the balance in mora count.

[o] Reading the sequence of *mûnaḥ* in 2:12b, followed by *ʾazlâ* on the word *ʾaryēh* ("lion"), as disjunctive.

[p-p] Reading *gōrāyw* in 2:13a with 4QpNah in place of *gōrōṯāyw*, which is found no-where else in *Codex L* (BHS).

[q] Reading the *mûnaḥ* on the word *ṭerēp̄* ("torn flesh") in 2:13b as disjunctive.

[r] Reading the conjunctive accent *ʾazlâ* in 2:14a with Letteris (1880) in place of the disjunctive *paštâ* in L (BHS) on the word *nəʾūm* ("utterance").

[s] Reading the *paštâ* on the word *mēʾereṣ* ("from the land") in 2:14b as conjunctive.

[t-t] Following the marginal *qere'*, reading *wəkāšəlû* ("and they stumbled") in 3:3 rather than the *kethiv* *yəkāšəlû* ("they will stumble") in BHS.

[u] Reading *hannōkeret* ("who acquires [nations]") in place of *hammōkeret* ("who sells [nations]") in 3:4b with Pinker 2003c: 5.

[v] The *ṭip̄ḥâ* on *wəśamtîk* ("and I will make of you") in 3:6 is read as conjunctive.

[w] Adding the word *kol* ("all") in 3:10b with LXX. This is the one missing word in L (see discussion under "Logoprosodic Analysis and the Book of Nahum." Reading the *ʾazlâ* on the word *hinnēh* ("behold") in 3:13a as disjunctive.

[y] Reading *mûnaḥ* on the word *šaʿărê* ("gates") in 3:13d, preceded immediately by *gaʿyâ* (= *meteḡ*) in Letteris (1880) and Ginsberg (1894), as disjunctive. BHS omits *gaʿyâ* (= *meteḡ*).

[z] Reading *mêrəkâ* on the word *haḥăzîqî* ("strengthen") in 3:14d, preceded immediately by *gaʿyâ* (= *meteḡ*) in Letteris (1880) and Ginsberg (1894), as disjunctive. BHS omits *gaʿyâ* (= *meteḡ*).

[aa] Reading the *yəṯîḇ* on the word *šām* ("there") in 3:15a as conjunctive.

[bb] Reading the *mêrəkâ* on the word *wəʾên* ("and there is none") in 3:18b as disjunctive.

[cc] Reading the *mûnaḥ* on the word *kēhāh* ("[there is no] assuaging") in 3:19a as disjunctive.

## SUMMARY TOTALS FOR THE BOOK OF NAHUM

| | | |
|---:|---|---|
| 2254 | letters | [**2254** = **23** × 2 × 7 × 7] |
| 2166 | morae | |
| 559 | words | [**559** = (**17** + **26**) × 13] |
| 351 | SAS units | |
| 181 | briques (primary SAS units) {153/181 = 84.5% marked with 3 major accents} | |
| 81 | versets | [middle verset = 2:11ab] |
| 47 | verses | |
| 41 | strophes | |
| 7 | cantos | |

| | |
|---|---|
| Middle verse: | 2:10 [9] with 23 verses on either side |
| Middle 2 words (*Codex L*): | *ûp̄ənê k̲ullām* ("and all their faces") in 2:11b [10b] |
| Middle word (adjusted): | *k̲ullām* ("[and the faces of] all of them") in 2:11b [10b] |
| Middle 2 letters (*Codex L*): | middle 2 letters in *ûp̄ənê* ("and the faces") in 2:11b [10b] |
| Middle 2 letters (adjusted): | last 2 letters in *ûp̄ənê* ("and the faces") in 2:11b [10b] |

☐    indicates middle word in that canto
⬚    indicates total number of words in that canto

| Text | Scansion in SAS Units | Total SAS Units |
|---|---|---:|
| 1:1–10 | (9.4).(5.5).(4.4).(4.4).(4.4).(5.5).(4.9) | 70 |
| 1:11–14 | (5.4).(5.5).(4.5) | 28 |
| 2:1–11 [1:15–2:10] | (5.4).(7.6).(4.4).(6.6.6).(4.4).(6.7).(4.5) | 78 |
| 2:11–14 [10–13] | {5.4}.(4.4).(4.4).(4.5) | 25 |
| 3:1–7 | (3.4).(3.3).(4.5).(4.4).(5.4).(3.3).(4.3) | 52 |
| 3:8–13 | (4.5).(6.6).(2.2).(6.6).(5.4) | 46 |
| 3:14–19 | (4.4).(4.6).(6.4.6).(6.4).(4.4) | <u>52</u> |
| | | 351 |

# INTRODUCTION

At first glance, the "angry God" we meet in Nahum seems far removed from the God revealed elsewhere in the Old Testament, and even farther removed from the God of the Greek New Testament. When read in isolation from its larger literary context, the book is sometimes interpreted as a vengeful nationalistic expression of glee over the destruction of a bitter enemy. Consequently some scholars dismiss Nahum as an example of perhaps the best of the "false prophets" Jeremiah opposed. They describe the book as ethically and theologically deficient and not worthy of inclusion in the canon of sacred Scripture (Marti 1903: 305–6; Staerk 1908: 179–80; J. M. P. Smith 1911: 281). Spronk (1997: 14) quotes R. A. Mason as follows: "Will any of us ever have the courage to admit . . . that the book really is rather a disgrace to the two religious communities of whose canonical Scriptures it forms so unwelcome a part?" Spronk also cites Mason (1991: 82–83) for a more moderate stance. For the most part, the book of Nahum has been ignored within both the Christian church and the Jewish synagogue. Within traditional Judaism, no lectionary reading is taken from Nahum (Pinker 2004a: 148).

Much of this fate, however, is not deserved, for Nahum is at home among the oracles against foreign nations in the prophetic literature, especially in Isaiah and Jeremiah. And as Spronk has argued (1997: 15), "Instead of accusing him of being a false prophet, we have to assume that in the later prophetic tradition the book of Nahum was accepted as a perfect example of true prophecy." Spronk is thinking explicitly in terms of the definition of the true prophet in Deuteronomy 18:21–22, which says that a prophet has rightly spoken in the name of YHWH when his word comes to pass as predicted.

Nahum is a book about God's justice within the context of the "wars of YHWH" as a theological construct. It is best read as a literary complement to Jonah and as an introduction to Habakkuk. Nahum and Jonah are closely connected in the Book of the Twelve Prophets—as literary complements, as books perhaps even from the same hand, and at least in terms of their numerical composition. These two books are the only ones in the entire Bible that end in a question, and both are closely connected structurally with what follows them: Jonah with Micah, Nahum with Habakkuk. Moreover, both Nahum and Jonah have Nineveh as their subject. This is remarkable in the case of Jonah, because according to 2 Kings 14:25, he ministered in the days of Jeroboam II (ca. 786–746 BCE) against the Aramean threat centered in Damascus and Hamath (2 Kings 14:28)—before the rise of Tiglath-pileser III (ca. 745–727 BCE; "King Pul" of 2 Kings 15:19) and the expansion of the Neo-Assyrian Empire in the Levant. Moreover, the ancient city of Nineveh did not become the capital until later yet, when Sennacherib (704–681 BCE) chose it as his new capital, which he transformed through extensive building projects.

Sennacherib built a magnificent palace in Nineveh and cut a great street through the heart of the city from that palace to the bridge crossing the Tigris. He constructed an elaborate system of aqueducts and canals to bring water into the city, where he built extensive gardens and pools, sparing no expense in his attempt to make Nineveh a wonder of the ancient world. Nonetheless, the great city of Nineveh disappeared altogether less than seventy years after Sennacherib's death, as described in vivid poetic imagery in the forty-seven verses that make up the book of Nahum.

The word Nahum (naḥûm) means "showing consolation, compassionated." The prophet's name draws attention to an aspect of God's character that is muted here and highlighted in Jonah—namely his compassion for friend and foe alike. The prophet's name is a note to observant readers reminding them not to interpret the book independent of its intended literary context within the Book of the Twelve Prophets.

Nothing is known about the prophet Nahum, and even the place of his hometown, Elkosh, remains unidentified (see the later discussion of 1:1). The conclusion reached by some scholars, that Nahum was a central prophet working within the context of the Jerusalem Temple personnel, is based on comparative study of the literary form of his book, which is an extended oracle against a foreign nation. As such, its original composition may have been motivated, at least in part, by political aims—perhaps to encourage a revolt on the part of the kingdom of Judah against Assyrian domination in the middle of the seventh century BCE. Once again, however, we must acknowledge that conclusions on the social location of the prophet Nahum, like that of the geographical location of Elkosh, are little more than scholarly guesses. When it comes to facts, we know almost nothing about the personal life and ministry of Nahum.

Nineveh was the capital of Assyria at its height, from the reign of Sennacherib to its destruction in 612 BCE. It was not the capital of Assyria in the days of Jeroboam II, the historical setting of Jonah, who is also associated with Nineveh. Moreover, there was never a time when it was appropriate to speak of the ruler of Assyria as "king of Nineveh" (Jonah 3:6) outside the book of Jonah. The person in question was ruler of the Assyrian Empire. Nineveh is mentioned in Isaiah 37:37 (and in 2 Kings 19:36) as the home of Sennacherib, where he was assassinated and succeeded by his son Esarhaddon.

Jonah and Nahum present complementary aspects of God's nature, his mercy and his justice (expressed in "anger"), with Jonah focusing on God's steadfast covenant love (*ḥeseḏ*) and Nahum on God's justice and wrath. Jonah presents God as one who is "compassionate, gracious . . . (and) abounding in steadfast love" (Exodus 34:6–7a), whereas Nahum presents God as the "one who punishes sons and grandsons to the third and fourth generations for the iniquity of their fathers" (Exodus 34:7b). In short, Nahum focuses on what some might call the "dark side" of God, while Jonah portrays God's mercy and compassion toward the same wicked city. Both aspects are essential for an understanding of the divine nature.

The word *YWNH* ("Jonah") in Hebrew means "dove," a primary symbol for Israel. Though the story of the book so named concerns a man named Jonah, the reader must never lose sight of the fact that the poetic work itself is to be read with a corporate "Jonah" in mind as well — the people of Israel. It was the nation of Israel who fled from YHWH's call to be a blessing to all peoples and was swallowed by an evil monster in a watery plunge to the depths of darkness and despair.

The name *Nineveh* in the story of Jonah was apparently selected for its symbolic value. The word *Ninuwa* and the alternate form *Nina*, in the cuneiform sources, refer to an enclosure with a fish inside. The letter *nun* actually means "fish" in Hebrew. The word *Nineveh* would be written *NYNWH*. If the initial *nun* ("fish") is removed, the letters that remain are *YNWH*. All one needs to do to get the word *YWNH* ("Jonah") is to metathesize the two central letters. In other words, *Jonah* is already *in Nineveh* — if we remove the "fish"! Though there is no comparable relationship between the name *Nahum* and Nineveh, the subject of "compassion" implied in the prophet's name appears in muted fashion in 1:3 ("YHWH is slow to anger") and 1:7 ("Good is YHWH; indeed a stronghold in the day of distress; and he knows those who take refuge in him").

Nahum and Habakkuk are so closely connected in both content and context that the two may be outlined as a single literary entity:

| | | |
|---|---|---|
| A | Hymn of theophany—a "bent" acrostic with a hidden message | Nahum 1 |
| B | Taunt song against Nineveh [in five cantos] | Nahum 2–3 |
| C | Habakkuk's prayers and YHWH's initial response | Habakkuk 1:1–2:3 |
| X | **The righteous will survive by faith(fullness)** | Habakkuk 2:4 |
| C′ | The "wicked one" will not endure—the tables are turned | Habakkuk 2:5 |
| B′ | Taunt of the nations—five "woes" on the "wicked one" | Habakkuk 2:6–10 |
| A′ | Hymn of theophany—the Psalm of Habakkuk | Habakkuk 3 |

There are only two hymns of theophany in the entire prophetic corpus (Former Prophets and Latter Prophets), which function as "bookends" in the combination of Nahum and Habakkuk as a literary unit. The "bent" acrostic in Nahum 1:1–10 is the only example of an acrostic "psalm" in the prophetic literature, and Habakkuk 3 is the only true psalm as such, though both Jonah 2:3–10 and Nahum 1:1–10 may also be classified in that literary category. The Psalm of Habakkuk includes all the rubrics we associate with the Psalms, including the only occurrences of the word *Selah* (three times) outside the Psalter. Within the "bookends" of parallel hymns of theophany in Nahum 1 and Habakkuk 3 we find parallel taunt songs, each of which features five major sections—with five (of the seven) "cantos" in the poetic literary structure of Nahum set over against the five "woes" in Habakkuk. The combined literary work focuses on the issue of theodicy. And in the center we find the fundamental theological instruction that divine justice is inexorable and will come in due time; in the meantime, the righteous will live by faith (Habakkuk 2:2–4).

## LOGOPROSODIC ANALYSIS AND THE BOOK OF NAHUM

This study of Nahum is by no means the first attempt to explore its poetic nature in detail, nor is it the first attempt to reconstruct its prosodic structure, nor will it be the last. In 1783, W. Newcome published his "metrical arrangement" of the entire Book of the Twelve Prophets. A decade later, E. Greve (1793) tried to prove that Nahum was written in a regular iambic meter. And a century later, at the tail end of a heated debate on related issues, which focused largely on the so-called acrostic hymn in the first chapter of Nahum, P. Haupt chose the book of Nahum as the topic of his presidential address to the Society of Biblical Literature, which was published separately as *The Book of Nahum: A New Metrical Translation with an Introduction, Restoration of the Hebrew Text and Explanatory and Critical Notes* (1907b). The subtitle of Haupt's work suggests that there were numerous other such attempts before him to reconstruct the prosodic structure of Nahum; still others were yet to come — including this commentary. Unlike me in the study presented here, however, these three earlier scholars showed no hesitation in correcting the Hebrew text of Nahum to agree with their own understanding of its metrical structure.

Following the discovery of the so-called acrostic of Nahum by G. Frohnmeyer, which was first reported by F. Delitzsch in his *Biblischer Commentar über die Psalmen* (published in 1867), the book of Nahum played a peculiar role in the study of Hebrew prosody as the focus of attention for a significant debate on methodology, which attracted some of the best-known Old Testament scholars of that era. Because acrostics provide external control in determining poetic structure, they have long attracted attention in the study of Hebrew prosody. In 1880, G. Bickell published his first of five studies (1880, 1880/81, 1882, 1886, 1894) dealing with this newly discovered acrostic poem, in which he championed a "syllabic theory" of Hebrew poetry. He was subsequently challenged by H. Gunkel (1893; see Cobb 1905: 83–107, 169–84, for a survey of this debate on method), who saw the key to Hebrew meter in the number of word stresses rather than in syllable count, according to the system of prosodic analysis advanced by J. Ley (1875, 1887), who, at the same time, continued to recognize the mora basis of Hebrew poetry.

The work of Ley was expanded in a series of significant studies on the part of E. Sievers (1901–7), who rejected the mora basis in the meter of Hebrew poetry (as did E. König 1914, J. Rothstein 1905, and others). As Isaacs noted, the objection to the use of mora count on the part of E. König was essentially that the matter had been decided in favor of the accentual basis and that "the subject is closed" (Isaacs 1918: 25). The Ley-Sievers System, which focuses on the counting of word-stress units, remains the dominant position in Old Testament scholarship and is used by L. Bliese (1995) in his current work on chiastic metrical structures in Nahum and other texts.

The stage for the methodological debate between Bickell and Gunkel was set earlier in the nineteenth century, when W. Gesenius and others discredited an older methodology that focused on mora count, which goes back to J. Alting in the middle of the seventeenth century — and remained the dominant theoretical position in terms of prosodic analysis in Old Testament scholarship for more than two hundred years, until it was eventually replaced by the Ley-Sievers System at the end of the nineteenth century. Alting (1654) was apparently the first to propose the *systema morarum*. That system was expanded into the *system trium morarum* by J. Danz (1699) and was known as the Alting-Danzian System. B. Spinoza (1677), J. Bellermann (1813), and J. Saalschütz (1825) were among those who used this methodology. H. Grimme (1896–97) illustrated the culmination of this trend in increasing complexity in his system of analysis, which Isaacs described as follows: "Grimme distinguishes three grades of tone, a main tone, a secondary tone, and a weak tone. He also distinguishes four degrees of morae, syllables with four, three, two, and one mora. These are combined in certain ways. At first glance this system appears theoretically logical. It is, however, impracticable" (Isaacs 1918: 25, citing Grimme 1896: 539–40).

The methodology of mora-counting was discredited because its advocates over-refined the system. Long before the middle of the nineteenth century, the system of mora-counting was already being applied to the wrong ends and had become too complex to be readily understood in the public sphere. But even though the system of mora-counting was discredited and ultimately replaced by the Ley-Sievers System, with the focus on word-stress patterns, the older system of mora-counting never completely died out. Isaacs notes that even Ley believed that Hebrew poetry "has a mora basis" (Isaacs 1918: 24). Sievers, however, rejected the mora basis of Hebrew poetry. He also refused to make any sharp distinction between poetry and prose, including narrative parts of such "prose" texts as Genesis, Kings, and Jonah in his *Metrische Studien* (Isaacs 1918: 27, n. 2).

For more than forty years now, F. M. Cross and D. N. Freedman have cautiously advanced a new version of the method of syllable-counting as a more effective means for analyzing the structure of Hebrew poetry than the more commonly accepted word-stress notation of the Ley-Sievers System. As early as 1960, Freedman utilized syllable count in his study of structural balance in early Hebrew poetry (1960: 101–7); but the method itself was not applied systematically to the study of prosodic structure in a more general sense until the publication of Freedman's article "The Structure of Job 3" (1968: 503–8). A spate of related articles followed on the part of Cross, Freedman, and a number of their students, particularly from 1970 to 1976 (see Longman 1982a: 232–33, notes 11 and 12). But as early as 1972, Freedman turned his attention to statistical approaches where emendation of the text is not necessary (1972: 367–92).

Meanwhile, in 1976 the study of Hebrew poetry took a quantum leap of sorts with two independent and simultaneous publications: D. Stuart's (1976) systematic assessment of Cross's approach to archaic Hebrew poetry and A. M. Cooper's Ph.D. dissertation at Yale (1976), which was based on the work of J. Kurylowicz. Kurylowicz suggested an important modification in methodology, which is followed, at least in part, in this commentary. By pay-ing careful attention to the Masoretic accentual system, Kurylowicz devised a system of "Syntactic Accentual Meter" (this terminology is that of Longman 1982a: 238). At the same time, Kurylowicz (1973: 176) addressed another significant issue when he wrote, "Parallelism of members etc. are adornments proper to poetic style, but must be left out of consideration in the analysis of metre." This statement needs qualification, for it is only with meter in the classical sense of a particular form of prosodic arrangement constituting a "foot" (a group of syllables constituting a metrical unit of a verse) that "parallelism of members" is not significant. Parallelism in the matter of the length of corresponding cola in their understanding of the structure of Hebrew poetry is what attracted the interest of Freedman and Cross in the first place. Some aspects of parallelism are described quantitatively in logoprosodic analysis and are, in fact, definitive in the determination of prosodic boundaries.

J. Fokkelman's dissertation on Genesis was published in 1975 and subsequently led to a series of significant publications on both Hebrew narrative and poetry (Fokkelman 1975, 1981, 1999, 2003). P. van der Lugt (1980, 2005) reviewed the study of Hebrew poetry from the time of Saalschütz (1825) to the present and attempted an ambitious synthesis, which he applied to fifty-seven psalms in his study of strophic structure. Because Van der Lugt's original work was published in Dutch and he was exploring a new set of questions within the context of the so-called Kampen school, his work took longer to make its impact in the expanding discussion of Hebrew poetry.

In 1978, T. Collins published his dissertation, *Line-Forms in Hebrew Poetry: A Grammatical Approach to the Stylistic Study of the Hebrew Prophets*, which is based on the modern linguistic theory of generative grammar. Working independently, S. Geller (1979) applied principles from modern linguistic theory to the subject of parallelism in his Harvard dissertation. A year later, M. P. O'Connor (1980) published a synthesis of modern linguistic theory and traditional classic description of Hebrew poetry (an expansion of his 1978 Ph.D. thesis at the University of Michigan). J. Kugel (1981) followed with his study of parallelism, which also addresses the fundamental question regarding the terms *poetry* and *prose* in relation to the Bible. There is no clear distinction between these two categories, because we are apparently dealing with some sort of continuum (see Christensen 1985a). Building on the linguistic theory of R. Jakobson (1966), A. Berlin (1985) carried the discussion of parallelism further when she combined the study of modern linguistics with earlier studies in word pairs in a comprehensive linguistic description.

Biblical parallelism has been center stage in the study of Hebrew poetry since R. Lowth published his *Lectures on the Sacred Poetry of the Hebrews* (1753). Subsequent studies of parallelism from that time until the work of Kugel (1981) refined the work of Lowth, with the primary focus on the basic sameness of parallel lines. Two impulses shaped the development in this field of study in the twentieth century: the study of the newly discovered corpus of Ugaritic poetry, with particular interest in sets of parallel terms or fixed word pairs, and the work of M. Parry (1933–35) and A. Lord (1950–51) in oral poetry and the techniques of oral composition used in Greek and Yugoslavian poetry by the traditional singer of tales (see Lord 1960). The list of word pairs grew long and soon numbered more than a thousand. Kugel (1981), however, rejected the notion of the synonymity of parallel lines and replaced it with the notion of continuity: "A, what's more, B." In like manner, R. Alter (1985) described the "consequentiality" of parallel lines. The focus thus shifted by putting the primary emphasis on the *difference* between parallel lines.

My study of the "Oracles against the Nations," which includes Nahum, was written as a doctoral dissertation using Cross's methodology based on syllable-count (Christensen 1972, published in 1975a). That method was altered substantially in 1982, with the substitution of counting morae instead of syllables, and again in 1984, with the addition of SAS units, as defined by Kurylowicz (Christensen 1984). This revised methodology was applied in a second article on the acrostic of Nahum, which demonstrates the proper boundaries of the "bent" alphabetic acrostic in Nahum 1:3–8 (Christensen 1987a) and the study of the literary structure of Nahum as a whole in *Harper's Bible Commentary* (Christensen 1988a: 736–38). A further revision in methodology, which adds the matter of word count, is presented in this commentary. The acrostic poem in Nahum 1:3–8 is the central part of a larger concentric structure that includes the whole of 1:1–10 as the first of seven "cantos" in the book of Nahum.

The concept of counting verses, words, and letters in the text of the Tanakh (Hebrew Bible) goes back to ancient times (see Andersen and Forbes 1992: 297–318). Within the Masoretic tradition, the number of verses in each book of the Former Prophets and the Latter Prophets is recorded, along with the number of readings (*sedarim*), in marginal notes and at the end of each book. For the Torah and the five Festal Scrolls (*Megilloth*) this tradition also includes the word count, and for the Torah the letter count as well. Careful study suggests that the word count is significant for the Book of the Twelve Prophets and for Nahum in particular (see the website www.bibal.net).

Earlier study indicates that Deuteronomy was carefully crafted as a numerical composition of exactly **14,300** (= **26** × **55** × **10**) words. The number was apparently chosen as a theological statement to describe the nature of that text (see Christensen 2001: ci–cvii). The number **26** is the numerical value of the divine name YHWH (10 + 5 + 6 + 5). The number **55** is triangular "10" (that is, the sum of the numbers 1 through 10) and the sum of two numbers associated with the Hebrew word *glory* (when written with the vowel letter *waw* as *kbwd*), **55 = 23 + 32**. The number 10 refers to the "Ten Commandments," or what Deuteronomy presents as the "ten words." The concept of ten is reinforced by multiplying the number by triangular 10. In Jewish tradition, the name of Deuteronomy is "These are the Words"—namely, the words of YHWH, which are summarized in the "Ten Words" (that is, the Ten Commandments).

A somewhat parallel phenomenon was reported earlier for the Rig Veda, which was apparently composed to have 432,000 (= $2^7 \times 3^3 \times 5^3$) syllables (McClain 1976: 75). A closer parallel of importance to biblical studies is found much later in Plato's *Ion*, which was composed in exactly 7776 syllables to correspond with "Apollo's Number" ($60^5 = 777,600,000$). This number is also YHWH's number when the tetragrammaton יהוה (10.5.6.5) is read exponentially as $10^5 \times 6^5 = 60^5$ (see Bremer 2005: 299–328).

The Book of the Twelve Prophets presents a parallel situation to that of Deuteronomy, with the grand total of 14,355 words in *Codex L*. The word count in the original canonical (that is, numerically composed) version of the Book of the Twelve Prophets appears to have been: **14,352 = (26 × 23 × 12) × 2**. The Book of the Twelve Prophets is presented as the word of YHWH (**26 = 10 + 5 + 6 + 5**, the numerical value of YHWH); the book was written to the "glory of YHWH" (**23** = numerical value of the Hebrew word *kbwd*, "glory"); and there are twelve books in this particular literary work.

The numerical structure of the Book of the Twelve Prophets in its presumed original canonical form may be outlined as follows:

| | *Total words* | | *before* <br> *ᵓaṭnaḥ* | | *after* <br> *ᵓaṭnaḥ* | |
|---|---|---|---|---|---|---|
| Hosea | 2380 | = | 1283 + | 1097 | 2380 = | 17 × 140 {140 = sum of squares 1 through 7} |
| Joel | 952 | = | 510 + | 442 | 442 = | 17 × 26; 510 = 17 × 30 |
| Amos | 2040 | = | 1130 + | 910 | 2040 = | 17 × 12 × 10; 910 = 26 × 35 |
| Obadiah | 291 | = | 174 + | 117 | 289 = | 17 × 17 {without heading, 2 words} |
| Jonah | 688 | = | 380 + | 308 | 688 = | (17 + 26) × 16; 680 = 17 × 40 {without 1:1} |
| Micah | 1394 | = | 744 + | 650 | 1394 = | 17 × 82; 650 = 26 × 25 |
| Nahum | 559 | = | 299 + | 260 | 559 = | (17 + 26) × 13; 260 = 26 × 10 |
| Habakkuk | 676 | = | 364 + | 312 | 676 = | 26 × 26; 364 = 26 × 14; 312 = 26 × 12 |
| Zephaniah | 768 | = | 384 + | 384 | 384 = | 32 × 12 |
| Haggai | 598 | = | 368 + | 230 | 598 = | 26 × 23; 368 = 23 × 16; 230 = 23 × 10 |

| | Total words | before ʾaṯnaḥ | | after ʾaṯnaḥ |
|---|---|---|---|---|
| Zechariah | 3128 = | 1768 + | 1360 | 3128 = $17 \times 23 \times 8$; $1768 = 17 \times 26 \times 4$; $1360 = 17 \times 80$ |
| Malachi | 878 = | 448 + | 430 | 430 = $(17 + 26) \times 10$ |
| Totals | 14,352 = | 7852 + | 6500 | all three numbers divisible by 26 |

$$14,352 = (26 \times 23 \times 12) \times 2 \text{ and } 650 = 26 \times 5 \times 5 = \text{sum of squares 1 through 12}$$

Building on the pioneering work of C. Schedl (1974), C. Labuschagne (2000: 88–92) has shown the significance of the four primary compositional numbers **17**, **23**, **26**, and **32** in the numerical composition of the Tanakh. The numbers **17** and **26** represent both the divine name YHWH and the numerical value of the Hebrew word for "glory."

**kbd "glory"**
alphabetical place value (22 gematria):    $(k = 11) + (b = 2) + (d = 4) = \mathbf{17}$
as numerical signs (400 gematria):    $(k = 20) + (b = 2) + (d = 4) = \mathbf{26}$

**yhwh, "YHWH"**
alphabetical place value:    $(y = 10) + (h = 5) + (w = 6) + (h = 5) = \mathbf{26}$
sum of digits:    $(y = 1 + 0) + (h = 5) + (w = 6) + (h = 5) = \mathbf{17}$

Labuschagne suggests that the number **17** is associated with God's personal name in terms of the numerical value of *ʾahweh*, which is analogous to the archaized form of *yahweh*. The first person singular form *ʾehyeh* occurs in Exodus 3:14, where the divine name is revealed and defined—"I am who I am" (NRSV). The numerical value of the archaic word *ʾahweh* is **17**. It is thus possible to read the combination of **17** and **26** as representing the "glory of YHWH" as well as the combination of the two numbers for the divine name (see Labuschagne 2000: 89).

The word count for Nahum in *Codex L* is $558 = 299 + 259$. In its original numerical composition, Nahum apparently had $\mathbf{559} = 299 + 260$ words. The missing word appears to be the word *kol* ("all") in Nahum 3:10b, which is preserved in the LXX (see the appropriate files on the website www.bibal.net). The number $\mathbf{559}$ (= $43 \times 13$) may have been selected for its symbolic value, because $\mathbf{43}$ (= $17 + 26$) is the sum of the two numbers for the divine name and the number 13 is associated with the Hebrew word *ʾeḥad* ("one"). YHWH alone is the true God, and he tolerates no rival.

The purpose of numerical composition is twofold. In the first place, putting the numbers for the divine name in the text is a symbolic way of saying that the text is the "Word of God." Another practical purpose concerns the protection of the text from inadvertent errors in transmission through the vicissitudes of time. Recovering specific numerical patterns in relation to what we call the "meaningful center" of a given text reveals the addition or subtraction of even a single word and provides specific information as to the location of any error in transcription within that text. This helps to explain why scribes included information about the number of verses, words, and even letters of texts in the Tanakh.

In many cases within the Masoretic textual tradition, the middle verse, and sometimes even the middle word and/or letter of a given text, is marked with a marginal note. A note in Genesis calls attention to the fact that the words Isaac says to Esau in Genesis 27:40, "By your sword you shall live," constitute the center of the book. And at the end of the five books of the Torah we find these words in *Codex L* (and *BHS*):

Sum of the verses of the Torah: 5845
Sum of the words of the Torah: 79,856
Sum of the letters of the Torah: 400,945

A marginal note indicates that Micah 3:12 is the center of the Book of the Twelve Prophets, and each of the twelve books concludes with a note giving the number of verses contained in it.

There are 47 verses in Nahum, and the middle verse is 2:10 [2:9], with **23** verses on either side. Nahum has **559** (= [**17** + **26**] × 13) words, and the middle word, which is found in 2:11b [10b], is *kullām* ("all of them"), with 279 words on either side of it. There are 2252 letters in Nahum in *Codex L*. At the same time, there are five marginal readings (1:3; 2:1 [1:15], 2:4 [3], 2:7 [6], and 3:3), three of which affect the letter count (1:3, 2:1 [1:15], and 2:4 [3]). If the proposed correction in 3:10b is accepted (see the following commentary) and the marginal readings are ignored, we have **2254** (= 23 × 7 × 7 × 2) letters in Nahum. The middle two letters in Nahum in *Codex L* (*BHS*), with the addition of the word *kol* ("all") in 3:10b, are the last two letters in the word *ûpānê* ("and the faces") in 2:11b [10b], with 1125 (= 3 × 3 × 5 × 5 × 5) letters on either side of the absolute center, which falls between the letters *nun* and *yodh* in this word.

Adjustments in terms of optional vowel letters appear to have been a relatively late aspect of the numerical composition of the Hebrew text in the Tanakh. One of its purposes may have been symbolic—to put the divine name YHWH back into the fabric of an already corrupted text without making substantive changes in that text, which would have violated the canonical injunction of Deuteronomy 4:2 not to add or to subtract anything. Though it was forbidden to restore missing words, it was possible to adjust the letter count using optional vowel letters so as to achieve numbers divisible by one of the four primary compositional numbers.

The method of logoprosodic analysis, which is applied here in the detailed study of the Hebrew text of the entire book of Nahum, involves the counting of three distinct elements: (1) morae (as a measurement of relative length of prosodic subunits); (2) SAS units, as defined in the Masoretic accentual system to assess the rhythmic or musical structure of the text; and (3) words (hence the term *logo*-prosodic). The data from each category reveal something different, and the interplay of the three reveals the prosodic structure of the poetic work as a whole.

## Summary of Basic Terminology in Logoprosodic Analysis

1. Letters—the 22 letters in the Hebrew alphabet plus 5 additional letters (final *ḵap̄, mêm, nûn, pēh, ṣāḏēh*), for a total of 27 letter forms. These letter forms also constitute numbers in two primary systems of notation:

    a. Place value (22 gematria): the 22 letters represent the numbers 1 through 22.

    b. Normal 400 gematria:

    | | |
    |---|---|
    | *ʾalep̄* through *ṭēṯ* | 1, 2, 3, . . . 9 |
    | *ḵap̄* through *ṣāḏēh* | 10, 20, 30, . . . 90 |
    | *rēš* through *tāw* | 100, 200, 300, 400 |
    | {final *ḵap̄, mêm, nûn, pēh, ṣāḏēh* | 500, 600, 700, 800, 900} |

    The 27 [22 + 5] letter forms supply the numbers for counting from 1 to 999. Adding a dot above one of these 27 letters or numbers indicates that the letter is a number. Adding two dots above each letter takes us to 1000, 2000, 3000, and so on.

2. Mora (plural morae)—a subdivision of the syllable; a syllable with a short vowel is one mora, and a syllable with a long vowel is two morae.

3. Words are made up of a grouping of syllables (open [ending in a vowel] and closed [ending in a consonant]).

4. Word-stress units—words joined with *maqqeph* constitute a single word stress.

5. SAS units—groupings of words between two successive disjunctive accent marks.

6. Brique—significant grouping of SAS units (more or less equivalent to what others call a "colon").

7. Verset—grouping of briques into dyads and triads, sometimes a dyad plus a pivot. A verset is thus similar to what others call a "verseline."

8. Strophe—a grouping of briques into binary (two-part) groups, except at the center of a canto, where the strophe may be a ternary (three-part) structure. In some instances, a strophe may consist of a single verset.
9. Canto—a significant grouping of strophes.

Note that the boundaries of strophes are marked in the logoprosodic analysis by the underlining that extends through all five columns of numbers in the right margin. Underlining of the first two columns indicates only the boundary of major subdivisions within a given strophe on the basis of balance in terms of mora count, which does not necessarily coincide with the concept of the verset as such.

There are many other aspects of Hebrew poetry that make up the stylistics of a given work. This hierarchy of building blocks, however, constitutes the essence of the formal structure of Hebrew poetry in terms of prosodic units. Poets in ancient Israel were conscious of number at all levels in terms of prosodic structure.

## Illustration of the Logoprosodic Analysis Using Nahum 1:3

It is useful to illustrate the concepts presented here in terms of the text of Nahum 1:3, which is the second strophe in the first canto (1:1–10). Note that the boundary at the end of this strophe is marked by underlining that extends under all five columns of numbers in the right margin.

| | | | *SAS* | *Word* | |
|---|---|---|---|---|---|
| | | *Morae* | *units* | *count* | |
| 1:3 | Yhwh / is slow to anger / but great in power / | 16 3 | 5 | 5 | 0 |
| | and he does not leave the guilty / unpunished // | _9 2_ | 3 | 3 | 0 |
| | 1:1b–2b | | 26 | 16 | 10 |
| | Yhwh / | _4 1_ | 1 | 0 | 1 |
| | 1:2–3c | | 23 | 16 | 7 |
| | In the whirlwind and in the storm / is his way / | 15 2 | 3 | 0 | 3 |
| | and clouds / are the dust of his feet // | 10 2 | 3 | 0 | 3 |
| | 1:1–3 | | 35 | 18 | 17 |

The word count in the Hebrew text (column 3 of the 5 columns) is divided into two parts: words before ʾaṭnaḥ (column 4) plus words after ʾaṭnaḥ (column 5). Nahum 1:3 is transliterated as follows (the mark ´ indicates the location of the stress):

| 1:3 | Yhwh / ʾereḵ ʾappáyim / ûḡəḏol-kóaḥ / | 16 3 | 5 = 5 + 0 |
|---|---|---|---|
| | wənaqqéh / lóʾ yənaqqéh ^ | _9 2_ | 3 = 3 + 0 |

| | SAS | Word |
|---|---|---|
| | *Morae* | *units* | *count* |
| YHWH / | _ 4 1_ | 1 = 0 + 1 |
| bəsûpā̂h ûḇiśʿārā̂h / darkô / | 15 2 | 3 = 0 + 3 |
| wəʿānā̂n / ʾăḇáq raḡláyw : | 10 2 | 3 = 0 + 3 |

The pronunciation of the divine name YHWH in antiquity is not known. It is arbitrarily assigned a value of four morae and two (or possibly three) syllables in this method of analysis. In this particular strophe, the second occurrence of the divine-name YHWH functions as a "pivot" and belongs to each of the two versets—completing one and beginning the other.

This strophe (1:3) contains

59 letters in *Codex L* (BHS) as written (*kəṯîḇ*) – וגדול ("and great")

58 letters, with the marginal (*qərēʾ*) reading of *Codex L* – וגדל ("and great")

54 morae [= (16 + 9) + 4 + (15 + 10)] = 25 + 4 + 25

33 syllables [+ 2 occurrences of YHWH] = YHWH + 17 ∥ YHWH + 16
   {with 13 long vowels, 20 short vowels, and 2 occurrences of YHWH}

15 words [= (5 + 4) + (3 + 3)]

14 word-stress units [= (4 + 4) + (3 + 3)]

10 SAS units [= (3 + 2) + (3 + 2)]

4 briques (two ending with *zāqēp̄ qāṭôn*, one with *ʾaṯnaḥ* and one with *sôp̄ pāsûq*).

2 versets (with the second occurrence of YHWH read as part of each verset):

| | |
|---|---|
| YHWH is slow to anger but great in power; | 16 morae |
| YHWH does not leave the guilty unpunished. | 13 morae |

   {In Hebrew the sentence above begins and ends with YHWH.}

| | |
|---|---|
| YHWH, in the whirlwind and in the storm is his way; | 19 morae |
| and clouds are the dust of his feet. | 10 morae |

The total word count from the beginning of the second part of the heading (not including the two-word incipit) is 26. The word count from the beginning of 1:2 to the end of the first verset in 1:3 is **23** words. The word count from the beginning of 1:2 to the end of the third brique (primary SAS units) in 1:3 is **26** words, and the total number of words after *ʾaṯnaḥ* from the beginning of Nahum to the end of 1:3 is **17**. The telestich [= the final letter of successive lines] that spells out the name YHWH ends at the *ʾaṯnaḥ* in 1:3 (that is, at the end of the first verset). The bent acrostic in 1:1–10 includes the initial **yoḏ** of the first occurrence of the divine name YHWH and the second occurrence of the word YHWH in its entirety, reading "I am YHWH."

The prosodic structure of the Hebrew text is revealed through careful study of the numbers in columns 1 and 2 in the right margin of the logoprosodic analysis and translation of Nahum. The mora count for a given line in the Hebrew text, which appears in column 1, is found by counting the syllables and adding one additional count for each long vowel. Mora count is essentially a measure of relative line length and thus becomes a quantitative assessment of the phenomenon of parallelism in Hebrew poetry. Groupings of SAS units form balanced structures in terms of total mora count, in which the parts of a given strophe are arranged in dyads or triads, often with a pivot joining the two "halves" of that strophe. A dyad or triad plus the pivot, if one is present, constitute a verset. If there is no pivot, each of the two (or three) sections of any given strophe is a verset. On occasion, a verset may consist of a pair of dyads (3:18, 19c–f) or even a single dyad (3:9, 11, 12). In such instances, the verset is sometimes identical with the strophe.

Column 2 gives the number of SAS units in that particular line. The boundary of each of these SAS units is marked by a disjunctive accent in the Masoretic accentual system. For a convenient list of both the conjunctive and disjunctive accents in this complex system of musical notation, see Fascicle 18 in *BHQ* (*Megilloth*) (2004: xcix–c). The presence of a disjunctive accent appears for the *ʾaṭnaḥ* and the *sôp̄ pasûq* (end-of-verse marker). The words included between successive disjunctive accents constitute the SAS units, which are essentially musical phrases in the chanting tradition of the performance of the Hebrew text in antiquity. The SAS units are distributed in discernible concentric patterns in which the prosodic structure of each parallel strophe is a mirror image of the other. Each strophe is a binary unit in terms of the distribution of SAS units, which frequently correspond with the verses, though not always. For the most part, each strophe represents a single unit of thought, though the principle of enjambment sometimes applies to carry the thought across a prosodic boundary.

Logoprosodic analysis reveals that the boundaries of all subunits in the prosodic structure of Nahum are marked in terms of word count by multiples of the four primary compositional numbers (**17**, **23**, **26**, and **32**) in one or more of three categories: total word count, words before *ʾaṭnaḥ*, and words after *ʾaṭnaḥ*. In the analysis presented here, these numbers make up the last three columns of numbers in the right-hand margin. The first of these columns (column 3) is the total word count, which is the sum of the numbers in the fourth and fifth columns (the number of words before and after *ʾaṭnaḥ*).

Pairs of strophes are normally arranged around a central "core" strophe, which is occasionally ternary in structure (that is, in three parts), as in Nahum 2:5–7 [4–6] and 3:17. Within each central strophe there is normally a "meaningful center," often at the level of both word count and letter count. By "meaningful center" I mean a statement that makes sense consisting of an exact number of words or letters arranged on either side of the "absolute center" of that prosodic unit.

The strophes are grouped into larger structures, which I call "cantos," though I define this term somewhat differently from scholars in the Kampen school (cf. van der Meer and de Moor 1988). Nahum has seven cantos, as follows:

| | | | |
|---|---|---|---|
| 1. | 1:1–10 | (9.4).(5.5).(4.4).(4.4).(4.4).(5.5).(4.9) | The Psalm of Nahum: YHWH's Vengeance |
| 2. | 1:11–14 | (4.4).(5.5).(4.4) | The Defeat of Belial |
| 3. | 2:1–11 | (5.4).(7.6).(4.4).(6.6.6).(4.4).(6.7).(4.5) | The Sack of Nineveh |
| 4. | 2:11–14 | {5.4}.(4.4).(4.4).(4.5) | Dirge on the Lions' Den |
| 5. | 3:1–7 | (3.4).(3.3).(4.5).(4.4).(5.4).(3.3).(4.3) | Taunt: Nineveh's Shame Will Be Seen by the Nations |
| 6. | 3:8–13 | (4.5).(3.3).(3.3).(2.2).(3.3).(3.3).(5.4) | Taunt: Like Thebes, Nineveh Will Be Sacked |
| 7. | 3:14–19 | (4.4).(2.2).(4.4).(4.2.4).(4.4).(2.2).(4.4) | The Locust Dirge: An Image of Imminent Ruin |

Five of the seven cantos have seven strophes, but they range from 46 to 78 SAS units. The second canto (1:11–14, Column 3), which has **26 SAS units** arranged in three strophes [(4.4).(5.5).(4.4)], is a relatively short transitional canto that is closely tied to what precedes and follows. Thus 1:9c–2:1 [1:15] constitutes a unit of another sort with its two references to Belial within a five-part concentric strophic structure. Nahum 1:11 is closely tied to 1:1–10 in a different way, as suggested by the positioning of the *setuma* layout marker after 1:11. The fourth canto, which is also relatively brief, with **34 SAS units** arranged in four strophes, constitutes the center of Nahum in terms of the menorah structure of the seven cantos. The opening verse here (2:11 [10] functions both as the concluding strophe of the third canto (2:1–11 [1:15–2:10]) and as the opening strophe of the fourth canto (2:11–14 [10–13]) and actually functions as the structural center of the book of Nahum as a whole on other grounds. It is also closely tied to 1:9–10 of the opening canto (1:1–10). The sixth canto has an extremely short center, which is framed on either side by double repetition of the emphasizing particle *gam*. This canto has **46** (= **23** × 2) SAS units.

A further complexity in the prosodic structure of Hebrew poetry is the fact that groupings of SAS units are arranged in larger musical phrases, which we call briques (or primary SAS units). In Nahum, 84.5 percent of these units have *sillûq*, *ʾatnah*, or the accent *zaqēp qatôn* at their boundaries. The briques are grouped into larger units called versets, which consist of dyads or triads plus the pivot, if one is present. A verset may also consist of a quatrain (a pair of dyads), which is often synonymous with a verse as marked in the Masoretic tradition (that is, what lies between two successive occurrences of *sōp̄ pasûq*, the end-of-verse marker). It is often difficult to distinguish between two adjacent dyads as two versets and a quatrain as a single verset. One key in making this distinction is whether the boundary between the two dyads is marked in terms of word count. A second criterion is whether the pair of dyads presents two parallel thoughts (that is, two versets) or a continuation of the same thought in a manner that indicates parallelism on a higher level in terms of balance in mora count within a two-part quatrain (that is, a pair of dyads as a single verset).

## THE INTERPRETATION OF NAHUM IN HISTORY

Interpretation of the book of Nahum through the centuries has focused on the need to trust God in the presence of tyranny. YHWH remains a dependable refuge for the people of Israel in the face of national injustice, whether at the hands of Assyria, Babylon, or Rome. Within the mainstream of interpretation, most scholars conclude that even the most powerful oppressor will ultimately be overthrown.

### Jonah and Nahum as
### Midrashic Reflection on Exodus 34:6–7

Jonah and Nahum may be read as midrashic reflection on the so-called attribute formula in Exodus 34:6–7, with Jonah focusing on God's compassion and Nahum on God's anger. As Fishbane observes (1985: vii–viii), original terms of compassion are transformed in Nahum into terms of violence and war (see also Spiekermann 1990: 1–18). The phrase "who maintains kindness (*nōṣēr*)" becomes "who rages (*nōṭēr*) against his enemies" (cf. Leviticus 19:18); "great in kindness (*rab̲ ḥesed*)" becomes "mighty in power (*gād̲ōl kōaḥ*)"; and "slow to anger (*'erek 'appayim*)," which appears in both contexts, takes on the meaning of "long of anger" in Nahum. In short, the book may be read as a reinterpretation of a central text in the Torah in a moment of need so far as Israel's national security is concerned.

Though YHWH is merciful and slow to anger, this time his patience toward those who flout him has run short. Nahum focuses on one aspect of God's character, while Jonah portrays the opposite—toward the same evil city of Nineveh. Both aspects are essential for an understanding of God's nature. Moreover, a close reading of Nahum reveals that both aspects are found here as well. Though the positive side of God's character is muted in Nahum, it is by no means absent. Besides the meaning of Nahum's name as "compassionated," we read that "YHWH is slow to anger" (1:3) and "a refuge in times of trouble" (1:7).

## Early Interpretation of Nahum in Judaism and Christianity

In the first century BCE, the community at Qumran apparently held the book of Nahum in high esteem. A number of the Psalms of Thanksgiving (1QH) show the influence of the language of the hymn in Nahum 1:2–10 (see Spronk 1997: 16–17). Moreover, the authors of the Dead Sea Scrolls produced a commentary on Nahum, the Qumran pesher 4QpNah (4Q169), which reads the book as a prediction of impending disaster for their opponents (Horgan 1979: 158–59; Doudna 2001: 601–25).

One Greek tradition of Tobit 14.4 (Codex Sinaiticus), which has its fictional setting in Nineveh, cites the prediction of Nineveh's fall by Nahum (elsewhere by Jonah) as fulfilled by Nebuchadnezzar and Ahasuerus (both names used anachronistically). This same understanding of the text as distant prophetic prediction subsequently fulfilled is found in Josephus (*Ant.* 9.11.3). The Aramaic Targum of Nahum emphasizes God's faithfulness to his people while looking to the ultimate destruction of the nations who have ravaged Israel and its Temple. Nahum is here presented as later than Jonah, which reflects the Hebrew ordering of the individual books within the Book of the Twelve Prophets.

Nahum is quoted only once in the New Testament (Romans 10:15; cf. Nahum 1:15, Isaiah 52:7); though the description of the whore of Babylon in Revelation 17:2 may contain an allusion to Nahum 3:4 (see Coggins 1985: 14). Among the Church Fathers, the book is cited infrequently: by Tertullian (twice), Clement of Alexandria (once), Eusebius (eight times), Epiphanius (ca. 315–403; five times), Cyril (twice), Hippolytus Romanus (ca. 170–ca. 236; twice), Melito of Sardis (once), and John Chrysostom (twice). Jerome presents a spiritual interpretation in which the book speaks of the certain destruction of those who oppose God and reject the church (J. Kelly 1975: 163–66).

Josephus mistakenly places Nahum in the context of the eighth-century prophets and then quotes Nahum 2:8–13 verbatim (*Ant.* ix.11.3). According to Coggins (1985: 15), this is the only extended quotation from the Old Testament to be found in Josephus. Coggins (1985: 14) also notes the curious fact that this particular passage in Nahum is also found in the Qumran fragment, which the Qumran commentary applies to rulers of the second century BCE.

The book of Nahum receives relatively little attention in early Jewish scholarship, with eight references in the Babylonian Talmud and thirty-one in Midrash Rabbah. The interpretation of the medieval exegetes Rashi (d. 1105), Ibn Ezra (d. 1167), and Kimchi (d. 1235) focused on the judgment of God on Israel's national enemies (see Rosenberg 1988; Gordon and Cathcart 1989).

Tanhum (d. 1291), who is often compared to Ibn Ezra, discussed various traditional Jewish sources and explains his preferences.

## Interpretation of Nahum from ca. 1500 to 1800 CE

Isaac Abarbanel (d. 1508) wrote an extensive body of biblical commentary that ranks among the classic works in Jewish biblical scholarship. His work is notable for its interpretation of the Bible in terms of its historical and social background and for his liberal quotation of Christian commentaries. His own writings were in turn condensed and translated by Christian scholars of the following two centuries (personal communication from Aron Pinker, from his forthcoming commentary on Nahum to be published by BIBAL Press).

Like the mainstream of Jewish exegetes before him, Martin Luther (1525) assumed a historical approach while at the same time linking the days of Nahum to his own situation, in the spirit of the Nahum Pesher at Qumran. Note, in particular, the reference cited by Spronk (1997: 17): "Also today the pope is being destroyed by the word of God." Nahum is taken as a contemporary of Isaiah, who spoke in light of the suffering of Judah under Sennacherib, the preservation of a righteous remnant, and the coming destruction of Nineveh. Thus Nahum, true to the meaning of his name, brought "comfort" to God's people in time of need. Few interpreters have expressed the essential message of Nahum more clearly than Luther when he wrote: "The book teaches us to trust God and to believe, especially when we despair of all human help, human powers, and counsel, that the Lord stands by those who are His, shields His own against all attacks of the enemy, be they ever so powerful" (taken from W. A. Maier 1959: 86).

Although Calvin's commentary is more detailed, it is also theological in orientation and largely grammatical and historical in focus. A characteristic quotation from Calvin declares that Nahum's message "teaches us in general, that the ungodly, whenever they harass the Church, not only do wrong to men, but also fight with God himself; for He so connects us with himself, that all who hurt us touch the apple of his eye. . . . We may then gather invaluable comfort from these words; for we can fully and boldly set up this shield against our enemies" (taken from Spronk 1997: 17).

Yehiel Altshuler (1753) completed the commentary begun by his father David Altshuler, which is divided into explanation of content and explanation of words. Nahum plays a prominent role in the theory of Kalinsky (1748), which posits two different destructions of Nineveh based on reports of Greek writers, especially Diodorus Siculus. This theory influenced Michaelis and others but was soon overtaken by archaeological facts after the discovery of ancient Nineveh at Tell Küyünjik in the nineteenth century.

## Interpretation of Nahum in the Nineteenth Century

Archaeology provided a significant impulse to the study of Nahum, which resulted in the works of Strauss (1853, 1855), Breiteneicher (1861), Vernier (1891), Billerbeck/Jeremias (1895), and Feuchtwang (1897) and to sermons and other edifying works pointing out the fulfillment of Nahum's prophecy (see Keith 1853; Oosterzee 1856; Spurgeon 1981 [reprint]).

Bishop Robert Lowth (1839: 281) singled out the book of Nahum for its aesthetic brilliance. With the subsequent development of historical criticism in the nineteenth century, attention shifted to the question of the precise historical and geographical origin of the book as the key to its interpretation. Supposed reference to the invasion of Sennacherib and linguistic ties to Isaiah led some to posit a date late in the reign of Hezekiah. But the discovery that Thebes fell to Assyria in 663 BCE (see Nahum 3:8–10) led scholars to suggest an earlier date of composition, with most critical scholars arguing for a setting close to the actual fall of Nineveh in 612 BCE.

Until 1893, no one doubted the unity of Nahum. According to G. A. Smith (1928: 81), Kuenen wrote in 1889 that "Nahum's prophecy is a whole," and in 1892 Wellhausen described Nahum 1 as an introduction that leads "in no awkward way to the proper subject of the prophecy." Meanwhile, however, an apparent acrostic poem in 1:2–10 was discovered that became the focus of numerous studies. G. Frohnmeyer, who discovered the acrostic pattern, made no claim for a complete acrostic as such but simply noted that the sequence of the letters of the alphabet influenced the arrangement of the prophet's thought in Nahum 1:3–7 (see Delitzsch 1867: 107). The first detailed study of this acrostic pattern appeared in 1880, shortly after the death of Frohnmeyer, when G. Bickell (1880) found the entire alphabet in Nahum 1: 2–10, which he reconstructed in 16 bicola in a clever manner. Bickell was an advocate of the so-called syllabic theory of Hebrew meter of that time, which was subsequently challenged by Gunkel (1893), who saw the key to Hebrew meter in the number of word stresses rather than in syllable count. In 1894, Bickell modified his position, accepting Gunkel's view that the acrostic poem continued throughout Nahum 1:2–2:3 and that it was a postexilic eschatological poem secondarily incorporated into the earlier work of the prophet Nahum. Gunkel reconstructed a series of twenty-three "distichs" in which he found twenty of the twenty-two successive letters of an alphabetical acrostic. Gunkel (1893: 223–25) also found what he considered the probable name of the author, Shobai (cf. Ezra 2:42; Nehemiah 7:45; 2 Samuel 17:27). Bickell continued to hold to his "syllabic theory," however, though the "accentual theory" eventually carried the day, gaining wide acceptance, especially as later modified by Sievers (1901–7). In 1895, Gunkel restated his position, adopting some of Bickell's suggestions and filling in some of the gaps he had left in his original reconstruction (102–3). Though Wellhausen (1898) insisted that the reconstructions of both Bickell and Gunkel must be rejected as total failures, scholarly attempts to find the rest of the alphabetic sequence continued to appear.

## Interpretation of Nahum in the Twentieth Century and Beyond

W. R. Arnold (1901: 256) concluded that only a "distorted fragment of an alphabetic poem" in 1:2–10 and 12b remains, with 16 of the 22 letters accounted for. Arnold was correct in recognizing that the original acrostic pattern had been "bent" to a new purpose, but his conclusions about the author must be rejected. Arnold concluded that the poem was supplied by "a late redactor, of little intelligence, resourcefulness, and taste," whose "contribution consists of (1) a slightly distorted fragment (about two-thirds) of an alphabetical poem, (2) some *memoriter* quotations from the prophetic writings, and (3) a few original reflections of the redactor" (256). These remarks tell us more about Arnold and the time in which he wrote than they do about the text of Nahum.

Budde (1901b) concluded that there was once a complete acrostic, but he noted that any attempt to restore it in its entirety "cannot be rewarded with full success" (see G. A. Smith 1928: 83; so also Nowack 1922). Marti (1903), Haupt (1907b), and J. M. P. Smith (1911) carried the alphabetic sequence through the letter *samech* and 1:10. Guthe (1923) suggested the possibility that the acrostic pattern was superimposed by a later scribe whose efforts failed when he reached 1:8 and the letter *kaph*.

Haupt (1907b: 18) explained the omission of the last seven lines (ע through ת) as "not quoted by the compiler of this festal liturgy for the celebration of Nikanor's Day, because they did not suit his purpose." Like Wellhausen before him, Humbert (1926: 267) insisted that the acrostic is limited to 1:2–8 and that it contains precisely half of the Hebrew alphabet. He cited as a parallel text Psalm 8, which also ends with the letter כ to form half an acrostic, and also cited the work of I. Elbogen for further examples of incomplete acrostics in Jewish poetic liturgy.

Although many interpreters continued to read the book as witnessing to God's just rule in history, others noted the nonreligious character of the poetry in Nahum 2–3 and the prophet's failure to address the sins of Judah. Consequently, some scholars judged Nahum as a nationalistic prophet, perhaps even allied with the "false prophets" condemned by Jeremiah (J. M. P. Smith 1911). Such views continue to be held in some circles.

Haupt (1907b) argued that the book of Nahum was not prophecy at all but rather the festival liturgy composed for the celebration of the Day of Nikanor on the 13th day of Adar, 161 BCE. Though the Maccabean date was subsequently rejected in light of the discovery of the Dead Sea Scroll commentary on Nahum, the idea that the book was a festival liturgy had profound influence in academic circles. In 1926 Humbert argued that the book was a prophetic liturgy used at the New Year festival in Jerusalem in 612 BCE to celebrate the fall of Nineveh. And in 1946 Haldar argued that it was the work of cultic prophets who used the language of ritual combat in the New Year festival as a curse on Israel's political enemies, the Assyrians.

Haldar (1947: 11) anticipated recent attempts to resolve the impasse in the study of Hebrew prosody in light of the Ugaritic texts. As he put it, "The poetic structure of Ugaritic deserves a detailed investigation, which . . . would correct some of the current misconceptions regarding Hebrew poetry" (quotation from Gordon 1940: 79).

My first study of the acrostic hymn in Nahum 1 was based on the theory of syllable count proposed by F. M. Cross and D. N. Freedman (Christensen 1975b). This study brought research on the acrostic of Nahum around full cycle and laid the groundwork for the logoprosodic analysis presented in this commentary. In the first detailed study of Nahum 1 in 1880, Bickell advanced a "syllabic theory" and turned to the study of acrostic poems as an obvious place to test his hypothesis. Though acrostics are certainly not typical of Hebrew poetry, they do present an objective control for the analysis of prosodic structure. Bickell's approach to the Hebrew text was arbitrary, however, and, like his opponents who favored the "accentual theory," he resorted to frequent and sometimes radical conjectural emendation. This arbitrariness subsequently led Nyberg (1941: 38–43), and Haldar after him (1947: 11), to stress most emphatically the impossibility of textual emendation on the basis of metrics.

Subsequent studies placed the book of Nahum in the sphere of international politics in premonarchic Israel, as reflected in the larger tradition of oracles against foreign nations in the prophetic literature. Perhaps the most attractive hypothesis along these lines was made in 1975 by Watts, who suggested that Nahum, along with Habakkuk and Obadiah, was a liturgical expression of foreign prophecies that was part of the "Day of YHWH" section of the Royal Zion Festival in ancient Jerusalem. Nonetheless, Eaton (1981: 14–21) has shown that there is no simple distinction between so-called cultic and noncultic prophecy in ancient Israel.

The study of Nahum in relation to holy war in ancient Israel raises new questions. Cathcart (1975) and I (1975a: 166–75) make a distinction between holy war as a military institution and the "wars of YHWH," which reflect symbolic speech in reference to cultic events in the worship experience of ancient Israel. This distinction points the way toward an important new impulse in the study of Nahum—namely, the shift from attempts to recover the historical setting that produced the book to a focus on the received literary text itself within the canonical process that produced the Book of the Twelve Prophets as one of four primary sections of the Latter Prophets (see Nogalski 1993a, 1993b, 1993c).

Nahum is to be read in conjunction with other oracles against foreign nations, particularly those of Isaiah 13–23, as Coggins has shown (1982: 7794). The first heading, *maśśāʾ Nînəwēh* (Nahum 1:1a), may well be an invitation to associate the book with this Isaiah material. The book may also be interpreted in relation to the wider oral and literary traditions of Hebrew prophecy (Coggins 1982: 79–85). Moreover, as Childs argues (1979: 440–46), its final form testifies to God's ultimate triumph over all foes. He believes that traditional critical assessments miss the authoritative hermeneutical role of this "canonical shaping."

In its poetic form the book of Nahum has no superior within the prophetic literature of the Tanakh. The vivid and rapid succession of images gives it a peculiar power. It delineates the swift and unerring execution of divine fury against the merciless foes of God and of God's people. At the same time, it also points rather sharply to God as the sure refuge and security of those who obey and trust him. Careful analysis of the poetry in Nahum reveals an elegant literary structure; the best way to explain its remarkable structural symmetry is to posit musical influence (Christensen 1989a: 159–69).

Floyd (1994) argues that the hypothesis of an acrostic in Nahum 1:2–8 should be discarded altogether. Spronk (1998) argues against Floyd's conclusions on stylistic grounds. Bliese (1995) tries to show the original unity of the acrostic and the entire book of Nahum in terms of a detailed analysis of what he calls "a cryptic chiastic acrostic" on metrical grounds. Weigl (2001: 87) sides with Floyd on the matter of the presumed acrostic and suggests that the task of interpretation should not be concerned with the "cryptic messages" of poetic structures.

An increasing number of studies on poetic devices and imagery suggest that Nahum is valued for its brilliance in literary style even more today than in times past, even to the point where difficult texts are seen to be the result of the "originality of the poet and not . . . a corruption of the text" (Spronk 1997: 6; see also Charles 1989 and Patterson and Travers 1990, references taken from Weigl 2001: 87). The poet used a wide range of poetic devices, including alliteration, chiastic and envelope structures, and so on (see Allis 1955; Patterson and Travers 1988 and 1990; and the many references to Nahum by Watson 1986). The author coined new words and introduced the name acrostic and the telestic form in Hebrew literature (see Spronk 1997: 6). The many direct and indirect references to Assyrian treaty texts and royal annals indicate that Nahum was familiar with this literature (Cathcart 1973a; Machinist 1983: 735–36; Johnston 1992: 330–98). Moreover, Gunkel (1893, 1895) and many scholars after him have noted affinities with the language of the Psalms, and others find similar affinities with the words of Isaiah (Kleinert 1910: 520–21; Armerding 1985: 453–55; Spronk 1997: 7–8).

An original worship setting or subsequent use of the book in liturgical contexts cannot be ruled out. Nonetheless, the book is to be read within the larger literary context of the Book of the Twelve Prophets as a whole. We have here an example of prophecy with a didactic purpose, much of which is hidden from the view of the casual reader. One needs to know something of the language and literary culture of ancient Israel within the context of scribal activity in the ancient world to read Nahum with understanding.

Current predilection for a "synchronic" reading of the book of Nahum reflects the same shifting methodological paradigms that can be observed in all fields of Old Testament exegesis (Weigl 2001: 88). Scholarly dispute on the proper methodological stance has led to an impasse of sorts. On the one hand, we find outright rejection of traditional literary criticism in the refusal to consider any secondary editorial activity, with open refutation of the idea of successive growth of the biblical text through time in the traditional redactional model (Longman 1993: 769). This is essentially the conclusion reached in this commentary as well. At the same time, traditional dissection of the text into the smallest possible literary units in an attempt to understand the guiding principles of the editor(s) continues in some circles (Seybold 1989a, 1991; Hieke 1993a, 1993b; Lescow 1995). As Weigl (2001: 88–89) notes, two basic principles stand behind this methodology: "First, the idea that the prophet himself uttered only short oracles using various forms of prophetic speech which later necessitated extensive editorial activity; and second, a profound mistrust of the Masoretic tradition of the Hebrew text." Spronk (1995a: 167) correctly insists that the synchronic and diachronic points of view "seem to be totally incompatible."

Weigl (2001: 89) is probably correct in his assessment that "the history of research on the book of Nahum . . . in the 1990s will be remembered for the maintenance of embattled positions, as well as for attempts to shake off totally more than a century of historical-critical research, without much dialogue between the proponents of the seemingly incompatible methodological approaches." In spite of some efforts on the part of Sweeney (1992), Becking (1993, 1995a, 1996), and Spronk (1995a, 1995b, 1997), little has been done to reconcile the differences. This commentary may contribute something of worth on this issue by providing a different stance from which to view the end product of that editorial process in terms of authorial design in the numerical (and musical) composition of Nahum within the context of the Book of the Twelve Prophets as a whole.

## ARCHAEOMUSICOLOGY
## AND THE STUDY OF NAHUM

Current research in the cosmology and mythology of the ancient Middle East, from ancient Vedic texts to detailed mathematical puzzles in Plato's Dialogues (as well as in both testaments of the Bible and extending into the common era in various circles), demonstrates how prevalent apparent "cryptic" information was in ancient texts and why (McClain 1976, 1978, 1981, 2002, 2004; Crickmore 2003; Bremer 2005; on the subject of archaeomusicology, see Dumbrill 1998). What appears hidden and obscure to modern eyes was not necessarily perceived that way in antiquity, at least in terms of matrix arithmetic and musical metaphor in relation to concepts developed from the tuning of musical instruments. Nahum is the product of a skilled scribal craftsman. Within ancient Israel, scribes adapted established principles to their own ends in the numerical (and musical) composition of the biblical text, which was intended from the outset to be recited as sacred Scripture.

McClain (1976: 129–52; 1981: 125–45) argues that the protoscience of ancient harmonics developed initially as "Sumerian grain piles" and eventually became Mesopotamian "holy mountains" limited to multiplicative products of 2, 3, and 5; it was acquired by Jewish scribes in Babylon in highly sophisticated forms. The "pebble mountains" he posits in his understanding of matrix arithmetic are essentially multiplication tables of the numbers 3 and 5, which functioned as an early form of logarithmic reflection on the phenomenon of tones in the theoretical understanding of music. His work develops musical insights of Ernst Levy and Siegmund Levarie into Pythagoreanism in general and the work of Plato in particular. Pythagorean thought has its origins in ancient Mesopotamia and Egypt, particularly in Babylon of the sixth century BCE, where it shaped biblical thought within Jewish circles in a different direction.

The system of musical metaphor was subsequently described in some detail by Plato. Nonetheless, it is still not commonly known in the mainstream of classical studies or in the field of biblical studies due to lack of understanding of the field of musicology (see McClain 1978). Sumerian genius is displayed in Plato's "reduced" matrices, in which factors of 2 are suppressed until the total tonal possibilities are isolated, for in musicology all doubling is "octave equivalence" or "matrix identity" (and indicated by the repetition of "tone names"). Greek tetrachord theory, profoundly influenced by Aristoxenus (fl.

fourth century BCE), deliberately destroyed this initial Sumerian "simplicity," uncovered by Plato's realization that "symbolic marriages" are made in the *prime* of life (McClain, personal communication).

The matrix is essentially a multiplication table of "tone numbers" in which the "twin" forces of the enemy (paired base 60 reciprocals) are utterly defeated by YHWH's "ambidextrous" fighters in base 10 arithmetic, as he "overturns" the enemy in the marvelous theological world of Jewish matrix arithmetic. It is not yet clear how this system of thought eventually disappeared within the mainstream of Jewish and Christian thought. It was well understood by Philo (d. 40 CE) and apparently by the authors of the Greek New Testament, especially in the book of Revelation (McClain 1976: 107–28), and it was apparently still understood, at least in part, by the medieval Jewish scholar Rashi (d. 1105 CE).

McClain sees the book of Nahum as an exercise in literary and musical metaphor in praise of the Hebrew matrix over its predecessors in Mesopotamia. The vivid metaphors in Nahum have symbolic tonal "cosmological" meaning that survives translation of the Hebrew text in any language. Nahum is a powerful reminder of YHWH's absolute power over the extravagant and misaligned forces of Nineveh that fail to meet the musical standards of either Marduk's throne in Figure 1 or the more severe limitations of YHWH's "Magen David," the familiar six-pointed star associated with Judaism, seen in Figure 2. YHWH's pride is in the "arithmetical reductionism" of the Hebrew matrix from that of its immediate predecessor, the Marduk matrix (McClain 1976: 77, Chart 15).

El Shaddai (the "Mountain God" in Exodus 6:3), whose name in Hebrew sums to 345 (= 1 + 30 + 300 + 4 + 10) in agreement with Plato's formula of "4:3 mated with 5" (McClain 1978: 18) generalizes the formula while removing *any* integer ceiling whatever. Factors of 3 increase from left to right as factors of 5 increase vertically to Marduk's limit; then all are doubled sufficiently to locate the "throne" as the largest integer and the fourth value in the eighth row. Rotation of the matrix by 180 degrees aligns paired arithmetical reciprocals at equal distances on all rays through the throne, symbolized here, as pitch class "D," as universal tonic and generalized cosmological *geometric mean*. Bible authors suppress most details except the flood depth of 15 units (Genesis 7:20). Hindu sources preserve both the limit of 8,640,000,000 and its half at 4,320,000,000 as years in the Brahma and Kalpa cycles. In the Bible the matrix is glossed eloquently as the "Tower of Babel," destroyed to contain human arrogance. Under the ecumenism of the Prophets, Judaic Christianity multiplied this ancient Babylonian limit by 200 into the "cube" of New Jerusalem as $12,000^3 = 1,728,000,000,000$ for a Savior who symbolically atones for the contradictory meanings that surface for incommensurable ratios in harmonic theory. See "Marduk's throne" in Figure 1.

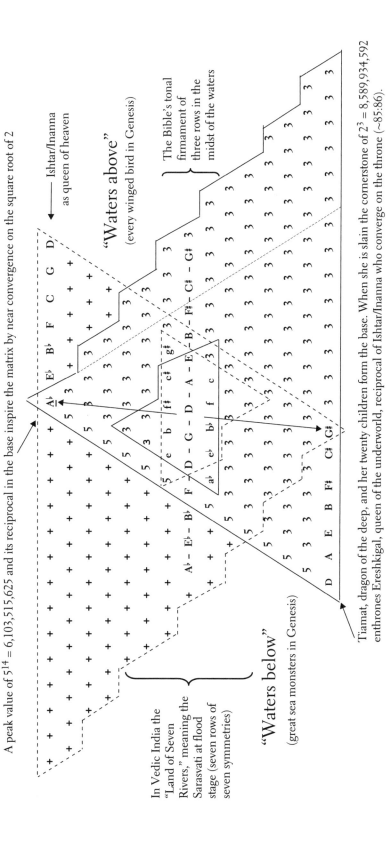

Figure 1. The Marduk / El Shaddai "universal flood" matrix for 8,640,000,000 = $2^{12}3^5 5^7$.

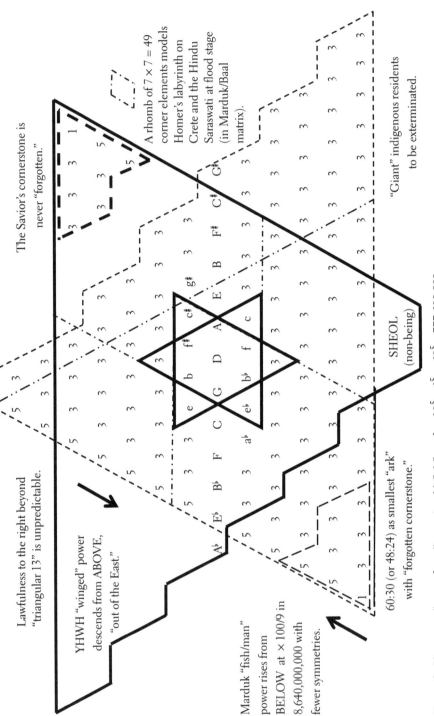

The Savior's cornerstone is never "forgotten."

A rhomb of $7 \times 7 = 49$ corner elements models Homer's labyrinth on Crete and the Hindu Saraswati at flood stage (in Marduk/Baal matrix).

"Giant" indigenous residents to be exterminated.

Lawfulness to the right beyond "triangular 13" is unpredictable.

YHWH "winged" power descends from ABOVE, "out of the East."

Marduk "fish/man" power rises from BELOW at $\times 100/9$ in 8,640,000,000 with fewer symmetries.

SHEOL, (non-being)

60:30 (or 48:24) as smallest "ark" with "forgotten cornerstone."

Figure 2. YHWH as a "man of war," meaning 10.5.6.5 read as $10^5 \times 6^5 = 60^5 = 777,600,000$.

The Marduk / El Shaddai / Platonic "pentatonic" throne, which is pictured as a "net of the gods" 30, 40, 50, and 60 (McClain 1978: 18) and described as a "seat with a back support" (Heidel 1942: 48, Tablet VI, line 53) to honor Marduk, is rejected by Judaism in favor of a more modest throne of much greater power under Yhwh (displayed in Figure 2). Marduk calls on "thirteen winds" to inflate Tiamat and her children to twenty-one elements of enormous size before he kills her and slices her lengthwise "like a fish for drying" to make *above* and *below* nearly coincide on their seventh tones. Only the basic thirteen tones of the spiral of fifths and fourths are notated here. The Bible and Jewish Midrash preserve the memory of Behemoth and Leviathan from this "flood" mythology, inspired by the elusive square root of 2 required for the precise middle of an octave 2:1.

The unpronounceable tetragrammaton for Yhwh as 10.5.6.5 is interpreted as $10^5 \times 6^5 = 60^5$ in agreement with Apollo (at Delphi) as "E," meaning "5" ($= 60^5$) in base 60 arithmetic. This is the special "tribal" name in which the four number values can be manipulated to dethrone all older ancient deities and also to correct "throne" values to near perfection with modern equal temperament while avoiding internal commas in the Marduk / El Shaddai / Platonic throne of Figure 1. This matrix achieves five pairs of invariant symmetries on either side of tone D in the central horizontal axis, plus an asymmetric twelfth tone (G-sharp, in the "tail") that becomes A-flat and thirteenth (but really "first" in the complete system) under reciprocation; thus the comma never arises between them. This artful construction makes Apollo "far-shooter" in Greece, and in Israel it ensures Yhwh's superiority over all earlier conceptions. Prime factors of 3 and 5 are displayed (as "reduced" integers) except where applicable as pitch names. The five pairs of symmetries from E-flat to C-sharp are defined by Abram's reciprocal value of $243 = 3^5$ as he is sent to "explore the Holy Land" of perfect inverse symmetry, indifferent to both "right and left" and "up and down." Jacob's family is elevated to the "throne" as "fewest of all peoples" but "leaders of millions."

The Yhwh matrix, like that of Marduk, is a two-dimensional grid that is compressed to only 9 *percent* of the latter's value of 8,640,000,000 but contains more internally paired symmetries—ten instead of six on the central axis, with forty-one pairs surrounding the self-symmetric throne on D. (Canaanite mythology treated the bottom row as "muck" or mud; Sumer considered the bottom row as an underworld desert beneath the freshwater ocean under the earth. It was dark, dusty, and unpleasant.) This matrix also appears to model Priam's tower at Troy for Homer, besieged by the Greeks assaulting with Marduk extravagance, illustrating the Platonic principle that a city that is "more of unity" is impregnable except from within. Judaism is concerned to build "a watchtower in the soul" as a moral example for all mankind. From present evidence, it is not possible to judge how well Athens and Jerusalem may have understood what each other was doing, but New Testament narrative must be assumed to be fully informed by Greek philosophy and science. Platonic principles decode Revelation most easily because of the wealth of deeply correlated detail (see McClain 1976: 107–28).

In base 60 science the formula reads 777,600,000, but the 777 here in base 10 is a humorous allusion to the 21 (= $3 \times 7$) elements in the extravagant base of the Marduk / El Shaddai matrix. Jewish authors never pretend that more than about 600,000 "brick makers" are fleeing Pharaoh's service in this primitive arithmetic, and only two survive to enter the Promised Land with 40,000 young men who mature "in the wilderness." That adventure must be displayed separately. "Sheol" simply lies "outside the number field" in a realm of "non-being." The "shoulders" on the matrix give its inversion the optical illusion of a "great eagle" watching over his people.

The index limit for the matrix of Nineveh is given in the concluding verse of Jonah, which reads: "As for me, should I not have compassion on Nineveh, that Great City, which has in it more than 120,000 humans, who cannot discern between their right and their left" (Jonah 4:11). The model of Nineveh is formed by building the matrix for 120,000 as the multiplication table for $3 \times 5$ that produces male "fighting men." To that limit there are exactly 48 counters in the matrix, which is also the number of verses in Jonah. YHWH's numerical value as 10.5.6.5 sums to 26, and 120,000 is $2^6$ (= 64) $\times$ 1875. His great power (*dynamis*) is exponential power. This "reduced matrix" for 120,000 (Figure 3) exposes Abram, whose Hebrew letters sum to 243 [= 1 + 2 + 200 + 40], as the first "ambidextrous" explorer of the Holy Land. The ten paired symmetries on either side of Abram in the bottom row are the maximum possible in any twelve-tone tuning system limited to rational numbers.

The next step in the process of reading the matrix is to double all "male, fighting men" to the limit of 120,000 within its octave half at 60,000 (Figure 4). The ascent along the left is accomplished by quintupling (doubling each integer twice and adding it to itself to determine the next). Progress to the right is achieved by tripling (doubling each integer in succession and adding it to itself). For many purposes in studying tonal consequences, no further arithmetic is required. Rotation of the matrix exposes the tonal meanings that survive arithmetical reciprocation. This initial multiplication was achieved by means of "Egyptian duplatio" of very great antiquity, and it remains a ready tool for exhausting tonal patterns within a given numerical limit. Reciprocation, however, is symmetric around $1875 \times 64 = 120,000$ as pitch class D and constant reference, and base 60 provides a new set of "twin" values that are suppressed here. Davidic musicology, instead, merely assumes double meanings and "maps" reciprocals by rotating the matrix 180 degrees.

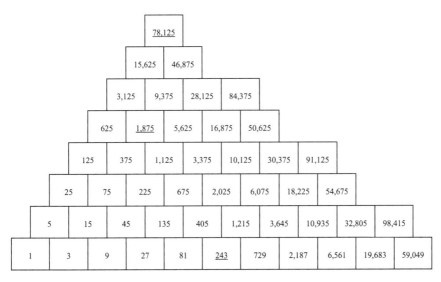

Figure 3. The "reduced" Nineveh matrix for 120,000 (= 64 × 1875) with 48 counters.

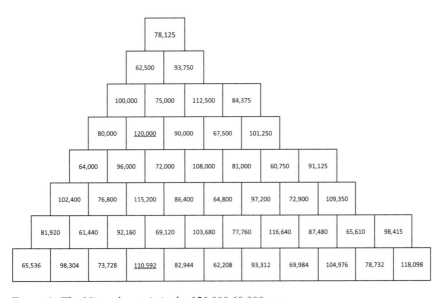

Figure 4. The Nineveh matrix in the 120,000:60,000 octave.

Only the fourth row, containing the "index" (120,000), and its immediate neighbors above and below are relevant to tuning theory. The first three rows are the "waters below," and rows 7 and 8 belong to the sky, the "waters above," where birds "swim" above this "firmament" (rows 4, 5, and 6 in this context). Other features of the matrix are as follows:

1. In row 3, the "head" digits of the first seven numbers (1024 to 729) "seal" the seven "white-key" heptatonic scales in the smallest integers for their characteristic *modal* octaves (on F C G D A E B, in that order). Here they are inflated by common factors of 100 (4 × 25 [Jonah's initial value as "dove"]).

2. In row 4, the "head" digits of the first five numbers (64 to 81) "seal" the five pentatonic modal patterns as "leaders of thousands" (great sea monsters in this context), and 108 is the favored Buddhist and Chinese pentatonic seal.

3. In row 5, the first four values display the index limit of 120,000 framed by the harmonic means 80,000 and 90,000 in the octave 120,000: 60,000. They constitute the basic musical proportion of 12:9::8:6, expanded here by David's minimal "ten thousands" and required for temperament because of restrictions in the fourth value (67,500) that prove determinate.

4. The peak offers an improved square root of 2 in relation to the fourth counter in the base, reducing the Marduk peak in Figure 1 to the square root of its original flood value as $5^{14}$. The number 110,592/78,125 is a slightly excessive Marduk square root of 2 as 1.4155 and is admittedly better than the simpler one of 7/5 = 1.4 but inferior to the inferred Jesus "good shepherd" ratio of 99/70 = 1.4142. Jewish concern is not with "power" but with "wisdom," displayed here to mock Marduk with more practical "Diophantine approximations."

With a little imagination, we can see that details in the story of Jonah take on fresh perspective in the matrix model (Figure 5). The prophet Jonah (with an index limit of 48) is an adaptation of the matrix on "god 50" (Ellil/Enlil) in Mesopotamian mythology—an active leader in the base 60 octave 2:1 = 60:30. This goes back ultimately to ancient Sumer, where it is mythologized in the Gilgamesh epic. It is subsequently compressed by Plato to "4:3 mated with the 5." Within the more severe limit of 48, the first counter in the third row cannot be doubled. Thus Jonah (25) becomes in one sense a sort of "passenger" on the "Jonah boat" (of the octave on 60:30) as it prepares to leave Joppa en route to distant Tarshish in the prophet's flight from the presence of YHWH. At the same time, Jonah is the Jewish version of Ellil/Enlil, god 50 and leader of the Mesopotamian pantheon.

The "throne of heaven" for Jew and Greek alike is the musical mode made famous as Plato's "World Soul," and the wicked "Fish City" of Nineveh is disorganized by everyone's musical standards, which are visible to the eye at first glance when the reader is familiar with either the Marduk throne of Figure 1 or the YHWH throne of Figure 2. Scholars know this mode as a "Just" tuning of the Greek Dorian, Plato's "true Hellenic mode," and usually present it on the "white keys," falling from E to E' or rising inversely from C to C' (through

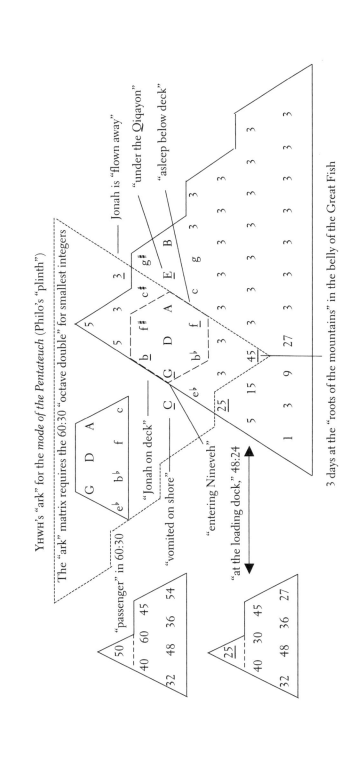

Figure 5. Jonah's travels in the Nineveh matrix for 120,000.

two similar tetrachords at intervals of the *tone, tone, semitone*). It was discovered to be the ancient *mode of the Pentateuch* by Idelsohn (1929) and his colleagues early in the twentieth century. I notate it here as falling D c b-flat A, G f e-flat D together with its opposite, rising D e f-sharp G, A b c-sharp D to make clear that Bible musicology always assumes double meanings so that this *heptatonic* pattern defines *two* modern modes for us.

The only numerical novelty of interest to Judaism in Nineveh's 120,000 people lies in the first four values of row 5 (G D A E) in Figure 5, which are required for a temperament calculation that is of secondary importance to a gracious deity (McClain, personal communication). A great deal of information is suppressed here, which is discussed in detail elsewhere. See the paper titled "Ancient Harmonics and the Book of Jonah" by McClain and Christensen (2005: 55–59).

The smallest numerical "ark" (the so-called "Jonah boat") that defines it to ancient satisfaction is displayed here with Jonah as an interloper because his 25 (= 50-100-200-400 and so on) in a cyclic musicology is "naturally" present in its smallest octave, 60:30, and if the niceties of the tetrachord are ignored under a gracious deity, it can be defined with 48:24. But in *any* matrix Jonah is third in *rising* order from the "cornerstone" below but in falling order from its reciprocal above. Thus Jonah's locus depends on how we view the matrix. The "ark" (Philo fortunately described it as a "plinth") can move right or left and up or down either upright or capsized anywhere *within* the borders of a particular matrix limit but not within Nineveh proper, which is not yet disciplined by YHWH. The limit of 120,000 "seals" four numbers required for a Jewish temperament, but the choir of 144,000 male virgins in Revelation 14:4 "saves" them in a better context. We are looking on a Socratic model, "put in motion to exhibit its powers." Every event is within the same matrix, and it is imagination that must move.

With the "Jonah boat" (Philo's "plinth") sailing at high sea, it is possible to envision the prophet on deck headed west in his flight from YHWH, fleeing in the opposite direction from the city of Nineveh ("Fish City"). Jonah then "went down into the farthest reaches of the vessel" (Jonah 1:5b)—that is, apparently from the first counter in row 6 to the third counter in row 4 (by reciprocation), which is below the water line. There Jonah "went deep into sleep," where the sailors found him in the midst of the storm. When Jonah (50) was subsequently thrown overboard to take his place among the great sea monsters of the lower three rows, he went down to the "roots of the mountains" (2:7) to spend three days and three nights in the "belly/womb" of the Great Fish—presumably to the third counter in row 2 (the number 45). The Hebrew word for fish appears in the feminine form in Jonah 2:2, and the word "belly" may be translated as "womb," for this Great Fish was a place of "rebirth" for Jonah. In short, the "Great Fish" that swallowed Jonah was a friendly one, but Jewish Midrash subsequently transferred him to a less friendly fish, which was pursued by Leviathan.

The Great Fish eventually vomited out Jonah upon the dry land (2:11) outside the city or matrix of Nineveh, on tone C in the axis of rotation—that is, on the first counter to the left of tone G in row 5—to begin the second half of the story, as Jonah entered the city of Nineveh ("Fish City") from the west. Jonah's experience in Nineveh ("Fish City") may be envisioned in a second reading of the same matrix on the octave 120,000:60,000. The matrix reciprocates on tone D (the second counter in row 5) to reveal Nineveh as a journey of three pebbles or days across in any direction. The hexagonal center of Nineveh here anticipates the Magen David form that will be seen in the Nahum matrix of Figure 6.

Jonah began his second three-day journey "by going into the city a journey of one day" (3:4a), apparently to the first counter in row 5, where he delivered his fateful five-word prophecy: "There remain but forty days and Nineveh shall be 'overturned'" (3:4b). Directly in front of Jonah at this point in the matrix, we see the city center on D and the tones D A E B extending to the right (eastward). In the lowest integers, these tones are $1 + 3 + 9 + 27$, and they sum to 40, which constitutes the forty-day forecast, counting from the throne D as "1." According to Jonah 4:5a, the prophet then went "east of the city," presumably to the fourth counter in the fifth row (tone E). There "he built himself a *Sukkah* (booth), and he sat down beneath it in its shade until he should see what would become of the city" (4:5b). In the meantime, God had his own plans, which unfolded in the reciprocation of the matrix that night, for a "*Qiqayon*-tree" was appointed by God "to deliver Jonah from his evil" (4:6), namely his anger.

Jonah wanted to "fly away" (that is, to reciprocate from *below* in the lower left corner to *above* in the upper right), but he was foiled, as he should have known would happen in his stubbornness as an "upright" (*Jeshurun*) Jew. The allegory thus invites reading as a gentle self-parody of Orthodox Judaism, never intended for the eyes of an enemy. The matrix rotates on "D" as the second counter in row 5, defined first by $3 \times 625 = 1875$, then doubled six times (multiplied by $2^6$ [another guise of YHWH's sum to 26] = 64, which is also the "eye of Horus" value guarding the throne of Egypt) to reach the matrix limit of 120,000. The 50 was deified as Ellil/Enlil, god 50 (Bull on the Mountain) in Mesopotamia but dethroned in Israel as the limit in years of the Jubilee calendar. The story can be read as perhaps the most perfect self-image Judaism ever discovered for its ironic male self. The Marduk square root that invited Noah's flood is preserved between the peak and the fourth value in the base (row 1, the bottom of the sea and the "roots of the mountains"), where Jonah was swallowed by the Great Fish in the first half of the story. Its eleven tones are the maximum symmetries possible among twelve tones.

The universe rotates day and night, and Nineveh with it, and so—as the matrix defined by 120,000—it rotates on the second counter in its fifth row to illustrate how Jonah, who originally appeared as $5^2 = 25$ (first counter in the third row) was taught a much-needed lesson at this later point in the story. The inverted Nineveh matrix now becomes the *Qiqayon*-tree, which temporarily shaded him from the quiet or burning east wind (*Hamsin*) and the heat of the noonday sun (Jonah 4:8). The *Qiqayon* grew up in a night to shade our weary prophet but unfortunately perished in a night as well in the rhythm of the matrix (4:10b). All arithmetical meaning *reciprocates*, while all musical meaning *inverts*, except for three invariant symmetric tones (G D A) on the central axis of the Jonah matrix on octave 48:24. This tonal algebra helps in tracking arithmetical transformations.

When the shade of the *Qiqayon* was removed, "the sun smote on Jonah's head and he grew faint and asked that he might die" (4:8). The story ends with Jonah in misery and anger and with God posing his final question: "And as for me, should I not have compassion on Nineveh that Great City with its population of more than 120,000 humans?" The reader/hearer is invited to supply the missing ending.

The book of Nahum functions as a commentary of sorts on the book of Jonah, and the meaning of Nineveh is found in reading the books of Jonah and Nahum together as parallel texts within the context of the Book of the Twelve Prophets as a whole. The primary key in determining the index limit for Nahum was found in the observation that there are 2250 (= 2 × 1125) consonantal letters in the book. In the "reduced" matrix for 72,000 (= 64 × 1125), the number 1125 (= $3^3$ × 125) falls on the third counter of row 4 (that is, on tone D in the axis of rotation; Figure 6).

When Jonah (25) "flies away" from the smallest "ark" (the so-called "Jonah boat") on the left, it loses the "peaks" above and below to become Philo's "plinth" (cf. Figure 5). Either "upright" (*Jeshurun*) or inverted "down in Egypt," its content defines the *mode of the Pentateuch* together with its reciprocal (modern major). Jonah as "25" is present here as the *forgotten cornerstone* (a-flat) and also as its reciprocal (g-sharp)—paired "tritone" approximations to the square root of 2 in the middle of the octave that music never wants together anyway. The Magen David naturally excludes the tritone conflict between them and also the commas at C:c and E:e. This essential "Jewish" arithmetic descends from the Sumerian "brick" constant of 720 ("days plus nights" in a biblical year) down through history and Egyptian arithmetic, when 720 is a factor of the "enthroned" limit. See McClain (1976), p. 51 for the brick constant of 720, p. 62 for limits of 3600 and 216,000, and p. 74

The enduring presence of Jonah as Yнwн's "dove" in Bible harmonics as the Nahum matrix remains centered to anticipate the choir of 144,000 male virgins

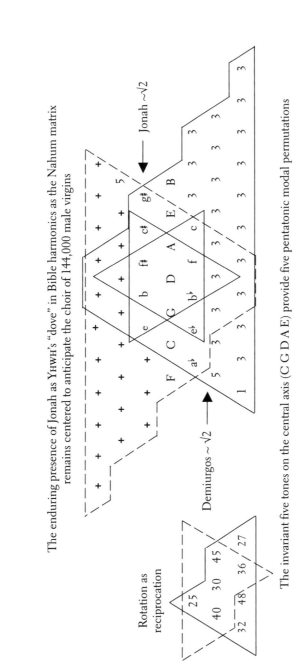

The invariant five tones on the central axis (C G D A E) provide five pentatonic modal permutations

Figure 6. The Nahum matrix on the octave 72,000:36,000.

for the Kali Yuga "dark age" of 432,000, and see Figures 1 and 2 of this introduction for the later Marduk and YHWH thrones. Thus 48 (the Bible's "Cities of Refuge") is *necessarily* the smallest integer that can ground this numerology from the ancient Egyptian calendar down through the Bible to Revelation and its doubled limit in the choir of 144,000 "male virgins" (Revelation 14:4). The Nahum matrix for 72,000 is a fitting foundation (lower bound) for this celestial choir of 144,000 male virgins. It is difficult to imagine a finer comment on Jonah; the Nahum matrix protects the severe discipline of the Chosen to merit their roles in heaven.

The Magen David "upright" pattern is necessarily shifted one place to the right to accommodate reciprocation by rotation (verifiable by eye in Figure 2) and lifted to *only* the fourth row here to center it between *excess* and *defect* vertically, which is verifiable by testing the ascent along the left arithmetically. Three "increases" of 5:4 (via 64-80-100-125) obviously fall short of doubling by three units in three steps (125:128), so that this modest elevation ensures that accepting it as the appropriate "throne" row for "Salem" (as the "City of Peace" in the soul) centers it perfectly between *excess* in the first row and *defect* in the seventh row. Here the "cornerstone" unit for 72,000 must be doubled sixteen times, to $2^{16} = 65,536$, while the seventh row reaches $5^6 \times 4 = 62,500$, as opposed to C in the fourth row as $125 \times 512 = 64,000$. (And that 512 encodes the 888 meaning $8 \times 8 \times 8$ as the Savior in Greek gematria.) The second counters in rows 1 and 7 also share the same ratios with "G" in the *pentatonic center of all systems* (for all matrix relations are "transitive," passed along in the matrix, so that the simplest "counters" in a straight line carry the meaning "do it again," no matter what one did first, as in Jonah's travels).

The word אשור ("Assyria") appears as an acrostic of the initial letters of four consecutive words in Nahum 1:12. In place value gematria (where the letters of the alphabet are numbered consecutively 1 through 22), these four Hebrew letters have the numerical value of $1 + 21 + 6 + 20 = 48$, which is the number of counters in the matrix of the Nineveh octave 120,000:60,000 and also the number of verses in the book of Jonah.

The word *Nineveh* appears three times in the book of Nahum with normal spelling נינוה (1:1, 2:9, 3:7) and once without the final *he'* in an acrostic made up of the initial letters in four successive half-lines in Nahum 3:18. The numerical value of the word *Nineveh* in place value gematria, without the final *he'*, is $14 + 10 + 14 + 6 = 44$, and there are 44 counters in the Nahum matrix on the octave 72,000:36,000.

The numerical value of the word *Nineveh* in its normal spelling (with *he'*) is $44 + 5 = 49$, which is the number of counters in the matrix of the octave 144,000:72,000 (that is, the double octave of Nahum at 72,000:36,000). The number of counters common to both the upright matrix and its inverted form of the Nahum matrix for 72,000 centered symmetrically on D is 25, which is the number for Jonah in the Nineveh matrix for 120,000. The matrix on the octave 144,000:72,000 subsequently plays a major role in the shaping of biblical tradition in the matrix arithmetic for the choir of 144,000 male virgins in Revelation 14:4, within the context of the "New Jerusalem" (= $12,000^3$), as Ernest McClain has shown (1976: 114, Chart 26).

## Reading Nahum as Literature

The book of Nahum, like many other texts in the Tanakh, is sometimes regarded as a collection of originally separate literary units (see Wehrle 1995: 894; Zenger 1995: 412). This point of view goes back at least as far as Gunkel (1893), who saw the presumed acrostic poem in chapter 1 as a secondary editorial addition to the text. Opinions are still divided on the literary nature of Nahum 1:1–10 and the relation of this opening section to the rest of the book. Among those who see the book as the end result of a gradual process of editorial expansion starting from some original core, there is little agreement on matters of detail. Some see the redactional process as completed soon after the destruction of Nineveh in 612 BCE (Rudolph 1975: 144–45), but others think that the process extended well into the exilic or even the postexilic period (Elliger 1949: 2–3). Seybold (1989a) and Lescow (1995) find at least three different editions of the original poems in the redactional process. Nogalski (1993a, 1993b) finds an extensive reediting of the book within the formation of the Book of the Twelve Prophets. Others see no successive stages of redactional growth at all and argue that the book was written by a single author at some given point in time, after the fall of Thebes to the Assyrians in 663 and before the fall of Nineveh in 612. But once again, there is no agreement among scholars who share this view as to the specific nature of the work as such.

Sweeney (1992) sees the prophet himself as the editor of the text sometime after the fall of Nineveh, with the fall of that city marking the termination of the prophetic activity as such. In some respects Sweeney takes a step beyond the current impasse in the synchronic and diachronic approaches to the text. It may be useful to take this argument a step further by drawing a distinction between the setting in which the author intended the book to be read and the actual historical setting of that same person at the time the text was written. Someone can write a meaningful poetic account of a given moment in the American Civil War without its being necessary for us to place the composition of that poem within that specific time context. Whatever historical process lies behind the text of Nahum as we now have it, that very text bears the stamp of numerical composition as an integral part of a much larger text, with its own agenda, which was intended from the outset to be preserved for all time as canonical Scripture.

## The Literary Genre of Nahum

The question of the literary genre of Nahum remains unresolved. In fact, some scholars argue that Nahum is a collection of prophetic speeches and poems that are lumped together simply because they all relate in some way to the fall of Nineveh, though there is no particular genre in the overall arrangement of the document (see Seybold 1989a: 19; Roberts 1991: 9–11, 37–38). Becking (1978: 122–24) sees the book as simply the prophet's way of communicating to the public his revelations concerning Nineveh's doom.

Spronk (1997: 1) does not take a specific position on the matter of genre as such in his argument that Nahum is a poetic composition written in Jerusalem by a royal scribe (ca. 660 BCE), one that was intended "to encourage the people of Judah groaning under the tyranny of the Assyrians." In contrast, Sweeney identifies the book of Nahum as a prophetic refutation speech, a component of the larger disputation genre (cf. Murray 1987: 95–121)—"an argumentative rhetorical form which is designed to examine contrasting points of view and to make a decision as to which represents the better position, point of view or option for action" (Sweeney 2000: 425; see also 1992: 364–77).

Though Floyd (2000: 10–13) rejects Sweeney's position, he nonetheless argues that each of the two main parts of the book "bears the stamp of the prophetic historical exemplum." Floyd follows Weis (1986), who argues that the term *maśśāʾ* is "a genre term that applies to both a type of prophetic speech and a type of prophetic literature" (Floyd 2000: 14). Though this genre shows diversity, Floyd finds a cluster of basic elements: (1) oracular speech of YHWH, (2) reports of past and/or present events, and (3) commands and/or prohibitions directly addressed to the audience. In short, "a *maśśāʾ* is a kind of revelation that interprets the present applicability of a previous revelation."

Other genres have been suggested. Haupt (1907b) argued that the book is not prophecy at all but a festal liturgy composed for the celebration of the Day of Nikanor in the Maccabean era. Humbert (1932: 3–4) also identified Nahum as a form of liturgy intended for a victory celebration at the New Year festival in Jerusalem in 612 BCE (cf. Fohrer 1968: 449–51). Engnell (1969: 167) argued that Nahum belongs to what he calls the "liturgical type," as opposed to the *dīwān* type—by which he means the collected words of a poet, in the sense of the whole collection of sayings attributed to a certain prophet. More recently, Watts (1975: 5–6) described the book as a liturgical expression of foreign prophecies used in the Royal Zion Festival in Jerusalem.

Haldar (1947: 147–49) believed that Nahum is a propagandistic tract written within cultic circles of the Jerusalem Temple in the late seventh century and intended to foment popular opposition to Assyrian domination. A number of others find in Nahum an extended eschatological hymn (see Schulz 1973: 99–101; Renaud 1987b: 213–18). Like the personified figure of Babylon in the book of Revelation, the personification of Nineveh becomes the symbol of evil, and the destruction of Nineveh represents the defeat of the forces of evil at the end of time (see Childs 1979: 443–46).

Henshaw (1958: 149) described Nahum as "a song of triumph" over a bitter enemy. Seybold sees the book as "soldier's songs, which have been put into the framework of a traditional religious text" (see Spronk 1995a: 160). Van der Woude (1977a: 124) concludes that the book is a letter written by an exile from northern Israel living in Assyria, presumably written to fellow Israelites in Judah to comfort them during the reign of Manasseh. But no addressee or sender is named, and nothing in the literary form of the book indicates that it is a letter as such.

Sasson suggests that the book of Nahum is close in genre to the *Curse of Agade* (see J. S. Cooper 1983), a Sumerian composition that purports to witness the destruction of an important capital city. As Sasson puts it (1990: 22, n. 20), "Both texts include vivid, often figurative descriptions of the fortification and fall of cities, divine curses against them, and laments over their demise." Dobbs-Allsopp (1993: 128–31) develops this idea further in his study of the "City-Lament Genre" but fails to demonstrate a convincing connection with the book of Nahum. Berlin (1995: 319) summarizes Dobbs-Allsopp's thesis as positing "the existence of an Israelite genre of city laments which, although probably influenced by the Mesopotamian genre, stood independent from it." Berlin also wants to see some kind of relationship to Nahum but is uncomfortable with the notion of a genre as such. At the same time, Dobbs-Allsopp (2000: 626) insists that "we have evidence for knowledge of city laments in Israel for a period of at least two hundred years and that as encountered in the Hebrew Bible the genre shows every sign of having long been internalized within and understood as an inherited part of the Israelite literary tradition." Nonetheless, we are simply unable to track the journey of literary genres through space and time with any real specificity.

## The Literary Structure of Nahum

There is no scholarly consensus in regard to the literary structure of Nahum. Floyd (2000) finds two major parts, which constitute a prophetic challenge to Yhwh's opponents in general (1:2–2:11 [10]) and to Nineveh's hubris in particular (2:12 [13]–3:19). Clark and Hatton (1989: 1) also see two parts:

Yhwh's vengeance against Nineveh (1:1–2:1 [1:1–15]) and a description of the fall of Nineveh (2:2–3:19 [2:1–3:19]). Sweeney (1992) sees three main sections (1:2–10; 1:11–2:1 [1:15]; and 2:2 [1]–3:19), which constitute a refutation speech challenging the assumption that Yhwh is powerless. Roberts (1991: 37–38) sees four major sections (1:2–2:1 [1:15]; 2:2–14 [1–13]; 3:1–17; 3:18–19), which together constitute a repeated announcement of impending judgment on Assyria (cf. O'Brien 2002: 1:2–10, 11–14; 2:1–14 [1:15–2:13]; 3:1–19). Renaud (1987b) sees five sections (1:2–8; 1:9–2:3 [2]; 2:4–11 [3–10]; 2:12 [11]–3:17; 3:18–19), whereas Mason (1991: 62) sees six sections (1:2–8; 1:9–2:3 [2]; 2:4–13 [3–12]; 2:14 [13]; 3:1–4; 3:5–19). Sponk (1997) finds three "cantos" (1:1–11; 1:12–2:14 [13]; 3:1–19), which include seven subcantos (1:1–11; 1:12–2:3 [2]; 2:4–8 [3–7]; 2:9–14 [8–13]; 3:1–7; 8–11; 12–19), and Coggins (1985: 7) also posits a seven-part structure (1:1–8; 9–11; 1:12–2:1 [1:15]; 2:2–3 [1–2]; 2:4–13 [3–12]; 2:14 [13]; 3:1–19). Mason (1991: 63) sees the book "as an 'anthology' of prophetic and cultic material which has been shaped for a particular purpose" and notes that "a number of commentators have argued for more small subdivisions in their conception of the plan of the book" than the six sections he suggests.

Logoprosodic analysis indicates that there are seven cantos and reveals the curious phenomenon in which 2:11 [10] plays an ambiguous role, completing the third canto and beginning the fourth canto, while belonging to both. The content of the book of Nahum as a whole may be outlined in a menorah pattern, which is determined primarily on prosodic grounds, as follows:

### Outline of the Book of Nahum in a Menorah Pattern

| | | |
|---|---|---|
| A | Yhwh's vindicating wrath—an acrostic hymn of theophany | 1:1–10 |
| B | Yhwh announces the defeat of Belial (the Wicked One) | 1:11–14 |
| C | Vision of the sack of Nineveh | 2:1–2:11 [1:15–2:10] |
| **X** | **Dirge on the lions' den** | 2:11–14 [10–13] |
| C′ | Taunt song: "Woe to the city of bloodshed!" | 3:1–7 |
| B′ | Taunt song: "Are you better than Thebes?" | 3:8–13 |
| A′ | Locust dirge—an image of imminent ruin | 3:14–19 |

This outline is simply a listing of the seven cantos within the framework of a seven-part menorah pattern, and, as such, it is only one way of looking at the literary structure of Nahum. In this reading, the outermost frame opens with a portrayal of the appearance of Yhwh as Divine Warrior in a hymn of theophany (1:1–10), and it closes with a concluding dirge, which Achtemeier (1986: 27) describes as "the complementary piece to 1:2–11." In the center we find a

remarkable dirge on the lions' den (2:11–14 [10–13]), with its implied presence
of Yʜᴡʜ as the "lion of Judah" (that is, the Divine Warrior Yʜᴡʜ) making
prey of wicked Assyria, who is portrayed as another lion, together with its
pride. The second frame opens with an announcement of the defeat of Belial
(1:11–14), and concludes with the taunt song portraying Nineveh as no better than Thebes, the greatest monument city of the ancient world, which was
conquered by Assyria (3:8–13). The innermost frame moves from the vivid
portrayal of the sack of Nineveh (2:1–11 [1:15–2:10]) to the taunt song proclaiming woe to that city of bloodshed (3:1–7).

Spronk (1997: 5) explores one aspect of the concentric structure of Nahum
2–3 in a listing of parallel words and phrases:

a.   הרים "mountains" (2:1aA)
 b.   שמע the verb "to hear" (2:1aB)
  c.   חגי "celebrate your festivals" (2:1bA)
   d.   פוץ "a scatterer has come up" (2:2aA)
    e.   Imperatives (2:2aB–b)
     f.   שערי נהרות נפתחו "gates of the rivers are opened" (2:7)
      g.   אמהתיה "her maidens" (2:8)
       h.   מים "water" (2:9 with Nineveh)
        i.   איה "where?" (2:12)
         j.   הנני אליך נאם יהוה צבאות "Behold I am against you" (2:14)
         j′.   הנני אליך נאם יהוה צבאות "Behold I am against you" (3:5)
        i′.   מאין "where?" (3:7)
       h′.   מים "water" (3:8 with No)
      g′.   נשים "women" (3:13aA)
     f′.   פתוח נפתחו שערי ארצך "gates of your land are opened" (3:13B)
    e′.   imperatives (3:14)
   d′.   פוש "your people are scattered" (3:18)
  c′.   תקע כף "clap your hands" (3:19bB)
 b′.   שמע verb "to hear"(3:19bA)
a′.   הרים "mountains" (3:18b)

Though some aspects of this nesting of words and phrases is probably coincidental, the overall pattern is in keeping with what is found in the present logoprosodic analysis.

The idea of arranging things symmetrically from the center was widely
known in antiquity, as noted by Kathleen Freeman, who cites an ancient para-
phrase of Philolaus, the first Pythagorean writer (fifth century ʙᴄᴇ), who was

supposedly Plato's source, as follows: "The universe is one, and it began to come into being from the centre, and from the centre upwards at the same intervals as those below. For the parts above from the centre are in inverse relationship to those below; for the centre is to what is below as it is to what is above, and so with all the rest; for both stand in the same relationship to the centre, except in so far as their positions are reversed" (Freeman 1966: 76; I am grateful to Ernest McClain for this reference). This pattern of concentric inverted literary structure is dominant throughout the Book of the Twelve Prophets and, for that matter, the Bible as a whole (see Christensen 2003a).

When 2:11 [10] is read in conjunction with the cipher hidden in the modified acrostic pattern of 1:2–8, which continues in a different form in 1:9–10, we find an apt reiteration of the central message of Nahum:

> I am the exalted YHWH, and (I am) in the presence of sin;
>     in an overflowing torrent (I am) bringing a full end—completely.
> What will you devise against YHWH?
>     A full end he himself will make.
> Distress will not arise a second time;
>     for while (they are) like thorns matted together—
> And like their drunken state, soaked with "drink"—
>     consumed (they will be) like dry stubble—completely.
> Destruction and desolation and disintegration,
>     and hearts grow faint, and knees give way—
> And anguish is in all loins, and (on) all their faces;
>     they are gathered as fuel (for burning).

The person addressed here is Nineveh, the capital of the Neo-Assyrian Empire and the focus of judgment on the part of the Divine Warrior.

Another way to look at the literary structure of Nahum is to place the book within the content of the Book of the Twelve Prophets as a whole in a nested menorah pattern:

### Outline of the Book of the Twelve Prophets in a Menorah Pattern

| A | Hosea | Israel's unfaithfulness and God's judgment |
|---|---|---|
| B | Joel | Day of YHWH—the enemy from the north |
| C | Amos | Israel and the nations—judgment and hope |
| X | **Obadiah–Zephaniah** | **YHWH's "vengeance"—destruction and salvation** |
| C′ | Haggai | Rebuilding the Temple in Jerusalem |
| B′ | Zechariah | Day of YHWH and the restoration of Judah |
| A′ | Malachi | Israel's unfaithfulness and God's judgment |

## Second Level: Yʜwʜ's "Vengeance" — Destruction and Salvation (Obadiah–Zephaniah)

| | | |
|---|---|---|
| A | Obadiah | Day of Yʜwʜ — against Edom and Judah |
| B | Jonah | Salvation of Nineveh |
| C | Micah | Salvation of Israel |
| **X** | **Micah 7:18–20** | **Confession of faith (cf. Exodus 34:6–7)** |
| C' | Nahum | Destruction of Nineveh |
| B' | Habakkuk | Destruction of Judah |
| A' | Zephanah | Day of Yʜwʜ — against Judah and the nations |

The outermost frame in the previous nested menorah pattern begins with the powerful imagery of redeeming love in the account of the prophet Hosea and his faithless wife Gomer (Hosea 1–3). It continues with a message of judgment against Israel for her perfidy, with the hope of ultimate restoration (Hosea 4–14). This same dual theme appears in the book of Malachi, in the other half of the outermost frame. The book of Malachi begins with the words "'I have loved you,' says Yʜwʜ" (Malachi 1:2). The ensuing words about the coming day of judgment in Malachi are climaxed with a remarkable vision of hope: "Behold, I will send you Elijah the prophet before the great and terrible Day of Yʜwʜ comes. And he will turn the hearts of fathers to their children and the hearts of children to their fathers, lest I come and smite the land with a curse" (Malachi 3:23–24 [4:5–6]).

The second frame in this nested menorah pattern presents Joel and Zechariah, which focus on the destructive aspects of the Day of Yʜwʜ. Once again we find hope within the context of gloom, for both books include words of hope and restoration. God's promise of restoration is in the structural center, where Joel depicts the Day of Yʜwʜ as a time of devastation for Judah and the nations (see Joel 2:18–29 and 3:18–21). The center of Zechariah includes words of hope that focus on the rebuilding of the Temple in Jerusalem by "the man whose name is the Branch" (Zechariah 6:9–15).

The third frame in this nested menorah pattern sets the book of Amos over against that of Haggai. The book of Amos ends with specific prophecies concerning the restoration of the Davidic dynasty and the glorious age to come (Amos 9:11–15). The book of Haggai, which focuses on the building of the Second Temple in Jerusalem, more than two hundred years after the time of Amos, concludes with a promise to Zerubbabel, governor of Judah (and a descendant of David), that God will again redeem his people. Like Amos, Zechariah links Israel's earlier traditions with the coming messianic age (Haggai 2:20–23). The remaining six books in the Book of the Twelve Prophets constitute the second-level menorah pattern, which is essentially an expansion of the great confession of faith in Exodus 34:6–7, to show the two sides of YHWH's nataure—his anger (Exodus 34:7) and his steadfast covenant love (Exodus 34:6).

The Day of YHWH is a dominant theme in Obadiah and Zephaniah, which constitute the outer frame in this menorah pattern. In the structural center of the Book of the Twelve Prophets, we find a confession of faith (Micah 7:18–20) that echoes Exodus 34:6–7. In the second frame, Jonah is set over against Habakkuk. The message of Jonah focuses on the salvation of Israel's most repugnant enemy, the city of Nineveh. Habakkuk, on the other hand, takes up the subject of theodicy in an explicit manner. After raising his complaint, the prophet asks God how long he can look on faithless people and do nothing "when the wicked swallow up the one more righteous than they" (Habakkuk 1:13). In the third frame, Micah is set over against Nahum. Most of the central part of Micah focuses on Zion's glorious future and the restoration of the Davidic kingdom (Micah 4–5). In contrast to this focus on the salvation of Israel, Nahum presents a moving picture of the destruction of Nineveh in the hands of YHWH, the God of vengeance, which, at the same time, constitutes YHWH's restoration of Judah (Nahum 2:3 [2]).

The attribution of "vengeance" to God's character is a source of misunderstanding. As Mendenhall has shown (1973: 69–104), the root *nqm* is properly translated in terms that designate punitive vindication in a judicial sense and should not be construed as "malicious retaliation for inflicted wrongs." As a result, YHWH is depicted in Nahum as a suzerain, one who demands exclusive devotion of his vassals, for he is utterly intolerant of rivals of any sort. The point becomes clearer when this opening Psalm of Nahum in 1:1–10 is outlined in a menorah pattern on prosodic grounds, as follows:

### Canto 1: The Psalm of Nahum: YHWH's Vengeance (1:1–10)

| | | | |
|---|---|---|---|
| A | YHWH takes vengeance against his foes: he is *ba^cal* ("lord") of wrath | [8.4] | 1:1–2 |
| B | YHWH is slow to anger but great in power | [5.5] | 1:3 |
| C | YHWH acts with cosmic consequences | [4.4] | 1:4 |
| X | **The earth and its inhabitants reel before YHWH** | [4.4] | 1:5 |
| C' | No one can endure YHWH's wrath | [4.4] | 1:6 |
| B' | YHWH is good and a refuge in the day of distress | [5.5] | 1:7–8 |
| A' | YHWH will bring complete destruction—"a *full end* (*kālāh*)" | [4.8] | 1:9–10 |

The opening verse (1:2) is set over against vv 9–10; both focus on the so-called dark side of YHWH, namely, his jealous anger that leads to punishment. Vv 3 and 7–8 present the other side of YHWH, one who is "slow to anger" (cf. Exodus 34:6–7), for in biblical usage "God's vengeance" has a redemptive quality.

His punishment often takes the form of discipline, however harsh it may appear to the recipient at the time.

The second canto (1:11–14), which functions as a literary "bridge" connecting the opening hymn of theophany with the detailed account of the destruction of Nineveh that follows, may also be outlined in a menorah pattern on prosodic grounds, as follows:

### Canto 2: The Defeat of Belial (1:11–14)

| | | | |
|---|---|---|---|
| A | From you (Nineveh) the counselor (of) Belial has departed | [5] | 1:11 |
| B | Yʜᴡʜ: "Are the Assyrians not strong and ever so numerous?" | [4] | 1:12ab |
| C | Even so, they will be sheared and they will pass on | [2] | 1:12c |
| X | **Yʜᴡʜ: "I will afflict you (Judah) no more"** | [3.3] | 1:12d |
| C′ | Yʜᴡʜ: "I will snap apart your (Judah) bonds" | [2] | 1:13 |
| B′ | Yʜᴡʜ has determined that you will have no descendants | [4] | 1:14ab |
| A′ | I will cut off false idols and prepare your (Assyria's) grave | [5] | 1:14c–d |

The concentric structure here focuses on Yʜᴡʜ's declaration that he will afflict Judah no longer (1:12d). The outermost frame presents the basis for this expression of hope; the "counselor (of) Belial" has departed from Nineveh (v 11), and Yʜᴡʜ is about to cut off false gods as he prepares Assyria's grave (v 14c–d). The second frame moves from the acknowledgment of Assyria's strength and numbers (v 12ab) to Yʜᴡʜ's determination that Assyria's king will be without descendants (v 14ab). The innermost frame underscores the twofold nature of Yʜᴡʜ's action: (1) Assyria will be "sheared" as sheep are sheared, and they will pass on (v 12c) (2) as Yʜᴡʜ removes Judah's shackles (v 13).

In the third canto (2:1–11 [1:15–2:10]), we find another carefully structured literary unit, which can be outlined in a menorah pattern on prosodic grounds, as follows:

### Canto 3: The Sack of Nineveh (2:1–11 [1:15–2:10])

| | | | |
|---|---|---|---|
| A | Celebrate your festivals, O Judah, for Belial is utterly cut off | [5.4] | 2:1 |
| B | Yʜᴡʜ has come against Nineveh to restore Israel | [7.7] | 2:2–3 |
| C | The warriors and chariots are prepared for battle | [4.4] | 2:4 |
| X | **Mayhem in Nineveh and the palace collapses in the flood** | [6.6.6] | 2:5–7 |
| C′ | Nineveh is destroyed and her people carried away in exile | [4.4] | 2:8 |
| B′ | Nineveh drains away and the city is plundered | [7.7] | 2:9–10 |
| A′ | The destruction is total: "They are gathered as kindling" | [4.5] | 2:11 |

Here the focus of the concentric literary structure is on the mayhem in Nineveh, with chariots jostling about in the streets (2:5–7 [4–6]). The innermost frame in this structure expands the imagery of destruction, with a description of the preparation of chariots and warriors for the ensuing battle (2:4 [3]) that is set over against a summary statement of the destruction of Nineveh portrayed as a woman of nobility carried into exile (2:8 [9]). The second frame presents the coming of the Divine Destroyer against Nineveh to restore the past glory of his chosen people (2:2–3 [2:1–2]), which is set over against the portrayal of Nineveh draining away, as water from a pool, and the plundering of the fallen city (2:9–10 [8–9]). And the outermost frame, which opens with Yhwh's command to Judah to celebrate her pilgrimage feasts once again because Belial is utterly cut off (2:1 [1:15]), continues with the summary description of Nineveh's utter destruction (2:11 [10]).

The fourth canto (2:11–14), like the second (1:11–14), functions as a literary "bridge" connecting two major sections in the book of Nahum. At the same time, the unit has literary integrity of its own, the content of which may be outlined in a menorah pattern on prosodic grounds, as follows:

### Canto 4: Dirge on the Lions' Den (2:11–14 [10–13])

| | | | |
|---|---|---|---|
| A | There is utter destruction—hearts grow faint and knees give way | [5] | 2:11a–c |
| B | They are in anguish for they are gathered as fuel for burning | [4] | 2:11de |
| C | Where is the lions' den? | [4] | 2:12ab |
| X | **The lion has torn sufficient prey—with none to disturb** | [4.4] | 2:12c–13b |
| C′ | The lion has filled his dens with torn flesh | [4] | 2:13cd |
| B′ | Yhwh speaks: "I will burn in smoke her chariots" | [4] | 2:14ab |
| A′ | The sword will devour your young lions—I will cut you off! | [5] | 2:14c–f |

The focus here is on the image of the lion as a metaphor for Assyria, which has torn sufficient prey with none to disturb (2:12c–13b). This unit is closely tied to the outermost frame, in which we find the powerful image of utter destruction in 11a–c set over against a concluding statement that Yhwh's sword will "devour your lions," as Yhwh himself declares: "I will cut you off" (2:14c–f). The second frame sets the prophet's announcement "They are gathered as fuel (for burning)" (2:11de) over against Yhwh's words as he declares: "I will burn in smoke (Assyria's) chariots" (2:14ab). The innermost frame opens with a rhetorical question: "Where is the lions' den?" (2:12ab), and concludes with a brief description of the current situation: the lion (Assyria) has filled his den with torn flesh (2:13cd), namely the despoiled nations she has conquered. The day of reckoning has come, as the lion of Assyria now faces Yhwh, the lion of Judah.

The fifth canto (3:1–7) may also be outlined in a menorah pattern on prosodic grounds, as follows:

## Canto 5: First Taunt: Nineveh's Shame Will Be Seen by the Nations (3:1–7)

| A | Woe to the bloody city—all of it filled with deceit and pillage | [3.4] | 3:1 |
|---|---|---|---|
| B | The sounds of war resound in the streets | [3.3] | 3:2 |
| C | The carnage is enormous—there is no end to the corpses | [4.5] | 3:3 |
| **X** | **The end has come because of Nineveh's harlotry** | **[4.4]** | **3:4** |
| C′ | YHWH speaks: "I will expose your shame to the nations!" | [5.4] | 3:5 |
| B′ | YHWH's spectacle of contempt: "I will pelt you with filth!" | [3.3] | 3:6–7a |
| A′ | Observers say: "Nineveh is in ruins! Who will grieve for her?" | [4.3] | 3:7b–d |

The focus this time is on the destruction of Nineveh, which has come because of the "harlotries of the harlot" (3:4). This central verse is closely connected with the outermost frame, which opens with the prophet voicing words of lamentation: "Woe to the city of bloodshed . . . never without prey!" (3:1), which is set over against the words of a fugitive from the destroyed city, who declares: "Nineveh is in ruins, who will mourn for her?" (3:7b–d). The second frame opens with a vivid description of the sounds of battle that have come to Nineveh (3:2). It continues with YHWH's declaration that he will make of Nineveh a spectacle of contempt (3:6–7a). The innermost frame presents the city filled with human gore and no end to the corpses (3:3), which is set over against YHWH's declaration that he is showing the nations Nineveh's shame (3:5).

The sixth canto (3:8–13) presents another taunt song against Nineveh in which the city is compared with Thebes in Egypt. Once again, the content of this canto may be outlined in a menorah pattern, which is determined primarily on prosodic grounds:

## Canto 6: Second Taunt—Like Thebes, Nineveh Will Be Sacked (3:8–13)

| A | To Nineveh: "Are you better than Thebes on the Nile?" | [4.4] | 3:8 |
|---|---|---|---|
| B | Thebes had a strong ally in Cush who "was her strength" | [3.3] | 3:9 |
| C | She went into captivity with her infants dashed to pieces | [3.3] | 3:10a–d |
| **X** | **The leaders of Thebes were carried away in chains** | **[2.2]** | **3:10ef** |
| C′ | Nineveh addressed: may you become drunk and seek refuge | [3.3] | 3:11 |
| B′ | Your fortresses will fall like first-ripe figs to be eaten | [3.3] | 3:12 |
| A′ | To Nineveh: "Look at your people—they are like women!" | [4.4] | 3:13 |

In the structural center we find a simple dyad describing the plight of the nobles and dignitaries of Thebes, who are bound in fetters (3:10ef). On either side we find strophes that highlight the double use of the emphasizing particle *gam* ("also"). In the first instance, the particle introduces the pronoun "she" (Thebes), who was carried into exile, with the slaughter of her children in the streets of the city (3:10a–d). The second half of this structure addresses

Nineveh in the 2nd pers. f. sg., expressing the desire that she now become inebriated with the cup of YHWH's wrath so as to share the very fate she inflicted on others in times past (3:11). The outermost frame opens with a rhetorical question, "Are you better than Thebes?" (3:8), and concludes with a vivid display of the negative response to this question—your people and your gates are wide open to violation and destruction (3:13). The second frame, which opens with a brief description of the strength of Thebes through her allies, which was to no avail (3:9), concludes with a vivid description of the fortresses around Nineveh falling as ripe figs into the mouth of the "eater" who has come to devour the hapless city (3:12).

The book of Nahum concludes with a funeral dirge using the image of a scourge of locusts. This seventh and concluding canto (3:14–19) may be outlined in a menorah pattern, as follows:

### Canto 7: The Locust Dirge: An Image of Imminent Ruin (3:14–19)

| | | | |
|---|---|---|---|
| A | Prepare for the siege—strengthen your defenses! | [4.4] | 3:14 |
| B | Fire will devour you and the sword will cut you off | [2.2] | 3:15a–c |
| C | It will devour you like a plague of locusts | [4.4] | 3:15d–16 |
| X | **Your palace officials fly away in the heat like locusts** | [4.2.4] | 3:17 |
| C' | Your shepherds are asleep and the people scattered | [4.4] | 3:18 |
| B' | Your wound is incurable | [2.2] | 3:19ab |
| A' | All rejoice at your fall; for on whom has not come your evil? | [4.4] | 3:19c–f |

The focus in this concentric literary unit is on the action of the palace officials in Nineveh, who flee when the heat of military opposition threatens them (3:17). The innermost frame expands this theme, starting with the image of locusts growing in size and number and then taking flight (3:15d–16). It continues with the image of the shepherds (rulers) of the people asleep and the people scattered upon the mountains (3:18). The second frame opens with a description of fire and sword devouring Nineveh like locusts (3:15a–c), which is set over against a parallel statement that describes Nineveh's wound as incurable (3:19ab). The outermost frame opens with a satirical summons to battle addressed to Nineveh, who is told to prepare for the siege by strengthening the defenses of the city (3:14). It concludes with a description of the response of those who hear the news of Nineveh's collapse—they clap their hands in joy (3:19cd). The book itself concludes with a rhetorical question: Who has not felt Nineveh's evil unceasingly (3:19ef)?

## Nahum and the Book of the Twelve Prophets

There is no real evidence that the book of Nahum ever circulated independently in antiquity as a separate book rather than as part of the Book of the

Twelve Prophets. In recent years it has become increasingly clear that the book of Nahum cannot be adequately interpreted when it is read independent of this larger literary context (see House 1990, 1996; Ben Zvi 1996b).

Coggins (1994: 64) argues that the overall shape of the Book of the Twelve Prophets resembles other prophetic books, which begin with words of doom against their own sinful people (Hosea–Micah; cf. Isaiah 1–12, 24–34; Jeremiah 1–25; Ezekiel 1–24). Then follows a section concerning foreign nations (Nahum–Zephaniah 2; cf. Isaiah 13–23, 34; Ezekiel 25–32), and a third major section includes words of hope for restoration of the community (Haggai–Malachi; cf. Isaiah 40–66; Ezekiel 33–48). D. N. Freedman (1991: 49–52) posits a further parallel on chronological grounds: Hosea, Amos, and Micah correspond to Isaiah 1–39; Nahum, Habakkuk, and Zephaniah are roughly contemporary with Jeremiah; and Haggai, Zechariah, and Malachi have many parallels with Ezekiel.

House argues for unity of the Book of the Twelve Prophets from a synchronic reading (1990: 88–96, 1996) that is similar to that of Patterson (1990). He explores genre, characterization, theme, and plot movement as indicators of the close connection between Nahum, Habakkuk, and Zephaniah along the following lines of inquiry: (1) they stem from the same era, (2) they share a strong thematic interest in impending or fulfilled judgment, (3) they are approximately the same length, (4) they have been placed together in all extant traditions, and (5) they use alternating speakers. House (1996: 203) finds evidence for a dramatic coherence among these three books: "God and the prophets begin with denunciation in Nahum, move to a shared understanding of the future in Habakkuk, and close with a vision of renewal in Zephaniah. God appears, then, as regal, merciful, kind, just, wrathful, and forgiving. The prophets are heralds, messengers, revelatory partners, and friends." For a somewhat similar approach, see Neef 2000. Weigl (2001: 98) rejects the significance of House's arguments for any "dramatic coherence" among these three books and suggests that the evaluation of how the nations are presented in the three books might lead to more significant conclusions, though it is not clear what these conclusions might be.

Nogalski (1993a, 1993b, 1993c) argues that the secondary editing of Nahum 1 was motivated by a desire to adapt it to the concluding chapter of Micah. He lists thirteen different words that he believes were repeated in Nahum 1 to tie these two books together. On the other hand, Zapff (1999a, 1999b) argues that Micah 7 was shaped in the light of Nahum 1, because the catch words shared between the two texts are an integral part of the acrostic pattern in Nahum 1:2–8 but are secondary accretions in Micah 7. Logoprosodic analysis lends support to arguments for a close editorial connection between the ending of Micah and the beginning of Nahum. The wide divergence of opinion on the unity of the Book of the Twelve Prophets supports Weigl's conclusion that any final agreement on the relationship between the canonical shape of Nahum and the formation of the Book of the Twelve Prophets will not be reached in the near future (Weigl 2001: 99–100). Evidence from the study of word-count patterns throughout the Book of the Twelve Prophets as a whole suggests that there is much more yet to be said on this subject.

In the LXX the book of Jonah appears immediately before Nahum, suggesting that the books were closely connected because of their common theme as regards Nineveh. Jones (1995: 239) argues that this juxtaposition of Jonah and Nahum in the LXX "may have been motivated by an attempt to balance the portrait of divine justice toward the nations that is contained in the books of Joel, Obadiah, and Nahum with the message of Yahweh's sovereign mercy in the Book of Jonah." The Targum adds the heading in Nahum 1: "Previously Jonah, son of Amittai, the prophet from Gath-Hepher, prophesied against her and she repented of her sins; and when she sinned again there prophesied once more against her Nahum of Beth Koshi, as is recorded in this book." As Spronk notes (1997: 10), the new sins referred to here probably refer to Micah 5:4–5, which speak of Assyria entering the territory of Judah.

Recent research continues to explore the relationship between Nahum and Jonah (Weissbleit 1993; Zapff 1999a; Ego 2000). Agreement between the books is cited in differing ways, starting with the obvious fact that both books are concerned with the same city of Nineveh, which in each is given a message of doom but with a completely different outcome. In both books God is described as being "slow in anger" (Jonah 4:2 and Nahum 1:3). The verbal root *nḥm* ("change of heart, regret") appears in Jonah 4:2, whereas in Nahum 3:7 there are "no comforters" (*mənaḥămîm*)—and Nahum's name comes from this same root. The two books pose questions about Nineveh (see Glasson 1969): Nahum asks, "Upon whom has not come your evil continually?" And Yhwh says to Jonah: "And I, should I not pity Nineveh that great city, in which there are more than 120,000 persons who do not know their right hand from their left, and also much cattle?" The focus has shifted from the innocent inhabitants of Nineveh to the innocent victims of Assyria (Spronk 1995a: 159).

## The Historical Setting of Nahum and Nineveh

Though the city of Nineveh is an apt symbol for the power of the Assyrian Empire, a symbol that lived on long after the destruction of Nineveh at the hands of the Medes and Babylonians in 612 BCE, it was actually the capital of Assyria for a relatively brief period of time, less than a century. It was Sennacherib (704–681 BCE) who made Nineveh the capital of his vast empire at the end of the eighth century BCE. His impressive building program laid the foundation for the greatness that was Nineveh. He described the new palace he built there as "the palace without rival" (Spronk 1997: 29).

The city of Nineveh was located east of the Tigris River, a short distance downstream from the confluence of the Tigris and the Great Zab. In ancient times, the Tigris was closer to the city of Nineveh on its southwestern side than it is to the ruins today. In more recent times, the city of Mosul was built on this strategic site, with its agricultural potential at the very crossing of the north–south and east–west trade routes. The modern city of Mosul spreads over to the west bank of the Tigris. At the same time, however, remembrance of the ancient city of Nineveh remains alive in the name of a mound covering the ruins of the ancient citadel. This mound is known as Nebi Yunus, the "prophet Jonah," which is a village around this Muslim shrine associated with the traditional grave of Jonah. A second hill nearby, which is known by the Turkish name Küyünjik, proved to be the palace mound of ancient Nineveh. Beginning with the excavations of Emille Botta (1842–45) and Sir Austen Henry Layard (1845–47), archaeological excavations here produced the treasures of ancient Assyria, which constitute the core of the great museum collections in the Louvre in Paris and the British Museum in London. Excavations continued in the twentieth century, most recently by the University of California (UC) at Berkeley under David Stronach, but were interrupted by the Gulf War known as Desert Storm (1990–91). See the surveys by Wiseman (1979), Scott and Maginnis (1990), and Stronach and Lumsden (1992).

Archaeology confirms the fact that Nineveh was indeed a "Great City," as presented in the book of Jonah (1:2, 3:2; cf. Genesis 10:12). Its double wall measures twelve kilometers, and the city itself covered about 750 hectares (Spronk 1997: 29). Billerbeck (1895: 126) computed the length of the north wall of Nineveh as 2000 meters (6561 feet), that of the south wall as 800 meters, and that of the east wall north to south at 5000 meters, and he conjectured that the city was large enough for 300,000 inhabitants (see also Davidson 1920: 29). G. A. Smith (1928: 97) described the city as "the largest fortified space in Western Asia." The excavations have revealed magnificent buildings with impressive reliefs and sculptures—and thousands of written texts on clay tablets, particularly from the famous library of Ashurbanipal. In the eyes of many, these texts and relief drawings help us to understand specific references to Nineveh in the book of Nahum. The UC Berkeley excavations at the Halzi gate revealed evidence of refortification in anticipation of an assault on the city and the bones of more than a dozen defenders of the city where they had fallen in battle (Stronach and Lumsden 1992: 227–33).

The historical setting of the work of Nahum as a prophet is the fifty-year period between 663 and 612 BCE. These dates are fixed by reference to the fall of Thebes in 663 BCE, which is described as an event in the past (3:8), and by the fact that Nineveh was destroyed in 612 BCE. Even with this relatively narrow window of time, however, the quest to recover the historical setting that produced the book of Nahum has produced at least six options:

1.  Soon after the fall of Thebes to Ashurbanipal in 663 BCE
2.  Around the time of Ashurbanipal's death (ca. 630 BCE)
3.  Just before the fall of Nineveh in 612 BCE
4.  Shortly after the fall of Assyria
5.  After the fall of Assyria in the exilic and/or postexilic period
6.  The Maccabean period (ca. 175–165 BCE)

Spronk (1997: 1) argues "that the book of Nahum was written in Jerusalem, ca. 660 BCE, by a talented royal scribe . . . to encourage the people of Judah groaning under the tyranny of the Assyrians" (for similar views see W. A. Maier 1959: 36–37 and Keller 1971). The date suggested by Spronk is influenced by the reference in Nahum 3:8 to the fall of Thebes, which appears to be a familiar and recent event to the audience for which this book was written. It is also possible to see the historical setting a decade or so later, within the context of the revolt of King Manasseh against Assyria in ca. 652–648 BCE, cited in 2 Chronicles 33:11. A number of scholars have argued for some connection between Nahum and the revolt of Shamash-shumukin in 652 (Goslinga 1923: 16; van der Woude 1978a; Dietrich 1994b: 740). At an earlier point in time, I argued that the basis for a revolt on the part of Manasseh (ca. 652 BCE) would have been the conviction that Assyria's days were numbered (see Christensen 1975a: 173–75). The content of the book of Nahum—the assurance that Assyria's fall was certain, in fact that it was ordained of God the Divine Warrior—presents that message and may have been used to persuade the Judean king to take part in such a revolt. The book would then have taken on deeper meaning as part of the theological basis for the subsequent resurgence of Judean independence under King Josiah, especially after the death of Ashurbanipal in ca. 630 BCE. The final destruction of Nineveh in 612 would have been the ultimate fulfillment of this prophecy and would thus explain the book's inclusion in the canon of sacred Scripture according to the law on true and false prophets in Deuteronomy 18:22: "If what a prophet proclaims of the LORD does not take place or come true, that is a message the LORD has not spoken."

Roberts (1991: 38–39) prefers a date in the decade between 640 and 630 BCE. Like Spronk, Roberts insists that the very evidence that establishes the outer limits of 663–612 BCE "suggests an earlier date rather than a later one." The city of Thebes in Egypt recovered its independence from Assyria, and by

616 BCE, if not earlier, Egypt had become Assyria's ally. But the Egypt of Dynasty 26 (the Saite Dynasty) is not the same as the Egypt of Dynasty 25 (the Nubian Dynasty), which controlled Thebes before Ashurbanipal's conquest in 663 BCE. Egypt in the time of Psammeticus (Psamtek) I (663–609 BCE) was centered in the delta at the city of Sais (Memphis), not at Thebes in Upper Egypt. Roberts argues that the later one goes in the fifty-year time slot, the less compelling would the example of Thebes have been for the original hearers of Nahum's message; but this is not necessarily true. The sack of Thebes lived on in popular tradition as the zenith of Assyrian expansion, just as did the sack of Nineveh as an apt symbol of the demise of Assyria and the end of an era. The sack of Rome by Alaric the Visigoth in 410 CE represents another such memorable moment in history, as does the "day of infamy" (December 7, 1941) at Pearl Harbor—and, more recently, the destruction of the World Trade Center in New York City on September 11, 2001, which is commonly referred to as simply 9/11. Roberts says the need to reassure the people and leadership in Judah of YHWH's imminent judgment against Assyria would have been more intense in the earlier part of this time frame. After the abdication of Ashurbanipal (ca. 635 BCE), factional disputes emerged in Assyria on the matter of a successor. And when Babylon successfully revolted against Assyria ca. 625 BCE, the fall of Assyria would no longer have seemed beyond possibility. In fact, the desire to throw off the Assyrian yoke appears to have been one of the motivating factors in Josiah's reform movement in 622 BCE.

A number of older scholars dated the book of Nahum to ca. 630–625 BCE, including Hitzig (1881: 241–42), Kuenen (1875), and Budde (1901b). They argued that Nahum speaks of the yoke of Assyria as still heavy on Judah, though it will be lifted soon (see G. A. Smith 1928: 86). Eybers (1969a: 10) suggested a date about 630, with Nahum as an "instrument in the hand of God to encourage Judah" (cf. also Van Gemeren 1990: 164). Ridderbos dates Nahum shortly after the reformation of Judah in 622 because of the positive attitude expressed toward Judah, as the measures of Josiah's reforms seem to meet with approval (see Spronk 1997: 12). Others, however, have dated the book in conjunction with the fall of Nineveh ca. 612 BCE. Wellhausen (1892: 17) said, "Apart from Herodotus, it would never have occurred to anybody to doubt that Nahum's prophecy coincided with the fall of Nineveh" (reference taken from G. A. Smith 1928: 87; so also Sweeney 2000: 422).

Within critical scholarship, most scholars tend to date the book of Nahum just prior to 612 BCE, because the historical situation would have been clear by then. In short, they tend to see Nahum's "prophecy" as political-military insight. Thus Sweeney (2000: 422) says, "The book of Nahum is to be dated to 612 BCE, either immediately before or after the actual fall of Nineveh to the

Babylonians and Medes." Humbert (1932) placed the book immediately after the fall of Nineveh.

Jeremias (1970: 14) argues that the book of Nahum belongs to the late exilic or early postexilic period and that the prophet's words were originally directed against his own people. His conclusions are based in large part on parallels to the so-called Second Isaiah, where he finds dependence on that literary figure. The direction of literary dependence, however, is always a difficult matter to determine. Schulz (1973) traces a more complex redactional process for the book of Nahum, which Mason (1991: 75) describes as "a *reductio ad absurdum* of the method" itself. At the same time, however, Mason himself (1991: 79) champions a complex redactional model of growth for the book of Nahum as we now have it. Haupt's attempt (1907b: 1–53) to place the book of Nahum in a Maccabean setting as a festal liturgy composed for the celebration of the Day of Nikanor on the 13th day of Adar, 161 BCE, was justifiably put to rest by the discovery of the Qumran commentary on Nahum (4QpNah).

Though the traditional approach to dating the composition of Nahum remains useful in terms of explaining the historical setting against which the book is to be read, it fails to adequately deal with its literary composition as a numerical and musical composition within its present context in the Latter Prophets. The book of Nahum was ultimately written as a numerical composition in the context of the Babylonian Exile or shortly thereafter, for it is an integral part of the Book of the Twelve Prophets in matters of compositional detail. In one sense, then, the redactor of that larger work became the "author" of the book of Nahum, as we now have it, and the historical prophet was lost within the canonical process itself.

In short, there are two different historical settings that the interpreter of the book of Nahum must examine: the setting in which the author intended us to place the content of the book as we read or hear it and the setting in which the author wrote the numerical and musical composition we have in our hands. There is a significant difference between these two historical settings, which helps to explain the diversity among interpreters of the book—both past and present—in dating it. The usual way to talk about this particular problem is to raise with Weigl (2001: 88) the question "Synchronic or Diachronic?" But these very categories are misleading. There is a reason why "historical-critical approaches are definitely on the decline," as Weigl has put it; for we are in the midst of a paradigm shift that requires new ways of thinking about old problems.

Evidence from logoprosodic analysis of the Book of the Twelve Prophets indicates that the question of authorship so far as the book of Nahum is concerned is part of a larger problem—the "authorship" of the Book of the Twelve Prophets itself (see Redditt 2001: 47–80). The book of Nahum has no real history apart from its context as the seventh of twelve "books" within this literary context, for there is no way to demonstrate that the book of Nahum ever existed independently as a document written within the time span reflected in the content of the book itself. If there ever was a prophet in ancient Israel by the name of Nahum who worked in the days of the Neo-Assyrian Empire, we know next to nothing at all about him—and his presumed literary work is beyond recovery on our part. Moreover, that presumed literary work is certainly not this meticulously contrived numerical and musical masterpiece that we have at our disposal to study within the context of the Book of the Twelve Prophets.

Even though it is not essential to know the details of the historical setting in which the book of Nahum is to be read, knowing something about that background does enhance our understanding. The army of King Esarhaddon of Assyria (680–668 BCE) briefly occupied Memphis in Egypt and routed Pharaoh Taharqa (Tirhakah) in 671. But when the Assyrian army departed, Tarharqa revolted, and it was Esarhaddon's son, King Ashurbanipal (668–627 BCE), who conquered Thebes in 663, an event to which Nahum makes specific reference (3:8). The Assyrian conquest of Thebes brought the Assyrian Empire to the height of its power in the ancient Near East.

Much nearer its home base in Mesopotamia, Assyria soon faced a growing challenge from Babylon, which had been a mighty political power a thousand years earlier in the days of Hammurabi and his successors and was destined to succeed Assyria as the next great imperial power in the ancient Near East. Esarhaddon tried to resolve the problem by placing Ashurbanipal's older brother Shamash-shumukin (667–648 BCE) on the throne in Babylon. The arrangement worked for a while after Ashurbanipal began his reign in 668, but Shamash-shumukin led a revolt against his brother in 652, which included King Manasseh of Judah in the coalition. The revolt was quelled four years later, after a long and bloody war. The war took its toll by depleting the resources of the Assyrian Empire as a whole, and Egypt broke free from Assyrian domination. By the time of Ashurbanipal's death (ca. 627), the decline of Assyria had gained momentum.

In 626 Babylon revolted under Nabopolassar, and the political picture becomes somewhat murky until the actual fall of Nineveh in 612 BCE. Nineveh fell, according to Greek sources (Diodorus Siculus and Xenophon), when the waters of the Tigris River were diverted so as to flood the city. In the eyes of many readers, these very events are in view in Nahum's description of the fall of the city in 2:7 [6], 9 [8]. At this point, Nabopolassar emerged as king of the new Babylonian Empire, assisted by his son Nebuchadrezzar, who subsequently destroyed the city of Jerusalem.

It is useful to place these specific events, which constitute the historical background of the fall of Nineveh, within the larger setting that provides perspective for reading the biblical text and the secondary literature on the book of Nahum.

## The Pax Assyriaca (ca. 700–640 BCE)

The emergence of the Ethiopian Dynasty 25 (ca. 710–663) in Egypt set the stage for one of the great power struggles in antiquity. With a direct clash of interest in Lower Egypt and southern Palestine, an eventual confrontation with Assyria was inevitable. As Gardiner (1966: 345–46) noted: "It had long become clear that a decision between the equally pertinacious Assyrian and Ethiopian rulers would have to be reached, but in point of fact there was a third party to the dispute and it was with this that the ultimate victory was destined to lie. As in the time of Pi‘ankhy [Piye], Lower Egypt and a part of Middle Egypt had disintegrated into a number of petty princedoms always ready to side with whichever of the two great powers would be the more likely to leave them their independence. One of these was to prevail before long, but for the moment it was Assyria which held the upper hand." The third party to which Gardiner refers is the royal house of Sais, which, under Psammetichus (Psamtek) I (663–609 BCE), produced the Saite Dynasty 26. The campaigns of Esarhaddon and Ashurbanipal from 675 to 663, climaxed by the sack of Thebes, mark the crest of Assyrian expansion. To defeat the Ethiopians, Ashurbanipal apparently used the royal house in Sais to unify Lower Egypt against the Ethiopian king (*ANET* 294–95). In so doing the Assyrians set the stage for a second phase in the power struggle.

The so-called Saite revival in art, painting and architecture, literature and religion—a nostalgic attempt to re-create the forms and styles of the Old Kingdom of Egypt—reached its height during the fifty-four-year reign of Psammeticus I. After a decade on the throne, Psammeticus shook off the restraint and supervision of the resident Assyrian officials and allied himself with Gyges of Lydia in a successful revolt against Assyria. When Ashurbanipal had finally settled affairs with Elam and the Arab tribes (Qedar) around 640, the independence movement of Psammeticus had gone so far that the Assyrian monarch did not care to risk opposing it. When revolt broke out in Babylon in 652 under Shamash-shumukin, the brother of Ashurbanipal, the conspiracy included Psammeticus in Egypt. Judah was part of this conspiracy against Assyria (2 Chronicles 33:10–15), as was the case earlier in 701 and probably in ca. 688 as well.

Throughout the Neo-Assyrian period, the kings in Nineveh faced what has been aptly called "the Babylonian Problem" (von Voigtlander 1963: 2). As early as 689, Sennacherib found it necessary to destroy the rebellious city of Babylon and to install his son Esarhaddon there as vice regent. On ascending the Assyrian throne in 681, Esarhaddon continued a pro-Babylonian policy

(Olmstead 1923: 347–50, 352). In 672 he designated his sons Ashurbanipal and Shamash-shumukin to succeed him as kings of Assyria and Babylon, respectively. His intention seems to have been to create a double line of kings with an independent entity in Babylonia ruled by an Assyrian line of kings.

Esarhaddon's plan, like that of the anomalous Ausgleich compromise in the Dual Monarchy of Austria-Hungary, was doomed to failure. As von Voigtlander (1963: 4, n. 8) put it: "Assurbanipal . . . retained military control of Nippur, probably on advice of councilors who had distrusted the 'brother kings' arrangement from the first. He also retained the prerogative of placing his name as king of Assyria on the temple restorations and religious dedications of the period." After a period of amicable relations, the experiment came to its predictable end. Stung by increasing encroachments on his autonomy, Shamash-shumukin formed a widespread alliance with Elam, the Chaldeans and Arameans, Qedar, and distant Egypt in revolt against his brother. In three years of bitterly fought campaigns, Ashurbanipal regained control of Babylonia. His brother Shamash-shumukin died in the conflagration that marked the end of the siege of Babylon in 648. Ashurbanipal then installed Kandalanu, who ruled as nominal king of Babylon for at least twenty years.

In the past a number of scholars conjectured that Kandalanu was, in fact, Ashurbanipal ruling under a Babylonian throne name in the tradition of his predecessors Tiglath-pileser III (Pulu) and Shalmaneser V (Ululaia) (see von Voigtlander 1963: 5; cf. Babylonian King List A in *ANET* 272). Von Voigtlander (1963: 7–8; 27, n. 20) presented a more convincing case for the identity of Kandalanu with Asshuretililani, the son and successor of Ashurbanipal: "The experience of the early Sargonids had shown that an empty throne in Babylon created a political vacuum destined to be filled by a local aspirant inimical to Assyrian interests. The Assyrians had tried the solution of nominating and supporting a local puppet only to discover that weaklings were frequently faithless. The most satisfactory solution yet found had been the later policy of Sennacherib. His son Assur-etil-ilani, who was probably still a minor, was therefore nominated to the Babylonian throne, reigning under his by-name Kandalanu." It is possible that in the early years of his kingship, Kandalanu remained in Assyria, exercising only nominal kingship in Babylon. Two letters, however, both demonstrably addressed to a son of Ashurbanipal ruling in Babylon, give evidence that at some subsequent time Kandalanu/Asshuretililani was actively engaged in administration in Babylon (von Voigtlander 1963: 27–28, n. 22).

## The Regnum Davidicum Redivivum (ca. 640–609 BCE)

Little is known concerning the history of Babylon and Assyria for the decade from 640 to 630 BCE. The eponym (*limmu*) lists run only until 648. After that date it is necessary to reconstruct a chronological list from the *limmu* as they appear on documents. A number of indications suggest that the last years of Ashurbanipal were troubled ones. By the end of the decade the growing weakness of Assyria was clearly evident in the West, as shown by Josiah's reform movement in Jerusalem, which had its inception in 632.

The chronology of the transition between the end of Assyrian rule in Babylon and the rise of Nabopolassar to power in 626 is a vexed problem. The latest tablet from Ashurbanipal's reign comes from Nippur and is dated in the third month of this thirty-eighth year (June 631) (von Voigtlander 1963: 10; see also A. J. Sachs, in Wiseman 1956: 92). The so-called Harran inscriptions of Nabonidus's mother, discovered in 1956, gives forty-two years to Ashurbanipal (Gadd 1958: 35–92). In this inscription, the mother of Nabonidus named the seven kings under whom she lived out her 104 years, carefully counting the years of each king. Von Voigtlander (1963: 226–27) drew the following conclusion from her careful analysis of the inscription in question: "It is useless to approach the above statements from the view of absolute chronology. Let us instead consider that they report what a very aged woman believed to be her birthdate and her, and probably her son's, statement of her age. Superimposed on this is the effort of the redactor to correlate these statements with his understanding of Assyro-Babylonian chronology."

Ashurbanipal probably died in or about 627 and was succeeded by his son Asshuretililani, whose latest document is from Nippur, dated 4/VII/1 (October 627). By the end of 627 Sinsharishkun had eliminated his brother Asshuretililani, and shortly thereafter a certain Sinshumlishir, commander of the Nippur garrison, laid claim to the throne of Assyria (von Voigtlander 1963: 16; 30, n. 40). Von Voigtlander suggested that Sinsharishkun and Sinshumlisher are in fact two names for the same individual, the latter being a throne name. He also described the year 627/26 as "the year in which there was no king in the land" (1963: 14). In the year 626, the diadem of Babylon passed from the hands of Assyria to the Chaldean Nabopolassar (626–605), who organized a new dynasty in Babylon. The death throes of the once mighty Assyrian Empire were near at hand.

With the decline of Assyria after the middle of the seventh century BCE, the stage was set for the resurgence of Judah among the nations. With the outbreak of hostilities in Syria and Mesopotamia from 652 to 648, pressure no doubt mounted on Manasseh to bring Judah into the widespread revolt. As Wright (1957: 176) noted, "This would have been the most natural occasion for the revolt of Manasseh as described in II Chron. 33:11." If indeed, Manasseh was taken by the commanders of the army of the king of Assyria with hooks and bound with fetters of bronze and brought to Babylon, he was subsequently restored to his throne as an Assyrian vassal.

From 648 to his death in 642, Manasseh remained a loyal vassal of Assyria, and his son Amon (642–640) apparently continued his father's policy. When Elam, the Arab confederacy, and Tyre were again in revolt against Assyria in 640, pressure was once more exerted on Judah to join in as well. The assassination of Amon was probably an attempt on the part of the rebel extremists to force Judah to throw off the Assyrian yoke. Instead, a more moderate group, the "people of the land," regained control in Judah, executed the kings' murderers, and installed the eight-year-old Josiah (640–609) as king of Judah. This action apparently staved off Assyrian intervention in Judah, though it seems that the advisers to the young king were merely seeking a more opportune time to restore the "kingdom of David."

According to 2 Chronicles 34:3, in the eighth year of his reign Josiah "began to seek the God of David his father." In other words, as early as 632 Josiah repudiated the gods of his Assyrian overlords (Cross and Freedman 1953b: 57). Four years later he annexed the Assyrian provinces to the north— Samaria, Megiddo, and probably Gilead. According to Ginsberg (1950: 347–68): "Josiah, then, reconquered even Israelite Transjordan, or part of it, and in so doing came into conflict with the children of Ammon. . . . It is, moreover, not out of the question that Josiah, in restoring the ancient empire of king David, brought not only practically all of the former territories of Judah and Israel under his direct rule but also the three Transjordan states (minus such territories) under his suzerainty." Of the three Transjordan states only Moab, which was but a shadow of her former self, escaped direct territorial incursion on the part of Judah. The Negev in particular was wrested from Edomite control.

Unfortunately for Judah, however, the international situation in the Levant in the seventh century was only superficially similar to that of the tenth century, such that it was quite impossible to restore the empire of David for any length of time. Egypt was again seeking an Asian empire of her own, and the temporary vacuum formed by the demise of Assyria was soon to be filled by another great power in Mesopotamia—the Neo-Babylonian Empire. Josiah met his death at Megiddo in 609 at the hands of Necho II (609–594), who was on his way north to Harran to check the progress of the Medo-Babylonian alliance against Assyria (see Nelson 1983: 186–89).

## The Rise of Babylon and the Fall of Nineveh (626–612 BCE)

The accession of Nabopolassar to the Babylonian throne in 626 marked the beginning of a new era in the history of the ancient Near East. Portrayed as an Assyrian commander, perhaps by birth a Chaldean, Nabopolassar took advantage of the Assyrian dynastic troubles to set up a Babylonian state (see von Voigtlander 1963: 17–18). The Babylonian Chronicle for 626 begins with a revolt in Babylon in which Nabopolassar routed the Assyrian garrison established by Sinsharishkun. The insurrection gained momentum, and by the end of 626 Nabopolassar also held Uruk. On the 26th day of Arahsamnu (November 23, 626), Nabopolassar was formally seated as king in Babylon (Wiseman 1956: BM 25127, 14–15). As his first official act in the Chronicle was that of returning to Susa the gods carried off to Uruk by the Assyrians some twenty years earlier, it is clear that he either had or hoped to have Elamite (or Persian) support in his struggle against Assyria.

Despite the testimony of the king list, which gives Nabopolassar an uninterrupted twenty-one-year reign, possession of Babylon was in dispute for some time. By November 624, Uruk was retaken by the Assyrian forces of Sinsharishkun (von Voigtlander 1963: 20). In 623 the Assyrians extended their military operations still farther to deal with a revolt in Der, a key city east of the Tigris. Because Der controlled one of the main routes into Elam, it seems likely that Elam was in league with Babylon in revolt against Assyria. Later in 623, Sinsharishkun, with his army, finally appeared in Babylonia. Though the Chronicle account unfortunately breaks off at this point, there seems little reason to doubt von Voigtlander's conclusion that Nabopolassar's hold on Babylon was secure by the end of 623. By midsummer of 621, Nabopolassar was again recognized in Uruk. Nippur probably also succumbed to the overwhelming Babylonian pressure at this time (von Voigtlander 1963: 22–23, 68).

After the fall of Nippur, Nabopolassar turned his attention to the middle and upper Euphrates in an attempt to force a passage through to the Mediterranean. Moving up the Euphrates, Nabopolassar engaged the Assyrians on July 23, 616. The Assyrian forces fled in disorder after the initial attack. In a second encounter in September, the "army of Egypt" appeared along with the Assyrians in opposition to Nabopolassar (see Wiseman 1956: BM 21901, 10–11). Because Egyptian forces had not appeared in Syria since the conspiracy against Sargon by the Egyptian (or Ethiopian) general Re'u a century earlier (in 720), this reference to the "army of Egypt" has invited speculation. Assyrian domination in Egypt came to an end with the energetic policies of Psammeticus I (see Drioton and Vandier 1952: 576). The penetration of an Egyptian force so far into Syria in 616 can only mean that the Egyptians were aware of the growing weakness of Assyria and perhaps also of Nabopolassar's intention to establish Babylonian control there. As von Voigtlander (1963: 72) argued, "It is not necessary to suppose that the Egyptians and Assyrians were allies at this time. Following this, there is no mention of the presence of Egyptian forces in the area for six years. It is difficult to believe that the fate of Assyria itself concerned the Egyptians directly. Their interest lay in control of the provinces between Egypt and Assyria." At this point Egypt was probably nothing more than an interested neutral party in the power struggle to the north.

However one interprets the Egyptian presence in Syria in 616, it is clearly evident that a notable weakening of Assyria had occurred. The following year the Medes joined Babylon and Egypt in the power struggle to succeed decadent Assyria. Von Voigtlander argues that this weakening of Assyria was not due to Babylonian pressure alone. Warfare between factions within Assyria itself apparently contributed to Assyrian decline. Sinsharishkun's belated foray into Babylonia in 623 appears to have been the action "of a man, hard pressed elsewhere, who snatches time for temporary measures to control a local insurrection" (von Voigtlander 1963: 73). It is also probable that the Medes had already begun their series of incursions into Assyrian territory (cf. Herodotus 1921: I, 102).

Aware that Egypt was now a potential enemy to any force pushing into Syria, Nabopolassar allied himself with the Medes to destroy the great citadels of Assyria along the Tigris. The Medes may not have welcomed Nabopolassar's intrusion into Assyria with much enthusiasm, for they had their own plans of conquest and expansion. Nonetheless, the threat of a possible alliance between Assyria and Babylon against them was adequate reason to convince the Medes to go along with the Babylonian venture.

In May 615, Nabopolassar laid siege to Asshur but was forced to retreat before the Assyrian forces of Sinsharishkun. By midsummer of 614, an army of Medes was advancing toward Nineveh (Wiseman: 1956: BM 21901, 26–28). Turning downstream along the bank of the Tigris, the Medes attacked Asshur, which was poorly defended because Sinsharishkun had gone to the defense of Nineveh. The city was sacked and its inhabitants massacred. The destruction of Asshur was such a shocking violation of international practice of the time, which usually permitted a city to ransom itself unless it could be termed "rebellious," that even the Babylonian chronicler took pains to dissociate Nabopolassar from this act of savagery. The Chronicle specifically states that although Nabopolassar was coming to assist the Medes, he did not arrive until after the sack (Wiseman 1956: BM 21901, 26–28). Nabopolassar and Umak-ishtar, king of the Medes, then concluded an alliance of "peace and cordial relations" that apparently remained in effect through the major campaigns against Nineveh (612) and Harran (610). After 609 the Medes disappear from the extant chronicles.

After two unsuccessful assaults on Nineveh and a three-month siege in 612, the wall of the city was finally breached and the Medes and Babylonians poured into the city. Sinsharishkun died, as had Shamash-shumukin before him, in the ruins of the city (von Voigtlander 1963: 85, n. 43). Though Nineveh was utterly destroyed, Sinsharishkun's son Asshuruballit II (611–609) did manage to escape and made his way to Harran, the final bastion of Assyria. Between 612 and 610, Egypt formed an alliance with the badly shattered Assyrians at Harran. Egypt had no intention of restoring the Assyrian Empire as such; rather the object was to keep Syria and the Mediterranean littoral from falling into Babylonian hands. In 610 the combined armies of Babylonia and the Medes marched against the Assyrians and an Egyptian contingent at Harran. The Egyptian force was a garrison awaiting reinforcements from Pharaoh Necho's army, which was apparently delayed at Megiddo by Josiah in 609. Josiah was killed in that encounter with the army of Pharaoh Necho. The Assyrians and Egyptians fled from Harran, evidently without a struggle, and the city was taken. A vain attempt on the part of Asshuruballit to retake Harran in 609 with Egyptian help failed (*ARAB*, 2:1182). The final curtain had fallen on Assyrian power in the ancient Near East.

## The Text of the Book of Nahum

The Hebrew text within the Masoretic tradition has been transmitted with great care and relatively little evidence of textual corruption. The text of *Codex L*, as published in *BHS*, has four instances of marginal corrections (*kǝtîb-qǝrê* readings), and there is a fifth such occurrence in 2:4 in the MT, which is not indicated in *BHS*:

| | | | | |
|---|---|---|---|---|
| 1:3 | *wǝgādôl koaḥ* | is read as | *ûgǝdal-kōaḥ* | omitting *waw* |
| 2:1 | *laʿǎbāwr bāk* | is read as | *laʿǎbor-bāk* | omitting *waw* |
| 2:4 | *pǝlādôt* | is read as | *pǝlādōt* | omitting *waw* |
| 2:6 | *bahǎlikāwtām* | is read as | *bahǎlîkātām* | omitting *waw* and adding *yod* |
| 3:3 | *yǝkāšǝlû* | is read as | *wǝkāšǝlû* | reading *waw* in place of *yod* |

With the exception of minor details, the text of *Codex L* is supported by the scroll of the Twelve Prophets found at Wadi Murrabbaʿat (= Mur) and the commentary on the book of Nahum found at Qumran (= 4QpNah).

The Greek translation of the LXX differs from the MT in a number of places, but these differences can be explained as misunderstanding or interpretive glossing on the part of the translator rather than as the use of a different Hebrew text as such. The Greek translations of Aquila, Symmachus, and Theodotion stay closer to the MT. The Greek scroll of the Minor Prophets from Naḥal Ḥ-ever (= Ḥ-ev) appears to be an early revision of the LXX, which for the most part supports the reading of the MT.

The Syriac Peshiṭta, which is dated "shortly before the final fixation of MT," agrees with the MT, though there is evidence of some influence from the LXX (Gelston 1988: 98). On some minor points, such as the added *waw* conjunction in 3:3, 11, the Syriac agrees with variant readings in 4QpNah (Spronk 1997: 2). According to Gordon (1994: 67), the variant readings of Nahum in the Targum "provide no evidence of a divergent Hebrew *Vorlage*." The same appears to be the case for the Latin Vulgate.

A glance at the footnotes in *BHS* suggests that the Hebrew text of Nahum is poorly preserved, with 103 possible emendations suggested in 47 verses (for an average of more than 2 suggested emendations per verse). The initial impression is that the transmitted text is almost hopelessly corrupt. This impression is underscored by a survey of the older commentaries, especially as regards the presumed alphabetic acrostic at the beginning of the book, which is sometimes restored by complex text-critical gymnastics. Though the extreme position on this matter taken by Gunkel (1893), Bickell (1894), Arnold (1901), and others was ultimately abandoned, scholars continue to "improve" the text by way of emendation. Roberts (1991) proposes a total of 36 emendations in his commentary, and the NRSV has 10 emendations, 9 with appropriate footnotes—4 on the basis of the LXX (1:8a; 2:4a [3a], 9 [8]; 3:9) and 5 conjectural (2:2 [1], 8 [7], 12 [11], 14 [13]; 3:4)—and an additional conjectural emendation without a footnote (1:4a), where the same Hebrew word is translated with two different English words.

In sharp contrast to authors of earlier commentaries, Spronk (1997: 3) reaches the following conclusion: "Most problems can be solved on the basis of the structural analysis of the text and a close examination of the extraordinary style of the poet." Spronk proposes five slight emendations (1:4b, 6a, 12a, 13a; 3:9b) plus the removal of a total of twenty-eight words in three instances of what he calls "early explanatory glosses" (2:1c; 3:16b–17a, 19b). An increasing number of scholars today share similar beliefs, which favor the general integrity of the MT (see Weigl 2001: 87).

The logoprosodic analysis presented here posits eight emendations, other than the necessary choice in the case of the four marginal *kǝtîb-qǝrê* readings in the MT (1:3a; 2:1b, 6a; 3:3b), and most of these changes have little effect on the meaning per se:

| | |
|---|---|
| 1:4b | reading the plural form of the verb *ʾumlǝlû* to match the plural subject |
| 1:12a | reading the plural form of the verb *wǝʿābārû* ("and they will pass on") with Tg in place of the singular form *wǝʿābār* ("and he will pass on") in *BHS* |
| 1:13a | reading *maṭṭēhû* ("his rod") with LXX, Vg, Syriac, Tg, and some Heb. Mss in place of *mōṭēhû* ("his yoke") in *BHS* |

2:9      Reading *mêmệhā hāwʾû hēmmāh nāsîm* ("her waters fall / they flee") in place of *mîmê hîʾ wǝhēmmāh nāsîm* ("from of old she is / and they flee") in *BHS*

2:12a    reading *ûmǝʿārāh* ("and the cave") in place of *ûmirʿeh* ("and the feeding place") in *BHS*

2:13a    reading *gōrāyw* rather than *gōrôṯāyw* with 4QpNah

3:4b     reading *hannōḵereṯ* for *hammōḵereṯ* with Pinker 2004c: 5 (cf. Rashi)

3:10b    adding the word *kol* ("all") with LXX

In three instances (2:14a; 3:13d; 3:14d), the reading of the accentual system in the Ginsberg Bible (1894: 1089), which is also found in the popular Letteris edition (1880), is followed in place of what appears in *BHS*. In 2:14a, Ginsberg and Letteris have the conjunctive accent *ʾazlâ,* whereas *BHS* has the disjunctive accent *pašṭâ* on the word *nǝʾūm* ("utterance"). In 3:13d, Ginsberg and Letteris have a *gaʿyâ* (= *meṯeḡ*) on the word *šaʿărê* ("gates"), whereas *BHS* omits the *gaʿyâ*. The addition of the *gaʿyâ* here transforms the *mûnaḥ* on this word into a disjunctive accent in the logoprosodic analysis of the text. In 3:14d, Ginsberg and Letteris have a *gaʿyâ* (= *meṯeḡ*) on the word *hahăzîqî* ("make strong"), whereas *BHS* omits the *gaʿyâ*. The addition of the *gaʿyâ* here transforms the *mêrǝḵâ* on this word into a disjunctive accent in the logoprosodic analysis of the text. In short, the received Hebrew text of Nahum in the MT stands among the better-preserved texts in the entire Tanakh.

In seventeen instances, specific accent signs (*ṭǝʿamîm*) are read differently from what is suggested in current usage elsewhere:

| | |
|---|---|
| 1:14b; 3:13a | *ʾazlâ* is read as disjunctive |
| 2:3b, 5b; 3:6 | *ṭipḥâ* is read as conjunctive |
| 2:3c, 5c, 14b | *pašṭâ* is read as conjunctive |
| 2:8a, 12b, 13b; 3:15b, 19a | *mûnaḥ* is read as disjunctive |
| 2:9a, 11a; 3:18a | *mêrǝḵâ* is read as disjunctive |
| 3:15a | *yǝṯîḇ* is read as conjunctive |

It remains to be seen whether these readings constitute emendations as such. There is still much we do not know about the distinction between conjunctive and disjunctive status among the Masoretic accents in terms of their function as musical notation.

# Bibliography

.

The bibliography here is not intended to be a complete listing of the literature on the book of Nahum. For the most part, it provides references to sources referred to in the Notes and Comments. Terms abbreviated are spelled out under "Principal Abbreviations" near the front of the book. References cited in the text solely by their abbreviations appear only in the list of abbreviations, with full bibliographical information there.

## Commentaries

Abarbanel, Isaac (1437–1508) [also: Abrabanel, Abravenal]
    n.d.    *Perush Abarbanel Hashalem.* Jerusalem: Mifalei Sepharim
                LeYetzu. Year not provided. Photostat of 2nd ed.
Achtemeier, Elizabeth R.
    1986    *Nahum–Malachi.* Interpretation: A Bible Commentary for
                Teaching and Preaching. Atlanta: John Knox.
Alonso Schökel, Luis (with the literary collaboration of
  José María Valverda)
    1966    *Doce profetas menores.* Madrid: Ediciones Cristiandad.
Altshuler, Yehiel Hillel
    1753    Metzudot. In *Mikraoth Gedolah / Neviim Ahronim.* Jerusalem
                1959. Metzudot is the commentary of Y. H. Altschuler, who
                lived in Prag and Galicia in the eighteenth century. He com-
                pleted the commentary begun by his father, David Altschuler.
Armerding, C. E.
    1985    Nahum. Pp. 447–89 in *The Expositor's Bible Commentary,*
                vol. 7. Grand Rapids, Mich.: Zondervan.

Austel, Hermann J.
  1989    Nahum. Pp. 659–65 in *Evangelical Commentary on the Bible*, ed. Walter A. Elwell. Grand Rapids, Mich.: Baker.
Baker, David W.
  1988    *Nahum, Habakkuk and Zephaniah.* Tyndale Old Testament Commentaries. Downers Grove, Ill.: Inter-Varsity.
Barker, Kenneth L., and Waylon Bailey
  1998    *Micah, Nahum, Habakkuk, Zephaniah.* Vol. 20 of the New American Commentary: An Exegetical and Theological Exposition of Holy Scripture. Nashville, Tenn.: Broadman and Holman.
Bennett, T. M.
  1969    *The Books of Nahum and Zephaniah.* Grand Rapids, Mich.: Baker.
Bernini, Giuseppe
  1970    *Osea, Michea, Nahum, Abacuc.* Rome: Edizioni Paoline.
Bévenot, Hugh
  1937    *The Old Testament, Nahum and Habakkuk.* In Westminster Version of the Sacred Scriptures. London, New York, and Toronto: Longmans, Green.
Blaiklock, E. M.
  1986    Nahum. Pp. 938–42 in *The International Bible Commentary.* Grand Rapids, Mich.: Zondervan. 1st edition, 1979.
Boice, James Montgomery (1938–)
  1986    *The Minor Prophets*, vol. 2. Grand Rapids, Mich.: Zondervan.
Bolle, M.
  1990    Sepher Nahum. In *Tere ꜤAsar im Perush Daat Mikra*, vol. 2. Jerusalem: Mosad ha-Rav Kuk.
Brandenburg, Hans
  1963    *Die Kleinen Propheten*, vol. 1. Das Lebendige Wort, 10. Basel/Giessen: Brunnen.
Buber, Martin, and Franz Rosenzweig
  1934    *Die Schrift, zu verdeutschen unternommen.* Berlin: Schocken.
Butterworth, Mike
  1994    Nahum. Pp. 834–39 in *New Bible Commentary: 21st Century Edition*, ed. D. A. Carson, R. T. France, J. A. Motyer, and G. J. Wenham. Downers Grove, Ill.: Inter-Varsity. Rev. ed. of *The New Bible Commentary*, 1953.
Calvin, John (1509–64)
  1559    *Prelectiones in duodecim prophetas (quos vocant) minores.* Geneva: Eustathium Vignon, 1581.
  1948    *Commentaries on the Twelve Minor Prophets.* Vol. 3. Trans. J. Owen. Edinburgh: Printed for the Calvin Translation Society.
  1950    *Commentaries on the Twelve Minor Prophets.* Vol. 3. Trans. John Owen. Grand Rapids, Mich.: Eerdmans.

1986     *Commentary on the Twelve Minor Prophets.* The Geneva series of commentaries. Edinburgh and Carlisle, Pa.: Banner of Truth Trust.

Christensen, D. L.
1988a    Nahum. Pp. 736–38 in *Harper's Bible Commentary,* ed. J. L. Mays. San Francisco: Harper and Row.

Clarke, Adam (1762–1832)
1817     Nahum. Pp. 730–39 in vol. 4 of *The Holy Bible Containing the Old and New Testaments.* 6 vols. New York: Daniel Hitt and Abraham Paul.

Coggins, Richard
1985     *Israel among the Nations: A Commentary on the Books of Nahum and Obadiah / Richard J. Coggins; And [on] Esther [by] S. Paul Re'emi.* Pp. 1–63 in *In Wrath Remember Mercy: A Commentary on the Book of Nahum; Israel among the Nations,* ed. R. J. Coggins and S. P. Re'emi. International Theological Commentary. Grand Rapids, Mich.: Eerdmans.

Cohen, A. (ed.)
1985     *The Twelve Prophets.* London and New York: Soncino.
1994     *The Twelve Prophets.* Rev. A. J. Rosenburg. London and New York: Soncino.

Craigie, Peter C.
1985     *Twelve Prophets.* Vol. 2 of the Daily Study Bible Series. Philadelphia, Pa.: Westminster.

Davidson, Andrew Bruce (1831–1902)
1896     *Nahum, Habakkuk and Zephaniah.* Cambridge Bible. Cambridge: Cambridge UP.
1920     *The Books of Nahum, Habakkuk and Zephaniah.* Adapted to the text of the Revised Version with some supplementary notes by H. C. O. Lanchester. Cambridge: Cambridge UP.

Deissler, Alfons
1984     *Zwölf Propheten II: Obadja, Jona, Micha, Nahum, Habakuk.* NEB. Würzburg: Echter.

Delcor, M.
1961     Nahum. Pp. 369–87 in *Les petits prophètes,* ed. A. Deissler and M. Delcor. SBPC 8/1. Paris: Letouzey and Ané.

De Vries, Simon J.
1971     The Book of Nahum. Pp. 491–93 in *The Interpreter's One-Volume Commentary on the Bible,* ed. Charles M. Laymon. Nashville, Tenn.: Abingdon.

Driver, S. R.
1906     *The Minor Prophets.* The New-Century Bible. New York: Henry Frowde. Edinburgh: T. C. and E. C. Jack.

Duhm, Bernard
    1910     *Die Zwölf Propheten.* Tübingen: J. C. B. Mohr (Paul Siebeck).
    1912     *The Twelve Prophets: A Version in the Various Poetical Measures of the Original Writings.* London: Adam and Charles Black.
Dupont-Sommer, A.
    1987     Commentaires bibliques 1: Habacuc, 2, Nahum, 3, Psaume XXXVII. Pp. 333–80 in *La Bible: Ecrits intertestamentaires,* ed. A. Dupont-Sommer and M. Philonenko. Bibliothèque de la Pleiade. Paris: Gallimard.
Eaton, J. H.
    1961     *Obadiah, Nahum, Habakkuk and Zephaniah.* TBC. London: SCM.
Edelkoort, A. H.
    1937     *Nahum, Habakuk, Zefanja: Drie profeten voor onzen tijd.* Amsterdam: H. J. Paris.
Elliger, K. (1901–77)
    1949     *Das Buch der zwölf Kleinen Propheten, II: Die Propheten Nahum, Habakuk, Zephanja, Haggai, Sacharja, Maleachi.* ATD 25/II, 3rd ed. Göttingen: Vandenhoeck and Ruprecht. 3rd ed., 1955; 6th ed. 1967.
    1959     *Das Buch der zwölf kleinen Propheten,* 4th ed. Göttingen: Vandenhoeck and Ruprecht.
Ewald, G. H. A. von (1803–75)
    1840     *Die Propheten des alten Bundes erklärt.* 5 vols. Göttingen: Vandenhoeck and Ruprecht. 2nd ed., 1867.
    1878     *Commentary on the Prophets of the Old Testament,* vol. 3. J. Trans. Frederick Smith. London and Edinburg: Williams and Norgate. Translation of Ewald, 1867.
Fabry, Heinz-Josef
    2006     *Nahum.* Herders Theologischer Kommentar zum Alten Testament. Freiburg, Basel, and Vienna: Herder.
Ferreiro, Alberto, and Thomas C. Oden
    2003     *The Twelve Prophets.* Downer's Grove, Ill.: Inter-Varsity Press.
Floyd, M.
    2000     *Minor Prophets, Part 2,* pp. 1–78. FOTL 22. Grand Rapids, Mich.: Eerdmans.
Gandell, R.
    1901     Nahum. Pp. 637–49 in *The Speaker's Commentary* [*The Holy Bible According to the Authorized Version with an Explanatory and Critical Commentary and a Revision of the Translation by Bishops and Other Clergy of the Anglican Church*], vol. 6, ed. F. C. Cook. New York: Charles Scribner's Sons.
García-Treto, F. O.
    1996     The Book of Nahum: Introduction, Commentary, and Reflections. Pp. 591–619 in *New Interpreter's Bible, VII: Introduction*

*to Apocalyptic Literature, Daniel, The Twelve Prophets*, ed.
L. E. Keck et al. Nashville, Tenn.: Abingdon.

Gebhardi, Julio Justo
1737    *D. Brandani Henrici Gebhardi . . . Gründliche einleitung in die*
        *zwölff kleinen Propheten, zuvor eintzeln ans licht gegeben, nun-*
        *mehro aber bey dieser 2. auf. zusammen degruckt, nebst einer*
        *vorrede von dem lebens-lauff und gesammten schrifften des sel.*
        *herrn autoris*. Braunschweig: L. Schröders sel. wittwe.

George, A.
1958    *Michée, Sophonie, Nahum*, 2nd ed. SBJ. Paris: Editions du
        Cerf.

Gordon, A. R.
1929    Nahum. Pp. 564–65 in A *Commentary on the Bible*, ed. Arthur
        S. Peake. London: T. C. and E. C. Jack.

Greve, Egbert Jan (1754–1811)
1793    *Vaticinia Nahum et Habacuci: Editio metrica*. Amsterdam:
        P. den Hengst.

Guthe, H.
1923    Der Prophet Nahum. Pp. 66–71 in *Die Heilige Schrift des*
        *Alten Testaments*, 4th ed. Ed. E. Kautzsch. Tübingen: J. C. B.
        Mohr. 1st ed. 1909.

Hailey, M.
1972    A *Commentary on the Minor Prophets*. Grand Rapids, Mich.:
        Baker.

Happel, Otto
1902    *Das Buch des Propheten Nahum erklärt*. Würzburg: Gogel and
        Scherer.

Haupt, Paul
1907a   *The Book of Nahum: A New Metrical Translation with an Intro-*
        *duction, Restoration of the Hebrew Text and Explanatory and*
        *Critical Notes*. Baltimore, Md.: Johns Hopkins UP.

Heflin, J. N. Boo
1985    *Nahum, Habakkuk, and Haggai*. BSC. Grand Rapids, Mich.:
        Zondervan.

Henderson, Ebenezer (1784–1858)
1845    *The Book of the Twelve Minor Prophets*. London: Hamilton,
        Adams.

Henry, Matthew (1662–1714)
1829    *An Exposition of the Old and New Testament*. 6 vols. Philadel-
        phia, Pa.: Towar and Hogan.

Hinton, Linda B.
1994    *Micah, Nahum, Habakkuk, Zephaniah, Haggai, Zechariah,*
        *and Malachi*. Nashville, Tenn.: Abingdon.

Hitzig, Ferdinand
    1881    *Die zwölf kleinen Propheten*, 4th ed. KEHAT, ed. Heinrich
            Steiner. Leipzig: Hirzel.
Holland, M.
    1986    *Die Propheten Nahum, Habakuk und Zephanja.* Wuppertaler
            Studienbibel. Wuppertal, Germany: R. Brockhaus.
Horst, Friedrich
    1938    Nahum. Pp. 153–66 in *Die zwölf kleinen Propheten, Nahum
            bis Maleachi*, 2nd ed. HAT. Tübingen: Mohr, 1954. 3rd ed.,
            1964.
Hyatt, J. P.
    1962    Nahum. Pp. 635–36 in *Peake's Commentary on the Bible*, ed.
            H. H. Rowley. London: Thomas Nelson and Sons.
Ibn Ezra, Abraham ben Meir (1092–1167)
    1989    *The Twelve Prophets.* Ed. Uriel Shimon. Ramat Gan, Israel:
            University Bar-Ilan. In Hebrew.
Jamieson, R., A. R. Fausett, and D. Brown
    1872    Nahum. Pp. 698–701 in *A Commentary, Critical and Explana-
            tory, on the Old and New Testaments.* Hartford, Conn.: S. S.
            Scranton.
Junker, Hubert
    1938    *Die zwölf kleinen Propheten, II, Hälfte: Nahum, Habakuk,
            Sophonias, Aggäus, Zacharias, Malachias.* Heilige Schrift des
            Alten Testamentes, Bd. 8, Abt. 3:2. Bonn: Peter Hanstein.
Justi, Karl Wilhelm (1767–1846)
    1820    *Nahum neu übersetzt und erläutert.* Leipzig: Barth.
Kaiser, W. C.
    1992    *Micah–Malachi.* The Communicator's Commentary Series,
            Old Testament, 21. Dallas: Word.
Keil, Carl Friedrich (1807–88)
    1888    *Biblischer Commentar über die zwölf kleinen Propheten.*
            Biblischer Commentar III/4. Leipzig: Dörffling und
            Franke.
    1949    Nahum. Pp. 1–48 in *The Twelve Minor Prophets*, vol. 2:
            *Nahum-Malachi.* Trans. James Martin. Biblical Commentary
            on the Old Testament. Reprinted Grand Rapids, Mich.:
            Eerdmans. 1st published in German, 1868.
    1995    *Biblical Commentary on . . . the Twelve Minor Prophets.* Trans.
            James Martin. Edinburgh: T. and T. Clark.
Keil, Carl Friedrich, and F. Delitzsch
    1971    *Biblical Commentary on the Old Testament: The Twelve Minor
            Prophets*, vol. 2. Trans. James Martin. Grand Rapids, Mich.:
            Eerdmans.

Keller, Carl-A.
1971    *Nahoum.* Pp. 93–134 in *Michée, Nahoum, Habacuc, Sophonie*,
        by René Vuilleumier and Carl-A. Keller. CAT 11B. Neuchâtel:
        Delachaux et Niestlé.
Kelley, Page H.
1984    *Micah, Nahum, Habakkuk, Zephankiah, Haggai, Zechariah,
        Malachi.* Nashville, Tenn.: Broadman.
Kimchi, David (d. 1235)
1927    *Der Kommentar des David Kimchi zum Propheten Nahum*,
        ed. Walter Windfuhr. Rabbinische Übungstexte I. Gießen:
        Töpelmann.
Kleinert, Hugo Wilhelm Paul (1837–1920)
1874    *The Book of Nahum.* Trans. and enlarged by Charles Elliott.
        New York: Scribner, Armstrong. German version, 1868.
Knabenbauer, Joseph (1839–1911)
1886    *Commentarius in prophetas minores.* Paris: Lethielleux.
Kraeling, E. M.
1966    *Commentary on the Prophets*, II. Camden, N.J.: T. Nelson.
Kraft, Charles F., and Charles M. Laymon
1983    *The Minor Prophets and the Apocrypha: A Commentary on
        Hosea, Joel, Amos, Obadiah, Jonah, Micah, Nahum, Habakkuk,
        Zephaniah, Haggai, Zechariah, Malachi, the Old Testament
        Apocrypha.* Nashville, Tenn.: Abingdon.
Laetsch, Theo
1956    Nahum. Pp. 293–312 in *Bible Commentary: The Minor
        Prophets.* St. Louis, Mo.: Concordia.
Lehrman, S. M.
1948    Nahum: נחום. In *The Twelve Prophets*, ed. A. Cohen. SBBS,
        vol. 8. New York: Soncino.
1970    נחום Nahum. Pp. 190–208 in *The Twelve Prophets*. SBBS.
        London: Soncino.
Lehrman, S. M., and A. J. Rosenberg
1994    Nahum: נחום . Pp. 190–208 in *The Twelve Prophets*, ed.
        A. Cohen and rev. by A. J. Rosenberg. SBBS, rev. 2nd ed.
        1st ed. 1948.
Lippl, Joseph (1876–1935)
1937    *Die zwölf kleinen Propheten.* Bonn: Hanstein.
Longman, Tremper III
1993    Nahum. Pp. 765–829 in *The Minor Prophets: An Exegetical
        and Expository Commentary*, ed. T. E. McComiskey, vol. 2.
        Grand Rapids, Mich.: Baker.
Machinist, Peter
2000    Nahum. Pp. 665–67 in *HarperCollins Bible Commentary*, ed.
        J. L. Mays et al. San Francisco: Harper.

Maier, W. A.
  1959      *The Book of Nahum: A Commentary.* St. Louis, Mo.: Concordia.
Marks, H.
  1987      The Twelve Prophets. Pp. 207–33 in *The Literary Guide to the Bible,* ed. R. Alter and F. Kermode. Cambridge, Mass.: Belknap Press of Harvard UP.
Marti, Karl (1855–1925)
  1903      *Das Dodekapropheton.* KHAT 13. Tübingen: Mohr.
Mason, R.
  1991      Nahum. Pp. 57–84 in *Micah, Nahum, Obadiah.* Old Testament Guides. General editor R. N. Whybray. Sheffield, England: JSOT Press.
Metzudot
  18th c.   See Y. H. Altshuler.
Michaelis, Johann David
  1782      *Johann David Michaelis deutsche Uebersetzung des Alten Testaments mit Anmerkungen für Ungelehrte: Theil 11 Welcher die zwölf kleinen Propheten enthält.* Göttingen: Dieterich.
Murphy, R. T. A.
  1968      Nahum. Pp. 293–95 in *The Jerome Biblical Commentary,* ed. R. E. Brown, J. A. Fitzmyer, and R. E. Murphy. Englewood Cliffs, N.J.: Prentice Hall.
Newcome, William
  1783      *An Attempt towards an Improved Version, a Metrical Arrangement, and an Explanation of the Twelve Minor Prophets.* London: Printed for J. Johnson . . . and G. G. J. and J. Robinson . . . and P. Elmsly.
Nötscher, Friedrich
  1948      *Zwölfprophetenbuch oder Kleine Propheten.* Würzburg: Echter.
Nowack, Wilhelm
  1922      *Die kleinen Propheten, übersetzt und erklärt.* Handkommentar zum Alten Testament, III. Abteilung. Prophetischen Bücher, 4. Bd 3, neu bearb. Göttingen: Vandenhoeck und Ruprecht, 1922. 1st ed. 1897.
Nowell, I.
  1990      Nahum. Pp. 258–61 in *The New Jerome Biblical Commentary,* ed. R. E. Brown, J. A. Fitzmyer, and R. E. Murphy. Englewood Cliffs, N.J.: Prentice Hall.
O'Brien, Julia Myers
  2002a     *Nahum.* New York and London: Continuum.
  2002b     *Nahum: Readings; A New Biblical Commentary.* Ed. John Jarick. London and New York: Sheffield Academic Press (a Continuum imprint).

Orelli, Conrad von (1846–1912)
  1896    *Die zwölf kleinen Propheten,* 3rd ed. Kurzgefasster Kommentar
          zu den Heiligen Schriften Alten und Neuen Testaments.
          Munich: Becksche.
  1897    *The Twelve Minor Prophets.* Trans. J. S. Banks. Edinburgh:
          T. and T. Clark.
Pereman, Jacob (1881–1960)
  1956    *Sefer Naḥum.* Tel Aviv: Hotsaʾat sefarim be-Yiśraʾel le-madaᶜe
          ha-Mizraḥ he-ᶜatiḳ.
Procksch, O.
  1910    *Die kleinen prophetischen Schriften vor dem Exil:* Erläuterung
          zum Alten Testament. 3. Teil. Calwer and Stuttgart: Vereins-
          buchhandlung.
Pusey, Edward Bouverle (1800–1882)
  1860    *The Minor Prophets.* Oxford: J. H. and J. Parker. Reprinted
          1950, Grand Rapids, Mich.: Baker.
Rashi (d. 1105)
  ca. 1100  See A. J. Rosenberg.
Renaud, Bernard
  1987a   *Michée, Sophonie, Nahum.* Sources Bibliques. Paris: J. Gabalda.
Ridderbos, J.
  1963    *De kleine profeten II.* KVHS. Kampen, Netherlands: Kok.
Riessler, Paul
  1911    *Die kleinen Propheten oder das Zwölfprophetenbuch.* Rotten-
          burg: Bader.
Roberts, J. J. M.
  1991    *Nahum, Habakkuk, and Zephaniah: A Commentary.* OTL.
          Louisville, Ky.: Westminster / John Knox Press.
Robertson, O. Palmer
  1990    *The Books of Nahum, Hakakkuk, and Zephaniah.* NICOT.
          Grand Rapids, Mich.: Eerdmans.
Robinson, George L. (1864–1958)
  1955    *The Twelve Minor Prophets.* Grand Rapids, Mich.: Baker.
Rosenberg, A. J.
  1986    *Twelve Prophets: A New English Translation.* Trans. of text by
          Rashi and commentary by A. J. Rosenberg. New York: Judaica.
  1988    תרי עשר *The Book of the Twelve Prophets* (מקראות גדולות),
          vol. 2. New York: Yuda'ika.
  1994    *The Twelve Prophets: Hebrew Text and English Translation.*
          New York: Soncino.
Rudolph, W.
  1975    *Micha, Nahum, Habakuk, Zephanja: Mit Einer Zeittafel von
          Alfred Jepsen.* KAT. Gütersloh: G. Mohn.

Sanderson, J. E.
  1992      Nahum. Pp. 217–21 in *The Women's Bible Commentary*, ed.
            C. A. Newsom and S. H. Ringe. London: SPCK; Louisville,
            Ky.: Westminster / John Knox.
Schüngel-Straumann, Helen
  1975      *Israel, und die Andern? Zefanja, Nahum, Habakuk, Obadja,
            Jona.* Stuttgart: Katholisches Bibelwerk.
Schwemer, Anna Maria
  1995–96   *Studien zu den frühjüdischen Prophetenlegenden Vitae
            prophetarum: Einleitung, Übersetzung und Kommentar.*
            Tübingen: J. C. B. Mohr.
Scott, Thomas (1747–1821)
  1823      *The Holy Bible Containing the Old and New Testaments.*
            5 vols. Boston: Samuel T. Armstrong.
Sellin, E.
  1930      *Das Zwölfprophetenbuch übersetzt und erklärt,* 3rd ed. KAT 12:
            1. Leipzig: A. Dichtersche Verlagsbuchhandlung D. Werner
            Scholl.
Seybold, K.
  1991      *Nahum, Habakkuk, Zephanja.* Zürcher Bibelkommentare.
            Zurich: Theologischer Verlag.
Shy, H.
  1991      *Tanhum Ha-Yerushalmi's Commentary on the Minor Prophets.*
            Jerusalem: Magnes.
Simon, Uriel (ed.)
  1989      See Ibn Ezra.
Slavitt, David R.
  2000      *The Book of the Twelve Prophets.* Trans. David R. Slavitt. New
            York: Oxford UP.
Smith, George Adam
  1898      *The Book of the Twelve Prophets.* New York: A. C. Armstrong.
  1903      The Book of Nahum. Pp. 579–87 in *An Exposition of the Bible,*
            vol. 4. Hartford, Conn.: S. S. Scranton.
  1928      Nahum. Pp. 75–113 in *The Book of the Twelve Prophets,* vol. 2,
            new and revised edition. New York and London: Harper and
            Brothers.
Smith, John Merlin Powis
  1911      A Critical and Exegetical Commentary on Nahum.
            Pp. 265–363 in *A Critical and Exegetical Commentary on
            the Books of Micah, Zephaniah, Nahum, Habakkuk and Joel.*
            ICC. Edinburgh: T. and T. Clark / New York: Scribner.
Smith, Ralph L.
  1984      *Micah-Malachi.* WBC 32. Waco, Tex.: Word.

Spronk, Klaas
    1997    *Nahum.* Kampen, Netherlands: Kok Pharos.
Stonehouse, George G. V.
    1929    *The Books of the Prophets Zephaniah and Nahum.* Westminster
            Commentaries. London: Methuen.
Stuhlmueller, Carroll
    1986    *Amos, Hosea, Micah, Nahum, Zephaniah, Habakkuk.* College-
            ville, Minn.: Liturgical Press.
Sweeney, Marvin
    2000    Nahum. Pp. 417–449 in *The Twelve Prophets,* vol. 2. Berit
            Olam: Studies in Hebrew Narrative and Poetry. Collegeville,
            Minn.: Liturgical Press.
Tanhum, son of Joseph the Jerusalemite (d. 1291)
    ca. 1280  See Shy's critical edition of Tanhum's commentary.
Theodor of Cyros (Theodoretus Cyrensis; d. 457)
    1787–   *Interpretatio Nahum prophetae. PG* 81. In Greek
    1808
Van der Woude, Adam S.
    1978a   *Jona, Nahum.* De Prediking van het Oude Testament. Nijkerk:
            G. F. Callenbach.
Van Hoonacker, Albin (1857–1933)
    1908    *Les douze petits prophètes.* Paris: J. Gabalda.
Watts, John D. W.
    1975    *Joel, Obadiah, Jonah, Nahum, Habakkuk, and Zephaniah.*
            CBC. Cambridge: Cambridge UP.
Weiser, Artur
    1956    *Das Buch der zwölf kleinen Propheten.* Göttingen: Vanden-
            hoeck und Ruprecht.
Weissenstein, Eberhard
    1957    *Nahum-Habakuk-Zephanja.* Stuttgarter Bibelhefte. Stuttgart:
            Quell.
Wellhausen, Julius (1844–1918)
    1892    *Die kleinen Propheten übersetzt und erklärt.* Skizzen und
            Vorarbeiten, vol. 5, 4th ed. Berlin: Walter de Gruyter. Reprint
            of 4th ed., 1963.
    1898    *Die kleinen Propheten übersetzt und erklärt,* vol. 3. Berlin:
            G. Reimer.
Yerushalmi, Shmuel
    1989–90 *The Book of Trei-asar: Me'am lo'ez = Twelve Prophets.* Trans.
            and adapted Zvi Faier. Jerusalem: Moznaim.
Zer-Kavod, Mordechai
    1990    Tere `Asar. In Torah, Nevi'im, Ketuvim ʿim perush "Daʿat
            Miḳra." Jerusalem: Mosad ha-Rav Kuk.

## OTHER WORKS

Aberbach, D.
   1993       *Imperialism and Biblical Prophecy, 750–500 BCE.* New York: Routledge.

Abou-Assaf, A.
   1982       *La statue de Tell Fekherye et son inscription bilingue assyro-araméenne.* Paris: Sur Les Civilisations.

Ackroyd, P. R., and B. Lindars
   1968       *Words and Meanings.* Festschrift for D. W. Thomas. London: Cambridge UP.

Adler, M.
   1895       A Specimen of a Commentary and Collated Text of the Targum to the Prophets. Nahum. *JQR* 7: 630–57.

Aharoni, Y.
   1966a      Hebrew Ostraca from Tel Arad. *IEJ* 16: 1–7.
   1966b      The Use of Hieratic Numerals in Hebrew Ostraca and the Shekel Weights. *BASOR* 184: 13–19.
   1968a      Arad: Its Inscriptions and Temple. *BA* 31: 2–32.
   1968b      Trial Excavations in the "Solar Shrinen" at Lachish. *IEJ* 18: 157–69.
   1970       Three Hebrew Ostraca from Arad. *BASOR* 197: 16–42.

Ahlström, G. W.
   1974       אַדִּיר *ʾaddîr*; אַדֶּרֶת *ʾadderet*. *TDOT* 1: 73–74.

Albright, W. F.
   1922       The Earliest Forms of Hebrew Verse. *JPOS* 2: 69–86.
   1932a      The Seal of Eliakim and the Latest Preexilic History of Judah, with Some Observations on Ezechiel. *JBL* 51: 77–106.
   1932b      The North-Canaanite Epic of ʾAlʾêyân Baʿal and Môt. *JPOS* 12: 185–208.
   1936a      New Canaanite Historical and Mythological Data. *BASOR* 63: 23–32.
   1936b      The Song of Deborah in Light of Archaeology. *BASOR* 62: 30 ff.
   1936c      *Zabûl Yam* and *Thâpiṭ Nahar* in the Combat between Baal and the Sea. *JPOS* 16: 17–20.
   1941       Two Letters from Ugarit (Ras Shamrah). *BASOR* 82: 43–49.
   1942       Review of Pfeiffer, *Introduction to the Old Testament*. *JBL* 61: 110–26.
   1943       Two Little Understood Amarna Letters from the Middle Jordan Valley. *BASOR* 89: 7–17.
   1944       The Oracles of Balaam. *JBL* 63: 207–33.
   1945       The Old Testament and Canaanite Language and Literature. *CBQ* 7: 5–31.

1953    The New Assyro-Tyrian Synchronism and the Chronology of Tyre. *Annuaire de l'institut de philologie et d'histoire orientales et slaves* 13: 1–9.

1956    The Nebuchadnezzar and Neriglissar Chronicles. *BASOR* 143: 28–33.

1957    *From the Stone Age to Christianity*, 2nd ed. Garden City, N.Y.: Doubleday.

1963    Archaic Survivals in the Text of Canticles. Pp. 1–7 in *Hebrew and Semitic Studies: Presented to Godfrey Rolles Driver in Celebration of His Seventieth Birthday, 20 Aug. 1962*, ed. D. Winton Thomas and W. D. McHardy. Oxford: Oxford UP.

1968    *Yahweh and the Gods of Canaan: A Historical Analysis of Two Contrasting Faiths*. Garden City, N.Y.: Doubleday.

Allegro, J. M.
    1956    Further Light on the History of the Qumran Sect. *JBL* 75: 89–95.

    1962    More Unpublished Pieces of a Qumran Commentary on Nahum (4QpNah). *JSS* 7: 304–8.

Allen, Leslie C.
    1976    *The Books of Joel, Obadiah, Jonah and Micah*. NICOT. Grand Rapids, Mich.: Eerdmans.

Allis, O. T.
    1955    Nahum, Nineveh, Elkosh. *EvQ* 27: 67–80.

Alonso Schökel, Luis
    1988    *A Manual of Hebrew Poetics*. Susidia Biblica 11. Rome: Editrice Pontificio Istituto Biblico.

Alonso Schökel, Luis, and J. L. Sicre Diaz
    1963    *Estudios de poética Hebrea*. Barcelona: J. Flors.

    1980    *Profetas* (Nueva Biblia Española), vol. 2. Madrid: Ediciones Cristiandad.

    1988    *A Manual of Hebrew Poetics*. Rome: Editrice Pontificio Istituto Biblica.

Alter, Robert
    1985    *The Art of Biblical Poetry*. New York: Basic Books.

Alting, Jacob (1618–79)
    1654    *Fundamenta punctationis linguae sanctae*. Francofurti ad Moenum: Sumptibus F. Knochii et Filee, 1717.

Andersen, Francis I. (1925–)
    2001    *Habakkuk: A New Translation with Introduction and Commentary*. AYB 25. New York and London: Doubleday.

Andersen, F. I., and A. Dean Forbes
    ca. 1976  *Eight Minor Prophets: A Linguistic Concordance*. The Computer Bible, v. 10. Wooster, Ohio: Biblical Research Associates.

1983        "Prose Particle" Counts in the Hebrew Bible. Pp. 165–83 in
            *The Word of the Lord Shall Go Forth: Essays in Honor of David
            Noel Freedman in Celebration of His Sixtieth Birthday.* Winona
            Lake, Ind.: Eisenbrauns.

1992        What Did the Scribes Count? Pp. 297–318 in Appendix A of
            *Studies in Hebrew and Aramaic Orthography,* by D. N. Freed-
            man, F. I. Andersen, and A. Dean Forbes. Winona Lake, Ind.:
            Eisenbrauns.

Andersen, F. I., and D. N. Freedman
1980        *Hosea: A New Translation with Introduction and Commentary.*
            AYB 24. Garden City, N.Y.: Doubleday.

André, G.
1995        כָּשַׁף *kāšap*; כֶּשֶׁף *kešep*; כַּשָּׁף; אשׁף; יִדְּעֹנִי; לחשׁ; לָחַשׁ;
            נחשׁ; נחשׁ; עִנֵּן; שׁחר *šāḥar* I magic. TDOT 7: 360–66.

Arnold, W. R.
1901        The Composition of Nahum 1: 2–2: 3. ZAW 21: 225–65.
1905        The Word פָּרָשׁ in the Old Testament. JBL 24: 45–53.

Asmusin, J. D.
1963        Ephraïm et Manassé dans le Péshèr de Nahum (4QpNah).
            *RevQ* 4: 389–96.

1977        The Reflexion of Historical Events of the First Century B.C. in
            Qumran Commentaries (4Q161; 4Q169; 4Q166). HUCA 48:
            123–52.

Assemanius, J. S.
1719        *Bibliotheca orientalis. Clementino-Vaticana I.* Rome.

Astour, Michael
1963        Un texte d'Ugarit récemment découvert et ses rapports avec
            l'origine des cultes bachiques. *RHR* 164: 6.

Athenaeus of Naucratis (ca. 170–ca. 230 CE)
1967–       *The Deipnosophists,* vol. v, Books 11–12. Trans. Charles
1980        Burton Gulick. Loeb Classical Library. Cambridge Mass.:
            Harvard UP.

Aune, D. E.
1983        *Prophecy in Early Christianity and the Ancient Mediterranean
            World.* Grand Rapids, Mich.: Eerdmans.

Avigad, Nahman
1965        Seals of Exile. IEJ 15: 223–32, esp. no. 4, the seal of Nahum.
1966        A Hebrew Seal with a Family Emblem. IEJ 16: 50–52.
1986        *Hebrew Bullae from the Time of Jeremiah: Remnants of a Burnt
            Archive.* Jerusalem: Israel Exploration Society.

Baker, David
1980        Further Examples of the *Waw Explicativum.* VT 30: 129–36.
1992        Put: P. 560 in *AYBD,* vol. 5.

Balaban, M.
    1962      Proto-Nahum und die Geschichtsphilosophie. *Communio viatorum* 5: 234–43.

Ball, E.
    1997      Interpreting the Septuagint: Nahum 2:2 as a Case-Study. *JSOT* 75: 59–75.
    1999      "When the Towers Fall": Interpreting Nahum as Christian Scripture. Pp. 211–30 in *In Search of True Wisdom: Essays in Old Testament Interpretation in Honour of Ronald E. Clements*, ed. E. Ball. JSOTSup 300. Sheffield, England: Sheffield Academic Press.

Bamberger, B. J.
    1969      The Changing Image of the Prophet in Jewish Thought. Pp. 301–23 in *Interpreting the Prophetic Tradition*, ed. H. M. Orlinsky. Cincinnati, Ohio: Hebrew Union College Press.

Barrick, W. B., and H. Ringgren
    2004      רָכַב *rākab;* רֶכֶב *rekeb;* רַכָּב; מֶרְכָּבָה *ride. TDOT* 13: 485–91.

Bartelmus, R.
    2003      פָּתַח *pātaḥ;* פֶּתַח; פְּתִיחָה; מִפְתָּח; מַפְתֵּחַ; פִּתּוּחַ; פִּתָחוֹן *open. TDOT* 12: 173–91.

Barth, C.
    1980      זמר *zmr;* זָמִיר *zāmîr;* זִמְרָה *zimrāh;* מִזְמוֹר *mizmôr. TDOT* 4: 91–98.
    1995      כָּשַׁל *kāšal;* כִּשָּׁלוֹן; מִכְשׁוֹל; מִכְשֵׁלָה *fall. TDOT* 7: 353–61.
    1999      נָתַץ *nātaṣ. TDOT* 10: 108–14.

Barthélemy, D.
    1963      *Les Devanciers d'Aquila: Première publication intégrale du texte des fragments du dodécaprophéton.* VTSup 10. Leiden: Brill.
    1992      *Critique textuelle de l'Ancien Testament,* tome 3: *Ezéchiel, Daniel et les 12 Prophètes.* OBO 50/3. Göttingen: Vandenhoeck und Ruprecht.

Barthélemy, D., A. R. Hulst, N. Lohfink, W. D. McHardy, H. P. Rüger, and J. A. Sanders
    1980      *Preliminary and Interim Report on the Hebrew Old Testament Text Project,* vol. 5. Prophetical Books II: Ezekiel, Daniel, Twelve Minor Prophets. New York: United Bible Societies.

Baudissin, W. von
    1897/98  The Original Meaning of "Belial." *ExpTim* 9: 40–45.

Baumann, A.
    1997a    מוּג *mûg. TDOT* 8: 149–52.
    1997b    מוט *mwṭ;* מוֹט *môṭ;* מוֹטָה *môṭâ totter. TDOT* 8: 152–58.

Baumann, Gerlinde
    1998      Das Buch Nahum: Der gerechte Gott als sexueller Gewalttäter. Pp. 347–53 in L. *Kompendium Feministische Bibelauslegung,*

ed. Schottroff and M. T. Wacker. Gütersloh, Germany: Chr.
Kaiser. 2nd ed. 1999.

1999      Connected by Marriage, Adultery and Violence: The
          Prophetic Marriage Metaphor in the Book of the Twelve and
          in the Major Prophets. SBLSP 38: 552–69.

2003a     Die Eroberung Ninives bei Nahum und in den neubabylonis-
          chen Texten: Ein Motivvergleich. Pp. 5–19 in *Einen Altar von
          Erde macht mir . . . Festschrift für Diethelm Conrad zu seinem
          70. Geburtstag*, ed. Johannes F. Diehl u.a. KAANT 4/5.
          Waltrop, Germany: Hartmut Spenner.

2003b     Die prophetische Ehemetaphorik und die Bewertung der
          Prophetie im Zwölfprophetenbuch: Eine synchronie und
          diachronie Rekonstruktion zweier thematischen Fäden.
          Pp. 214–31 in *Thematic Threads in the Book of the Twelve*,
          ed. P. L. Redditt. Berlin and New York: Walter de Gruyter.

2004      Gott als vergewaltigender Soldat im Alten Testament? Ein
          Vergleich von Jes 47,2f und Nah 3,4–7. Pp. 55–67 in *Macht-
          beziehungen, Geschlechterdifferenz und Religion*, ed. B.
          Heininger. Münster: Lit.

2005      *Gottes Gewalt und Wandel: Traditionsbeschichtliche und inter-
          textuelle Studien zu Nahum 1,2–8*. Neukirchen-Vluyn, Ger-
          many: Neukirchener.

Baumgart, Hildegard
1990      *Jealousy: Experiences and Solutions*. Trans. Manfred and
          Evelyn Jacobson. Chicago: University of Chicago Press.

Baumgärtel, F.
1961      Dir Formel $n^{e}$'*um jahwe*. ZAW 1961: 277–90.

Beck, J. T.
1899      *Erklärung der Propheten Nahum und Zephanjah*. Gütersloh,
          Germany: Bertelsmann.

Becking, B.
1978      Is het boek Nahum een literaire eenheid? *NedTTs* 32:
          107–24.

1980      Bee's Dating Formula and the Book of Nahum. *JSOT* 18:
          100–104.

1993      Goddelijke toorn in het boek Nahum. Pp. 9–19 in *Kleine
          encyclopedie van de toorn*, ed. A. de Jong et al. Utrechtse theol-
          ogische reeks, 21. Utrecht: Faculteit der Godgeleerdheid.

1995a     Divine Wrath and the Conceptual Coherence of the Book of
          Nahum. *SJOT* 9: 277–96.

1995b     A Judge in History: Notes on Nahum 3,7 and Esarhaddon's
          Succession Treaty 47: 452. *ZABR* 1: 111–16.

1995c     Protectors. Cols. 1259–61 in *Dictionary of Deities and Demons*,
          ed. K. van der Toorn et al. Leiden: Brill.

1996 Passion, Power and Protection: Interpreting the God of Nahum. Pp. 1–20 in *Reading Prophetic Texts: Gender Specific and Related Studies in Memory of Fokkelien van Dijk-Hemmes,* ed. B. Becking and M. Dijkstra. BibIs 18. Leiden: Brill.

Bee, Ronald E.

1979 An Empirical Dating Procedure for Old Testament Prophecy. *JSOT* 11: 23–25.

1980 Dating the Book of Nahum: A Response to the Article by Bob Becking. *JSOT* 18: 104.

Begg, C. T.

1987 The Non-mention of Zephaniah, Nahum and Habakkuk in the Deuteronomistic History. *BN* 38–39: 19–25.

1988 The "Classical Prophets" in Josephus' Antiquities. *Louvain Studies* 13: 341–57.

1995 Josephus and Nahum Revisited. *REJ* 154: 5–22.

Bellermann, J. J.

1813 *Versuch über die Metrik der Hebräer.* Berlin: Maurerschen.

Bellis, Alice Ogden (ed.)

1995 The Book of Nahum / Oracle in the Style of Nahum. Pp. 47–53 in *Many Voices: Multicultural Responses to the Minor Prophets.* Lanham, Md.: UP of America.

Benoit, P., et al.

1961 Rouleau des douze prophètes. Pp. 181–205 in *Les grottes de Murabba‘at.* DJD 2. Oxford: Clarendon.

Ben Uzziel. See Jonathan ben Uzziel.

Ben Yahuda, E.

1917 Three Notes in Hebrew Lexicography, 3: Nahum 2.14. *JAOS* 37: 327.

Benyus, J. M.

1992 *Beastly Behaviors: Pandas Turn Somersaults, and Crocodiles Roar; A Watcher's Guide to How Animals Act and Why.* Reading, Mass.: Addison-Wesley.

Ben Zvi, E.

1993 History and Prophetic Texts. Pp. 109–120 in *History and Interpretation: Essays in Honour of J. H. Hayes,* ed. M. P. Graham et al. JSOTSup 173. Sheffield, England: JSOT Press.

1996a Studying Prophetic Texts against Their Original Backgrounds: Pre-Ordained Scripts and Alternative Horizons of Research. Pp. 125–35 in *Prophets and Paradigms: Essays in Honor of Gene Tucker,* ed. S. B. Reid. JSOTSup 229. Sheffield, England: Sheffield Academic Press.

1996b Twelve Prophetic Books or "The Twelve": A Few Preliminary Considerations. Pp. 125–56 in *Forming Prophetic Literature: Essays on Isaiah and the Twelve in Honor of John D.W. Watts,* ed. J. W. Watts and P. R. House. JSOTSup 235. Sheffield, England: Sheffield Academic Press.

Berger, P. R.
   1970    Zur Bedeutung des in den akkadishen Texten aus Ugarit bezeugten Ortsnamens Hīlu (Hl). *UF* 2: 340–46.
Bergman, J., and G. J. Botterweck
   1986    יָדַע *yādaᶜ*. *TDOT* 5: 448–81.
Bergman, J., and B. Kedar-Kopfstein
   1978    דָּם *dām*. *TDOT* 53: 234–50.
Bergman, J., and Magnes Ottosson
   1974    אֶרֶץ *ʾereṣ*. *TDOT* 1: 388–405.
Bergman, J., Joachim Kretcher, and Vinzenz Hamp
   1974    אִשֶּׁה *ʾēš*. *TDOT* 1: 418–28.
Bergman, J., H. Ringgren, and R. Mosis
   1975    גָּדֵל *gādal*; גָּדוֹל; גְּדֻלָּה; גֹּדֶל; → מִגְדָּל. *TDOT* 2: 390–416.
Bergman, J., W. von Soden, and P. R. Ackroyd
   1986    יָד *yad*; זְרוֹעַ; יָמִין; כַּף; אֶצְבַּע. *TDOT* 5: 393–426.
Berlin, Adele
   1985    *The Dynamics of Biblical Parllelism.* Bloomington: Indiana UP.
   1995    Review of F. W. Dobbs-Allsopp, *Weep, O Daughter of Zion: A Study of the City-Lament Genre in the Hebrew Bible. JAOS* 115: 319.
Berlin, M.
   1901    Nahum I and the Age of Alphabetic Acrostics. *JQR* 13: 681–82.
Berlinerblau, J.
   1996    *The Vow and the "Popular Religious Groups" of Ancient Israel: A Philological and Sociological Inquiry.* JSOTSup 210. Sheffield, England: JSOT Press.
Berrin, Shani L.
   2000a   Lemma/Pesher Correspondence in Pesher Nahum. Pp. 157–69 in *The Dead Sea Scrolls Fifty Years after Their Discovery: Proceedings of the Jerusalem Congress, July 20–25, 1997*, ed. L. Schiffmann et al. Jerusalem: Israel Exploration Society.
   2000b   Pesharim. Pp. 644–47 in *Encyclopedia of the Dead Sea Scrolls*, vol. 2, ed. L. H. Schiffman and J. C. VanderKam. Oxford: Oxford UP.
   2000c   Peshar Nahum. Pp. 653–55 in *Encyclopedia of the Dead Sea Scrolls*, vol. 2, ed. L. H. Schiffman and J. C. VanderKam. Oxford: Oxford UP.
   2001    4QpNah (4Q169, Pesher Nahum): A Critical Edition with Commentary, Historical Analysis, and In-depth Study of Exegetical Method. Ph.D. diss., New York University, New York.

Beuken, W. A. M., and U. Dahmen
    2004        רֹאשׁ *rōʾš;* רֹאשָׁה ;רֵאשִׁית מְרַאֲשׁוֹת *head. TDOT* 13: 248–61.
Bewer, J. A.
    1950        Textkritische Bemerkungen zum A.T. Nah 1,10. Pp. 68–69 in
                *Festschrift für Alfred Bertholet zum 80. Geburtstag,* ed. Walter
                Baumgartner et al. Tübingen: J. C. B. Mohr (Paul Siebeck).
Beyse, K.-M.
    1995        כְּלִי *kelî container; tool; weapon. TDOT* 7: 169–75.
    1999        סוּפָה *sûpâ storm wind. TDOT* 10: 196–99.
    2004        קַשׁ *qaš;* קְשֹׁשׁ *qšš straw. TDOT* 13: 180–82.
Bibliander, Th.
    1534        *Propheta Nahumiuxta veritatem Hebraicum.* Zurich: Tiguri.
Bič, Miloš
    1968        *Trois prophètes dans un temps de ténèbres:*
                *Sophonie–Nahum–Habaquq.* Lectio divina 48. Paris: Cerf.
Bickell, Gustav (1838–1906)
    1880        Die hebräische Metrik. ZDMG 34: 557–63.
    1880–81 *Die hebräische Metrik.* Leipzig: F. A. Brockhaus.
    1882        *Carmina Veteris Testamenti Metrice: Notas criticas et disser-*
                *tationemm de re metrica Hebraeorum adjecit.* Oeniponte:
                Sumptibus Libraria Wangeriani.
    1886        Exegetischkritische Nachlese zu den alttestamentlichen Dich-
                tungen (Nah. 1,2–10). *ZKT* 10: 550.
    1894        Beiträge zur hebräischen Metrik, I: Das alphabetische Lied in
                Nahum 1:2–2:3. *Sitzungsberichte der philosophisch-historischen*
                *Klasse der Kaiserlischen Akademie der Wissenschaft* 131/5:
                1–12. Vienna.
Billerbeck, A., and A. Jeremias
    1895        Der Untergang Ninives und die Weissagungsschrift des
                Nahum. *Beiträge zur Assyriologie* 3: 87–188.
Bird, P.
    1989        "To Play the Harlot": An Inquiry into an Old Testament
                Metaphor. Pp. 75–94 in *Gender and Difference in Ancient*
                *Israel,* ed. P. L. Day. Minneapolis, Minn.: Augsburg-Fortress.
Birkeland, Harris
    1938        *Zum hebräischen Traditionswesen: Die Komposition der*
                *prophetischen Bücher des Alten Testaments.* Oslo: J. Dybwad.
    1940        *Akzent und Vokalismus im Althebräischen.* Oslo: J. Dybwad.
Black, Jeremy A., and Anthony Green
    1992        *Gods, Demons and Symbols of Ancient Mesopotamia.* Austin:
                University of Texas Press.
Black, Jeremy A., G. Cunningham, E. Robson, and G. Zólymi (eds.)
    2004        *The Literature of Ancient Sumer.* Oxford and New York:
                Oxford UP.

Blenkinsopp, J.
  1996    *A History of Prophecy in Israel from the Settlement in the Land to the Hellenistic Period.* Philadelphia, Pa.: Westminster.
Bliese, Loren F.
  1982    Metrical chiasmus, peak and structural symmetry in Hosea. A paper presented to the 1982 United Bbible Societies Afrescot Workshop in Kenya, rev. 1992. Parts of this paper have been published in *Discourse Perspectives on Hebrew Poetry in the Scriptures,* ed. Ernst Wendland. New York: United Bible Societies.
  1988    Metrical Sequences and Climax in the Poetry of Joel. *Occasional Papers in Translation and Textlinguistics* 2/4: 52–84.
  1993    Chiastic and Homogeneous Metrical Structures Enhanced by Word Patterns in Obadiah. *JTT* 6/3: 210–27.
  1994    Symmetry and Prominence in Hebrew Poetry in the Scriptures. Pp. 67–94 in *Discourse Perspectives on Hebrew Poetry in the Scriptures,* ed. Ernst Wendland. New York: United Bible Societies.
  1995    A Cryptic Chiastic Acrostic: Finding Meaning from Structure in the Poetry of Nahum. *JTT* 7 (3): 48–81.
  1999    The Poetics of Habakkuk. *JTT* 12: 47–75.
  2003a   The Key Word "Name" and Patterns with 26 in the Structure of Amos. *BiTr* 54 (1): 121–35.
  2003b   Numerical and Lexical Patterns in the Structure of Micah. *JTT* 16: 119–43.
  2004    Metrical and Word Patterns in the Structure of Zephaniah. *JTT* 17: 36–68.
Boadt, Lawrence
  1975    The A:B:B:A Chiasm of Identical Roots in Ezekiel. *VT* 25: 693–99.
  1982    *Habakkuk, Zephaniah, Nahum.* Old Testament Message 10. Wilmington, Del.: Glazier.
  1987    Nahum: God Rules over All Nations. *TBT* 25: 272–77.
Boehmer, Julius
  1908    Ein alphabetisch-akrostichisches Rätsel und ein Versuch es zu lösen. *ZAW* 28: 53–57.
Boer, P. A. H. de
  1948    An Inquiry into the Meaning of the Term *Massa. OTS* 5: 197–214.
Bosshardt(-Nepustil), Erich
  1987    Beobachtungen zum Zwölfprophetenbuch. *BN* 40: 30–62.

1997 *Rezeptionen von Jesaja im Zwölfprophetenbuch: Untersuchungen zur literarischen Verbindung von Prophetenbüchern in Babylonischer und Persischer Zeit.* OBO 154. Fribourg: Universitätsverlag; Göttingen: Vandenhoeck und Ruprecht.

Botta, M.
1849– *Monument de Ninive.* 5 vols. Paris: Imprimerie Nationale.
50

Botterweck, G. J.
1972 Gott und Mensch in den alttestamentlichen Löwenbildern. Pp. 117–28 in *Wort, Lied und Gottesspruch: Festschrift für J. Ziegler,* ed. J. Schreiner. Würzburg: Echter Verlag.
1977 אֲרִי *ʾărî*; גּוּר *gûr*; כְּפִיר *kĕpîr*; לָבִיא *lābîʾ*; לַיִשׁ *layiš*; שַׁחַל *šaḥal*. Pp. 374–388 in *TDOT,* vol. 1, rev. ed. Grand Rapids, Mich.: Eerdmans.

Box, George Herbert
1911 Nahum. P. 153 in *Encyclopaedia Britannica,* 11th ed. New York: Encyclopaedia Britannica Co.

Brandt, Peter
2001 *Endgestalten des Kanon: Das Arrangement der Schriften Israels in der jüdischen und christlichen Bibel.* BBB 131. Berlin: Philo.

Breiteneicher, Michael
1861 *Ninive und Nahum: Mit Beziehung der Resultate der neuesten Entdeckungen historisch-exegetgisch bearbeitet.* Munich: J. J. Lentner.

Bremer, John
2005 *Plato's Ion: Philosophy as Performance.* North Richland Hills, Tex.: BIBAL Press.

Brenner, A.
1982 *Colour Terms in the Old Testament.* JSOTSup 21. Sheffield, England: JSOT Press.
1995 *A Feminist Companion to the Latter Prophets,* ed. A. Brenner. FCB 8. Sheffield, England: Sheffield Academic Press.

Bright, John
1965 *Jeremiah.* AYB 21. Garden City, N.Y.: Doubleday.

Brockelmann, C.
1941 Zur Syntax der Sprache von Ugarit. *Or* n.s. 10: 223–40.

Brockington, L. H.
1973 *The Hebrew Text of the Old Testament.* London: Oxford UP.

Brongers, H. A.
1963 Der Eifer des Herrn Zebaoth. *VT* 13: 269–84.
1965 Bemerkung zum Gebrauch des adverbialen *weʿattāh* im Alten Testament. *VT* 15: 289–99.
1969 Der Zornesbecher. *OTS* 15: 177–92.

Brooke, G. J.
  1991    The Kittim in the Qumran Pesharim. Pp. 135–59 in *Images of Empire*, ed. A. Loveday. JSOTSup 122. Sheffield, England: JSOT Press.
Brownmiller, S.
  1975    *Against Our Will: Men, Women and Rape.* Toronto: Bantam.
Brug, J. F.
  1990    Biblical Acrostics and Their Relationship to Other Near Eastern Acrostics. Pp. 283–304 in *The Bible in the Light of Cuneiform Literature*, ed. W. Hallo et al. Scripture in Context III. Lewiston, N.Y.: E. Mellen.
Brunner, H.
  1952    Eine assyrisches Relief mit einer ägyptischen Festung (cf. Nah. 3,8ss). *AfO* 16: 253–62.
Bruno, Arvid
  1957    *Das Buch der Zwölf: Eine rhythmische und textkritische Untersuchung.* Stockholm: Almqvist and Wiksell.
Budde, Karl (1850–1935)
  1901a   Elkoshite, The. Pp. 1281–82 in *Encyclopaedia Biblica*, vol. 1, ed. T. K. Cheyne et al. New York: Macmillan.
  1901b   Nahum. Pp. 3259–63 in *Encyclopaedia Biblica*, vol. 2, ed. T. K. Cheyne et al. New York: Macmillan.
Buhl, F.
  1885    Einige textkritische Bemerkungen zu den Kleinen Propheten. *ZAW* 5: 179–84.
Bühlmann, Walter, and Karl Scherer
  1994    *Stilfiguren der Bibel: Von Assonanz bis Zahlenspruch; Ein Nachschlagewerk.* 2nd ed. Giessen: Brunnen.
Bullinger, E. W. (1837–1913)
  1898    *Figures of Speech Used in the Bible, Explained and Illustrated.* New York: E. and J. B. Young. Republished 1968, Grand Rapids, Mich.: Baker.
Burkert, Walter
  1976    Das hunderttorige Theben und die Datierung des Ilias. *Wiener Studien* 89 n.s. 10: 5–21.
Burney, C. F.
  1903    *Notes on the Hebrew Text of the Book of Kings.* Oxford: Clarendon. Reprinted in 1970 in the Library of Biblical Studies, ed. Harry M. Orlinsky. New York: Ktav.
  1920    *The Book of Judges: With Introduction and Notes*, 2nd ed. London: Rivingtons.
  1926/27 Conjectures on Some Minor Prophets. *ExpTim* 38: 377–78.
Cannon, W. W.
  1925    Some Notes on Nahum I–II,3. *Expositor* 9/3: 280–86; 9/4: 102–10.

Caquot, A.
1978      גָּעַר *gāʿar. TDOT* 3: 49–53.
Carroll, R.
1982      Eschatological Delay in the Prophetic Tradition? *ZAW* 94: 47–58.
1983      Poets Not Prophets. *JSOT* 27: 25–31.
1988      Inventing the Prophets: Essay in Honour of Professor Jacob Weingreen to be Presented on the Occasion of his 80th Birthday. *IBS* 10: 24–36.
Cassuto, Umberto
1915      La patria del profeta Nahum. *Giornale della Società Asiatica Italiana* 26: 291–302.
1971      *The Goddess Anath.* Jerusalem: Magnes.
1973      On the Formal and Stylistic Relationship between Deutero-Isaiah and Other Biblical Writers. Pp. 141–77 in *Biblical and Oriental Studies*, vol. 1: *Bible.* Jerusalem: Magnes.
Cathcart, K. J.
1968      Notes on Micah 5,4– 5. *Biblica* 49: 511–14.
1973a     *Nahum in the Light of Northwest Semitic.* BibOr 26. Rome: Pontifical Biblical Institute.
1973b     Treaty Curses and the Book of Nahum. *CBQ* 35: 179–87.
1975      The Divine Warrior and the War of Yahweh in Nahum. Pp. 68–76 in *Biblical Studies in Contemporary Thought: The Tenth Anniversary Commemorative Volume of the Trinity College Biblical Institute*, ed. M. W. Ward. Somerville, Mass.: Greeno, Hadden.
1978      Kingship and the "Day of YHWH": in Isaiah 2:6–22. *Hermathena* 125: 48–59.
1979      More Philological Studies in Nahum. *JNSL* 7: 1–12.
1992      Nahum. Pp. 998–1000 in *AYBD*, vol. 4.
Cathcart, Kevin J., and Robert P. Gordon
1989      *The Targum of the Minor Prophets.* The Aramaic Bible, 14. Wilmington, Del.: M. Glazier.
Cazelles, H.
1957      La Titulaire du Roi David. Pp. 131–36 in *Mélanges bibliques rédigés en l'honneur de André Robert.* Paris: Bloud et Gay.
Ceresko, A. R.
1975      The A:B:B:A Word Pattern in Hebrew and Northwest Semitic with Special Reference to the Book of Job. *UF* 7: 73–88.
1985      The ABCs of Wisdom in Ps xxxiv. *VT* 35: 99–104.
Cerný, Ladislav
1948      *The Day of Yahweh and Some Relevant Problems.* Prace z Vedeckých ústava, 53. Prague: Nákl. Filosofické fakulty Univ. Karlovy.

Charles, J. D.
  1989      Plundering the Lion's Den—A Portrait of Divine Fury
            (Nahum 2,3–11). *GTJ* 10 (2): 183–201.
Cheyne, T. K.
  1896      Notes on Psalm XXII 25 and Nahum II 8. *JBL* 15: 198.
  1896/97   The Origin and Meaning of "Belial." *ExpTim* 8: 423–24.
  1898a     Note on Mr. Gray's Article, "The Alphabetical Poem in
            Nahum." *Expositor* 45: 304–5.
  1898b     Influence of Assyrian in Unexpected Places. *JBL* 17: 103–7.
  1903–4    *Critica Biblica*. London: A and C. Black. Reprint Amsterdam:
            Philo Press, 1970.
Childs, Brevard S.
  1971      "Psalm Titles and Midrashic Exegesis." *JSS* 16: 137–50.
  1979      Nahum. Pp. 440–46 in *Introduction to the Old Testament as
            Scripture*. Philadelphia, Pa.: Fortress.
  1996      Retrospective Reading of the Old Testament Prophets. *ZAW*
            108: 362–77.
  2003      Critique of Recent Intertextual Canonical Interpretations.
            *ZAW* 115: 173–84.
Chisholm, R. B.
  1990      *Interpreting the Minor Prophets*. Grand Rapids, Mich.:
            Zondervan.
Christensen, D. L.
  1972      Studies in the Oracles against the Nations: Transformations
            of the War Oracle in Old Testament Prophecy. Ph.D. thesis,
            Harvard University, Cambridge, Mass.
  1974      Num 21:14–15 and the Book of the Wars of Yahweh. *CBQ* 36:
            359–60.
  1975a     *Transformations of the War Oracle in Old Testament Prophecy*.
            Harvard Dissertations in Religion 3. Missoula, Mont.: Scholars
            Press.
  1975b     The Acrostic of Nahum Reconsidered. *ZAW* 87: 17–30.
  1976      The March of Conquest in Isaiah X 27c–34. *VT* 26: 385–99.
  1984      Two Stanzas of a Hymn in Deuteronomy 33. *Bib* 65: 382–89.
  1985a     Prose and Poetry in the Bible: The Narrative Poetics of
            Deuteronomy 1, 9–18. *ZAW* 97: 179–89.
  1985b     The Song of Jonah: A Metrical Analysis. *JBL* 104: 217–31.
  1985c     Nahum, the Book of; Nineveh. Pp. 681, 707–8 in *Harper's
            Bible Dictionary*, ed. P. J. Achtemeier. San Francisco: Harper
            and Row.
  1985d     Andrzej Panufnik and the Structure of the Book of Jonah:
            Icons, Music and Literary Art. *JETS* 28: 133–40.
  1987a     The Acrostic of Nahum Once Again: A Prosodic Analysis of
            Nahum 1,1–10. *ZAW* 99: 409–16.

1987b   Narrative Poetics and the Interpretation of the Book of Jonah.
        Pp. 29–48 in *Directions in Biblical Hebrew Poetry*, ed. Elaine
        R. Follis. JSOTSup 40. Sheffield, England: Sheffield Academic
        Press.

1988b   A New Israel: The Righteous from among All Nations.
        Pp. 251–59 in *Israel's Apostasy and Restoration: Essays in
        Honor of Roland K. Harrison*, ed. Avraham Gileadi. Grand
        Rapids, Mich.: Baker.

1988c   The Book of Nahum: The Question of Authorship within the
        Canonical Process. *JETS* 31: 51–58.

1989a   The Book of Nahum as a Liturgical Composition: A Prosodic
        Analysis. *JETS* 32: 159–69.

1989b   Nahum. Pp. 166–75 in *Prophecy and War in Ancient Israel:
        Studies in the Oracles against the Nations in Old Testament
        Prophecy.* BIBAL Monograph Series 3. Berkeley, Calif.: BIBAL
        Press. Book is a reprint of *Transformations of the War Oracle in
        Old Testament Prophecy,* listed earlier.

1990    The Masoretic Accentual System and Repeated Metrical
        Refrains in Nahum, Song of Songs, and Deuteronomy.
        Pp. 31–36 in *VIII: International Congress of the International
        Organization for Masoretic Studies, Chicago 1988,* ed. E. J.
        Revell. Masoretic Studies 6. Missoula, Mont.: Scholars Press.

1996a   The Book of Nahum: A History of Interpretation. Pp. 187–94
        in *Forming Prophetic Literature: Essays on Isaiah and the
        Twelve in Honor of John D. W. Watts,* ed. J. W. Watts and P. R.
        House. JSOTSup 235. Sheffield, England: Sheffield Academic
        Press.

1996b   Nahum, the Book of; Nineveh. Pp. 731–32, 759–60 in *The
        HarperCollins Bible Dictionary,* ed. P. J. Achtemeier. San
        Francisco: Harper.

1999    Nahum, Book of. Pp. 199–201 in *Dictionary of Biblical Inter-
        pretation,* vol. 2. Nashville, Tenn.: Abingdon.

2001    *Deuteronomy 1:1–21:9,* rev. WBC 6A. Nashville, Tenn.:
        Thomas Nelson.

2003a   The Book of the Twelve Lesser Prophets. Pp. 124–29 in *Unity
        of the Bible: Exploring the Beauty and Structure of the Bible.*
        New York and Mahwah, N.J.: Paulist Press.

2003b   Letter Count and the Phenomenon of *Matres Lectionis.* Paper
        read at the meeting of the International Organization for
        Masoretic Studies, November 2003, in Atlanta, Georgia. Avail-
        able for downloading at www.bibal.net.

2005    Paul's "Cloak" and the Completion of the Tanakh. Pp. 106–20
        in *Text and Task: Scripture and Mission; Essays for John Olley.*
        Carlisle, England: Paternoster Press.

Christianakis, P. E.
    1971    Ἡ ἐν Ναουμ 1,9 αρχη του δεδικασμενου των υπο του Θεου κριθεντων. *Deltion biblikōn meletōn* 1: 148–53.
Clark, David J., and Howard A. Hatton
    1989    *A Translator's Handbook on the Books of Nahum, Habakkuk, and Zephaniah.* New York: United Bible Societies.
Clements, R. E.
    1968    Baal-Berith of Shechem. *JSS* 13: 21–32.
    1977    Patterns in the Prophetic Canon. Pp. 43–56 in *Canon and Authority*, ed. G. W. Coats and B. O. Long. Philadelphia, Pa.: Fortress.
    1982    The Form and Character of the Prophetic Woe-Oracles. *Semitics* 8: 17–29.
    1995    כּוֹכָב *kôkab* star. TDOT 7: 75–85.
Clements, R. E., and G. J. Botterweck
    1975    גּוֹי *gôy.* TDOT 2: 426–33.
Clements, R. E., and H.-J. Fabry
    1997    מַיִם *mayim* water. TDOT 8: 265–88.
Clermont-Ganneau, Charles
    1883    Epigraphes hébraïques et grecques sur des ossuaires juifs inédit. *Revue archéologique* (NS) 3: 257–276.
Clifford, Richard J.
    1966    The Use of *Hôy* in the Prophets. *CBQ* 28: 458–64.
Cobb, W. H.
    1905    *A Criticism of Systems of Hebrew Metre: An Elementary Treatise.* Oxford: Clarendon.
Cogan, Mordechai
    1974    *Imperialism and Religion: Assyria, Judah and Israel in the 8th and 7th Centuries B.C.E.* SBLMS 19. Missoula, Mont.: Society of Biblical Literature; distributed by Scholars Press.
    1993    Judah under Assyrian Hegemony. *JBL* 112: 403–14.
Coggins, R. J.
    1982    An Alternative Prophetic Tradition. Pp. 77–94 in *Israel's Prophetic Tradition: Essays in Honour of Peter R. Ackroyd*, ed. R. Coggins, A. Phillips, and M. Knibb. Cambridge: Cambridge UP.
    1994    The Minor Prophets: One Book or Twelve? Pp. 57–68 in *Crossing Boundaries: Essays in Biblical Interpretation in Honour of Michael D. Goulder*, ed. S. E. Porter et al. BibIS, 8. Leiden: E. J. Brill.
Collins, T.
    1978    *Line-Forms in Hebrew Poetry: A Grammatical Approach to the Stylistic Study of the Hebrew Prophets.* Rome: Biblical Institute Press.

1993    *The Mantle of Elijah: The Redaction Criticism of the Prophetical Books.* BibSem. Sheffield, England: JSOT Press.

Conrad, Edgar W.

1997a    The End of Prophecy and the Appearance of Angels/Messengers in the Book of the Twelve. *JSOT* 73: 65–79.

1997b    Reading Isaiah and the Twelve as Prophetic Books. Pp. 3–17 in *Writing and Reading the Scroll of Isaiah: Studies of an Interpretive Tradition,* ed. C. C. Broyles and C. A. Evans. VTSup 70. Leiden: Brill.

2003    Forming the Twelve and Forming Canon. Pp. 90–103 in *Thematic Threads in the Book of the Twelve,* ed. P. L. Redditt and A. Schart. BZAW 325. Berlin and New York: Walter de Gruyter.

Conrad, J.

1998    נָכָה *nkr;* מַכָּה *makkâ;* נְכֵה; נכא *nkʾ strike.* TDOT 9: 415–23.

2004    שָׁחַת *šāḥat.* TDOT 14: 583–95.

Cooke, G. A.

1903    *A Textbook of North-Semitic Inscriptions.* Oxford: Clarendon.

Cooper, Alan M.

1976    Biblical Poetics: A Linguistic Approach. Ph.D. diss., Yale University, New Haven, Conn.

Cooper, Jerrold S.

1983    *The Curse of Agade.* Baltimore, Md.: Johns Hopkins UP.

Cornill, C. H.

1907    Die literarhistorische Methode und Jeremia Kap, I. ZAW 27: 100–110.

Craigie, Peter C.

1983    *Psalms 1–50.* WBC 19. Waco, Tex.: Word.

Crickmore, Leon

2003    A Re-valuation of the Ancient Science of Harmonics. *Psychology of Music* 31: 391–403.

Cross, Frank Moore

1950    Studies in Ancient Yahwistic Poetry. Ph.D. thesis, Johns Hopkins University, Baltimore, Md. Republished Missoula, Mont.: Scholars Press for the Society of Biblical Literature, 1975.

1966    The Divine Warrior in Israel's Early Cult. Pp. 11– 30 in *Studies and Text III: Biblical Motifs,* ed. A. Altmann. Cambridge, Mass.: Harvard UP.

1969    New Discoveries in the Study of Apocalyptic. *JThC* 6: 157–65.

1970    The Cave Inscriptions from Khirbet Beit Lei. Pp. 299–306 in *Near Eastern Archaeology in the Twentieth Century: Essays in Honor of Nelson Glueck,* ed. J. A. Sanders. Garden City, N.Y.: Doubleday.

1973    *Canaanite Myth and Hebrew Epic: Essays in the History of the Religion of Israel.* Cambridge, Mass.: Harvard UP.

1998    *From Epic to Canon: History and Literature in Ancient Israel.* Baltimore and London: Johns Hopkins UP.

Cross, F. M., and D. N. Freedman

1952    *Early Hebrew Orthography: A Study of the Epigraphic Evidence.* American Oriental Series 36. New Haven, Conn.: American Oriental Society.

1953a    A Royal Psalm of Thanksgiving: II Samuel 22 = Psalm 18. *JBL* 72: 15–34. Reprint, pp. 125–58 in *Studies in Yahwistic Poetry.* Missoula, Mont.: Scholars Press for the Society of Biblical Literature, 1975.

1953b    Josiah's Revolt against Assyria. *JNES* 12: 56–58.

1955    The Song of Miriam. *JNES* 14: 237–50.

Dahood, M. J.

1955    Review of T. H. Robinson, F. Horst, *Die Zwölf kleinen Propheten. CBQ* 17: 103–4.

1957    Northwest Semitic Words in Job. *Biblica* 38: 306–20.

1959    The Value of Ugaritic for Textual Criticism. *Bib* 40: 160–70.

1961    *Psalms I.* AYB 16. Garden City, N.Y.: Douleday.

1963    Hebrew-Ugaritic Lexicography I. *Bib* 44: 289–303.

1964a    Review of *Das Hohelied* by Gillis Gerlemen. *Bib* 45: 287–88.

1964b    Hebrew-Ugaritic Lexicography, II. *Bib* 45: 393–412.

1965    *Ugartic-Hebrew Philology.* BibOr 17. Rome: Biblical Institute Press.

1966a    *Psalms I. 1–50.* AYB 16. Garden City, N.Y.: Doubleday.

1966b    Hebrew-Ugaritic Lexicography IV. *Bib* 47: 403–19.

1968    *Psalms II. 51–100.* AYB 16B. Garden City, N.Y.: Doubleday.

1969a    Review of J. M. Allegro, with the collaboration of A. A. Anderson, *Discoveries in the Judean Desert of Jordan, V, Qumran Cave 4, I (4Q158–4Q186). Biblica* 50: 270–72.

1969b    Hebrew-Ugaritic Lexicography, VII. *Bib* 50: 337–56.

1970a    *Psalms III. 101–50.* AYB 17A. Garden City, N.Y.: Doubleday.

1970b    Hebrew-Ugaritic Lexicography, VIII. *Bib* 51: 391–404.

1970c    The Independent Personal Pronoun in the Oblique Case in Hebrew. *CBQ* 32: 86–90.

1971    Causal *Beth* and the Root NKR in Nahum 3,4. *Bib* 52: 395–96.

1974    Northwest Semitic Notes on Genesis. *Bib* 55: 76–82.

1976    Hebrew Lexicography: A Review of Baumgartner's *Lexicon,* vol. 2. *Or* 45: 327–65.

1983    The Minor Prophets and Ebla. Pp. 47–67 in the *Word of the Lord Shall Go Forth: Essays in Honor of David Noel Freedman in Celebration of His Sixtieth Birthday*, ed. Carol L. Meyers and M. O'Connor. Winona Lake, Ind.: Eisenbrauns.

Dalman, Gustaf (1855–1941)
1964 *Arbeit und Sitte in Palästina.* 2 vols. Hildesheim, Germany: Georg Olms. 1st ed. 1928.

Danz, Johann Andreas (1654–1727)
1694 *Turgeman, sive, Interpres Ebaeo-Chaldaeus: Omnes vtrivsque lingvae idiotismos dexterè explicans; Ad genvinvm Scriptvrae Sacrae sensuvm rite indagandum accompdatus.* Jena, Germany: Sumtu Ioh. Bielckii, bibliopolae, litteris Ioh. Zach. Nisii.
1699 *Ioh. Andr. Danzii Medakdek = sive Compendium grammaticae ebraeo-chaldaicae: Utriusque linguae Vet. Test. institutionem harmonice ita tradens, ut cuncta, firmas superstructa fundamentis, innotescant scientifice.* Francofurti ad Moenum: Sumtu Dan. Christiani Hechtelii, 1751 (editio novissima).

Davidson, A. B.
1902 *Hebrew Syntax.* Edinburgh: T. and T. Clark.

Davies, G. H.
1962 Vows. *IDB* 4: 792–93.

Davis, J. D.
1911 Nahum. Pp. 526–27 in *A Dictionary of the Bible*, 3rd ed. Philadelphia, Pa.: Westminster, 1921.
1944 Nahum. Pp. 416–17 in *The New Westminster Dictionary.* London and New York: Collins.

Day, J.
1985 *God's Conflict with the Dragon and the Sea.* University of Cambridge Oriental Publications, 35. Cambridge and New York: Cambridge UP.

Delcor, Mathias
1964 Nahum. Pp. 361–87 in *L.*
1973 Homonymie et Interprétation de l'Ancien Testament. *JSS* 18: 40–54.
1977 Allusions à la Déesse Ištar en Nahum 2:8? *Bib* 58:73–83.

Delitzsch, Franz (1813–90)
1867 *Biblischer Commentar über die Psalmen.* Leipzig: Dörffling und Franke.
1970 *Biblical Commentary on the Psalms.* 3 vols. Trans. Francis Bolton (from the second edition, revised throughout). Reprinted Grand Rapids, Mich.: Eerdmans.

Delitzsch, Friedrich
1920 *Die Lese- und Schreibfehler im Alten Testament.* Berlin and Leipzig: Vereinigung wissenschaftlicher Verleger.

Dentan, Robert C.
1963 The Literary Affinities of Exodus XXXIV 6 f. *VT* 13: 34–51.

de Rossi, Giovanni Bernardo (1742–1831)
    1786    *Variae Lectionis Veteris Testament*, vol. 3. Parma: Regio
           typgrapheo.
DeVries, L. F.
    1997    Nineveh. Pp. 31–34 in *Cities in the Biblical World*. Peabody,
           Mass.: Hendrickson.
De Vries, S. J.
    1966    The Acrostic of Nahum in the Jerusalem Liturgy. *VT* 16:
           476–81.
Dhorme, E.
    1956    *La Bible: Edition publiée sous la direction d'Edouard Dhorme*.
           Paris: Gallimard.
Dhorme, P.
    1931    *La poésie biblique*. La vie chrétienne 6. Paris: B. Grasset.
Dietrich, M., and O. Loretz
    1968    Zur ugaritischen Lexicographie (III). *BO* 25: 100–101.
Dietrich, Walter
    1976    Rache: Erwägungen zu einem alttestamentlichen Thema. *EvT*
           36: 450–72.
    1994a   Der Eine Gott als Symbol politischen Widerstandes: Religion
           und Politik im Juda des 7. Jahrhunderts. Pp. 463–90 in *Ein
           Gott allein? JHWH-Verehrung und biblischer Monotheismus
           im Kontext der israelitischen und altorientalischen Religions-
           geschichte*, ed. W. Dietrich and A. Klopfenstein. OBO 139.
           Göttingen: Vandenhoeck und Ruprecht.
    1994b   Nahum. *TRE* 23: 737–42.
Dietrich, Walter, and Christian Link
    1995    *Die dunklen Seiten Gottes*. Bd. 1, Willkür und Gewalt.
           Neukirchen-Vluyn, Germany: Neukirchener.
    2000    *Die dunklen Seiten Gottes*. Bd. 2, Allmacht und Ohnmachat.
           Neukirchen-Vluyn, Germany: Neukirchener.
Dijkstra, M.
    1995    Is Balaam also among the Prophets? *JBL* 114: 43–64.
Dillard, Raymond B., and Tremper Longman III
    1994    Nahum. Pp. 403–8 in *An Introduction to the Old Testament*.
           Grand Rapids, Mich.: Zondervan.
Dimant, D.
    1994    A Quotation from Nahum 3–10 in 4Q385#6. Pp. 31–37 in *The
           Bible in the Light of Its Interpreters*, ed. S. Japhet. Jerusalem:
           Magnes. In Hebrew.
Diodorus Siculus (ca. 80–20 BCE)
    1950    *Diodorus Siculus: Library of History*, I–II (Books 1–2.34 and
           2:35–4.58). Trans. C. H. Oldfather. Loeb Classical Library.
           Cambridge, Mass.: Harvard UP.

Dobbs-Allsopp, F. W.
1993 *Weep, O Daughter of Jerusalem: A Study of the City-Lament Genre in the Hebrew Bible*. BibOr 44. Rome: Biblical Institute Press.
2000 Darwinism, Genre Theory, and City Laments. *JAOS* 120: 625–30. A response to A. Berlin's review of Dobbs-Allsopp's book in *JAOS*.

Dohmen, Christoph
1990 Eifersüchtiger ist sein Name (Ex 34,14): Ursprung und Bedeutung der alttestamentlichen Rede von Gottes Eifersucht. *BZ* 46: 289–304.
1998 נָסַךְ *nāsak;* נֶסֶךְ ; מַסֵּכָה II *massēkâ* מַסֵּכֶת ;סוּךְ; אָסוּךְ ' *image, idol.* TDOT 12:30–38.
2003 פסל *psl;* פָּסִיל; פֶּסֶל *image, idol.* TDOT 12: 30–38.
2004 רעע *rᶜᶜ;* רַע; רֹעַ; רָעָה; מֵרַע *evil.* TDOT 13: 560–93.

Dohmen, C., and D. Rick
2004 רעע *rᶜᶜ;* רַע *raᶜ;* רֹעַ *rōaᶜ;* רָעָה *rāᶜ;* מֵרַע *mēraᶜ evil.* TDOT 13: 560–88.

Dohmen, C., and P. Stenmans
1995 כָּבֵד *kābēd* I; כָּבֵד *kābēd* II; כֹּבֶד *kōbed;* כְּבוּדָה;כָּבֵד *be heavy, honor.* TDOT 7: 13–22

Döller, Johannes
1908 "Ninive gleich einem Wasserteiche" (Nah 2,9). *BZ* 6: 164–68.

Dommershausen, W.
1975 גּוֹרָל *gôrāl.* TDOT 2: 450–56.
1980 חָלַל *ḥālal* I and II. TDOT 4: 409–21.

Doudna, Gregory L.
2001 *4Q Pesher Nahum: A Critical Edition.* JSPSup, 35. Sheffield, England: Sheffield Academic.

Doutreleau, L.
1976 *Origène: Homélies sur la Genèse.* Paris: Éditions du Cerf.

Drioton, E., and J. Vandier
1952 *L'Egypte,* 3rd ed. Paris: Presses Universitaires de France.

Driver, Godfrey Rolles (1892–1975)
1931 Studies in the Vocabulary of the Old Testament, III. *JTS* 32: 361–65.
1933 Studies in the Vocabulary of the Old Testament, VI. *JTS* 34: 375–85.
1935 Studies in the Vocabulary of the Old Testament, VIII. *JTS* 36: 293–301.
1938 Linguistic and Textual Problems: Minor Prophets, II. *JTS* 39: 260–73.
1940 Hebrew Notes on Prophets and Proverbs. *JTS* 41: 162–75.
1956 *Canaanite Myths and Legends.* Edinburgh: Clark.

1964        Farewell to Queen Huzzab! *JTS*, n.s. 15: 296–98.
1967        Hebrew Homonyms. Pp. 50–64 in *Hebräische Wortforschung: Festschrift zum 80. Geburtstag von Walter Baumgartner.* VTSup 16. Leiden: Brill.

Driver, Samuel Rolles
1913        *An Introduction to the Literature of the Old Testament,* 11th ed. Edinburgh: T. and T. Clark.

Duhm, B.
1911        Anmerkungen zu den zwölf Propheten, V: Buch Náhum. *ZAW* 31: 100–107.

Dumbrill, Richard Jean
1998        *The Musicology and Organology of the Ancient Near East.* London: Tadema.

Dupont-Sommer, A.
1963a       Le Commentaire de Nahum découvert près de la mer morte (4QpNah): Traduction et Notes. *Sem* 13: 55–88.
1963b       Observations sur le commentaire découvert près de la mer morte. Pp. 242–43 in *CRAIBL,* issue 3 in 107th annual series of meetings.
1964        Observation sur le commentaire de Nahum, note addit. *RB* 71: 298–99.

Duval, Y.-M.
1984        Jérôme et Origène avant la querelle origéniste. La cure et la guérison ultime du monde et du diable dans Nahum. *Augustinianum* 24: 471–94.
1985        Jérome et les prophètes: Histoire, prophétie, actualité et actualization dans les commentiares de Nahum, Michée, Abdias et Joel. Pp. 108–31 in *Congress Volume: Salamanca 1983,* ed. J. A. Emerton. VTSup 36. Leiden: E. J. Brill.

Eaton, J. H.
1978        *Readings in Biblical Hebrew* 2. Ed. J. H. Eaton. Birmingham, England: University of Birmingham.
1981        *Vision in Worship: The Relation of Prophecy and Liturgy in the Old Testament.* London: SPCK (Society for Promoting Christian Knowledge).

Ebach, Jürgen
1993        Der Gott des Alten Testaments—Ein Gott der Rache? Pp. 81–93 in *Biblische Erinnerungen Theologische Reden zur Zeit.* Bochum, Germany: SWI.

Ecker, Jakob (1851–1912)
1883        *Prof. Dr. Bickell's "Carmina Veteris Testamenti metrice."* Munster: Theissing'sche Buchhandlung.

Edelkoort, A. H.
1937        *Nahum, Habakuk, Zefanja: Drie profeten voor onzen tijd.* Amsterdam: H. J. Paris.

Ego, B.
    2000      The Repentance of Nineveh in the Story of Jonah and Nahum's
                Prophecy of the City's Destruction: Aggadic Solutions for an
                Exegetical Problem in the Book of the Twelve. Pp. 243–53 in
                *Society of Biblical Literature 1999 Seminar Papers*, 39. Atlanta:
                Society of Biblical Literature.
Ehrlich, Arnold B. (1848–1919)
    1912      *Randglossen zur Hebräischen Bibel: Textkritisches, Sprachliches
                und Sachliches.* Vol. 5: *Ezekiel und die kleinen Propheten.*
                Hildesheim, Germany: G. Olms (reprinted from the 1912
                Leipzig edition).
Eichhorn, J. G. (1752–1857)
    1816      *Die Hebräischen Propheten,* 3 vols. Göttingen: Vandenhoeck
                und Ruprecht. Here Eichhorn arranged Nahum in strophes.
Eiselen, F. C.
    1915      Nahum, The Book of. Pp. 2109–11 in *The International
                Standard Bible Encyclopedia*, vol. 4, ed. James Orr. Chicago:
                Howard-Severance.
Eising, H.
    1980a     זָכַר *zāḵar;* זֵכֶר *zēḵer;* זִכָּרוֹן *zikkārôn;* אַזְכָּרָה *ʾazkārāh.*
                *TDOT* 4: 64–82.
    1980b     חַיִל *ḥayil. TDOT* 4: 348–56.
Eissfeldt, O.
    1965      *The Old Testament: An Introduction.* Trans. P. R. Ackroyd.
                Oxford: Basil Blackwell.
Eitan, Israel
    1937–38 A Contribution to Isaiah Exegesis. *HUCA* 12/13: 55–88.
Elbogen, Ismar (1874–1943)
    1924      *Der jüdische Gottesdienst in seiner geschichtlichen Entwicklung,*
                2nd ed. Frankfurt am Main: J. Kauffmann.
Elliger, K.
    1970      *Liber XII Prophetarum.* Fascicle 10, in *Biblia Hebraica
                Stuttgartensia*, ed. K. Elliger and W. Rudolph. Stuttgart: Würt-
                tembergische Bibelanstalt.
Ellis, M.
    1997      *Unholy Alliance: Religion and Atrocity in Our Time.*
                Minneapolis, Minn.: Fortress.
Ellison, H. L.
    1966      *The Old Testament Prophets.* Grand Rapids, Mich.: Zondervan.
Englander, H.
    1942/43  A Commentary on Rashi's Grammatical Comments. *HUCA*
                17: 427–98.
Engnell, Ivan
    1969      Prophets and Prophetism in the Old Testament. Pp. 123–79
                in *A Rigid Scrutiny: Critical Essays in the Old Testament*

*by Ivan Engnell*, ed. J. T. Willis. Nashville, Tenn.: Vander-
bilt UP.

Ephal, I.
  1996      *Siege and Its Ancient Near Eastern Manifestations.* Jerusalem:
            Magnes.
Erlandsson, S.
  1970      *The Burden of Babylon: A Study of Isaiah 13,2–14,23.* Con-
            BOT 4. Lund, Sweden: C. W. K. Gleerup.
  1980      זָנָה *zānâ;* זְנוּנִים; זְנוּת; תַּזְנוּת. *TDOT* 4: 99–104.
Eslinger, L.
  1992      Inner-Biblical Exegesis and Inner-Biblical Allusion: The
            Question of Category. *VT* 42: 47–58.
  1995      The Infinite in a Finite Organical Perception (Isaiah VI 1–5).
            *VT* 45: 145–73.
Eybers, I. H.
  1969a     Note Concerning the Date of Nahum's Prophecy. *OTWSA*
            12: 9–12
  1969b     The *Pèšèr*-Commentaries on Habakkuk and Nahum and the
            Origin of the Qumran Sect. *OTWSA* 12: 75–90.
Fabry, Heinz-Joseph
  1999      שַׂעַר *sāʿar;* סַעַר *saʿar;* סְעָרָה *səʿārāh;* שָׂעַר *śāʿar* II;
            *śaʿar;* שְׂעָרָה *śəʿār* storm wind, whirlwind. *TDOT* 10: 291–96.
  2002      Die Nahum- und Habakuk-Rezeption in der LXX und in
            Qumran. Pp. 159–90 in *"Wort JHWHs, das gescha . . ."*
            *(Hos 1,1): Studien zum Zwölfpropheten Buch,* ed. E. Zenger.
            HBS 35. Freiburg and New York: Herder.
  2003a     צַר *ṣar* I; צרר *ṣrr* I; צָרָה *ṣārâ* I; צְרוֹר *ṣᵉrôr;* מֵצַר *mēṣar;*
            מָצוֹר *māṣôr* enemy. *TDOT* 12: 455–64.
  2003b     The Reception of Nahum and Habakkuk in the Septuagint and
            Qumran. Pp. 241–56 in *Emmanuel: Studies in Hebrew Bible,*
            *Septuagint and Dead Sea Scrolls in Honor of Emanuel Tov,*
            ed. S. M. Paul et al. VTSup 94. Leiden and Boston: Brill.
Fabry, H.-J., and N. van Meeteren
  2006      תבל *tēbel* world. *TDOT* 15: 557–64.
Fabry, H.-J., E. Blum, and H. Ringgren
  2004      רִבּוֹא/רְבוֹא; רָבָה; רִבְבָה; רֶבַב; רוֹב/רֹב; רַב *rab;* רַב *rab* II;
            תַּרְבִּית; מַרְבִּית; מַרְבֶּה; אַרְבֶּה; רְבִיבִים *be large/many.*
            *TDOT* 13: 272–98.
Feliks, J.
  1962      *The Animal World of the Bible.* Tel-Aviv: Sinai.
Fensham, F. Charles
  1963      Common Trends in Curses of the Near Eastern Treaties and
            Kudurru-Inscriptions Compared with Maledictions of Amos
            and Isaiah. *ZAW* 75: 157–59.

1969      Legal Activities of the Lord According to Nahum. *OTWSA* 12: 13–20.

Feuchtwang, D.
1897      Assyriologische Studien II: Nahum. *Monatsschrift für Geschichte und Wissenschaft des Judentums* 41: 385–92.

Fishbane, M.
1977      Torah and Tradition. Pp. 275–300 in *Tradition and Theology in the Old Testament*, ed. D. A. Knight. Philadelphia, Pa.: Fortress.
1985      *Biblical Interpretation in Ancient Israel.* Oxford: Oxford UP.
1988      Use, Authority and Interpretation of Mikra at Qumran. Pp. 339–77 (esp. 354–55) in *Mikra: Text, Translation, Reading and Interpretation of the Hebrew Bible in Ancient Judaism and Early Christianity*, ed. M. J. Mulder. Compendia Rerum Judaicarum ad Novum Testamentum. Assen: Van Gorcum; Philadelphia, Pa.: Fortress.

Fisher, L. R., and F. B. Knutson
1965      An Enthronement Ritual at Ugarit. *JNES* 28: 157–67.

Fitzmyer, J. A.
1956      *l^e* as a Preposition and a Particle in Micah 5,l. *CBQ* 18: 10–13.

Florit, D. E.
1932      Ripercussioni immediate della caduta de Nineve sulla Palestina. *Bib* 13: 399–417.

Floyd, M.
1994      The Chimeral Acrostic of Nahum 1,2–10. *JBL* 113: 421–37.
2002      The משׂא (*Maśśāʾ*) as a Type of Prophetic Book. *JBL* 121: 401–22.

Flusser, D.
1981      Pharisäer und Essener in Pescher Nahum. In *Qumran*, ed. K. E. Grözinger et al. Wege der Forschung 160. Darmstadt: Wissenschaftliche Buchgesellschaft.

Fohrer, G.
1968      *Introduction to the Old Testament.* Trans. D. E. Green. Nashville, Tenn.: Abingdon.
1980      Neue Literatur zur alttestamentlichen Prophetie. *ThR* 45: 193–225.

Fokkelman, J. P.
1975      *Narrative Art in Genesis: Specimens of Stylistic and Structural Analysis.* Studia Semitica Neerlandica. Assen: Van Gorcum. Reprinted 1991, Sheffield, England: JSOT Press.
1981      *Narrative Art and Poetry in the Books of Samuel: A Full Interpretation Based on Stylistic and Structural Analyses.* Studia Semitica Neerlandica 20. Assen: Van Gorcum.
1999      *Reading Biblical Narrative: An Introductory Guide.* Trans. I. Smit. Louisville, Ky.: Westminster Fort Knox.

2003        *Major Poems of the Hebrew Bible: At the Interface of Hermeneu-
           tics and Structural Analysis.* Studia Semitica Neelandica 37.
           Assen: Van Gorcum

Fowler, Jeaneane D.
1988        *Theophoric Personal Names in Ancient Hebrew: A Comparative
           Study.* JSOTSup 49. Sheffield, England: JSOT Press.

Fox, N. S.
1995        Clapping Hands as a Gesture of Anguish and Anger in
           Mesopotamia and in Israel. *JANES* 23: 49–60.

Freedman, David Noel
1960        Archaic Forms in Early Hebrew Poetry. *ZAW* 72: 101–7.
1962        The Law and the Prophets. *VT* 9: 250–65.
1968        The Structure of Job 3. *Bib* 49:503–8.
1972        Acrostics and Metrics in Hebrew Poetry. *HTR* 65: 367–92.
1976        Canon of the OT. Pp. 130–36 in *IDBSup.* Nashville, Tenn.:
           Abingdon.
1983        The Earliest Bible. *Michigan Quarterly Review* 22: 16–75.
1985        Prose Particles in the Poetry of the Primary History. Pp. 49–62
           in *Biblical and Related Studies Presented to Samuel Iwry,* ed.
           A. Kort and S. Morschauser. Winona Lake, Ind.: Eisenbrauns.
1986        Acrostic Poems in the Hebrew Bible: Alphabetic and Other-
           wise. *CBQ* 48: 408–31.
1987        Headings in the Books of the Eighth-Century Prophets. *AUSS*
           25: 9–26.
1990        Formation of the Canon of the Old Testament. In *Religion and
           Law: Biblical-Judaic and Islamic Perspectives,* ed. E. B. Firmage
           and B. G. Weis. Winona Lake, Ind.: Eisenbrauns.
1991        *The Unity of the Bible.* Ann Arbor: University of Michigan Press.

Freedman, David Noel, and A. Welch
2004        שָׁדַד *šāḏaḏ;* שֹׁד *šōḏ devastate.* TDOT 14: 412–18.

Freedman, David Noel, B. E. Willoughby, and H.-J. Fabry
1997        מַלְאָךְ *malʾāḵ messenger.* TDOT 8: 308–25.
2001        עָנָן *ʿānān cloud.* TDOT 11: 253–57.

Freedman, David Noel, J. R. Lundbom, and H.-J. Fabry
1986        חָנַן *ḥānan;* חֵן *ḥēn;* חנון;חנינה;תחנה;תחנון. TDOT 5: 22–36.

Freedman, David Noel, M. P. O'Connor, and H. Ringgren
1986        יהוה *YHWH.* TDOT 5: 500–521.

Freedman, David Noel, B. E. Willoughby, H.-J. Fabry, and H. Ringgren
1999        נָשָׂא *nāśāʾ;* מַשְׂאֵת *maśʾēṯ;* מַשָּׂא *maśśōʾ;* מַשָּׂאָה *maśśāʾâ;* נְשִׂיא
           II *nāśîʾ* II; שְׂאֵת *śʾēṯ;* שִׂיא *śîʾ;* מַשָּׂא *maśśāʾ to lift, carry, bear.*
           TDOT 10: 24–40.

Freeman, James M.
1972        *Manners and Customs of the Bible.* Plainfield, N.J.: Logos
           International.

Freeman, Kathleen
    1966    *Ancilla to the Pre-Socratic Philosophers.* Cambridge, Mass.: Harvard UP.

Frevel, C.
    2004    רָדַף *rāḏap. TDOT* 13: 340–51.

Friedrich, Thomas
    1898    *Nineve's Ende und die Ausgänge des Assyrischen Reiches.* Pp. 13–52 in *Festgaben zu Ehren Max Büdingers von seinen Freunden und Schülern.* Innsbruck: Wagner.

Fuhs, H. F.
    1999    עָבַר *ʿāḇar. TDOT* 10: 408–25.
    2001    עָלָה *ʿālâ;* עֲלִיָּה ;עֲלִי ;עֵלִי ;תַעֲלָה ;מַעֲלָה ;מַעֲלֶה ;מֹעַל ;מַעַל go up, raise up. *TDOT* 11: 76–95.
    2004    רָאָה *rāʾâ;* מַרְאָה ;רְאוּת ;רְאִי ;רְאִי ;רֹאֶה *marʾeh see. TDOT* 13: 208–42.

Fuller, R.
    1996    The Form and Formation of the Book of the Twelve: The Evidence from the Judean Desert. Pp. 86–101 in *Forming Prophetic Literature: Essays on Isaiah and the Twelve in Honor of John D. W. Watts,* ed. J. W. Watts and P. R. House. JSOT-Sup 235. Sheffield, England: Sheffield Academic Press.

Gadd, C. J.
    1923    *The Fall of Nineveh.* Oxford: Oxford UP.
    1958    The Harran Inscriptions of Nabonidus. *Anatolian Studies* 8: 35–92.

Gamberoni, J.
    1986    חָסָה *ḥāsâ;* מַחֲסֶה *maḥᵃseh* חָסוּת *ḥāsût. TDOT* 5: 64–74.
    2003    קוּם *qûm. TDOT* 12: 589–612.

Garcia-López, F.
    1999    סבב *sbb;* סָבִיב ;מוּסָב ;מֵסַב ;נְסִבָּה ;סַבָּה *turn around, surround. TDOT* 10: 126–39.
    2001    פֶּה *peh mouth. TDOT* 11: 490–503.

Gardiner, Sir Alan Henderson
    1966    *Egypt of the Pharaohs.* A Galaxy Book. Oxford: Clarendon (ca. 1961).

Garsiel, M.
    1991    *Biblical Names: A Literary Study of Midrashic Derivations and Puns.* Ramat Gan, Israel: Bar-Ilan UP.

Gaster, T. H.
    1937a    Notes on the Minor Prophets. *JTS* 38: 163–65.
    1937b    The Battle of the Rain and the Sea: An Ancient Semitic Nature Myth. *Iraq* 4: 21–32.
    1942    A Canaanite Magical Text. *Or* n.s. 11: 41–79.

1944      Two Notes on Nahum: 1. Nahum 1,12. 2. Nahum 2,4. *JBL* 63: 51–52.
1962      Belial. P. 377 in *IDB*, vol. 1. Nashville, Tenn.: Abingdon.
1966      *Thespis: Ritual, Myth, and Drama in the Ancient Near East,* rev. ed. New York: Doubleday.
1969      *Myth, Legend, and Custom in the Old Testament: A Comparative Study with Chapters from Sir James G. Frazer's "Folklore in the Old Testament."* New York: Harper and Row.
1972      Belial. Pp. 428–29 in *Encyclopedia Judaica*, vol. 4. Jerusalem: Macmillan, 1971. Reprinted pp. 289–90 in *Encyclopedia Judaica*, 2nd ed., vol. 3. Detroit; New York; San Francisco; New Haven, Conn.; Waterville, Maine; and London: Thomas Gale, 2007.

Geers, F. W.
1945      The Treatment of Emphatics. *JNES* 4: 65–67.

Gehman, Henry S.
1940–41  The "Burden" of the Prophets. *JQR* n.s. 31: 107–21.

Geller, S.
1979      *Parallelism in Early Biblical Poetry*. Missoula, Mont.: Scholars Press.

Gelston, A. (ed.)
1980      *Dodekapropheton*. Leiden Peshitta, vol. 3: 4. Leiden: E. J. Brill.
1987      *The Peshitta of the Twelve Prophets*. New York: Oxford UP.
1988      Some Readings of the Peshitta of the Dodekapropheton. Pp. 81–98 in *The Peshitta: Its Early Text and History*, ed. P. B. Dirksen and M. J. Mulder. Leiden: Brill.

George, A.
1960      Nahum. Cols. 291–301 in *Dictionnaire de la Bible: Supplément*, vol. 6. Paris: Letouzey et Ané.

Gerstenberger, Erhard
1962      The Woe-Oracles of the Prophets. *JBL* 81: 249–63.
2001      עָנָה II‘ānâ; עָנְוָה עֲנָוָה עָנָה תַּעֲנִית עֱנוּת עָנִי עָנוּ *debase, misery, poor.* TDOT 11: 230–52.

Gese, H.
1957      Die hebräischen Bibelhandschriften zum Dodekapropoheton nach der Variantensammlung des Kennicott. ZAW 69: 55–69.

Gevaryahu, H. M. I.
1975      Biblical Colophons: A Source for the "Biography" of Authors, Texts, and Books. Pp. 42–59 in VTSup 28. Leiden: Brill.

Gevirtz, S.
1961      West Semitic Curses and the Problem of the Origins of Hebrew Law. *VT* 11: 137–58.

Geyer, J. B.
1987      Twisting Tiamat's Tail: A Mythological Interpretation of Isaiah XIII 5 and 8. *VT* 37: 164–79.

Gibson, J. C. L. (ed.)
    1994     *Davidson's Introductory Hebrew Grammar Syntax.* Edinburgh: T. and T. Clark.

Ginsberg, C. D.
    1894     עשרים וארבעה ספרי הקדש. London: n.p.; Vienna: Carl Fromme.

Ginsberg, H. L.
    1929     Studies on the Biblical Verb: Masoretically Misconstrued Internal Passives. *AJSL* 46: 53–56.
    1935a   A Phoenician Hymn in the Psalter. Pp. 472–76 in *Atti del XIX Congresso Internazionale degli Orientalisti.* Rome: G. Bardi.
    1935b   The Victory of the Land-god over the Sea-god. *JPOS* 15: 327–33.
    1938     Baʿal and ʿAnat. *Or* n.s. 7: 1–11.
    1941     Did Anat Fight the Dragon? *BASOR* 84: 12–14.
    1942     The Rebellion and Death of Bavlu. *Or* n.s. 5: 161–98.
    1943     The Ugaritic Texts and Textual Criticism. *JBL* 62: 109–15.
    1946     *The Legend of King Keret: A Canaanite Epic of the Bronze Age.* BASOR Supplementary Series, nos. 2–3. New Haven, Conn.: American Schools of Oriental Research.
    1950     Judah and the Transjordan States from 734 to 582 B.C.E. Pp. 347–68 in *Alexander Marx Jubilee Volume.* English section. New York: Jewish Theological Seminary of America.
    1960     Studies in Hosea 1–3. Pp. 50–69 in *Yehezkel Kaufmann Jubilee Volume.* Jerusalem: Magnes.

Gitin, Seymour
    1989     Tel-Miqne-Ekron: A Type Site for the Inner Coastal Plain in the Iron Age II Period. Pp. 23–59 in *Recent Excavations in Israel: Studies in Iron Age Archaeology*, ed. S. Gitin and W. Dever. AASOR, 49. Winona Lake, Ind.: Eisenbrauns.

Glasson, T. F.
    1969/70  The Final Question—In Nahum and Jonah. *ExpTim* 81: 54–55.

Glück, J. J.
    1969     *Pārûr-pāʾrûr*—A Case of Biblical Paronomasia. *OTWSA* 12: 21–26.

Goldman, M. D.
    1954–55  The Root *nqy. ABR* 4: 49–55.

Gonen, Rivka
    1975     *Weapons of the Ancient World.* Cassell's Introducing Archaeology Series. London: Cassell.

Gordis, R.
    1954     Hosea's Marriage and Message: A New Approach. *HUCA* 27: 9–35.

Gordon, Alexander Reid (1872–1930)
  1916    *The Prophets of the Old Testament.* New York: Doran.
Gordon, Cyrus H.
  1940    *Ugaritic Grammar.* AnOr 20. Rome: Pontifical Biblical Insti-
          tute Press.
  1943    The Poetic Literature of Ugarit. *Or* n.s. 12: 31–75.
  1965    *Ugaritic Textbook.* AnOr 38. Rome: Pontifical Biblical Institute
          Press.
  1978    New Directions. *Bulletin of the American Society of Papyrolo-
          gists* 15: 59–66.
Gordon, P., and H. C. Washington
  1995    Rape as a Military Metaphor in the Hebrew Bible. Pp. 308–25
          in *A Feminist Companion to the Latter Prophets,* ed. A. Brenner.
          FCB 8. Sheffield, England: Sheffield UP.
Gordon, Robert P.
  1974    The Targum to the Minor Prophets and the Dead Sea Texts:
          Textual and Exegetical Notes. *RevQ* 8: 425–29.
  1983    Loricate Locusts in the Targum to Nahum III 17 and Revela-
          tion IX 9. *VT* 33: 338–39.
  1994    *Studies in the Targum to the Twelve Prophets from Nahum to
          Malachi.* VTSup 51. Leiden: Brill.
Gordon, R. P., and K. J. Cathcart
  1989    *The Targum of the Minor Prophets.* The Aramaic Bible, vol. 14.
          Edinburgh: T. and T. Clark.
Görg, Manfred
  1978    Eine formelhafte Metaphor bei Joel und Nahum. *BN* 6:
          12–14.
  1990    יָשַׁב *yāšaḇ;* מוֹשָׁב. *TDOT* 6: 420–38
  2004    שָׁכַן *šākān;* שֵׁכֶן *šāḵēn settle, dwell. TDOT* 14: 691–702.
Goslinga, C. J.
  1923    *Nahums Godsspraak tegen Nineve.* Zutphen, Netherlands:
          Nauta.
Gottwald, Norman K.
  1954    *Studies in the Book of Lamentations.* London: SCM Press.
  1964    *All the Kingdoms of the Earth: Israelite Prophecy and Inter-
          national Relations in the Ancient Near East.* New York: Harper
          and Row.
  1984    Tragedy and Comedy in the Latter Prophets. *Semeia* 32:
          83–96.
Gradwohl, R.
  1963    *Die Farben im Alten Testament.* BZAW 83. Berlin: A. Töpelmann.
Graetz, H.
  1893    *Emendationes in plerosque Sacrae Scripturae Veteris Testamenti
          libros.* Breslau [Wroclaw]: Schlesische Buchdr.

Graffy, A.
 1984 *A Prophet Confronts His People.* AnBib, 104. Rome: Pontifical
  Biblical Institute.
Graham, W. C.
 1927–28 The Interpretation of Nahum 1:9–2:3. *AJSL* 44: 37–48.
Gray, G. B.
 1898 The Alphabetic Poem in Nahum. *The Expositor,* 5th series 8:
  207–20.
 1915 The Alphabetic Poem in Nahum. Pp. 243–63 in *The Forms of
  Hebrew Poetry.* New York: Ktav, 1972. Reprint of Gray's 1898
  article with additions.
Gray, John
 1947/53 The Wrath of God in Canaanite and Hebrew Literature. *Journal of
  the Manchester University Egyptian and Oriental Society* 25: 9–19.
 1956 The Hebrew Concept of the Kingship of God: Its Origin and
  Development. *VT* 6: 268–85.
 1961 The Kingship of God in the Prophets and Psalms. *VT* 11: 1–29.
Grayson, A. K.
 1972 *Assyrian Royal Inscriptions.* Wiesbaden: O. Harrassowitz.
 1975 *Assyrian and Babylonian Chronicles.* New York: J. J. Augustin,
  ca. 1970.
 1987–90 *The Royal Inscriptions of Mesopotamia: The Assyrian Periods,*
  vols. 1–2. Toronto: University of Toronto Press.
 1991 Assyria 668–635 B.C.: The Reign of Ashurbanipal. *CAH* III/2:
  142–61.
 1992a Mesopotamia, History of (Assyria). Pp. 732–55 in *AYBD,* vol. 4.
  New York: Doubleday.
 1992b Nineveh. Pp. 1118–19 in *AYBD,* vol. 4. New York: Doubleday.
Green, A. See Black, J., and A. Green.
Green, W. H.
 1855 Review of "Nahum's Prophecy Concerning Nineveh
  Explained and Illustrated from Assyrian Monuments" by Otto
  Strauss. *Biblical Repertory* 27: 102–32.
 1877 *A Hebrew Chrestomathy.* New York: John Wiley and Son.
Greenfield, Jonas C.
 1985 The Meaning of *TKWNH\*.* Pp. 81–85 in *Biblical and Related
  Studies Presented to Samuel Iwry,* ed. Ann Kort and Scott
  Morschauser. Winona Lake, Ind.: Eisenbrauns.
Greenwood, D. C.
 1976 On the Jewish Hope for a Restored Northern Kingdom. *ZAW*
  88: 376–85.
Gressman, Hugo (1877–1927)
 1905 *Der Ursprung der israelitisch-jüdischen Eschatologie.* FRLANT
  6. Göttingen: Vandenhoeck und Ruprecht.

Griffin, W. P.
  1997      *The God of the Prophets: An Analysis of Divine Action.* JSOT-
             Sup 249. Sheffield, England: Sheffield Academic Press.
Grimme, Hubert
  1896–97   Abriss der biblisch-hebräischen Metrik. ZDMG 50: 529–84;
             51: 683–712.
Gross, W.
  1998      נָדַד *nādad* flee. TDOT 9: 227–31.
Grossouw, Willem Karel Maria
  1938      *The Coptic Versions of the Minor Prophets: A Contribution
             to the Study of the Septuagint.* Rome: Pontifical Biblical
             Institute.
Gry, L.
  1910      Un épisode des derniers jours de Ninive (Nahum II, 8). *RB*,
             n.s. 1: 398–403.
Guèrin, Victor (1821–91)
  1897      *La Terre Sainte, Jérusalem; et le nord de la Judée.* Paris:
             Librairie Pion.
Gunkel, Hermann (1862–1932)
  1893      Nahum 1. ZAW 13: 223–44.
  1895      *Schöpfung und Chaos.* Göttingen: Vandenhoeck und
             Ruprecht.
Gwaltney, W. C.
  1994      Assyrians. Pp. 77–106 in *Peoples of the Old Testament World,*
             ed. A. J. Hoerth et al. Grand Rapids, Mich.: Baker.
Haldar, Alfred
  1945      *Associations of Cult Prophets among the Ancient Semites.*
             Uppsala, Sweden: Almqvist and Wiksell.
  1947      *Studies in the Book of Nahum.* Uppsala, Sweden: Almqvist and
             Wiksell.
Halévy, J.
  1905      Le Livre de Nahum. *Revue Sémitique* 13: 97–123.
Hallo, William W., and William Kelly Simpson
  1971      *The Ancient Near East: A History.* New York: Harcourt, Brace,
             Jovanovich.
Halperin, David J.
  1981      Crucifixion, the Nahum Pesher, and the Rabbinic Penalty of
             Strangulation. *JJS* 32: 32–46.
Haney, Herbert M.
  1960      *The Wrath of God in the Former Prophets.* New York: Vantage.
Happel, O.
  1900      *Der Psalm Nahum (Nahum 1) kritisch untersucht.* Würzburg:
             Andreas Göbel.

Harper, Robert Francis
1892–   *Assyrian and Babylonian Letters Belonging to the Konyunjik*
1914    *Collections of the British Museum,* vols. 1–14. Chicago and
         London: University of Chicago Press.
Harris, J. Rendel
1887    *The Teaching of the Apostles.* Newly edited, with facsimile text
         and a commentary, for the Johns Hopkins University, Balti-
         more, from the MS. of the Holy Sepulchre (Convent of the
         Greek Church) Jerusalem. Baltimore, Md.: Publication
         Agency of Johns Hopkins University.
Harrison, C. R. Jr.
1988    The Unity of the Minor Prophets in the LXX: A Reexamina-
         tion. *BIOSCS* 21: 55–72.
Harrison, Roland K.
1969    The Book of Nahum. Pp. 926–30 in *Introduction to the Old
         Testament.* Grand Rapids, Mich.: Eerdmans.
Hasel, G. F.
1995    כָּרַת *kārat;* כְּרִתוֹת; כְּרִיתָת *cut (off).* TDOT 7: 339–52.
Haupt, P.
1907b   Eine alttestamentliche Festliturgie für den Nikanortag. ZDMG
         61: 275–97.
1907c   The Book of Nahum. *JBL* 26: 1–53. Published separately as
         *The Book of Nahum: A New Metrical Translation with an Intro-
         duction, Restoration of the Hebrew Text and Explanatory Criti-
         cal Notes.* Baltimore, Md.: Johns Hopkins UP.
1907d   Xenophon's Account of the Fall of Nineveh. *JAOS* 28: 99–107.
Hausmann, J.
1995    לַהַב *lahab;* להבה/לֶהָבָה; שַׁלְהֶבֶת *flame, lance.* TDOT 7: 469–73.
Hay, Lawrence C.
1960    The Oracles against the Foreign Nations in Jeremiah 46–51.
         Ph.D. thesis, Vanderbilt University, Nashville, Tenn.
Hayes, J. H.
1968    The Usage of Oracles against Foreign Nations in Ancient
         Israel. *JBL* 87: 81–92.
Hayward, Robert
1987    Saint Jerome and the Aramaic Targumim. *JSS* 32: 105–23.
Heelan, Patrick
1979    Music as Basic Metaphor and Deep Structure in Ancient Cul-
         tures. *Journal of Social and Biological Structures* 2: 279–91.
Heidel, Alexander
1942    *The Babylonian Genesis: The Story of Creation.* Chicago: Uni-
         versity of Chicago Press.
1946    *The Gilgamesh Epic and Old Testament Parallels.* Chicago:
         University of Chicago Press.

Helberg, J. L.
    1969    Nahum–Jonah–Lamentations–Isaiah 51–53. Pp. 46–55 in
            *Biblical Essays*, ed. A. H. van Zyl. Potchefstroom, South Africa:
            Pro Rege-Pers Bpk.
Held, Moshe
    1969    Rhetorical Questions in Ugaritic and Biblical Hebrew. *ErIs* 9:
            71–19.
    1971    Studies in Biblical Homonyms in the Light of Akkadian.
            *JANES* 3: 46–55.
Helfmeyer, F. J.
    1978    הָלַךְ *hālak;* הליכה. *TDOT* 3: 388–403.
    1986    חָנָה *hānâ;* מַחֲנֶה. *TDOT* 5: 4–19.
    1995    כָּלָה *kālâ* bring *to an end, complete. TDOT* 7: 157–64.
Hendel, R. S.
    1995    Serpent. Cols. 1404–12 in *DDD.*
Henshaw, T.
    1958    Nahum. Pp. 144–50 in *The Latter Prophets*. London: George
            Allen and Unwin.
Herdner, Andrée
    1963    *Corpus des Tablettes en Cunéiformes Alphabétiques Découvertes
            à Ras Shamra-Ugarit de 1929 à 1939.* Mission de Ras Shamra
            10. Paris: Imprimerie Nationale / Geuthner.
Hermann, Wolfgang
    1999    Rider-upon-the-clouds. Pp. 703–5 in *DDD*[2].
Herodotus (ca. 484–430 BCE)
    1921    *The Persian Wars*, vol. 1 (Books 1–2). Trans. A. D. Godley.
            Loeb Classical Library. London: W. Heinemann; New York:
            G. P. Putnam.
Heschel, A. J.
    1962    *The Prophets.* New York: Harper and Row.
Hesse, F.
    1980    חָזַק *hāzaq;* חָזַק; חֵזֶק; חֹזֶק; חֶזְקָה; הַזְקָה. *TDOT* 4: 301–8.
Hestrin, Ruth, and Michel Dayagi-Mendels
    1979    *Inscribed Seals.* Jerusalem: Israel Museum.
Hiebert, T.
    1986    *God of My Victory: The Ancient Hymn in Habakkuk 3.* HSM
            38. Atlanta: Scholars Press.
Hieke, Th.
    1993a   Der Anfang des Buches Nahum I: Die Frage des Textverlaufes
            in der jetzigen Gestalt; Ein antithetisches Prinzip. . . . *BN* 68:
            13–17.
    1993b   Der Anfang des Buches Nahum II: Wie begann die Prophetie
            Nahums ursprünglich? Ein Rekonstruktionsversuch. . . . *BN*
            69: 15–20.

Hillers, Delbert R.
1964     *Treaty-Curses and the Old Testament Prophets.* BibOr 16.
         Rome: Pontifical Biblical Institute Press.
1965     A Convention in Hebrew Literature: The Reaction to Bad
         News. ZAW 77: 86–89.
1983a    *Hôy* and *Hôy*-Oracles: A Neglected Syntactic Aspect.
         Pp. 185–88 in *The Word of the Lord Shall Go Forth: Essays
         in Honor of David Noel Freedman,* ed. Carol L. Meyers and
         Michael O'Connor. Winona Lake, Ind.: Eisenbrauns.
1983b    *Micah.* Hermeneia. Philadelphia, Pa.: Fortress.
Hilprecht, H. V.
1903     *Explorations in Bible Lands during the 19th Century.* Phila-
         delphia, Pa.: A. J. Homan.
Himmelfarb, M.
1968     Translating the Psalms. *Commentary* 45: 72–76.
Hirshler, J.
1930     Nahum. In *Torah Neri'im u–Khetuvim 'im perush mada'I,*
         ed. A. Kahane. Tel Aviv: Mekorot.
Hockerman, Jacob
1986     Etymologies in Biblical Hebrew. *Beth Mikra* 106: 220–26.
Hoenig, S. B.
1964     *Dorshé Halakot* in the Pesher Nahum Scrolls. *JBL* 83: 119–38.
1967     The Pesher Nahum "Talmud" (Nahum 3:4). *JBL* 86: 441–45.
Höffken, Peter
1977     Untersuchungen zu den Begründungselementen der
         Völkerorakel des Alten Testaments. Ph.D. diss., Bonn.
Hoffner, H. A.
1986     יָבֵל *ybl;* יָבוּל. *TDOT* 5: 364–67.
Holladay, William L.
1986     Pp. 647–53 in *Jeremiah 1: A Commentary on the Book of the
         Prophet Jeremiah Chapters 1–25.* Hermeneia—A Critical and
         Historical Commentary on the Bible. Philadelphia, Pa.: Fortress.
Holloway, S. W.
2000     Biblical Assyria and Other Anxieties in the British Empire.
         Paper delivered at the SBL Annual Meeting, Nashville, Tenn.,
         November 18–21.
Hommel, F.
1896/97  Belial and Other Mythological Terms. *ExpTim* 8: 472–74.
Horgan, M. P.
1979     *Pesharim: Qumran Interpretation of Biblical Books.* CBQMS 8.
         Washington, D.C.: Catholic Biblical Association of America.
Horst, Friedrich
1960     Die Visionsschilderungen der alttestamentlichen Propheten.
         *EvT* 20: 193–205.

Hossfeld, F. L., and E. Reuter
1999    סֵפֶר sēp̄er. TDOT 10: 326.
House, P. R.
1990    *The Unity of the Twelve.* JSOTSup 97. Sheffield, England: Almond.
1996    Dramatic Coherence in Nahum, Habakkuk, and Zephaniah. Pp. 195–208 in *Forming Prophetic Literature: Essays on Isaiah and the Twelve in Honor of John D. W. Watts,* ed. J. W. Watts and P. R. House. JSOTSup 235. Sheffield, England: Sheffield Academic Press.
Höver-Johag, I.
1986    טוֹב ṭôḇ; טוּב ṭûḇ; יטב yṭb. TDOT 5: 296–317.
Howard, G.
1971/72 Lucianic Readings in a Greek Twelve Prophets Scroll from the Judaean Desert. *JQR* 62: 51–60.
1974    The Quinta of the Minor Prophets: A First Century Septuagint Text? *Bib* 55: 15–22.
Hrouda, B.
1963    Der Assyrische Streitwagen. *Iraq* 25: 155–58.
Hudson, Michael
2000    Music as an Analogy for Economic Order in Classical Antiquity. Pp. 113–35 in *Karl Bücher. Theory, History, Anthropology, Non-Market Economies,* ed. Jürgen Backhaus. Marburg, Germany: Metropolis.
Huenergard, J.
1985    Biblical Notes on Some New Akkadian Texts from Emar (Syria). *CBQ* 74: 428–34.
Huesman, John
1956a   Finite Uses of the Infinite Absolute. *Bib* 37: 271–95.
1956b   The Infinitive Absolute and the Waw + Perfect Problem. *Bib* 37: 410–34.
Huffmon, H. B.
1966a   The Treaty Background of Hebrew YADAᶜ. *BASOR* 181: 31–37.
1966b   A Further Note on the Treaty Background of Hebrew YADAᶜ. *BASOR* 184: 36–38.
Hulst, A. R.
1960    *Old Testament Translation Problems.* Leiden: Brill.
Humbert, P.
1926    Essai d'analyse de Nahoum 1,2–2,3. *ZAW* 44: 266–80.
1927    Nahoum II, 9. *REJ* 83: 74–76.
1928    La vision de Nahoum 2,4–11. *AfO* 5: 14–19.
1932    Le problème du livre de Nahoum. *RHPR* 12: 1–15.

1933    Die Herausforderungsformel "hinnenî êlékâ." ZAW 1933: 101–8.

1936    Les Prophètes d'Israël ou les tragiques de la Bible. *RThPh* 24: 209–51.

Hummel, H. D.
1957    Enclitic *Mem* in Early Northwest Semitic. *JBL* 76: 85–107.

Hyatt, J. P.
1956    New Light on Nebuchadnezzar and Judean History. *JBL* 75: 277–84.

Idelsohn, A. Z.
1967    *Jewish Music: Its Historical Development.* New York: Schocken, 1967. 1st ed. 1929.

In der Smitten, W. T.
1980    חוֹמָה *ḥômāh. TDOT* 4: 267–71.

Irwin, W. H.
1974    Review of Kevin J. Cathcart, *Nahum in the Light of Northwest Semitic* (BibOr 26; Rome: Biblical Institute Press, 1973). *CBQ* 36: 397–98.

Isaacs, E.
1918    The Metrical Basis of Hebrew Poetry. *AJSL* 35: 20–54.

Jacob, E.
1912    Erklärung einiger Hiob-Stellen. *ZAW* 32: 278–87.

Jacobsen, T., and S. Lloyd
1935    *Sennacherib's Aqueduct at Jerwan.* OIP 24. Chicago: University of Chicago Press.

Jahnow, Hedwig
1923    *Das hebräische Leichenlied im Rahmen der Völkerdichtung.* BZAW 36. Giessen: A. Topelmann.

Jakobson, R.
1966    Grammatical Parallelism and Its Russian Facet. *Language* 42: 399–429.

Janzen, Waldemar
1972    *Mourning Cry and Woe Oracle.* BZAW 125. Berlin and New York: de Gruyter.

Jastrow, Marcus
1950    *A Dictionary of the Targumim, the Talmud Babli and Yerushalmi, and the Midrashic Literature.* 2 vols. New York: Pardes.

Jensen, P.
1890    *Die Kosmologie der Babylonier: Studien und Materalien.* Strassburg: Trübner.

Jeppesen, Knud
1984    The Verb *yāᶜad* in Nahum 1,10 and Micah 6,9. *Bib* 65: 571–74.

Jepsen, A.
1980    חָזָה *chāzāh*; חֹזֶה *chōze*; חָזוֹן *hāzôn*. TDOT 4: 280–90.
Jeremias, Alfred (1864–1935)
1895    See A. Billerbeck.
1930    *Das Alte Testament im Lichte des alten Orients.* Leipzig, J. C. Hinrichs. 1st ed. 1904.
Jeremias, Jörg
1965    *Theophanie: Die Geschichte einer alttestamentlichen Gattung.* WMANT 10. Neukirchen, Germany: Neukirchener.
1970    *Kultprophetie und Gerichtsverkündigung in der späten Königszeit Israels.* WMANT 35. Neukirchen-Vluyn, Germany: Neukirchener.
Johnson, A. R.
1935    The Role of the King in the Jerusalem Cultus. Pp. 73–111 in *The Labyrinth*, ed. S. H. Hooke. London: SPCK (Society for Promoting Christian Knowledge).
1944    *The Cultic Prophet in Ancient Israel.* Cardiff: University of Wales Press.
1962    *The Cultic Prophet in Ancient Israel*, 2nd ed. Cardiff: University of Wales Press.
1979    *The Cultic Prophet and Israel's Psalmody.* Cardiff: University of Wales Press.
Johnson, E., and Jan Bergman
1974    אָנַף *'ānap*; אַף *'ap* (*za'am, za'ap, chemah, charah, 'abhar, qatsaph, raghaz*). TDOT 1: 348–60.
Johnson, Gordon H.
1985    The Book of Nahum: An Exegetical, Rhetorical, and Theological Study. Th.M. thesis, Dallas Theological Seminary, Dallas, Tex.
Johnston, G. H.
1992    A Rhetorical Analysis of the Book of Nahum. Ph.D. dissertation, Dallas Theological Seminary, Dallas, Tex.
Jones, Brian C.
1996    *Howling Over Moab: Irony and Rhetoric in Isaiah 15–16.* SBLDS, 157. Atlanta: Scholars Press.
Jones, Barry A.
1995    *The Formation of the Book of the Twelve: A Study in Text and Canon.* SBLDS, 149. Atlanta: Scholars Press.
Joüon, P.
1911–12 Notes de critique textuelle, AT: Nahum 3,6. MUSJ 5: 485–86.
1924    *bəliyya'al* Belial. Bib 5:178–83.
1926    Notes de lexicographie hébraïque: Verbe מוג. Bib 7: 165–58.

Joüon, P., and T. Muraoka
    1993      A *Grammar of Biblical Hebrew*. Subsidia Biblica 14. Rome: Biblical Institute Press.

Kaiser, O.
    1986a    חָרַב *ḥārab* I; חָרֵב *ḥārēb;* הֹרֶב *ḥōreb;* חָרְבָּה *ḥorbâ;* חָרְבָה *ḥārābâ;* חֶרְבּוֹן *ḥᵃrābôn*. *TDOT* 3: 150–54.
    1986b    חֶרֶב *ḥereb;* חָרֵב II. *TDOT* 3: 155–65.

Kalinsky, Johann Gattlieb (fl. 1715–49)
    1748     *Vaticinia Chabacuci et Nahumi itemque nonnulla Iesaiea, Micheae et Ezechielis oracular observationibus historico-philologicis ex historia Diodori Siculi circa res Sardanapali ea methodo illustriata* etc. Vratislaviae, Poland: Iacobi Kornii.

Kapelrud, A. S.
    1986     טִיט *ṭîṭ*. *TDOT* 5: 322.
    2003     פָּרַח *pāraḥ;* פֶּרַח *peraḥ*. *TDOT* 12: 92–95.

Kasser, R.
    1979     Un lexeme copte oublié, TKHN a Khmimique (Nahum 3,19). *Bulletin de la Société d'Egyptologie* 1: 23–25.

Katzenelbogen, M. Y.
    2002     *Biur Ha-GRA Le-Nach*. Jerusalem: Mossad Harav Kook.

Kedar-Kopfstein, B.
    2003     קוֹל *qôl* voice. *TDOT* 12: 576–88.

Keith, A.
    1853     Pp. 234–40 in *De stipte en letterlijke vervulling der Bijbelsche profetieën*, 2nd ed. Amsterdam: Bij H. Hoëveker.

Keller, C. A.
    1972     Die theologische Bewältigung der geschichtlichen Wirklichkeit in der Prophetie Nahums. *VT* 22: 399–419.

Kellermann, D.
    1975     גָּאָה *gāʾāh;* גֵּאֶה; גַּאֲוָה; גֵּאוּת; גָּאוֹן; גֵּאָה; גֵּוָה . *TDOT* 2: 344–50.

Kelly, J. N. D.
    1975     *Jerome: His Life, Writings, and Controversies*. New York: Harper and Row.

Kelly, William
    1871     *Lectures Introductory to the Study of the Minor Prophets*. London: W. H. Broom.

Kennedy, James M.
    1987     The root *gᶜr* in the Light of Semantic Analysis. *JBL* 106: 47–64.

Kennedy, R. A. S.
    1902     Nahum. Pp. 473–77 in *Dictionary of the Bible*, vol. 3. New York: Charles Scribner's Sons.

Kennicott, Benjamin (1718–83)
   1776–80   *Vetus Testamentum Hebraicum cum variis lectionibus.* Oxford: Clarendoniano.
Kim, Y. I.
   1981   The Vocabulary of Oppression in the Old Testament. Ph.D. dissertation, Drew University, Madison, N.J.
Kirkpatrick, A. F.
   1912   Lecyture 8: Nahum. Pp. 239–57 in *The Doctrine of the Prophets,* 3rd ed. Warburtonian Lectures for 1886–1890. London: Macmillan.
Kitchen, K. A.
   1975   Thebes. Pp. 714–15 in *ZPEB,* vol. 5.
Kleinert, P.
   1910   Nahum und der Fall Ninives. *Theologische Studien und Kritiken* 83: 501–34.
Klopfenstein, M. A.
   1964   *Die Lüge nach dem Alten Testament.* Zürich: Gotthelf.
Knipping, B.
   2004   שָׁבַר *šābar;* שֶׁבֶר; מַשְׁבֵּר; מִשְׁבָּר *break.* TDOT 14: 367–81.
Kobayashi, Y.
   1992   Elkosh. P. 476 in *AYBD,* vol. 2.
Koch, K.
   1995   Nahum. Pp. 261–63 in *Die Propheten,* Bd. 1: *Assyrische Zeit, I,* rev. ed., ed. A. Schart. Urban Taschenbücher, 280. Stuttgart: Kohlhammer.
Koch, K., and H.-J. Fabry
   2003   קֶבֶר *qeber;* קָבַר; קְבוּרָה *grave, burial.* TDOT 12: 492–98.
Koenen, Klaus
   1994   *Heil den Gerechten—Unheil den Sündern! Ein Beitrag zur Theologie der Prophetenbücher.* BZAW 229. Berlin: W. de Gruyter.
König, Eduard (1846–1936)
   1914   *Hebräische Rhythmik: Die Gesetze des alttestamentlichen Vers- und Strophenbaues.* Halle, Germany: Waisenhauses.
Koole, Jan Leunis
   1990   *Jesaja* II/2. Commentar op het Oude Testament. Kampen, Netherlands: Kok Pharos.
Korpel, M. C. A.
   1990   *A Rift in the Clouds: Ugaritic and Hebrew Descriptions of the Divine.* Münster: Ugarit.
Korpel, Marjo, and Johannis de Moor
   1986   Fundamentals of Ugaritic and Hebrew Poetry. UF 18: 173–212. Republished pp. 1–61 in *The Structural Analysis of*

*Biblical and Canaanite Poetry,* ed. Willem van der Meer and Johannes C. de Moor, JSOTSup 74, 1988.

Kraay, C. M., and P. R. S. Moorey
1968    Two Fifth Century Hoards from the Near East. *Revue Numismatique* ser. 6, 11: 181–235.

Kraft, C. F.
1938    *Strophic Structure of Hebrew Poetry as Illustrated in the First Book of the Psalter.* Chicago: University of Chicago Press.

Kramer, S. N.
1949    *Lament over the Destruction of Ur.* Chicago: University of Chicago Press.

Krause, G.
1962    *Studien zu Luthers Auslegung der Kleinen Propheten.* Tübingen: Mohr.

Krauss, S.
1930    Mitteilungen. ZAW 48: 320–24.

Kreenen, E.
1808    *Nahumi vaticinium philologice et critice expositum.* Hardervici: Evarardi Tyhoff, Academiae Typographi.

Krenkel, M.
1866    Zur Kritik und Exegese der kleinen Propheten. *ZWTh* 9: 266–81.

Krieg, Matthias
1988    *Todesbilder im Alten Testament.* Zürich: Theologischer Verlag.

Kronholm, T.
1999    נָתַק *nātaq;* נֶתֶק *neteq tear loose.* TDOT 10: 115–19.

Kselman, J. S.
1979    *rb/kbd*: A New Hebrew-Akkadian Formulaic Pair. *VT* 29: 110–14.

Kuenan, Abraham (1828–91)
1877    *The Prophets and Prophecy in Israel: An Historical and Critical Enquiry.* Trans. from the Dutch by Adam Milroy. London: Longmans, Green.

Kugel, James L.
1981    *The Idea of Biblical Poetry: Parallelism and Its History.* New Haven, Conn.: Yale UP.

Kumalo, A. N. C.
1980    Red Our Colour. P. 58 in *Poets to the People: South African Freedom Poems,* ed. B. Feinberg. London: Heinemann.

Kurylowicz, Jerzy (1895–1978)
1973    *Studies in Semitic Grammar and Metrics.* London: Curzon.

Labat, R.
1935    *Le poème babylonien de la création.* Paris: Adrien-Maissonneuve.

Labuschagne, C. J.
1966    The Emphasizing Particle *Gam* and Its Connotations. Pp. 193–203 in *Studia Biblica et Semitica: FS T. C. Vriezen,*

ed. W. van Unnik and A. van der Woude. Wageningen, Netherlands: Veenman.

1973        The Particles הֵן and הִנֵּה *hinnēh*. OTS 18: 1–14.
1987–97     *Deuteronomium.* 3 vols. De Prediking van het Oude
            Testament. Nijkerk, Netherlands: Uitgeverij Callenbach.
1992        *Vertellen met getallen: Functie en symboliek van getallen in
            de bijbelse oudheid.* Zoetermeer, Netherlands: Uitgeverij
            Boekencentrum.
2000        *Numerical Secrets of the Bible: Rediscovering the Bible Codes.*
            North Richland Hills, Tex.: BIBAL Press.

Lambdin, T. O.
1953        Egyptian Words in Tell El Amarna Letter No. 14. *Or* 22: 362–69.
1962a       Ethiopia. Pp. 176–77 in *IDB*, vol. 2. Nashville, Tenn.:
            Abingdon.
1962b       Libya. Pp. 123–24 in *IDB*, vol. 3. Nashville, Tenn.: Abingdon.
1962c       Put. P. 971 in *IDB*, vol. 3. Nashville, Tenn.: Abingdon.
1962d       Thebes. Pp. 615–17 in *IDB*, vol. 4. Nashville, Tenn.: Abingdon.
1971        *Introduction to Biblical Hebrew.* New York: Charles Scribner's
            Sons.

Lambert, W. G.
1957        Ancestors, Authors, and Canonicity. *JCS* 11: 1 ff.
1962        A Catalogue of Texts and Authors. *JCS* 16: 59–77.
1979        Assyrians and Israel. *TRE* 4: 265–77.

Lambert, W. G., and A. R. Millard
1969        *Atra-Hasīs: The Babylonian Story of the Flood.* Oxford: Clarendon.

Landsberger, B., and Th. Bauer
1926/27     Zu neuveröffentlichten Geschichtsquellen der Zeit von
            Asarhaddon bis Nabonid. ZA 37: 61–98.

Langdon, S.
1923        *The Babylonian Epic of Creation: Restored from the Recently
            Recovered Tablets of Aššur.* Oxford: Clarendon.
1927        *Babylonian Penitential Psalms.* Paris: P. Geuthner.

Layard, A. Henry (1817–94)
1849        *Nineveh and Its Remains.* New York: G. P. Putnam.
1853        *Discoveries in the Ruins of Nineveh and Babylon.* London:
            J. Murray.
1856        *Popular Account of Discoveries at Nineveh.* New York: Derby
            and Jackson.

Leclerq, J.
1954        Nahum. Pp. 85–110 in *Etudes sur les prophètes d'Israël*, ed.
            Ph. Béguéri et al. Paris: Editions du Cerf.

Lee, A. Y.
1985        The Canonical Unity of the Scroll of the Minor Prophets.
            Ph.D. dissertation, Baylor University, Dallas, Tex.

Lee, H. W.
    1988    The Function of Figurative Speech in the Book of Nahum.
               Ph.D. dissertation, Southern Baptist Theological Seminary,
               Louisville, Ky.

Leeman, S.
    1996    The Atbash-Acrostic. *JBQ* 24: 43–45.

Leonardi, G.
    1968    Note su alcuni versetti del Salmo 104. *Bib* 49: 238–42.

Lescow, Th.
    1972    Redaktionsgeschichtliche Analyse von Micha 1–5. *ZAW* 84:
               61–64.
    1995    Die Komposition der Bücher Nahum und Habakuk. *BN* 77:
               59–85.

Leslie, E. A.
    1962    Nahum, The Book of. Pp. 498–99 in *IDB*, vol. 3. Nashville,
               Tenn.: Abingdon.

Letteris, Myer Levi
    1880    *The Hebrew Bible,* revised and carefully examined. New York:
               John Wiley and Sons.

Levarie, Siegmund
    1991    Philo on Music. *IJM* 9: 124–30.

Levenson, Jon D.
    1975    Textual and Semantic Notes on Nah. 1:7–8. *VT* 25: 792–95.

Lewis, Theodore
    1992    Belial. Pp. 654–56 in *AYBD*, vol. 1.

Ley, Julius
    1875    *Grundzüge des Rhythmus, des Vers- und Strophenbaues in der
               hebräischen Poesie.* Halle, Germany: Waisenhauses.
    1887    *Leitfaden der Metrik der hebräischen Poesie: Nebst dem ersten
               Buche der Psalmen; Nach rhythmischer Vers- und Strophen-
               abteilung mit metrischer Analyse.* Halle a. S., Germany:
               Waisenhauses.

Liagre Böhl, F. M. Th. de
    1966    Blüte und Untergang des Assyrerreiches als historisches Prob-
               lem. Pp. 204–20 in *Studia Biblica et Semitica* (FS Th. C.
               Vriezen). Wageningen, Netherlands: H. Veenman.

Lichtheim, Miriam
    1980    *Ancient Egyptian Literature,* vol. III: *The Late Period.*
               Berkeley, Los Angeles, and London: University of California
               Press.

Lidzbarski, M.
    1898    *Handbuch der nordsemitischen Epigraphik.* Weimar: G. Olms.

Linafelt, T.
2000        *Surviving Lamentations: Catastrophes, Lament, and Protest in the Afterlife of a Biblical Book*. Chicago: University of Chicago Press.

Lindblom, Johannes
1962a       *Prophecy in Ancient Israel*. Philadelphia, Pa.: Muhlenberg; Oxford: Blackwell.
1962b       Lot Casting in the Old Testament. *VT* 12: 164–78.

Lipiński, E.
1968        *La Royauté de Yahwé dans la poésie et le culte de l'ancien Israël*, 2nd ed. Brussels: Paleis der Academiën. 1st edition 1965.
1971        Nahum. Pp. 793–95 in *Encyclopedia Judaica*, vol. 12. Shaker Heights, Ohio: Judaica Multimedia.
1999        נָקַם *nāqam;* נָקָם *nāqam;* נְקָמָה *nəqāmâ. TDOT* 10: 1–9.
2004        רכל *rkl;* רָכִיל ;רְכֻלָּה ;רְכֻלָּה ;מַרְכֹלֶת *to trade; merchant. TDOT* 13: 498–99.

Lipiński, E., and H.-J. Fabry
1997        מכר *mkr sell. TDOT* 8: 291–96.
2001        עָזַר II עֵזֶר ;עָזִיר ;עֶזְרָה ;עֶזְרָה ;עֹזֵר; *'āzar;* *'āzar. help; leader. TDOT* 11: 12–18.

Lipiński, E., and W. von Soden
2001        עַם *'am people. TDOT* 11: 163–77.

Littauer, M. A., and J. H. Crouwel
1992        Chariots. Pp. 888–92 in *AYBD*, vol. 1.

Liwak, R.
2004        שֶׁטֶף *šṭp. TDOT* 14: 599–606.

Locher, C
2001        עָלַם *'ālam;* תעלמה *ta'ᵃlumâ (be) hidden. TDOT* 11: 147–54.

Lods, A.
1920        L'état actuel des recherches sur la métrique hebraïque. *RHR* 82: 122–32.
1931        Review of E. Sellin, *Das Zwölfprophetenbuch übersetzt und erklärt, deuxième et troisième édition, Zweite Haelfte: Nahum-Malachi*. RHPR 11: 211–13.

Loewenstamm, S. E.
1980        The Trembling of Nature during the Theophany. Pp. 173–89 in *Comparative Studies in Biblical and Ancient Oriental Literature*. AOAT 204. Neukirchen-Vluyn, Germany: Neukirchener.

Löfgren, O.
1930        *Das äthiopische Dodekapropheton: Jona, Nahum, Habakkuk, Zephanja, Haggai, Sacharja und Maleachi äthiopisch unter Zugrundelegung des oxforter MS; Huntington 625 nach*

*mehreren Handschriften herausgegeben von Oskar Löfgren.* Arbeten utgivna med understöd av Vilhelm Ekmans universitetsfond, Uppsala 38. Uppsala, Sweden: Almqvist and Wiksell.

Lohfink, N.
1983     "Gewalt" als Thema alttestamentlicher Forschung. Pp. 30–35 in *Gewalt und Gewaltlosigkeit im Alten Testament,* ed. N. Lohfink. Freiburg: Herder.
2001     עָצַם *ʿāṣam;* עָצוּם; עֹצֶם; עָצְמָה; תַּעֲצֻמוֹת (*be*) *numerous, mighty.* TDOT 11: 289–303.

Löhr, M.
1905     Alphabetische und alphabetisierende Lieder im Alten Testament. ZAW 25: 173–98.

Long, Burke O.
1976     Reports of Visions among the Prophets. *JBL* 95: 353–65.

Longacre, Robert
1983     *The Grammar of Discourse.* New York: Plenum.

Longman, Tremper, and D. Reid
1995     *God Is a Warrior.* Grand Rapids, Mich.: Zondervan.

Longman, Tremper III
1982a     A Critique of Two Recent Metrical Systems. *Bib* 63: 230–54.
1982b     The Divine Warrior: The New Testament Use of an Old Testament Motif. *WTJ* 44: 290–307.
1984     Psalm 98: A Divine Warrior Victory Song. *JETS* 27: 267–74.
1985     The Form and Message of Nahum: Preaching from a Prophet of Doom. *Reformed Theological Journal* 1: 13–24.
1987     *Literary Approaches to Biblical Interpretation.* Grand Rapids, Mich.: Zondervan.
1988     *How to Read the Psalms.* Downers Grove, Ill.: Inter-Varsity.
1994     See Dillard, Raymond B., and Tremper Longman III.

Lord, Albert B.
1960     *The Singer of Tales.* Harvard Studies in Comparative Literature 24. Cambridge, Mass.: Harvard UP. Republished in 1968 in paperback as *The Singer of Tales.* New York: Atheneum.

Loretz, O.
1960     Die Hebräische Nominalform qattāl. *Bib* 41: 411–16.

Lowden, John
1988     *Illuminated Prophet Books: A Study of Byzantine Manuscripts of the Major and Minor Prophets.* University Park: Pennsylvania State UP.

Lowth, Robert (1710–87)
1753     *De sacra poesi Hebraeorum.* Oxonii: Clarendoniano.
1839     *Lectures on the Sacred Poetry of the Hebrews.* Trans. G. Gregory. London: T. Tegg.

Luckenbill, D. D.
1928    *Ancient Records of Assyria and Babylonia*, vol. 2: *Historical Records of Assyria from Sargon to the End.* Chicago: University of Chicago Press.

Lugt, Hans
1975    Wirbelstürme im Alten Testament. *BZ* 19: 195–204.

Lund, N. W.
1932/33  Chiasmus in the Psalms. *AJSL* 49: 281–312.

Luther, M. (1483–1546)
The following are from *D. Martin Luthers Werke: Weimarer Ausgabe* (WA), *Abteilung 2: Deutsche Bibel,* by Martin Luther (Weimar: Böhlaus Nachfolger, 2001). Available through the electronic resource *Luthers Werke im WWW: Weimarer Ausgabe* (Ann Arbor, Mich.: ProQuest Information and Learning, 2001).
        *Vorrede auf den Propheten Nahum.* WA 11.2: 288–89.
        *Der Prophet Nahum.* WA 11.2: 290–97.
        *In Nahum.* WA 13: 344–94.
1832–57  *Sämmtliche Werke.* Erlangen and Frankfurt am Main: Heyder und Zimmer.
1975    *Lectures on the Minor Prophets.* Luther's Works, vol. 18. St. Louis, Mo.: Concordia.

Maag, V.
1965    B<sup>e</sup>lija<sup>c</sup>al im Alten Testament. *ThLZ* 21: 287–99.
1980    *Kultur, Kultkontakt und Religion.* Göttingen: Vandenhoeck und Ruprecht. Pp. 221–33 includes a reprint of Maag's 1965 article.

Machinist, P.
1983    Assyria and Its Image in the First Isaiah. *JAOS* 103: 719–37.
1995    The Fall of Assyria in Comparative Ancient Perspective. Pp. 179–95 in *Assyria 1995*, ed. S. Parpola and R. M. Whiting. Helsinki: Neo-Assyrian Text Corpus Project.

MacIntosh, A. A.
1969    A Consideration of Hebrew *g<sup>c</sup>r*. *VT* 14: 474 ff.

Madhloom, T. A.
1967    Excavations at Nineveh: A Preliminary Report (1965–1967). *Sumer* 23: 76–79.
1968    Nineveh: The 1967–1968 Campaign. *Sumer* 24: 45–51.
1969    Nineveh: The 1968–1969 Campaign. *Sumer* 25: 43–49.

Madl, H.
1998    נָטַר *nāṭar;* מַטָּרָה *maṭṭārâ. TDOT* 9: 402–6.

Magdalene, F. R.
1995    Ancient Near Eastern Treaty Curses and the Ultimate Texts of Terror: A Study of the Language of Divine Sexual Abuse in the Prophetic Corpus. Pp. 326–52 in *A Feminist Companion to the*

    *Latter Prophets*, ed. A. Brenner. FCB 8. Sheffield, England: Sheffield UP.

Mahler, E.
  1886    *Untersuchung einer im Buche Nahum auf den Untergang Ninives bezogenen Fisterniss.* Vienna.

Maiberger, P.
  2001    פגר *pāḡar;* פֶּגֶר *peḡer corpse. TDOT* 11: 477–82.

Maier, J.
  1962    Weitere Stücke zum Nahumkommentar aus der Höhle 4 von Qumran. *Judaica* 18: 215–50.

Maier, Walter A.
  1936    Recent Archeological Light on Nahum. *CTM* 7: 692–98.

Mandelkern, S.
  1896    *Veteris Testament, Concordantiae Hebraicae Atque Chaldaicae.* Leipzig: Veit et Com. Reprinted Jerusalem and Tel Aviv: Sumtibus Schocken, 1962.

Mann, Jacob (1888–1940)
  1956    *The Bible as Read and Preached in the Old Synagogue.* New York: Rinehart.

Marböck, J.
  2004    קלה *qlh* II; קָלוֹן *qālôn shame. TDOT* 13: 31–37.

Marcus, D.
  1977    Animal Similes in Assyrian Royal Inscriptions. *Or* 46: 86–106.

Marcus, R.
  1947    Alphabetic Acrostics in the Hellenistic and Roman Periods. *JNES* 6: 109–11.

Margolis, M. L.
  1911    Miscellen. *ZAW* 31: 313–15.

Margolit, B.
  1975    Introduction to Ugaritic Prosody. *UF* 7: 287–313.

Marks, Herbert
  1987    The Twelve Prophets. Pp. 207–33 in *The Literary Guide to the Bible*, ed. Robert Alter and Frank Kermode. Cambridge: Belknap Press of Harvard UP. See esp. pp. 214–19.

Martens, E. A.
  1996    God, Names of. Pp. 297–300 in *EDBT*. Grand Rapids, Mich.: Baker.

Mathys, Hans-Peter
  1994    *Dichter und Beter: Theologen aus spätalttestamentlicher Zeit.* OBO 132. Freiburg: Universitätsverlag.

Mayoral, J. A.
  1995    El uso simbólico-teológico de los animals en los profetas del exilio. *EstBib* 53: 317–63.

McClain, Ernest
    1976        *The Myth of Invariance: The Origin of the Gods, Mathematics
                and Music from the Ṛg Veda to Plato.* New York: Nicolas Hays.
    1978        *The Pythagorean Plato: Prelude to the Song Itself.* York Beach,
                Me.: Nicholas Hays.
    1981        *Meditations through the Quran: Tonal Images in an Oral Cul-
                ture.* York Beach, Me.: Nicolas Hays.
    1997        The "Star of David" as Jewish Harmonical Metaphor. *IJM* 6:
                25–49.
    2002        A Priestly View of Bible Arithmetic: Deity's *Regulative Activity*
                within Davidic Musicology. Pp. 429–43 in *Hermeneutic Philos-
                ophy of Science, Van Gogh's Eyes, and God: Essays in Honor of
                Patrick A. Heelan, S.J.,* by Patrick A. Heelan and Babette E.
                Babich. Studies in the Philosophy of Science 225. Dordrecht:
                Kluwer Academic Publishers.
    2004        The Forgotten Harmonical Science of the Bible. *Epigraphical
                Society Occasional Papers* 24: 150–68.
McClain, Ernest, with D. L. Christensen
    2005        Addendum: Ancient Harmonics and the Book of Jonah.
                Pp. 55–59 in *Reading Jonah in Hebrew,* by D. L. Christensen.
                Rodeo, Calif.: BIBAL Corporation. Available on the Internet
                at http://www.bibal.net/04/proso/psalms-ii/pdf/dlc_reading-
                jonah-b.pdf.
McClain, Ernest, and Siegmund Levarie
    1994        Temple Tuning Systems. *IJM* 3: 23–30.
McComiskey, Thomas E.
    1986        The Hymnic Elements of the Prophecy of Amos: A Study of
                Form-Critical Methodology. Pp. 105–28 in *A Tribute to Glea-
                son Archer,* ed. Walter C. Kaiser Jr. and Ronald F. Youngblood.
                Chicago: Moody.
McIntosh, A. A.
    1969        A Consideration of Hebrew נער. *VT* 19: 471–79.
McKane, William
    1980        משא in Jeremiah 23:33–40. Pp. 35–54 in *Prophecy, Essays
                Presented to Georg Fohrer on his Sixty-Fifth Birthday, 6 Septem-
                ber 1980,* ed. John A. Emerton. BZAW 150. Berlin: de Gruyter.
McWilliam, Thomas
    1902        *Speakers for God: Being Plain Lectures on the Minor Prophets.*
                London: H. R. Ellenson.
Meek, T. J.
    1929        The Structure of Hebrew Poetry. *JR* 9: 523–50.
Meier, S. A.
    1992        *Speaking of Speaking. Marking Direct Discourse in the Hebrew
                Bible.* VTSup 46. Leiden: Brill.

Melitz, A.
1991    אקרקסטיכון במקרא. *Beit Mikra* 36: 250–62.

Mendenhall, George E.
1973    The "Vengeance" of Yahweh. Pp. 69–104 in *The Tenth Genera-tion: The Origins of the Biblical Tradition*. Baltimore, Md.: Johns Hopkins UP.

Michaud, H.
1960    Review of J. B. Pritchard, *Hebrew Inscriptions and Stamps from Gibeon. VT* 10: 102–6.

Mihelič, Joseph L.
1948    The Concept of God in the Book of Nahum. *Int* 2: 199–207.

Milik, J. T., and F. M. Cross
1954    Inscribed Javelin-Heads from the Period of the Judges: A Recent Discovery in Palestine. *BASOR* 134: 5–15.

Miller, P. D.
1967    El the Warrior. *HTR* 60: 411–31.
1970    Ugaritic ǦZR and Hebrew ʿZR II. *UF* 2: 159–75.
1973    *The Divine Warrior in Early Israel*. HSM 5. Cambridge, Mass.: Harvard UP.

Mitchell, T. C.
1991    Judah until the Fall of Jerusalem. *CAH* 3 (2): 371–409.

Mittmann, S.
1978    Komosition und Redaktion von Psalm XXIX. *VT* 28: 172–94.

Moffatt, James
1954    *A New Translation of the Holy Bible Containing the Old and New Testaments*. New York, Hagerstown, San Francisco, and London: Harper and Row. 1st ed. 1922.

Möller, H.
1932    Strophenbau der Psalmen. *ZAW* 50: 240–56.

Montgomery, J. A.
1935a   Ras Shamra VI: The Conflict of Baal and the Waters. *JAOS* 55: 268–77.
1935b   Some Oracle Place Names. *JBL* 54: 61–62.

Moor, Johannes de
1975    בַּעַל *baʿal. TDOT* 2: 181–92.
1982    De goede herder. Oorsprong en vroege geschiedenis van de herdersmetaphoor. Pp. 36–45 in *Bewerken en bewaren: Festschrift Klaas Runia*. Kampen, Netherlands: Kok.
1986    The Ancestral Cult in *KTU* 1.17:I.26–28. *UF* 17: 407–9.
1987    *An Anthology of Religious Texts from Ugarit*. Leiden: Brill.
1990    *The Rise of Yahwism*. BETL 91. Leuven, Belgium: Uitgeverij Peters.

Moran, W. L.
    1950        The Use of the Canaanite Infinitive Absolute as a Finite Verb
                 in the Amarna Letters from Byblos. *JCS* 4: 169–72.
    1951        New Evidence on Canaanite *taqtulū(na)*. *JCS* 5: 33–35.
    1953        Amarna *šumma* in Main Clauses. *JCS* 7: 78–80.
    1961        The Hebrew Language in Its Northwest Semitic Background.
                 Pp. 54–72 in *The Bible and the Ancient Near East: Essays in
                 Honor of William Foxwell Albright*, ed. G. E. Wright. Garden
                 City, N.Y.: Doubleday.
Movers, Franz Carl
    1856        *Die Phönizier*, vol. 2 (in 3 parts). Berlin: F. Dummler.
Mowinckel, S.
    1926        *Jesaja-disiplene: Profetien fra Jesaja til Jeremia*. Oslo:
                 Aschehoug (Nygaard).
    1962        Drive and/or Ride in the Old Testament. *VT* 12: 278–99.
Muffs, Y.
    1969        *Studies in Aramaic Legal Papyri from Elephantine*. Leiden: Brill.
Muilenburg, J.
    1953        A Study in Hebrew Rhetoric: Repetition and Style. Pp. 97–111
                 in *Congress Volume: Copenhagen 1953*. VTSup 1. Leiden: Brill.
    1969        Form Criticism and Beyond. *JBL* 88: 1–18.
Mulder, M. J.
    1975        בַּעַל *baʿal*. TDOT 2: 192–200.
    1995a       כַּרְמֶל *karmel*. TDOT 7: 325–36.
    1995b       לְבָנוֹן *lᵉbānôn*. TDOT 7: 447–57.
    2004        רָקַד *rāqaḏ leap, dance*. TDOT 13: 643–45.
Müller, H.-P.
    1998        מַשָּׂא *maśśāʾ*. TDOT 9: 20–24.
Muraoka, T.
    1969        *Emphasis in Biblical Hebrew*. Doctoral thesis, University of
                 Jerusalem, Jerusalem.
    1985        *Emphatic Words and Structures in Biblical Hebrew*. Jerusalem:
                 Magnes.
    1989        In Defense of the Unity of the Minor Prophets. *Annual of the
                 Japanese Biblical Institute* 15: 25–36.
    1993        *A Greek-English Lexicon of the Septuagint (Twelve Prophets)*.
                 Louvain, Belgium: Peeters.
Murray, D. F.
    1987        The Rhetoric of Disputation: Re-examination of a Prophetic
                 Genre. *JSOT* 38: 95–121.
Nagel, W.
    1966        *Der mesopotamische Streitwagen und seine Entwicklung im
                 ostmediterranen Bereich*. Berliner Beiträge zur Vor- und
                 Frühgeschichte 10. Berlin: Hessling.

1990 Assyrian Chariotry and Cavalry. *State Archive of Assyria Bulletin* 4: 61–68.

Naudé, J. A.
1969 *Maśśā* [*sic*] in the Old Testament with Special References to the Prophets. *OTWSA* 12: 91–100.

Neef, H.-D.
2000 JHWH und die Völker: Beobachtungen zur Theologie der Bücher Nahum, Habakuk, Zephanja. *TBei* 31: 82–91.

Nelson, R. D.
1983 *Realpolitik* in Judah (687–609 B.C.E.). Pp. 177–89 in *Scripture in Context II: More Essays on the Comparative Method*, ed. W. W. Hallo, J. C. Moyer, L. G. Perdue. Winona Lake, Ind.: Eisenbrauns.

Nestle, G.
1879 Where Is the Birthplace of the Prophet Nahum to Be Sought? Pp. 136–38 in *Palestine Exploration Fund Quarterly Statement for 1879.*
1909 Miscellen: Nah 1,1. ZAW 17: 154.

Neusner, Jacob (trans.)
1982 *Sanhedrin and Makkot.* The Talmud of the Land of Israel, vol. 31. Chicago: University of Chicago Press.

Niehr, H.
2001 עֶרְוָה *ʿārâ;* מוֹרָה; מַעֵר *maʿar;* ערוה; עריה *(be) naked, empty. TDOT* 11: 343–49.
2003 פֶּרֶשׁ *pāraš horse; rider. TDOT* 12: 124–28.

Nissinen, Marty, C. L. Seow, and Robert K. Ritner
2003 *Prophets and Prophecy in the Ancient Near East.* Society of Biblical Literature Writings from the Ancient World 12. Atlanta: Society of Biblical Literature; Leiden: Brill.

Nogalski, J. D.
1993a The Redactional Shaping of Nahum 1 for the Book of the Twelve. In *Among the Prophets*, ed. D. J. A. Clines and P. R. Davies. JSOTSup 144: 193–202.
1993b *Literary Precursors to the Book of the Twelve.* BZAW 217. Berlin and New York: W. de Gruyter.
1993c *Redactional Processes in the Book of the Twelve.* BZAW 218. Berlin and New York: W. de Gruyter.
1996 Intertextuality in the Twelve. Pp. 102–24 in *Forming Prophetic Literature: Essays on Isaiah and the Twelve in Honor of John D. W. Watts*, ed. J. W. Watts and P. R. House. JSOTSup 235. Sheffield, England: Sheffield Academic Press.

Nogalski, James D., and Marvin Sweeney (eds.)
2000 *Reading and Hearing the Book of the Twelve.* SBL Symposium Series 15. Atlanta: Society of Biblical Literature.

Noguera Millán, M.
1993    El libro del profeta Nahum según las versions ladinadas de
        A. Asá y de Ferrara: Differencias léxicas. Pp. 279–84 in *IV Sim-
        posio Biblico Espanol (I Ibero-Americano): Biblia y Culturas, II:
        Area de Estudios Hebreos,* ed. J. Martinez et al. Granada: Uni-
        versidad de Granada.

Noll, K. L.
1996    Nahum and the Act of Reading. *Proceedings Eastern Great
        Lakes and Midwest Biblical Societies* 16: 107–20.

Noth, Martin
1928    *Die israelitischen Personennamen im gemeinsemitischen
        Namengebung.* Stuttgart: W. Kohlhammer.

Nyberg, H. S.
1941    *Hoseaboken: Uppsala Universitets Årsskrift* 7, 2. Uppsala,
        Sweden.

Oates, J.
1991    The Fall of Assyria (635–609 B.C.). *CAH* 3 (2): 162–93.

O'Connor, M.
1980    *Hebrew Verse Structure.* Winona Lake, Ind.: Eisenbrauns.

Oded, Bustenay
1979    *Mass Deportations and Deportees in the Neo-Assyrian Empire.*
        Wiesbaden: Harrassowitz.

Oesterley, W. O. E.
1904/05  The Old Latin Texts of the Minor Prophets. *JTS* 5: 378–86.

Olivier, J. P. J.
1969    The Concept Day in Nahum and Habakkuk. Pp. 71–74 in
        *Biblical Essays,* ed. A. H. van Zyl. OTWSA 12. Potchefstroom,
        Netherlands: Pro Rege-Pers Bpk.

Olmstead, A. T.
1923    *History of Assyria.* New York: Charles Scribner's Sons.

Orchard, William Edwin
1922    *Oracles of God: Studies in the Minor Prophets.* Boston: Pilgrim;
        London: J. Clarke.

O'Rouke, J.
1974    Review of *Nahum in the Light of Northwest Semitic,* by Kevin
        J. Cathcart. *CBQ* 36: 397–98.

Otto, B.
2001    עִיר *ʿîr* city. TDOT 11: 51–67.

Ottosson, Magnus
1974a   אֶרֶץ *ʾereṣ.* TDOT 1: 388–405.
1974b   אָכַל *ʾākal;* אֹכֶל ;אָכְלָה ;אֲכִילָה ;מַאֲכָל ;מַאֲכֶלֶת ;מַאֲכֹלֶת.
        TDOT 1: 236–41.

Otzen, Benedikt
1975        בְּלִיַּעַל *bᵉliyyaᶜal.* TDOT 2: 131–36.
2004        שָׁבָה *šābâ;* שְׁבִי; שִׁבְיָה; שָׁבִי; שְׁבִית *take captive; prisoner.*
            TDOT 14: 286–94.
Palumbo, A. E.
1992–93   A New Interpretation of the Nahum Commentary. *FO* 29:
            153–62.
Parpola, S.
1970–71   *Letters from Assyrian Scholars to the Kings Esarhaddon and
            Assurbanipal,* parts 1–2. AOAT 5. Kevelaer, Germany: Butzon
            und Bercker.
Parrot, A.
1953        *Ninive et l'ancient testament.* Neuchâtel: Delachaux et Niestlé.
1955        *Nineveh and the Old Testament.* New York: Philosophical
            Library.
1961        *The Arts of Assyria.* New York: Golden.
Paterson, John
1950        Nahum: Prophet of Vengeance. Pp. 109–25 in *The Goodly
            Fellowship of the Prophets.* New York: Charles Scribner's Sons.
Patterson, Richard D.
1990        A Literary Look at Nahum, Habakkuk and Zephaniah. *GTJ*
            11: 17–27.
Patterson, Richard D., and Michael E. Travers
1988        Literary Analysis and the Unity of Nahum. *JTR* 9: 45–58.
1990        Nahum: Poet Laureate of the Minor Prophets. *JETS* 33: 437–44.
Patton, J. H.
1944        *Canaanite Parallels in the Book of Psalms.* Baltimore, Md.:
            Johns Hopkins UP.
Paul, S. M.
1982        Two Cognate Semitic Terms for Mating and Copulation. *VT*
            32: 492–93.
Peckham, B.
1993        *History and Prophecy: The Development of Late Judean Literary
            Traditions.* New York: Doubleday.
Pedersen, Johs.
1926        *Israel: Its Life and Culture,* I–II. Copenhagen: Povl Branner.
Peels, H. G. L.
1993        "Voed het oud vertrouwen weder." *De Godsopenbaring bij
            Nahum.* Apeldoornse Studies, 28. Kampen, Netherlands: Kok.
1995        *The Vengeance of God: The Meaning of the Root NQM and the
            Function of the NQM-Texts in the Context of Divine Revelation
            in the Old Testament.* Leiden: E. J. Brill.

Peiser, F. E.
    1897      Miscellen: Nah 1,1. ZAW 17: 349.
Petersen, D. L.
    1998      The Book of the Twelve—The Minor Prophets: Hosea, Joel,
                 Amos, Obadiah, Jonah, Micah, Nahum, Habakkuk, Zepha-
                 niah, Haggai, Zechariah, Malachi. Pp. 95–126 in *The Hebrew*
                 *Bible Today: An Introduction to Critical Issues*, ed. S. L.
                 McKenzie and M. P. Graham. Louisville, Ky.: Westminster /
                 John Knox.
Pfeiffer, R. H.
    1957      Assyria and Israel. *Revista degli studi orientali* 32: 145–54.
Piepkorn, A. C.
    1933      *Historical Prism Inscriptions of Ashurbanipal.* Assyriological
                 Studies 5. Chicago: University of Chicago Press.
Pinker, Aron
    1998      Nimrod Found? *JBQ* 26: 237–45.
    2002      Castanets. ZAW 114: 618–21.
    2003a     Upon an Attack in Nahum 2,2. *JHS* 4, article 7 (www
                 .jhsonline.org).
    2003b     On the Meaning of *htkbd* in Nahum iii 15. *VT* 53: 558–61.
    2004a     Nahum's Theological Perspectives. *JBQ* 32: 148–57.
    2004b     Nineveh: An Isle Is She. ZAW 116: 402–5.
    2004c     The Hard "Sell" in Nah 3:4b. *JHS* 5, article 7 (www.jhsonline
                 .org).
    2004d     Shelter or Strength in Nahum 1, 7? ZAW 116: 610–13.
    2004e     Smoking Out the Fire in Nahum ii 14. *BN* 123: 45–48.
    2005a     Nahum 2,4 Revisited. ZAW 117: 411–19.
    2005b     Descent of the Goddess Ishtar to the Netherworld and Nahum
                 II 8. *VT* 55: 89–100.
    2005c     Nahum—The Prophet and His Message. *JBQ* 33: 81–90.
    2006a     Nahum 1: Acrostic and Authorship. JBQ 34: 97–103.
    2006b     Nineveh's Defensive Strategy and Nahum 2–3. ZAW 118:
                 618–25.
Pitard, W. T.
    1982      Amarna *ekemu* and Hebrew *naqam. Maarav* 3: 5–25.
    1992      Vengeance. Pp. 786–87 in *AYBD*, vol. 6.
Pope, M.
    1970      A Mare in Pharaoh's Chariotry. *BASOR* 200: 56–61.
Porten, Bezalel, and J. C. Greenfield
    1974      *Jews of Elephantine and Arameans at Syene: Aramaic Texts with*
                 *Translation.* Jerusalem: Hebrew University.
Porter, J. R.
    1981      Ancient Israel. Pp. 191–214 in *Oracles and Divination*, ed.
                 M. Loewe and C. Blacker. Boulder, Colo.: Shambhala.

Portman, J.
2000     *When Bad Things Happen to Other People.* New York: Routledge.
Preuss, H. D.
1975     בּוֹא *bôʾ.* TDOT 2: 20–49.
1980     זֶרַע *zāraᶜ;* זָרַע. TDOT 4: 143–62.
1986     יָבֵשׁ *yābēš;* יַבָּשָׁה *yabbāšâ;* יַבֶּשֶׁת *yabbwšet.* TDOT 5: 373–79.
1990     יָצָא *yāṣāʾ;* מוֹצָא; תּוֹצָאוֹת. TDOT 6: 225–50.
Pritchard, J. B.
1959     *Hebrew Inscriptions and Stamps from Gibeon.* Philadelphia,
          Pa.: University Museum, University of Pennsylvania.
Procksch, O.
1933     *Liber XII Prophetarum.* Fascicle 10 in *Biblia Hebraica,* ed.
          R. Kittel. Stuttgart: Württembergische Bibelanstalt.
Pseudo-Epiphanius (315–403)
1612     *Epiphanii liber de vitis prophetarum.* Schleusingue: Joachim
          Zehner.
Puech, E.
1995     "Lioness לבאת." Cols. 981–83 in *DDD.*
Rabbinowitz, I.
1978     The Meaning of the Key ("Demetrius") Passage of the Qumran
          Nahum-Pesher. *JAOS* 98: 394–99.
Rad, G. von
1965     *Old Testament Theology,* vol. 2. Trans. D. M. G. Stalker. New
          York: Harper and Row.
1967     *The Message of the Prophets.* Trans. D. M. G. Stalker. New
          York: Harper and Row.
Rahmer, Moritz
1861–    *Die hebräischen Traditionen in den Werken des Hieronymus:*
1902     *Durch eine Vergleichung mit den jüdischen Quellen.* Breslau,
          Germany: Schletter.
Rainey, Anson F.
1993     Manasseh, King of Judah, in the Whirlpool of the Seventh
          Century B.C.E. Pp. 147–64 in *Kinattutu sa darâti: Raphael*
          *Kutscher Memorial Volume,* ed. A. F. Rainey et al. Tel Aviv:
          Institute of Archaeology of Tel Aviv University.
Rankin, O. S.
1930     Alliteration in Hebrew Poetry. Review article of I. Gàbor, *Der*
          *Hebräische Urrhythmus* (BZAW 52 [Giessen 1929]). *JTS* 31:
          285–91.
Ratner, Robert
1988     Does a *t*-Preformative Third Person Masculine Plural Verbal
          Form Exist in Biblical Hebrew? *VT* 38: 80–88.
Rattray, S., and J. Milgrom
2004     קֶרֶב *qereḇ* interior. TDOT 13: 148–52.

Rawlinson, George
    1868        Huzzab. Pp. 1110–11 in *Dr. William Smith's Dictionary of the
                Bible*, vol. 2, ed. H. B. Hackett. New York: Hurd and Houghton.
Reade, J.
    1978a       Studies in Assyrian Geography, part 1: Sennacherib and the
                Waters of Nineveh. BZAW RA 72: 42–72.
    1978b       Studies in Assyrian Geography, part 2: The Northern Canal
                System. BZAW RA 72: 157–80.
Redditt, Paul L.
    1990        Nahum, Book of. Pp. 601–2 in *Mercer Dictionary of the Bible*,
                ed. W. E. Mills. Macon, Ga.: Mercer UP.
    2001        Recent Research on the Book of the Twelve as One Book.
                *CRBS* 9: 47–80.
Redditt, Paul L., and Aaron Schart (eds.)
    2003        *Thematic Threads in the Book of the Twelve*. BZAW 325. New
                York: Walter de Gruyter.
Redford, Donald B.
    1992        Thebes. Pp. 442–43 in *AYBD*, vol. 6.
Reider, J.
    1938        The Name of Ashur in the Initials of a Difficult Phrase in the
                Bible. *JAOS* 58: 153–55.
    1949        A New Ishtar Epithet in the Bible. *JNES* 8: 104–7.
    1952        Miscellanea Hebraica. *JJS* 3: 78–86.
Reif, S. C.
    1971        A Note on נער. *VT* 21: 241–44.
Reindl, J.
    1998        נצב/יצב *nṣb/yṣb*. *TDOT* 9: 519–29.
Reinke, Lorenz
    1867        *Zur Kritik der älteren Versionen des Propheten Nahum*. Münster:
                W. Niemann.
Reiterer, F.
    2003        פָּרַק *pāra;* פֶּרֶק *pereq pull off; tear away*. *TDOT* 12: 111–14.
Renaud, B.
    1963        *Je suis un Dieu jaloux*. Lectio Divina 36. Paris: Du Cerf.
    1987b       La composition du livre de Nahum. ZAW 99: 198–219.
Rendsburg, Gary
    1980        Janus Parallelism in Gen 49:26. *JBL* 99: 291–93.
Rendtorff, R.
    1994        El als israelitische Gottesbezeichnung. ZAW 106: 4–21.
Renner, E.
    1958        A Study of the Word *gôral*. Theology Dissertation, University
                of Heidelberg, Heidelberg.
Reuter, E.
    2004        קנא *qn²;* … קַנּוֹא *qannô². TDOT* 13: 47–58.

Ribera Florit, José
  1980    La versión armaica del Profeta Nahum. *Anuario de Filologie*
          6: 291–322.
Richardson, G. L.
  1927/28 The Jealousy of God. *ATR* 10: 47–50.
Richlin, A.
  1992    Reading Ovid's Rapes. In *Pornography and Representation in
          Greece and Rome*. New York: Oxford UP.
Richter, G.
  1914    *Erläuterungen zu dunklen Stellen in den kleinen Propheten.*
          Gütersloh, Germany: C. Bertelsmann.
Ridderbos, J.
  1963    Nahum. Pp. 119–43 in *De kleine profeten: Opnieuw uit den
          grondtekst vertaald en verklaard door J. Ridderbos.* Kampen,
          Netherlands: J. H. Kok.
Riede, P.
  1993    Denn wie der Mensch jades Tier nennen würde, so solltee es
          heißen. Hebräische Tiernamen und was sie uns verraten. *UT*
          25: 331–78.
Ringgren, Helmer
  1966    *Israelite Religion*. Philadelphia, Pa.: Fortress.
  1974    אֵיב *ʾāyaḇ;* אֹיֵב; איבה. *TDOT* 1: 212–18.
  1980    זָרַח *zārah;* מִזְרָח. *TDOT* 4: 141–43.
  1986    חֹמֶר *ḥmr;* חֹמֶר *ḥōmer;* חמר. *TDOT* 5: 1–4
  1990    יָם *yām. TDOT* 6: 87–98.
  1995a   כֹּח *kōaḥ* stength, power. *TDOT* 7: 122–28.
  1995b   לבן *lbn;* לְבָכָה; לָבָן; לְבֵנָה bricks; white; moon. *TDOT* 7:
          438–41.
  1997    מוּשׁ / מִישׁ *mûš / mîš* depart. *TDOT* 8: 184–85.
  1998a   נוּד *nûḏ* shake, wander, flee; show pity. *TDOT* 9: 271–72.
  1998b   נוּעַ *nûaʿ* shake, wander. *TDOT* 9: 293–95.
  2001    עָמַד *ʿāmaḏ* approach, stand. *TDOT* 11: 178–87.
Roaf, Michael
  1990    *Cultural Atlas of Mesopotamia and the Ancient Near East.*
          New York: Facts on File.
Robinson, E. S. G.
  1950    A "Silversmith's Hoard" from Mesopotamia. *Iraq* 12: 44–50.
Robinson, H. Wheeler
  1964    *Corporate Personality in Ancient Israel*. Philadelphia, Pa.:
          Fortress.
Robinson, Theodore Henry
  1923    *Prophecy and Prophets in Ancient Israel*. London: Duckworth.
Röllig, W.
  1986    Assur — Geißel der Völker. *Saeculum* 37: 116–28.

Rothstein, J. W.
    1905        Nahum. In *Biblia Hebraica*, ed. R. Kittel. Leipzig: J. C. Hinrichs.
Roux, G.
    1980        *Ancient Iraq*, 2nd ed. Harmondsworth, England: Penguin.
Rowley, H. H.
    1947        Review of A. Haldar, *Studies in the Book of Nahum*. BO 4:
                60–61.
    1956        4QpNahum and the Teacher of Righteousness. *JBL* 75: 188–93.
Ruben, P.
    1896        *Central Remarks upon Some Passages of the Old Testament*.
                London: Luzac.
    1898        An Oracle of Nahum. *PSBA* 20: 173–85.
    1899        Strophic Forms in the Bible. *JQR* 11: 431–79.
Ruppert, L.
    1990        יָעַץ *yāʿaṣ*; עֵצָה; מוֹעֵצָה. *TDOT* 6: 156–85.
Saalschütz, J. L.
    1825        *Von der Form der hebäischen Poesie: Nebst einer Abhandlung
                über die Musik der Hebräer*. Königsberg, Germany: Unzer.
Saggs, H. W. F.
    1965        *Everyday Life in Babylonia and Assyria*. London: Batsford;
                New York: G. P. Putnam's Sons.
    1969        Nahum and the Fall of Nineveh. *JTS* n.s. 20: 220–25.
    1984        *The Might That Was Assyria*. London: Sidgwick and Jackson.
Sanders, Henry A. (ed.)
    1927        *Facsimile of the Washington Manuscript of the Minor Prophets
                in the Freer Collection, and the Berlin Fragment of Genesis*.
                Ann Arbor: University of Michigan Press.
    ca. 1927   *The Minor Prophets in the Freer Collection and the Berlin Frag-
                ment of Genesis*, by Henry A. Sanders . . . and Carl Schmidt.
                New York and London: Macmillan.
Sarna, N. M.
    1959        The Interchange of the Preposition *Beth* and *Mem* in Biblical
                Hebrew. *JBL* 78: 310–16.
    1964        Ezekiel 8:17: A Fresh Examination. *HTR* 57: 347–52.
Sasson, Jack M.
    1990        *Jonah: A New Translation with Introduction, Commentary, and
                Interpretation*. AYB 24B. New York and London: Doubleday.
Sauer, G.
    1997        נקם *nqm* to avenge. Pp. 767–69 in *TLOT*, vol. 2.
Saydon, P. P.
    1955        Assonance in Hebrew as a Means of Expressing Emphasis. *Bib*
                36: 36–50, 287–304.
Scharbert, J.
    2004        קלל *qll*; קַל; קְלָלָה be small, light. *TDOT* 13: 37–44.

Schart, A.
1998       *Die Entstehung des Zwölfprophetenbuches: Neubearbeitungen
           von Amos im Rahmen schriftenübergreifender Redaktions-
           prozesse.* BZAW 260. Berlin: W. de Gruyter.
Schedl, Claus
1974       *Baupläne des Wortes: Einführung in die biblische Logotechnik.*
           Vienna: Herder.
Schiemann, R.
1967       Covenanting with the Princes: Neh VI 2. *VT* 17: 367–69.
Schiffman, L. H.
1993       Pharisees and Sadducees in *Pesher Nahum.* Pp. 272–90 in
           *Minhah le Nahum: Biblical and Other Essays Presented to
           Nahum M. Sarna in Honour of His 70th Birthday,* ed. M. Bret-
           tler et al. JSOTSup 154. Sheffield, England: JSOT Press.
Schlögl, Nivard
1912       *Die echte biblisch-hebräische Metrik.* Freiburg im Breisgau:
           Herder.
Schmidt, Dan
2002       *Unexpected Wisdom: Major Insight from the Minor Prophets.*
           Grand Rapids, Mich.: Baker.
Schmidt, H.
1923       Nahum. Pp. 170–77 in *Die grossen Propheten.* Göttingen:
           Vandenhoeck und Ruprecht.
Schmoldt, H.
2003       פָּשַׁט *pāšaṭ take off, shed. TDOT* 12: 129–32.
2004a      רָעַשׁ *rāʿaš;* רַעַשׁ *raʿaš. TDOT* 13: 589–93.
2004b      שָׁאַב *šāʾaḇ;* מַשְׁאַבִּים *mašʾabbîm. TDOT* 14: 229–32.
Schneider, D.
1979       The Unity of the Book of the Twelve. Ph.D. dissertation. Yale
           University, New Haven, Conn.
Schneider, Thomas
1988       Nahum und Theben: Zum topographisch-historischen Hinter-
           grund von Nah 3,8f. *BN* 44: 63–73.
Schulz, Hermann
1973       *Das Buch Nahum: Eine redaktionskritische Untersuchung.*
           BZAW 129. Berlin and New York: W. de Gruyter.
Schunck, K.-D.
1980       חֵמָה *chēmāh. TDOT* 4: 462–65.
1995a      כָּהָה *kāhâ;* כֵּהֶה *kēheh;* כהה *kēhâ grow weak. TDOT* 7:
           58–59.
1995b      כָּחַשׁ *kāḥaš;* כַּחַשׁ *;* כֶּחָשׁ *waste away; deny. TDOT* 7: 132–35.
Schüngel, Paul H.
1978       Noch einmal zu קבצו פארור Jo 2.6 und Nah 2,11. *BN* 7:
           29–31.

Schuurmans Stekhoven, J. Z.
1887    *De Alexandrijnsche vertaling van het Dodekapropheton.* Leiden:
        E. J. Brill.
Schwager, R.
1983    Der Zorn Gottes. *ZKT* 105: 406–14.
Scott, L., and J. Maginnis
1990    Notes on Nineveh. *Iraq* 52: 63–73.
Sebök, M.
1887    *Die Syrische Uebersetzung der zwölf kleinen Propheten und ihr*
        *Verhältnis zu dem massoretischen Text und zu den älteren Über-*
        *setzungen namentlich den LXX. und dem Targum.* Breslau,
        Germany: Preuss und Jünger.
Seebass, H.
1998    נָפַל *nāpal;* נֵפֶל; נְפִילִים *fall. TDOT* 9: 488–97.
Seibert, I.
1969    *Hirt–Herde–König: Zur Herausbildung des Königtums in*
        *Mesopotamien.* Berlin: Akademie.
Sellers, Ovid R.
1935–36 Stages of Locust in Joel. *AJSL* 52: 81–85.
Sendrey, Alfred, and Mildred Norton
1964    *David's Harp: The Story of Music in Biblical Times.* New York:
        New American Library.
Seybold, K.
1980    חָלָה *ḥālāh;* חֱלִי; חִלָּה פָנִים. *TDOT* 4: 399–409.
1985    *Satirische Prophetie: Studien zum Buch Zephanja.* SBS 120.
        Stuttgart: Katholisches Bibelwerk.
1986    חָשַׁב *ḥāšab;* חֹשֵׁב *ḥōšēb;* חֶשְׁבּוֹן *ḥešbôn;* חִשָּׁבוֹן *ḥiššābôn;*
        מַחֲשֶׁבֶת *maḥašebet. TDOT* 5: 228–45.
1989a   *Profane Prophetie: Studien zum Buch Nahum.* SBS 135.
        Stuttgart: Katholisches Bibelwerk.
1989b   Vormasoretische Randnotizen in Nahum 1. *ZAW* 101: 71–85.
1999    *Die Sprache der Propheten: Studien zur Literaturgeschichte der*
        *Prophetie.* Zurich: Pano.
Seybold, K., H. Ringgren, and H.-J. Fabry
1997    מֶלֶךְ *melek;* מָלַךְ *mālak;* מלוכה; מלכות; ממלכה; ממלכות
        *king, kingship. TDOT* 8: 346–75.
Siegel, J. L.
1929–30 *wᵊhuṣṣab gullᵊtāh hōᶜᵃlātāh,* Nah. 2:8. *AJSL* 46: 139–40.
Sievers, Eduard (1850–1932)
1901    *Metrische Studien I: Studien zur Hebräischen Metrik 2;*
        *Textproben.* Leipzig: B. G. Teubner.
Simian-Yofre, H., and H.-J. Fabry
1998    נחם *nḥm regret, repent; comfort. TDOT* 9: 340–55.

Simons, J.
1954    The "Table of Nations" (Genesis 10): Its General Structure and
        Meaning. *OTS* 10: 155–84. Reprinted pp. 234–53 in *"I Studied
        Inscriptions from before the Flood": Ancient Near Eastern Liter-
        ary, and Linguistic Approaches to Genesis 1–11,* ed. R. S. Hess
        and D. T. Tsumura. Winona Lake, Ind.: Eisenbrauns, 1994.

Sister, M.
1934    Die Typen der prophetischen Visionen in der Bibel. MGWJ
        78: 399–430.

Skehan, P. W.
1971    *Studies in Israelite Poetry and Wisdom.* CBQMS 1. Washing-
        ton, D.C.: Catholic Biblical Association of America.

Smith, C. C.
1995    "Aha, Assyria! Rod of My Fury, Very Stuff of My Sentencing-
        Curse." Pp. 182–206 in *Words Remembered Texts Renewed,*
        J. Davies et al. Fs. J. F. A. Sawyer. JSOTSup 195. Sheffield,
        England: Sheffield Academic Press.

Smith, Gary V.
1986    Nahum. Pp. 477–79 in *The International Standard Bible Ency-
        clopedia,* vol. 3, ed. G. W. Bromiley. Grand Rapids, Mich.:
        Eerdmans.
1994    *The Prophets as Preachers: An Introduction to the Hebrew
        Prophets.* Nashville, Tenn.: Broadmann and Holman.

Smith, R. H.
1965    Abram and Melchizedek (Gen 14:18–20). *ZAW* 77: 129–53.

Smith, Sidney
1924    *Babylonian Historical Texts Relating to the Capture and Down-
        fall of Babylon.* London: Methuen.

Snijders, L. A., and H.-J. Fabry
1997    מָלֵא *mālēʾ*; מִלֵּא, מְלֵאָה, מְלֵאִים; מְלוֹא; *fill, be full.* TDOT
        8: 297–308.

Snijders, L. A., H. Ringgren, and H.-J. Fabry
1998    נָהָר *nāhār river.* TDOT 9: 261–70.

Soden, Wolfram von
1963    Die Assyrer und der Krieg. *Iraq* 25: 131–44.
1967    *Hebräische Wortforschung.* VTSup 16. Leiden: Brill.
1986    Hebräisch *nāṭar* I und II. *UF* 17: 412–14.

Soggin, J. A.
1964    "Wacholderholz" 2 Sam VI 5a gleich "Schlaghölzer",
        "Klappern"? *VT* 14: 374–77.
1965    La "negazione" in Geremia 4, 27 e 5, 10a, cfr. 5, 18b. *Biblica*
        46: 56–59.
1989    *Introduction to the Old Testament.* Louisville, Ky.: Westminster /
        John Knox.

Soll, W. M.
   1988        Babylonian and Biblical Acrostics. *Bib* 69: 305–23.
Spalinger, A.
   1974        Assurbanipal and Egypt: A Source Study. *JAOS* 94: 316–28.
Specht, Franz Anton
   1871        *Der exegetische Standpunkt des Theodor von Mopsuestia und Theodoret von Kyros in der Auslegung Messianischer Weissagungen aus ihren Commentaren zu den kleinen Propheten.* Munich: J. J. Lentner.
Speiser, E. A.
   1964        *Genesis.* AYB 1.
Sperber, Alexander
   1945        Biblical Exegesis. Prolegomena to a Commentary and Dictionary to the Bible. *JBL* 64: 39–140.
   1962        *The Bible in Aramaic: The Latter Prophets,* vol. 3. Leiden: Brill.
Sperling, S. D.
   1995        Belial בְּלִיַּעַל "wickedness." Pp. 322–27 in *DDD*.
   1999        Belial בְּלִיַּעַל "wickedness." Pp. 169–71 in *DDD*².
Spiegelberg, W.
   1904        *Ägyptologische Randglossen zum Alten Testament.* Strassburg: Schlesier und Schweikhardt.
Spiekermann, Hermann
   1982        *Juda unter Assur in der Sargonidenzeit.* FRLANT 129. Göttingen: Vandenhoeck und Ruprecht.
   1990        "Barmherzig und gnädig ist der Herr . . . ." *ZAW* 102: 1–18.
Spinoza, Benedictus de
   1677        *Compendium grammatices linguæ Hebrææ.* Amsterdam: J. Rieuwertsz.
Spreafico, A.
   1998        Nahum I 10 and Isaiah I 12–13: Double Duty Modifier. *VT* 48: 104–10.
Spronk, K.
   1986        *Beatific Afterlife in Israel and in the Ancient Near East.* AOAT 219. Kevelaer, Germany: Butzon und Bercker.
   1995a       Synchronic and Diachronic Approaches to the Book of Nahum. Pp. 159–86 in *Synchronic or Diachronic: A Debate on Method in Old Testament Exegesis,* ed. J. C. de Moor. OTS 34. Leiden: E. J. Brill
   1995b       Noble Ones. Cols. 1194–95 in *Dictionary of Deities and Demons,* ed. K. van der Toorn et al. Leiden: Brill.
   1998        Acrostics in the Book of Nahum. *ZAW* 110: 209–22.
Spronk, K., and N. H. Ridderbos
   1995        *Worstelen met een wrekende God: De uitleg van het boek Nahum.* Kampen, Netherlands: Kok.

Spurgeon, C. H.
    1981    Mercy, Omnipotence and Justice (Nahum 1:3). *The Treasury of the Bible*, vol. 4. Grand Rapids, Mich.: Baker. Reprint.

Stade, B.
    1906    Die Drehzahl im Alten Testament. ZAW 26: 124–28.

Stadelmann, J.
    1970    *The Hebrew Conception of the World.* AnBib 39. Rome: Biblical Institute Press.

Staerk, Willy
    1908    *Das Assyrische Weltreich im Urteil der Propheten.* Göttingen: Vandenhoeck und Ruprecht.

Stahl, R.
    1992    "Deshalb trocknet die Erde aus und verschmachtet alle, die auf ihr wohnen . . . ": Der Versuch einer theologiegeschichtlichen Einordnung von Hos 4,3. Pp. 166–73 in *Alttestamentlicher Glaube und Biblischer Theologie: Festschrift für H. D. Preuß,* ed. J. Hausmann et al. Stuttgart: W. Kohlhammer.

Staples, W. E.
    1931    An Inscribed Scaraboid. Pp. 49–68 in *New Light from Armageddon,* by P. L. O. Guy. Oriental Institute Communication 9. Chicago: University of Chicago Press.

Stendebach, F. J.
    1999    סוּס *sûs* horse. TDOT 10: 178–87.
    1999    עוּף; עוֹף *ʿûp̄; ʿôp̄* to fly; bird. TDOT 10: 562–68.
    2004    רֶגֶל *regel.* TDOT 13: 309–24.

Stiglmair, A.
    1999    נָתַךְ *nātak̄* pour, melt. TDOT 10: 85–89.

Stol, M.
    1989    Malz. RLA 7: 322–29.
    1991    De Babyloniërs drunken bier. *Phoenix* 37: 24–29.

Stollz, F.
    1997    נשא *nśʾ* ' to lift, bear. Pp. 769–74 in *TLOT,* vol. 2.

Strassmaier, J. N.
    1886    *Alphabetisches Verzeichnis der assyrischen und akkadischen Wörter der Cuneiform Inscriptions of Western Asia,* vol. 2. Vorderasiatische Bibliothek 4. Leipzig: J. C. Hinrichs.

Strauss, Otto
    1853    *Nahumi de Nino vaticinium explicavit ex Assyriis monumentis illustravit.* Berlin: W. Hertz.
    1855    *Nineveh und das Wort Gottes.* Berlin: Wilhelm Hertz.

Strawn, Brent A.
    2005    *What Is Stronger Than a Lion? Leonine Image and Metaphor in the Hebrew Bible and the Ancient Near East.* OBO 212. Göttingen: Vandenhoeck und Ruprecht.

Streck, M.
1916      *Assurbanipal und die letzten assyrischen Könige bis zum Unter-
          gange Ninivehs.* Vorderasiatische Bibliothek 7: 1–3. Leipzig:
          J. C. Hinrichs.
Stronach, D., and S. Lumsden
1992      UC Berkeley's Excavations at Nineveh. *BA* 55: 227–33.
Strugnell, John
1969–71   Notes en Marge du Volume V des "Discoveries in the Judean
          Desert of Jordan." *RevQ* 7: 163–276.
Stuart, D.
1976      *Studies in Early Hebrew Meter.* Missoula, Mont.: Scholars
          Press for the Harvard Semitic Museum.
Sweeney, M.
1992      Concerning the Structure and Generic Character of the Book
          of Nahum. *ZAW* 104: 364–77.
1999      Zephaniah: A Paradigm for the Study of the Prophetic Books.
          *CRBS* 7: 119–45.
2005      *Form and Intertextuality in Prophetic and Apocalyptic Litera-
          ture.* FAT 45. Tübingen: Mohr Siebeck.
Talmon, S.
1978      הַר *har;* גִּבְעָה *gibʿāh. TDOT* 3: 427–47.
2004      קֵץ *qēṣ end. TDOT* 13: 78–86.
Tantlevskij, I. R.
1997      The Historical Background of the Qumran Commentary on
          Nahum (4QpNah). Pp. 329–38 in *Hellenismus: Beiträge zur
          Erforschung von Akkulturation und politischer Ordnung in den
          Staaten des hellenistischen Zeitalters; Akten des Internationalen
          Hellenismus-Kolloquiums 9.–14.d.1994, Berlin,* ed. B. Funck.
          Tübingen: Mohr Siebeck.
Tasker, R. V. G.
1951      *The Biblical Doctrine of the Wrath of God.* London: Tyndale.
Tawil, H.
1977      A Curse Concerning Crop-Consuming Insects in the Sefire
          Treaty and in Akkadian: A New Interpretation. *BASOR* 225:
          59–62.
Taylor, Charles
1956      The Book of Nahum: Introduction and Exegesis. Pp. 951–69
          in *The Interpreter's Bible,* vol. 6. Ed. George A. Buttrick et al.
          Nashville, Tenn.: Abingdon.
Thiel, W.
2003      צוּר *ṣûr;* מָצוֹר *māṣôr;* מְצוּרָה ;צוּרָה ;צִיר *bind, tie. TDOT*
          12: 306–11.

Thistlethwaite, S.
  1993    "May You Enjoy the Spoil of Your Enemies": Rape as a Biblical
          Metaphor for War. Pp. 59–75 in *Women, War, and Metaphor:*
          *Language and Society in the Study of the Hebrew Bible*, ed.
          C. Camp and C. Fontaine. *Semeia* 61.
Thomas, D. Winton
  1936    The Root *mkr* in Hebrew. *JTS* 37: 388–89.
  1938    The Language of the Old Testament. Pp. 374–402 in *Record*
          *and Revelation*, ed. H. Wheeler Robinson. Oxford: Clarendon.
  1952    A Further Note on the Root *mkr* in Hebrew. *JTS* 3: 214.
  1963    בְּלִיַּעַל in the Old Testament. Pp. 11–19 in *Biblical and Patris-*
          *tic Studies in Memory of Robert Pierce Casey*, ed. J. Neville
          Birdsall and Robert W. Thomsoln. Freiburg: Herder.
Thompson, J. A.
  1974    Translation of the Words for Locusts. *BiTr* 25: 405–11.
Thompson, R. C. (1876–1941), and R. W. Hutchinson
  1929    *A Century of Exploration at Nineveh*. London: Luzac.
Thomson, William M. (1806–94)
  1859    *The Land and the Book*. New York: Harper and Brothers.
Thureau-Dangin, F.
  1940    Une tablette bilingue de Ras Shamra. *RA* 37: 97–118.
Till, Walter
  1927    *Die achmimische Version der zwölf Kleinen Propheten (Codex*
          *rainerianus, Wien)*. Hauniae (Copenhagen): Gyldendal,
          Nordisk.
Tisdall, W. St. Claire
  1913–14 The Aryan Words in the Old Testament. *JQR* n.s. 4: 97–105.
Torczyner, H.; see also Naphtali H. (Naphtali Herz) Tur-Sinai
  1936    Presidential Address. *JPOS* 16: 1–8.
  1945    Yes, Haplography! *JBL* 64: 545–46.
Tournay, R.
  1958    Le Psaume de Nahum. Pp. 328–33 in Recherche sur la
          chronologie des Psaumes. *RB* 65: 321–57.
  1962    Review of J. H. Eaton, *Obadiah, Nahum, Habakkuk, Zepha-*
          *niah*. London: SCM.
  1965    Review of A. Deissler and M. Delcor, *Les Petits Prophètes*.
          Paris: Letouzey et Ané.
Tov, E., et al. (eds.)
  1990    *The Greek Minor Prophets Scroll from Naḥal Hever (8HevXIIgr)*.
          DJD 7. Oxford: Clarendon; New York: Oxford UP.
Tromp, Nicholas J.
  1969    *Primitive Conceptions of Death and the Netherworld in the Old*
          *Testament*. BibOr 21. Rome: Biblical Institute Press.

Tropper, J.
1994    Die enklitische Partikel -y im Ugaritischen. *UF* 26: 473–82.
Tsevat, M.
1975    בְּכוֹר *bəkôr;* בכר *bkr;* בְּכֹרָה; בִּכּוּרִים. *TDOT* 2: 121–27.
Tsumura, David T.
1983    Janus Parallelism in Nah 1:8. *JBL* 102: 109–11.
Tucker, G. M.
1977    Prophetic Superscriptions and the Growth of a Canon.
        Pp. 56–70 in *Canon and Authority: Essays in Old Testament
        Religion and Theology*, ed. G. W. Coats and B. O. Long.
        Philadelphia, Pa.: Fortress.
1978    Prophetic Speech. *Int* 32: 31–45.
Tur-Sinai, Naphtali H. (Naphtali Herz); see also H. Torczyner
1959    *Ha-Lashon ve-Haseper,* vol. 2. Jerusalem: Bialik Institute.
Ullendorff, E.
1958    The Moabite Stone. Pp. 195–99 in *DOTT,* ed. D. Winton
        Thomas. New York: Harper Torchbooks.
Uzziel, Jonathan ben, Jean Mercier, and Charles Estienne
1557–58 *Chaldaea Ionathae, Vzielies filii, interpretation in duodecim
        prophetas: Diligenter emendate, & punctis iuxta analogiam
        gra[m]maticam notata.* Paris: Caroli Stephani.
Van Buren, E. D.
1946    The Dragon in Ancient Mesopotamia. *Or* 15: 1–45.
Van der Lugt, Pieter
1980    *Strofische Structuren in de Bijbels-Hebreeuwse Poëzie.* Kampen,
        Netherlands: J. H. Kok.
2005    *Cantos and Strophes in Biblical Hebrew Poetry with Special
        Reference to the First Book of the Psalter.* OTS 53. Leiden: Brill.
Van der Meer, Willem, and Johannes C. de Moor (eds.)
1988    *The Structural Analysis of Biblical and Canaanite Poetry.*
        JSOTSup 74. Sheffield, England: JSOT Press.
Van der Merwe, Christo H. J.
1990    *The Old Hebrew Particle Gam: A Syntactic-Semantic Descrip-
        tion of gam in Gen–2 Kings.* Revised version of doctoral
        dissertation. TSAT 34. Emming, Germany: St. Ottilien.
Van der Toorn, K., Bob Becking, and Pieter W. van der Horst (eds.)
1995    *Dictionary of Deities and Demons.* Leiden: Brill.
Van der Wal, A. J. O.
1988    *Nahum, Habakkuk: A Classified Bibliography with a Special
        Paragraph Concerning Literature on the Qumran Commen-
        taries on Nahum and Habakkuk.* Amsterdam: Free UP.
Van der Westhuizen, J. P.
1969    A Proposed New Rendering of Nah. 1:5b. OTWSA 12:
        27–32.

Van der Woude, Adam S.
  1977a   The Book of Nahum: A Letter Written in Exile. *OTS* 20: 108–26.
  1977b   Hoe de Here naar Sion wederkeert . . . Traditio-historische
          overwegingen bij Jesaja 52:7–8. Pp. 188–96 in *De Knecht:
          Studies rondom Deutero-Jesaja*, FS J. L. Koole. Kampen,
          Netherlands: Kok.
  1978b   Nahum: Bericht uit de assyrische ballingschap. *Schrift* 59:
          163–98.
  1981    Bemerkungen zu einigen umstrittenen Stellen im
          Zwölfprophetenbuch, NAHUM 1:8b–c. P. 493 in *Mélanges
          bibliques et orientaux en l'honneur de M. Henri Cazelles*, ed.
          A. Caquot and M. Delcor. AOAT 212. Kevelaer, Germany:
          Butzon und Bercker.
  1984    Zacharia. POT. Nijerk, Netherlands: Uitgeerij Callenbach.
Van Dijk, H. J.
  1968    *Ezechiel's Prophecy on Tyre (Ez. 26,1 – 28,19): A New Approach.*
          BibOr 20. Rome: Biblical Institute.
Van Doorslaer, J.
  1949    No Amon. *CBQ* 11: 280–95.
Van Gemeren, W.
  1990    *Interpreting the Prophetic Word.* Grand Rapids, Mich.:
          Zondervan.
Van Leeuwen, F. C.
  1993    Scribal Wisdom and Theodicy in the Book of the Twelve.
          Pp. 31–49 in *In Search of Wisdom: Essays in Memory of
          John G. Gammie*, ed. Leo G. Perdue, Bernard B. Scott, and
          William J. Wiseman. Louisville, Ky.: Westminster / John Knox.
Vannoy, J. Robert
  1978    *Covenant Renewal at Gilgal: A Study of 1 Samuel 11:14–12:25.*
          Cherry Hill, N.J.: Mack.
Vanoni, G.
  2004    שִׂים *śîm;* תְּשׂוּמָה *set, put, place.* TDOT 14: 89–112.
Van Oosterzee, Johannes Jacobus (1817–82)
  1856    *Nineveh en de Heilige Schrift.* Rotterdam: Van der Meer en
          Verbruggen.
Van Selms, Adrian
  1969    The Alphabetic Hymn in Nahum 1. *OTWSA* 12: 33–45.
Van Wyk, W. C.
  1971    Allusions to "Prehistory" and History in the Book of Nahum.
          Pp. 222–32 in *De Fructu Oris sui: Essays in Honour of Adri-
          anus van Selms*, ed. I. H. Eybers et al. POS 9. Leiden: Brill.
Van Zijl, P. J.
  1969    A Discussion of the Root GA'*ar* ("Rebuke"): A Semasiological
          Study. *OTWSA* 12: 56–63.

Van Zyl, A. H. (ed.)
 1969     *Biblical Essays. OTWSA* 12. Praetoria: Potchefstroom.
Vaux, Roland de
 1961     *Ancient Israel: Its Life and Institutions.* New York: McGraw-Hill.
Vawter, B.
 1961     *The Conscience of Israel: Pre-exilic Prophets and Prophecy.* New
          York: Sheed and Ward.
Vegas Montaner , Luis
 1980     *Biblia Del Mar Muerto: Profetas Menores.* Madrid: Instituto
          "Arias Montano."
Vermeylen, J.
 1978     Le discourse prophétique en hôy. Pp. 603–52 in *Du prophète
          Isaïe à l'apocalyptique,* vol. 2. Paris: J. Gabalda.
Vernier, F.
 1891     *La ruine de Nineve et l'oracle de Nahoum: Etude historique,
          exégétique et critique.* Montauban, France: J. Granié.
Voigtlander, E. von
 1963     A Survey of Neo-Babylonian History. Ph.D. diss., University of
          Michigan, Ann Arbor.
Vycichi, W.
 1940     Agyptische Ortsnamen in der Bibel. ZAS 76: 79–93.
Wagner, M.
 1966     *Die lexikalischen und grammatikalischen Aramaismen im altest-
          mentlichen Hebräisch.* BZAW 96. Berlin: Walter de Gruyter.
Wagner, S.
 1975     בָּקַשׁ *biqqēš*; בַּקָּשָׁה. *TDOT* 2: 229–41.
 1986     טָרַף *ṭārap̄*; טָרָף טְרֵפָה טַרְף. *TDOT* 5: 350–57.
 2001     עֹזז *ʿzz*; עָזוּז *ʿzûz*; עַז *ʿaz*; עוֹז/עֹז *ʿōz/ʿōz*; מָעוֹז *māʿōz*.
          *TDOT* 11: 1–11.
Waldman, N.
 1975/76  A Comparative Note on Exodus 1:14–16. *JQR* 66: 189–92.
Wallis, G.
 2004     רָעָה *rāʿāh*; רֹעֶה *rōʿeh* graze; shepherd. *TDOT* 13: 544–53.
Waltke, Bruce K., and M. O'Connor
 1990     *An Introduction to Biblical Hebrew Syntax.* Winona Lake, Ind.:
          Eisenbrauns.
Wanke, G.
 1966     "ʾôy und hôy." ZAW 78: 215–18.
Warmuth, G.
 1998     נָקָה *nāqâ*; נָקִי *nāqî*; נִקָּיוֹן *niqqāyôn*. *TDOT* 9: 553–63.
Waschke,. E.-J.
 2004a    רָמַס *rāmas*; מִרְמָס *mirmās* tread. *TDOT* 13: 509–11.
 2004b    שׁוֹט *šûṭ*; שׁוֹט *šôṭ*; שַׁיִט שׁוֹט/מְשׁוֹט/מְשׁוֹט שְׁאָט. *TDOT* 14:
          528–32.

Watson, Wilfred G. E.
  1969      Shared Consonants in Northwest Semitic. *Bib* 50: 525–33.
  1976      The Pivot Pattern in Hebrew, Ugaritic and Akkadian Poetry.
            ZAW 88: 239–53.
  1980a     Gender–Matched Synonymous Parallelism in the Old Testa-
            ment. *JBL* 99: 321–41.
  1980b     Quasi-Acrostics in Ugaritic Poetry. *UF* 12: 445–47.
  1986      *Classical Hebrew Poetry.* JSOTSup 26, 2nd ed. Sheffield,
            England: JSOT Press. 1st ed. 1984.
Watts, J. D. W.
  2000a     A Frame for the Book of the Twelve. Pp. 209–18 in *Reading and
            Hearing the Book of the Twelve,* ed. J. D. Nogalski and M. A.
            Sweeney. Symposium, 15. Atlanta: Society of Biblical Literature.
  2000b     Superscriptions and Incipits in the Book of the Twelve.
            Pp. 110–24 in *Reading and Hearing the Book of the Twelve,*
            ed. J. D. Nogalski and M. A. Sweeney. Symposium, 15.
            Atlanta: Society of Biblical Literature.
Watts, J. W., and P. R. House (eds.)
  1996      *Forming Prophetic Literature: Essays on Isaiah and the Twelve
            in Honor of John D. W. Watts.* JSOTSup 235. Sheffield,
            England: Sheffield Academic Press.
Wehrle, J.
  1995      Nahum, Nahum (Buch). Pp. 893–97 in *Neues Bibellexikon,*
            vol. 3. Zürich: Benziger.
Weigl, Michael
  2001      Current Research on the Book of Nahum: Exegetical Method-
            ologies in Turmoil? *Currents in Research in Biblical Studies* 9:
            81–130.
Weill, J.
  1923      Nahoum ii, 9–12, et Josèphe (*Ant.* IX, xi, §239–241). *REJ* 76:
            96–98.
Weinfeld, M.
  1965      The Active-Passive (Factitive-Resultive) Sequence of Identical
            Verbs in Biblical Hebrew and Ugaritic. *JBL* 84: 272–82.
  1978      Late Mesopotamian Prophecies. *Schnaton Mikra* (Tel Aviv) 3:
            263–76.
  1987      Der Protest gegen den Imperialismus in der altisraelitischen
            Prophetie. Pp. 240–57 in *Kulturen der Achsenzeit,* vol. 1, ed.
            S. N. Eisenstadt. Frankfurt am Main: Suhrkamp.
Weingreen, J.
  1954      The Construct-Genitive Relation in Hebrew Syntax. *VT* 4: 50–59.
Weippert, M. H. E.
  1973      Die Kämpfe des assyrischen Königs Assurbanipal gegen die
            Araber. *WO* 7: 39–85.

1983        Nieuwassyrische profetieën. In *Schrijvend verleden,* ed. K. R.
            Veenhof. Leiden: Oriente Lux; Zutphen, Netherlands: Terra.
Weis, Richard D.
   1986     The Genre *Maśśāʾ* in the Hebrew Bible. Ph.D. diss., Clare-
            mont Graduate School, Claremont, Calif.
   1992     Oracle. Pp. 28–29 in *AYBD,* vol. 5.
Weiss, R.
   1963/64  A Comparison between the Massoretic and the Qumran Texts
            of Nahum III, 1–11. *RevQ* 15: 433–39.
Weissbleit, S.
   1993     God's Character in the Prophecies of Jonah and Nahum in
            Regard to Nineveh. *Beit Mikra* 38: 206–11. In Hebrew.
Wendland, E. R.
   1994     *Discourse Perspectives on Hebrew Poetry: With Examples from
            Hosea,* ed. Ernst Wendland. New York: United Bible Societies.
   1998     What's the Good News? Check Out "the Feet"! Prophetic
            Rhetoric and the Salvific Centre of Nahum's Vision. *OTE* 11
            (1): 154–81.
Wessels, W.
   1998     Nahum: An Uneasy Expression of Yahweh's Power. *OTE* 11
            (3): 615–28.
Westermann, Claus
   1967     *Basic Forms of Prophetic Speech.* Trans. Hugh C. White.
            Philadelphia, Pa.: Westminster.
   1987     *Prophetisch Heilsworte im Alten Testament.* FRLANT 145.
            Göttingen: Vandenoeckk und Ruprecht.
Wiklander, B.
   1980     עַזָ *zāʿam;* עַזָ *zaʿam.* TDOT 4: 106–11.
Wildeboer, G.
   1902     Nahum 3, 7. ZAW 22: 318–19.
Williams, D. T.
   1991     The Acrostic of Nahum: Call of the Prophet. *OTE* 4: 248–56.
Williams, James G.
   1967     The Alas-Oracles of the Eighth Century Prophets. *HUCA* 38:
            75–91.
Williams, Ronald J.
   1970     Energic Verbal Forms in Hebrew. Pp. 75–85 in *Essays on the
            Ancient Semitic World,* ed. J. W. Wevers and D. B. Redford.
            Toronto: University of Toronto Press.
   1976     *Hebrew Syntax: An Outline,* 2nd ed. Toronto: University of
            Toronto Press.
Wilson, Robert
   1980     *Prophecy and Society in Ancient Israel.* Philadelphia, Pa.: Fortress.

Windfuhr, Walter
1927        *Der Kommentar des David Kimchi zum Propheten Nahum.*
            Giessen: A. Töpelmann.
Winter, I. J.
1981        Royal Rhetoric and the Development of Historical Narrative
            in Neo-Assyrian Reliefs. *Studies in Visual Communication* 7
            (2): 2–38.
Wiseman, Donald J.
1956        *Chronicles of Chaldaean Kings (626–556 B.C.) in the British
            Museum.* London: BM.
1979        Jonah's Nineveh. *TynB* 30: 29–51.
1982        "Is It Peace?"—Covenant and Diplomacy. *VT* 32: 311–26.
Wit, C. de
1951        *Le rôle et le sens du lion dans l'Egypte ancienne.* Leiden: Brill.
Wolfe, R. E.
1935        The Editing of the Book of the Twelve. *ZAW* 53: 90–129.
Wolff, Maternus
1924        Nahum 1,5b. *BZ* 16: 92.
Woods, F. H., and F. E. Powell
1910        *The Hebrew Prophets for English Readers*, vol. 2. Oxford:
            Clarendon.
Wordsworth, W. A.
1939        *En Roeh, the Prophecies of Isaiah the Seer, with Habakkuk and
            Nahum.* Edinburgh: T. and T. Clark.
Wright, G. E.
1957        *Biblical Archaeology.* Philadelphia, Pa.: Westminster.
Xenophon (ca. 430–354 BCE)
1918–68   Book 3, chap. 4 in *Xenophon, III: Anabasis.* Trans. Carleton L.
            Brownson. Loeb Classical Library. London: W. Heinemann.
            New York: G. P. Putnam's Sons.
Yadin, Y.
1963        *The Art of Warfare in Bibical Lands: In the Light of Archaeo-
            logical Study.* 2 vols. New York: McGraw-Hill.
1981        Pesher Nahum Reconsidered. *IEJ* 21: 1–12. Reprinted
            pp. 167–84 in *Qumran*, ed. Karl Erich Grözinger et al.
            Wege der Forschung, 160. Darmstadt: Wissenschaftliche
            Buchgesellschaft.
Yéfer ben Ely
1992        Medieval manuscripts located in British libraries: Oxford
            Bodleian 2483 and Cambridge Trinity 37. The first is a com-
            mentary on the minor prophets and the second is a translation
            of a Hebrew manuscript located in Leiden (Or 4750). Reported
            by Barthélemy (1992: 807–8).

Yoder, Perry B.
    1971        A-B Pairs and Oral Composition in Hebrew Poetry. *VT* 21:
                470–89.
Zalcman, Lawrence
    2004        Intertextuality at Nahum 1,7. *ZAW* 116: 614–15.
Zapff, B. M.
    1999a       The Perspective of the Nations in the Book of Micah as a "Sys-
                tematisation" of the Nations' Role in Joel, Jonah, and Nahum?
                Reflections on a Context-Oriented Exegesis in the Book of the
                Twelve. Pp. 596–616 in *SBL 1999 Seminar Papers*, 38. Atlanta:
                Scholars Press.
    1999b       Die Völkerperspektive des Michabuches als "Systematisierung"
                der divergierenden Sicht der Völker in den Büchern Joel, Jona
                und Nahum? *BN* 98: 86–99.
Zawadzki, Stefan
    1988        *The Fall of Assyria and Median-Babylonian Relations in Light
                of the Nabupolassar Chronicle.* Delft: Adam Mickiewicz UP.
Zenger, E.
    1995        *Einleitung in das Alte Testament.* Stuttgart: W. Kohlhammer.
    1998        Das Buch Nahum. Pp. 509–12 in *Einleitung in das Alte
                Testament*, 3rd enlarged and completely revised edition,
                ed. E. Zenger et al. Stuttgart: Kohlhammer.
Ziegler, Joseph
    1967        *Septuaginta: Duodecim Prophetae*, vol. 13. Göttingen: Vanden-
                hoeck und Ruprecht.
Zimmern, H.
    1905        *Babylonische Hymnen und Gebete.* Leipzig: Hinrichs.
Zobel, H.-J.
    1975        גָּלָה *gālāh*; גּוֹלָה גָּלוּת. *TDOT* 2: 476–88.
    1978        הוֹי *hôy. TDOT* 3: 359–64.
    1986        יְהוּדָה *yəhûḏâ. TDOT* 5: 482–99.
Zorell, F.
    1984        *Lexicon Hebraicum et Aramaicum Veteris Testamenti.* Rome:
                Pontifical Biblical Institute.
Zyl, P. J.
    1969        A Discussion of the root *gāʿar* ("rebuke"): A Semasiological
                Study. *OTWSA* 12: 56–63.

# NOTES AND COMMENTS

# I. Heading (1:1)

1:1    The exposition of Nineveh;
       The scroll of the vision of Nahum the Elkoshite.

## INTRODUCTION

In Jewish tradition, titles are often incipits, taken from the first words of the literary work in question. Here in Nahum, however, the six-word superscription stands apart from the text of the poem that follows. The two-part heading in v 1 is similar to other headings in the prophetic literature and in the Psalms. Childs (1971: 137) argues that, at least for the Psalter, "the titles represent an early reflection of how the Psalms as a collection of sacred literature were understood. The titles established a secondary setting which became normative for the canonical tradition. In this sense the titles form an important link in the history of exegesis." Focusing his attention specifically on the prophetic literature, Tucker (1977: 57–58) also finds the primary function of headings in the Tanakh (Hebrew Bible) within the canonical process itself.

The situation of the headings in the Book of the Twelve Prophets is like that in the Psalter, for the title of Nahum is used to tie the book to the ending of Micah in terms of specific totals in cumulative word count (see the section of the introduction headed "Logoprosodic Analysis and the Book of Nahum"). In some respects the heading in Nahum is similar to that of Psalm 3:1, which also has a two-part heading consisting of a title ("A Psalm of David") plus a descriptive statement ("when he fled from before Absalom his son"). In Psalm 3, as here in Nahum, the initial two-word title stands outside the prosodic structure of what follows in terms of balance in mora count. In Psalm 3:1a, the two-word title integrates that text into its larger canonical context in matters of numerical composition—in relation to the ending of the same psalm, in terms of what we call a "meaningful framework" (see my file on Psalm 3 at www.bibal .net) in relation to the ending of Psalm 2.

The heading of the book of Nahum includes two distinct titles, which are juxtaposed: "the exposition (*maśśāʾ* ) of Nineveh" and "the scroll of the vision (*sēper ḥāzôn*) of Nahum the Elkoshite." The first of these titles stands outside the prosodic structure in terms of balanced dyads and triads on the basis of mora count. These two words were apparently added by the author or composer of this text to achieve two specific goals: that of tying together the books of Micah and Nahum as numerical compositions and that of achieving specific totals in cumulative word count in the opening "Psalm of Nahum" in 1:1–10 (see the following discussion of 1:10). The four words in the second part of the heading (1:1b), which stand within the prosodic structure of what follows, are carefully contrived with v 2 to form a balanced triad of 16 ‖ 14 ‖ 16 morae. The fact that the close connection between these opening two verses is authorial in design is demonstrated by the telestich that spells out the divine name YHWH in the final letters of four successive lines, beginning with the final letter in v 1b. In short, the logoprosodic analysis indicates that the two-part heading is an integral part of the book of Nahum at the point of its numerical composition, which took place within the context of the composition of the Book of the Twelve Prophets.

## NOTES

1:1. *The exposition of Nineveh.* Scholars in times past have interpreted the two-part heading in Nahum as composite (see G. A. Smith 1928: 77), with the words *maśśāʾ nînəwēh* (*exposition of Nineveh*) and *sēper* (*scroll*) as later additions to a presumed original title: *Vision of Nahum the Elkoshite* (so Budde 1901a, Marti 1903, and others). Spronk (1997: 28) argues that the heading in v 1 should not be regarded as a later prosaic addition. As he puts it: "It is part of the poetic structure and is itself a bicolon with two corresponding halves." The second half of this "bicolon" also functions as the initial element in a balanced triad in which the first and third parts end with the letters *yod* and *he'* to spell the name "Yah," which begins the telestich in vv 1–3a that spells out the divine name YHWH using the final letters of four successive lines.

In his attempt to define the word *maśśāʾ* more precisely in relation to the form and function of the texts to which the term is applied, Weis (1992: 28) demonstrates that the translation "prophetic exposition of divine revelation" is preferable to "oracle." The word oracle refers to information transmitted from the deity to humans, which pertains to the deity's will or knowledge (that is, the prior revelation). The *maśśāʾ*, however, refers to the prophet's exposition of what God has revealed (cf. the word *massāh* = "essay" in modern Hebrew). Weiss (1986; 1992: 28) argues that the term *maśśāʾ* may be interpreted to mean "prophetic interpretation of revelation" (cf. Floyd 2000: 14).

In short, for Weis a *maśśā'* is a specific literary genre. Floyd (2000: 14; 2002: 401–22) attempts to carry this argument further in his conclusion that "a *maśśā'* is a type of prophetic literature that is defined in terms of a previously existing prophecy, and it is thus a literary genre whose compositional form often incorporates within it some citation of this previous prophecy."

In the present context, the word *maśśā'* ("exposition") corresponds with *sēper ḥāzôn* ("scroll of vision") to form a parallel word pair (cf. the linking of the word *maśśā'* ["oracle, exposition"] with the verb *ḥāzāh* ["have a vision, see"] in Isaiah 13:1; Habakkuk 1:1; Lamentations 2:14). The word *maśśā'* appears here in a construct relationship with the proper noun *Nineveh* as the name for a revealed "prophetic oracle" (Müller 1998: 23), "revelation" (Tanhum ca. 1280; see Shy 1991: 188; reference from Pinker), "prophecy" (Altshuler 1753; Bolle c. 1990; references from Pinker), "verdict, sentence" (Naudé 1969: 98), or "charge" (Soggin 1989: 303, 325).

De Boer (1948: 214) questioned the usual interpretation of *maśśā'* to mean "utterance, oracle" and argues that the term refers specifically to "a heavy burden, a judgment of God." For some who take this point of view, an oracle is "Yʜᴡʜ's burden" in the sense that it belongs to him and is entrusted to the prophet to present to God's people. The message is not the prophet's "burden" as such, which is carried by him; rather the "burden" belongs to Yʜᴡʜ. The difference in English translation is thus split among translating the word *maśśā'* as "oracle" (RSV, NRSV), "burden" (ASV, KJV), or perhaps "pronouncement" (JPS Tanakh).

Andersen argues that the description of a prophetic utterance as *maśśā'* could derive from the expression *nāśā' qôl*, "lift up the voice (in speech)" (AYB 25; 2001: 87). Therefore, the meaning overlaps that of *māšāl* ("proverb") in Habakkuk 2:6 and its usage in connection with the prototypical visionary Balaam (Numbers 23:7, 18; 24:3, 15, 20, 21, 23). The term *maśśā'* sometimes appears in the phrase *maśśā' Yʜᴡʜ* (Jeremiah 23:33, 34, 36, 38) or *maśśā' dəbar Yʜᴡʜ* (Zechariah 9:1; 12:1; Malachi 1:1). Proverb 30:1 uses the word *maśśā'* in reference to the words of Agur, son of Jakeh. In the Hebrew Prophets, *maśśā'* is a technical term for the message the prophet presents (Isaiah 14:28). Naudé (1969) argues that the word marks the beginning of a prophetic oracle to denote a prophetic pronouncement predicting divine retribution on a foreign nation. Mason (1991: 63) calls attention to the fact that in Isaiah the term *maśśā'* is repeatedly used in the oracles against foreign nations and that Nahum itself is strikingly similar to the kind of material in this body of literature within the three major prophetic books. In addition to its use in the oracles against foreign nations in Isaiah 13–23, the term *maśśā'* introduces collections of prophetic material that begin at Nahum 1:1; Habakkuk 1:1; Zechariah 9:1 and 12:1; and Malachi 1:1. In the latter three instances, the term connotes not the object of the oracle's concern but rather the symbolic nature and content of the message itself as the "word of YHWH."

The prophet Jeremiah expressed unhappiness with the prophetic use of the term *maśśāʾ* in his day at some length (Jeremiah 23:33–40). At first glance, it appears that Jeremiah expressly forbids the use of the term *maśśāʾ* altogether: "You shall not say, the burden (*maśśāʾ*) of YHWH" (Jeremiah 23:38 NRSV). In spite of this injunction, however, the term is used repeatedly as the title of oracles in Isaiah (13:1; 15:1; 17:1; 19:1; 21:1, 11, 13; 22:1; 23:1; 30:6); Ezekiel (12:10); Nahum (1:1); Habakkuk (1:1); Zechariah (9:1; 12:1); and Malachi (1:1). There is no clear explanation of how this term came to carry the technical denotation we find in these several texts. Bright (1965: 153) argued that the point Jeremiah is making (23:33) hinges on a pun on the word *maśśāʾ*, for the same word has two distinct meanings. On the one hand, the word carries the force of a lifting up of the voice in the sense of a prophetic utterance, from the root *nśʾ* ("to lift up"). On the other hand, the word signifies something physical to be lifted up, a "burden." In Jeremiah 23:34–40, Bright said, "the wordplay is developed in a somewhat different direction. It appears that some have been using the word sarcastically, in the sense that Yahweh's utterance is a burden to them; they are therefore forbidden to use the word at all."

Wilson (1980: 249, 257) suggests the possibility that the term *maśśāʾ* was applied to a particular type of oracle characteristic of Jerusalem as opposed to what he calls the Ephraimite tradition in the northern kingdom of Israel. O'Brien (2002: 43) argues that "the *maśśāʾ* form announces a reversal of fortunes (the enemy is about to be routed and we are about to be saved)." For Sweeney (2000: 424–25), the *maśśāʾ*, at least in the book of Nahum, functions within a refutation speech as part of the effort to convince the audience to abandon a prevailing viewpoint and to persuade them to adopt an alternate view.

Two traditional explanations have been given for the turn in meaning from *maśśāʾ* as "burden," in the sense that Jeremiah is using the term, and its use as a technical term for a prophetic pronouncement. According to Holladay (1986: 650), Jerome argued "that an oracle is called a 'burden' because it is a heavy and menacing prediction laid on the hearer." Luther and Calvin maintained this point of view, as did Gehman (1940–41). Michaelis, however, took a different position, arguing that the term is used for oracles that have nothing to do with doom (such as that in Zechariah 12) and that the term *maśśāʾ* has to do with the "lifting up" of the voice, which is also the view of Kimchi and his father before him (for all these points of view, see Holladay 1986: 650). This is the position taken in BDB 672 and *HALOT* 604.

Weis (1992: 28) argues that "the initiative for a *maśśāʾ* lies not with deity or the prophet, but with the prophet's community—or a member thereof—

which asks the question to which the *maśśāʾ* is a response." The later texts of the Old Testament that belong to this genre refer to previously communicated revelations. Following this line of reasoning, an old problem takes on new meaning in light of recent interpretation of Nahum as symbolic speech designed to demonstrate the absolute power of YHWH over the gods of Mesopotamia (symbolized in the figure of Nineveh). Here the previously communicated revelation concerns what McClain calls the *matrix* of the "Marduk cosmos" (see 1976: 77, Chart 15, a modified version of which is reproduced in the section of the introduction to this book headed "Archaeomusicology and the Study of Nahum"). In this instance, the previous "prophecy," which is being exposited, is the way in which cosmology itself was understood. The old cosmology (the "Marduk" cosmos) is replaced by a new model in which YHWH occupies the "throne of deity," replacing all the gods of Mesopotamia. One might describe the change as that of moving from mythology to theology.

The book of Nahum is the exposition on a cosmic scale of the meaning of YHWH's "Holy War," in which all rival deities are subsumed in the God who is the great *One*. In this reading of the *matrix* we find the triumph of Yahwistic theology over an older mythos of Mesopotamian cosmology. As McClain (personal communication) puts it: "The paired base 60 reciprocals are utterly defeated by YHWH's 'ambidextrous' fighters in base 10 as he 'overturns' the enemy leaving only the seven values of the Menorah model 'fixed' in all this turmoil. The 'clouds above' are 'the dust of his feet' below, and 'the earth' between them is 'laid waste before him' as the 'rocks are broken asunder in Abram's arithmetic that follows from the numerical value of his name — 243 [= 3 × 3 × 3 × 3 × 3]." This summary statement assumes prior knowledge of harmonics, which was the norm for scribes in antiquity, who were schooled in what subsequently became known in the Middle Ages as the quadrivium (arithmetic, geometry, astronomy, and music).

The noun "exposition" is qualified by the name *Nineveh*, the object of the prophecy but not the direct recipient of the message, for an oracle of judgment against Nineveh would be a positive word to Judah. The key word *Nineveh* appears explicitly three times in the book of Nahum, once in each chapter (1:1; 2:9 [8]; 3:7), as noted by Bliese (1995: 49), who calls attention to similar distributions of key words in Amos (2003a: 123), Hosea (1994: 69), Joel (1988: 74), Obadiah (1993), Micah (2003b), Habakkuk (1999: 48), and Zephaniah (2004). Spronk (1997: 112–13, 141–43) locates a fourth implicit occurrence of the word *Nineveh* in the form of an acrostic in the initial letters of four successive clauses in 3:18. He also calls attention to the fact that in the Tanakh the name *Nineveh* is associated with proud and powerful rulers like Nimrod (Genesis 10:8–12) and Sennacherib (2 Kings 19:36 = Isaiah 37:37), and the prophet Zephaniah (2:15) describes Nineveh as boasting of its incomparable greatness (Spronk 1997: 29). At the same time, we do well to remember that Nineveh carried symbolic meaning from the outset, for Nineveh symbolized all that might stand in opposition to Yhwh's power and, as such, it was a symbol that was easily applied in similar situations through the centuries (see Coggins 1985: 13, 17).

The word for Nineveh in cuneiform sources goes back to an earlier form, *Ninuwa*, which would seem to underlie the received biblical writing. In addition to the syllabic spelling, the cuneiform texts occasionally use a pseudo-logographic form, *Nina*, which is the combination of two Sumerian signs (AYB + KHA) representing an enclosure with a fish inside. This reading is of interest in light of the prophet Jonah's being swallowed by a large fish (Jonah 2:1 [1:17]). Another line of folk interpretation is found in Greek literature, where the city of Nineveh is called "Ninos." Some say that "Ninos" (or "Ninus") is a name for a lineage of thirteen generations down from Nimrod. Moreover, Pinker (1998) argues that Nimrod is the god Marduk.

Nineveh (Akkadian *Ninuwa, Ninua, Ninâ*), which is located on the east bank of the Tigris opposite Mosul and near the mounds of Nebi Yunus and Tell Küyünjik, was founded in approximately 5000 BCE and enjoyed a checkered history until Sennacherib (704–681 BCE) made it the capital of the Assyrian Empire. Sennacherib spent twenty-five years restoring and enlarging the old city of Nineveh, building temples, palaces, gardens, and aqueducts. The watering system was enormous in scope, as revealed by archaeological excavation. Water was brought from the mountains to the north to the small river Khoser, which flows through the city of Nineveh. The city itself is situated a few kilometers downstream from the foothills of the Kurdish mountains and not far from the confluence of the Tigris with the river Great Zab. In ancient times the Tigris was closer to the southwest city wall of ancient Nineveh at Tell Küyünjik than it is now.

Memory of Assyrian greatness at Nineveh was kept alive, at least in part, by the mound Nebi Yunus ("the prophet Jonah") in a village around a Muslim shrine associated with a traditional grave of Jonah. That hill turned out to be the palace mound, which began to reveal its secrets of the distant past in 1840, starting with Emille Botta and continuing in successive excavations until the eve of the first Gulf War ("Desert Storm") in 1991 (see Wiseman 1979; Scott and Maginnis 1990; Stronach and Lumsden 1992).

Sennacherib was followed by two able kings, who in turn were also great builders, his son Esarhaddon (680–668 BCE) and grandson Ashurbanipal (668–627 BCE). This was Assyria's golden age; her empire covered the whole of the Fertile Crescent, from the Persian Gulf to Egypt. The palaces in Nineveh were filled with the wealth of subject nations, and behind its double line of ramparts, the city appeared to be invulnerable. So Nineveh became the symbol of Assyrian power in the ancient Near East.

In the second part of the heading in Nahum, this "exposition" is described as a *ḥăzôn* ("vision"), which is similar to what appears in the book of Habakkuk "that the prophet saw" (Habakkuk 1:1) or to what Isaiah saw (Isaiah 13:1). As Andersen (2001: 88) observes, the combination of seeing and hearing is inherent in the psychology of perception itself: "We read body language. . . . In common idiom, while 'I hear you' recently had some vogue, when we understand what someone says we say 'I see.'" Sweeney (2000: 423) thinks the inclusion of the term *ḥăzôn* ("vision") in the heading here indicates "an interest in explicating the meaning of the semi-acrostic Psalm in Nah 1:2–8, in which the Psalm constitutes the *maśśā'* and the rest of the book constitutes the *ḥăzôn*, which explains the meaning of the Psalm in relation to the fall of Assyria."

*The scroll of the vision of Nahum the Elkoshite.* Technically speaking, a *sēp̄er* is not a book, at least in the modern sense, with pages sewn together in a quire of pages (that is, a codex). With reference to antiquity, the word *sēp̄er* refers to a written document—on any suitable material: a stone stela, an ostracon, sheets of papyrus, or a scroll. It may even refer to a received oral tradition in the form of an epic poem that was transmitted in song, as in the case of the "Book (*sēp̄er*) of the Wars of Yhwh" in Numbers 21:14 (Christensen 1974: 359–60). The codex, as such, did not appear until the time of the apostle Paul in the era of the Greek New Testament (see Christensen 2005: 112). The term "scroll" (*sēp̄er*), which appears only here in a prophetic superscription, was chosen to indicate the literary nature of this composition as a written document. The specific reference to Nahum as a "scroll of (the) vision" suggests that we have here a work that was written from the outset, not merely a work written to preserve the spoken words of the prophet. The reader is invited to know what God has revealed by reading the words that follow.

Speculation varies on the original form of the *sēp̄er* in question. Some see Nahum as a liturgy of thanksgiving following the final destruction of Nineveh, but such a view ignores the prophetic nature of the text. It has even been described as a "Cantata on Nineveh" (see Craigie 1985: 60). Watts (1975: 100) sees the original "book" as that of a sermon text intended to be preached, or perhaps as a play script. Van der Woude (1977a) argues that the book is a letter written in exile, but as Spronk (1997: 30) notes, the document makes no reference to the sender, the addressee, or their relationship. Edelkoort (1937: 280) described the book as a "pamphlet" that was circulated during the Assyrian oppression in the reign of Manasseh in Judah. In a similar manner, Spronk (1997: 30) argues that the poet wrote down his message, "like his great model Isaiah (cf. Isaiah 30:8), convinced that time would prove that he was not a false prophet (cf. Deuteronomy 18:22)." All of these proposals assume that Nahum was a written document within the context of the Assyrian Empire. There is no real evidence, however, that the book ever existed in antiquity independent of its present context in the Book of the Twelve Prophets.

The word ḥăzôn ("vision"), which also appears in the title of Isaiah and Obadiah, sometimes refers to a prophet's characteristic activity as a visionary (see Ezekiel 7:26). In a narrow sense, however, the word denotes a specific type of prophetic revelation, such as that presented in the vivid description of battle in Nineveh in 2:4–10 [3–9] and 3:1–3 (see Horst 1960; Sister 1934). O'Brien (2002: 41) points out that in the Tanakh the word is used almost exclusively to refer to prophecy and that it refers not to data registered by the eye but to truth made known by revelation from YHWH, as Jeremiah 23:16 indicates in these words: "(False prophets) speak visions of their own minds, not from the mouth of Yahweh." In later literature the term took on a specialized focus, as in the book of Daniel, where its usage (eleven times) implies a vision into the heavenly realm.

Jepsen (1980: 283) argues that the term ḥăzôn designates "a nocturnal audition." The revelation of a spoken word is involved, but it comes when the prophet is in a deep sleep—"he sees something that he cannot recognize, and in the silence he hears a voice." In the course of time, however, the term apparently came to mean little more than "prophecy" (see Hillers 1983b: 13).

The verb ḥāzāh ("to see a vision") appears in contexts in which the emphasis is on the prophet's message and not on the reception of that message (Isaiah 30:10; Zechariah 10:2; Lamentations 2:14). The term "vision" here suggests that the book of Nahum has more to do with the world of the imagination than it does with any memory of political history per se, as Haldar suggested (1947). The phrase "to see a vision" describes the prophetic function of revealing what is otherwise unseen or unknown. The usage here functions as a clue to the reader to look for hidden meaning in the literary work that follows, for dimensions of that text that carry us into the world of cosmology and mythology, and perhaps also into that of musical and mathematical allegory in the scribal world of matrix arithmetic and what some call theological harmonics.

Spronk (1997: 30) calls attention to a useful parallel to the heading in Nahum 1:1 in the Deir ʿAlla inscription, which begins (see Dijkstra 1995):

ysry spr [b]lʿm [brbʿ]r    Warning from the writing of Balaam, son of Beor,
ʾš ḥzh ʾlhn hʾ               A man of vision of the gods is he.

That text was written in a Canaanite dialect, akin to Aramaic, on a wall about 800 BCE in what is now the country of Jordan. With many commentators,

Spronk concludes that it is not necessary to assume a double heading in Nahum 1:1, for in this example the heading also combines a reference to the contents of the oracle with a reference to the way in which it was received, followed by the name of the writer. The nature of the two-part heading in Nahum, however, is more complex than Spronk has seen (see discussion in the following "Comment" section).

The word *Nahum* (*naḥûm*) means "showing consolation, compassionated," and the books of Nahum and Jonah have much to do with the interplay between the themes of divine judgment and compassion. The name comes from the root *nḥm* ("to be sorry, console oneself, have compassion"). In the Hebrew language, the name *naḥûm* is intensive in its grammatical form. Like *rāḥûm,* "full of compassion," and *ḥannûn,* "full of grace," the name *naḥûm* means "full of comfort."

The same root appears in the biblical names *Nehemiah, Nahamani* (Nehemiah 7:7), *Tanhumeth* (Jeremiah 40:8), and *Menahem* (2 Kings 15:14–23). Though the name *Nahum* appears only here in the Tanakh, the root *nḥm* is attested in personal names on seals and seal impressions from the seventh and sixth centuries BCE (see Avigad 1965: no. 4; 1986, nos. 77, 121, 153, 176, 202; Hestrin and Dayagi-Mendels 1979: no. 17) and on Jewish ossuaries (Clermont-Ganneau 1884). The vocalization of the name as *naḥûm* is confirmed in the Elephantine texts as N*ḥwm* (Porten and Greenfield 1974: 64, 66, 72). The name appears frequently in Northwest Semitic inscriptions; once in the Arad ostraca (seventh century BCE; Aharoni 1966a: 4; 1966b: 14–16; 1968a: 14); once in a bulla from Lachish with the Hebrew seal impression *lnḥm bn ᶜnnyhw,* "belonging to Nahum son of ᶜAnanyahu" (Aharoni 1968b: 166); and in the Ebla tablets (in *MEE* 2, 30 obv. I 7; Dahood 1983: 59). It occurs often in the Mishnah.

The name has been explained as a shortened form of *nḥmyh* (Nehemiah), meaning "YHWH has comforted" (Noth 1928: 175; Rudolph 1975: 148; Fowler 1988: 107, 351; Roberts 1991: 41), or perhaps of *nḥmʾl,* "El [God] is a comforter" (Haldar 1947: 148; Cathcart 1973a: 37). Spronk (1997: 33) suggests a connection between Nahum and the person many identify as Deutero-Isaiah, with many commonalities between Nahum and Isaiah 40–66. Note in particular the opening words of Isaiah 40:1, with the twofold repetition of the verbal root *nḥm* in the statement: "Comfort (*naḥămû*), O comfort [my people]."

The gentilic term "Elkoshite" apparently designates Nahum's hometown (Elkosh), the location of which is not known. Four other prophets are identified in reference to their hometowns: Amos, from Tekoah; Micah, from Moresheth; Jeremiah, from Anathoth; and Jonah, from Gath-hepher (2 Kings 14:25). Attempts to locate the town of Elkosh have focused on at least six different possibilities (two in Mesopotamia, two in northern Israel, and two in Judah).

In eastern medieval tradition, Elkosh has been identified as al-Kush, a site twenty-six miles north of modern Mosul, on the Tigris River opposite the ruins of Nineveh (Assemanius 1719: 525; Billerbeck-Jeremias 1895: 92–93). There are traditional burial places of both Nahum and Jonah in this area. According to G. A. Smith (1928: 78), the tradition locating Nahum's tomb at this site cannot be traced earlier than the sixteenth century CE. In 1165, Benjamin of Tudelah reported that he was shown the tomb of Nahum elsewhere in what is now the country of Iraq—in ᶜAin Japhata, a small town south of Babylon (G. A. Smith 1903: 579, citing Bohn's "Early Travels in Palestine," p. 102; J. M. P. Smith 1911: 286).

According to G. A. Smith (1898: 79), Jerome located Elkosh in Galilee close to the border of Lebanon, identifying it with Helkesei or Elkese, which may be modern el-Kauzeh near Ramieh, southwest of Tibrin. Van der Woude (1977a: 113) agrees with Jerome, arguing that Nahum was an exiled northern Israelite who wrote his letter to Judah from Assyria. Hitzig (1881: 244) and Davidson (1896: 12) claimed that Elkosh was the original site of Capernaum, on the north shore of the Sea of Galilee, which means "Nahum's city" (Caper-*naum*).

According to W. A. Maier (1959: 25), Cyril of Alexandria and Pseudo-Epiphanius (fourth century CE) located Elkosh near Eleutheropolis in Judah about twelve miles northeast of Lachish and twenty miles southwest of Jerusalem, near the modern village of Beit Jibrin (see W. A. Maier 1959: 25–26). An ancient well at the upper end of the Wadi es-Sur bears the name Bir el K-ûs, which means "Well of the Bow" according to Guèrin (see G. A. Smith 1928: 80, n. 3). According to Harrison (1969: 926), who preferred this view, the site is near Begebar, the modern Beit Jibrin (Nestle 1879: 136–38; Cassuto 1915: 291–302). The same tradition is reflected in the *Lives of the Prophets*, where Elkosh is identified with Beth-gabre in the tribe of Simeon, which G. A. Smith traced to the Syriac translation of the Old Testament by Paul of Tella, 617 CE (1928: 79, n. 4). A further possibility is suggested by Roberts (1991: 41), who notes: "The place name *ʾlqwš* may contain the Edomite divine name *Qauš*, 'Qauš / Qôš -is-God,' and if so, one should look for a site in the south of Judah near the border with Edom" (see also G. A. Smith 1903: 580; Procksch 1937: 301).

Cheyne (1903–4: 164) solved the problem by emending the text to read *ʾškly,* "Eskol" (cf. Numbers 13: 23–24). T. Schneider (1988: 73) emends the text to read *ᶜlqšt*, "head of the archers," and suggests that Nahum was an officer in Israel's army. Happel (1900: 10–11) suggested that the acrostic in 1:2–10 has as its opening word *ʾēl* ("El, God") and ends with *qaš* at the beginning of the last clause in 1:10. The second part of the heading in 1:1 thus refers to "the vision of Nahum from *ʾēl* to *qaš.*" He suggested that the word is an editor's note added to indicate that only part of the original alphabetic acrostic was preserved and translates the word *ʾelqōšî* as a statement: "God collects stubble" (that is, the enemies) to be burnt.

The fact that the location of Elkosh is not known suggests the possibility that the name itself was selected by the author for literary reasons, and perhaps the same is true for the name of the prophet Nahum ("compassionated") as well (so conclude Haldar 1947: 148; Hyatt 1962: 635; Keller 1971: 108, n. 3; Spronk 1997: 32–33). Allis (1955: 76) reads the word *ʾlqšy* as suggesting to the reader the word *ʾl* ("God") and *qšh* ("severe"). He supports his argument with variant readings in medieval manuscripts, which have *ʾl-qšy* or *ʾl-qwšy* (cf. Kennicott 1776–80; Budde 1901a: 1280; see also Montgomery 1935b: 61–62). In a similar manner, O'Brien (2002: 42–43) suggests that "the designation 'Elkoshi' may be a literary play on the themes of Nahum," because the word "is comprised of two elements: *ʾel*, 'God'; and *qāšâ*, 'be hard,' the same root used throughout Exodus to describe the 'hardening' of Pharaoh's heart." Though it cannot be determined what the precise nuance of the word may be, she argues, by way of association with other texts and contexts, that its meaning is "evocative in such a 'hard,' 'burdensome' book." Spronk (1997: 32) remains open to the possibility of reading the text here in the manner suggested by Allis and O'Brien, arguing that the word *ʾelqōšî* offers a nice transition to the next line beginning with *ʾēl qannôʾ*, because *qšh* and *qnʾ* appear as a parallel pair elsewhere (cf. Cant. 8:6). As a good parallel he cites Isaiah 21:1–2, where a pronouncement (*maśśāʾ*) is presented as a stern vision (*ḥāzôn qāšeh*) of coming destruction (cf. Nahum 3:7).

The Targum interprets the text as the prophet's family name: "from the house of Koshi." Gordon and Cathcart (1989: 131, n. 5; 1994: 142) explain that here the Targum is attempting to avoid any connection with the Jewish-Christian sect of the Elchasaites, but as Spronk (1997: 31) observes: "It is more likely that the Targumist also did not know a place called Elkosh." According to Rosenberg (1988: 438), Abarbanel relates the Hebrew word *hāʾelqōšî* to the verbal root *lqš* ("to succeed") and the word for "latter rain" (*mlqwš*) — in the sense that Nahum succeeded Jonah as God's prophet to Nineveh.

Allis (1955: 75–78) sees wordplay between the name *Nahum* ("compassionated") and the word *nōqēm* ("avenger"), which is repeated three times in v 2. He argues that the connection is strengthened by a second wordplay between the name of Nahum's hometown, *Elkosh*, and the description of God as *ʾēl qannôʾ* ("jealous God"). He also notes that it is possible to hear in the Hebrew word *ʾēlqōšî* ("Elkoshite") the words *ʾēl qāšeh* ("the severe God"), the other side of the portrayal of God as "merciful and gracious, slow to anger, and abounding in steadfast love and faithfulness" in Exodus 34:6. In short, both proper nouns may reflect symbolic meaning more than historical reference to an otherwise unknown person and place.

## COMMENT

Though sometimes described as comparable to a title page in a modern book (Longman 1993: 786), the opening verse in Nahum 1:1 is integrally connected with what follows and much more than a mere title, which today is often assigned by the publisher rather than the author. The concluding word in this superscription introduces the first letter of the divine name YHWH, which is spelled out in the form of a telestich as the final letter of four consecutive lines in 1:1, 1:2a, 1:2b, and 1:3a. But, even more important, this superscription is written in "poetic" form even though virtually all English translations suggest otherwise, for this verse is an essential part of the numerical composition of the opening "canto" (1:1–10). Each word of this so-called title page is carefully chosen to foreshadow what follows. In short, the superscription is much more than an afterthought on the part of some publisher; it was composed by the author as a fitting introduction to the whole of his literary work, which focuses its attention on Nineveh.

The diversity within the headings of prophetic books in the Old Testament has been the focus of study from different points of view. Andersen and Freedman present a detailed and useful discussion in their commentary on Hosea (1980: 143–45; see also Freedman 1987). Of the fifteen prophetic books of the Latter Prophets, three begin abruptly in narrative style without a formal title, namely Jonah, Haggai, and Zechariah. Among these three, Jonah is distinct in its resemblance to stories about the prophets embedded in 1–2 Kings. Among the twelve remaining prophetic books with titles, Andersen and Freedman (1980: 144) find at least eight features in their headings, although no single book has all of them:

1. A name for the work
2. The prophet's name
3. The prophet's patronymic
4. His hometown
5. A reference to his call, however vague
6. The time of his activity
7. A precise date (of his call or first oracle)
8. The subject matter of his prophecy

For a somewhat different way of comparing the prophetic superscriptions, with six categories (vehicle of inspiration, family information, locale, political setting, target/recipient, other information), see O'Brien (2002: 44–45).

Andersen and Freedman (1980: 144) find enough similarity in the headings of Amos, Hosea, Isaiah, and Micah to conclude that "they were shaped by a common editorial tradition. Yet each shows its own peculiarities, suggesting that the editor(s) devised and applied the front matter for each book with care and deliberation." The titles of Zephaniah, Jeremiah, and Ezekiel (in part), have features similar to the four eighth-century prophets, but they are markedly different in other respects. The books of Joel, Obadiah, Nahum, and Habakkuk have "meager titles" in contrast to the ample information provided by the first seven features of titles mentioned earlier, while Malachi is unique.

In the heading of Nahum is the expression "the vision of Nahum the Elkoshite," which includes three of the first four items in the list above — though nothing further is known about the town Elkosh. There is nothing in the heading about the other items in the list, except for the designation of the book as a "*maśśāʾ Nînəwēh*" ("an exposition of Nineveh").

In his form-critical approach, Tucker (1977: 59) assumes that "the superscriptions are not in any way grammatically attached to what follows; the body of the book simply begins after the superscriptions." The logoprosodic analysis does not support this conclusion, however, nor does the telestich pattern in 1:1–3, as reported by Spronk (1998: 216). Tucker (1977: 62) identifies three distinct categories of titles in the prophetic corpus:

1. A word identifying the book, followed by the name of the prophet
2. The title or phrase "The word of YHWH," followed by the relative clause "that came to . . ."
3. A title beginning *maśśāʾ* ("an oracle") but not following a fixed syntactical pattern

Tucker (1977: 65) assumes that "it is all but self-evident that the superscriptions were not created by the prophets themselves." This statement is misleading, however, for there is no reason to conclude that the presumed "historical prophet" is the "author" of the text as we now have it. If the text is a numerical composition, and if the text is also an integral part of the Book of the Twelve as a whole, the "author" (or composer) may have conceived of the heading as an integral part of the text of Nahum from the outset within the canonical process.

Gevaryahu (1975: 42–43) calls attention to a number of possible ancient Near Eastern parallels and advances more than one thesis to explain the origin and history of the prophetic superscriptions. He finds significant connections with Akkadian colophons and argues that the superscriptions once stood at the end of the prophetic books and only later were transferred to the beginning. The logoprosodic analysis makes this conclusion extremely unlikely for the book of Nahum, and Tucker (1977: 66) concurs, writing: "There is no direct evidence that the prophetic superscriptions originally were colophons at the end of the books." As Tucker also notes, the differences between the biblical superscriptions and the Akkadian colophons are more striking than the similarities. An Akkadian colophon frequently provides data concerning the scribe who copied it, as well as its sponsor or owner, and almost never includes the name of an author (Lambert 1957: 1). Tucker (1977: 66) calls attention to a number of Sumerian texts in which the colophons describe the composition of each in terms of its genre and/or its use (cf. *ANET* 1967: 577–79, 583, 591).

The closest parallels to the biblical superscriptions are found in Egyptian "wisdom" texts. In particular, Tucker (1977: 67) calls attention to "The Instruction of the Mayor and Vizier Ptah-Hotep, under the majesty of the King of Upper and Lower Egypt; Izezi, living forever and ever" (cf. *ANET* 412). Here we find a work identified in terms of itself and its author, whose occupation and date are provided. Tucker correctly concludes that the genre in question may be attributed to scribal activity.

Labuschagne (private communication) has studied the headings of the twelve individual books in the Book of the Twelve Prophets in terms of the numerical composition of the Tanakh. The data he has compiled suggest a different grouping of the books from that found by Andersen and Freedman, which was determined on the basis of the presumed date of prophetic activity of the prophet(s) in question. Labuschagne finds at least four groupings of the headings in terms of patterns in cumulative word count:

| Prophetic books | Total number of words in the headings |
|---|---|
| Hosea, Joel, and Amos | $52 = 26 \times 2$ |
| Obadiah–Zephaniah | $51 = 17 \times 3$ |
| Obadiah–Nahum | 26 |
| Nahum, Habakkuk, and Zephaniah | $51 = 17 \times 3$ |

In this arrangement, the book of Nahum (the seventh book) occupies a pivotal position. The focus of attention here is on the order of the books within the Book of the Twelve Prophets as a literary whole, not on the historical setting per se of each individual prophet. Andersen and Freedman (1980: 146–57) conclude that the works of Amos, Hosea, Isaiah, and Micah "show signs of common editing . . . as parts of the same corpus." There is also a growing body of evidence to suggest that the entire corpus of the Book of the Twelve Prophets was carefully edited as a numerical composition into a single literary entity that takes its rightful place alongside the three Major Prophets (Isaiah, Jeremiah, and Ezekiel).

As a form of literary art, there is no composition in the whole of the Tanakh that surpasses the book of Nahum in terms of its technical achievements as a work of Hebrew poetry at virtually any level one chooses to explore—and the heading is an integral part of that numerical composition. At first glance, the first two words in the heading to the book of Nahum appear to be outside the prosodic structure of what follows. But when we count the words in the Hebrew text of Nahum, including the first two, we observe an interesting convergence. The numerical value of the prophet's name *nḥwm* is

| *nun* | *ḥet* | *waw* | *mem* | $= 50 + 8 + 6 + 40 = 58 + 46 = 104,$ |
|-------|-------|-------|-------|------|

where $104 = 26 \times 4$; $58 = 26 + 32$; and $46 = 23 \times 2$. In the logoprosodic structure of Nahum, the 104th word falls on the 4th word in 1:10, which marks the middle of the concluding pair of dyads—in the middle of the two pairs of troublesome words *sîrîm səbūkîm* and *ûkəsābəʾām səbûʾîm* (see the following discussion on 1:10), which are $14 + 12 = 26$ morae in length, in balance with the following balanced dyad with $13 + 14 = 27$ morae. The compositional formula at this point is $104 = 58 + 46$ in terms of word count. In other words, the totals at this point, counting from the beginning of Nahum, are **58** words before *ʾatnaḥ* and **46** words after *ʾatnaḥ*. This implicit (coded) appearance of the name *Nahum* (twice in v 10) in terms of cumulative word count forms an inclusion with the explicit occurrence of the prophet's name in the heading (v 1). Careful numerical analysis of this sort helps to explain some of the peculiarities in the headings of individual books within the Book of the Twelve Prophets as a whole.

Though Nineveh was the capital of Assyria for less than a century, the city retained a position of dominance in biblical history and beyond as a paradigmatic enemy of God's people (note that Holofernes, general of Nebuchadnezzar, is from Nineveh in the book of Judith and that Tobit is a God-fearing Jew in Nineveh). In the half century from Sennacherib's devastating campaign against Judah in 701 BCE to the revolt of Babylon on the part of Ashurbanipal's brother Shamash-shumukin in 652–648 BCE, the Assyrian domination of Judah was harsh. Babylon's revolt apparently suggested the beginning of the end of Assyrian power, and if we give credence to the account in 2 Chronicles 33:10–13, Manasseh of Judah was drawn into that conflict. Nonetheless, Assyria reasserted its control in the Levant until ca. 635–630 BCE, when further troubles led to greater freedom on the part of Josiah, king of Judah (640–609 BCE). Twenty years later, the city of Nineveh was destroyed by the Medes and Babylonians (612 BCE), and three years later King Josiah was killed at Megiddo by Egyptian forces to end an era in Judah as well as in Assyria.

For the prophet Nahum, Nineveh took on a meaning that transcended that of the Nineveh of history. In the inscriptions recovered from ancient Nineveh, we find written accounts and detailed pictures carved in stone that tell us even more than words the nature of Assyria's rule by terror—including piles of human hands, and heads, and the portrayal of defeated foes impaled for public display. The glee of her victims over the fall of Nineveh is easy to comprehend, particularly in light of the scourge of modern-day rulers like Adolf Hitler, Joseph Stalin, Idi Amin, and radical Muslim extremists who behead innocent victims and seem to take pleasure in terror itself. On tablets of stone Assyrian kings boasted of their acts of terror—how they dragged women and children away from the corpses of their dead husbands and fathers as spoils of conquest and took them to the fortress of Nineveh. Their annals reflect pride in the human suffering they inflicted in the total devastation of their enemies. As Craigie (1985: 58) puts it: "Of all the oppressive powers that have stained the pages of human history from the past to the present, Assyria claims a place of pre-eminence among evil nations."

Though there has never been any doubt on the identity of Nineveh within the historical situation addressed in Nahum, later readers have had little difficulty applying the text to their own time and circumstances. Like Babylon in the book of Revelation, Nineveh is easily regarded as a symbol of the forces of evil. Thus the oldest known commentary on Nahum, written at Qumran in the first century BCE, explained the text as a prophecy that YHWH would bring to an end the Roman occupation of Israel. Near the end of the fourth century CE, Jerome interpreted the text in relation to the comfort that Roman emperors like Valerian found in the promise that eventually God will deal with the forces of evil. Cyril of Alexandria found reference to the final judgment in Nahum 1:2 and 9. Haymo of Halberstadt, who studied under Alcuin (ninth century CE), and Bibliander (1534) after him interpreted Nahum in reference to God's protecting the church against heretics like Marcion. Luther found here a parallel in "the empire of the pope being shaken by the word of God" (see Spronk 1997:20).

But having said this, there is a timeless message here. Watts (1975: 120) describes the symbolic meanings of Ninevah and Assyria as well as any when he says: "Nineveh is no ordinary city for the prophet, nor is Assyria just another degenerating civilization. They stand for the ultimate supernatural evil that frustrates and suppresses the purposes and people of God, and the basis for hope that his power and justice will ultimately conquer all evil."

# II. THE PSALM OF NAHUM: YHWH'S VENGEANCE (1:1–10)

| | Morae | units | SAS | Word | count |
|---|---|---|---|---|---|
| **A. YHWH Takes Vengeance against His Enemies (1:1–2)** | | | | | [9.4] |
| 1:1 The exposition / of Nineveh // | 8 | 2 | 2 | 2 | 0 |
| Mic 7:17–Nah 1:1a | | | 52 | 28 | 24 |
| The scroll of the vision / of Nahum / the Elkoshite // י | _16 | 3_ | 4 | 0 | 4 |
| Mic 7:16–Nah 1:1 | | | 67 | 33 | 34 |
| 1:2 א A zealous and avenging God (ʾEl) / is YHWH / | _14 | 2 | 4 | 4 | 0 |
| Mic 7:17–Nah 1:2a | | | 60 | 32 | 28 |
| Avenging is YHWH / and a lord (Baʿal) of wrath // ה | 16 | 2 | 4 | 4 | 0 |
| Mic 7:18–Nah 1:2b | | | 51 | 29 | 22 |
| ב Avenging is YHWH / against his foes / | _13 | 2_ | 3 | 0 | 3 |
| 1: 1–1:2c | | | 17 | 10 | 7 |
| And he rages / against his enemies // ו | _13 | 2 | 3 | 0 | 3 |
| Mic 7:17–Nah 1:2 | | | 70 | 36 | 34 |
| **B. YHWH Is Slow to Anger but Great in Power (1:3)** | | | | | [5.5] |
| 1:3 ר YHWH / he is slow to anger / [a]but great in power[a] / | 16 | 3 | 5 | 5 | 0 |
| and the guilty / he does not acquit // ה | _9 | 2 | 3 | 3 | 0 |
| 1:1b–3b | | | 26 | 16 | 10 |
| * YHWH / | _4 | 1 | 1 | 0 | 1 |
| 1:2–3c | | | 23 | 16 | 7 |

| | Morae | SAS units | Word count | | |
|---|---|---|---|---|---|
| In the whirlwind and in the storm / is his way / | 15 | 2 | 3 | 0 | 3 |
| and clouds / are the dust of his feet // | 10 | 2 | 3 | 0 | 3 |
| 1:1–3 | | | 35 | 18 | 17 |
| **C. YHWH Acts with Cosmic Consequences (1:4)** | | | | | [4.4] |
| 1:4 ב He blasts the Sea / and he dries it up / | 14 | 2 | 3 | 3 | 0 |
| and all the Rivers / he desiccates // | 12 | 2 | 3 | 3 | 0 |
| 1:1–4b | | | 41 | 24 | 17 |
| א They[b] wither away (that is) Bashan / and Carmel / | 12 | 2 | 3 | 0 | 3 |
| and the green of Lebanon / withers // | 13 | 2 | 3 | 0 | 3 |
| 1:1–4 | | | 47 | 24 | 23 |
| **D. The Earth and Its Inhabitants Reel before YHWH (1:5)** | | | | | [4.4] |
| 1:5 ה Mountains / quake before him / | 14 | 2 | 3 | 3 | 0 |
| and the hills / melt away // | 14 | 2 | 2 | 2 | 0 |
| 1:4–5a | | | 17 | 11 | 6 |
| ו And the earth reels / before him [/] | 14 | 2 | 3 | 0 | 3 |
| and the world / and all who dwell in it // | 14 | 2 | 4 | 0 | 4 |
| 1:2–5 | | | 53 | 27 | 26 |
| **E. YHWH Acts with Cosmic Consequences (1:6)** | | | | | [4.4] |
| 1:6 [ז] In the presence of his fury / who can stand? / | 12 | 2 | 4 | 4 | 0 |
| and who can rise up / in the heat of his anger? // | 15 | 2 | 4 | 4 | 0 |
| 1:4–6a | | | 32 | 19 | 13 |
| ח His wrath / is poured out like fire / | 13 | 2 | 3 | 0 | 3 |
| and the rocks / are broken asunder by him // | 14 | 2 | 3 | 0 | 3 |
| 1:5–6 | | | 26 | 13 | 13 |
| **F. YHWH Is Good and a Refuge in the Day of Distress (1:7–8)** | | | | | [5.5] |
| 1:7 ט Good is YHWH / | 6 | 1 | 2 | 2 | 0 |
| indeed a stronghold / in the day of distress // | 12 | 2 | 3 | 3 | 0 |
| 1:3–7b | | | 58 | 32 | 26 |
| [י] And he knows / those who take refuge in him // | 12 | 2 | 3 | 0 | 3 |
| 1:5–7 | | | 34 | 18 | 16 |
| 1:8 And in the sweeping torrent / | 7 | 1 | 2 | 2 | 0 |
| [כ] a full end (kālāh) / he will make of her place // | 12 | 2 | 3 | 3 | 0 |
| And his enemies / he pursues into darkness // | 12 | 2 | 3 | 0 | 3 |
| 1:3–8 | | | 69 | 37 | 32 |

|  | | SAS | Word | | |
|---|---|---|---|---|---|
|  | *Morae* | units | count | | |

**G. YHWH Is Bringing Complete Destruction—A Full End (1:9–10)** [4.9]

| | Morae | units | count | | |
|---|---|---|---|---|---|
| ¹⁹מ Whatever you (f. pl.) devise / against YHWH / | _11 2_ | | 4 | 4 | 0 |
| 1:6–9a | | | **34** | 22 | 12 |
| **A full end** (*kālāh*) / he himself is making // | 9 2 | | 3 | 3 | 0 |
| 1:7–9a | | | **23** | 17 | 6 |
| ל Distress / will not arise a second time // | _14 2_ | | 4 | 0 | 4 |
| 1:7–9 | | | 27 | 17 | 10 |
| 1:10 For / while like thorns matted together / | _12 2_ | | 4 | 4 | 0 |
| 1:1–10a | | | **04** | 58 | 46 |
| And *in* a drunken state / soaked with "drink" // | _11 2_ | | 2 | 2 | 0 |
| 1:1b–10b | | | **04** | 58 | 46 |
| א Devoured they will be / like dry stubble / **completely** // | _14 3_ | | 4 | 0 | 4 |
| 1:7–10 | | | 37 | **23** | 14 |
| 1:1–10 | | | [110] | 60 | 50 |

## Scansion of the "Bent" Acrostic Psalm of Nahum (1:1–10)

| | | SAS | Word |
|---|---|---|---|
| | *Morae* | units | count |
| 1:1 *maśśāʾ / nînəwēh* ^ | 8 2 | | 2 = 2 + 0 |
| *sēp̄er ḥăzôn / naḥûm / hāʾelqōšî* : | 16 3 | | 4 = 0 + 4 |
| 1:2 *ʾēl qannôʾ / wənōqēm YHWH /* | 14 2 | | 4 = 4 + 0 |
| *nōqēm YHWH / ûḇaʿal ḥēmāh* ^ | 16 2 | | 4 = 4 + 0 |
| *nōqēm yhwh / ləṣārāyw /* | 13 2 | | 3 = 0 + 3 |
| *wənôṭēr hûʾ / ləʾōyəḇāyw* : | 13 2 | | 3 = 0 + 3 |
| 1:3 *YHWH / ʾerek ʾappáyim / ûḡəḏol-kôaḥ /* | 16 3 | | 5 = 5 + 0 |
| *wənaqqēh / lôʾ yənaqqéh* ^ | _ 9 2_ | | 3 = 3 + 0 |
| *YHWH /* | 4 1 | | 1 = 0 + 1 |
| *bəsûp̄āh ûḇiśʿārāh / darkô /* | 15 2 | | 3 = 0 + 3 |
| *wəʿānān / ʾăḇaq raḡláyw* : | 10 2 | | 3 = 0 + 3 |
| 1:4 *gôʿēr bayyām / wayyabḇəšēhû /* | 14 2 | | 3 = 3 + 0 |
| *wəkol-hannəhārôṯ / heḥĕrîḇ* ^ | _12 2_ | | 3 = 3 + 0 |
| *ʾuml<əlû>ᵇ bāšān / wəkarmél /* | 11 2 | | 3 = 0 + 3 |
| *ûp̄ēraḥ ləḇānôn / ʾumlál* : | _12 2_ | | 3 = 0 + 3 |
| 1:5 *hārîm / rāʿăšû mimménnû /* | 13 2 | | 3 = 3 + 0 |
| *wəhaggubāʿôṯ / hiṯmōḡāḡû* ^ | _14 2_ | | 2 = 2 + 0 |

|  | Morae | SAS units | Word count |
|---|---|---|---|
| *wattiśśáʾ hāʾāreṣ / mippānāyw /* | 14 | 2 | 3 = 0 + 3 |
| *wǝtēḇēl / wǝkol-yōšǝḇê ḇáh* : | 14 | 2 | 4 = 0 + 4 |
| 1:6 *lip̄nê zaʿmô / mî yaʿămôḏ /* | 12 | 2 | 4 = 4 + 0 |
| *ûmî yāqûm / bahărôn ʾappô* ^ | 15 | 2 | 4 = 4 + 0 |
| *ḥămāṯô / nittǝkāh ḵāʾēš /* | 13 | 2 | 3 = 0 + 3 |
| *wǝhaṣṣūrîm / nittǝṣû mimménnû* : | 14 | 2 | 3 = 0 + 3 |
| 1:7 *ṭôḇ YHWH /* | 6 | 1 | 2 = 2 + 0 |
| *lǝmāʿôz / bǝyôm ṣārāh* ^ | 12 | 2 | 3 = 3 + 0 |
| *wǝyōḏēaʿ / ḥôsê ḇô* : | 12 | 2 | 3 = 0 + 3 |
| 1:8 *ûḇǝšeṭep̄ ʿōḇēr /* | 7 | 1 | 2 = 2 + 0 |
| *kālāh / yaʿăśeh mǝqômāh* ^ | 12 | 2 | 3 = 3 + 0 |
| *wǝʾōyǝḇāyw / yǝraddep̄-ḥōšek* : | 12 | 2 | 3 = 0 + 3 |
| 1:9 *mah-tǝḥaššǝḇûn / ʾel-YHWH /* | 11 | 2 | 4 = 4 + 0 |
| *kāláh / hûʾ ʿōśeh* ^ | 9 | 2 | 3 = 3 + 0 |
| *lōʾ-ṯāqûm paʿămáyim / ṣārāh* : | 14 | 2 | 4 = 0 + 4 |
| 1:10 *kî /ʿaḏ-sîrîm sǝḇûkîm /* | 12 | 2 | 4 = 4 + 4 |
| *ûḵǝsāḇǝʾ ām / sǝḇûʾîm* ^ | 11 | 2 | 2 = 2 + 2 |
| *ʾukkelû / kǝqáš yāḇēš / mālēʾ* : | 14 | 3 | 4 = 0 + 4 |
| 1:1–10 |  |  | 110 = 60 + 50 |

## NOTES

a–a The marginal *qǝrēʾ*, reading *ûḡǝḏol-kōaḥ* ("and great in power" —7 morae), is read in place of *wǝḡāḏôl kōaḥ* (8 morae) in 1:3a, which reduces the letter count by one.

b The verb *ʾumlal* in 1:4b is emended to read *ʾumlǝlû* so as to agree with the plural subject and to improve the balance in terms of mora count.

SAS units:

$$[(9 + 4) + (5 + 5)] + [(4 + 4) + (4 + 4) + (4 + 4)] + [(5 + 5) + (4 + 9)] = 70$$
$$[13 + 10] + [8 + 8 + 8] + [10 + 13] = 23 + 24 + 23 = 70 \text{ SAS units}$$

Meaningful center: eight words on either side of the arithmological center:

| 5 | *hārîm rāʿăšû mimmennû* | Mountains quake before him; |
|---|---|---|
|  | *wǝhaggǝḇāʿôṯ hiṯmōḡāḡû* | and the hills melt away. |
|  | *wattiśśáʾ hāʾāreṣ mippānāyw* | And the earth reels before him; |
|  | *wǝtēḇēl wǝkol-yōšǝḇê ḇāh* | and the world and all who dwell in it. |
| 6 | *lip̄nê zaʿmô mî yaʿămôḏ* | In the presence of his fury who can stand? |

Strophic units as shown by balance in mora count:

| – | 1:1a | first title (2 words) | stands outside the prosodic structure of the poem | | |
|---|------|------------------------|---------------------------------------------------|---|---|
| A | 1:1b–2 | balanced triad | [16 + 14 + (8 + 8)] | = | 16 + 14 + 16 morae |
| B | 1:3 | 2 balanced dyads + pivot | [16 + 9] + 4 + [15 + 10] | = | 25 + 4 + 25  morae |
| C | 1:4 | 2 balanced dyads | [14 + 12] + [12 + 13] | = | 26 + 25      morae |
| D | 1:5 | 2 balanced dyads | [14 + 14] + [14 + 14] | = | 28 + 28      morae |
| E | 1:6 | 2 balanced dyads | [12 + 15] + [13 + 14] | = | 27 + 27      morae |
| F | 1:7–8 | 2 balanced dyads | [18 + 12] + [19 + 12] | = | 30 + 31      morae |
| G | 1:9–10 | balanced dyad | [11 + 9] | = | 11 + 9       morae |
|   |        | 2 balanced dyads | [14 + 12] + [11 + 14] | = | 26 + 25      morae |

Word count:

| 1:1–3 | 17 | words after ʾaṭnaḥ |
|-------|-----|--------------------|
| 1:1–4 | 23 | words after ʾaṭnaḥ |
| 1:2–5 | 26 | words after ʾaṭnaḥ |
| 1:5–6 | 26 | words |
| 1:5–7 | 34 | (= 17 × 2) words |
| 1:3–8 | 69 | (= 23 × 3) words |
| 1:7–9 | 17 | words before ʾaṭnaḥ |
| 1:7–10 | 23 | words before ʾaṭnaḥ |

## INTRODUCTION

The seven strophes in Nahum 1:1–10 may be outlined in a menorah pattern, which is determined primarily on prosodic grounds, as follows:

### Canto 1: "Bent" Acrostic Psalm of Nahum on Yʜwʜ's Vengeance (1:1–10)

| A | Yʜwʜ takes vengeance against his foes: he is *baʿal* of wrath | [8.4] | 1:1–2 |
|---|----------------------------------------------------------------|-------|-------|
| B | Yʜwʜ is slow to anger but great in power | [5.5] | 1:3 |
| C | Yʜwʜ acts with cosmic consequences | [4.4] | 1:4 |
| X | **The earth and its inhabitants reel before Yʜwʜ** | [4.4] | 1:5 |
| C′ | No one can endure Yʜwʜ's wrath | [4.4] | 1:6 |
| B′ | Yʜwʜ is good and a refuge in the day of distress | [5.5] | 1:7–8 |
| A′ | Yʜwʜ will bring complete destruction—"a *full end* (*kālāh*)" | [4.8] | 1:9–10 |

In terms of the distribution of SAS units in Nahum 1:1–10, the seven strophes are arranged in perfect symmetry with v 5 in the center:

$$[8 + 4] + [5 + 5] + [4 + 4] + 4 + 4 + [4 + 4] + [5 + 5] + [4 + 8]$$

The numbers in the previous outline, which appear in an inverse symmetrical pattern, represent the distribution of SAS units as indicated in the Masoretic accentual system. Vv 1–2 [8 + 4 SAS units] are set over against vv 9–10 [4 + 8 SAS units], in which both sets of verses focus on the "negative side" of YHWH, namely on his zealous anger that leads to punishment. Vv 3 [5 + 5 SAS units] and 7–8 [5 + 5 SAS units] present the other side of YHWH, one who is "slow to anger" (cf. Exodus 34:6–7) and "a refuge in time of distress." There are only two places in the entire book of Nahum (other than in the meaning of the prophet's personal name, "Consolation") where we find this muted theme of the character of God as described in Exodus 34:6—namely, here in v 3 [4 + 4 SAS units] and again in vv 7–8 [5 + 5 SAS units]. Elsewhere the book focuses attention sharply on God's justice and the theme of judgment, as reflected in Exodus 34:7.

Bliese (1995) considers 1:2–11 as the proper prosodic unit here. His analysis has v 6a, with its rhetorical questions and inverted parallelism, as the central peak. Chiastic balance is defined metrically by the length of paired lines on each side of the peak. Bliese allows some differences from MT hyphenation. When his methodology of metrical chiasm is applied to 1:1–10, based on the distribution of word stresses (that is, counting accents), no such symmetry is found. Instead we have the following: [6 + 8 + 6] + [7 + 7] + [5 + 6] + 5 + 6 + [8 + 6] + [8 + 7] + [8 + 9].

The scansion requires the inclusion of the heading (1:1) in the structure of 1:1–10 as a whole; and the presence of the telestich, which spells out the divine name YHWH using the final letters of four successive lines in the first three verses, confirms this observation. It is important to observe the role of word count in determining the prosodic structure of this text. The primary compositional numbers are **17**, **23**, **26**, and **32** (see "Logoprosodic Analysis and the Book of Nahum" earlier). These numbers, or multiples of them, are used to mark the boundaries of prosodic subunits except for the opening strophe in 1:1–2, where the word-count totals are too small. And here the word count appears to be contrived in a manner that ties the beginning of Nahum to the ending of Micah—much the same as each psalm in the Psalter is tied to the preceding psalm in carefully contrived totals in terms of cumulative word count (see the psalm files at www.bibal.net).

The examples cited here represent but a sampling of numerous ways in which the four compositional numbers **17**, **23**, **26**, and **32** are woven into the fabric of this text (see Labuschagne 2000: 88–92). This phenomenon in "numerology" is a scribal adaptation from the ancient science of harmonics, which was widely known in antiquity throughout the Middle East (see McClain 1976, 1978, 2005; Crickmore 2003). Harmonics, which was the theoretical underpinning of the tuning of musical instruments in antiquity, can be traced back to ancient Sumer at least as early as ca. 2650 BCE (McClain 2004). As Crickmore (2003: 391) puts it: "Harmonics probably emerged amongst our stone-age ancestors, matured in ancient India, Babylon and Egypt, and flourished in Greece, which is the source of our earliest surviving records of it." In antiquity it was widely believed that the planets circle the heavens in mathematical proportions similar to those of the musical scale and to corresponding geometric structures, and that by analogy this also corresponds to powers in the human psyche. The early science of harmonics survived until the seventeenth century CE. Only recently, however, have musicologists made a breakthrough to a more comprehensive understanding of its coherence and cultural significance. The science of harmonics applies to the fields of geometry, philosophy, and music—and to cosmology and mythology in general. In ancient Near Eastern culture, the world of musical harmonics and mythology were one and the same. Scribes in ancient Israel were exposed to the Babylonian understanding of harmonics in matters of cosmology, and they apparently adapted that protoscience to their own purposes in the system for the numerical composition of sacred Scripture.

There are seven prosodic subunits (that is, strophes) in the first canto (1:1–10) of Nahum, which are carefully contrived in terms of balance in mora count except for the first two words in v 1, which stand outside the prosodic structure of the poem itself in terms of balance in mora count. The strophic structure of 1:1–10 is closely related to the prosodic boundaries within these subunits, as revealed by the dyadic and occasional triadic parallelism.

The final letters in the first four lines of the book of Nahum (vv 1, 2a, 2b, and 3a) are *yod* / *he'* / *waw* / *he'*, which spell out the name YHWH in a telestich, which was first observed by Labuschagne (see Spronk 1997: 25, n. 8). The telestich pattern is found in four successive half-lines (vv 1b–3a), which include a total of **26** words, the sum of the four letters in question ([*yod* = 10] + [*he'* = 5] + [*waw* = 6] + [*he'* = 5] = **26**). The name YHWH appears explicitly seven times in the opening canto: in vv 2 (3 times), 3 (twice), 7, and 9. The telestich in vv 1–3a constitutes the eighth occurrence, and all eight appear in the two outermost frames in the previously illustrated menorah pattern, with a particular high density in vv 2–3. These same two verses include the opening sentence acrostic, the statement "I am YHWH."

My second study of the "bent" acrostic hymn of theophany in Nahum 1 (Christensen 1987a), which emerged in conjunction with the publication of my brief commentary on Nahum in *Harper's Bible Commentary* (Christensen 1988a), was an attempt to move beyond the impasse in methodology between those who champion "syllabic theory" and those who prefer the older "accentual theory" of Ley-Sievers by modifying and combining both approaches in light of the concept of mora-counting and SAS units as described by the Polish linguist Kurylowicz (1973). That earlier form of prosodic analysis is combined here with Labuschagne's method of logotechnical analysis (focusing on word count) to form what I now call logoprosodic analysis (see www.bibal.net), in which three variables are counted: morae, words, and SAS units—and word count is further divided into the categories of words before and words after ʾaṭnaḥ (the major verse divider among the ṭaʿamîm).

Meanwhile, another discovery emerged at the University of Groningen, which culminated in an article by van der Woude (1977a), which in some ways picks up on the observation of Arnold, who long before recognized that an original acrostic pattern was "bent" to new ends in Nahum 1 (cf. Arnold 1901). The big difference, however, is in the level of sophistication achieved by the author-composer, for van der Woude and Labuschagne have found here a coded message that would have been known only to the author himself and to those who were privy to his hidden intent. Noting the irregularities in the presumed acrostic in 1:2–8, van der Woude (1977a: 123) says: "When one accepts (one) small change of the text, it turns out that the first letters of each line together with *lpny* in verse 6a constitute a sentence: *ʾny gʾh wlpny ḥty*, 'I am the Exalted One and confronting them who commit sin against me.'" He continues: "If the letters of the individual lines are chosen deliberately, it follows also that they are a literary composition from the outset, since the peculiarity of the text would remain unnoticed if spoken publicly. Meanwhile, the initial letters summarize in a condensed way the basic preaching of Nahum's writing." In short, van der Woude (1977a: 108–26) argues that it is better to read the Hebrew text as received and to see here a deliberate modification of the underlying acrostic poem to produce the cipher:

> *ʾny* Yhwh *gʾh welipnê ḥṭ(ʾ)* / *ûbešeṭep ʿōḇēr kālāh mālēʾ*
> I, Yhwh, am exalted and (I am) in the presence of sin;
>    and in an overflowing torrent (I am) bringing a full end—completely.

The only thing van der Woude and Labuschagne did not see is the fact that the hidden message apparently continues throughout the whole of 1:2–10 and picks up again for its conclusion in the enigmatic structural center of the book of Nahum, in 2:11 [10]. The cipher in 1:2–8, when combined with vv 9–11, presents a reiteration of the central message of the book of Nahum itself, as follows:

| | |
|---|---|
| *ʾny yhwh gʾh wliḇnê ḥṭ* | I, Yhwh, am exalted and (I am) in the presence of sin; |
| *wbšṭp ʿḇr kālāh* | and in a sweeping torrent (is) a full end. |
| *mah-təḥašḇûn ʾel-yhwh* | What will you devise against Yhwh? |
| *kālāh hûʾ ʿēśeh* | A full end he himself will make. |

| | |
|---|---|
| *lō<sup>ʾ</sup>-ṭāqûm paʿămayim ṣārāh* | Distress will not come a second time; |
| *kî ʿad-sîrîm səḇūḵîm* | for while (they are) as thorns matted together, |
| *ûḵəsāḇəʾām səḇûʾîm* | and like (their) drunkenness soaked with "drink"— |
| *ʾukkəlû* | They are consumed, |
| *kəqaš yāḇēš mālēʾ* | like dry stubble, completely! |

The key word, *mālēʾ* ("completely"), which appears as the final word in v 10, also appears as a word acrostic in vv 9–10 to complete the cipher in the first line; for YHWH is about to bring a *full end—completely—*to the city of Nineveh.

The first two strophes (vv 1–3) include the statement "I am YHWH" in an acrostic pattern at the beginning of the second through the fifth versets, and the name YHWH in a telestich at the end of the first four versets. Moreover, the first half of v 3 (that is, the fourth verset) begins with *yod* and ends with *he'*, which constitutes the normal abbreviation for the divine name YH(WH), or "Yah." This final *he'* also concludes the telestich of the name YHWH in vv 1–3a. The concluding two strophes (vv 7–10) include the bulk of the hidden re-iteration of the central message of the book, starting with v 8 and the words "in the sweeping torrent," which stand immediately before the *kaph* word that completes the first half of the alphabet. The coded message in the "bent" acrostic then becomes the focus of attention in the concluding word acrostic on *mālēʾ* ("completely"), with which the canto ends. The placement of the *aleph* line at the very end appears to have been determined by the poet's desire to code the numerical value of the name *Nahum* twice at this climactic point in the structure (see the later discussion of 1:10).

As discussed in detail in the section of the introduction headed "The Interpretation of Nahum in History," the matter of the presumed alphabetic acrostic in Nahum 1 has dominated scholarly discussion for the past century. Though the attempt on the part of Floyd (1994) to lay the matter to rest has attracted some following (see Weigl 2001: 85–86; O'Brien 2002: 47), the problem itself is not likely to fade away, for Gunkel's attempt to reconstruct a complete alphabetic acrostic continues to exert its influence. Recently, Krieg (1988: 518–19) made an attempt to revive Gunkel's work with some modifications. Earlier attempts along this line were made by Nowack (1897); Berlin (1901: 681–82); Happel (1902); Kennedy (1902: 475); Van Hoonacker (1908: 418–32); Davis (1911); Richter (1914: 120–29); Alonso Schökel (1980: 1081–82), at least in part; Holland (1986: 26); and others. All this, in spite of Wellhausen's convincing arguments in 1898 (159) that one should not look for more than the sequence from *aleph* to *kaph* in Nahum 1:2–8 (so also Löhr

1905: 174–75; Kleinert 1910: 525–6; Cannon 1925, 9/4: 104–5; Humbert 1926: 267; Graham 1927–28: 43; Christensen 1975a, 1975b; and others). Various attempts to trace the alphabetic pattern beyond the letter *kaph* have been made, ending with the following:

| | |
|---|---|
| *mem:* | Gray (1898); Fohrer (1968: 449); Van Wyk (1971: 231); Spronk (1995a: 183–84). |
| *samek:* | Marti (1903); Haupt (1907b: 278–79; 1907c: 8–9); J. M. P. Smith (1911: 296); Horst (1938: 156); *BH²* (1905) and *BH³* (1937); Lipiński (1971: 794); Alonso Schökel (1980: 1078–79); Seybold (1989b: 75). |
| *'ayin:* | Duhm (1911: 100–101); Edelkoort (1937: 18–19); Dhorme (1956: 794). |
| *qoph:* | Sievers (1901); Brockington (1973: 257–58). |

From the beginning, theories about an alphabetic acrostic in Nahum 1 encountered opposition because of the many proposed emendations of the Hebrew text. One response to such criticism was to propose the theory that an existing alphabetic acrostic poem was "bent" to new purposes by the author and/or redactor of the book of Nahum. In some respects, this idea was proposed as early as 1901 by Arnold, who suggested that a redactor cited the poem from memory, forgetting or confusing some lines. The idea of a "bent" acrostic was taken up in different ways by Kleinert (1910: 525–26); Cannon (1925, 9/4: 109–10); Jeremias (1970: 16–19); van der Woude (1977a); Christensen (1987a); Seybold (1989b: 81–82); and Nogalski (1993a), among others.

A telestich pattern in which the divine name YHWH is spelled out with the final letters of the first four lines of the poem was first observed by Labuschagne and published by Spronk (1997: 25; 1998); this has added a welcome new dimension to the picture, along with the acrostic of the personal pronoun *ʾny* ("I") at the beginning of the same lines used to spell the divine name YHWH in the telestich pattern. This observation is expanded here to include a similar acrostic on the word *mlʾ* ("completely") at the end of the hymn in vv 9–10 (see following discussion). Though there are traces of a true alphabetic acrostic in Nahum 1, that pattern was apparently "bent" to achieve a level of sophistication in design that matches the intricacy of the numerical composition of the text, which is explored in detail in this commentary. The scribal craftsmanship displayed in the book of Nahum is a tour de force, unsurpassed elsewhere in the whole of the Tanakh (Hebrew Bible).

## NOTES

1:2. *A zealous and avenging God (ʾEl) is YHWH.* Though the KJV reads this line as two parallel clauses, "God is jealous, and the LORD revengeth" (as does the LXX), the two verbal forms are joined with the conjunctive accent *məhuppak̲*, which confirms the decision on the part of Cathcart (1973a: 29), Roberts (1991: 42), Longman (1993: 787), and Spronk (1997: 19), as well as the NRSV, NIV, JPS Tanakh, and others to see here a single clause with Yʜᴡʜ as the subject. The Hebrew word *ʾēl* ("God") frequently occurs with adjectives to express attributes of God—"a great God" (Deuteronomy 7:21; cf. Nehemiah 9:31, "gracious and merciful God"); "living God" (Hosea 2:1 [1:10]); and "a gracious God" (Jonah 4:2). It is also the name of the Canaanite deity El. Cathcart (1973a: 40) argues that there is conscious allusion to the Canaanite gods "El" and "Baal" here, for Yʜᴡʜ is also described as a "lord (*Baʿal*) of wrath" (see also Tournay 1958: 330 and cf. Gray 1956: 280; 1961: 16–17). Coggins (1985: 21) goes even further in translating the three successive phrases as "jealous El, avenging Yahweh, angry Baal." He argues that we have here "a deliberate dramatic device" in which "the two great Canaanite deities, El and Baal, are used as alternative designations of Yahweh."

The word *qannôʾ* ("jealous, zealous") occurs only twice in the Tanakh, here and in Joshua 24:19. Spronk (1997: 28) observes, however, that the adjective *qāšāh* ("severe, vehement, intense") modifies the noun *qinʾāh* ("jealousy, zeal") in Song of Songs 8:6 ("jealousy is as severe as Sheol"). He concludes that the words *ʾelqōšî* ("Elkoshite") and *ʾēl qannôʾ* ("a jealous God") are in fact "a parallel pair" (cf. Allis 1955: 76 and Longman 1993: 766). At the same time, the verbal root from which Nahum's name is derived, *nḥm* ("be sorry, console, have compassion"), and the root *nqm* ("avenge") are linked in a somewhat similar manner in Isaiah 1:24 and 61:2 to form another parallel pair in Hebrew poetry. The same is true for the words *ḥēmāh* ("wrath") in v 2a and *ʾappayim* ("anger") in v 3a, and also for the words *nōqēm* ("avenging") and *ʾerek̲ ʾappayim* ("slow to anger"), as shown by parallel usage in Jeremiah 15:15.

Each word in the opening verses of the book of Nahum is carefully selected with nuances that defy easy translation in English. The threefold repetition of the word *nōqēm* ("avenging") is easy to convey, but the alliteration with the word *qannôʾ* ("zealous") is difficult to capture (see Alonso Schökel 1980). The phrase *ʾēl qannôʾ* ("a jealous God") also appears in Joshua 24:19, and it appears in modified form as *ʾēl qannāʾ* ("a jealous God") in Exodus 20:5, 34:14; Deuteronomy 4:24, 5:9, 6:15. As de Moor (1990: 227–29) and Rendtorff (1994: 7–10) have shown, this phrase appears only in conjunction with the use of the name Yʜᴡʜ, whose jealousy is an essential aspect of his covenant with Israel (Fensham 1969: 14–15), for the divine suzerain tolerates no rivals. As Spronk notes (1997: 34), Nahum 1:2 is the only place where Yʜᴡʜ's jealousy "is indicated as the root of his anger against the enemies of Israel" (see also Renaud 1963: 112–18, 148, and Reuter 2004: 53–55). Spronk traces the development of this change in reference to include the enemies of Israel in Psalm 79:5–6 and especially in Isaiah 59:17–18.

The Hebrew root *nqm* ("to avenge, take vengeance") takes on a specialized meaning with YHWH as its subject and should not be construed as involving malicious retaliation for inflicted wrongs. YHWH is depicted as a ruler who demands exclusive devotion from his subjects, for he is utterly intolerant of rivals (Lipiński 1999: 8–9). The threefold occurrence of the phrase *nōqēm yhwh* ("avenging is YHWH") has attracted the attention of exegetes through the centuries. Rashi (d. 1105) saw a reflection of the threefold vengeance of YHWH: in the beginning of Israel's history, in the prophet's own time, and in the future, when Israel was to be deported to Babylon. Abarbanel (d. 1508) saw an allusion to the three times that Assyria had invaded and devastated Israel. Gebhardi (1737), Michaelis (1782), and Pusey (1860) found here an allusion to the three persons of the Trinity (see Strauss 1853: 9–10; J. M. P. Smith 1911: 297). Kalinski (1748: 230–33) used this reference in support of his theory that Nineveh was destroyed by YHWH twice after a first act of revenge when YHWH broke the Assyrian siege of Jerusalem (2 Kings 19; this reference is taken from Spronk 1997: 34, n. 18). Spronk (1997: 34) compares the repetition here to the threefold use of "holy is He, YHWH" in Isaiah 6:3 and Psalm 99:3, 5, and 9 (cf. Stade 1906: 124–28).

*Avenging is YHWH and a lord (Baʿal) of wrath.* The dyad in the first half of v 2 presents a striking example of chiastic structure. The eight words are arranged in four pairs in an a:b::b:a pattern, with total repetition at the center. The opening two words, *ʾel qannôʾ* ("a God [ʾEl] of jealousy"), are set over against the final two words, *ûbaʿal ḥēmāh* ("a lord [Baʿal] of wrath"). The words *qinʾāh* ("jealousy") and *ḥēmāh* appear in numerous other texts (Deuteronomy 6:15; Ezekiel 5:13; 16:38, 42; 23:25; 36:6; Zechariah 8:2; Proverb 27:4). Both of these words appear together with the root *nqm* in Isaiah 59:17 and Proverb 6:34. According to Longman 1993: 88), the use of the phrase *baʿal ḥēmāh* ("lord of wrath") is similar to the use in Akkadian of the word *bēlu*, which appears in compound phrases with a variety of words (*agê*, *kakki*, and so on) to signify "holder of, responsible for, entitled to" (*CAD* II [B] 198b). De Moor (1975: 181–82) says that the Akkadian word *bēl* signifies "owner of"; in more idiomatic expressions it is used to describe an activity or characteristic. Like jealousy or zeal, "wrath" (*ḥēmāh*) denotes intense and passionate feelings that constitute a divine characteristic a human being faces when the terms of a covenant relationship are violated (Schunck 1980: 464–65). With an abstract noun, the word *baʿal* expresses attribution, describing the one who possesses the object or quality named by the noun—with the word *ḥēmāh* ("wrath"), a possessor of wrath (GKC §128 u; *IBHS* §9.5.3.b).

In light of the use here of the word *ʾēl* ("God, El"), and the apparent literary allusions to the Canaanite deities Sea (*Yam*) and Rivers (*Nǝhārôt*) in v 4, it is likely that the author is making at least a subliminal allusion to the proper noun *Baʿal* here (Becking 1995a: 287; Spronk 1997: 35). Becking (1993: 15) suggests that the use of the words *ʾēl* and *baʿal* here reminds the reader that only Yʜᴡʜ is to be regarded as God and Lord. At the same time, as Roberts shows (1991: 43), the description of Yʜᴡʜ's anger here has no necessary connection with any Canaanite deity as such, for we are dealing with a common idiom. The phrase *baʿal ḥēmāh* ("lord of wrath") appears in Proverb 29:22 in poetic parallelism with the phrase *ʾîš ʾap̄* ("a man of anger"), and Roberts cites other synonymous expressions as well. It is important to remember that Yʜᴡʜ's wrath is not arbitrary but rather provoked by his adversaries (Becking 1993: 15–17; 1995a: 288; Spronk 1997: 35). The noun "lord" (*baʿal*) in this construction describes a person's outstanding characteristic or attribute (cf. Genesis 37:19; 1 Samuel 28:7; 2 Kings 1:8; Proverbs 1:17; 18:9; 22:24; 23:2; 24:8; Ecclesiastes 7:12; 8:8; 10:11, 20; Isaiah 41:15; 50:8; Daniel 8:6, 20; see *IBHS* §9.5.3.b). As Spronk notes (1997: 34), parallel usage in the book of Proverbs does not indicate that being a "possessor of wrath" has anything to do with self-control as such: "It simply means that Yʜᴡʜ can become angry."

Baʿal is the epithet of the Canaanite deity Hadad. Though Tournay (1958) was careful not to draw any firm conclusions about the juxtaposition of the names "El" and "Baal" here, it is important to note the similarity between the portrayal of Yʜᴡʜ in these verses and that of the Canaanite storm god Baʿal. The parallel is so close that Gray (1956: 280; 1961: 16–17) and Gaster (1966: 143; 1969: 662–63) regarded the hymn here as basically a Canaanite poem of Baʿal. Miller (1967: 428–31) maintained that Baʿal and Yʜᴡʜ shared common characteristics, and Ringgren (1966: 42, n. 6) identified *baʿal bǝrît* (Judges 8:33) with *ʾēl bǝrît* (Judges 9:46; see also Clements 1968: 21–32).

*Avenging is Yʜᴡʜ against his foes; and he rages against his enemies.* Spronk (1997: 35) observes that the verb *nṭr* ("to rage") appears without a preposition in Leviticus 19:18 together with the verb *nqm* ("to avenge"), which curiously ends with the same words (*ʾny yhwh* ["I am Yʜᴡʜ"]) that are found in the acrostic of vv 1–3. There are two meanings of the root *nṭr* in the Tanakh: "to preserve, keep, guard" and "to be angry" (Madl 1998: 404–5). Some scholars have posited the existence of an Akkadian cognate *nādaru* ("to rage"), which refers to a violently raging or seething anger (Roberts 1991: 43; so also G. R. Driver 1931: 361–63; Thomas 1938: 394; M. Held 1969: 73, n. 19; 1971: 46–55; Cathcart 1973a: 42–44). Though Longman (1993: 788) insists that the Akkadian letter *d* does not normally correspond to Hebrew *ṭ*, he nonetheless still finds the same meaning here, which he explains as "a contextually determined extension" of the primary meaning of the root (788–89). Von Soden (1986: 412–14) argues that there are two different roots to deal with, the one related to *nṣr* ("to be angry") and the other to the root *wṭr* (cf. Arabic *waṭar* ["to aim, purpose"]; reference from Spronk 1997: 36). Spronk (1997: 36) resolves the problem by finding here a sort of "dialectical pun" on the expression *nṣr ḥsd l* ("maintaining grace to") in Exodus 34:7. The poet used the same expression (with the preposition *l*), but he changed *nṣr* into *nṭr* because of the standard word pairing with *nqm*. The pronoun *hûᵓ* ("he") here is a direct reference to Yʜᴡʜ, as the poetic parallelism demonstrates.

The long-term anger expressed in the term *nôṭēr* (1:2b) functions as a bridge of sorts to the following statement that Yʜᴡʜ "is slow to anger." Though he exercises great patience, he will in due course burst forth to express the full fury of his wrath. The word pair *ləṣārāyw* ("his foes") and *ləᵓōyəbāyw* ("his enemies") occurs in Ugaritic poetry as well as the Tanakh, though as Longman (1993: 789) notes, the order is normally the reverse of what we find here. The LXX translation ἐξαίρον ("he lifts up, takes away") for the Hebrew word *nôṭēr* is a rather loose translation, or perhaps the translators were reading the Hebrew word *nôṭēl*, as Roberts suggests (1991: 43).

1:3. *(As for) Yʜᴡʜ, he is slow to anger but great in power.* In the Old Testament, words for anger are connected with God three times as often as they are with human beings, and some words (*ᵓānap* and *ḥārôn*) are used exclusively with God as subject (Johnson and Bergman 1974: 356). Longman (1993: 789) observes that all other occurrences of the phrase *gədol-kōaḥ* ("great in power") extol God's grace. Here the context is that of divine justice and judgment. The article here has adversative force: "*but* of great power." In his note in *BHS*, Elliger (1970) suggested that the word *ḥesed* ("covenant-love") be read in place of the word *kōaḥ* ("power") (as did Gunkel 1893; J. M. P. Smith 1911; Nowack 1922; Guthe 1923; and others), but there is no textual support whatsoever for this proposed change. Our task is to explain what the poet has written, not to rewrite the poem in the light of our own presuppositions about it. The same judgment applies to those who choose to regard the text here as a later addition, which disturbs the acrostic pattern and introduces the theme of the delay of Yʜᴡʜ's vengeance (Nogalski 1993c: 199–200; van Leeuwen 1993: 47–48).

*And the guilty he does not acquit.* Most recent English translations emend the MT by relocating the *ᵓaṭnaḥ* so as to make the divine name Yʜᴡʜ the subject of this clause. Though the LXX reads the text in this manner, the other ancient versions (the Syriac, Vulgate, and Targum) do not. Evidence from the logoprosodic analysis supports the MT as it stands without emendation. The name Yʜᴡʜ has the accent *rəbîaᶜ*, which is a relatively strong disjunctive that adds further emphasis to its function as the subject of the clause it introduces in the second half of this verse. As Spronk observes (1997: 36), the name YHWH here functions as a *casus pendens* (a grammatical element isolated outside a clause) exactly the same as does the occurrence of the same word with the same accent at the beginning of v 3. In both instances the word is followed by two successive words beginning with the same letter of the alphabet—first *aleph*, then *beth*:

YHWH—*ʾereḵ ʾappayim* ("YHWH, who is slow in anger")
YHWH—*bəsûp̄āh ûḇiśʿārāh* ("YHWH, who is in the whirlwind and in the storm")

The root *nqh* ("to acquit") is repeated twice for emphasis (see GKC §75.hh; *IBHS* §35.3.1). The words "the guilty" are not in the Hebrew text, but they are implied when the idiom is used (cf. Exodus 34:7; Numbers 14:18).

Haldar (1947: 18) interpreted the particle *lōʾ* here as a misunderstood emphatic lamed and finds support in the parallel text in Jeremiah 4:27, where Soggin (1965: 59) also read *lōʾ* as an emphatic lamed. Nonetheless, the negative particle *lōʾ* makes good sense here, especially in view of similar usage in Exodus 34:7 and Numbers 14:18. The phrase *wənaqqēh lōʾ yənaqqeh* ("and he will not leave the guilty unpunished") presents the Piel infinite absolute with the finite verb expressing emphasis (GKC §113 l). Goldman (1954–55: 52) suggested the translation "and will surely not wipe out" (cf. also Haldar 1947: 18). Longman (1993: 789) reads the inf. abs. with the finite verb to express emphasis and translates the passage "will assuredly not leave [the enemy] unpunished" (cf. Warmuth 1998: 556–57). Parallel use of the root *nqh* appears in Inscription B of the Cave inscriptions from Khirbet Beit Lei (seventh or sixth century BCE), which Cross (1970: 299–306) translates as follows:

*nqh yh ʾel ḥnn*   Absolve (us), O Merciful God!
*nqh yh yhwh*   Absolve (us), O Yahweh!

Sweeney (2000: 427–28) notes that vv 2–3a seem to emphasize words that begin with the letter *nun*, which is also the first letter of the names *Nineveh* and *Nahum*, and Cathcart (1973a: 47) calls attention to the fact that the consonants *n* and *q* are juxtaposed in vv 2–3a no fewer than six times. As Muilenburg (1953: 99) once put it: "Repetition serves to center the thought, to rescue it from disparateness and diffuseness, to focus the richness of varied prediction upon the poet's controlling concern. . . . Repetition serves too to give continuity to the writer's thought; the repeated word or phrase is often strategically located, thus providing a clue to the movement and stress of the poem" (reference taken from Cathcart 1973a: 47).

YHWH, *in the whirlwind and in the storm is his way; and clouds are the dust of his feet.* The image here is that of the Divine Warrior marching forth to battle (Exodus 15:1–12; Deuteronomy 33:2; Judges 5:4–5; Psalms 18:7–15; 68:4–10, 32–35; 77:16–19; Micah 1:3–4; Habakkuk 3:3–15). Many recent translations follow the editorial suggestion of Elliger (1970) in *BHS* and ignore the *ʾatnaḥ* in v 3 or relocate it (as do the NRSV, NIV, NASB, and JPS Tanakh, as well as Cathcart 1973a: 45; Roberts 1991: 42; Longman 1993: 787; and others). The translation presented here is similar to those of the KJV, the ASV, the older JPS Version, and the old Roman Catholic Douay Version, along with those of W. A. Maier (1959: 156), Spronk (1997: 36), and others, which read the MT as it stands without emendation. The statement "In the whirlwind and in the storm is his way" directs attention to the ancient tradition of YHWH's "Holy War," with the Divine Warrior marching in the vanguard of his hosts in battle (Exodus 15:1–12; Deuteronomy 33:2; Judges 5:4–5; Psalms 18:7–15; 68:4–10, 32–35; 77:16–19; Micah 1:3–4; Habakkuk 3:3–15; cf. Beyse 1999: 198). The word pair *sûpāh* ("destructive wind") and *śəʿārāh* ("gale") appears in Isaiah 29:6 and other contexts (see H. Lugt 1975). Allusions to the story of the Exodus from Egypt are present here, as noted by numerous commentators. Longman (1993: 789) calls attention to allusions to the Exodus story in v 4 and sees in v 3 "a reference to God's use of the wind to divide the Red Sea." The LXX apparently understood *sûpāh* ("whirlwind") to be the word *sûp*, meaning "end," in the translation ἐν συντελεια ("in the end / completion"; see Rudolph 1975: 151; Roberts 1991: 34). Harrison (1988: 67, n. 13) relates the word *bəsûpāh* to ἐν συσσεισμῷ.

The words *wəʿānān ʾăbaq raglāyw* ("and clouds are the dust of his feet") in v 3d should be compared with *waʾărāpel taḥat raglāyw* ("a storm-cloud under his feet") in Psalm 18:10 (cf. Psalm 97:2 and Exodus 19:9; on the word "cloud," see Freedman, Willoughby, and Fabry 2001: 254–55). Compare also the divine title *rōkēb baʿărābôt* ("Rider in the Clouds") in Psalms 68:5, 34; 104:3; cf. also Deuteronomy 33:26 and Isaiah 19:1 and the similar phrase in Ugaritic, *rkb ʿrpt* ("Rider of the Clouds"; cf. Korpel 1990: 601; Hermann 1999: 703–5). Numerous associations in Nahum 1:3–6 to the Canaanite god Baal have been noted (Spronk 1997: 39). We find Baal's battle with the god Yam ("Sea"), which makes reference to the "Highness Yam (sea) Judge Nahar (river)" (*KTU* 1.2.IV). Baal's voice makes the earth quake (*KTU* 1.4.VII: 30–33). When Baal was temporarily defeated by the god Mot ("death"), nature itself languished as Baal took his clouds, winds, thunderbolts, and rain with him into the Netherworld (*KTU* 1.5.V: 7–9). The reference to God's "feet" (*raglāyw*) is language typical of a theophany (cf. Psalm 18:10 [9]; Zechariah 14:4; Isaiah 60:13; see Stendebach 2004: 321).

In the Assyrian version of the Atrahasis epic, the Babylonian story of the flood, the storm god Adad is described as riding on the winds (see Lambert and Millard 1969: 123). Gaster (1969: 662–63) discussed parallels in Mesopotamian texts to Adad, Marduk, and Ninurta, but they are less clear than those in the Canaanite texts. We are dealing here with familiar imagery from the world of ancient Near Eastern cosmology.

1:4. *He blasts the Sea and he dries it up; and all the Rivers he desiccates.* On the word *gôʿēr*, Kennedy (1987: 59) argues persuasively for the meaning "to blast" rather than the weaker "to rebuke." The root has "strong connotations of forceful and destructive movement of air accompanied by loud, frightening noise." When the verb *gʿr* has an object, the object often takes the preposition *b*, as it does here, though van Zijl (1969: 61) showed that at times the verb takes the simple accusative. In the context of a military attack, the term reflects a battle cry intended to strike fear in the enemy so as to drive them away (cf. 2 Samuel 23:16; Psalms 18:15; 76:6; 80:17; 104:7). A parallel Ugaritic term is used when Baʿal utters a battle cry against Yam before the two gods fight it out to the death. The "sea" is personified as an antagonistic enemy representing the forces of chaos (Psalms 66:6; 72:8; 80:12; 89:26; 93:3–4; Isaiah 50:2; Micah 7:12; Habakkuk 3:8; Zechariah 9:10). The terms *Yam* (Sea) and *Nahar* (River) are frequently paired in both biblical poetry (Isaiah 48:18; 50:2; Psalms 24:2; 66; 72:8; 80:12; 89:26; 98:7–8; Habakkuk 3:8) and in Ugaritic poetry, where Prince Sea and Judge River appear as deities (*UT*, 68:16–20; 51:II:6–7; 68:12–30; 129:7–23; 137:22–44; *ʿnt*:III:36).

The verb *wayyabbašēhû* ("and he made it very dry") is a Piel intensive from the root *ybš* ("to dry up"). In this context, it follows a participle and is used as a predicate in present time, depicting characteristic (present-time) action or imminent future action (see *IBHS* §33.3.5.c). The pronominal suffix *-hû* is archaic in form. The fact that Yhwh dries up the rivers is part of a theophany of judgment (Preuss 1986: 377). The difference between the roots *ḥārab* ("dry") and *yābēš* ("become dry") is well illustrated in Genesis 8:13a and 14b, where *ḥārab* designates the process and *yābēš* the result (Speiser 1964: 53; Kaiser 1986a: 151). The verb *heḥĕrîb* ("he desiccates") is a Hiphil from the root *ḥrb* ("to dry up"). These two verbs often occur together in parallel, as do *yām* ("sea") and *nahār* ("river") in both Ugaritic texts and the Tanakh (Snijders et al. 1998: 264). Note that these latter two terms are also the names of Canaanite deities, like the allusions to the gods Baʿal and El in v 2. The two verbs in question here are both perfects, and some have translated them into English as past tense, seeing a reference here to mythological events (as did Gaster 1969: 663). The context, however, calls for the present tense. On the difficulties of translating verbal tenses in Hebrew poetry, see Craigie (1983: 110–13).

*Bashan and Carmel wither away; and the green of Lebanon withers.* In the Tanakh, the names *Bashan* and *Carmel* refer to places associated with luxurious fertility. Bashan is the fertile land east of the Sea of Galilee. Carmel is the promontory terminating the central mountain range in Israel, where the modern city of Haifa is located. Here *Lebanon* refers to a chain of mountains along the coast of ancient Syria that was famous for its cedar forests. Along with Lebanon, these places are cited as parts of the whole (a figure of speech known as synecdoche), for it is indeed the whole earth that is shaken by an angry God (Longman 1993: 790). On the *peraḥ* ("bloom") of Lebanon, compare Sirach 50:8 and the reference to the work of the high priest Simon, which is described as a "green shoot of Lebanon on a summer day" (Kapelrud 2003: 94). The devastation inflicted on the beauty of the mountains of Lebanon in this theophanic visitation is associated with an earthquake and other natural phenomena (Mulder 1995b: 454). Note the contest between Yhwh and Baʿal on Mount Carmel in the story of the prophet Elijah (1 Kings 18). Bashan, Carmel, and Lebanon are commonly associated with fertility so that their withering is a cosmic reversal in keeping with the theophanic images elsewhere in this poem (cf. Isaiah 19:5–7; see Mulder 2003: 335, 454).

Spronk (1997: 41) relates the reference to Bashan here to Isaiah 2:12–13 and the Day of Yhwh:

> Against all that is proud and lofty,
>     and against all that is lifted up and low;
> Against all the cedars of Lebanon, lofty and high,
>     against all the oaks of Bashan.

Spronk argues that this text had a direct influence on the words of Nahum. Nogalski (1993b: 108–9) finds a metaphor here to depict the political weakness of northern Israel caused by the Assyrians. For Spronk (1998: 41), the reference is to natural phenomena in a more general sense, and he calls attention to Isaiah 33:9, where the same imagery is taken up and expanded further (cf. Stahl 1992: 169–70).

The verb *ʾumlal* ("it withers, languishes") is a Pulal perfect from the root *ʾml*, an unusual verbal form. The same term appears in Isaiah 24:4, which describes the reaction of the earth to the coming of the Divine Warrior. When Yhwh makes war, natural forces and the earth itself collapse and crumble before him (Longman 1993: 790). Most critical scholars, including me at an earlier point (Christensen 1975b), have read *dālălû* here from the root *dll* ("to be low, languish"), though Rudolph (1975: 151) prefers the reading *dāʾēb,* with a similar meaning. This commonly accepted emendation is nothing but a scholarly guess based on the conviction that the *dālet* line in the presumed acrostic pattern must be restored. 4QpNah has *ʾmll* in both places (*DJD* II: 197), and so do all other extant textual witnesses. The ancient versions use two different verbal forms, but this proves nothing other than that these ancient translators felt the same pressure as modern ones to "correct" the text they had in their hands. And the fact that the verb *dālal* appears in a related context in Isaiah 19:6 proves nothing either, so far as the text here in Nahum 1:4 is concerned. An acrostic poem with such a *dālet* word was probably used as a primary source in writing the "bent" acrostic poem in question, but that source itself is no longer available to us and beyond any attempt on our part to reconstruct it with confidence. As Spronk observes (1997: 40, n. 29), even scholars who are not trying to reconstruct an alphabetic sequence propose emendations here to explain the different verbs in the versions. Buhl (1885: 181) suggested reading the root *ʾbl* ("to mourn"), which appears together with *ʾmll* in Isaiah 33:9 and Joel 1:10 (see also Goslinga 1923: 164). The repetition of the same verb at the beginning and the end of 1:4b was a deliberate move on the part of the author of this text, which may originally have been intended as a "glaring" marker to suggest that the hearer or reader needs to pause and take a closer look to see what is going on at a deeper level.

Logoprosodic analysis suggests that the initial use of the word *ʾumlal* ("it languishes") in v 4b should be emended to read *ʾumləlû* ("they languish"; cf. Jeremiah 14:2). The so-called *paʿlēl* verbal form is rare, and in all cases such forms appear in the perfect with no corresponding Qal form (GKC §55d). If the original word in the acrostic poetic source was *dāləlû* ("they languish"), as Spronk (1997: 40) and many others argue, it seems likely that the restored word in the bent acrostic would be equivalent in length (that is, 5 morae). Lengthening the vowel in both verbal forms strengthens the balance in terms of mora count, with two balanced dyads $[(14 + 12) \| (12 + 13)] = 26 \| 25$ morae. Because the subject of the verb in question is plural ("Bashan and Carmel"), it is almost universally agreed among those who choose to restore the presumed missing *daleth* word that the verb in question is 3rd pers. m. pl.—that is, *dālǝlû* ("they languish"), according to Spronk and many others before him (including Gray 1898: 215; Duhm 1911: 101; J. M. P. Smith 1911; Sellin 1930; Tournay 1958: 330; and others); *dāʾăbû* ("they languish"), according to Gunkel (1893: 227) and others; or *dukkǝʾû* ("they are crushed"), according to Arnold (1901: 260). These proposed emendations support the decision to read a plural form here.

Spronk (1997: 40) finds the text in v 4 influenced by Isaiah 19:5–7, citing Psalm 104:7, a hymn on Yhwh as creator of heaven and earth, as a useful parallel text. He calls attention to the combination here of the verbs *gʿr* ("rebuke") and *ḥrb* ("dry up"), which also appear in describing the miracle at the crossing of the sea in Psalm 106:9—"He rebuked the Sea of Reeds and it turned dry" (cf. also Isaiah 51:10 and Psalm 66:6). The focus here is on Yhwh's victory over the sea, with strong allusions to the crossing of the sea in the Exodus from Egypt (Psalms 66:6; 106:9; cf. Isaiah 51:10; cf. also Day 1985: 60–61 and Mittmann 1978: 187–90). The association between Nahum

1:4 and the Exodus narrative was observed in the Talmud (Hagiga 12a) and by Kimchi and Luther (see Spronk 1997: 40). Tertullian (*Against Marcion,* IV.20.3) used Nahum 1:4 in his argument against Marcion that the God of the Tanakh is not the same as God the Father of Jesus Christ in the Greek New Testament, for Christ's power over wind and sea (Luke 8:22–39) is attested in the Tanakh (cf. also Habakkuk 3:10 and Psalm 29:3).

As Spronk (1997: 41) observes, the region of Bashan is cited here not only as a symbol of fertility (cf. Micah 7:14) but even more as a symbol of pride that so often accompanies wealth (cf. Isaiah 2:12–13; cf. Cathcart 1978: 52):

> For the LORD of hosts has a day against all that is proud and lofty,
>     against all that is lifted up and high;
> Against all the cedars of Lebanon, lofty and lifted up;
>     and against all the oaks of Bashan.

Nogalski (1993b: 108–9) argues that Nahum 1:4 is used metaphorically to depict the political weakness of the northern kingdom of Israel caused by the Assyrians. It is more likely, however, that the references to Bashan, Lebanon, and Carmel here are to be taken quite literally, as does Spronk (1997: 41; cf. also Stahl 1992: 169–70, who argues for a connection between Isaiah 33:9 and Nahum 1:4–5).

1:5. *Mountains quake before him; and the hills melt away.* The trembling of the earth is a common image in descriptions of the theophany, and there are many parallels in the Old Testament (e.g., Exodus 19:18; Isaiah 29:6; Psalm 18:8; Job 26:11), in Ugaritic literature (cf. *KTU* 1.4.VII: 30), and in Mesopotamian literature (see Loewenstamm 1980: 181–89). The definite article at the beginning of v 5 is present in the Wadi Murabbaʿat scroll, the LXX, and the Targum (Gordon 1994: 68). Moreover, the definite article appears on this same word in Nahum 2:1 and 3:18. Though it is easy to explain the loss of the initial letter *h* by simple haplography, we must note, with Haldar (1947: 77), that the definite article is expressly written only fourteen times in the entire book of Nahum (chap. 1, four times; chap. 2, six times; and chap. 3, four times); besides, the definite article is not common in archaic Hebrew poetry, as Freedman (1985: 49–62) and Andersen and Forbes (1983) have shown (the article by D. N. Freedman was actually written before the article by Andersen and Forbes appeared). In terms of places where the vocalization of the particles *b*, *k*, and *l* imply the article, Haldar lists the following typical examples: 2:5 (*kallappîḏîm, kabbərāqîm*), 2:10 (*lattəkûnāh*), 2:12 (*lakkəpîrîm*), 2:14 (*beʿāšān*), 3:3 (*laggəwîyāh*), 3:10 (*laggōlāh, baššebî*), 3:14 (*baṭṭîṭ, baḥōmer*), 3:15 (*kayyāleq, kayyeleq, kāʾarbeh*), and 3:17 (*kāʾarbeh*). This relatively rare usage of the definite article is only one example of the archaizing style, which also includes the almost complete absence of the *nota accusativa* particle. It appears only once, in 2:3 (*ʾt gʾwn yᶜqb*). Haldar also calls attention to the obsolete pronominal suffix *hw* (for the later *w*) in 2:4, as well as two occurrences of the enclitic *m* (1:10 and 1:14).

The subject of the verb *rᶜš* ("quake, tremble") is usually *ʾereṣ* ("earth"), and it is used only here and in Jeremiah 4:24 and Psalm 46:4, in each case with *hārîm* ("mountains"); however, in all three instances the word *ʾereṣ* ("earth") is present in the immediate context. The preposition *mimmennû* is taken in a causal sense ("because of him") by the JPS Tanakh and the NASB, but it is taken in a locative sense ("before him") by the KJV, NKJV, NRSV, and NIV. The parallelism with *mippānāyw* ("before him") favors the locative sense. Longman (1993: 790) interprets the preposition *min* in the word *mimmennû* with causal rather than spatial force and reads "because of him" rather than "before him," as does the NRSV (see R. J. Williams 1976: §319). There are many parallels to such physical movement in nature in theophanic descriptions in the Tanakh (see Exodus 19:18; Isaiah 29:6; Psalm 18:8), in Ugaritic mythology (cf. *KTU* 1.4.VII: 30 ff), and in Mesopotamian literature (Loewenstamm 1980: 181–86; cf. Gaster 1969: 663 ff).

The verbal form *hitmōḡāḡû* ("melt away") is the Hithpael from the root *mwg* ("to melt"), which is frequently used in a metaphorical sense. In parallel with the verb *rāᶜăšû* ("they quaked"), these words describe typical reactions of nature to the appearance of the Divine Warrior. But they also frequently apply to people, who shake (Ezekiel 38:20) and melt (usually said of the human heart; see Exodus 15:15; Joshua 2:9; 24; Amos 9:13; Nahum 2:7) in the presence of God's judgment. According to A. Baumann (1997a: 152), the verbal root *mwg* occurs seventeen times in the Tanakh and shows clear evidence of a shift in meaning as the word was drawn into the context of Yhwh's struggle with the nations and with chaos. Its original meaning focuses on the notion of the rolling sea or of ground becoming soft because of moisture; hence the concept of the hills melting away.

As A. Baumann (1997a: 150) says: "There is a fluid transition from the notion of the surging sea to that of an earthquake. When the convulsions of the earth assume cosmic proportions, then not only the masses of water surge, but also the seemingly immovable mountains threaten to sink into the sea, and that means: into chaos." Thus the notions of earthquakes and surging seas become two sides of the same coin, and the LXX translation of the term *hitmōḡāḡû* here as "(the hills) were shaken (ἐσείσθησαν)" makes good sense, particularly when the parallel phrase is *hārîm rāᶜăšû* ("the mountains quaked"). At the same time, it is clear that *hitmōḡāḡû* is better translated here with its primary meaning "(the hills) melt away" (as by Cathcart 1973a: 52 and Longman 1993: 787, along with the KJV, NRSV, NIV, and JPS Tanakh). A similar expression is found in Micah 1:4 using a synonym, *nāmēs*, from the root *mss*, which means "to melt"—*wənāmassû hehārîm* ("and the mountains melt"; cf. also Psalm 97:5). Those who live in Bangladesh, in some parts of the Philippines, or even in California in the rainy season know well what it means to see the water-saturated soil of the hills literally dissolve and flow away with massive destructive force. As Spronk (1997: 42) observes, the choice of the root *mwg* ("to melt") here was perhaps influenced by the poet's desire to use alliteration with repetition of the letter *gimel* in this SAS unit (cf. Allis 1955: 73).

Sronk (1997: 43) cites an interesting parallel text in a Mesopotamian hymn to Adad (see Zimmern 1905: 12; Langdon 1927: 13; Loewenstamm 1980: 183):

> In the Lord's anger the heavens will shake,
>   in Adad's anger the earth will tremble,
>   the great mountains will crumble.

Here we find a striking resemblance to the wording of Nahum 1:5–6; both texts speak of divine anger, the shaking of mountains and the earth, and the crumbling (or shattering) of mountains (or rocks). In the Akkadian text the verb *nāšû(m)* is used to denote the trembling of the earth. The Hebrew root *nś²* is normally related to Akkadian *nāšû(m)*, "to lift" (*HALOT* 683), but the context here in v 5 and the clear parallel in this Akkadian text lend strong support to this interpretation (cf. Ottosson 1974a: 396–97). As Spronk (1997: 43) puts it: "With a poet who in other places also appears to be so familiar with Mesopotamian literature this would not seem to be too unlikely."

The terms *har* ("mountain") and *gibʿāh* ("hill) are a frequently occurring word pair in Hebrew and Ugaritic and express inherent mythical qualities of mountains: they are the oldest things in creation (Proverb 8:25; Job 15), and they last forever (Genesis 49:26; Habakkuk 3:6). These aspects culminate in the concept of the "holy mountain," which in biblical tradition refers to Jerusalem and the Temple mount (Talmon 1978 :430). The concept of the "holy mountain," however, is by no means limited to the Bible and in the cultures of the ancient Middle East reflects numerical traditions and mythology that have to do with tonal images in oral cultures (see McClain 1981: 125–61). In thirty-one of sixty occurrences in the Tanakh, the word *gibʿāh* ("hill") is used in apposition or parallel to *har* ("mountain"), often in contexts that have to do with theophany with mythical allusions to cosmology (Talmon 1978: 430, 436–42). Though the verb *rʿš* ("to quake") also has much to do with the concept of theophany in the Tanakh, it also refers to the clatter of (war) chariots (Jeremiah 47:3) and the rumble of their wheels (Nahum 3:2; see Schmoldt 2004a: 590–92). Though the verb *rʿš* ("to quake, shake") often has the sense of undulating motion, like that of grain waving in the wind (Psalm 72:16), it is sometimes used to describe the reaction of natural phenomena to the destructive power of God (cf. Isaiah 13:13) or other powerful forces (Jeremiah 8:16)—"the mountains quake."

*And the earth reels before him.* The word ***wattiśśāʾ*** ("[the earth] heaves"), which is a 3rd pers. f. sg. Qal imperfect from the root *nśʾ* ("to lift, carry"), is the most frequently discussed word in v 5 (see van der Westhuizen 1969). The primary problem is that the direct object is missing and the intransitive use of this root is rare, though present elsewhere in Habakkuk 1:3 and Psalm 89:10 [9]. The text may represent an idiom such that the object is left unexpressed by ellipsis (Rudolph 1975: 150; Ratner 1988: 84). The unnamed object has been identified as a pillar of smoke (Rashi d. 1105; cf. Judges 20:38, 40), a fire (Kimchi d. 1235; cf. Deuteronomy 29:22–23; 2 Samuel 5:21), a voice (Strauss 1855; G. R. Driver 1933: 384; Rudolph 1975: 151, n. 5; cf. Isaiah 3:7; Psalm 93:3), a head (Breiteneicher 1861), or feet (van der Westhuizen 1969; cf. Genesis 29:1). As it stands, the text means that the earth "lifts itself up, rises up," in reference to the heaving motion associated with earthquakes (cf. Gandell 1901: 638). Roberts (1991: 44) calls attention to the similar use of the root *ʿlh* ("to go up") in related theophanic texts, such as Amos 9:5 and Jeremiah 46:7–8.

In my first publication on this text (Christensen 1975b: 22), I followed Cathcart and others in reading ***wattiśśāʾeh,*** from the root *śʾh* ("crash into ruins"), rather than ***wattiśśāʾ,*** from the root *nśʾ* ("to lift"). This reading involves changing the dot above the letter so as to read *šin* rather than *śin.* Longman (1993: 791) accepts this emendation and suggests that the Vulgate and Syriac "support the proposed change." Roberts (1991: 44), on the other hand, says the renderings of the LXX, Vulgate, and Syriac support the MT as it stands. The NRSV and the JPS Tanakh render the MT as it stands, with: "The earth heaves before him." The same thought is captured in the translation: "The earth reels before him." I now see no compelling reason to emend the text in the manner I argued thirty years ago.

Spronk (1997: 43) cites a pertinent parallel text from Mesopotamian literature in a hymn to Adad, which reads as follows (cf. Zimmern 1905: 12; Langdon: 1927: 13; Loewenstamm 1980: 183):

> In the Lord's anger the heavens will shake,
>> in Adad's anger the heavens will tremble,
>> the great mountains will crumble.

The resemblance to Nahum 1:5–6 is indeed striking, as both texts deal with divine anger, trembling of mountains and the earth, and crumbling or moving of mountains or rocks. The Mesopotamian text uses the Akkadian verb ***našu(m)*** to denote the trembling of the earth. Spronk's argument that we have here "a unique connection" with that Akkadian word makes good sense.

Other proposed emendations include reading the following:

1. *wattāšām* ("is desolated"), from the root *šmm,* with Stonehouse (1929)
2. *wattišaḥ* ("and the earth sinks"), from the root *šḥh,* with Duhm (1911) and Sellin (1930)
3. *wattāšaḥ* ("the earth moves/melts before him"), from the root *šwḥ,* with George (1958)
4. Niphal imperfect *wattinnāśēʾ* ("and the earth is lifted up"), from the root *nśʾ,* with Happel (1900)
5. Hophal *wattuśśāʾ,* from the root *nśʾ,* with Orelli (1897)
6. *wattiḡ͑aš* ("and [the earth] sways"), from the root *g͑š,* with Graetz (1893)

*And the world and all who dwell in it.* The word *tēḇēl* ("world"), which is often used in parallel with or apposition to *ʾereṣ* ("earth"), tends to be associated with its inhabitants (cf. 1 Samuel 2:8; Isaiah 26:9, 34:1; and elsewhere). Cathcart (1973a: 53) argues that the usage here is common in Hebrew poetry: cf. Isaiah 14:17; 18:3; 24:4; 26:9, 18; 34:1; etc., stressing the universal dimensions of God's acts of judgment (cf. Psalms 33:8; 98:7; Lamentations 4:12). Stadelmann (1970: 129–30) discussed the Hebrew word *tēḇēl* in relation to Akkadian in the expression *eli tabali,* "by land." Nonetheless, there are attempts to emend the text, including these:

1. Wolff (1924: 92) read *wayyibbəlû* ("they sink away").
2. Elliger (1970) suggested reading either *waʾāḇəlû kol* ("and [all the inhabitants in it] mourned") or perhaps *wayyaʾāḇlû kol,* with similar meaning (cf. Amos 9:5).
3. Albright (1945: 23) read *wattēḇal kol yôšəḇê ḇāh* ("and all its inhabitants drooped").
4. Moran (1951: 33–35; 1961: 62–63 and 71, n. 108) read *tēḇālû* for *tbl w* and cites Nahum 1:5 as an example of the 3rd pers. pl. m. *taqtulû(na)* form.

The *waw* conjunction on the word *wətēḇel* ("and the world") is omitted in the LXX and some Heb. Mss (cf. Gese 1957: 61). Spronk (1997: 43–44) reads the MT as it stands because of the consistent use of the *waw* conjunction to connect each of the eight dyads in the alphabetic acrostic. Careful study of the letter count in the book of Nahum supports Spronk's position (see discussion in the introduction). Spronk also calls attention to the connection between the references to the withering of the earth or world together with its inhabitants in Isaiah 24:4.

1:6. *In the presence of his fury who can stand; and who can rise up in the heat of his anger?* Those who insist on restoring the presumed acrostic poem to its original form usually emend the word order here so as to get the "*zayin* word" at the beginning of the line. Though logical arguments have been given to explain the presumed "genesis of the present text" (see Tournay 1958: 331; Bliese 1995: 55; Spronk 1997: 44), no such emendation is needed, for we have here a "bent" acrostic pattern in which the change is authorial in design.

The poet asks a rhetorical question with the implied answer "No one" (see Coggins 1985: 25). In eighteen of its twenty-four occurrences, the noun *zaʿam* ("indignation, wrath") is connected directly with action on the part of YHWH in the form of punishment (Wiklander 1980: 110). According to Longman (1993: 791), the word *zaʿmô* ("his fury") may be translated either "curse" or "indignation." Longman translates the text "Before his curse who can stand?" His arguments for interpreting *zaʿmô* as "his curse," however, are not persuasive, for we are not dealing here with a legal setting in the manner he assumes. The position of most English translations (the KJV, NRSV, JPS Tanakh, NASB, NIV and others), which render the word *zaʿmô* to mean "his indignation, wrath," is more likely the correct interpretation. Schulz (1973: 15) argues that the verb *yaʿămôd* ("he can stand") has legal force here, in the sense that no one is able to endure the force of YHWH's judicial judgment. The setting, however, is not that of a legal court proceeding as such but rather that of a theophanic visitation on the part of the Divine Warrior in awesome power, with cosmic overtones. In military contexts the verb *ʿāmad* ("he stood") refers to holding one's ground against an enemy (Judges 2:14; Joshua 10:8; 21:44; 23:9; 2 Kings 10:4; Daniel 11:16; Amos 2:15). The Divine Warrior is about to attack his enemies, and none will be able to take a stand against him so as to hold their ground (cf. Psalms 76:8 [7]; 147:17; Malachi 3:2). As Ringgren has shown, the question as to who can stand before YHWH belongs to the common stock of phrases in Old Testament usage (2001: 183). Spronk (1997: 44–45) compares the text here with that of Psalm 76:8—"Yes, terrible are You, and who can stand before You?" (see also Mathys 1994: 274–75).

The words *zaʿam* and *(hărôn) ʾap* constitute a normal word pair (see Cathcart 1973a: 54). The closest parallels appear in Psalms 2:5, 12; 69:25; 78:49; cf. also Zephaniah 3:8. As Spronk observes (1997: 45), the double question with *mî* ("who?") appears in many places in the Tanakh, usually in describing the differences between YHWH and human beings (cf. Exodus 4:11; 2 Kings 19:22; Isaiah 14:27; 33:14; Jeremiah 49:19; Amos 3:8; Psalm 15:1; Job 9:12; 21:31; 36:23; and other instances). On its use with the verbal root *qwm* ("to rise"), see Psalm 24:3:

> Who shall ascend the hill of the LORD?
> And who shall stand (*qwm*) in his holy place?

On its use with the verbal root *ʿmd* ("to stand"), see Jeremiah 50:44 and Malachi 3:2.

The expression *mî yāqûm baḥărôn* could be translated "Who can rise up *against* his anger?" (cf. Job 16:8; Micah 7:6; Psalm 27:12). The expression carries with it the idea of resistance, as noted in the NET Bible. Longman's (1993: 791) translation of the verb *yāqûm* as "(who can) rise up" continues the theme of judicial usage as he understands it. The image is more that of a reference to the inability to get up off the ground at all in the presence of such awesome power. Hence the translation "who can endure?" with the NRSV, JPS Tanakh, NIV, NASB, and others.

*His wrath is poured out like fire.* Repetition of the word *ḥēmāh* ("wrath") here in v 6 forms an inclusion with its use in v 2, which also marks a significant juncture in the prosodic structure (see later discussion). Coggins (1985: 25) calls attention to the fact that the likening of divine wrath to fire is comparable to the familiar words in Handel's *Messiah:* "Who can endure the days of his coming, and who can stand when he appears? For he is like a refiner's fire" (cf. also Jeremiah 4:26).

The use of the root *ntk* ("to pour out") here picks up a semantic component influenced by its use in metallurgy (Stiglmair 1999: 87). The word *nittəkāh* ("poured out") presents a familiar image of God's wrath "pouring out" on his enemies (Jeremiah 7:20; 42:18; Ezekiel 22:20–22). The root *ntk* ("to pour out") is found in Ugaritic and Akkadian. Cathcart (1973a: 55) cites a useful parallel in Panammū I, *KAI*, 214: 23: "May Hadad pour out wrath upon him." But here wrath is poured out "like fire," and some interpreters find difficulty with that image. The poet's choice to use the rare verbal root *ntk* may have been governed by the principle of alliteration, as suggested by Spronk (1997: 45–46). The LXX apparently misread the text altogether, reading the word *rō˒š* ("head") rather than *kā˒ēš* ("like fire"). Though the words seem to be quite different in the consonantal text, the only difference would be the initial *r* instead of *k*. The letters are not so dissimilar in the ancient script. The power of YHWH's devastating wrath is portrayed as fire in Deuteronomy 32:22: "For fire is kindled by my anger and it burns to depths of Sheol, devours the earth and its increase, and sets on fire the foundations of the mountains." And anyone who has observed volcanic activity knows the appropriateness of a reference to God's judgment being "poured out as fire." On the theophany as a volcanic outburst, see Exodus 19:18 and Jeremiah 51:25–26.

*And the rocks are broken asunder by him.* The term *wəhaṣṣūrîm* ("the rocks") is perhaps to be interpreted as "the boulders" or even "the cliffs," in the sense of huge stones, as does Longman (1993: 792). There is no reason to emend the text to read *haṣṣārîm* ("his enemies"), as did Krenkel (1866: 276).The verbal form *nittəṣû* ("are broken asunder, demolished") is often found in military contexts in reference to the tearing down of towers, temples, or high places (see Barth 1999: 112–14). There is no need to emend the text to read *niṣṣaṭû,* from the root *yṣt* ("to be burnt"), as suggested in the *BHS* note, though the same metathesis is attested in Jeremiah 4:26. As Spronk (1997: 45) points out, the only text that can be cited as evidence of this reading is a single medieval Hebrew manuscript (cf. Barthélemy 1992: 787). Though rare, the preposition *min* (with pronominal suffix) is here understood with agentive force and translated "by him" (see R. J. Williams 1976, §320), as in the NRSV. On the parallel description of Adad's anger making the mountains crumble, see the discussion above at 1:5b.

1:7. *Good is* Yhwh, *indeed a stronghold in the day of distress.* The opening phrase *ṭôḇ* Yhwh ("good is Yhwh") concludes the alphabetic sequence and sets the stage for the focus on the nature of Yhwh's response, in which he brings about "a full end" (*kālāh*), with repetition of that word in vv 8 and 9. The destruction itself is to be "complete" (*mālēʾ*), with that word picked up as an initial letter in a word acrostic in vv 9–10 and repeated at the very end of this opening canto (1:1–10).

The two triads in this strophe (1:7–8) present the contrast among those who place their trust in Yhwh, who experience his goodness, and those who oppose him and face the consequences. O'Brien (2002: 50) makes this important observation: "In the rhetorical world of the Divine Warrior texts, . . . the deity's ability and willingness to act in decisive ways *is* the hallmark of goodness." Though the term *ṭôḇ* ("good") plays an important role in covenantal and legal terminology, its use here falls within the category of "the good" par excellence in that it is personified and identified with Yhwh as "the Good One" (cf. Psalms 16:2; 104:28; 119:122; Proverb 13:21; see Höver-Johag 1986: 311, 314–15). The noun *māʿôz* denotes the semantic elements of protection and refuge and also those of security and strength, which may be imagined concretely in the form of an inaccessible stronghold or citadel built on a rock (S. Wagner 2001: 9; cf. also Nahum 3:11, discussed later).

Many interpreters ignore the strong disjunctive accent *zaqēp qaṭon* and assume that the opening clause here includes three words. Van der Woude suggests emending the text to read *ləmēʿîz,* Hiphil of the root *ʿwz,* which he renders "To those who seek refuge in him" (see Cathcart 1979: 4; reference from Spronk 1997: 47). Others emend the text with the LXX (ὑπομένουσιν, "they wait") by adding the word *ləqōwāw* so as to read "Yhwh is kind to those who wait for him" (cf. Lamentations 3:25). The word *mʿwz* is not deleted but read as the beginning of the next clause (Bickell 1880: 560; Gunkel 1893: 229; Goslinga 1923). Rudolph (1975: 151–52) suggests the loss of the word *lqwyw* or *limqawwāyw,* and Elliger (1970) suggests the loss of *limḥakkê.* Roberts (1991: 45) argues that the Hebrew text read by the Greek translator would have lost *mḥkyw* by haplography. Levenson (1975: 793) thinks a scribe misread the original *lmqwyw* for *lmʿwz* and argues against adding a word to the MT (cf. Duhm 1911: 101).

My earlier suggestion (Christensen 1975: 22) that the *lamed* be interpreted as asseverative or emphatic is followed by a number of scholars (see Cathcart 1975: 6; Becking 1996: 18; Spronk 1997: 46; *HALOT* 485–86; NET Bible): "Yʜᴡʜ is good, indeed a fortress." Dahood (1965: 30) took the *lamed* as a comparative *lamed*, which was discussed at some length by Fitzmyer (1956: 10–13) and Albright (1963: 2). The presence of the accent *zaqēp̄ qāṭon* on the word Yʜᴡʜ, however, suggests a stronger disjunctive break at this point, which supports the reading I proposed thirty years ago. Vv 7–8 scan as follows in terms of mora count: $(6 + 12 + 12) \parallel (7 + 12 + 12) = 30 \parallel 31$ morae. Yʜᴡʜ is portrayed elsewhere as a "fortress" (*māʿôz*) protecting his people (Psalms 27:1; 28:8; 31:3, 5; 37:39; 43:2; 52:9; Isaiah 17:10; 25:4; Joel 4:6; Jeremiah 16:19; Nehemiah 8:10; Proverb 10:29).

Following the suggestion of Levenson (1975: 792), Longman (1993: 792) emends *ləmāʿôz* to read "to those who wait on him" with the LXX, which he thinks reflects something like *ləqōrāyw*. The NET Bible, however, notes (p. 1681) that the Hiphil participle *ləmēʿîz* of the root *ʿwz* ("to seek refuge") is the more likely source of the LXX reading, and its translators were forced to supply a missing direct object. Roberts (1991: 42, 45) goes further, arguing that the original text of 1:7 had *ṭôb yhwh limḥakkāyw māʿôz bəyôm ṣārāh* ("Yahweh is good to those who wait for him, A place of refuge on the day of affliction"). He thinks that the "MT lost *mḥkyw* by haplography due to homoioarchton while the Hebrew Vorlage of LXX lost the following *mʿwz* for the same reason." His reasoning is clever, but the motivation is the misguided effort to restore the *yod* line (cf. Rudolph 1975: 152). Logoprosodic analysis suggests rather strongly that the MT is correct as it stands in regard to word count at this point. There is a missing word in the Hebrew text of *Codex L*, but that word is located after *ʾatnaḥ,* and it appears to be the word *kol* ("all") in 3:10b. Restoring the word *limḥakkāyw* here destroys the balance in terms of mora count in 1:7–8 (noted earlier), and it destroys carefully contrived patterns in terms of word count at the boundaries of vv 7–10. It is better to read the MT as it stands.

Spronk (1997: 47) argues that the problem in the LXX is the same as that encountered by many modern interpreters in that the translator failed to recognize "the sudden shift in the Hebrew text to shorter lines." C. R. Harrison (1988: 66–70) gives further examples of similar errors on the part of the Greek translator by "ignoring the basic sentence structure and thought division of the *Vorlage*" in 1:4, 11, 12; 2:1, 3, 8, 10; 3:6.

The expression *bəyôm ṣārāh* ("day of distress") refers to situations in which God's people are oppressed by a foreign foe (Psalms 50:15; 77:3 [2]; Isaiah 33:2; Jeremiah 14:8; 15:11; 16:19; Obadiah 12). Some scholars see a reference here to Sennacherib's invasion in 701 BCE, in which YHWH protected his people within the fortress walls of Jerusalem (2 Kings 18–19 = Isaiah 36–37; 2 Chronicles 32; see NET Bible, p. 1681). Longman (1993: 792) notes: "In some contexts 'day of distress' is similar to 'day of the LORD' (Jeremiah 30: 7)." Though the definite article is not present here, this is frequently the case with "the Day of YHWH" (Amos 5:18–20; Zephaniah 1:7; Jeremiah 30:7; and elsewhere) and in the parallel expression in 2:4 [3] ("a day of preparation"). Spronk (1997: 48) calls attention to the close parallel between *mᶜwz mywm ṣrh* ("a stronghold in the day of trouble") here and *mᶜwzm bᶜt ṣrh* ("their refuge in the time of trouble") in Psalm 37:39. In both places the phrase appears next to the expression *ḥsh bw* ("the one who takes refuge in him"; cf. also Joel 4:16).

*And he knows those who take refuge in him.* The verbal form *wəyōdēaᶜ* ("and he knows") sometimes means "cares for, is friendly with" (Cathcart 1973a: 55–56; 1979: 4–5; 1992: 998; Bergman and Botterweck 1986: 468; Longman 1993: 792; Spronk 1997: 48, n. 40; see Genesis 39:6; Job 9:21; Psalm 31:8). The term *ḥōsê ḇô* ("the one who takes refuge in him"), from the verbal root *ḥsh* ("to seek refuge"), is an active participle constructed with the preposition *b*, which occurs primarily in the Psalms (Gamberoni 1986: 65, 71).

YHWH's knowledge of those who take refuge in him is more than mere intellectual awareness; it is an active caring (Longman 1993, 792). Nonetheless, it is better to use the normal meaning of the Hebrew verb in question: "He knows." The ambiguity in meaning is fitting for this poetic context. When the subject of this verb is a king (suzerain) and the object is a servant (vassal), the meaning often carries covenantal overtones referring to the king's obligation to protect his vassal. Thus a letter from Abdi-Ashirta, governor of Ammuru, to the Egyptian king Amenophis III ends with a plea for protection against the Mittani: "May the king my lord *know* [= protect] me" (*EA* 60: 30–32; see also Huffmon 1966a: 31–37; 1966b: 36–38; reference taken from NET Bible, p. 1681). At the same time, when Adam "knew" Eve (Genesis 4:1) she subsequently bore a son. Here we find a more intimate meaning of what it means "to know" someone. YHWH "knows" those who take refuge in him.

The attempt to restore the presumed missing *yod* line of the acrostic poem has led both Rudolph and Roberts on a path to futility. Roberts himself (1991: 45) concludes that "the possibilities are too numerous to permit a convincing restoration." The futile efforts of many other scholars (including me) in an earlier era speak volumes on this matter. It is not possible to reconstruct the

acrostic poem that the author used in Nahum 1:2–10 with any confidence;
even if we were to succeed in doing so, all we would have is the source behind
the text as we now have it and not the carefully crafted "bent" acrostic poem
in the MT as it stands, which requires no emendation.

Attempts to interpret the words *ṭôḇ* ("good") and *ydᶜ* ("to know") here as
covenant terminology, as suggested by Fensham (1969: 18) and Van Gemeren
(1990: 471, n. 30), add no real substance to the interpretation of the text (see
Spronk 1997: 47, n. 39). The word *ṭôḇ* ("good") appears at the beginning of
the *ṭet* line within alphabetic acrostics in Psalm 119:65–72 and Lamentations
3:25, and the reference to YHWH's knowing his people appears in Psalms 1:6;
31:2, 4, 8; 37:18; and 144:2–3.

1:8. *And in the sweeping torrent, a full end he will make of her place.* This
verse poses serious difficulties to those who try to reconstruct the acrostic pattern beyond the letter *ṭet* in v 7. The "sweeping torrent" is a metaphor for
YHWH's anger expressed against his enemies; cf. Proverb 27:4—"Anger is overwhelming; and who can stand before jealousy?" The words here call to mind
Isaiah's description of the coming of the king of Assyria against Judah, which
"will sweep on into Judah as a flood, and, pouring over, it will reach . . ." (Isaiah 8:8; cf. also Jeremiah 47:2 in reference to the Philistines). Logoprosodic
analysis supports the reading of the Masoretic division of the text with parallel
triads in vv 7 and 8 (cf. Spronk 1997: 48; Floyd 1994: 425–26).

A further problem is whether to read the first two words in relation to the
preceding verse, to connect it with what follows, or to find some kind of
double-duty usage in relation to both (Tsumura 1983; Longman 1993: 793).
The noun *šeṭep̄* ("flood, torrent") emphasizes the divine dominion over the
seas and rivers. At the same time, God causes the flood to overwhelm his adversaries. In sharp contrast, the *ḥāsîḏ* ("godly one" or "devout one") who prays at
the proper time is assured of being left untouched by the rush of mighty
waters (*šeṭep̄ mayim rabbîm*) in Psalm 32:6 (Liwak 2004: 605). The verbal
form *ᶜōḇēr* ("going over/beyond") is a Qal active participle from the root *ᶜbr* ("to
cross over"), which connotes movement that is purposeful or goal-oriented
(Fuhs 1999: 413). In this instance the goal is destructive, for the "torrent"
(*šeṭep̄*) overflows and overwhelms YHWH's enemies.

In his discussion of the phenomenon of Assyrian propaganda and reaction to
it in the book of Isaiah, Machinist (1983: 735) calls attention to the language
of Isaiah 8:7–8 in reference to "the waters of the River," in which Assyria "will
overflow and sweep over" Judah. This same image is picked up in Nahum as
an instrument of YHWH to erase Nineveh and the whole empire in Nahum
1:8—"With a flood sweeping over, he will make a complete devastation of her
(= Nineveh's site)." The first two words, *ûḇašeṭep̄ ᶜōḇēr* ("and in the sweeping
torrent"), are often connected with the previous verse, with the addition of a

verb. Thus Gunkel (1893: 230) added either *yəmallaṭēm* ("he caused them to escape") or *yaṣṣîlēm* ("he delivered them") so as to find here a statement that Y<small>HWH</small> saved his people from the flood. Bickell (1886: 550) added *yišmərēm* ("he keeps them"), and Procksch (note to Nahum 1:8 in *BH*³) added *yaʿăḇîrēm* ("he let them pass through"; see also the note in *BHS*). Duhm (1911: 101) read *yaʿăḇîrēm* ("he let them pass through") in place of the MT *ʿbr*. Sellin (1930) added *yastîrēm* ("he hid them"), and Rudolph (1975: 152) reads *yaʿăzōr* ("he helps"). Sperber (1945: 133) read the consonantal text of the MT, taking *ʿbr* as the masculine equivalent of *ʿbrh* ("wrath"), and translates the passage "And with a flood of wrath." Haldar (1947: 26) rejected Sperber's interpretation, arguing that the overflowing flood as an instrument of destruction is a common motif in contexts of this sort.

The term *šeṭep̄* ("torrent") frequently carries a metaphorical sense, depicting the rush of distress (Psalm 32:6), anger (Proverb 27:4), events (Daniel 9:26), and the like (Longman 1993: 792). Only in Job 38:25 does it have the literal sense of a flood or torrent of water. The phrase *ûḇəšeṭep̄ ʿōḇēr* is difficult to translate. Hillers (1964: 70–71) found possible Akkadian and Egyptian inspiration in the likening of a conqueror to a flood. At the same time, he correctly notes that in the Tanakh flood imagery of this sort must be derived from the mythological combat between the deity and the primeval waters (cf. Day 1985). As Spronk (1997: 48) puts it: "The 'overwhelming flood' is a metaphor for Y<small>HWH</small>'s anger over his enemies; cf. Prov 27:4."

Logoprosodic analysis indicates that this two-word phrase marks the beginning of a new poetic line (contrary to what is indicated in the layout of *BHS*, which is followed by the NRSV, the NIV, and Longman 1993: 787). This translation fits well with the imagery of 2:9 [8] and the understanding on the part of classical sources (Diodorus and Xenophon) that Nineveh was destroyed by water. Logoprosodic analysis also suggests the possibility that the initial *waw* conjunction may have been added to the text, perhaps as a simple dittography. Those who seek to attach these words to the end of v 7 are forced to remove this conjunction or to explain it as a late prosaic insertion or an emphatic *waw*. As Longman (1993: 793) notes: "This line may be an example of intentional ambiguity that lends richness to poetic language":

> He cares for those who seek refuge in him
> > in an overflowing torrent.
> [With an overflowing torrent]
> > he makes an end to those who rise up against him

This reference to "an overwhelming flood" anticipates 2:9 [8] and the manner in which the walls of Nineveh were destroyed by floodwaters in the diverting of the Tigris River, as reported by Greek sources (Diodorus Siculus,

*Bibliotheca Historica*, 2.27.1–3; Xenophon, *Anabasis*, 3.4.12) and modern archaeological evidence (Gadd 1923: 18). The concept of Yhwh appearing in "an overwhelming flood" in order to "make an end of Nineveh" should be compared with the frequent boasting of the Assyrians themselves that they overwhelmed their enemies like a flood (see ARAB, 2:32–33, 39, 68, 133, 151, 253–54, 317, 328, 339, 345, 522, 561, 563, 587, 644, 651, 859, 865, 906, 926; reference taken from the NET Bible, p. 1684).

The translation of the word *ʿōbēr* as "overflowing," "passing," or "sweeping" has significant connotations. Within the Tanakh the verb *ʿbr* ("to pass over") is essentially a technical term for the crossing of the Red Sea in the Exodus from Egypt and the crossing of the Jordan River into the Promised Land. In the text here, the imagery points in a different direction, for the raging waters themselves are sweeping over the enemies of God's people, much as the waters of the Red Sea buried the Egyptians who pursued the people of Israel as they left the land of Egypt in the narrative of Exodus 14.

The so-called **kaph** line in 1:8 begins with the word **kālāh** ("a full end, annihilation"), which is repeated in 1:9 in the context of another acrostic on the word *mlʾ* ("completely"; see the later discussion of 1:9). In the repetition of the words **kālāh** ("a full end") and **mālēʾ** ("completely") in 1:8–10, the focus is on the finality of Yhwh's judgment. This statement is set over against the hidden message in 1:1–3, which is spelled out as an acrostic in the first letters of three consecutive lines, followed by the divine name itself at the beginning of each half of v 3. That message reads: "I am Yhwh." The Divine Warrior's patience with wicked Nineveh has run out, and the nature of his vindicating wrath is spelled out in what follows.

The feminine noun **kālāh** means "complete destruction," and the expression **kālāh yaʿăśeh** means "to annihilate" (cf. Isaiah 10:23; Jeremiah 30:11; 46:28; Ezekiel 11:13; 20:17; Zephaniah 1:18; Haldar 1947: 26; Helfmeyer 1995: 162). In other contexts, however, this phrase must be interpreted as "to restrain" or the like (cf. Jeremiah 4:27; 5:10, 18). Because the phrase is often followed by *b* elsewhere, carrying an accusative sense, Elliger (1970) suggested that the following word be read *bəqāmāyw* ("against his foes"). Haldar (1947) read the MT without emendation and interprets the following word as an accusative without *ʾet* so that there is no need to insert the initial *b*, as do many interpreters.

The term **məqômāh** in 1:8 presents serious difficulties for many interpreters. As Roberts (1991: 45) points out: "The context offers no antecedent for the feminine suffix, and 'place' provides a poor parallel for 'his enemies' in the next line." In one sense, Roberts is correct, at least on the surface, for the identification of the antecedent for the feminine suffix takes us all the way back to the second word in Nahum—"Nineveh," as Machinist observes (1983: 735,

n. 102). This becomes clearer in the 2nd pers. f. pl. form *taḥšəḇûn* ("you will devise") at the beginning of v 9a, for we have here the initial instance of the phenomenon of enallage in Nahum to announce the approach of a significant prosodic boundary at the end of v 10, with another change to 3rd pers. f. sg. in the verb *tāqûm* ("it will [not] arise") in 1:9b. This phenomenon is characteristic of the book of Nahum as a whole.

The LXX reads ἐπεγειρομένους ("those who rise up against him"), which suggests that the LXX read a plural participle from the root *qwm*. According to Roberts (1991: 45), the suggested emendations here include *qāmāyw* ("his foes"), *bəqāmāyw* ("against his foes"; Buhl 1885: 181), and *miqqāmēhû* ("from his foes"; Albright 1945: 23). Cathcart (1973a: 57) proposed reading *miqqômēhû*. Roberts (1991: 45) rejects Cathcart's proposal, arguing: "It cannot be supported by the vocalization of the Hithpolel in Psalm 59:2 [1]." A further argument against the emendations suggested by Albright and Cathcart is that they increase the mora count by two and so produce prosodic imbalance. The text of 1:7–8 as it stands in the MT scans as follows: (6 + 12 + 12) ∥ (7 + 12 + 12) = 30 ∥ 31 morae, two balanced triads. Rudolph (1975: 152) argued for an abstract noun with the same pointing as the MT reading, without the mappiq, namely *məqômāh* ("opposition"). Roberts (1991: 45) accepts this proposal but in a revised form, reading *məqûmāh*, which he thinks could be represented by the same consonantal text as in the MT. A half century earlier, G. R. Driver (1935: 300–301) said that *mqwmh* here means "opposition," based primarily on certain Arabic nouns. Haldar (1947: 27) follows G. R. Driver (as do De Vries 1966: 479 and Rudolph 1975: 152). Van Dijk represented a similar approach, interpreting *mqwmh* as *māqôm* + the 3rd pers. m. sg. suffix *-ōh*; hence *məqômōh*, "his enemies"—and thus *məqômōh* is an abstract noun with concrete meaning (Van Dijk 1968: 19). Van der Woude (1981: 493) reads the final syllable (without *mappiq*) as a locative ending and *māqôm* as a reference to the grave, in parallel with the darkness in the next clause.

It seems best to interpret the text as does Rudolph, without emendation other than perhaps the removal of the *he'* mappiq, or to interpret the mappiq itself as a more general marker to call attention to the unusual usage of the word in question (as also does Floyd 1994: 425–26). Floyd (2000: 36) reads the f. sg. suffix with reference to the nearest preceding f. sg. noun, that is, *ṣārâ* ("opposition"; RSV, "trouble") in v 7a and translates the passage "He will put an end to the place [of opposition]." Longman (1993: 793) follows Tsumara (1983) in translating the term *məqômāh* as "those who rise against him" by reading instead something like *bəqāmāyw*, as in the *BHS* note. There are four aspects to Tsumara's proposal (cf. also Buhl 1885: 181; G. R. Driver 1938: 269):

1.  "The *mater lectionis* ו can sometimes represent *qāmeṣ* in Biblical Hebrew."
2.  An "*m* and *b* are often interchangeable in Hebrew spelling."
3.  "The verbal idiom עָשָׂה כָלָה can appear with or without the preposition בְּ before its object."
4.  "קוּמָה is probably like אֵיבָת and יֹשֶׁבֶת a feminine abstract noun . . . which experienced a secondary semantic development to the meaning 'opposer(s)' or 'rebel(s)' in a collective sense."

The argument is clever and without flaw, but there is no real reason to dismiss the traditional reading that leaves the MT intact, as have most translators and interpreters past and present. The text as it stands is supported by the Dead Sea Scrolls (4QpNah), *mqwmh* ("her place"), and Symmachus τῇ τόπου αὐτοῦ ("his place"). The fact that the LXX translators read the text in the manner Tsumara proposes does not necessarily indicate that this was the original authorial intent.

It should be noted that the traditional reading "in *her* place" (with *he'* mappiq) presents the contrast between YHWH as a place of refuge in 1:7 and "*her* place" (that is, Nineveh) here in 1:8; obviously Nineveh is anything but a place of refuge in the day of trouble. The context produces the reading proposed here as a deliberate poetic ambiguity. In short, the MT is to be retained as it stands, but note the surprising depth in poetic meaning that the word *məqômāh* takes on in this particular context, for the meaning of the word shifts when the reader or hearer moves on to the next word. This is essentially what the phenomenon of "Janus parallelism" is all about, which Tsumara (1983) has correctly observed.

*And his enemies he pursues into darkness.* Nineveh is destined for total destruction, for YHWH "will pursue his enemies into darkness" itself. The term *yəraddēp* ("he will pursue, chase") is Piel intensive (GKC §52f, k) and frequently connotes military action. In the present context, the verb denotes a durative action rather than a one-time military pursuit (see Frevel 2004: 347). The word *ḥōšek* ("darkness") is directive: "He will pursue his enemies into darkness," in which case YHWH is the pursuing subject (according to Seybold 1989a: 77), or it is the subject: "And darkness will pursue his enemies." Like Cathcart, Roberts (1991: 45) interprets "darkness" as an adverbial accusative rather than as the subject of the verb, which is also the position taken in the translation presented here (as in that of Spronk 1997: 48, who describes it as an "accusative of place or direction" with Joüon and Muraoka 1993: §126h).

The suggested emendation in the *BHS* note to read *yehdōp* ("he will thrust away, drive away"), or perhaps *yndp* (with Wellhausen 1898; G. A. Smith 1928: 92), is clever but arbitrary, with no real textual support. The syntax of the concluding clause here is ambiguous. The LXX takes "darkness" as the subject, reading the passage "Darkness pursues his enemies." Some interpreters take "God" as the understood subject (as in the NRSV, NIV, NASB, and JPS Tanakh). Cathcart (1973a: 31) translates the passage "His foes he will pursue into Darkness." Keil (1949: 12) rendered the text "to pursue with darkness," with *ḥōšek* ("darkness"), an accusative either of place or of more precise definition, used in an instrumental sense. Others see the enemies of God chasing darkness (Longman 1993: 793), and the KJV has "darkness shall pursue his enemies" (as does the LXX). Haldar (1947: 28) thought the verb *rdp* here means "to expel," as suggested earlier by G. R. Driver (1935: 297), and rendered the phrase: "He expels into darkness." The NET Bible (p. 1681) translates the passage "He will drive his enemies into darkness."

1:9. *Whatever you devise against Y*HWH, *a full end he himself is making.* The enemy is addressed directly for the first time in 1:9, but the author does not yet tell us who he is. The interrogative pronoun *mah* is rendered three different ways by interpreters:

1. What? (KJV, NKJV, ASV; Longman 1993, Spronk 1997, Sweeney 2000: 431)
2. Why? (NRSV, NJPS; W. A. Maier 1959; Cathcart 1973a; Roberts 1991)
3. Whatever? (NIV, NASB; NET Bible; R. Smith 1984: 1976)

The indefinite use of *mah* in the sense of "whatever" is well attested (see *IBHS* §18.3.e; GKC §137.c; BDB 553 1.e) and makes good sense in this context. The subject of the verb *təḥaššəbûn* ("you will devise") is the enemy of Y HWH, who is not formally identified. Some scholars think the addressee here is Judah (among them Goslinga 1923; W. A. Maier 1959: 186; Robertson 1990: 72–73; Westermann 1987: 93), but others have thought the prophet is addressing the Assyrians or Nineveh (J. M. P. Smith 1911: 293; Ridderbos 1930; Becking 1978: 111–13) or both Judah and Assyria (Sweeney 1992: 373). But because the third part of this verse refers to current circumstances as "a second time" (*paʿămayim*), the earlier plotting may be interpreted with Van Wyk (1971: 225–27) as referring to the Assyrians in the time of Sennacherib in 701 BCE). Gunkel's (1893: 232) proposed addition of the word *rʿh* ("evil") is unnecessary.

The verbal root *ḥšb* ("to plan, devise, think") appears frequently in Wisdom aphorisms (Seybold 1986: 236), and the context determines the nature of the thought, which may be taken in a hostile sense as directed against Y HWH (with Cathcart 1973a: 59; Longman 1993: 794; Bliese 1995: 49–50; Spronk 1997: 51; and others), or in a nonhostile sense (with W. A. Maier 1959: 184). Roberts (1991: 42) translates the preposition as "against," but at the same time he says: "The context suggests that this reflection on Yahweh was negative in character, but it does not necessarily imply an active, hostile plotting against God" (1991: 46). The preposition is used in a hostile sense elsewhere when followed by the preposition ʾel, as it is here (Jeremiah 49:20; 50:45; Hosea 7:15), but note that the verb is followed by the preposition ʿal in Nahum 1:11, and one might expect a difference in meaning in the present context. Bliese (1995: 49–50) argues that the preposition ʾel is one of two words that appears once only in each of the three "parts" of Nahum (1:1–2:3 [2]; 2:4–14 [3–13]; 3:1–19) and that it means "against" in all three instances. The other occurrences are in 2:14 and 3:5, both of which have the word ʾēlayik ("against you") in the same repeated phrase: "Behold I am against you, utterance of YHWH of hosts." Bliese discusses the meaning of the preposition as significant in relation to the other keyword, Nineveh, which also appears once only in each of his three "parts" of Nahum. Cathcart (1973a: 59) notes that the verb ḥāšab is found with three different prepositions: ʾel (v 9), ʿal (v 11), and lə (Psalm 41:8). The interchange of the latter two prepositions is also found in Ugaritic (cf. UT 99–100, §10.13). The interchange of the first two prepositions here in Nahum may be shaped by the change in subject from the 2nd pers. m. pl. "you" of direct address with the verb təḥaššəbûn ("you will devise [against YHWH]") to the m. sg. participle ḥōšēb ("he is plotting [against YHWH]").

Haldar followed the ancient versions, which took the preposition ʾel here as equivalent to ʿal, meaning "(think) against" (1947: 28). The expression ḥaššēb ʾel is used in Hosea 7:15 in a slightly different form, together with the accusative complement raʿ ("evil"), in the sense of "plotting evil against." As Roberts notes (1991: 46; so also W. A. Maier 1959: 4), without that complement the expression could mean simply "to meditate, reflect on, consider" (Psalms 73:16; 77:6 [5]). The context suggests that the thoughts are negative in nature but not necessarily hostile, plotting against God in the manner suggested by Cathcart. As Longman (1993: 794) points out, it is possible to interpret the text here to mean "Whatever you may think about Yahweh, he always brings everything to a conclusion." Keil (1949: 12) argued that the meaning of mah-təḥaššəbûn ʾel-yhwh in 1:9 is "What think ye [that is, Judah] of Jehovah?" and that the meaning of ḥōšēb ʿal-yhwh is "Who meditated evil against Jehovah?" (cf. also W. A. Maier, "meditate," 1959: 4 and Rudolph, "doubt," 1975: 151).

The Hebrew word klh ("a full end"), which marks the conclusion of the cipher in 1:2–8, is repeated here. The literary form of a short question with a 2nd pers. subject followed by the answer given in the 3rd pers. is closely paralleled in Psalm 52:3, as Spronk observes (1997: 52). Humbert (1926: 269–71) found an even closer relationship to the Psalms here in his proposed reading of təšabbəḥûn from the root šbḥ ("to praise") rather than təḥaššəbûn ("you will devise"). Though still mentioned in HALOT 346 (under the root ḥšb), there is no textual support for this emendation. The use of the 3rd pers. m. sg.

pronoun *hûʾ* ("he") makes it clear that it is YHWH himself who is acting here. The pronoun is not to be deleted as it was by Graham (1927/28: 46), who argued: "It adds nothing new to the text."

*Distress will not arise a second time.* The translation presented here is essentially the same as that of the KJV, NKJV, ASV, NASB, and NIV. The confusion in the LXX translation, as Spronk (1997: 52) observes, comes from the fact that the translator apparently confused the roots *qwm* and *nqm* and slightly paraphrased the word *pʿmym* ("a second time"; cf. Hulst 1960: 245–46; C. R. Harrison 1988: 66, 68; Barthèlemy 1992: 791–92). Both Symmachus and Theodotion translated a text that was much closer to the MT. G. A. Smith (1928: 93) followed the LXX and emended *tāqûm* to read *yiqqôm,* translating the passage "Not twice hath He to avenge Him on His foes." It is better to see here a more general meaning, with Spronk (1997: 53), in the sense that "the enemies brought down by YHWH do not get the opportunity to recover (cf. Psalm 18:39)."

The grammatical form of the word *paʿămayim* ("two times, twice") is dual, despite the arguments of Sperber (1945: 62–63) to the contrary. Some scholars try to find specific reference to events here in the time of Sennacherib (van Wyk 1971: 225–27; Rudolph 1975) or earlier in reference to the fall of Samaria (Graham 1927/28: 46). Origen interpreted the text in 1:9 to mean that God does not punish the sinner twice for the same offense (see Doutreleau 1976: 287–90; reference from Spronk 1997: 53, n. 49). In his understanding, all sinners, and even the devil, will be given their original purity. Jerome accepted this view at first but later abandoned it under the influence of Jewish exegetes (Christianakis 1971; Duval 1984). Jerome's Hebrew mentor explained the verse to mean that God would not hand over Judah and Jerusalem to the Assyrians in the way the ten tribes and Samaria were given into their hands (R. P. Gordon 1994: 45). The Targum, however, applies the text to a much later period of time than that of the historical realities of 70 CE and subsequently, when the second "affliction" did befall Jerusalem and the Jewish state. In this setting interpretation shifts to the matter of a second "relief" from affliction: "Tg's statement that 'relief after affliction will not be established twice for you as for the house of Israel' implies that Israel had already suffered a second 'affliction' involving the destruction of the Jerusalem Temple, in which case the perspective is that of someone living after the events of A.D. 70" (R. P. Gordon 1994: 42).

Cathcart (1973a: 59–60) argues from parallel examples, especially that of Psalm 54:9 (where *ṣārāh* = "my adversaries," balancing *ʾōyəbay,* "my enemies") that *ṣārāh* is an abstract noun with a concrete meaning and that the pronominal suffix is not needed. Roberts (1991: 46) also interprets *ṣārāh* as an abstract noun, meaning "hostility," which can be used concretely as a substitute or synonym for "adversary, enemy" (see CTA 2.4[68].9; 3 [ʿNT].3.34;

3[ʿNT].4.48, 50; cf. Exodus 23:22; Psalms 54:9 [7]; 138:7). As Longman (1993: 795) notes, however, this interpretation implies a minor emendation to read ṣārāyw ("his foes," as suggested in the *BHS* note) rather than ṣārāh ("hostility, distress") in the MT as it stands. Albright (1945: 23) emended the text to read ṣārêhū, "his adversaries." G. A. Smith (1928: 93) emended it to read ṣārāyw, "his foes." Gaster (1969: 665) chose an older interpretation that leaves the MT intact as it stands, by interpreting ṣārāh with the notion of "rebellion" or "opposition." For an earlier view of ṣārāh with the meaning "hostilities, enmity," on the basis of Akkadian ṣarrātu, "hostilities," see G. R. Driver 1938: 269, which was accepted by Haldar (1947: 31).

1:10. *For while (they are) like thorns matted together*. The particle *kî* in this verse underscores one of Muilenburg's primary points in his presidential address to the Society of Biblical Literature in November 1968 (1969: 13–14), for this little word plays a major role in Hebrew poetry and occurs at strategic points. In this instance it introduces the climax of the opening canto, the hymn of theophany in Nahum 1:1–10. There are differences of opinion on how to interpret the preposition ʿaḏ in this context, which has been taken as a comparative of degree by most interpreters (BDB 735 [3]; *HALOT* 787 [5]; NASB, NRSV, JPS Tanakh; W. A. Maier 1959: 192; R. L. Smith 1984: 76; Patterson 1990: 42; and others—along with Aquila [128 CE], Symmachus [late 2nd century CE], and Theodotian [230–240 CE]). Longman (1993: 796) suggests a locative sense, "by the entangled thorns," whereas W. A. Maier (1959: 192) argued for a comparative meaning.

The MT reading sîrîm səḇuḵîm ("thorns matted together") is supported by the Dead Sea text from Murabbaʿat (*DJD* 1: 197). The noun sîr means "thornbush" (BDB 696; *HALOT* 752; cf. Isaiah 34:13; Hosea 2:8; Ecclesiastes 7:6). The verb **səḇuḵîm** is a Qal passive participle from the root *sbk* ("to interweave"), which is related to Assyrian *sabaku* ("to entwine"). The MT is supported by Symmachus ("like an intertwined plant"), Aquila (like a thornbush intertwined"), Theodotion ("like thorn-bushes intertwined"), and the Latin Vulgate among ancient versions. The Syriac Peshitta translates the passage "Your princes are rebels," and somewhat similar confusion is apparent in Origen: "His foundation shall be laid bare," which seems to reflect **yəsōḏāh yəḵabbēs,** caused by orthographic confusion of *d* for *r* and transposition of consonants (according to the NET Bible, p. 1682). Following a variant reading in the LXX, G. R. Driver (1938: 269) emended the MT to read **yswdm ykbsm** ("to the foundation he shall be laid bare") in place of **syrym sbkym** ("thorns matted together"), with the verbal root **sbk** ("to interweave"). Haldar (1947: 32) interpreted the MT to mean "For into the very meshes [that is, "a (woven) net"] they are interwoven."

The expression *kî ʿaḏ sîrîm səḇūkîm ûḵəsoḇʾām səḇûʾîm* has been described as one of the most difficult clauses to interpret in the entire Bible (Haldar 1947: 31; Cathcart 1973a: 60). De Vries (1966: 479) described the text here as "surely one of the most obtuse passages in the Old Testament." Both Wellhausen and van der Woude considered it wise to refrain from attempts to explain the present text in detail (see Spronk 1997: 54). J. M. P Smith (1911: 294) said: "No translation affording any connected sense is possible within the limits of ordinary grammatical interpretation."

The many variant readings listed by Kennicott (1776–80) and De Rossi (1786) indicated that we have here a very old problem. Schulz (1973: 12, n. 34) provides a useful summary of some of the past attempts in interpretation. The list of proposed emendations is extensive, including several attempts to relocate the text in various ways. Spronk (1997: 54, n. 50) calls attention to the conclusion of Seybold on the matter as perhaps the "most extravagant" of them all. Seybold (1989b: 80–81) "assumes that this verse is a remark written in the margin, about the state of the alphabetic acrostic: 'complete until *sameḥ*, complete until 'they were consumed like dried stubble.'" W. A. Maier (1959: 193–94) discusses the following proposed emendations:

1. Gunkel (1893), Guthe (1923), Sellin (1930), and others proposed *sîrîm kəsûḥîm* ("thorns cut off").
2. Stonehouse (1929) eliminated the difficult words and reads "Like a thicket of thorns are they consumed."
3. Horst (1938) proposed "His enemies are intertwined thorns."
4. Graetz (1893) read *śārîm səḇûʾîm ûḇəsoḇʾām* ("princes drunken in their wine").
5. Van Hoonacker (1908) read *səḇûḵîm kəsîrîm* ("interwoven as thorns").
6. Orelli (1897) read *kəsôḏîm səḇûḵîm kəsōḇāḵ* ("foundations interwoven like a thicket").
7. Riessler (1911) read "for they are destroyed to their foundation."
8. Duhm (1912) suggested *sîrîm səḇûḵîm ʾaḵ lô* ("interwoven thorns will surely be to him").
9. Haupt (1907a) found "wine jars" here that represent Antiochus Epiphanes and his nephew Demetrius I, both noted drunkards

Cathcart (1973a: 61) reads the particle *ʿôḏ* ("again"). Roberts (1991: 42, 46) emends the text to read *kî <y>aʿar sîrîm səḇūkîm*, which he translates "though a thicket of entangled thorns." He posits a concessive understanding of the word *kî*. In light of the reading of the rest of this verse presented here, the preposition *ʿaḏ* together with the particle *kî* in this context has the "temporal sense" of "while" (see R. J. Williams 1976: §497). In a *BHS* note, Elliger

(1970) suggested reading *hôy ʿîr* ("woe to the city!") or perhaps *yibʿărû k* ("they will burn like"). Though the text is difficult, it remains more plausible than any of these conjectural emendations.

*And in the likeness of their drunken state, soaked with "drink"; devoured they are like dry stubble — completely!* A. M. Cooper notes the deliberate use of alliteration in the sibilants in v 10 and "suggests that the alliteration imitates the stumbling speech of a drunk person" (the words quoted here are those of Longman 1993: 796; see A. M. Cooper 1976: 86–93). Cooper's conclusion on the matter is apropos in light of the reading of the verse in question that is presented here. The "confused nature of the language" that Longman (1993: 796) observed was apparently intentional. O'Brien (2002: 51) observes much the same phenomenon from another perspective as she concludes: "The verse, like the images it employs, twists and staggers" in a drunken manner.

The MT as it stands is supported by Symmachus ("and as those drinking their drink with one another") and is reflected in the Syriac ("in their drink"). The first word in this two-word phrase, *ûkəsobʾām,* is a noun with a 3rd pers. m. pl. suffix and two prefixes — the *waw* conjunction and the preposition *kə.* The second word, *səbûʾîm,* is a passive participle from the same verbal root *sbʾ* ("to drink"; BDB 685 [a]), which conveys the image of being drunk. According to the NET Bible (p. 1682), the verb *ʾukkəlû* ("they were consumed") "is frequently used in comparisons of consuming liquor and being consumed like chaff."

De Vries (1966: 480) emended the text from *ûkəsobʾām səbûʾîm* to *ûkə-sōbəbîm səbûkîm* and translates it "And as intertwining brambles, devoured like completely dried-out chaff." This suggestion is clever but no more convincing than the several other conjectural emendations of this sort made in times past, which have no textual support. Reider (1952: 79) interpreted the first *mem* as enclitic and translates the passage "As the drunken are getting drunk." The Akkadian cognate is *sābû / sābî,* and Cathcart cites several examples that show a clear connection with "taverns" and "alehouses" and thus with drunkenness. Unable to make sense out of the text by taking *sbʾ* as meaning of "to drink," Haldar (1947: 32) found another root, *spʾ,* which he thinks has the meaning "to eat," though Cathcart (1973a: 61) finds this questionable. Haldar's subsequent translation (1947: 81) is a bit strange: "And as they consume a consuming, they are eaten as chaff wholly dry." Roberts (1991: 46) observes that the root *sbʿ* "is associated with the excessive consumption of alcoholic beverages," which in his understanding "does not seem to fit the context"; but, to the contrary, it is the main point. Roberts emends the text from *ûkəsobʾām* ("and like their liquor") to read *ûbəsobʾām* ("and with their liquor"), and he suggests the possibility of a different emendation so as to read *ûkəsōbəʾîm* ("and like drunkards they are well-liquored").

One thing is clear at the outset, as Longman (1993:796) says: "As it stands, the Masoretic Text describes the enemy by using two similes: drunkenness and thorns"; or, as Roberts (1991: 46, n. 19) puts it: "A double metaphor is involved in these two lines." The problem is how to put these two similes together, for the poet has done so in highly compressed form—in only four words. The meaning of the first word, *sîrîm,* is relatively clear. Though the noun can refer to a large water jar or pot (BDB 696), it clearly has a second meaning that applies here, namely that of "thorns" (cf. Ecclesiastes 7:6 on the sound of thorns crackling as they burn under the pot). The second word, *səbûkîm,* is more problematic. The verbal root *sbk* means "to interweave," and thus the Pual passive participle means "interwoven (entangled) thorns" (BDB 687), which I have rendered "matted thorns." What we have is highly combustible material commonly used as fuel. But how does this fit with what follows in the next two carefully chosen words? BDB (684) translates the parallel occurrence in Hosea 4:18 as their "liquor (that is, their drunkenness) is gone" (cf. Andersen and Freedman 1980: 344, 378). According to Isaiah 1:22, the "liquor" in question is the *strong* kind that readily induces drunkenness. The Hebrew root *sbʾ* should be compared with the Akkadian *sabû* ("to make beer"). As Spronk (1997: 56) observes: "The inhabitants of Mesopotamia were known in the ancient Near East as beer drinkers" (see Stol 1989).

The image is clear, but how do we attach this meaning to the fourth word in the series—*səbûʾîm,* which comes from the same verbal root? The first two words in the series set the stage for understanding the primary meaning of the text—the matted thorns will be "consumed like dry stubble—completely!" It is the two words in between that create the poetic tension, for the image is that of heavy drinking and drunkenness, with the implied "soaking" of the fuel to render it noncombustible (cf. Davidson 1920: 22–23). Ewald (1878, quoted by Keil 1949: 13) rendered the text "As it were drowned in wine, so that fire can do no more harm than to anything else that is wet." Arnold (1901: 240) rendered it as "thickets ever so drenched." In short, the matted thorns are sopping wet with liquor and/or the consequence of heavy drinking—that is, the vomit of those who are inebriated.

The simile contained in the MT as it stands compares the imminent destruction of Nineveh to the burning of a mass of dry matted thorns, which are highly combustible and used as fuel (Ecclesiastes 7:6, "the crackling of thorns under a pot"). The verbal form *ʾukkəlû* ("they were consumed") is an example of the old Qal passive perfect 3rd pers. pl., which is vocalized in the MT as Pual perfect (cf. Exodus 3:2; Nehemiah 2:3, 13; Isaiah 1:20; Nahum 1:10; and see Ginsberg 1929: 53–56; Joüon-Muraoka 1993: §58; *IBHS* §375, n. 36). The image of fire "consuming" with the verbal root *ʾkl* ("to eat, consume") appears again in Nahum 3:13.

The term *mālēʾ* ("fully, completely") functions as an adjective modifying the phrase *kəqaš yābēš* ("like fully dried stubble"). Keil (1949: 14) argued that the word "is not to be taken, as Ewald supposes (§279, a), as strengthening *yābēš*, 'fully dry,' but is to be connected with the verb adverbially, and is simply placed at the end of the sentence for the sake of emphasis." Coggins (1985: 29) argues that the word *mālēʾ* ("fully, completely") here "makes no apparent sense in the context" and emends the text with the note in *BHS* to read *hălōʾ* ("Has not . . . ?") and connects it with the next line "Has not one plotting evil marched out from you?" This suggestion is mere conjecture with no textual support, for the MT is supported by 4QpNah and the ancient versions.

The idea of God's enemies being consumed like chaff or stubble in a fire is easy to understand in light of parallel texts like Exodus 15:7: "In the greatness of your majesty you overthrew your adversaries, you sent forth your fury, it consumed them like stubble" (cf. Isaiah 33:11–12; 47:14). On the linking of "drunkenness," "thorns," and "stubble," see Obadiah 16–18, where "drunkenness" is followed by the "burning" of the faithless and worthless "house of Esau" (v 18). The completeness of Yhwh's destruction of this enemy is underscored by the final word *mālēʾ* ("completely"), which is emphasized by repetition in the form of an acrostic *mlʾ* at the beginning of the first, second, and concluding poetic lines in 1:9–10.

Confusion on how to read the four key words in the first half of v 10 has led to difficulties on the part of many translators in making sense out of the conclusion of the verse, especially in regard to the final word, as a glance at almost any of the standard English translations quickly reveals. The RSV takes the verb "to fill" and attaches it to the following verse, but emends the text so that v 11 begins with a negative *lōʾ*, presumably taking the *mem* as an enclitic. The NRSV seems not to reflect the presence of the word in question at all. The NIV also ignores the presence of this word. The NASB at least attempts to read the text of the MT as it stands, as does the JPS Tanakh, but without grasping its full meaning. It is best to read the word *mālēʾ* as an adverb with an intensive sense of being "fully consumed" (as does Longman 1993: 796) or "completely," as rendered here: "Consumed they are like dry stubble — completely!"

The motif of drunkenness belongs to the theme of the cup of Yhwh's wrath, which in Jeremiah 25:25–29 is proffered to the nations, who must drink it— and stagger and vomit (cf. Isaiah 19:14; 51:17; and later discussion of 3:11). The metaphor of entangled thorns is also a judgment motif (see Isaiah 33:11–12). Here the two metaphors are mixed, for the entangled thorns are matted and soaked with wine and vomit. Nonetheless, what appears to be not flammable will be utterly consumed with the fire of Yhwh's wrath—as though it were dry stubble. Though the concluding word, *mālē<sup>ɔ</sup>* ("completely"), appears at first glance to be out of place, it is in fact the climax of the matter, which reiterates the content of the closing acrostic in vv 9–10, made up of the same word.

## COMMENT

The opening Psalm of Nahum is the key to understanding the book, for as Achtemeier (1986: 8) notes: "We have here only a little less than a complete presentation of the biblical witness to God's person: the testimony to his covenant love and to his patient mercy; his intimate knowledge of his own and his protection of them; his just lordship over his world and his might in maintaining his rule; his specific but also eschatological defeat of all who would challenge his sovereignty." It is not to be taken as just a later orthodox addition made to render the profane soldier's songs acceptable for religious purposes, as Seybold (1991, 1999) suggests. The theological tone established here sets the tone that rings throughout the book as a whole.

### Nahum 1:1–10, the Psalms, and the Phenomenon of Acrostics
An acrostic is a device employed in poetry in which the initial letters of successive lines constitute a name, a word, a phrase, a clause, a sentence, or an alphabetic pattern. Acrostic poems on the order of the twenty-two letters of the Hebrew alphabet appear with some frequency among the Psalms (9–10 [altered], 25, 34, 37, 111, 112, 119, 145), the best known of which is Psalm 119, with eight successive verses beginning with each letter of the alphabet so that we have 176 (= 22 × 8) verses in all (the longest chapter in the Bible, more than twice as long as the entire book of Nahum). Other examples appear in Proverb 31:10–31 and Lamentations 1–4. The "bent" acrostic hymn of theophany in Nahum 1:2–10 is the only example of this poetic genre in the Former and Latter Prophets. Tur-Sinai (1959: 179) found the beginning of an alphabetic acrostic in Proverb 24:1–7 (reference from the manuscript of a forthcoming commentary on Nahum by Aron Pinker to be published by BIBAL Press).

A "normal" alphabetic acrostic would have twenty-two verses, each of which would begin with a successive letter of the alphabet. This is true of Proverbs 31:10–31 and Lamentations 1, both of which follow the usual order of the letters of the alphabet. The acrostic pattern in Psalm 37 is based on alternate verses, and in Psalms 111 and 112 it is based on each half-verse. Lamentations 2 and 4 transpose the *ayin* and the *peh*. Lamentations 3 has 66 verses, with threefold repetition of each letter and the same transposition of *ayin* and *peh*. Psalm 145 lacks the *nun*, which is added in the LXX and the Dead Sea Psalms Scroll. Psalms 25 and 34 omit the *waw* verse and add a second *peh* line in the concluding verse. Leeman (1996: 43–44) explains the replacement of the *waw* by *peh* as an application of the atbash principle. Skehan (1971: 74) explains the addition of final *peh* as an acrostic within an acrostic, with the letter *aleph* (ʾ*lp̄*) spelled out with the beginning, middle, and final letters of a twenty-three-letter acrostic poem. An alternate way of explaining departures from the presumed original acrostic pattern in the Psalter is presented in my files on these Psalms (www.bibal.net) in terms of the principles of numerical composition in the final "canonical" form of the Psalter as we now have it. For detailed study of acrostic poems in the Hebrew Bible, see the work of D. N. Freedman (1972: 367–92; 1986: 408–31).

A number of reasons have been suggested for the use of the acrostic pattern, including aesthetics, mnemonics, organization, completeness, the demonstration of an author's prowess (R. Marcus 1947; reference from Pinker 2006a: 97). Ceresko (1985: 102) argues that the acrostic pattern in some of the psalms appears to be used to achieve order among verses that otherwise are not intrinsically related. He connects the acrostic with "a characteristic concern of the wisdom writers: that effort to wrest some kind of order and coherence out of the variety and seeming disconnectedness of the experiences of everyday life and to express that order in language, especially language in its written form" (reference from Pinker 2006a). Gottwald (1954: 27) thought that the primary reason for the acrostic pattern was to highlight the idea of completeness of expression—the idea of totality, "from A to Z." In a Midrash we read: "Adam translated the whole law from *Aleph* to *Taw*," and again: "Abraham kept the whole law from *Aleph* to *Taw*" (reference taken from J. R. Harris 1887: 93 n). D. N. Freedman (personal communication) calls attention to the common belief that the town in Southern California called Azusa is an abbreviation of "A to Z in the U.S.A." Melitz (1991: 261) thinks the acrostic pattern was motivated by a wish to create something unique, singular, and attractive, as dictated by the topic or circumstance (reference from Pinker 2006).

Floyd's (1994) arguments against the presence of an acrostic here in Nahum are based on three claims on his part: that to maintain the alphabetic sequence one must (1) propose lines of very different lengths, (2) emend the text, and (3) ignore the way in which 1:9–10 fits into the section's larger argument. Though Floyd correctly identifies the proper prosodic boundary at the end of v 10, his arguments do not demonstrate his conclusion. The argument that the poem has poetic lines of different lengths must be balanced against the fact that we have here a more complex situation than Floyd assumes, and his presuppositions about the nature of Hebrew poetry itself are in error. There is more than one acrostic pattern here, and a telestich as well in vv 1b–3a. The primary acrostic pattern has been "bent" and extended so as to form a larger statement that includes vv 9–10 and concludes in 2:11 [10], and there is no need to emend the text at all. In short, Floyd's arguments against the presence of an acrostic in Nahum 1:1–10 are without substance.

The opening canto (1:1–10) is often described as a hymn, comparable to Psalm 97 (Löhr 1905: 174), which is one of several psalms praising Y<small>HWH</small> as king. Others in this series include Psalms 47; 93; 96; 98; and 99. Spronk singles out Psalm 99 as perhaps the most interesting parallel (1997: 27), for there we find specific reference to "avenging" as a divine characteristic (cf. Psalm 99:8 with Nahum 1:2; see also Peels 1995: 277–79). At the same time, Spronk (1997: 27) points out that certain elements in the hymn as a literary form are missing here in Nahum 1, for the poem lacks the usual call to praise (Rudolph 1975: 154; Floyd 1994: 435), and Y<small>HWH</small> is not addressed directly. Spronk explains these aberrations in terms of the prophetic context in which the hymn form is embedded: "Apparently, the poet was inspired by hymns about Y<small>HWH</small> as king, when he wrote the introduction to the prophecy, especially vv 2–6."

Logoprosodic analysis reveals other parallels between Nahum's opening hymn of theophany and the book of Psalms. As noted earlier, the two-part heading in 1:1 parallels that of the headings in the Psalms in that the heading is carefully contrived to achieve the same specific ends we find in the "editing" of the 150 psalms in the Psalter. The six words in the heading balance the six words at the end of this opening canto to form a structural inclusion that reiterates the central message of the book as a whole:

> The exposition of Nineveh,
>> the scroll of the vision of Nahum the Elkoshite.
> And in a drunken state, soaked with "drink,"
>> devoured they are like dry stubble—completely!

The poetic image here is conveyed in two carefully chosen words that may have been coined by the poet to communicate what he wanted to say in a mixed metaphor. The cup of Y<small>HWH</small>'s wrath is proffered to Nineveh, who will consume that cup of "wine" and reel in a drunken stupor (cf. Jeremiah 25:15–26 for a subsequent adaptation of this same image in reference to Babylon). In that drunken state, inebriated and soaked with vomit, Nineveh will be consumed by Y<small>HWH</small>'s fire as if she were dry stubble—completely! The final word in this opening canto is "completely," which in Hebrew is the word *mālē'*. That same word is spelled out as the initial letter in the concluding lines of this poem:

> 1:9 מ  Whatever you devise against Y<small>HWH</small>,
>> **a full end** (*kālāh*) he himself will make.
>
> ל  It will not arise a second time, namely distress—
> 1:10    for while like thorns matted together,

and in a drunken state soaked with "drink"—

א    Devoured they are like dry stubble—**completely** (*mālē'*).

The first line starts with the words *mah-təḥaššəbûn* ("whatever you devise"), the second line begins with the words *lō'-tāqûm* ("it will not arise"), and the third line begins with the word *'ukkəlû* ("they will be consumed"). The initial letter of these three lines spells out the word *ml'* ("completely") in Hebrew, and that word is repeated at the end of this poetic unit. Note also the repetition in the first line of the word *kālāh* ("a full end"), which also appears in the previous verse—"*a full end* (*kālāh*) he will make of her place." That is what the book of Nahum is about, the destruction of Nineveh.

The same image appears in the center of the book in 2:11 [10] in the striking image of boughs gathered as fuel for burning—in the total destruction of Nineveh, which is described with unforgettable alliterative force: *bûqāh ûməbûqāh ûməbullāqāh* ("destruction and devastation and destitution"). The poet Nahum had a love affair with words, which he used and coined with power.

The first canto in the book of Nahum begins with an even more impressive acrostic structure, which includes a telestich as well. In four consecutive lines, the poet constructs an acrostic sentence:

1:2   א      A zealous and avenging God (*'ēl*) is Yhwh,
           avenging is Yhwh and a lord (*ba'al*) of wrath.

     ב      Avenging is Yhwh against his foes;
           and he rages against his enemies.

1:3   י     Yhwh is slow to anger but great in power;
           and the guilty he does not acquit!

    *     Yhwh—in the whirlwind and in the storm is his way;
           and clouds are the dust of his feet.

The first line starts with the word *'ēl* ("God"), the second line starts with the word *nōqēm* ("avenging"), and the third line starts with the word *yhwh* ("Yhwh"). The first letter of these three words spells out the word *'ny* ("I [am]"). The first word of the fourth line is the word *yhwh* ("Yhwh"), so that the acrostic sentence reads: "I am Yhwh!" At the same time, this same word *yhwh* ("Yhwh") appears as a telestich made up of the final letter in each of the first four lines, including the heading. To reinforce this same idea, there are 17 words after *'atnaḥ* in vv 1–4, and Yhwh is described in terminology that includes allusion to the Canaanite deities El and Ba'al (v 2). The image of a mass of sopping wet, matted thorns burning like dry stubble is striking. The fire of Yhwh's wrath knows no limitations, as the prophet Elijah demonstrates so vividly on Mount Carmel in his contest with the prophets of Ba'al (1 Kings 18).

Sandwiched between these two carefully contrived acrostic structures at the beginning and the end of the first canto of the book of Nahum, we find another "bent" acrostic that ends with the letter *kaph* in the first occurrence of the word *kālāh* ("a full end") in v 8. It appears that the poet borrowed an existing alphabetic acrostic poem, at least in part, and "bent" it to serve a new purpose within the design of his own book. The alphabetic sequence in vv 3–7 extends from the letter *gimel* through *ṭet* in seven dyads. The sequence of these seven consecutive letters of the Hebrew alphabet was altered twice as the poet bent the acrostic pattern into another acrostic statement. The *daleth* line was changed to an *ʾaleph* line by substituting the corresponding verb in the second part of v 4b, and the *zayin* word was pushed back and thus replaced by adding the preposition *lipnê* ("in the presence of") at the beginning of v 6. The resulting acrostic statement reads *gʾh wəlipnê ḥṭ(ʾ)* ("exalted and in the presence of sin"). When combined with the opening acrostic in vv 2–3 and the content of vv 8–9a, we have

> I am the exalted Yʜᴡʜ,
> > and I am in the presence of sin.
> In the sweeping torrent, a full end (*kālāh*) he will make of her place;
> > and his enemies he pursues into darkness.
> What will you devise against Yʜᴡʜ?
> > A full end (*kālāh*) he himself will make.

The initial letters in the first three lines of 1:4–5a spell out the word *gʾh* ("exalted") in a prosodic unit made up of **17** words. The first half of v 5 functions in a pivot pattern, completing the three-part description of the reaction of the cosmos to the appearance of the Divine Warrior and introducing an expansion of that same idea in the four-part poetic unit in 1:5–6, which is made up of **26** words.

These two numbers for the divine name, **17** and **26**, are woven into the text in what follows in a variety of ways. In some ways this observation is somewhat trivial, and thus I will not draw attention here to the details in this process of numerical composition. Nonetheless, these numerical observations highlight the fact that we are dealing here with a sophisticated work of literary art in which the composer demonstrated great skill within the context of narrow restraints, like that of Japanese haiku poetry. In short, it should be noted that God's presence in this text is expressed symbolically from the outset by the careful and deliberate counting of each word in relation to the position of the *ʾatnaḥ* marker in each verse.

The 12-word "meaningful framework" in the first canto (1:1–10), which is discussed earlier, is nested within a larger 34-word framework, as follows:

| | |
|---|---|
| ¹ *maśśā² nînəwēh* | The exposition of Nineveh, |
| *sēper ḥāzôn naḥûm hā²elqōšī* | the scroll of the vision of Nahum the Elkoshite. |
| ² *²ēl qannô² wənōqēm yhwh* | A zealous and avenging God is YHWH; |
| *nōqēm yhwh ûba²al ḥēmāh* | avenging is YHWH and a lord of wrath, |
| *nōqēm yhwh ləṣārāyw* | avenging is YHWH against his foes. |
| ⁹ *kālāh hû² ²ōśeh* | A full end he himself is making; |
| *lō² tāqûm pa²ămayim ṣārāh* | distress will not arise a second time. |
| ¹⁰ *kî ²ad-sîrîm səbūkîm* | For while they are like thorns matted together, |
| *ûkəsob²ām* | and in likeness to their drunken state |
| *səbû²îm* | soaked with "drink" |
| *²ākəlû kəqaš yānēš mālē²* | they are consumed like dry stubble, completely. |

The outer framework, which is highlighted in gray, consists of 6 words at the beginning and ending of this literary unit. A second framework consists of 11 words on either side. The third such framework consists of 17 words in each part of the Hebrew text. This phenomenon of nesting of "meaningful frameworks" is also found in each of the 150 psalms in the Psalter (see the Psalm files at www.bibal.net).

In Psalm 1, the 14-word "meaningful framework" is nested within a larger 30-word framework, as follows:

| | |
|---|---|
| ¹ *²ašrê hā²îš* | Happy is the man, |
| *²ăšer lō² hālak ba²ăṣat rəšā²îm* | who does not walk in the counsel of the wicked. |
| ² *ûbəderek ḥaṭā²îm lō² ²āmād* | And in the way of sinners he does not stand; |
| *ûbəmôšab lēṣîm lō² yāšāb :* | and in the camp of scorners he does not sit. |
| *lō² yāqûmû rəšā²îm bammišpāṭ* | The wicked will not arise in the judgment |
| *wəhaṭṭā²îm ba²ădat ṣaddîqîm* | and sinners in the congregation of the righteous. |
| ⁶ *kî yôdēa² yhwh derek ṣaddîqîm* | For YHWH knows the way of the righteous, |
| *wəderek rəšā²îm tō²bēd* | but the way of the wicked shall perish. |

The outer framework, which is highlighted in gray, consists of 7 words at the beginning and ending of this literary unit. A second framework consists of 15 words on either side.

The same phenomenon is found in Psalm 2, where the 8-word "meaningful framework" is nested within a larger 32-word framework, as follows:

| | |
|---|---|
| ¹ *lāmmāh rāgəšû gôyīm* | Why do they conspire, (that is) nations |
| *²ûlə²ummîm yehgû rîq* | and peoples snarl in vain? |
| ² *yityaṣṣəbû malkê ²ereṣ* | The kings of the earth take their stand; |
| *wərôzənîm nôsədû yāḥad* | and the rulers take counsel together, |
| *²al yhwh wə²al məšîḥô* | against YHWH and against his anointed one. |

| | |
|---|---|
| *wəgîlû birᶜādāh* | And rejoice with trembling; |
| 12 *naššəqû bar pen yeˀĕnap̄* | Kiss the son lest he be angry |
| *wətōˀbəḏû ḏerek* | and you perish in the way |
| *kî yibᶜar kimᶜaṭ ˀappô* | for his anger flares up quickly; |
| *ˀašrê kol ḥôsê bô* | Blessed are all who seek refuge in him. |

The outer framework, which is highlighted in gray, consists of 4 words at the beginning and ending of this literary unit. A second framework consists of 16 words on either side. This phenomenon of a nested "meaningful center" is found in all 150 psalms in the Psalter, when all the words are counted, including those in the headings and rubrics like the word "Selah."

A further parallel with the Psalms is found in the concept of a "meaningful center." Each of the 150 psalms in the Psalter is carefully contrived in terms of total word count so as to have a "meaningful center," which is sometimes nested two or more levels in depth. These statements are made up of exactly the same number of words before and after the "arithmological center" of that psalm. These statements normally highlight the central meaning of the poem in question. The same is true for the opening canto in Nahum 1:1–10, which has 110 words. The "arithmological center" falls between the eighth and ninth words in v 5, with 55 words on either side. The meaningful center consists of 8 words on either side of the arithmological center, as follows:

| | |
|---|---|
| 5 *hārîm rāᶜăšû mimmennû* | Mountains quake before him; |
| *wəhaggəbāᶜôṯ hiṭmōḡāḡû* | and the hills melt away. |
| *wattiśśāˀ hāˀāreṣ mippānāyw* | And the earth reels before him; |
| *wəṯēḇēl wəkol-yōšəḇê ḇāh* | and the world and all who dwell in it. |
| 6 *lip̄nê zaᶜmô mî yaᶜămôḏ* | In the presence of his fury, who can stand? |

This 16-word statement stands at the center of Nahum 1:1–10 and highlights the central message of this opening canto. Yʜwʜ is appearing in all his cosmic power, and the physical universe itself reels before him. The statement concludes with a rhetorical question: "In the presence of his fury, who can stand?" One thing is certain. Nineveh cannot stand in the presence of Yʜwʜ's wrath: "In the sweeping torrent, a full end he will make of her place" (v 8).

A larger "meaningful center" is formed with 14 words on either side. A still larger such center consists of 20 words on either side of the absolute center of this passage in terms of word count. This same phenomenon of the nesting of meaningful centers on the basis of word count is present in each of the 150 psalms in the Psalter (see the Psalm files at www.bibal.net). In terms of the principles of numerical composition, the hymn of theophany here in Nahum 1:1–10 was constructed in the same manner as the collection of poems in the

Psalter and was perhaps written in the same circles under the same general guidelines—as a numerical composition.

In terms of the 67 words in Psalm 1, the arithmological center falls on the word בְעִתּוֹ ("in its season") in 1:3a, with 33 words on either side. The meaningful center of Psalm 1 consists of 7 words on either side of the arithmological center, as follows:

| ³ šātûl ʿal palḡê māyim | He is planted by streams of water; |
| ʾăšer piryô yittēn ba‿ʿittô | which its fruit it gives in its season. |
| wǝʿālēhû lōʾ yibbôl | And its leaf does not wither; |
| wǝkōl ʾăšer yaʿăśeh yaṣlîaḥ | and all that he does prospers. |

This 15-word statement stands at the center of Psalm 1 and highlights its central message. Labuschagne (www.labuschagne.nl/psalms.htm) notes that the structural pattern is thus in the form of "a perfectly concentric menorah pattern":

$$67 = 26 + 4 + 3 + \boxed{1} + 3 + 4 + 26.$$

In terms of the 92 words in Psalm 2, the arithmological center falls between the words אָמַר אֵלַי ("he said to me") in v 7, with 46 words on either side. These two words may be considered a meaningful center. Labuschagne notes the appropriateness of this formula introducing God's words addressed to the king at the structural center of Psalm 2. He also calls attention to the fact "that the total number of words attributed to God amount to exactly **26** (7 in vv 6 and 19 in vv 7–9)," as is also true of the number of words addressed to the rebellious kings in vv 10–12, which totals **26** words.

The meaningful center may be expanded to include 11 words on either side of the arithmological center, as follows:

| ⁶ waʾănî nāsaktî malkî | I have set my king |
| ʿal ṣîyôn har qōdǝšî | upon Zion, mountain of my holiness. |
| ⁷ ʾăsappǝrāh ʾel ḥōq | Let me recount concerning a decree: |
| yhwh ʾāmar ʾēlay bǝnê ʾattāh | Yнwн himself said to me: "You are my son" |
| ʾănî hayyôm yǝlidtîkā | I myself today have begotten you. |
| ⁸ šǝʾal mimmennî | Ask of me |
| wǝʾettǝnāh gôyīm naḥălāṭekāk | and I will give the nations as your inheritance. |

This 22-word statement stands at the center of Psalm 1 and highlights its central message.

## Nahum 1:1–10 and Its Larger Literary Context

The description of Yнwн in Nahum 1:2 contains the Hebrew name of the Canaanite gods El ("God") and Baʿal ("Lord"), and the terms "the sea" and "rivers" in 1:4 allude to deities of the same names in Canaanite lore. Nahum 1:4–6 presents the reaction of the cosmos to the appearance of the Divine Warrior and includes a number of allusions to Canaanite mythology. The Assyrian army generally waged war in the spring after the Tigris and Euphrates had receded from flood stage, thus allowing them to cross more readily. Yнwн, as the Divine Warrior par excellence, dries up the rivers so that his "hosts" cross on dry ground to attack Assyria.

Spronk (1997: 49) calls attention to the fact that this opening clause in 1:8 marks a divide of sorts in the structure of Nahum; from this point on we find fewer references to the Psalms (as is also the case at the center of the Psalm of Jonah). Coinciding with this shift, the content itself shifts from praising Yнwн's might to a presentation of the destruction of Nineveh. From this point on there are more and more direct and indirect references to Mesopotamian literature and in particular to that of the Assyrian royal annals and vassal treaties (cf. Machinist 1983: 735–36; Johnston 1992: 330–98).

Assyrian kings boast that they destroy the cities of their enemies "like a flood" (Machinist 1983: 726–27; *CAD* A, 76–77). Spronk (1997: 49) cites as an example Sargon II, who "says of Hamat that he, as if he were a god, completely brought down the city 'like a flood'" (*TUAT* I/4, 385). And Sennacherib describes the capture of Babylon in similar language, saying that he "dug canals through the midst of that city, flooding its site with water, and destroyed the structure of its foundation" (*ARAB*, 152). A common curse in the vassal treaties of Esarhaddon reads "May a flood, an irresistible deluge, come up from the earth and devastate you" (*ANET* 539; cf. Hillers 1964: 70). Ashurbanipal says much the same about the fall of Thebes, for his army "conquered this city completely, (and) smashed (it as if by) a floodstream" (*ANET* 297). The reference to "her place" in Nahum 1:8 indicates that the same fate now awaits Nineveh (cf. 2:7 [6]); for Nineveh is indeed no better than Thebes (No-of-Amon). The prophet Isaiah describes the Assyrian onslaught against Judah in the same imagery: like the water of the river, which "will overflow and pass on" (*šāṭap̄ wəʿābar*, Isaiah 8:8; cf. Jeremiah 47:2 about the Philistines).

Spronk (1997: 37) calls attention to Jeremiah 30:11 and how the prophet Jeremiah apparently reused the words of Nahum. Jeremiah declared: "I will make an end (*ʿśh klh*; cf. Nah 1:8–9) of all the nations among which I scattered you, but of you I will not make an end. I will chastise you in just measure, and I will by no means leave you unpunished (*nqh lʾ ʾnqk*)." The punishment of both Nineveh and Babylon does not absolve Israel from facing the consequences of her own sins.

Spronk (1997: 54–55) correctly relates the content of 1:10 to that of 2:11 [10] and the phenomenon of alliteration: "Both describe the total destruction of the enemy." The connection is even closer than Spronk has seen, however, as shown in the later discussion of 2:11 [10], which constitutes the completion of the cipher presented in the bent-acrostic poem in 1:1–10. The coming of YHWH as a devastating flood in 1:8a has parallels in the Assyrian royal annals, as shown earlier, and so does the comparison of the defeated enemies with "thorns and thistles" (*kima balti u ašagi; CAD* B, 65). Moreover, as Spronk observes, the influence of Isaiah 10:17 on the text here is readily apparent:

> The light of Israel will become a fire, and his Holy One a flame;
>   and it will burn and devour his thorns and briers in one day.

The big difference here is the brilliant mixing of metaphors with the addition of the image of drunkenness and the cup of YHWH's wrath. But even when the Ninevites' drunken condition makes such a burning unlikely from a human point of view, it makes no difference at all. They will still be consumed as is dry stubble—completely, as shown in the paraphrased version preserved in the Targum.

Some scholars find a connection between the reference to drunkenness in Nahum 1:10 and the report of the Greek historian Diodorus of Sicily, who wrote that "the king of the Assyrians . . . had become elated over his past successes, turned to indulgence and divided among his soldiers . . . great quantities of wine . . . the whole army was carousing" (Diodorus Siculus 1950: II.26.4; W. A. Maier 1959: 191–92; Spronk 1997: 56). A similar report was recorded by Ktesias (cf. Kleinert 1910: 524–25; Gaster 1969: 665). A parallel event appears in Daniel 5:1–4 when King Belshazzar saw the handwriting on the wall before the fall of Babylon to Darius the Mede. In that instance the vessels that Nebuchadnezzar had taken from the Temple in Jerusalem were desecrated by the drunken guests at Belshazzar's festival.

Spronk (1997: 55) calls attention to the key role of the verbal root ʾkl ("to eat, consume, devour"), which is introduced in 1:10 and taken up again in 2:14a and 3:15a (*bis*). At first glance, there is no reference in 1:10 to an active subject of the verb in question. A closer look, however, reveals that the subject is the Divine Warrior YHWH. The acrostic pattern in the first two strophes of this opening canto makes it clear who the subject is: "I am YHWH" (1:1–3). That identity is underscored in the telestich pattern of 1:1–3a, in which the name YHWH is spelled out. Moreover, the two sides of YHWH's character are carefully depicted: YHWH is an avenging God who rages against his enemies (v 2). At the same time, however, YHWH is slow to anger (v 3a). In the concluding two strophes, these same two aspects of YHWH's personality appear again, in reverse order: "Good is YHWH, and a stronghold in the day of trouble" (v 7). But at the same time he is bringing "a full end—completely" (vv 8–10). Another acrostic pattern highlights the nature of God's action, reiterating the word *mlʾ* ("completely"), and in the first word of the concluding line of this acrostic we find our key verb: "They were devoured" (*ʔukkəlû*). In 2:14a, the inhabitants of Nineveh are burned and killed like young lions "devoured" by the sword. And in 3:15a, the same parallel between fire and sword appears again, combined with a third metaphor: "There the fire will devour you; the sword will cut you off; it will devour you like the locust."

The focus of interest in the second half of the opening canto in 1:1–10 is the question raised in v 9 ("What will you devise against YHWH"), which plays a prominent role for those scholars who regard this passage as a "prophetic interrogation" (Floyd 1994: 436) or see the entire book as a "prophetic refutation speech" (Sweeney 1992: 374–75). Spronk (1997: 27–28) calls attention to similar questions in the Psalms (cf. Psalm 52:3), for the statement "YHWH is good, indeed a stronghold in the day of distress" is at home in the world of psalmody as well (cf. Coggins 1985: 9–10, 19–20). Spronk observes that vv 7–10 is "a first application of the description of YHWH in vv 2–6. It emphasizes the difference between the friends and the foes of YHWH."

### The Vengeance of YHWH
Though the book of Nahum opens with a threefold declaration that YHWH is one who exercises vengeance, revenge is not the major theme. Vengeance is only one aspect of the presentation of YHWH as judge (see Peels 1995). His anger is the just response to gross injustice in human affairs, and the message of his judgment is intended as comfort to the oppressed and a source of hope for those who cower in the presence of invincible power (Edelkoort 1937: 52–53). As the context shows, the power is not "invincible" but only claims to be as part of its strategy of intimidation. It is clear that "invincibility" is a relative term, for from Israel's point of view, only YHWH is invincible.

Writing in 1948 while looking back at the atrocities of World War II, Mihelič (1948: 199–200) observed: "If the critics of Nahum had lived in the last decade and witnessed the brutality that had been visited upon the helpless people in the European and Asiatic concentration camps, they would rather have joined their voices with Nahum in his joy over the fall of the 'bloody city,' than have condemned his righteous indignation in the comfort and the security of their ivory tower" (reference taken from Spronk 1997: 15). In light of more recent events in Cambodia, Bosnia, Serbia, Uganda, Rwanda, Darfur in Sudan, and elsewhere, it is clear that terrorism remains political policy in the modern world as it was in ancient Assyria and that many such atrocities remain unavenged.

Until the rise of modern biblical scholarship in the nineteenth century, interpreters had little difficulty with the concept of YHWH as an avenger full of wrath. The apparent contradiction with other texts such as Leviticus 19:18 ("You shall not take vengeance") and Isaiah 27:4 ("I have no wrath") was handled in both Jewish and Christian circles by distinguishing between human vengeance and God's avenging evil. Human vengeance entraps the avenger in a hopeless cycle of violence, whereas God's vengeance brings hope to the oppressed. The confession of YHWH as avenger is an essential part of seeing him as judge and protector of his people (Chisholm 1990: 179–81; Becking 1995a, 1995b; Peels 1995: 205–8; Spronk 1997: 21).

The concepts of jealousy and holiness appear together for the first time in Joshua 24:19, where they are presented as attributes of God's nature (Reuter 2004: 55). Here in Nahum 1:2, the word "jealous" is used as a synonym of *nōqēm* ("avenging") and is qualified further by *ḥēmāh* ("wrath") and *nôṭēr* ("raging"; see Schulz 1973: 9–11). The adjectives *qannāʾ* ("jealous") and *qannôʾ* ("jealous") are used solely in reference to God and primarily in the context of his self-revelation at Sinai (Exodus 20:5; 34:14 [*bis*]; Deuteronomy 4:24; 5:9; 6:15). The more usual form *ʾēl qannāʾ* refers to the fact that God demands exclusive loyalty from his people, as spelled out in the first and second Commandments (see Loretz 1960: 413–14; Fensham 1969: 14–15). The second Commandment in both Exodus 20:5 and Deuteronomy 5:9 contains God's self-assertion of jealousy. In Exodus 34: 14 the designation of God as "jealous" indicates exclusivity of worship. Albright (1957: 309) insisted that the "outstanding concept of God in the Prophetic Age was his character as a 'jealous God.'"

Mendenhall (1973: 78, 88–95) argues: "The root NQM signifies the executive exercise of power by the highest legitimate political authority for the protection of his own subjects" (cf. also Dietrich 1976: 450–72; Lohfink 1983: 30–35; Peels 1995). In this context the sense of "vengeance" is essentially that of "punitive vindication." At times YHWH's "vengeance" is directed against his own people as well—so as to bring about their repentance. As a judicial function, "vengeance" belongs solely to God and his ordained representatives (cf. Exodus 21:20–21; Numbers 31:2–3; Joshua 10:13; Esther 8:13). Human beings are expressly forbidden to exercise their own vengeance on enemies (Leviticus 19:18).

Pitard's (1992: 786) article on vengeance stresses the difference between human vengeance and divine vengeance, which always carries positive weight in the Hebrew Bible. His argument that vengeance is YHWH's righting of wrongs is similar to earlier arguments by Mendenhall (1973: 69–104), for whom YHWH's vengeance was essentially that of punitive vindication. For Peels (1995: 204), YHWH's vengeance is a "continuing quality or characteristic (virtually a 'function')" of YHWH. Nonetheless, it cannot be denied that YHWH is presented here as the perpetrator of violence.

The wrath of YHWH is presented in terms of full repetitive parallelism carried through three successive poetic lines that are reminiscent of ancient Canaanite poetry that predated the prophet Nahum by hundreds of years:

A vengeful God (El), Y*HWH takes vengeance;*
Y*HWH takes vengeance;* he is a "Lord (Baal)" of wrath;
Y*HWH takes vengeance* on his foes.

This sequence of abc:bcd:bce is an adaptation of ancient Canaanite repetitive style (see Albright 1968: 4–10). The abc:abd pattern of the second two lines is paralleled in the archaic Song of the Sea in Exodus 15: 6, 11, 16. It should be noted, however, that Nahum did not in fact succeed in this attempt to re-create the climactic parallelism of ancient Canaanite poetry. The chiastic relationship between the first two lines and the fact that these three lines are part of a quatrain (four-part structure) gives the poet away. What we have here is archaizing on the part of a seventh- or sixth-century poet, not the quotation of older material.

The language here is taken from Exodus 34:6–7, a text to which other books in the Book of the Twelve Prophets make allusion as well (cf. Joel 2:13; Jonah 4:2; Micah 7:18–19). In that same context (Exodus 34:14) one also finds specific reference to Y*HWH* as *ʾel qannāʾ* ("a jealous God"). Elsewhere in the Tanakh, the words "slow to anger" are followed by affirmations of divine love (see Exodus 34:6; Numbers 14:18; Nehemiah 9:17; Psalms 86:15; 103:8; 145:8; Jeremiah 15:15; Joel 2:13). There is a clear connection of the phrase *ʾereḵ ʾappayim* ("long-suffering"; lit. "long of nose [= two nostrils, reflecting the dual form])" with Exodus 34:6 (cf. also Numbers 14:18; Nehemiah 9:17; Psalms 86:15; 103:8; 145:8; Jeremiah 15:15; Joel 2:13), where the phrase is followed by affirmations of divine love or fealty rather than an affirmation of God's greatness, *ûḡaḏol-kōaḥ* ("great in power"). The *kəṯîḇ* reading *wgdwl-kḥ* ("and great in power") is probably shaped by parallel usage in Exodus 32:11 (*bkh gdwl,* "in great power") and elsewhere (Deuteronomy 4:37; 9:29; 2 Kings 17:36). The *qərēʾ* reading *ûḡaḏol-kōaḥ* ("and great in power") achieves closer balance in mora count [25 + 4 + 25], which highlights the use of the divine name Y*HWH* in a pivot pattern—completing one statement, beginning another, and belonging to both.

Spronk (1997: 37) calls attention to an interesting parallel text in Psalm 145:8, where "we find a mixture of Exodus 34:6 and Nahum 1:3: וגדל־חסד ארך אפים" ("slow to anger and great in covenant-love"). He concludes that the phrase *ḡaḏol-kōaḥ* ("great in power") serves to counterbalance *ʾereḵ ʾappayim* ("slow to anger") in Nahum 1:3 and thus prepares the way to the next clause, with its focus on the certainty of punishment. He also notes the fact that the writer carefully omitted any reference to Y*HWH*'s forgiving sin (cf. Exodus 34:7); in this instance, Nineveh will not be forgiven. Elsewhere in the Tanakh, God's *kōaḥ* ("power") is normally associated with creation or the deliverance of the people of Israel from Egypt, and thus Ringgren (1995a:

126–27) wonders if perhaps the text here in Nahum 1:3 should be emended to read "great in *ḥeseḏ* ("covenant love"), as suggested by others in times past.

The poet presents Nineveh as the symbol of Yʜᴡʜ's enemy, and thus the work testifies to Yʜᴡʜ's power over the forces of evil. Thus Keller (1972: 418) speaks of "Relativierung und Mythisierung der Geschichte" (cf. van der Woude 1978a: 127). Others carry this line of thinking further in finding Nahum's influence in later apocalyptic literature (Schulz 1973; Renaud 1987a; Spronk 1997: 8), in particular the image of the Day of Yʜᴡʜ (Cathcart 1975).

**The Grace of Yʜᴡʜ**
Though vengeance is a dominant motif in the opening Psalm of Nahum and the book as a whole, that theme is balanced by specific reference to God's grace. In v 7 we read that Yʜᴡʜ is good, with the emphasis on good. D. N. Freedman (personal communication) sees this clause as the central theme of the whole Hebrew Bible, and he also calls attention to what he sees as the longest-range envelope construction in the Hebrew Bible: Genesis 1:1–2:4 is all about "God" and "Good," while the concluding two words in Ezra–Nehemiah, which he sees as the original ending of the Hebrew Bible, are also about "God" and "Good." Achtemeier (1986: 9) thinks the English word "God" is a shortened form of "good" and bears witness to the fact that all good comes from God. As the psalmist puts it: "Yʜᴡʜ is good to all, and his compassion is over all that he has made" (Psalm 145:9). Even in times of great trouble, faith declares: "God is good all the time; and all the time God is good!" And thus, Nahum, at the turbulent end of an era in human history, with armies in conflict and empires tottering on the brink of destruction, affirms the eternal truth "Good is Yʜᴡʜ."

Nahum gives two reasons to substantiate this claim. In the first place, God is "a stronghold in the day of distress" (v 7b), a mighty fortress so that we need not fear, "though the earth should change, though the mountains shake in the heart of the sea" (Psalm 46:1–2). God's protection is eternal. He provides peace in the midst of the raging storm. Second, God is good because "he knows those who take refuge in him" (v 7c). And that knowledge implies intimacy—tender loving care, like that of a husband for his cherished wife (see the earlier discussion of the term *baʿal* at 1:2) or of a father for his child. God knows their needs, their wants, their desires, and their sufferings. He cares for his own and sustains them in time of need with his loving presence.

God is slow to anger, but "he does not leave the guilty unpunished" (v 3ab); "in the sweeping torrent a full end he will make . . . and his enemies he will pursue into darkness" (v 8). God opposes those who defy him, and that too is part of his goodness, for God will not allow evil to triumph but will pursue it until it disappears into the dark, lifeless realm of chaos itself—into emptiness and nothingness, until it is completely destroyed and God's goodness alone remains.

The fact that God is patient and long-suffering in the face of human sin is a mark of his goodness. Like the mighty lion, he waits patiently before he acts. The weak lash out in response to every insult. The strong smile and wait, for they know that the enemy has no real power and cannot prosper indefinitely. God gives us time to turn to him. Spurgeon put it well (ca. 1890) when he wrote: "He doth not even threaten the sinner by his conscience, until the sinner hath oft-times sinned. He will often tell the sinner of his sins, often urge him to repent; but he will not make hell stare him hard in the face, with all its dreadful terror, until much sin has stirred up the lion from his lair, and made God hot in wrath against the iniquities of man. He is slow even to threaten" (quoted from 1981 [reprint]: 689; reference taken from Achtemeier 1986: 12). And even when he threatens, he is slow to pass sentence; when he passes sentence, he is slow to carry it out. Great cities of the past like Nineveh, Babylon, Rome, and Jerusalem all lived in their glory for hundreds of years before God, whose wrath is hard to kindle, finally swept them aside.

We do well to remember that God's hesitancy is due not to any lack of power on his part, for he is "great in power" (v 3a), but to his goodness. God does not ignore Assyria's evil out of weakness, for it is the God of creation itself that Nahum addresses (vv 3c–5). As Calvin (1948: 427) put it: "The world cannot for a moment stand, except as it is sustained by the favour and goodness of God" (reference taken from Achtemeier 1986: 12). Nahum presents God's power in awesome images. The mighty tornado is nothing but air stirred up as he strides along. The clouds are the dust kicked up by his feet. The mountains quake before him, and the hills melt away. The earth is laid waste together with all its inhabitants.

There are some who would soften Nahum's words as he speaks of God's destruction of evil. But if God does not destroy the evil that willful humans have brought into being, the world itself can never experience the wholeness God intended in creation itself. As Achtemeier (1986: 10) puts it: "To divest God of his function as destroyer of wrong is to acquiesce to the present corrupt state of the world—to accept the sinful status quo and simply to put up with whatever is done by selfish and prideful and corrupted men and women." If God's kingdom is to come on earth, evil must be dealt with by God in the manner Nahum describes. As Kleinert wrote long ago (1874: 21): "Our hearts must learn to give way to the wrath of God." We must learn to step aside and allow God's destruction of evil to unfold, and not take matters into our own hands. Here there is a fine line for us to walk, for we must learn to pray: "Deliver us from evil," and, at the same time, we must love the enemies of God's goodness. This does not mean that we must be passive toward sin and evil any more than it means that we can replace God as redeemer in his world. Achtemeier (1986: 11) put it well when she said: "In dealing with evil, in our world and in our enemies and in ourselves, we are to rely on God's action and not on our own, as he works through both his covenant people and the affairs of nations. 'Not my will, but thine be done' is here too the rule of faith."

# III. The Defeat of Belial (1:11–14)

|  | | SAS | Word |  |  |
|---|---|---|---|---|---|
|  | Morae | units | count |  |  |
| **A. The Counselor (of) Belial Has Departed** | | | | | |
| **Despite Assyria's Numbers (1:11–12b)** | | | [5.4] | | |
| 1:11 From you (f. sg.) he has departed / | 7 | 1 | 2 | 2 | 0 |
| a plotter (m. sg.) of evil / against YHWH // | 13 | 2 | 4 | 4 | 0 |
| 1:2–11b | | | 10 | 64 | 46 |
| (He is) the counselor (of) / Belial //   ס | 10 | 2 | 2 | 0 | 2 |
| 1:1–11 | | | 18 | 66 | 52 |
| 1:12 Thus / says YHWH / | 9 | 2 | 3 | 3 | 0 |
| "Are they not strong / and ever so numerous? / אִ שׁ וֹ ר[a] | 12 | 2 | 4 | 4 | 0 |
| 1:9–12b | | | 36 | 26 | 10 |
| **B. YHWH Addresses Judah: "I Will Remove** | | | | | |
| **the Rod of Assyria" (1:12c–13)** | | | [5.5] | | |
| But even so they shall be sheared / and they[b] will pass on // | 16 | 2 | 3 | 3 | 0 |
| though I afflicted you (f. sg.) / I will afflict you / no more  ⟦//⟧ | 14 | 3 | 4 | 0 | 4 |
| 1:8–12 | | | 51 | 34 | 17 |
| 1:13 And now / I will break his rod[c] / from upon you (f. sg.) // | 19 | 3 | 4 | 4 | 0 |
| and your (f. sg.) bonds / I will snap apart" // | 13 | 2 | 2 | 0 | 2 |
| 1:10–13 | | | 36 | 26 | 10 |

225

|  |  | SAS | Word |
|---|---|---|---|
|  | Morae | units | count |

**C. YHWH Addresses Assyria: "I Will Prepare Your Grave"**
**(1:14)** [4.5]

| | | Morae | SAS units | Word count | | |
|---|---|---|---|---|---|---|
| 1:14 And YHWH / has commanded concerning you (m. sg.) / | | 13 | 2 | 3 | 3 | 0 |
| "Seed from your (m. sg.) name will not be sown / | | | | | | |
| again // | | 11 | 2 | 4 | 4 | 0 |
| | 1:8–14b | | | 64 | 45 | 19 |
| From the house of your (m. sg.) gods / | | 9 | 1 | 2 | 0 | 2 |
| | 1:4–14c | | | 112 | 69 | 43 |
| I will cut off the graven image /^d and the cast idol / | | 12 | 2 | 3 | 0 | 3 |
| I will prepare your grave / for you are worthless" // ‏פ | | 13 | 2 | 4 | 0 | 4 |
| | 1:11–14 | | | [44] | 27 | 17 |

## Scansion of YHWH's Announcement of the Defeat of Belial (1:11–14)

| | | SAS | Word |
|---|---|---|---|
| | Morae | units | count |

| | Morae | SAS units | Word count |
|---|---|---|---|
| 1:11 *mimmḗk yāṣāʾ / hōšēḇ ʿal- YHWH / rāʿāh* ^ | 20 | 3 | 6 = 6 + 0 |
| *yōʿēṣ / bəlîyāʿal :* ‏ס | 10 | 2 | 2 = 0 + 2 |
| 1:12 *kōh / ʾāmár YHWH /* | 9 | 2 | 3 = 3 + 0 |
| *ʾim-šəlēmîm / wəkēn rabbîm /* ‏ר ו שׁ אַ^a | 12 | 2 | 4 = 4 + 0 |
| *wəkēn nāgōzû / wəʿāḇár<û>^b* ^ | 16 | 2 | 3 = 3 + 0 |
| *wəʿinnīṯik / lōʾ ʾăʿannḗk /ʿôd* [:] | 14 | 3 | 4 = 0 + 4 |
| 1:13 *wəʿattāh / ʾešbōr m<a>ṭḗhû^c / mēʿālāyik* ^ | 19 | 3 | 4 = 4 + 0 |
| *ûmôsərōṯáyik / ʾănattḗq :* | 13 | 2 | 2 = 2 + 2 |
| 1:14 *waṣiwwāh ʿālêka / YHWH /* | 13 | 2 | 3 = 3 + 0 |
| *lōʾ-yizzāraʿ miššimkā / ʿôd* ^ | 11 | 2 | 4 = 4 + 0 |
| *mibbêṯ ʾĕlohêkā /* | 9 | 1 | 2 = 0 + 2 |
| *ʾakrîṯ pésel /^d ûmassēkāh /* | 12 | 2 | 3 = 0 + 3 |
| *ʾāśîm qiḇrékā / kî qallôta :* ‏פ | 13 | 2 | 4 = 0 + 4 |
| 1:11–14 | | | 44 = 27 + 17 |

## NOTES

^a These letters indicate that the word *Assyria* is spelled out with the initial Hebrew letters of four successive words in this line.

^b Reading the plural form *wəʿāḇārû* ("and they will pass on") with Tg in place of *wəʿāḇār* ("and he will pass on") in BHS in 1:12a, with either the loss of *waw by* haplography or the "sharing of a consonant" (Watson 1969: 532).

<sup>c</sup> Reading *maṭṭēhû* ("his rod") with LXX, Vg, Syriac, Tg, and some Heb. Mss in place of *mōṭēhû* ("his yoke") in BHS in 1:13a.

<sup>d</sup> Reading the sequence of *ʾazlâ* plus *dargâ* here in 1:14b as disjunctive.

SAS units:

$$[5 + 4] + [5 + 5] + [4 + 5] = 9 + 10 + 9 = 28 \quad \text{SAS units}$$

Meaningful center: four words on either side of the arithmological center:

| | |
|---|---|
| *wəʿinnīṯīḵ lōʾ ʾăʿannēḵ ʿôḏ* | And I have afflicted you; I will afflict you no more; |
| *wəʿattāh ʾešbōr maṭēhû mēʿālāyik* | And now I will break his rod from upon you. |

Strophic units as shown by balance in mora count:

| | | | | | | |
|---|---|---|---|---|---|---|
| A | 1:11–12b | 2 balanced dyads + pivot | [7 + 13] + 10 + [9 + 12] | = | 20 + 10 + 21 | morae |
| B | 1:12c–13 | 2 balanced dyads + pivot | [16 + 14] + [19 + 13] | = | 30 + 32 | morae |
| C | 1: 14 | 2 balanced dyads + pivot | [13 + 11] + 9 + [12 + 13] | = | 24 + 9 + 25 | morae |

Word count:

| | | |
|---|---|---|
| 1:1–11 | 52 | (= 26 × 2) words after *ʾaṯnaḥ* |
| 1:8–12 | 51 | = 34 + 17   [compositional formula—all divisible by 17] |
| 1:10–13 | 26 | words before *ʾaṯnaḥ* |
| 1:11–14 | 17 | words after *ʾaṯnaḥ* |

## INTRODUCTION

The content of the meaningful center highlights the central message of Yʜᴡʜ's announcement of the defeat of Belial (the Wicked One) in the second canto as a whole. The destruction of this enemy is indeed "good news" (2:1 [1:15]) to Judah, for the days of her affliction under Assyrian domination are finally coming to an end.

The content of the three strophes in the second canto (1:11–14) may be outlined in a five-part concentric pattern that is determined on prosodic grounds as follows:

### Canto 2: Yʜᴡʜ Announces Assyria's Defeat and Israel's Deliverance (1:11–14)

| | | | |
|---|---|---|---|
| A | From you (f. sg. = Nineveh) the counselor (of) Belial has departed | [5] | 1:11 |

| B | YHWH says: "Are the Assyrians not strong and ever so numerous?" | [4] | 1:12ab |
|---|---|---|---|
| X | **YHWH: "I will remove Assyria's rod from you"** (f. sg. = Judah) | [5.5] | 1:12c–13 |
| B′ | YHWH says: "You (m. sg. = Assyria) will have no descendants" | [4] | 1:14ab |
| A′ | YHWH says: "I will prepare your grave (m. sg. = corporate Assyria)" | [5] | 1:14c–e |

In terms of the distribution of SAS units in Nahum 1:11–14, the three strophes are arranged in perfect symmetry, with vv 12c–13 in the center: [5 + 4] +⟦5 + 5⟧+ [4 + 5] SAS units. The statement that the "counselor (of) Belial" has departed (1:11), which is marked with the *setuma'* layout marker at the end of v 11, is set against a word of judgment announcing the king's fate as YHWH declares that he is preparing Assyria's grave (1:14c–e). YHWH speaks about Assyria in the two segments of the inner frame in this structure in contrasting ways, in the first raising the question of Assyria's strength and numbers (v 12ab) and in the second declaring that Assyria will be without descendants (v 14ab). And in the center (1:12c–13) we find an oracle directed to Judah ("you"—f. sg.) announcing that YHWH is removing the rod of Assyrian oppression.

When Bliese's methodology of metrical chiasm (1995: 53) is applied to 1:11–14, based on the distribution of word stresses (that is, counting accents), we have the following: [7 + 6] +⟦7 + 6⟧+ [6 + 9]. This three-part structure can be read in symmetrical balance by combining *lōʾ-ʾăʿannēk* ("I will not afflict you") in v 12 and the words *bêt-ʾělōhêḵā* ("house of your gods") and *kî-qallôṯā* ("for you are worthless") in v 14 so as to have the following symmetrical pattern in word stress units: [7 + 6] +⟦6 + 6⟧+ [6 + 7]. Bliese himself (1995: 56–60) analyzes vv 12–13 and 14 as separate metrically chiastic poems. These are balanced by 2:3 [2] and 2:4 [3], with 2:2 [1] the high point in the center of a larger unit of 17 lines from 1:12 to 2:4 [3]. Each of the five poems in his analysis switches its addressee in turn between Judah and Nineveh.

The three strophes in Nahum 1:11–14 are part of a larger concentric structure that extends from the latter part of the seventh strophe in the first canto (1:1–10) to include the first strophe of the third canto (2:1–11 [1:15–2:10]). The content of this larger structure may be outlined in a similar menorah pattern that is determined on prosodic grounds as follows:

## YHWH Announces the Defeat of Belial (1:9c–2:1 [1:15])

| A | Distress will not arise a second time—they will be consumed | [4.5] | 1:9c–10 |
|---|---|---|---|
| B | From you (f. sg. = Nineveh) the counselor (of) Belial has departed | [5] | 1:11 |

| C | Though strong and numerous, Assyria will be sheared and pass on | [4] | 1:12ab |
|---|---|---|---|
| X | **Yнwн's word to Judah: "I will afflict you** (f. sg.) **no more"** | [5.5] | 1:12c–13 |
| C′ | To Assyria: "Seed from your (m. sg.) name will be no more" | [4] | 1:14ab |
| B′ | To Assyria: "I will remove idols and prepare your (m. sg.) grave" | [5] | 1:14c–e |
| A′ | Good news announced: Belial (m. sg.) will be utterly cut off | [5.4] | 2:1 [1:15] |

The numbers in this outline, which appear in an inverse symmetrical pattern, represent the SAS units. The structure begins in the middle of v 9, following the repetition of the word *kālāh* ("a full end" in vv 8 and 9), which plays a significant role in the structure of the "bent" acrostic pattern in 1:2–8. The structure continues through the second reference to Belial in 2:1 [1:15]. What we have here is a carefully crafted transitional canto that connects the first and third cantos in the book of Nahum (that is, 1:1–10 and 2:1–11 [1:15–2:10]). These four verses in 1:11–14 also function as a transition in the overall content of the book, as announced at the outset in the two-part heading. The *maśśāʾ* ("oracle") constitutes the psalm (hymn of theophany) in 1:1–10. The remaining two chapters focus on the *ḥāzôn* ("vision") to describe the imminent fate of Nineveh in graphic detail, as seen by the prophet (cf. Sweeney 2000: 423).

The *petuchah* layout marker at the end of v 14 in *BHS* marks the end of Yнwн's speech and also the chapter division of the Hebrew text. English translations, however, follow the chapter break of the LXX, which comes one verse later. In terms of the numerical composition of the text, the break falls at the end of v 14 with the Masoretic chapter division. At the same time, however, the reference to Belial in v 11 anticipates the second use of this same word in 2:1 [1:15], forming an inclusion around 1:11–2:1 [1:15] as previously outlined.

Spronk (1997: 68) believes that the *setumah* marker at the end of v 11 and the *petuchah* marker at the end of v 14 are used "for the obvious reason that Yнwн is said to be speaking here." Even if this should prove to be the correct explanation for the presence of these two markers here, and they do not appear as mere coincidence, this does not justify Spronk's decision to place the boundary between the first two cantos at the end of v 11, for the logo-prosodic analysis indicates that the boundary falls at the end of v 10. There is much we do not know about the use of these two layout markers, which are not so easily explained in other contexts (cf. Nahum 2:14; Habakkuk 1:17; 2:8,

14, 17, 18; and many other places). The function of the *setumah* at the end of v 11 may have something to do with marking the prosodic boundary in the literary structure along different lines, together with the phenomenon of enallage. The sudden change to the 2nd pers. f. pl. "you" in 1:9 announces the prosodic boundary that falls at the end of 1:10, as Cathcart argued (1973a: 30–31), along with others on other grounds.

The phenomenon of enallage in 1:11–14, however, is more complex. In v 11 the 2nd pers. f. sg. "you" refers to Judah, and the 3rd pers. m. sg. "he" refers to the "counselor (of) Belial," who is presumably the king of Assyria, or perhaps to Assyrian might personified as an individual person in v 13, as Keil (d. 1888) suggested long ago ([reprint] 1949: 16). In v 12 the 3rd pers. m. pl. "they" refers to Assyria in a collective sense, and that word is coded into the text in a name acrostic of the initial letters of the first four consecutive words of YHWH's speech. The 2nd pers. f. sg. "you" in v 12 continues to refer to Judah through the end of v 13. The 2nd pers. f. sg. "you" then shifts in v 14 to m. sg., as the "you" becomes the king of Assyria (that is, the "counselor [of] Belial" of v 11). And in 2:1 [1:15] the 2nd pers. m. sg. "you" shifts back to f. sg. in reference to Judah. All of the prosodic boundaries of the three strophes in 1:11–14 are marked by the phenomenon of enallage.

Somewhat comparable occurrences of enallage are noted in my commentary on Deuteronomy, where the word *Numeruswechsel* is used to describe a narrower version of the same phenomenon in the frequent change between 2nd pers. sg. and pl. forms. See in particular "The *Numeruswechsel* in Deuteronomy" in Christensen (2001: xcix–ci) and specific examples of places where this happens more than one time in the same location (Deuteronomy 1:20–22; 3:21–22, 26; 4:1–4, 19–24, 25–26; 5:1–5, 22; 6:2–3, 16–17; 7:4–8; 8:19–20; 9:12–17; 10:15–20; 11:10–21, 26–31; 12:1–7; 13:2–6 [1–5]; 14:1–4; 19:18–19; 22:23–24; 23:4–5 [3–4]; 24:8–9, 14–15; 25:12–13, 17–18; 27:1–4; 28:61–63; 29:1–5 [2–6], 9–14 [10–15]; 30:18–19; 31:5–6, 26–27).

A more common approach used in times past to explain the bewildering shift of pronouns and forms of address in 1:11–2:3 was to follow the assumption of Wellhausen (1892) that we have here a composite text that must be taken apart in some manner. Wellhausen saw the promises of salvation for Judah (1:13; 2:1, 3) as secondary additions to the original text. Other scholars (Wolfe 1935: 93; J. Jeremias 1970: 14–19; Schulz 1973: 12–21; Seybold 1989a: 20–21; Hieke 1993b: 15; Lescow 1995: 70–71) have dismissed vv 9–10 and 12 as secondary. There are many variations along these same lines to explain the apparent disorder in the text as it stands. Some scholars express little, if any, hope that the problems of the text can ever be resolved. Sellin (cited by Spronk 1997: 64) posited a theory of despair in his suggestion that two columns of an oracle to Judah (1:12–14; 2:1, 3) and an oracle against Nineveh (1:10–11; 2:2, 4–14), which were originally written next to each other, were somehow intermingled (cf. J. M. P. Smith 1911; J. Jeremias 1970: 18; and Coggins 1985). Rudolph (1975) retains the MT as it stands in regard to 1:9–2:1.

Though any sort of scholarly consensus appears remote at this point in time, an increasing number of scholars are quick to point out that proposals along the lines suggested by Wellhausen a century ago remain hypothetical, with no support in the ancient versions. And some are coming to the defense of the MT on stylistic and other grounds. J. Ridderbos (1930: 26) suggested that these verses represent a survey of the prophet's thoughts. Eaton (1961: 63; 1981: 17) thought that "the recitation of the poem was originally accompanied by dramatic action," so hearers of the text would have had no difficulty with the changes in the person addressed (quote from 1981: 17). At an earlier point in time, Humbert (1926, 1928), who also interpreted the text on liturgical grounds, handled the difficulties in a somewhat similar manner.

Though S. J. de Vries (1966: 481) also posited a liturgical reading, he still found it necessary to assume later additions to the text. At the same time, as Spronk points out (1997: 65), Becking (1978: 111–14) uses the arguments of de Vries to defend the unity of the passage. Sweeney (2000: 432) builds on the work of Becking to come up with a form-critical solution in which he interprets the m. pl. form in v 9 as a reference to both the king of Assyria and Judah, who express doubts about Yʜwʜ's power as described in the preceding psalm (hymn of theophany). In Sweeney's opinion, the rest of the book deals with a refutation of these doubts: in 1:11–2:1, Judah is addressed in regard to its deliverance; and in 2:2–3:19 Nineveh and its king are addressed announcing their downfall. Spronk (1997: 65–66) correctly observes, however, that 1:9 does not clearly state that the people of Judah consider Yʜwʜ powerless, and the division of the text in the manner Sweeney assumes remains in question (cf. Zenger 1995: 412).

Nahum 1:12–14 appears to have been shaped by Isaiah 10:5–27c, which condemns Assyria for oppressing the people of Judah with rod and staff. At the same time, these verses appear to have been used to shape the account in Jeremiah 27–28, where the prophet Jeremiah appears in the streets of Jerusalem wearing a yoke to symbolize his belief that Judah must submit to Babylon (see Sweeney 2000: 433–34).

## NOTES

**1:11.** *From you he has gone forth.* There are differences of scholarly opinion on the identity of both the 2nd pers. f. sg. suffix in the word *mimmēḵ* ("from you") and the 3rd pers. m. sg. subject of the verb *yāṣāʾ* ("he has gone forth").

Most interpreters think the 2nd pers. f. sg. pronoun refers to Nineveh as the hometown of Y_HWH's enemy (as have Keil 1949: 14; Spronk 1997: 58; and many others). The NIV inserts the word *Nineveh* at this point. Logoprosodic analysis indicates that we have a two-part strophe in 1:11–12b, with the prosodic boundary at the end of the word acrostic in v 12, which ends with the sixth word. The phenomenon of enallage is at work here; therefore, the one who has departed is the personification of Assyrian power, namely the corporate personality designated here as Belial (see the following discussion), so that the "he" (m. sg.) in the verb *yāṣāʾ* ("he went forth") is to be identified with the m. pl. referent in the four-word name acrostic in the final four words of the strophe. The feminine addressee at the outset is the city of Nineveh, whence the evil one (that is, Assyrian power) has gone forth in the prophet's vision.

Those who have sought consistency in the use of pronouns here (Graham 1927–28: 45–46; S. J. de Vries 1966: 160) have drawn a connection with 1:12 and 2:1 [1:15], where Judah is addressed in the 2nd pers. f. sg. Graham thought that the text here refers to a specific opponent of the prophet Nahum, perhaps Jeremiah, or one who shares his views. Others (Rudolph 1975: 157; Becking 1978: 113; Renaud 1987b: 203) argue that the evil one has left Judah, or perhaps Jerusalem, and translate the verb *ysʾ* with the sense "He marched off." This could then be a reference to the Assyrian king Sennacherib when he was forced to give up the siege of Jerusalem according to 2 Kings 19 (according to Halévy 1905: 105; J. M. P. Smith 1911: 310–11; G. A. Smith 1928: 104; Rudolph 1975: 158; and Floyd 2000: 57) or perhaps to King Ashurbanipal on his way back from the conquest of Egypt (Peels 1993: 27). Jeremias (1970: 20–25) argued that the person addressed here (and also in v 14) is King Manasseh in Jerusalem.

Cathcart (1973a: 62) links v 11 with v 9 in the repetition of the verbal root *ḥšb* ("to think, devise"), even though the verse here does not belong to the introductory psalm that ends in vv 9–10. Much as the repetition of the noun *kālāh* ("a full end") together with the verbal root *ʿśh* ("to do, make") ties together vv 8 and 9, the verbal root *ḥšb* with the prepositional phrase *ʾel Y_HWH* ("you devise against Y_HWH") becomes "plotting evil against Y_HWH" (*ḥōšēb ʿal Y_HWH*) in v 11. The primary difference, however, is in the subjects of the verbal forms, which shift from 2nd pers. f. pl. ("you will devise against Y_HWH") to 3rd pers. m. sg. ("he is devising against Y_HWH"), which might be explained as a further instance of the phenomenon of enallage.

Van der Woude (cited by Spronk 1997: 57) emends the pointing of the word in the MT so as to derive *mmk* from the root *mkk* ("to humiliate") and translates: "The oppressor shall disappear completely." J. Jeremias (1970: 20–25) saw v 11 as addressed to King Manasseh in Jerusalem, who was responsible for the idols in the Temple. This interpretation is accepted by W. Dietrich (1994a: 470; 1994b: 740), who translates the phrase in question as "counselor of Belial" and identifies him as the high priest advising Manasseh or Manasseh advising the king of Assyria.

Longman (1993: 794) argues that v 11 "speaks of YHWH's departure from the sinful city of Nineveh" and calls attention to the fact that the verb *yṣ*ʾ ("to go forth, depart") is used elsewhere (Lamentations 1:6; Ezekiel 10:18–19) in reference to God's abandonment of a city. In short, he understands the "you" of v 11 to be a reference to Nineveh and the "he" to refer to YHWH, as in v 9 (though the pronoun is plural in v 9 and singular in v 11). Longman understands v 10 as a subordinate clause introduced by the particle *kî* ("for"), with v 11 continuing the subject established in v 9 (which is Assyria there and here is the city of Nineveh, as the capital of Assyria), in spite of the grammatical change in both the gender and number for the word "you."

The prosodic boundary between vv 10 and 11 between the two cantos, as well as between strophes, makes Longman's interpretation unlikely, though not impossible, at least as regards the grammatical connection between vv 9 and 11. That connection probably does not extend across this boundary. The principle of enallage suggests that we should look forward to what follows in this passage to understand the abrupt change in person and gender in the opening word of a new strophe (and canto). A further problem with Longman's reading (1993: 794) is in the gender of the two participles, which he renders "you who plan evil . . . you who counsel wickedness." The "you" at the beginning of this verse is feminine, and thus one would expect feminine forms of the two participles if the poet intends us to see Nineveh as the subject here as well; but the gender of both participles is masculine.

Even if we reject Longman's interpretation in matters of detail, it is not easy to dismiss outright his intuition in regard to seeing Nineveh as the person addressed using the 2nd pers. f. sg. suffix in the word *mimmēk* ("from you") at the beginning of v 11. This is how the NIV and the NET Bible read the text, both of which insert the word "Nineveh" in their translation at the beginning of v 11 by way of clarification. The problem is how to interpret the 3rd pers. m. sg. subject of the second word, *yāṣāʾ* ("he has gone forth"). It is preferable to see here the same person we find in the 3rd pers. m. sg. suffix to the word *maṭṭēhû* ("his rod") in v 13. That person is probably not the king of Assyria as such, who is apparently addressed in v 14 in the 2nd pers. m. sg. as one who faces death as the object of YHWH's wrath. Instead we have here a reference to "the Assyrian power personified as a single man" (using the words of Keil 1949: 16 in his discussion of 1:14). In this text we are dealing with the concept of what H. W. Robinson (1964) described as a corporate personality. Achtemeier (1986: 14) sees this as a reference "not to one Assyrian conqueror but to all of them, and Nineveh's sin, manifested in her cruelty toward sub-jugated nations, is finally sin against God." The personification of evil here is described as "a plotter of evil against YHWH" who is "the counselor (of) Belial" (v 11). This same person is subsequently described as Belial in 2:1, where the prophet declares that he will never again invade Judah, for "he is utterly cut off," which raises the question as to whether the words *yōʿēṣ bəlîyaʿal* might be read in apposition to "(the) counselor Belial." In Isaiah 9:5 the *peleʾ yôʿēṣ* ("wonder of a counselor") apparently refers to the prediction of an ideal ruler (as in BDB 419). The ruler referred to in Nah 1:11 is subsequently described as "worthless" and destined for a grave that YHWH has already prepared for him (see v 14).

A *plotter of evil against YHWH (he is) the counselor (of) Belial.* The one plotting evil against YHWH is interpreted by many scholars to be the king of Assyria. And so they conclude that the departure mentioned in Nahum refers to his departure from Judean territory. The perfect form of the verb is the prophetic perfect, and the sense is that the Assyrian presence in Judah is about to be removed. YHWH is destroying Assyrian hegemony in the land, and Judah will never again suffer under this particular oppressor (cf. Isaiah 33:18–19).

According to Sperling (1995: 324; cf. Pedersen 1926: 431), the word *bəlîyāʿal* is the combination of the negative *bal* followed by a word related to the verbal root *yʿl* ("to be of value"). A second possibility is that achieved by combining the negative particle with the verbal root *ʿālâ* ("to go up"), mean-ing "that which does not come up," or unsuccessful, along with Cross and Freedman (1953a: 22, n. 6), who argued that the word comes from *\*bal(i) yaʿl(ê)*, "[place from which] none arises, a euphemism for Hades or Sheol." A third possibility is that of deriving the word from the root *blʿ* ("to swallow"), along with Dahood (1966a: 105; cf. Tromp 1969: 125–28), which has the sense of "the swallowing abyss." In rabbinic usage, corrupt individuals were described as being "yokeless" (*balî ʿōl*) in the sense of being uncontrollably lawless (*Sanhedrin* 111b, a tractate of the Talmud; see Neusner 1982). Since Dahood's time, a number of other popular etymologies have been proposed (see Thomas 1963: 11–17; Otzen 1975: 131–33). It has also been suggested that the word is a Hebrew adaptation from *Belili*, a Babylonian goddess (see Achtemeier 1986: 16). In short, the origin of the word cannot be traced with certainty.

Though many (Longman 1993: 794, NRSV, NIV, etc.) interpret the word *bəlîyāʿal* as "wickedness," the word appears again in 2:1 [1:15], where it clearly represents a person (or people) rather than an abstract concept of "wickedness" or "worthless counsel" (as does Sweeney 2000: 432). The NASB is closer to the truth in translating the word as "the wicked one" in 2:1 [1:15]. Haldar (1947: 33) also argued that the meaning of the term must be "in some degree personified." Writing specifically in terms of its appearance in 2:1 [1:15], Gaster (1962: 377) said: "The word is used absolutely to designate a malevolent power, either human or demonic." It is better to recognize that the term represents a personification of evil that is used in reference to the power of Assyria as a collective personality, or perhaps as an epithet for the king of Assyria, who is counselor (of) Belial.

It is best to leave the term *bəlîyāʿal* untranslated here, as Otzen (1975: 131–36) suggests for other contexts, and to render the text "counselor (of) Belial" so as to call the reader's attention to the mythic overtones the word takes on elsewhere. The term refers to the personified leader of the enemy forces. Taken literally, the name apparently means something like "no value," worthlessness," "confusion," or "chaos." The concluding words in v 14 in fact describe this very person as one who is "worthless" (see the following discussion for the word *qallôṭā*, "You are worthless"). The word *Belial* subsequently took on a life of its own in Jewish literature, particularly in the Pseudepigrapha and in the Qumran texts, and it is also found in the Greek New Testament as a term for the devil (as *beliar* in 2 Corinthians 6:15). It is used as a proper noun to designate Satan in the Testimony of the Twelve Patriarchs, The Ascension of Isaiah, and Jubilees, and in the Sibylline Oracles it is applied to Nero (see J. M. P. Smith 1911: 308).

W. Dietrich (1994a: 470; 1994b: 740) identifies the "counselor of Belial" with the high priest advising Manasseh (= Belial) or perhaps with Manasseh advising the king of Assyria. Haldar (1947: 33) argued that the hostile power referred to in this pronoun "is neither Nineveh nor its king." Instead Haldar found "an allusion to the planning of the power hostile to Yahweh . . . so we have there an equivalent of *Bəlîyaʿal*," which he compares to the power of Kingu in *Enuma Elish*. In that epic poem, the goddess Tiamat gives the *malikūṭu* of all the gods to Kingu, "that is, He is their *maliku*, 'prince' or 'counselor'" (114).

Haldar (1947: 33) followed Burney (1903: 246) in deriving the term *bəlîyāʿal* from the root *blʿ* ("to swallow up") with a formative *lamed*, and Thomas derives the word from the same verbal root (1963: 18–19). Burney understood the *yod* as the mark of the diminutive and posited an original *\*bulaiʿāl*, which perhaps became *bəlîʿōl,* with the meaning "engulfing ruin" or "perdition." Haldar (1947: 33) added this comment: "It must only be added that this notion can be almost personified." He went on (108) to identify this person as "the leader of the hostile forces" and argues that he "seems to play a role equivalent to that of Kingu," who is killed and with his blood humankind is fashioned in the Babylonian epic Enuma Elish (VI II. 31 ff). Arguing from the references to Belial in Nahum 1:14 and 2:1 [1:15], Haldar concluded that, like Kingu, Belial as leader of the hostile forces is "cut off" by Yʜwʜ, who makes an end of opposition or enmity (1:9). Here he found parallels to Marduk in Enuma Elish II 1. 95 and again in regard to Tammuz, who is said to throw down enmity like a hero (see AnOr 10, p. 454, l. 17).

It is possible to find here a double entendre in which the meaning shifts as the reader or hearer moves on to the text that follows. The abrupt usage of the 2nd pers. f. sg. form at the outset announces the beginning of a new prosodic unit and at the same time raises the image of a city being addressed. Moreover, the stage is now set for the delineation of the prophet's vision (ḥăzôn) about the impending destruction of Nineveh, which was intimated in the heading in 1:1; thus the antecedent of the pronoun "you" is Nineveh from the opening words of the book in 1:1, as Spronk argues (1997: 58). So the recipient of the words of this text hears two complementary messages at the outset: from you, O Nineveh, YHWH has departed—in the sense Longman suggests—and from you, O Nineveh, the "counselor (of) Belial" has gone forth—for the last time.

The possibility of finding in the 2nd pers. f. sg. usage a reference to Judah as well emerges more slowly as we move into the second half of v 12, which is also the beginning of the second strophe of this transitional canto. Here a new identity for the person addressed is established, as YHWH himself declares: "Though I afflicted you (f. sg.), I will afflict you (f. sg.) no more." The addressee is no longer in doubt (though scholars such as J. M. P. Smith 1911; Ewald 1878; Hitzig 1881; G. A. Smith 1898; and Eaton 1961 have still managed to see Nineveh as the addressee here as well), because these words are addressed to Judah (according to Roberts 1991: 53 and many others). As Keil observed long ago (cited by Spronk 1997: 73), it is not likely that Assyria would have been addressed with the promise "I will afflict you no more." The punishment leveled against Assyria is more severe. "It is not a matter of humbling, but of complete destruction."

Sweeney's (2000: 432) conclusions on the meaning of the text are shaped by presuppositions as regards the disputation genre. He argues that the phrase yōʾēṣ bəlîyāʿal means "worthless counsel," and he translates the verse "From you has gone forth thinking about YHWH evil, worthless counsel" or, in more idiomatic English: "Evil thinking, worthless counsel, has gone forth from you about YHWH." In short, Sweeney sees 1:11 as "the thesis that [the author] intends to dispute within the context of the disputation genre, viz., the people think ill of YHWH and the prophet intends to demonstrate that YHWH indeed has acted on their behalf."

Spronk (1997: 56–57) notes that deities other than YHWH are deemed worthless elsewhere (cf. Jeremiah 16:19–20). Spronk's interpretation of the text is shaped by his assumptions about the structure of the text as a whole, with v 11 forming the conclusion of the opening hymn, as he follows the layout of the text as given in *BHS*. However, his conclusion that he is in fact merely following the Masoretes, who used the *setumah* layout marker here to mark the boundary, moves beyond the evidence at hand. The meaning of such layout markers may yield to other explanations as we come to understand the nature of the numerical composition of the text in greater detail. If the *setumah* marker is used here to mark a boundary, it may be more subtle in nature, as the logoprosodic analysis suggests.

The prosodic boundary at the end of v 10 is marked by the emphatic use of the word *mālē'* ("completely"), which reiterates the acrostic pattern of this same word in vv 9–11, and by the principle of enallage in the first word of v 11. Moreover, the text scans perfectly in vv 11–12, with the *setumah* marking a secondary prosodic boundary immediately before Yhwh's direct speech, which begins with another carefully constructed acrostic on the word *'šwr* ("Assyria") in the initial letters of the first four words attributed directly to Yhwh in the book of Nahum. This reported speech of Yhwh, which is exactly 17 words in length, continues to the end of v 13 (the end of the second strophe in the second canto) and contains three more instances of the 2nd pers. f. sg. pronoun, which appears first in the opening word of this canto (vv 11–14).

1:12. *Thus says* Yhwh: "*Are they not strong (with allies), and ever so numerous?*" This opening expression is essentially what Westermann (1967: 100–115) called the "messenger formula," where the prophet appears as a messenger of God's salvation, a formula that is frequently used to introduce prophetic speeches (cf. Jeremiah 2:5; Ezekiel 2:4; Amos 1:3). According to Haldar (1945: 114–15; 1947: 34), this phrase is used to introduce oracles pronounced by a priest-prophet in the name of Yhwh. The message of salvation is that God will destroy their enemy, however numerous they and their allies may be. Translation of the next seven words after this opening rubric, however, poses serious difficulties. J. Jeremias (1970: 15) found the text here totally corrupt, and Sellin (1930: 363) insisted "that it defies all explanation." According to Sponk (1997: 64), Sellin found the text so confused that he posited that two columns, one with an oracle to Judah (1:12–14; 2:1, 3) and another with an oracle against Nineveh (1:10–11; 2:2, 4–14), were originally written next to each other and were erroneously intermingled. Consequently, numerous possible corrections have been proposed.

Sponk (1997: 59, 69) calls attention to what he calls a name acrostic of the word *'šwr* ("Assyria") in the initial letters of four consecutive words at the beginning of this judgment oracle in 1:12, which was apparently first observed by Reider (1938: 154), who noted what he describes as a statement that is "acrological in character, the initial letters yielding the name Ašur." In this instance the acrostic names the addressee of Nahum's oracle and the opponent Yhwh will destroy. Sponk (1997: 70, n. 8) calls attention to a parallel phenomenon observed by van der Wal (cited by Spronk) in Jeremiah 31:8–9, where the first letters after the word *hinənî* ("Behold I") spell out the word *mᵊmṣ* ("he who strengthens"), namely Yhwh who restores Israel. This observation helps to explain the unusual grammatical construction in v 12; as Spronk puts it: "In this line grammar was subordinate to the wordplay" (70).

The word *šəlēmîm* has a wide range of potential meaning. Longman (1993: 798) translates the phrase *ʾim šəlēmîm* as "although intact" or perhaps even "strong." Others focus their attention on the aspect of strength in translations such as "though they are at full strength" (NRSV, NASB) or on the sense of being complete in "though they are full" (JPS Tanakh), whereas the NIV has "though they are unscathed" and the KJV reads "though they be quiet." Cathcart (1973a: 63) interprets the word *šəlēmîm* as "strong" with the sense of "hale, healthy," citing parallels in Ugaritic. Spronk (1997: 71) interprets the word *šəlēmîm* in light of parallel usage in Zechariah 8:12 and finds here the image of chaff blown away by the wind (cf. van der Woude 1984: 142).

Roberts (1991: 42) translates the line as "Even if they are strong and just so numerous," but he argues incorrectly: "The first *wᵊkēn* refers back to the thicket of interwoven thorns mentioned in v 10" (46–47). The word *šəlômî* ("my friend") sometimes refers to friends or allies (Psalms 7:5 [4]; 41:10 [9]), and the noun *šelem* is used in reference to a sacrifice for alliance or friendship with God (1 Samuel 11:15); Nahum refers to the allies of the Assyrians in 3:15–17 using different terminology. It thus seems possible to hear a double entendre here; if the poet wanted to stress Assyrian might, he could easily have chosen a different word. The word *wəkēn* ("and moreover, thus") is an emphatic comparative adverb of degree (BDB 486; *IBHS* §39.3.4.c, e). This is sometimes called an "A; what's more, B!" form of parallelism: "They are strong; what's more, they are many!"

Haldar (1947: 34) presented an interesting explanation of the LXX rendering ("ruler of many waters"), which appears to be based on a Hebrew text in which the word *wəkēn* ("and [ever] so [numerous]") was missing. Haldar's reconstruction of the presumed original text is close to what Ruben suggested earlier (cf. Ruben 1898: 174) in *ʾmšl mym rbym*, which he translated "I shall cause to flow mighty waters." Haldar (1947: 35) differed from Ruben in his interpretation of the verbal root *mšl* as meaning "to resemble," the causative form meaning "to make similar," which becomes "to divide a thing into two equal parts, to split." He thus translates the clause "I shall split great waters." He understood this as an allusion to Yhwh's victory in the crossing of the Sea (114–15). But all this is based on removing the word *wəkēn* ("and so") and fails to recognize the fact that the initial letters of these four words form an acrostic on the word "Assyria."

The four words *ʾim-šəlēmîm wəkēn rabbîm* are usually considered the concessive protasis of a conditional statement meaning something like "even though they are at full strength and numerous." The second clause, *wəkēn nāḡōzû wəʿāḇār*, would then be the logical apodosis of a comparative statement: "Nevertheless they will be cut off and pass away." In light of both the acrostic in the initial letters of the first four words and the logoprosodic analysis, it is better to translate these four words as a complete statement and not merely as the protasis in a comparative clause that is completed in the next three words, as in most English translations. The *ʾim* is to be read as an interrogative particle: "Is it the case that?" (see *DCH* I:305), and the four words should be translated as follows: "Are they not strong [that is, with allies], and thus all the more numerous?"

W. A. Maier (1959: 203–4) discussed each one of the following "substitute readings" for the four words in question:

1. Gunkel (1893), Nowack (1897), and Marti (1903) proposed *ʾak šāləmû wəkēn rabbîm* ("Verily the days of my contention are completed").
2. J. M. P. Smith (1911) proposed *ʾak šāləmû yəmê rîḇî* ("Verily the days of my contention are completed") or *ʾak šāləmû yāmîm rabbîm* ("Verily many days have been completed").
3. Wellhausen (1892) suggested *ʾim šāləmû mayim* ("If many waters are ever so full"), which was followed by G. A. Smith (1898) and in essence by G. R. Driver (1906).
4. Haupt (1907b) read *ʾim mayim məlaʾîm* ("if the waters are filling").
5. Junker (1938) read *ʾim šəlamîm wəʾim rabbîm* ("if they are complete and if they are numerous").
6. Van Hoonacker (1908) proposed *mōšēl mārôm* ("the ruler of the heights").
7. Ruben (1898) read *ʾămaššēl mayim rabbîm* ("I shall cause many waters to flow").
8. Haupt (1907b) read *mōšēl mayim* ("He rules the water").
9. Riessler (1911) proposed *mōšēl mayim rabbîm* ("ruler of great waters").
10. Horst (1938) read *hinnēh mōšəlîm mayim rabbîm* ("Behold, tyrants are mighty waters"), which was followed by Sellin (1930, based on Bickell [1894]), who said: "Tyrants, like powerful waters, are dangerous; but they run off quickly and pass away."
11. Duhm (1910) read *ʾim šālam yôm ʿannōṯēk* ("if the day of thine affliction is complete").
12. Stonehouse (1929) suggested "Though thou rulest over peoples."

13.   Gaster (1944) had "what though great waters gushed" (reading *šallû*
      from the root *šll*, "to gush").

*But even so they shall be sheared; and they will pass on.* The second use of
the word *wəkēn* ("and moreover") in v 12 differs slightly from its earlier usage
in this same verse; here the word emphasizes that the action described will
occur immediately (cf. 1 Kings 20:40; Psalm 48:6). The three Hebrew words
should be rendered "But even so, they are cut off; and they pass on." The
word *nāgōzû*, which the NRSV translates "they will be cut off" (cf. NIV and
KJV) is ordinarily used to describe the process of "shearing" sheep (Genesis
31:19; 38:12–13; Deuteronomy 15:19; 18:4; 1 Samuel 25:2, 4, 7, 11; 2 Samuel
13:23–24; Job 31:20; Isaiah 53:7) and "cutting hair" (Jeremiah 7:29; Micah
1:16; Job 1:20). It is used here in a figurative sense to describe the destruction
of the Assyrian army (BDB 159). This is an example of implied comparison
because the Assyrians made frequent use of sheep imagery when boasting
of the brutality with which they defeated their enemies (see Marcus 1977:
92–93). Thus Sennacherib brags: "I cut their throats like lambs" (*ARAB*, 254).
Tiglath-pileser III writes: "I butchered their troops like sheep" (Grayson
1987–90: 2:25, 37). In short, the Assyrians face the same fate they boasted of
inflicting on others.
     W. A. Maier (1959: 205–6) discussed seven proposed emendations of the
word *nāgōzû* ("they are cut off"):

1.   *gazzû* ("they shall pass away") by J. M. P. Smith (1911)
2.   *yāgûzû* ("they shall pass away") by Wellhausen (1892) and Sellin
     (1930)
3.   *gāzal* ("he tears away") by Newcome (1783)
4.   *nigzərû* ("they shall be cut off") by Happel (1902)
5.   *nāgôz* ("cut off") by Gunkel (1893)
6.   *nāgôzû* (Niphal of the root *gwz*, "they are destroyed") by Friedrich
     Delitzsch (1920)
7.   *yigzərû* ("they disappear") by Wellhausen (1892; alternate possibility)

The word *waʿābār* ("and he passes on") is emended here with LXX, Syriac,
and Targum to read as a 3rd pers. pl. form of the verb *ʿābar<û>* ("they shall
pass away"). The word appears in 1:8 and again in 2:1 [1:15], whereas it refers
to the departure of the one plotting evil against Yhwh in v 11. The verb may
be read as an indefinite personal subject for the 3rd pers. m. sg. *ʿābar* with the
sense of "they" (see GKC §144d). Haldar (1947: 35) reached the same conclusion, arguing that emendation is not necessary to obtain the translation
"And so they are cut off and pass away." It is also possible to read the *waw* at
the beginning of the verb *wəʿinnītīk* ("although I have afflicted you") as a

shared consonant (cf. Watson 1969: 532). Rudolph (1975: 159) transfers the *waw* from the beginning of the next word (as do Roberts 1991: 47 and Spronk 1997: 69–71) to achieve this same end. Logoprosodic analysis supports emending the text in this instance, which adds at least one and possibly two morae to this dyad. Some scholars interpret the singular form as a collective: "Yet did they pass away" (W. A. Maier 1959: 200) or "with special emphasis" (Keil 1949: 15). The NET Bible (p. 1683) explains the singular verbal form *ʿābār* in terms of a rhetorical, stylistic device used for emphasis (see Genesis 29:27; Numbers 22:6; 32:25; Job 12:7; 18:2; Esther 9:23; Psalm 73:7; Proverb 14:1, 9; cf. Bullinger 1898: 525 [4.5]). This is another way of describing the phenomenon of enallage.

*Though I have afflicted you, I will afflict you no more.* Keil (1949: 15) argued that the address here turns to Judah, whereas Abarbanel (d. 1508), Grotius (d. 1645), Ewald (1878), and Hitzig (1881) understood it as applying to the Assyrians. Spronk (1997: 72) prefers to read the text here as two independent clauses, even though the conditional relationship implied by simple juxtaposition, which is reflected in the translation presented here, is the more natural reading (cf. Joüon and Muraoka 1993: §167a; see also Haldar 1947: 36). Because of his assumptions about the nature of Hebrew prosody, Spronk (1997: 59, 72) finds a prosodic boundary here that separates v 12 into two distinct parts, with the break occurring with the *ʾatnaḥ*. Logoprosodic analysis indicates that the break falls at the end of the name acrostic, which is marked with the accent *zaqēp qaṭan*.

Though the meaning of this line in Hebrew is fairly clear, the text suffered in times past from those determined to restore a complete alphabetic acrostic. Some scholars have interpreted the text to mean that Nineveh is addressed here rather than Judah (Ewald 1878; Hitzig 1881; G. A. Smith 1898; J. M. P. Smith 1911; Eaton 1961). Ruben (1898: 176) understood the verb here to mean "to sound" and translated the passage "and the sound of thy name shall no longer resound." Wellhausen (1892) read a masculine instead of a feminine personal pronoun because of the imperative masculine form in 2:2. Roberts (1991: 47) notes that the LXX reading ("And your report will not be heard again") appears to be based on reading the Hebrew root *ʿnh* I ("to answer") instead of *ʿnh* II ("to oppress, afflict").

1:13. *And now, I will break his rod from upon you; and your bonds I will snap apart.* The particle *waʿattāh* ("and now"), which is used to make a contrast between a past condition, as described in 1:12, and what will happen in the immediate future (Brongers 1965: 289–99; cf. Genesis 11:6; 2 Samuel 2:6; 2 Kings 12:8), carries an emphatic disjunctive force (*IBHS* §39.3.4f). The pointing of the Hebrew text is emended here to read *maṭṭēhû* ("his rod") with LXX (τὴν ῥάβδον), the Vulgate (*virgam*, "his scepter"), and some Hebrew

manuscripts listed by de Rossi (1786) rather than *mōṭēhû* ("his yoke") with
Cathcart (1973a), Rudolph (1975), van der Woude (1978a), and others. Spronk
(1997: 73) presents a strong argument for this same change in light of parallel
texts (primarily in Isaiah 10:5 and 30:31), which is followed here on prosodic
grounds (to achieve balance in terms of mora count). Nonetheless, the MT as
it stands also makes good sense (and is supported by the Syriac). The reading
in the MT is followed by the NRSV, NIV, and JPS Tanakh, as well as Roberts
(1991: 47, n. 23), Longman (1993: 794), and others. It should be noted that
a "yoke of iron" is the agent of covenantal discipline in Deuteronomy 28:48,
and Isaiah makes reference to the Assyrian "yoke" as YHWH's instrument of
discipline (Isaiah 28:22). It is easy to understand why the unpointed Hebrew
text would have been misread to find the word "yoke" here, but it is more difficult to explain the reading "rod" unless that is in fact the original text.

The term *ûmôsərōṭayik* ("your bonds, shackles"), which Longman (1993:
798) interprets as part of the yoke apparatus, is better understood as the shackles the Assyrians used to subdue prisoners. The word *môsərōṯ* ("bonds")
comes from the root *ʾsr* ("to tie, bind, imprison") and is translated "chains" by
Spronk (1997: 59; cf. Psalms 2:3; 107:14; Jeremiah 2:20; 5:5; 27:2; 30:8).

For examples in which breaking the yoke means release from political
oppression, see Leviticus 26:13; Jeremiah 28:10–14; and Isaiah 10:27 and
especially 14:25. The yoking of a beast of burden is used here as a metaphor
for the subjugation of a nation under a foreign power, that is, vassaldom (Jeremiah 27:2; 28:14; Ezekiel 30:18; 34:27). This same imagery has parallels in
Assyrian usage. In describing their subjugation of foreign nations, Assyrian
rulers frequently spoke of causing them "to pull my yoke." Sennacherib
describes his subjugation of Judah in 701 BCE in these words: "I laid waste the
large district of Judah and put the straps of my yoke upon Hezekiah, its king"
(ANET 288). Assyrian rulers frequently speak of causing subject nations to
"pull my yoke" (ARAB, 238–39, 308, 331, 347, 516–17, 662, 780, 786, 798,
833, 970).

1:14. *YHWH has commanded concerning you.* The break in the prosodic
structure with the introduction of a new strophe at the beginning of v 14 is
underscored by the change in content as the "tone becomes judgmental, and
the words are directed toward another person" (Longman 1993: 798). Gandell (1901: 640) understood this person to be the king of Assyria. Keil (1949:
16), however, argued that "it is not the king of Assyria who is addressed, but
the Assyrian power personified as a single man." The logoprosodic analysis
lends substance to Keil's argument in the presence of the phenomenon of
inclusion, in which the "he" here is to be identified with the "plotter of evil
against YHWH," who is also called "the counselor (of) Belial" in v 11. Moreover, we find here another instance of the phenomenon of enallage with the

shift from 2nd pers. f. sg. suffix forms to the 2nd pers. m. sg. because Yhwh is now addressing Assyria as a "corporate personality," to use the phrase of H. W. Robinson (1964) from another context.

According to Meier (1992: 197–201), the use of the verb *ṣwh* ("to command") with direct divine speech connotes greater authority on the part of the speaker. In this context, it highlights the contrast between Yhwh and the king of Assyria. Spronk (1997: 74) finds that this interpretation depends on the parallel text in Isaiah 10:5–6 about Yhwh commanding Assyria to act against the nation that aroused his wrath. The proposed emendation to read *ʿlyh* ("against her") in place of *ʿlyk* ("against you"), as argued by Rudolph (1975), is mere conjecture without textual support of any sort.

*"(Seed) from your name will not be sown again."* Taken literally, the expression *lōʾ yizzāraʿ miššimkā ʿôd* could be rendered "It will no longer be sown from your name again," which Keil (1949: 16) interpreted to mean "Thou wilt have no more descendants." It is not the king of Assyria only who is addressed here but the Assyrian state itself as a corporate personality. On the one hand, the meaning is that the king will have no descendants, or perhaps that his fame will die out. At the same time, the prophet is announcing the end of Assyrian domination on the world scene, but not in the manner assumed by Floyd (2000: 413) when he writes: "The Assyrians' departure from Jerusalem marked the beginning of their downfall." Floyd is thinking of the departure of Sennacherib in 701, which predated the expansion of Assyrian power in the days of Esarhaddon (680–668 BCE) and Ashurbanipal (668–627 BCE), when Assyrian power reached its zenith in the conquest of Thebes (663)—an event actually cited in the book of Nahum (3:8). It makes little sense to think of the beginning of Assyria's downfall before ca. 650 BCE, at the earliest. Like Floyd, other interpreters in times past identified the person addressed here with an Assyrian king—either Sennacherib (Pusey 1860; Henderson 1864; Kleinert 1874; Hitzig 1881) or Ashurbanipal (Rashi [d. 1105]; Michaelis 1782; see J. M. P. Smith 1911: 311).

Haldar (1947: 37) read the initial *mem* on the word *miššimkā* as enclitic (as have Hummel 1957: 85–107 and Cathcart 1973a: 65). Others render it partitively, as "One of your name" (Rudolph 1975: 159) or as "part of your name" (van der Woude 1978a). The word *šēm* ("name") here means "posterity, progeny, memory." There is certainly no reason to emend *yizzāraʿ* to read *yizzākēr* ("it will [not] be remembered") as suggested by Elliger in the *BHS* note (1970; cf. also Nowack 1922: 248; J. Jeremias 1970: 21).On the specific phrase in question, as Spronk (1997: 75) observes: "The destruction of the name and seed (*šumu u zeru*) from the land is mentioned more than once in the vassal treaties of Esarhaddon"; examples include 'May Zerbanitu, who gives name and seed, destroy your name and seed from the land,' and 'May

Nabu, who holds the tablets of fate of the gods, erase your name and destroy your seed from the land" (*ANET* 538, 541). Similar curses are found in later Aramaic texts. For example: "May Shachar, Shamash, Nikkal, and Nushku exterminate your name and your place from the living and kill you with an evil death and let your seed perish" (*KAI*, 225, seventh century BCE), and again: "May the gods of Tema exterminate him and his seed and his name from Tema" (*KAI*, 228, ca. 400 BCE).

The Assyrian royal annals frequently refer to memorials set up to preserve the king's name, such as the prism inscription of Ashurbanipal: "A memorial inscribed with my name, anoint it with oil, offer sacrifice; with the memorial inscribed with his name and the name of Sennacherib, my grandfather and strength to befall his position. Whoso destroys this memorial inscribed with my name . . . may the gods of heaven and earth curse him in wrath, smite down his kingship, eradicate his name, his seed out of the land" (Piepkorn 1933: 86–89). YHWH takes the place of the "great gods" of Assyria, because those famous kings are now subject to his curse. This theme is explored symbolically in the book of Nahum in terms of what Hudson (2000) has described as a "tuning metaphor." In terms of the matrix model as understood by McClain (1976), YHWH indeed takes his place on the "throne" in the place of the "great gods" of Assyria, who are understood as the numbers 10 (Marduk), 15 (Ishtar/Inanna), 20 (Shamash/Utu), 30 (Nanna/Sin), 40 (Ea/Enki), 50 (Enlil/Ellil), and 60 (Anu/An) in the sexagesimal system of Mesopotamian mythology (see McLain 1976: 132; 1994: 29; cf. Black and Green 1992). The three "greatest gods" (Ea-Enki = 40; Bel-Enlil = 50; and Anu-An = 60), in the ratio 4:5:6 "actually generate the whole tonal universe" (McClain 1976: 133). YHWH displaces them all and subsumes their various functions in the process, along with those of all the lesser gods as well. That is what the book of Nahum is about.

*From the house of your gods, I will cut off the graven image and the cast idol.* We are dealing here with a common motif and the fact that a curse on the Assyrian king implies a confrontation between YHWH and the gods of Assyria (Spronk 1997: 75). However, Keil (1949: 16) thought that the text concerns "the utter destruction of the Assyrian power, together with its idolatry, upon which that power rested." Armerding (1985: 469) notes that when the temple of Nabu at Nineveh was excavated, "the statue of Ishtar was discovered, prostrate and headless, amid the ruins of her temple, which had stood at Nineveh for almost fifteen centuries."

The expression *bêt ʾĕlōhệkā* has the general sense of "temple" (cf. Judges 18:31; Joel 1:13, 16; Daniel 1:2). Haldar (1947: 37) noted that the Syriac drops the preposition and the Targum indicates that the author is thinking of the gods of Assyria. The combination of *pesel* ("graven image") and *massēkāh* ("cast idol"), as in Deuteronomy 27:15, denotes every kind of idolatrous practice (Keil 1949: 16). W. Dietrich (1994a: 470) argues that it could have been only King Manasseh who was so closely associated with a house of God by Nahum. He thinks this text refers to the image of the goddess Asherah that Manasseh placed in the Temple in Jerusalem (2 Kings 21:7; cf. Keller 1971: 402–3).

*I will prepare your grave for you are worthless.* Spronk (1997: 76) argues that the MT, as it stands, "can only be read as announcing the coming death of the king." Nonetheless, there are differences of opinion as to whether the statement here is meant as a threat before or after death. As it stands, the MT announces the coming death of the king, or perhaps that of the Assyrian people as a corporate body (Barker and Bailey 1998: 189), for his grave is already prepared. Reflecting earlier scholarly opinion (that of Clarke 1817; T. Scott 1823; Henry 1829; and others), Jamieson et al. (1872: 696) understood 1:14 (as translated in the KJV) as referring "to the murder of Sennacherib twenty years after his return from Palestine." However, today a growing number of scholars prefer to see here a connection with the common curse that the corpse is to be left unburied (cf. Isaiah 5:25; 14:19–20; Jeremiah 9:21; 22:19; 25:33; 36:30; and many parallels in Mesopotamian texts; see Hillers 1964: 68–69). Spronk (1997: 76–77, quoting Heidel 1946: 156) cites an interesting parallel in the report of Ashurbanipal about his treatment of the kings of Elam: "The graves of their former and later kings who had not feared Asshur and Ishtar, my sovereigns, and who had harassed the kings my fathers, I ravaged, destroyed and exposed to the sun. Their bones I took to Assyria." In spite of the attractiveness of this hypothesis, there is no textual support for the necessary emendations, however slight they may be. And the verse makes perfect sense as it stands in the MT. On the "preparation of the grave" as one's "eternal home," see Ecclesiastes 12:5. Josiah took the cult image (*hā'ăšērāh*) from the Temple in Jerusalem, burned it, pounded it to dust, and scattered it on graveyards (2 Kings 23:6). This same fate awaits the king of Assyria, who trusts in his gods, because they are powerless in the presence of YHWH.

The Targum and the Syriac interpret the text with a double accusative construction, with the implied second object being "the house of your gods": "I will make it [the house of your gods] your grave." Cathcart's (1973a: 67) emendation of *'āśîm* ("I will prepare [your grave]") to read *'āšîm* ("I will devastate"), as suggested earlier (by Sellin 1930; Horst 1938; Gaster 1944; and Delcor 1961, as also by R. Coggins 1985: 33), is attractive and accepted by the NET Bible. The destruction of a grave, like the threat of no burial at all, was a common ancient Near Eastern treaty-curse (Cathcart 1973b: 180–81). This change involves only the difference as to over which side of the Hebrew letter one places the dot so as to read the letter *shin* (שׁ) rather than *sin* (שׂ). Nonetheless, it is better to leave the text as it stands with Longman (1993: 799),

Roberts (1991: 43), and others. Keil (1949: 16) took *qibrekā* ("your grave") as the object of the verb *ʾāśîm* ("I put, place, make, fashion") and translated the passage "I prepare your grave." This may be understood as a figure of speech (metonymy of effect) meaning that YHWH will destroy the king of Assyria. It is also possible to interpret *ʾāśîm* in the MT as "I will determine" or perhaps "I will mark out" (Cathcart 1973a: 67; see Leonardi 1968: 240–41).

Cathcart (1973a: 67) translated *kî qallôtā* in the MT as "because you are worthless" (as did Keil 1949: 16), from the root *qll* ("to appear trifling, lightly esteemed") or perhaps *qlh* II ("to be lightly esteemed"). More recently, Cathcart (1992: 998) suggested the translation "I will make your grave a refuse heap" on the basis of new evidence, especially in the Tell Fakhariyeh bilingual inscription (Abou-Assaf et al. 1982: 21, 36). A significant problem with reading <qî>qālôt in place of *kî qālôt* is the fact that it reduces the word count by one, which disturbs the carefully contrived totals in the numerical composition of the Hebrew text. Moreover, the confusion of *k* and *q* is not likely in Hebrew orthography. Spronk (1997: 77) notes that "there are no deviating readings in the Hebrew MSS, and that there is no support from the Versions for the proposed emendations. Moreover, the MT clearly makes sense."

Procksch prefers a noun to a verb and emends *qlwt* to read *qlwn* (see *BH*[3]). G. R. Driver (1938: 270), who proposed a noun *qlyt* that he described as "abstract with semi-concrete meaning" translated the passage "I will make thy grave as (a thing of) shame." Haldar (1947: 38) related the word to Ugaritic *qll* ("to fall") and translates the passage "Thou hast fallen." It is also possible to interpret the Hebrew root *qll* here in relation to the Assyrian word *qalu* ("accursed") with the NET Bible, because so much of the immediate context concerns vocabulary associated with treaty-curses (see von Soden 1967: 295). This reading, however, appears to be dependent on emending the verb *ʾāśîm* ("I will prepare [your grave]") to read *ʾāśîm* ("I will devastate"). It is preferable to go with the more traditional reading: "I will prepare your grave because you are worthless" (with Roberts 1991: 43; Longman 1993: 794; NRSV; and others). As Spronk (1997: 77) observes, the concluding reference to the Hebrew word *qlwt* ("worthless") has an instructive parallel in Job 40:4; "Job replies to God that he is of too little account (*qlty*) to argue any longer with such a mighty God."

## COMMENT

### The Phenomenon of Enallage and the Structure of Nahum 1:11–14

The phenomenon of enallage here should have alerted scholars long ago to the fact that v 11 marks the beginning of a new prosodic unit in the structure of Nahum (contra Spronk and others). Even if one chooses to recognize the subject in both v 9 and v 11 to be Assyria as the one plotting evil against YHWH,

one must still account for the change from plural to singular in the pronoun
"you." In this instance the difference is to be explained primarily as a boundary marker, like the sudden introduction of the second plural form at the
beginning of v 9. In that instance the subject shifts to a 3rd pers. m. pl. suffix
in v 10 so that the implied subject in the remainder of that verse remains 3rd
pers.—"they," as indicated in the earlier translation, where this pronoun
appears in parentheses. But here at the beginning of v 11 the subject abruptly
shifts to the 2nd pers. f. sg. suffix in the term *mimmēḵ* ("from you").

Vv 11 and 14, which are addressed to Nineveh, on the one hand (f. sg.), and
to the Assyrian state as a corporate personality, on the other (m. sg.), function
as a frame around the oracle, which is introduced by the formula "Thus says
YHWH." YHWH speaks first about Assyria (7 words in 1:12ab) and then in direct
address to Judah (10 words in 1:12cd–13). In this 17-word speech YHWH
announces that he will remove the rod of Assyria, which has afflicted his
people in Judah.

In terms of the 154 words in 1:1–14, the arithmological center falls between
the words *bəyôm ṣārāh* ("in the day of trouble") in 1:7a, with 77 words on
either side. The meaningful center is found by adding four words on either
side of the arithmological center, as follows:

| | |
|---|---|
| *ṭôḇ yhwh ləmāʿôz* | Good is YHWH, indeed a stronghold |
| <u>*bəyôm ṣārāh*</u> | in the day of distress; |
| *wəyōḏēaʿ ḥōsê ḇô* | and he knows those who take refuge in him. |

The opening words of 2:1 [1:15] are familiar because of the parallel passage
in Isaiah 52:7. There is "one who brings good news, who proclaims peace so
that Judah may celebrate (her) festivals" once again. Passover was celebrated
in Jerusalem under Josiah after the period of Assyrian domination came to an
end (see 2 Kings 23:21–25). The reader is called to "Look, there on the
mountains; for the feet of one who brings good news, who proclaims peace."
In Nahum, Judah is mentioned by name here for the first time, and the end
of her oppression is likened to the cessation of warfare. The command to "fulfill your vows" may refer to the tithe of what one receives from God, as with
Jacob in Genesis 28:20–22. In most cases, however, it is the sacred vow to
praise God for deliverance in time of need, which is expressed in the form of
specific acts of thanksgiving accompanied by appropriate sacrifices (cf. Jonah
1:16; 2:10 [9]).

The *scriptio defectiva* in the word *wəʿinnītīḵ* ("and afflicted you") raises
the question of why and when medial *matres lectionis* were introduced into
biblical Hebrew. Albright (1932a: 81) and Cross and Freedman (1952: 57)
argued that these vowel letters were introduced under the influence of Aramaic about the fifth century BCE. Aharoni (1970: 21) presented evidence that

prompts Cathcart (1973a: 64) to remark that "recent epigraphical discoveries in Israel may require a new appraisal of the situation." Manuscripts within the proto-Masoretic tradition appear to have been adjusted in terms of total letter count to achieve specific ideal totals in cumulative word count in the numerical composition of the Tanakh (Christensen 2003b). This phenomenon is evident in the Book of the Twelve Prophets and Nahum in particular—along with the Torah and the Megilloth (in the four earlier Festal Scrolls, excluding Esther).

### Nahum 1:11–14 as a Transitional Canto

The second canto (1:11–14) is a carefully contrived transitional structure that ties the opening psalm (1:1–10), which constitutes the *maśśāʾ* ("exposition") in the book of Nahum, to the *sēp̄er ḥāzôn* ("scroll of vision") that follows in chapters 2 and 3. This transition in content is achieved by means of a series of poetic devices that break the passage up into smaller entities in which the author highlights his central message in different ways. Looking back over the whole of chapter 1, the central message is highlighted in the meaningful center in v 7: "Yhwh is good; indeed he is a stronghold in the day of distress; and he knows those who take refuge in him." The statement marks the conclusion of the bent acrostic poem (1:2–7) in which Yhwh declares that he is in the presence of sin and that he will accomplish *a full end* for Assyria, which is about to be consumed as dry stubble is burned—completely. The concluding strophe of Nahum's psalm (vv 9–10) highlights the totality of Assyria's destruction; the day of distress will not be repeated. No second chance will be given to Assyria; her destruction is both certain and final.

The second canto itself is a chain of short statements linked by the phenomenon of enallage. The first strophe is a balanced dyad with a pivot tying together the two different but complementary statements:

| | | |
|---|---:|---:|
| From you has departed the one plotting evil against Yhwh, | 20 | 3 |
|   *a schemer—namely, Belial!* | 10 | <u>2</u> |
| *He is the schemer, Belial;* | 10 | 2 |
|   Thus says Yhwh: "Are they not strong and ever so numerous?" | <u>21</u> | <u>4</u> |

The end of the first statement is marked with the *setumah* layout marker, whereas the end of the second statement is marked by the name acrostic *ʾšwr* ("Assyria") in the initial letter of the first four words placed on the lips of Yhwh. The figure of Belial here is the personification of Assyrian power, which has gone forth from the city of Nineveh "plotting evil against Yhwh." Together with their allies, the Assyrians are strong and ever so numerous.

The second strophe (1:12c–13) is addressed to Judah, the victim of Assyrian aggression, who is informed that in spite of Assyria's apparent strength and great numbers, "They shall be sheared" like sheep "and they will pass on." Y<small>HWH</small> informs them that Assyria as the "rod of his anger" (cf. Isaiah 10:5) will be broken and Judah's bonds will be snapped asunder; though Y<small>HWH</small> has afflicted his people, he will afflict them no more.

In the concluding strophe (v 14), Y<small>HWH</small> addresses the Assyrian state directly as a corporate entity, or perhaps addresses the king of Assyria, in two balanced dyads connected by a pivot, which yield two parallel statements:

| | | |
|---|---:|---:|
| And Y<small>HWH</small> has commanded concerning you: | 13 | 2 |
|   "Seed from your name will not be sown again, | 11 | 2 |
|     *from the house of your gods.* | <u>9</u> | <u>1</u> |
| *From the house of your gods,* | 9 | 1 |
|   I will cut off the graven image and the cast idol; | 12 | 2 |
|     I will prepare your grave, for you are worthless." | <u>13</u> | <u>2</u> |

The concluding reference — to the fact that Assyria as a corporate body, or perhaps the king of Assyria, who represents the power of this evil empire, will go to his grave as "worthless" — carries us back to the root meaning of the term *Belial*, the plotter of evil against Y<small>HWH</small> concerning whom the canto began in v 11. The gods of Assyria are powerless, and in fact are no gods at all, in the presence of the Divine Warrior Y<small>HWH</small>.

The content of this transitional prosodic unit continues across the canto boundary in a form of enjambment so as to reach its conclusion in the second half of the opening strophe of the third canto in 2:1 [1:15], with a reiteration of the announcement that Belial will never invade Judah again, for "he is utterly cut off" (2:1b [1:15b]).

## Finding Contemporary Meaning in Nahum 1:11–14

The trial of Saddam Hussein in Iraq raised the issue of crimes against humanity, as did the Nuremburg trials against Nazi leaders after World War II. Crimes against humanity are in fact crimes against God, which God himself deals with in his own time. As E. Achtemeier notes (1986: 14), Pope Pius XII showed that he understood this well when he addressed a gathering of international leaders in the Sistine Chapel before Michelangelo's famous painting of the Last Judgment. On that last day there is no escape from God's judgment.

According to Isaiah (10:5–6), Assyria was an instrument of God's anger against his own people; but power corrupted Assyria, as it does all who believe that they are self-sufficient and in control of their own destinies. Like other nations, Assyria proudly declared: "By the strength of my hand I have done it, and by my wisdom, for I have understanding; I have removed the boundaries of peoples, and have plundered their treasures" (Isaiah 10:13). Assyria's pride became defiance of the power of the God of Israel as shown in the boasting of the Assyrian commander Rabshakeh in the days of Hezekiah: "Do not let Hezekiah mislead you saying, YHWH will save us. Has any of the gods of the nations saved their land out of the hand of the king of Assyria? Where are the gods of Hamath and Arpad? Where are the gods of Sepharvaim? Have they delivered Samaria out of my hand? Who among all the gods of these countries have saved their countries out of my hand, that YHWH should save Jerusalem out of my hand?" (Isaiah 36:18–20). Assyria's pride provoked God's anger, because God demands submission to his authority. As Achtemeier (1986: 15) puts it: "God will be king over us, and it is for us to decide whether he will exercise his kingship in love toward us or in wrath."

Though this psalm of Nahum is used to introduce the powerful words of judgment against Nineveh that follow, the poem itself (1:2–10) does not mention Nineveh or Assyria by name; this hymnic preface applies to all peoples in every age. The psalm bears witness to God's essential goodness and his incomparable power. It testifies to God's forbearance and to the fact that he will not continue to ignore evil in high places. There is a day of accountability.

The Christian church has used the words of Nahum in reference to the final judgment. Calvin (1559) illustrated this fact in his commentary when he paused after commenting on the first five verses to express this prayer: "Grant, Almighty God, that as thou settest before us here as in a mirror how dreadful thy wrath is, we may be humbled before thee, and of our own-selves cast ourselves down, . . . and be cleansed from our vices, until we shall at length appear in confidence before thee, and be gathered among thy children, that we may enjoy the eternal inheritance of thy heavenly kingdom, which has been obtained for us by the blood of thy Son. Amen" (trans. in Owen 1846–49: 3:427–28, cited by Achtemeier 1986: 15).

The message, however, applies to individuals and corporate bodies within the flow of history itself, not just to matters of eschatology. The book of Nahum constitutes an urgent call to repentance—a call to turn from our prideful ways and to seek refuge in God's goodness. Though we stand condemned under his sentence, for we know that he will not acquit those who are guilty, we also know his very nature. God is slow to anger and slow to carry out the just sentence of death and destruction, because he does not desire that any should perish.

In this transitional canto, Nahum quickly moves on to spell out the consequences of God's appearance in his own time for wicked Assyria, which faces imminent destruction. In forceful repetition, we are told that God will "shear" mighty Assyria as a sheep is sheared (v 12). YHWH declares that he will "cut off" Assyria's gods, which are nothing but worthless idols (v 14). In short, Belial himself will be "cut off" and will invade Judah no more (2:1 [1:15]). In

this instance, Belial is the personification of Assyria as the "wicked one." God
has uttered his decree against Assyria (v 12) in the "good news" long awaited
in Judah: "I will break [Assyria's] rod from upon you; and your bonds I will
snap apart" (v 13). The canto concludes with God's spoken words of judgment addressed to Assyria as personified in Belial. The God who created all
things by his spoken word also rules it by his word. As the psalmist puts it: "For
he spoke, and it came to be; he commanded, and it stood forth" (Psalm 33:9).
Assyria's name will not be sown again (v 14), which means she will have no
offspring; God is preparing Assyria's grave.

The image in v 13 is not that of a yoke, as the NRSV renders it, but that of
the upraised rod of a slave master. That punishing rod will be broken, and
Judah's bonds will be snapped asunder (cf. Isaiah 9:4; 10:27). This oracle of
judgment against Assyria is at the same time an announcement of good news
to the people of Judah; the days of Assyrian affliction are over forever. God
used Assyria as the rod of his anger in times past (see Isaiah 10:5–19), but he
will never use her in this manner again.

# IV. THE SACK OF NINEVEH
## (2:1–11 [1:15–2:10])

|  | Morae | SAS units | Words count |  |  |
|---|---|---|---|---|---|
| **A. Celebrate Your Festivals, O Judah, for Belial Is Utterly Cut Off (2:1 [1:15])** |  |  |  | [5.4] |  |
| 2:1 [1:15]Here now on the mountains / are the feet of a sentinel / | 16 | 2 | 5 | 5 | 0 |
| announcing peace / | _8 | 1_ | 2 | 2 | 0 |
| 1:11–2:1b |  |  | 51 | 34 | 17 |
| Celebrate, O Judah / your (f. sg.) festivals / | _12 | 2_ | 3 | 3 | 0 |
| 1:14–2:1c |  |  | 26 | 17 | 9 |
| Fulfill your vows (f. sg.) // | _10 | 1_ | 2 | 2 | 0 |
| 1:13–2:1d |  |  | 34 | 23 | 11 |
| For never again / will Belial invade you (f. sg.) / | 19 | 2 | 7 | 0 | 7 |
| he is utterly cut off // | 6 | 1 | 2 | 0 | 2 |
| 1:11–2:1 |  |  | 65 | 39 | 26 |
| **B. YHWH Has Come against Nineveh to Restore Israel (2:2–3 [1–2])** |  |  |  | [7.7] |  |
| 2:2 [1]A scatterer has come up / against you (f. sg.) / | 13 | 2 | 4 | 4 | 0 |
| guard the ramparts // | _9 | 1_ | 2 | 2 | 0 |
| 1:9–2:2b |  |  | 92 | 58 | 34 |
| Watch the road / gird the loins / | 11 | 2 | 4 | 0 | 4 |
| marshal strength / exceedingly // | 9 | 2 | 3 | 0 | 3 |
| 2:1–2 |  |  | 34 | 18 | 16 |

253

| | Morae | SAS units | Words count | | |
|---|---|---|---|---|---|
| 2:3 [2] For YHWH is restoring / the pride of Jacob / | 15 | 2 | 6 | 6 | 0 |
| indeed the pride of Israel // | 8 | 1 | 2 | 2 | 0 |
| 2:1–3b | | | 42 | 26 | 16 |
| For devastators / have devastated them / | 12 | 2 | 3 | 0 | 3 |
| and their vine-branches / they destroyed // | 13 | 2 | 2 | 0 | 2 |
| 2:2–3 | | | 26 | 14 | 12 |

### C. The Warriors and Chariots Are Prepared for Battle (2:4 [3])   [4.4]

| | Morae | SAS units | Words count | | |
|---|---|---|---|---|---|
| 2:4 [3] The shields of his warriors / are reddened / | 16 | 2 | 3 | 3 | 0 |
| (his) men of valor / are clad in scarlet / | 11 | 2 | 3 | 3 | 0 |
| 2:2–4d | | | 32 | 20 | 12 |
| Flashing as with fire are the [a]chariot coverings[a] / | 8 | 1 | 3 | 3 | 0 |
| on the day of its preparation // | 8 | 1 | 2 | 2 | 0 |
| 1:13–2:4d | | | 80 | 48 | 32 |
| Indeed the juniper arrows / are poisoned // | 12 | 2 | 2 | 0 | 2 |
| 2:3–4 | | | 26 | 19 | 7 |

### D. There Is Mayhem in Nineveh, and the Palace Melts Away (2:5–7 [4–6])   [(4.6).(6.4)]

| | Morae | SAS units | Words count | | |
|---|---|---|---|---|---|
| 2:5 [4] In the streets / the chariots run amok / | 15 | 2 | 3 | 3 | 0 |
| they rush to and fro / in the squares // | 10 | 2 | 2 | 2 | 0 |
| 2:1–5b | | | 65 | 42 | 23 |
| Their (f. pl.) appearance / is like torches / | 10 | 2 | 2 | 0 | 2 |
| 2:2–5c | | | 46 | 30 | 16 |
| Like lightning / they dart about // | 13 | 2 | 2 | 0 | 2 |
| 2:1–5 | | | 69 | 42 | 27 |
| 2:6 [5] His powerful ones / are brought to remembrance[b] / | 11 | 2 | 2 | 2 | 0 |
| 2:2–6a | | | 50 | 32 | 18 |
| They (m. pl.) stumble forward / as they go // | 13 | 2 | 2 | 2 | 0 |
| they hasten / to her wall / | 11 | 2 | 2 | 0 | 2 |
| 2:2–6c | | | 54 | 34 | 20 |
| But the mantlet / is (already) set up // | 9 | 2 | 2 | 0 | 2 |
| 2:5–6 | | | 17 | 9 | 8 |
| 2:7 [6] The gates of the rivers / are opened // | 15 | 2 | 3 | 3 | 0 |
| and the palace / melts away // | 10 | 2 | 2 | 0 | 2 |
| 2:4–7 | | | 48 | 31 | 17 |

|  | Morae | SAS units | Words count | | |
|---|---|---|---|---|---|

**E. Nineveh Is Destroyed, and Her People Are Carried Away into Exile (2:8 [7])** [4.4]

| | Morae | SAS units | Words count | | |
|---|---|---|---|---|---|
| 2:8 [7] And it is determined / she is stripped /^c (and) taken away // | 14 | 3 | 3 | 3 | 0 |
| *along with* her maidens / | 8 | 1 | 1 | 0 | 1 |
| 2:3–8c | | | 52 | 34 | 18 |
| *They are* moaning / like the sound of doves / | 12 | 2 | 3 | 0 | 3 |
| beating / on their breasts // | 12 | 2 | 3 | 0 | 3 |
| 2:6–8 | | | 23 | 10 | 13 |

**F. Nineveh Drains Away, and the City Is Plundered (2:9–10 [8–9])** [7.7]

| | Morae | SAS units | Words count | | |
|---|---|---|---|---|---|
| 2:9 [8] And Nineveh /^d is like a pool of water / | 12 | 2 | 3 | 3 | 0 |
| <her waters fall>^e // | 10 | 1 | 2 | 2 | 0 |
| 2:5–9b | | | 37 | 20 | 17 |
| They are /^f draining away / | 8 | 2 | 2 | 0 | 2 |
| "Stop! Stop!" (they cry) / but no one turns back // | 13 | 2 | 4 | 0 | 4 |
| 2:7–9 | | | 26 | 11 | 15 |
| 2:10 [9] Plunder silver / plunder gold // | 14 | 2 | 4 | 4 | 0 |
| 2:5–10a | | | 47 | 24 | 23 |
| Indeed there is no end / to the treasure / | 12 | 2 | 3 | 0 | 3 |
| 2:5–10b | | | 50 | 24 | 26 |
| Wealth / from all / its precious vessels // | 13 | 3 | 4 | 0 | 4 |
| 2:8–10 | | | 32 | 12 | 20 |

**G. The Destruction Is Total: They Are Gathered as Kindling (2:11 [10])** [4.5]

| | Morae | SAS units | Words count | | |
|---|---|---|---|---|---|
| 2:11 [10] Destruction /^g and desolation / and disintegration // | 19 | 3 | 3 | 3 | 0 |
| and hearts grow faint / | 7 | 1 | 2 | 0 | 2 |
| 2:5–11b | | | 59 | 27 | 32 |
| And knees give way / | 7 | 1 | 2 | 0 | 2 |
| 2:9–11c | | | 29 | 12 | 17 |
| And anguish / is in all loins / and (on) all their faces / | 19 | 3 | 5 | 0 | 5 |
| they are gathered as fuel (for burning) // | 8 | 1 | 2 | 0 | 2 |
| 2:1–11 | | | 128 | 64 | 64 |

## Scansion of Nahum's Vision of the Sack of Nineveh in 2:1–11 [1:15–2:10]

| | | Morae | SAS units | Words count |
|---|---|---|---|---|
| 2:1 [1:15] | hinnḗh ᶜal-hehārîm / raḡlê məḇaśśḗr / | 16 | 2 | 5 = 5 + 0 |
| | mašmîaᶜ šālôm / | _8 | 1_ | 2 = 2 + 0 |
| | ḥāggî yəhûḏāh / ḥaggáyik / | _12 | 2_ | 3 = 3 + 0 |
| | šalləmî nəḏāráyik ^ | _10 | 1_ | 2 = 2 + 0 |
| | kî lôʾ yôsîp̄ ᶜôḏ / laᶜăḇor-bāk bəlîyáᶜal / | 19 | 2 | 7 = 0 + 7 |
| | kullôh nikrāṯ : | _6_ | 1 | 2 = 0 + 2 |
| 2:2 [1] | ᶜālāh mēp̄îṣ / ᶜal-pānáyik / | 13 | 2 | 4 = 4 + 0 |
| | nāṣôr məṣūrāh ^ | _9 | 1_ | 2 = 2 + 0 |
| | ṣappēʾ-ḏérek / ḥazzēq moṯnáyim / | 11 | 2 | 4 = 0 + 4 |
| | ʾammēṣ kóaḥ / məʾôḏ : | _9 | 2 | 3 = 0 + 3 |
| 2:3 [2] | kî šāḇ YHWH / ʾeṯ-gəʾôn yaᶜăqôḇ / | 15 | 2 | 6 = 6 + 0 |
| | kiḡʾôn yiśrāʾēl ^ | _8 | 1_ | 2 = 2 + 0 |
| | kî ḇəqāqûm / bōqəqîm / | 12 | 2 | 3 = 0 + 3 |
| | ûzəmōrêhem / šiḥēṯû : | _13 | 2 | 2 = 0 + 2 |
| 2:4 [3] | māḡēn gibbōrêhû / məʾādām / | 16 | 2 | 3 = 3 + 0 |
| | ʾanšê-ḥáyil / məṯullāᶜîm / | _11 | 2_ | 3 = 3 + 0 |
| | bəʾēš- ᵃpildōṯ [hā]rékeḇᵃ /bəyôm hăḵînô ^ | 16 | 2 | 5 = 5 + 0 |
| | wəhabbərōśîm / horᶜālû : | _12 | 2 | 2 = 0 + 2 |
| 2:5 [4] | baḥûṣôṯ / yiṯhôləlû hārékeḇ / | 15 | 2 | 3 = 3 + 0 |
| | yištaqsəqûn / borḥōḇôṯ ^ | _10 | 2_ | 2 = 2 + 0 |
| | marʾêhen / kallappîḏim / | _10 | 2_ | 2 = 0 + 2 |
| | kabbərāqîm / yərôṣēṣû : | 13 | 2 | 2 = 0 + 2 |
| 2:6 [5] | <yizzākərû>ᵇ / ʾaddîráyw / | _11 | 2 | 2 = 2 + 0 |
| | yikkāšəlû / bahălîḵāṯám ^ | 13 | 2 | 2 = 2 + 0 |
| | yəmahărû / ḥômāṯāh / | _11 | 2_ | 2 = 0 + 2 |
| | wəhûḵan / hassōḵēḵ : | _9 | 2 | 2 = 0 + 2 |
| 2:7 [6] | šaᶜărê hannəhārôṯ / niptāḥû ^ | 15 | 2 | 3 = 3 + 0 |
| | wəhahêḵāl / nāmôḡ : | _10 | 2 | 2 = 0 + 2 |
| 2:8 [7] | wəhuṣṣaḇ / gulləṯāh /ᶜ hōᶜălāṯāh ^ | 14 | 3 | 3 = 3 + 0 |
| | wəʾamhōṯêha / | _8 | 1_ | 1 = 0 + 1 |
| | mənahăḡôṯ / kəqôl yōnîm / | 12 | 2 | 3 = 0 + 3 |
| | məṯōp̄əp̄ōṯ / ᶜal-liḇəḇēhen : | _12 | 2 | 2 = 0 + 2 |
| 2:9 [8] | wənînəwêh /ᵈ kiḇrēkaṯ-máyim / | 12 | 2 | 3 = 3 + 0 |
| | <mêmêhā hāwʾû>ᵉ ^ | _10 | 1_ | 2 = 2 + 0 |
| | wəhḗmāh /ᶠ nāsîm / | 9 | 2 | 2 = 0 + 2 |

|  |  | 14 | 2 | 4 = 0 + 4 |
|---|---|---|---|---|
| | ʾiməd̯ú ʾāmōd̯û / wəʾên map̄néh : | 14 | 2 | 4 = 0 + 4 |
| 2:10 [9] | bōzzû k̯ésep̄ / bōzzû zāhāb̯ ^ | 14 | 2 | 4 = 4 + 0 |
| | weʾên qéṣeh / lattək̯ûnāh / | 12 | 2 | 3 = 0 + 3 |
| | kāb̯ṓd̯ / mikkṓl / kəlî̄ ḥemdāh : | 13 | 3 | 4 = 0 + 4 |
| 2:11 [10] | bûqāh /ᵍ ûməb̯ûqāh / ûməb̯ullāqqāh ^ | 19 | 3 | 3 = 3 + 0 |
| | wəlēb̯ nāmḗs / | _7 | 1_ | 2 = 0 + 2 |
| | ûp̄îq birkáyim / | _7 | 1_ | 2 = 0 + 2 |
| | wəḥaḥālāh / bəkol-motnáyim / ûp̄ənê̄ k̯ullām / | 19 | 3 | 5 = 0 + 5 |
| | qibbəṣû pāʾrûr : | 8 | 1 | 2 = 0 + 2 |
| 2:1–11 [1:15–2:10] | | | | 128 = 64 + 64 |

## NOTES

ᵃ⁻ᵃ Reading *pildôt rek̯eb̯* ("chariot coverings"—5 morae) in place of *pəlād̯ôt hārek̯eb̯* ("coverings of the chariots"—9 morae) in the BHS.

ᵇ Reading a Niphal 3rd pers. m. pl. form *yizzāk̯ərû* ("they are brought to remembrance") in place of *yizkōr* ("he will remember") in 2:6a, with the LXX μνησθήσονται ("they bethink themselves") and the Syriac ("they are obedient to their officers").

ᶜ Reading the *mûnaḥ* in 2:8a on the word *gulləṭāh* ("she is stripped") as disjunctive.

ᵈ Reading the *mêrək̯â* on the word *wənînəwēh* ("and Nineveh") followed by *gaʿyâ* (= *meṭeg̱*) in 2:9a as disjunctive.

ᵉ Reading *mêmệhā hāwʾû hēmmāh nāsîm* ("her waters fall / they flee") in 2:9a in place of *mîmê hîʾ wəhēmmāh nāsîm* ("from of old she is / and they flee") in the MT.

ᶠ Reading the *mêrək̯â* on the word *wənînəwēh* ("and Nineveh") followed by *gaʿyâ* (= *meṭeg̱*) in 2:9b as disjunctive.

ᵍ Reading the *mêrək̯â* in 2:11a on the word *bûqāh* ("destruction") as disjunctive.

SAS units (2:1–11):

$$[(5 + 4) + (7 + 7) + (4 + 4)] + \boxed{(4 + 6) + (6 + 4)} + [(4 + 4) + (7 + 7) + (4 + 5)] =$$
$$[9 + 14 + 8] + \boxed{20} + [8 + 14 + 9] =$$
$$31 + 20 + 31 = 82 \text{ SAS units}$$

Meaningful center: one word on either side of the arithmological center (in v 5):

**yištaqšəqûn bārəḥōb̯ôt**    They (that is, chariots) rush to and fro in the squares.

Strophic units as shown by the balance in terms of mora count:

| A | 2:1 | 2 balanced triads | [(16 + 8) + 12] + [10 + (19 + 6)] | = | 36 + 35 | morae |
|---|-----|-------------------|-----------------------------------|---|---------|-------|
| B | 2:2 | 2 balanced dyads | [13 + 9] + [11 + 9] | = | 22 + 20 | morae |

|   | 2:3    | 2 balanced dyads          | [15 + 8] + [12 + 13]        | = | 23 + 25           | morae |
|---|--------|---------------------------|------------------------------|---|-------------------|-------|
| C | 2:4    | 2 balanced dyads          | [16 + 11] + [16 + 12]       | = | 27 + 28           | morae |
| D | 2:5–6a | 2 balanced dyads<br>+ pivot | [15 + 10] + 10<br>+ [13 + 11] | = | 25 + 10 + 24      | morae |
|   | 2:6b–7 | 2 balanced dyads<br>+ pivot | [13 + 11] + 9<br>+ [15 + 10]  | = | 24 + 9 + 25       | morae |
| E | 2:8    | 2 balanced dyads          | [14 + 8] + [12 + 12]        | = | 22 + 24           | morae |
| F | 2:9    | 2 balanced dyads          | [12 + 10] + [9 + 14]        | = | 22 + 23           | morae |
|   | 2:10   | balanced triad            | [14 + 12 + 13]              | = | 14 + 12 + 13      | morae |
| G | 2:11   | 2 balanced dyads<br>+ pivot | [19 + 7] + 7<br>+ [19 + 8]   | = | 26 + 7 + 27       | morae |

Word count:

| 1:13–2:1 | 23 | words before *'aṭnaḥ* |
| 2:1–2 | 34 | (= **17** × 2) words |
| 2:2–3 | 26 | words |
| 2:3–4 | 26 | words |
| 2:1–5 | 69 | (= **23** × 3) words |
| 2:1–6 | 46 | (= **23** × 2) words before *'aṭnaḥ* |
| 2:4–7 | 23 | words before *'aṭnaḥ* |
| 2:4–8 | 26 | words before *'aṭnaḥ* |
| 2:1–9 | 46 | (= **23** × 2) words *after 'aṭnaḥ* |
| 2:8–10 | 32 | words |

These examples are a sampling of numerous ways in which the compositional numbers **17**, **23**, **26**, and **32** are woven into the fabric of this text (see Labuschagne 2000:88–92).

## INTRODUCTION

The content of the seven strophes in Nahum 2:1–11 [1:15–2:10] may be outlined in a menorah pattern on prosodic grounds, as follows:

### Canto 3: The Sack of Nineveh in a Menorah Pattern (2:1–11 [1:15–2:10])

| A | Celebrate your (f. sg.) festivals, O Judah, for Belial is utterly cut off | [5.4] | 2:1 |
| B | YHWH has come against Nineveh to restore Israel | [7.7] | 2:2–3 |
| C | The warriors and chariots are prepared for battle | [4.4] | 2:4 |
| X | **There is mayhem in Nineveh and the palace melts away** | [4.6.6.4] | 2:5–7 |

| C′ | Nineveh is destroyed and her people carried away in exile | [4.4] | 2:8 |
| B′ | Nineveh drains away and no one turns back from plundering her | [7.7] | 2:9–10 |
| A′ | The destruction is total; they are gathered as fuel (for burning) | [4.5] | 2:11 |

In terms of the distribution of SAS units in Nahum 2:1–11 [1:15–2:10], the seven strophes are arranged in perfect symmetry, with the twenty SAS units of vv 5–7 in the center:

$$[5 + 4] + [7 + 7] + [4 + 4] + \boxed{(4 + 6) + (6 + 4)} + [4 + 4] + [7 + 7] + [4 + 5]$$

Bliese (1995) considers 2:4–14 [3–13] the proper prosodic unit here. When his methodology of metrical chiasm, based on the distribution of word stresses (that is, counting accents) is applied to 2:1–11 as a whole, however, no such symmetry is found.

## NOTES

2:1 [1:15]. *Here (now) on the mountains are the feet of a sentinel announcing peace.* The opening word, **hinnēh**, "here now, behold," appears more than a thousand times in the Tanakh (Old Testament) as a predicator of existence emphasizing the immediacy, the here-and-now-ness, of a given situation (Lambdin 1971: 168). This interjection, which constitutes the normal introduction to a prophetic vision (Spronk 1997: 79), marks the transition to a new canto in which the theme changes from that of judgment on Assyria to salvation for Judah. Longman (1993: 800) sees the word as a signal announcing "a sudden transition from judgment to salvation." The mountains are the hills of Judah that surround the city of Jerusalem (cf. Psalm 125:2). The reference to the messenger's feet highlights the fact that he is running swiftly (cf. 2 Samuel 18:20–27). As Longman (1993: 800) notes, evidence from Ugarit shows that the root **bśr** ("message") can refer to a message that is bad as well as one that is good, depending on the context. In this instance, it is good tidings, but the reader or hearer does not know this until the message itself is presented at the end of the poetic line. The word **šālôm** means "peace and salvation" (Keil 1949: 16) or "wholeness, completeness, total well-being" (Heflin 1985: 49), which implies "peace with justice" (Barker and Bailey 1998: 192).

This image of a military sentinel running home from the battlefield to inform the people about what happened was adapted in a somewhat different manner in Isaiah 52:7, and the apostle Paul developed it in still another manner centuries later in Romans 10:15. Some scholars have assumed that Nahum borrowed these words from Second Isaiah (see Arnold 1901: 257–58; J. Jeremias

1970: 13–14; Renaud 1987b: 205; Nogalski 1993b: 97–98; Lescow 1995: 69). Though it is difficult to demonstrate with certainty the direction of the borrowing, Spronk (1997: 80) is probably correct in his belief that it is more likely that the words of Nahum 2:1 were subsequently adapted by the author of Isaiah 40–66 (so also Keller 1972: 404; Rudolph 1975: 163; van der Woude 1978a: 190–91; Koole 1990: 186–87; and others). Spronk cites other passages in Isaiah that appear to be dependent on Nahum. He concludes: "The book of Nahum was a source of inspiration for the Second Isaiah and other members of the 'school of Isaiah.'"

*Celebrate, O Judah, your festivals.* For the first time in the book of Nahum, Judah is mentioned explicitly here in 2:1 [1:15]. Celebration in this instance is the "return to God's house to keep the festivals in the way God commanded" (Barker and Bailey 1998: 192). With the cessation of war, the people are free to resume regular observance of the annual pilgrimage festivals in Jerusalem. In grammatical form we have here an imperative Qal f. sg. verb with an object from the same root with a 2nd pers. f. sg. suffix, which is followed by another imperative with a similar 2nd pers. f. sg. suffix. The combination has a sense of poetic symmetry that carries over into the sort of rhyming verse familiar in English poetry. Logoprosodic analysis suggests that these two clauses are in successive halves of a larger poetic unit that includes the whole of 2:1 [1:15].

Humbert (1926: 279–80; 1932: 14–15) interpreted the text as an invitation to the New Year festival in the autumn of 612 BCE, shortly before the fall of Nineveh (cf. Sellin 1930; J. Gray 1961: 17). Keller (1972: 410) has shown that the events are not described as accurately as Humbert assumed. Spronk (1997: 80) argues that Humbert ignored the fact that we are dealing here with a prophetic vision and that the many parallels with Mesopotamian texts indicate that the poet was using common expressions. The term *ḥaggayik* ("your festivals") refers to the three annual pilgrimage festivals, which were feasts of thanksgiving for the blessings of salvation: Passover, Shavuot (Weeks), and Sukkoth (Booths). These three holidays celebrate not only the stages of the agricultural year but also YHWH's deliverance of Israel from Egypt (Passover), YHWH's revelation of the Torah at Sinai (Weeks), and YHWH's guidance of Israel through the wilderness (Booths).

*Fulfill your vows.* The term *nᵊdārāyik* ("your vows") refers to an essential part of those celebrations in which offerings of the people were brought to YHWH in gratitude for his benefits. On the translation of the root *šlm* as "fulfill a vow" rather than "pay a vow," see Berlinerblau (1996: 179). When people were in distress in ancient Israel, they often made vows to YHWH promising to do certain things in return for a positive answer to their prayers (cf. Genesis 28:20; 31:13; Leviticus 7:16; Judges 11:30, 39; 2 Samuel 15:7–8; Psalms 22:25

[26]; 50:14–15; 56:12–13; 61:6 [5]; 66:1–14 [2–15]; 116:12–14, 18; Ecclesi-astes 5:4 [3]; Jonah 2:10 [9]).

*For never again will Belial invade you; he is utterly cut off.* The particle *kî* ("for") introduces the reason for the great change in Judah that restored the opportunity to observe the pilgrimage festivals in Jerusalem. On the meaning of the term *bəlîyaᶜal* as the personification of wickedness in the leadership of Assyria, see the earlier discussion on 1:11 (cf. Maag 1965; 1980). Davidson (1920: 24–25) correctly interpreted Belial as "Assyria personified or the king of Assyria." The verse here in 2:1 [1:15] picks up a number of words and expressions from the previous canto, including *lōᵓ ᶜôd* ("never again"; cf. 1:12, 14); the verb *ᶜbr* ("cross over, invade"; cf. 1:12); *bəlîyaᶜal* ("Belial"; cf. 1:11), and the verb *krt* ("cut off"; cf. 1:14). One reason for this repetition is that 2:1 functions as a transitional strophe, completing the second canto (1:11–2:1 [1:15]), beginning the third (2:1–11 [1:15–2:10]), and belonging to both. Spronk (1997: 81) notes that for the most part these words are used here in a different way, especially the verb *ᶜbr* ("cross over, invade"). Van der Woude (1978a; citation taken from Spronk 1997: 81) sees the verse here as a scribal gloss on the term *bəlîyaᶜal* ("Belial"), and Spronk (1997: 80) argues that what he translates as "never again shall the wicked come over you" is a gloss. Seybold (1991: 25) also removes both *bəlîyaᶜal* and *kullōh niḵrāt* as glosses. All of these proposals are based on questionable presuppositions about the prosodic nature of the text. There is no compelling reason to change the text here at all other than to make the necessary choice in the matter of the *kethiv* or *qere'* reading of the word *lᶜbwr*, which is here interpreted as the Qal inf. const. *laᶜăḇor-bāḵ* ("to invade you"). From a prosodic point of view, the Hebrew text of 2:1 scans perfectly—both as the concluding strophe of the extension of the second canto (1:11–14), so as to include this verse in a larger transitional prosodic unit, 1:9c–2:1 (see the earlier discussion in the intro-duction to the section on 1:11–14), and as the first strophe in the third canto (2:1–11 [1:15–2:10]).

Elliger (1970) suggested a possible emendation to read *ben bəlîyaᶜal* ("son of Belial"), as did Procksch (1937), with a question mark. Roberts (1991: 47–48) uses this observation, at least in part, to correct the MT by making *bəlîyaᶜal* the subject of the verb at the end of 2:1, ignoring the conjunctive accent at the end of the expression *laᶜăḇor-bāḵ* ("to invade you"), but the cor-rectness of this reading is highly unlikely.

The word *kullōh* ("all of him/it, utterly, totally"), which is a combination of the adverb *kōl* ("all") and the 3rd pers. m. sg. pronominal suffix (see GKC, §91e), was apparently confused in the LXX with the verbal form *kālāh* (read-ing "it will be completed") in 1:8 and 1:9. For parallel usage of *kullōh* ("all of him/it") to emphasize a preceding noun in the same line, see Jeremiah 48:31; Ezekiel 11:15; 20:40; 36:10; Hosea 13:2). The word *nikrāt* is not a Niphal participle but a perfect verbal form in pause.

2:2 [2:1]. *A scatterer has come up against you.* The term *mēpîṣ* ("a scatterer"), which is a Hiphil participle from the verbal root *pwṣ* ("to scatter"), normally has YHWH as its subject. The Qal stem is used in Numbers 10:35 and Psalm 68:2 to characterize YHWH's effect on his enemy, and in a later reversal of holy war imagery in Jeremiah 18:17 the Hiphil stem is used to describe the flight of God's people before their enemy. Spronk (1997: 83) cites parallel usage in Jeremiah 9:15, especially in Jeremiah 13:24, where YHWH warns the people that he will scatter them like chaff flying away in the desert wind. Longman (1993: 801) reaches the same conclusion when he says: "We must leave open the possibility, however, that the 'scatterer' refers not to these nations, but to God himself, who is the Divine Warrior. Behind the battles of the nations, it is he who will destroy Nineveh (Ezek 29:12)."

The term *mēpîṣ* ("a scatterer") was emended to read *mappēṣ* ("war-club") by G. A. Smith (1928: 104), as in Jeremiah 51:20 (see *BHS* note); however, as Haldar (1947: 40–41) pointed out, the term *mappēṣ* denotes an instrument of war by which YHWH crushes his enemy, and the term *mēpîṣ* here denotes a person (cf. Cathcart 1973a: 80). Haupt (1907c: 10, 17, 27) combined these two ideas by reading the term "Hammer" (*mappēṣ*), referring to Judas Maccabeus.

Coggins (1985: 35) finds what he considers better parallels in Jeremiah supporting the MT, and Spronk (1997: 84) points out that the proposed emendations have no support in the ancient versions. The image is that of the scattering of people after their defeat in battle (1 Samuel 11:11; 2 Kings 25:5; Isaiah 24:1), though perhaps the best known example of YHWH's scattering a people is in the story of the Tower of Babel (Genesis 11:8–9). Haldar (1947: 41) was probably correct in offering his word of caution that the translation "crusher, destroyer" rather than "scatterer" remains possible without emending the text, because both concepts are common expressions of smiting an enemy.

In light of 2:14 [13], Roberts (1991: 56) identifies the "scatterer" as YHWH and sees the epithet as a particularly appropriate one, "given Nahum's glorification of the deity in the traditional language and imagery of the Divine Warrior." Others translate the verb in the past tense and look for a specific historical person to whom the abstract term makes reference. Graham (1927–28: 46) suggested that the "scatterer" is Necho. According to Spronk (1997: 83), Jerome (d. 420), Abarbanel (d. 1508), Calvin (1559), and Kleinert (1874: 8–12, 24) identified the "scatterer" with Nebuchadnezzar, and Cyril of Alexandria (ca. 370–444) identified him with Cyrus. In an argument in which he interprets the verse as directed against Judah rather than Nineveh, van Wyk (1971: 225) identifies the "scatterer" with Sennacherib (as did Rashi [d. 1105] and Kimchi [d. 1235]). On the basis of Greek sources, some scholars identify the person in question with a king in Media: Arbacus (Michaelis 1782), Cyaxares (Greve 1793; J. M. P. Smith 1911: 312–13), or Phraortes (Ewald 1878), or even with the Medo-Chaldean army (Eichhorn 1816; Justi 1820; Hitzig 1881: 251). Haupt (1907c: 17, n. 21) opted for Judas Maccabeus in a much later historical setting. More recent commentaries have tended to leave the question open as to whether the "scatterer" is a king or an army, for in one sense he is YHWH himself (W. A. Maier 1959: 222; Keller 1971: 119–20; Spronk 1997: 83; and others), acting through whatever human agency he chooses.

According to Spronk (1997: 83), the medieval Jewish commentators Rashi (d. 1105) and Kimchi (d. 1235) interpreted the pronominal suffix "you" here to refer to Judah rather than Nineveh (see Lehrman and Rosenberg 1994); this possibility was also considered by Calvin (1559). This interpretation is shaped by the identity of the 2nd pers. f. sg. pronominal suffix in the previous verse, which refers to Judah, and by the subtle contrasting comparison with 2:1 [1:15], where Judah is directed to look at the approaching herald of peace, which is followed by a series of commands.

Van der Woude (1977a: 116–17) thinks the reference "must" be to Judah, as in 2:1 [1:15] (cf. also Graham 1927–28: 45–46). On this observation, van der Woude builds his theory that *mēpîṣ* refers to "the dispersed" exiles of the northern kingdom, seeing v 3 [2] as a promise of the restoration of the northern kingdom of Israel. This theory is accepted by Becking (1978: 115–18; 1996: 19) and rejected by Peels (1993: 33–34), W. Dietrich (1994b: 738), and Spronk (1997: 84). Pointing to the parallel with 3:14, Spronk insists that "2:2 refers to the anxious awaiting of the enemy and not to the joyful expectation of former exiles" (cf. J. Jeremias 1970: 25–26). Bliese (1995: 58–59) also sees the addressee in 2:2 as Nineveh. He analyzes 1:12–2:3 [2] as a chiastic unit of five poems in which the first, middle, and last are addressed to or focus on Judah, while 1:14 and 2:2, between them, are addressed to Nineveh.

Although the phrase *ʿal pānayiḵ* ("against you") has the 2nd pers. f. sg. suffix, the change in content indicates that the announcement here is no longer addressed to Judah, as in 2:1 [1:15], but to Nineveh—for Judah has just been promised that she will not be attacked, and the verse here announces that the addressee is under attack (see Floyd 2000: 55–56). Keil (1949: 18) also argued that the phrase *ʿal pānayiḵ* ("against thy face") cannot be addressed to Judah as in 2:1 [1:15] and that we have here a sudden change in the person addressed, as in 1:11–12 and 13–14. He understood the phrase as referring to the pitching of enemy tents opposite the city of Nineveh. The 2nd pers. f. sg. suffix appears twice, in *ḥaggayiḵ* ("your feasts") and *nəḏārayiḵ* ("your vows"), followed by the 2nd pers. m. sg. suffix in *bāk* ("[will he] invade you") in 2:1 [1:15], in another instance of the phenomenon of enallage.

J. Jeremias (1970: 27) emended the text to read *ᶜal pinnayik* ("wider deine 'Zinne' [= pinnacle, battlement]"), from the noun *pinnāh* ("corner"), in place of *ᶜal pānayik* (as did Duhm 1911: 103; Humbert 1926: 275; Sellin 1930: 366; and Brockington 1973: 258). Ruben (1898: 176), Ewald (1878: 8), Hitzig (1881: 251), and others have emended the text to read *pānêkā* ("your face"), with a 2nd pers. m. sg. suffix. Roberts (1991: 57) argues that the pronominal suffix here "was probably mispointed as a feminine due to the influence of the 2 f. sg. forms in 2:1 [1:15]." At the same time, he acknowledges that "these forms have a different referent." Logoprosodic analysis indicates that there is a strophic boundary at the end of 2:1 [1:15], which suggests that the shift in identity is related to the larger phenomenon of enallage observed elsewhere in Nahum. The masculine person addressed in 1:14 is the king of Assyria, or perhaps Assyria as a corporate personality, and the feminine person addressed in 2:2 [1] is Nineveh as the personified capital of Assyria. Note the change to 3rd pers. pl. forms in the second half of 2:3 [2], which announces another strophic boundary.

*Guard the ramparts, watch the road, gird the loins, marshal strength exceedingly.* The people of Nineveh are warned of their impending doom as the sack of the city is described in vivid detail. Haldar (1947: 42, 121), however, read the infinitives as a continuation of the perfect introducing the sentence and translates the passage "A scatterer ascendeth upon thy summits, he watcheth the watch, he looketh along the way, he girdeth his loins, and strengtheneth his force firmly." The term *nāṣôr* ("guard [the ramparts]") is a Qal inf. abs. from the root *nṣr* ("watch, guard, keep"), which is read as imperative (see GKC 113 bb; ,356; *IBHS* §35.5.1). In like manner, the following three inf. abs. forms are also read as imperatives: *ṣappē᾿* ("watch [the road]"), *ḥazzēq moṯnayim* (literally, "gird the loins"), *᾿ammēṣ koaḥ* ("marshal strength"). The term *maṣūrāh* refers to the enclosure of a city, hence the wall or fortification (Keil 1949: 18–19). Based primarily on his understanding of the LXX translation, Roberts (1991: 56) follows the lead of Wellhausen (1898: 161) and emends *maṣūrāh* ("rampart") to read *maṣṣārāh* ("guard, guard post"), from the root *nṣr*. This change in pointing would give the cognate accusative: "Guard the guard post," that is, "Set the guard" or "Man the guard post" (this approach is also taken by Delcor 1964: 375, following Ruben 1898: 176; Marti 1903: 315; Junker 1938: 19; Horst 1938: 158; Elliger 1970: 1046; and others). The suggestion is attractive but not necessary, for the text makes good sense as it stands, and the word appears as *mṣwrh* in many Hebrew Mss (cf. de Rossi 1786). Moreover, the word *maṣṣārāh* appears nowhere in the Tanakh, while the MT reading *maṣūrāh* ("rampart, fortification") and the related noun *māṣôr* ("rampart") appear frequently (Psalms 31:22; 60:11; Habakkuk 2:1; Zechariah 9:3; 2 Chronicles 8:5; 11:5, 10, 11, 23; 12:4; 14:5; 21:3; 32:10).

For a similar exhortation to "watch the road" (*sappēh-derek*), see Jeremiah 48:19 and an oracle against Moab. The sense is to watch carefully so as to repulse or prevent the enemy from entering the city. G. R. Driver (1940: 172) showed that the expression *ḥazzēq motnayim* means "gird [your] loins" and not "strengthen the loins" or "grasp the loins," as the ancient versions rendered it (cf. Isaiah 22:21; Wagner 1966: 54, no. 99). It is suggested by some that this refers to the practice of tucking the ends of the long cloak (outer garment) into the belt so as to prepare oneself for activities such as running and fighting in battle. Another possibility is to interpret the clause as meaning to prepare oneself physically for the coming onslaught of the enemy; the NASB renders it "Strengthen your back." Longman (1993: 801) observes that we have here a "satirical call to battle." He says: "The infinitive form is used here rather than the imperative to signal that these are satiric commands that were not really delivered to the Assyrians (that is, 'Do the best you can, but you do not stand a chance')."

Parallel texts of interest include the account in 1 Kings 20:22 of Elisha encouraging the king of Israel to be strong against the king of Aram, who has come up against him. The verbal roots *ḥzq* ("be strong") and *ʾmṣ* ("to fortify") appear together as words of encouragement in Deuteronomy 31:6–7 and Joshua 1:6–9. In Isaiah 35:4 the same two words appear together with the root *nqm* ("to avenge") announcing the restoration of "the glory of Lebanon" and "the majesty of Carmel" (35:2)

2:3 [2]. *For YHWH is restoring the pride of Jacob, indeed the pride of Israel.* The particle *kî* ("for") introduces the reason for the turn of events. YHWH is now at work restoring the former splendor or majesty of his people. The term *šāb* ("is restoring") is Qal m. sg. participle from the root *šwb* ("to turn, return"), in the sense of turning around or returning something to a person—that is, the restoration of Jacob's eminence. Though the Qal usage of this verb is not normally transitive in nature, it does have this meaning elsewhere (see *HALOT*, 1328; cf. in particular Psalm 85:5). W. A. Maier (1959: 233) emended the text here to find the root *šbb* ("to cut off"), but the evidence he presents is meager and late. Moreover, he ends up replacing a well-known Hebrew word with a *hapax legomenon* (word that occurs only once in the Tanakh).

The term *gaʾôn* has both positive connotations ("splendor, majesty, glory, pride [as the opposite of humiliation]") and negative ones ("pride [as arrogance]"). The context determines the specific meaning. Rudolph (1975: 160) presents an interesting combination of these two points of view. He thinks the verse was originally negative in its connotation, with the meaning "to cut off," as suggested by W. A. Maier (1959: 233), and thus part of the "announcement against Nineveh" in 2:2. When the *maśśāʾ* ("oracle") was combined with the hymn, however, the verse would also have been read positively, with the sense of "to restore," and related to 2:1. So in its present context it has a double function.

The *gəʾôn yaʿăqōḇ* ("pride of Jacob") here denotes the land, as in Psalm 47:5 [4], where the phrase appears in parallel with *naḥălāh* ("inheritance"; cf. Kellermann 1975: 348). The humiliation that is ending is the loss of the land to the Assyrian Empire (2 Kings 17:1–6), and the expression here may be interpreted as a message of hope for a restored northern kingdom in Israel (Greenwood 1976: 377). As Spronk observes (1997: 86), there is no reason to see in the double name Jacob/Israel a reference to the United Monarchy of the more distant past (as have Goslinga 1923; Elliger 1959: 9–10; and Schulz 1973: 23) or to remove the reference to Israel here as a gloss, as does van der Woude (1978a) and Rudolph (1975).

The *k* prefixed to the phrase "pride of Israel" is interpreted as emphatic (along with Irwin 1974: 398; O'Rouke 1974: 397; Cathcart 1979: 6; Longman 1993: 794; and Spronk 1997: 86). In short, the words *Jacob* and *Israel* here are both honorific titles for Judah as the whole of Israel (the twelve tribes), as Longman points out (1993: 802). It would make little sense to say that Judah would be restored "as" the pride of Israel if one were referring to the northern kingdom of Israel in the middle of the seventh century BCE. The former kingdom of Israel was no longer in existence. Cyril (quoted by Keil 1949: 18) expressed the matter well: "Jacob is the natural name which the people inherited from their forefather, and Israel the spiritual name which they had received from God." In short, God is restoring to his people the lofty eminence of their divine calling. The text here is not a prediction of the return of the exiles, as van der Woude argues (1977a: 118–19). Moreover, his understanding of the relation between Isaiah 52:8, which refers to the watchmen seeing the return of Yhwh to Zion, and the text here may be interpreted with Spronk (1997: 86) as a further example of "a reinterpretation of the prophecy in the book of Nahum."

A number of scholars have emended *gəʾôn* to read *gepen* ("vine") before both *Jacob* and *Israel* (Delcor 1964: 374, following Sellin 1930: 363; Horst 1938: 158; Junker 1938: 19; Nötscher 1948; and George 1958: 88; see also J. M. P. Smith 1911: 305; G. A. Smith 1928: 94; Kraeling 1966: 236; Murphy 1968: 294). In spite of the fact that this proposed emendation has had such a long shelf life among so many otherwise competent scholars, Cathcart (1973a: 84) is surely correct in his assessment: "It seems to the present writer that the emendation of *gəʾôn* to *gepen* is audacious."

*For devastators have devastated them; and their vine-branches they destroyed.* There is ambiguity here. On the one hand, it is easy to interpret the "devastators" as the Assyrians who destroyed Israel's "vine-branches" (that is, her former economic well-being), and restoration of Judah's "pride" was needed because of this past humiliation. Spronk (1997: 87), however, interprets the passage in a completely different manner, finding here another reference to the coming destruction of Assyria: "For destroyers shall ruin them (that is, Assyria) and they shall ruin their branches" (as have Graham 1927–28: 45–46; van der Woude 1977a: 116–17; and Becking 1995c: 1260). Holland (1986: 32) interprets the text as referring to the Babylonians plundering the Assyrians. Cathcart (1973: 73) suggests that the text refers to the exiles being plundered on their way home, which is also how Becking (1995c: 1260) understands the verse (see the discussion by Spronk 1997: 88, n. 32). Spronk bases his argument primarily on the presence of the poetic device of inclusion within his understanding of 1:12–2:3 as a "subcanto." It is more likely, however, that vv 2–3 constitute the second strophe in a seven-part canto (2:1–11 [1:15–2:10]), in which the restoration of Judah in v 3 is a minor part. The canto itself has the sack of Nineveh as its primary subject, and YHWH's destruction of that city serves to restore the pride of Jacob/Israel, who was humiliated in times past when "devastators devastated them" and destroyed their vine-branches.

Bliese (personal communication) sees 2:3 in the context of all three of the poems he identifies in 1:12–2:3, with a focus on Israel. Each of the three has a reference to restoration after they had been destroyed by Assyria. In 1:12–13 YHWH "afflicted" Israel, but now he promises: "I will break his yoke from off you, and will burst your bonds." In 2:1 it is: "For it will not happen again that the wicked pass through you." Here in 2:3, YHWH "restores" Israel after the Assyrian "plunderers" "plundered" and "ruined" them.

The combination of the words *bəqāqûm bōqəqîm* ("devastators devastate them") has an alliterative effect in the repetition of sounds (cf. also 2:11 [10], where the same verbal root(s), *bqq / bwq* ["lay waste, devastate"] appear). A similar repetition of the verbal root *bqq* appears in Isaiah 24:3: "[the earth] will be completely laid waste." The effect is produced by using the Qal perfect 3rd pers. pl. with the 3rd pers. pl. suffix from the root *bqq* ("to devastate"), followed by a Qal active participle from the same root. Sweeney (2000: 437) argues that the verb *bqq* actually means "to empty, depopulate" and thus recalls the Assyrian practice of deporting native populations.

The noun *ûzəmōrêhem* is almost always translated "and their vine-branches," from the root *zmr* ("to prune"), as in the LXX and the Vulgate. Citing Psalm 80:8–19 as a parallel (cf. also Isaiah 5:1–7), Gandell (1901: 641) argued that the people of Israel are spoken of as a vine and that the branches are cities of the land. Sweeney (2000: 437) suggests that the portrayal of Israel's ruined branches may reflect Assyria's use of the Shephelah region and the coastal plain for olive production (cf. Gitin 1989: 25–58).

Cathcart (1973a: 85–86) takes the word *ûzəmōrêhem* in relation to an Ugaritic cognate *ḏmr* ("soldier, some class of troops") with the translation "And their soldiers they slaughtered." Van der Woude (1977a: 119) argues that the word *zəmōrêhem* should be repointed to read *zōmərêhem,* with "their soldiers." Becking (1995c: 1260) thinks the word is better translated with "their protectors," which he sees as a reference to military aid that may include "a reminiscence of ancestral deities." Cathcart (1973a: 85, n. 38) also notes the fact that the Ugaritic counterpart to Hebrew *zmr* ("to sing, make music") is *ḏmr*, not *zmr* as in *HALOT* 262. The key text in this regard is *UT*, 602: 3–4, *dyšr wyḏmr bknr*: "He sings and makes music on the lyre." The relation between Hebrew *zmr* and Ugaritic *ḏmr* is discussed by Cross and Freedman (1955: 243), Cazelles (1957: 135–36), and Sarna (1964: 347–52).

Graham (1927–28: 46) argued that the term translated "vine-branches" here is also used to designate "suckers" that grow out of the roots of a tree and divert the sap to their own sustenance. He thinks that "nothing could better describe Egypt's relations to Assyria at this time, nor could there be more strikingly expressed Nahum's conviction that Egyptian power would end with Assyria's defeat."

A more attractive option is given by Longman (1993: 802), who turns to the much more common meaning of the root *zmr* ("to sing, make music"). Longman calls attention to "the frequent motif that songs cease during warfare." In the picture of destruction in Isaiah 24:8–9, we read: "The mirth of the timbrels is stilled, the noise of the jubilant has ceased, the mirth of the lyre is stilled. No more do they drink wine with singing." Barth (1980: 91) calls attention to the fact that "the root *zmr* II ['prune'] does not occur within the sphere of Akkadian, where *zmr* I (*zamāru*, "sing, play") appears to originate." Isaiah 25:5 mentions *zəmîr ʿārîṣîm* ("triumph songs of tyrants"), and Job 35:10 has *zəmîrôṯ ballāylāh* ("songs in the night"). Barth (1980: 94) lists four certain occurrences of *zimrāh* I ("song"; Isaiah 51:3; Amos 5:23; Psalms 91:3 [2]; 98:5).

But in spite of all this, use of the noun *zəmôrāh* for a "branch" of a grapevine is well attested in one of the most familiar images of the entire Tanakh, in Numbers 13:23, where it was used to describe a branch (*zəmôrāh*) with a single cluster of grapes so huge that it was carried on a pole between two men (cf. also Ezekiel 8:17; 15:2; Isaiah 17:10). There is no way that the original hearer or reader of Nahum's words could have missed this connection, even if the more subtle nuances suggested by Longman were also intended. Consequently, I have chosen to go with the majority of interpreters past and present and translate the text as "Their vine-branches are destroyed (*šiḥēṯû*)." Some support for this traditional reading is found in the interpretation of 2:11 [10] that appears later, where the same verbal root(s), *bqq* or *bwq*, "lay waste,

An archer (Kouyunjik). From Layard (1849: 268).

A spearman (Kouyunjik). From Layard (1849: 268).

A spearman of Sennacherib's army. From Yadin (1963: 293).

devastate," appear in a context where we find reference to prunings from the vines serving as fuel for burning. The term *zəmōrêhem* ("their vine-branches") is a figurative expression representing the field of agriculture (that is, an example of synecdoche, use of a part to represent the whole).

When Yʜwʜ is the subject of verb *šḥt* ("to destroy"), his destructive action "moves mercilessly and vehemently against the guilty party" (Conrad 2004: 590). Though the object in such cases is normally Israel, Judah, or Jerusalem, in the context here in Nahum 2:3 [2] the object of Yʜwʜ's destruction is the city of Nineveh.

2:4 [3]. *The shields of his warriors are reddened; (his) men of valor are clad in scarlet.* The focus of attention here shifts to the task of finding the correct antecedent for the 3rd pers. m. sg. suffix on the word *gibbōrêhû* ("his warriors"). The nearest possibility is Yʜwʜ, the subject of 2:3 [2]; but Spronk (1997: 89) is also correct in insisting that the pronoun in question "can only refer to the 'scatterer' in 2:1," for the two are one and the same person. The Divine Warrior Yʜwʜ's "mighty men" are now arrayed for battle against Nineveh, and that battle has cosmic overtones, as Haldar has shown. Spronk understands this, at least in principle, to judge from his observation that the word *gibbōrê* ("mighty ones") in Psalm 103:20 is used for angels.

Bliese (1995: 63) interprets the "his" in 2:4 [3] as referring to the same person as the pronominal suffix "he" in 2:6 [5] and the masculine "you" suffixes in 2:14 [13]. He sees a unity in the masculine pronominal suffixes throughout the poem he identifies in 2:4–14 [3–13] and thus avoids having to explain any shift in the referent between vv 4 and 6. He believes that all of these references are to the Assyrian king. He argues that seeing 2:4–14 as a single poem encourages expectations of a change of referent at the beginning of the poem rather than internally. Bliese interprets 2:4–5 as a description of the confusion and bloody defeat of the defenders rather than referring to the frightening redness of the victors.

The *māgēn* ("shield") was a circular body shield held with the left arm and made of leather covering a wicker interior and coated with fat (2 Samuel 1:2; Isaiah 21:5), similar to that portrayed on the walls in the bas relief of Lachish (see de Vaux 1961: 244–45, and an artist's reconstruction of the siege of Lachish in Yadin 1963: 436–37).

Haldar (1947: 121–24) was correct in principle when he interpreted the army as YHWH's celestial army. If the pronoun refers to the "scatterer" of 2:1, his attacking army is meant. According to Keil (1949: 20), the shields are made red, not "radiant," as Ewald (1840) argued, and not with the blood of enemies (as Abarbanel [d. 1508] and Grotius [d. 1645] assumed; see Keil 1949: 20). Hitzig (1881: 252) agued that the red color refers to the copper or brass with which the shields were overlaid (see Davidson 1920: 26; cf. Josephus, *Ant.* xiii. 12, 5; cf. 1 Maccabees 6:39). Dahood's (1974: 78) suggested emendation to read *məgan* ("the general") in place of *māgēn* ("shield") is rejected by Cathcart (1979: 6).

The debate over whether the term *məʾāddām* ("reddened") refers to clothes made red with dye prior to battle or reddened with blood in battle is misleading. The ambiguity is intentional in that both concepts are present. The term *məʾāddām* ("are reddened"), which is a Pual from the root *ʾdm* ("to be red"), implies an external cause. Haupt (1907b: 17) interpreted the word to mean "bespattered with blood." Longman's (1993: 804) argument that the shields have been colored red is founded in large part on his assumption in regard to the nature of the poetic parallelism with the following clause, where the word *məṭullāʿîm* ("clad in scarlet") describes how the warriors are clothed. Ezekiel 23:14 informs us that the Babylonians wore *šāšar*, that is red garments. Spronk (1997: 89) is surely correct in his conclusion that "the poet does not intend to give a precise description of the red leather shields and the scarlet uniforms of the advancing army. These clothes are only mentioned to picture the right atmosphere of violence and expectation of the coming bloodshed (cf. Isa. 63:1–6)." Warriors apparently wore uniforms colored blood-red so as to strike fear in the hearts of their opponents (see Xenophon, *Cyropaedia* 6.4.1; J. Freeman 1972: 324).

On the use of color terms and the so-called psychology of colors, see Grad-wohl 1963: 73–76 and Brenner 1982: 110–11 (reference taken from Spronk 1997: 89, n. 34). According to Spronk (1997: 89), Kimchi (d. 1235) com-mented on the psychological effect of the color red on enemy soldiers. Spronk then makes a pertinent observation on a curse found in Esarhaddon's vassal treaties: "Just as this chariot is spattered with blood up to its running board, so may they spatter your chariots in the midst of your enemy with your own blood" (*ANET* 540).

The term *'anšê-ḥayil* ("men of valor") denotes the regular army (cf. 2 Samuel 17:10; Isaiah 5:22; Jeremiah 48:14). Scholarly opinion on how to interpret the word *maṯullāʿîm* ("clad in scarlet") varies widely in the literature. The word is a Pual participle derived from the substantive *tlʿ* ("scarlet"), which elsewhere refers to clothing dyed red or purple (Isaiah 1:18; Lamentations 4:5). Taylor (1956: 955) has "The mighty men are gleaming"; Gaster (1969: 661) has "His troops are incarnadined," with the comment "What the prophet means is that the shields and uniforms of the soldiers were bloodstained." But, by a clever choice of words, Gaster likens these braves to "princes stoled in scarlet." Kraeling (1966: 236) says: "The description of the foe is fantastic: red shields, scarlet clothes. In Hesiod 7.61 ff., several contingents in the international Persian army wear colorful garments, but scarlet is not mentioned." Cathcart (1973a: 87), however, calls attention to Ezekiel 23:5–6, where the Assyrian troops are described as "dressed in purple," and Ezekiel 23:14, where the Babylonians are presented in similar language: "Images of the Chaldeans are engraved in vermilion."

*Flashing as with fire are the chariot coverings.* Chariots were light two-wheeled carts pulled by a pair of horses with two or three people in them, one to drive and the others to fight.

The common translation of *bəʾēš-pəlāḏôṯ* as "the metal (on the chariots) flashes" is based on an Arabic cognate. The LXX and Vulgate understood it to refer to the reins of the horses, but this appears to be a mere guess based on the context. Margolis (1911: 314) argued that the Greek translator associated a damaged word in the Hebrew text with the Aramaic term *pgdt*. The Targum renders *pldt* as *pyly* ("plates"), but Jastrow (1950: 1163) translated *pyly* as "elephants." Pinker (2005a: 414) rejects this meaning for the Hebrew *pldt* because there is no evidence of elephants being in this region before the time of Antiochus Epiphanes. The elephants the Seleucids used in battle bore tur-rets with a number of soldiers in them (1 Maccabees 6:34–37). The Syriac and Symmachus apparently read *lāppîḏôṯ* ("torches"; compare *lāppîḏîm* in 2:5 [4]) instead of *pəlāḏôṯ*. On the basis of this observation, Elliger (1970) sug-gests emending the text to read *kəʾēš lappîḏôṯ* ("like torches of fire" or "like flaming torches") (as do the KJV and JPS Tanakh). The problem with this reading is that the plural of the masculine noun *lappîd* ("torch") is *lāppîdîm*, as shown in the next verse. Others rearrange the consonants to read *dlpwt*, from the root *dlp* ("to drip, trickle, leak"), and translate the passage as "like flickering fire" (NEB).

Dietrich and Loretz (1968: 100–101), Keller (1971:121), and Cathcart (1973a: 87–8) connect the word with the Ugaritic *pld* (*UT*, 1108.7; 1111.8, 12; 1112.1, 7; 1113.4, 7, 8; *CTA* 140 [98].4), which refers to some kind of garment or covering. Spronk's (1997: 89) translation, "Flaming-red are the coverings of the chariots," is perhaps as close as we can come (cf. Cathcart 1973a: 87). In Assyrian reliefs, chariots are sometimes portrayed with coverings (see Hrouda 1963: 155–58, esp. plate XXIX; Nagel 1966: 50–51, plates 46, 48, 65; Nagel 1990). Building his case on observations by Cathcart in Ugaritic texts, Longman (1993: 804) translates the word *pəlādôt* as "the caparisons of," arguing that we have here "an ornamental covering worn by an animal" (see Dietrich and Loretz 1968: 100–101; Keller 1971; Roberts 1991). Such a reading requires the translation of the word *rekeb* as "horse" rather than "chariot," which is possible (see 2 Samuel 8:4, where David hamstrung the *rekeb* captured from Hadadezer; cf. also Pope 1970: 56–61; Dahood 1970b: 396–97). Longman himself (1993: 804), however, admits: "The Ugaritic cognate is not perfectly clear." The unusual word *pəlādôt* was apparently selected by the author because of its assonance with the word *lāpîdôt* ("torches") in the next verse.

Some scholars interpret the text in light of the Persian word for "steel," as reflected in Syriac as *pūlād* or *pūlādaʾ*, and explain the word as referring to the metal decorations on the chariot and the gear worn by the horses (in the NRSV, NIV, and NASB; see Cathcart 1973a: 87 n. 49; Rudolph 1975: 167). According to Tisdall (1913–14: 102–3), steel was not called *pūlād* in Nahum's time but rather *pōurupāt* or *pōuruʿāt* in Avestic Persian and *parupat* or *paruvat* in Achaemenian Persian (reference taken from Pinker 2005a: 415, n. 19). Tisdall (1913–14: 102–4) considers *pldwt* (with a change of *r* to *l*) as derived from a root cognate with Akkadian *parādu* ("be impetuous, hasten") or *prdʾ* ("to be bright"). Pinker (2005a: 415, n. 19) argues that in the Tanakh the root *prd* never means "to be bright" and suggests the possible meaning "as sparks do the chariots separate" in the sense of their exit from the assembly area. Pereman (1956: 47) suggested that the chariots were made of steel, but Pinker (2005a: 415) rejects this interpretation, arguing that this would "make the chariot very expensive, too heavy, and the advantage of having such a vehicle is very doubtful." The NET Bible interprets the word *pəlādôt* ("steel") as referring "to the metallic pole attachments for the chariot spears, the side armor of the chariots, or the steel scythes fastened to the axle of a chariot" (see J. Freeman 1972: 325; also Michaelis, Ewald, and others according to Keil 1949: 20). This reading is based in part on Xenophon's description of the army of Cyrus, with chariots and the breastplates and thigh pieces of the chariot horses "flashing with bronze" (Xenophon, *Cyclopaedia* 6.4.1). The *BHS* note suggests that the Ugaritic *pld* means *tegimen* ("armor"), but chariots did not have vehicle armor of metal plates because the increased weight would have reduced their speed and restricted their maneuverability (Pinker 2005a: 414, 416).

A. Jeremias (1930: 98) suggested that *rkb pldt* means "battering rams" enclosed in a protective "armored" shield (reference from Pinker 2005a: 416). After a lengthy discussion of the word in question, Haldar (1947: 44–46) chose to leave the word untranslated. Rowley (1947: 60–61) mentioned the suggestion of Tisdall, that *bəʾēš-pəlāḏôt* means "like fire flash the chariots."

Roberts (1991: 57–58; with Nestle 1909) suggests emending the text from *bəʾēš* ("in fire") to *kəʾēš* ("like fire"), as in some Hebrew manuscripts (and also in G. A. Smith 1928: 104), which is not necessary, for Cathcart (1973a: 87) translates the term *bəʾēš* as "fiery," or "flaming-red," and explains the *b* here as a *beth essentiae* (cf. GHB, §133c). The word *hārekeḇ* ("the chariot") is a collective singular that refers to the chariots of the army as a whole, or the chariotry. The collective force is demonstrated by the plural form of the verb, with the same word in the next verse.

The prophet sees the armies as also the hosts of Yʜwʜ; they appear as chariots of fire coming with the force of the storm and the devastation of an earthquake. The specific battle against the city of Nineveh takes place in history, but the poetic imagery used here has cosmic dimensions as the chaotic powers of evil are subdued in the wars of Yʜwʜ (cf. Psalm 68:17; Joshua 5:13–15; Joel 2:1–11).

*On the day of its preparation.* The term *hăkînô* ("its preparation") is a Hiphil verbal form from the root *kwn* ("to be firm"), with the 3rd pers. m. sg. suffix. In the present context, "the day of its preparation" is the day of the preparation of the chariots for battle. The Hiphil of this verbal root is used elsewhere of equipping an army for battle (Jeremiah 46:14; Ezekiel 7:14, 38:7; 2 Chronicles 26:14; Psalms 7:14 [13]; 57:7 [6]). The one making the preparation is Yʜwʜ, as in the suffix on *gibbōrêhû* ("his mighty men"; cf. Isaiah 13:4, where Yʜwʜ raises an army for war against Babylon). Taylor (1956: 955, 962) emends *bəyôm* to read *kayyām* and translates the passage "The squadrons of chariots are spread like the sea," which Cathcart (1973a:89) dismisses as "quite strange."

*Indeed the juniper arrows are poisoned.* Scholars differ on how to interpret the words *habbərōšîm horʿālû*. Cathcart (1973a: 89) interprets *habbərōšîm* as meaning "the cypresses" or "the cedars," in reference to spears made of wood. G. R. Driver (1956: 101) supports his interpretation of *UT*, 51:VII:40–41 as follows: "Baʿal's eye is towards his hand when the spear swings in his right hand," in which he reads the word "cedar" as "spear," with Nahum 2:4 as a parallel. Following this same line of reasoning, Pinker (2005a: 417–18) explains *habbərōšîm* as a reference to "the spears, which were made of fir wood, sharpened at the end, and dried in a kiln" and were also tipped with poison. According to Pinker (2005a: 418), Abarbanel (d. 1641) noted that in his day, such spears made of wood were still used only in Africa, as in ancient times. Pinker lists the following possible interpretations of the word *horʿālû*: "poisoned" (Kimchi [d. 1235]); "covered" (Rashi [d. 1105]); "trembled" (Ibn Ezra [d. 1167]); "they are frenzied (that is, they run amok), run like mad" (Haupt 1907c: 40); "are upholstered" (Spronk 1997: 90); and "stand in row and rank" (Rudolph 1975: 165), among other possibilities. Pinker (2005a: 418) chooses the meaning "were poisoned" and translates an emended text to read "The spears/arrows in the chariot's quiver [ready] to shoot on the day of its [chariot] assembly, and the arrows are poisoned." The proposed emendation, however, is not necessary. The two words *wəhabbərōšîm horʿālû* are translated "And the 'junipers' [that is, wooden arrows] they poisoned." The image is that of chariotry mobilized in great haste, because the poisoning of the wooden arrows or spears would normally be delayed until just before the battle itself. The scene portrayed here is that of the preparation of the chariots and equipment for the coming battle.

Sweeney (2000: 438) thinks *habbərōšîm hārəʿālû* means "and the cypresses quiver," in reference to the central pole to which horses were harnessed (cf. Littauer and Crouwel 1992: 888–92). Fisher and Knutson (1965: 157–59, esp. n. 10) interpret the expression "tree of lightning" in *UT*, 603:4 [= RŠ.24.245] as a reference to Baʿal's spear, and they call attention to Wilson's translation of *Papyrus Leyden* 345, recto, iv 12–v 2 in *ANET* 249: "Baal smites thee with the cedar tree which is in his hand." Gaster (1944: 51–52) translates *habbərōšîm hārəʿālû* as "the fir-trees are rustled (as they pass)" (cf. Gaster 1969: 661). Longman (1993: 803) translates *habbərōšîm horʿālû* as "the spear shafts are made to quiver" (as does Roberts 1991: 55). The NRSV reading, "the chargers prance," is apparently based on the LXX, which has οἱ ἱππεῖ ("the horses, steeds"), but this involves changing *brš* to *prš* ("horseman"), which is unnecessary and unlikely, though accepted by Coggins (1985: 38). As Roberts (1991: 58) notes, this interpretation also involves reading the verbal root *rʿl* ("shake, reel, quiver") in reference to tumult and confusion among the cavalry or chariot horses, or we must assume a meaning of this verb not attested elsewhere in Hebrew.

The root *brš* refers to a tree (cypress, fir, or juniper), which is extended in this context to mean the frames of the chariots, or perhaps the juniper shafts of the spears. As Roberts (1991: 58) notes: "Such transference is attested with

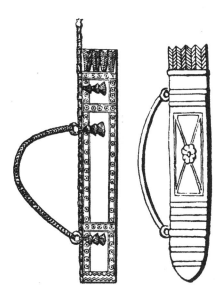

Left: An Assyrian quiver. Right: An
Elamite quiver. From Yadin (1963: 296).

the Akkadian cognate, *CAD* b, 328," and he notes similar phenomena in
other languages; however, he also finds merit in the suggestion of Leong
Seow (personal communication) that the word be taken as a reference to the
wooden framework of the chariots. The Akkadian phrase **narkabti burāši** is
translated "a chariot of juniper wood" (*CAD* b, 327). Spronk (1997: 90) thinks
the reference is to the parts of the chariot that keep something of the shape of
the tree, that is, the poles, and translates the phrase "the poles are upholstered." Roberts (1991: 58) reads the verb *horᶜālû* ("quiver shake") as the
Hophal perfect from the root *rᶜl* ("quiver, shake, reel"). If the word *habbərōšîm* is interpreted as the juniper framework of the chariots, the image is that
of the shaking, swaying, or quivering of the wooden structure as the chariot
rushes into battle. If the word *habbərōšîm* is taken as the brandished spears,
the image could be that "of a rippling or quivering effect in the sea of spears
held aloft by the advancing spearmen of the attacking army." Soggin (1964:
377) suggests a reference to clappers made of juniper wood and observes that
the *brwš* always refers to a tree or to its useful timber (cf. Pinker 2002). It is
better to translate the verb *horᶜālû* as "they poisoned" with Kimchi (d. 1235)
and Pinker (2005a: 417).

On the basis of the versions, a number of scholars emend *habbərōšîm*
to read *happārāšîm,* "and the steeds" (G. A. Smith 1928: 105). Rudolph's
interpretation (1975: 165, 167), "And the horses stand in row and rank," is

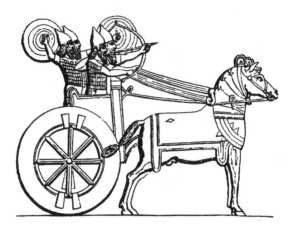

Chariot of Ashurbanipal's army. From Yadin (1963: 299).

thus based on the tenth conjugation of the Arabic root *r‘l*, which is not at all convincing.

2:5 [4]. *In the streets the chariots run amok; they rush to and fro in the squares.* At first glance the scene appears to shift from outside the besieged city to inside, with a description of chariots moving *baḥûṣôṯ*, "through the streets" of the city, and *bārəḥōḇôṯ*, "through the squares." As Keil (1949: 21) noted, the *ḥûṣôṯ* ("streets") are roads and open spaces inside the city (cf. Amos 5:16; Psalm 144:13–14; Proverb 1:20) or "in the suburbs surrounding the inner city or citadel." Because of this, some regard 2:5 [4] as a description of the defending army inside the city of Nineveh (Ewald 1878; Happel 1902; cf. the LXX), which suggests that the word *hārekeḇ* ("the chariot") in two successive verses refers to the chariots of two different armies.

Watson (1976: 243) finds what he calls a "pivot pattern" here. In a poetic context of this sort, the word pair "streets" and "squares" is traditional language used to heighten the immediacy of the imagery; the poet is portraying the action of this terrifying weaponry as near at hand. Thus it is appropriate to see here a description of what took place on the roads leading to Nineveh (Jeremias 1895: 100; Billerbeck and Jeremias 1895: 100; Humbert 1936: 16–17), on the plains near the city (J. M. P. Smith 1911: 330; Rudolph 1975: 171–72), or within the city itself. Van der Woude's (1978a) argument that the streets were too narrow for rushing chariots is contradicted by Assyrian records where Sennacherib boasts of his new capital with these words: "I widened the squares, made bright the avenues and streets; . . . I made its market streets wide enough to run a royal road." Moreover, he took measures "that there might be no narrowing of the royal roads" (*ARAB*, 162–63, 195; reference from Spronk 1997: 91). Spronk (1997: 92) presents a convincing argument to support his conclusion that the actions described here "do not take place after each other, but at the same time."

The verb *yiṯhôləlû* ("they act madly, rave," rendered here as "[the chariots] run amok") is the Hithpolel from the root *hll*, which is used in 1 Samuel 21:13 [14] to describe insane actions on the part of David before King Achish of Gath. When used in a military context, it describes the wild, furious action of war chariots charging to attack the enemy (Jeremiah 46:9; cf. 2 Kings 9:20). The *nun* ending on the verb *yištaqšəqûn* ("rushing back and forth") suggests additional energy and emphasis (Muilenburg 1953: 101; see *IBHS*, 516–17). The vivid imagery implies utter confusion and panic.

The word *yištaqšəqûn* is the Hithpalpel of the root *šqq* ("run, run about, rush"), which BDB 1055 translates "They rush to and fro." The verbal form suggests intense, furious, energetic action (cf. Deuteronomy 9:20; Jeremiah 5:22; see Muilenburg 1953: 101). Haldar (1947: 48–49), however, noted that the meaning of this word was not known to those translating the ancient versions and that in his day interpreters did not yet agree on its meaning. He interpreted the root *šqq* as "to abound," and Rowley (1947: 60) had "to reverberate." Roberts (1991: 58–59) suggests that the infixed *t* form here could be interpreted as reciprocal, "to race against one another" (cf. Rudolph 1975: 167). Spronk (1997: 91) calls attention to the play with sounds in an attempt to mimic the noise of chariots raging on (*yištaqšəqûn*) and flashing lightning (*yərôṣēṣû*) (cf. Coggins 1985: 38–39).

*Their appearance is like torches; like lightning they dart about.* Spronk (1997: 92) explains the 3rd pers. f. pl. suffix on *mar'êhen* ("their appearance") as a collective that can be regarded as abstract (see GKC §122q, 135p), along with others (Happel 1902; W. A. Maier 1959: 245). Keil (1949: 21) understood the plural suffix as referring "to everything in and upon the chariots." The word *lappîḏ* usually means "torch, flame" (cf. Genesis 15:17; Judges 7:16, 20; 15:4, 5; Isaiah 62:1; Ezekiel 1:13; Zechariah 12:6; Daniel 10:6), but it sometimes refers to "lightning bolts" (Exodus 20:18; Job 12:5), which is how the NET Bible (p. 1687) renders it here. Poetic parallelism, however, does not demand synonymity, as Kugel and others have shown (Kugel 1981; Alter 1985; A. Berlin 1985).

The expression *kabbərāqîm* "like lightning" suggests two images: that of brightness in the bright glitter of the chariots, and that of speed, in the swift destruction of the enemy (cf. Zechariah 9:14). The word *bārāq* ("lightning") conveys two different images: that of the brightness of an object, such as the glory of Yhwh (Ezekiel 1:13), the glitter of swords (Deuteronomy 32:41;

Ezekiel 21:15; Nahum 3:3; Habakkuk 3:11), the gleam of arrowheads (Job 20:25); and that of speed, such as the swift destruction of an enemy (Zechariah 9:14). Both images appear to be present here. The term *yərôṣēṣû* ("they dart about") is the only example of the polel of the verbal root *rwṣ* ("to run, charge"). The sequence of *yitḥôləlû* ("[the chariots] run amok"), *yištaqšəqûn* ("to rush to and fro"), and *yərôṣēṣû* ("to dart about") are instructive examples of what Muilenburg (1953: 101) meant when he said: "In such stems as P$^{ec}$al$^c$al, Pilpel and Hithpalpel, the verb is given a special energy or movement." Spronk (1997: 92) observes a progression in the references to fire in 1:4–5 in regard to the speed of the vehicles in question. The scene begins with chariots in preparation, "flashing as with fire" (2:4a [2:3a]). Then we see the chariots in motion, like the fire of burning torches (2:5b [4b]), and the speed increases, for now the fire is like lightning darting about (2:5b [4b]). The picture is that of quickly repeated flashes of lightning coming from different places in the heavens as the chariots go faster and faster. Spronk contrasts this with the progressive decline of the city of Nineveh in 2:6–9, with the "stumbling" of Nineveh's nobles, the setting up of the mantlet, the collapse of the city's defenses, and the "moaning" of "her maidens."

2:6 [5]. *His powerful ones are brought to remembrance.* With this verse the scene shifts abruptly from its earlier focus on the armies of the attackers in the two previous verses to that of the defenders of the besieged city (see Davidson 1920: 28; Keil 1949: 22). As the verse unfolds, the confusion of battle is caught up in the language itself, in which there is relatively little in the way of semantic parallelism of thought. The poetry itself is sustained by short staccatolike two-word clauses. But the content of the language adds confusion in matters of detail. Longman (1993: 895) suggests that "this is purposeful poetic ambiguity that . . . reflects the confusion of battle."

Attempts to read the Hebrew text as it stands, with the word *yizkōr* ("he remembers") in relation to *ʾaddîrāyw* ("his powerful ones"), vary widely in English translation. At first glance, the subject of the verb *yizkōr* ("he remembers") appears to be the "scatterer" of 2:2 [1], who is identified as the Divine Warrior YHWH in 2:3 [2]. And the verbal root *zkr* ("to remember") appears frequently in the Tanakh in reference to God's remembering (Eising 1980a: 69–72). Though God's remembering his people with favor plays a significant role, there are also passages in which the remembering is punitive (Hosea 7:2; 8:13; 9:9; Jeremiah 14:10). Here, presumably, he would be remembering the human leadership within the traditional "hosts of YHWH," who now include the unwitting forces of foreign troops arrayed against the city of Nineveh. But her once powerful military leaders now stumble forward under the burden of their siege equipment, which they are about to set up against this proud bastion of evil. God remembers, and he knows that the "full end" envisioned in

1:8–10 is about to be accomplished in the sack of Nineveh. If this is taken as the correct reading, it certainly presents serious problems in matters of detail.

Logoprosodic analysis indicates that something has apparently dropped out of the text at this point, for there is no way to achieve balance in mora count here with the text as it stands. It is better to add a missing vowel letter *waw* at the end of the verb so as to read a 3rd pers. pl. form, as is also the case in the LXX and Syriac. Thus we read the Niphal *yizzākərû* ("they are brought to remembrance") in agreement with the 3rd pers. pl. forms in the next two clauses of this same verse. This emendation increases the mora count by three so as to achieve balance in both halves of this central strophe of the third canto (2:1–11 [2:15–2:10]). Riessler (1911), Sellin (1930), and Horst (1938) read *yizzākərû* ("they are remembered," that is, his nobles are called up). G. R. Driver (1938: 270) also kept the consonantal text by reading *yiz-zakkərû* but with the meaning, "puff themselves up," though he later changed his mind and suggested *yizzākēr* or *yizzākərû*, "show themselves off" (1967: 54). Procksch (1937) suggested four different possible emendations, among which he preferred *yəkarkərû* ("they prance"), from the root *krr* II ("to dance"). Dahood (1961: 129; 1964b: 406) reads *yazkīrū* and understands it as a denominative verb from *zākār* ("male"), with the meaning "to be strong." Himmelfarb (1968: 74) emends the text to read *yəkarkərû ʾaddîrāyw* ("his nobles/officers prance/whirl") or *yidhărû ʾabbîrāyw* ("his war horses gallop"). Roberts (1991: 59) interprets the root *zkr* to mean "to command, assign, appoint," which he compares with the Akkadian *zakāru* (the NET Bible also interprets it this way [p. 1687], as does the JPS Tanakh; see *AHW*, 1503–4). However, the existence of the root *zkr* II ("to command") in Biblical Hebrew is not demonstrated. Following Dahood (1965: 126), Cathcart (1973a: 92–94) reads the text as *yazkīrū,* with the meaning "they are strong."

The English versions vary widely in their interpretations of the text. Thus we have "He shall recount his worthies" (KJV), "He calls his officers" (NRSV), "He summons his picked troops" (NIV), "He commands his burly men" (JPS Tanakh), "He remembers his nobles" (NASB), "The leaders display their prowess" (REB), and so on. An even more bewildering array of opinions is found in the scholarly literature on this verse. Gaster (1944: 52) described *yzkr* as an "Assyrianism" meaning "he musters" but later changed his mind and translated the text "He recalls (the past glories of) his braves" (1969: 662). Haldar (1947: 50–51) emended the text to find the root *zbr* ("to bestow upon") and found here "an allusion to the ritual meal." Taylor (1956: 963) somehow managed to find the word *ʿēṣîm* here and came up with "His nobles are felling timbers." Spronk (1997: 93, n. 43) observes that in some contexts the word *ʾaddîrîm* has a divine connotation, denoting mighty deified ancestors (cf. Spronk 1995b: 1194–95).

Among "many other renditions," W. A. Maier (1959: 247–48) discusses fourteen options in regard to the word *yizkōr* ("he remembers"):

1. G. A. Smith (1898: 106), J. M. P. Smith (1911: 316), and others read "he summons his nobles (for a council of war)."
2. Marti (1903: 317) and others drop the word altogether.
3. Graetz (1893) reads *yiškərû* ("they are intoxicated").
4. Orelli (1897: 230) reads *yəmahărû* ("they hasten").
5. Ruben (1898) reads *wəzûkak* ("and your infantry").
6. Duhm (1910: 75) reads *yidhărû* ("they rush forward").
7. Bevenot (1937: 13) reads "He runneth over the list of his mighty defenders."
8. Stonehouse (1929: 117) reads *yāʾûṣû* ("his majestic ones press forward").
9. Kautzsch and Guthe (1923: 69) read *yipqōd* ("he musters").
10. Ehrlich (1905: 295) reads *ûzəkūr ʾaddîrāyhā* ("and the best of their brave").
11. Van Hoonacker (1908) suggests the plural *yizkərû* ("they remember").
12. Junker (1938: 21) reads *yazkîr* ("he urges").
13. Haupt (1907a) reads *yizzākar* ("and he is remembered").
14. Sellin (1930: 368), Riessler (1911: 172), and Horst (1938: 160) read *yizzākərû* ("they are remembered," that is, his nobles are called up).

The logoprosodic analysis indicates that the central strophe (2:5–7 [4–6]) in this canto (2:1–11 [1:15–2:10]) is in two parts. The first half of this two-part strophe, which consists of two balanced dyads plus a pivot scanning 4 + 6 in SAS units [and 25 + 10 + 24 in mora count], presents the chaos and confusion in the streets as the chariots of the invading army run amok in the city squares (v 5 [4]). In the second part of this strophe, which also consists of two balanced dyads plus a pivot scanning 6 + 4 in SAS units [and 24 + 9 + 25 in mora count], the subject is that of the Assyrian defenders in the city of Nineveh. At the juncture of these two strophes, the once powerful officers are brought to remembrance. But now, in sharp contrast, "They stumble forward" in defense of the doomed city. Spronk (1997: 93) calls attention to 3:18, where these same "nobles" remain completely passive — in fact, they are slumbering! We are now in a position to resolve other problems in matters of interpretation.

*They stumble forward as they go.* The negative meaning of the verb *yikkāšəlû* ("they stumble") is no longer a problem. The defending officers stumble as they rush to defend the walls as the enemy prepares to breach them. The movement is not as such that of a military march that brings the army from distant places to the city of Nineveh. That march has already taken place. The movement portrayed here is that of those who make their way in haste in a hopeless cause to defend the city walls, which are about to be breached in the prophet's imagination.

Armerding's (1985: 475) interpretation, that the stumbling of the attacking army is caused not by their weakness but by the corpses of the Assyrian troops strewn in their path, shows good imagination, but it moves beyond the evidence at hand. There is no need to restore a presumed missing negation of the verb here (with the *BHS* note), nor is there any need to resort to philological gymnastics, with van der Woude (1978a) and others, to find a different verb here altogether in order to make sense of the text we have.

G. R. Driver (1938: 270) says: "I can only obtain sense by altering *yikkāšəlû* to *yiššāləkû*, when it will mean 'launched themselves on their way(s).'" Davidson (1920: 28) interprets the text as the defenders stumbling as they go, whereas Wellhausen (1898: 161) takes the verse as referring to the besiegers (cf. G. A. Smith 1903: 586; Sweeney 2000: 438). Cathcart (1973a: 94) renders the word "they stumble forward" and suggests: "Perhaps, the implication is that as the men head towards the ramparts, they stumble in their haste" (as does Longman). Following Dahood, Cathcart translates the *kethiv* reading *bahălîḵôtām* as "in their march." The NET Bible (p. 1688) suggests other possibilities as well: "in their trenches" or "in their columns," that is, "in their advance" (cf. *HALOT*, 246). The form of the noun in this instance is f. pl., which is also the case in all other occurrences of the word in the Tanakh. The *qere'* reading *bahălîḵātām* has the singular form of the noun *hălîḵāh* ("a going, way, walk") with the 3rd pers. pl. suffix, with the sense "in their going."

Rudolph (1975: 171) argues unconvincingly that v 6 cannot refer to the attacking army because the previous verse describes the battle inside the city of Nineveh—in her streets and her public squares. Such arguments presuppose that the poet was merely describing a historical event. As Haldar (1947: 121–27) and others have shown, there are cosmic and symbolic overtones to the entire visionary account presented here. It can be argued that the concentric structural design of the poetic canto in 2:1–11 [1:15–2:10] is more important than any sense of chronology as such. The portrayal of the mayhem of battle in Nineveh, with chariots storming in the streets, stands at the structural center of this canto in Nahum and is thus the focus of attention in the prophet's visionary account of the sack of Nineveh. The preparation for battle is described in v 4, and vv 5–7 present the action of the attacking force and the plight of Assyria, for her once mighty nobles are now described stumbling hopelessly forward to defeat and annihilation. The next verse (v 8) presents the ultimate consequences as the Assyrian captives are carried away into exile.

*They hasten to her wall; but the mantlet is (already) set up.* The subject "they" could be interpreted to be either the attackers or the defenders of Nineveh, but the context makes the latter view more likely (Gandell 1901: 642). The final *h*

Left: Typical siege shield of Tiglath-pileser's
army. Right: Ashurbanipal's siege shield.
From Yadin (1963: 295).

on the word *ḥômāṯāh* ("her wall") is sometimes interpreted as the *he' directionis*
(with some Hebrew Mss, the LXX, Targum, and Syriac; see Dahood 1965: 33)
or omitted altogether with the *BHS* note. But neither is needed. As Spronk
(1997: 94) observes, the use of the 3rd pers. f. sg. pronoun also appears in 1:8
without an antecedent in the immediate context. What we have here can be
interpreted as accusative of place or the adverbial accusative of direction (cf. R. J.
Williams 1976: §54; *IBHS* §10.2.2.b). The poet chose to use names sparingly
as a means of heightening tension. At the same time, however, it is possible to
find here a reference to Nineveh or to Ishtar, with J. D. W. Watts (1975: 113).

Cathcart's (1973a: 95) emendation of *wəhūkan* ("and [it] is set up") to read
*wəhākēn* ("and they set up"), which has no effect on the mora count, remains
attractive but is not really necessary. Cathcart notes that the three preceding
verbs are active, and thus one expects an active sense here. This is achieved
by reading the Hiphil inf. abs., which continues a preceding phrase with a finite
verb. On this construction in Northwest Semitic, see Moran (1950) and Huesman (1956a, 1956b). At the same time, the MT as it stands makes good sense,
as Spronk argues (1997: 94). The passive perfect (Hophal) form denotes an
action already taken and one taken by other persons. This reading is supported by the ancient versions and fits the context well. The shift from active to
passive verbs to mark a cause-result sequence is a common phenomenon
(Psalms 24:7; 69:14 [15]; Jeremiah 31:4; Hosea 5; see Weinfeld 1965: 272–82).

A *hassōkēk* ("the mantlet") was the siege shelter used by the Assyrians as a protective cover for soldiers besieging a fortified city, which was often portrayed on Assyrian reliefs (see *ANEP*, plates 368, 369, 373). These movable shelters were used by besieging armies as a protective cover for sappers and troops manning the battering rams to shield them from missiles coming down from the city wall (see the picture of the relief from Ashurbanipal's palace in Nineveh, now in the British Museum; Yadin 1963: 462). According to Clark and Hatton (1989: 31), the battering ram was normally a large tree trunk with an iron tip in the shape of an ax head. The battering ram was mounted to a frame that allowed it to be swung at the walls or gates of the city. Though the noun appears only here in the Hebrew Bible, the verbal root *skk* III ("to cover, protect") appears in Psalm 140:8 [7], as noted by Cathcart (1973a: 95), in a verse that confirms the reading here: "Yhwh, my Lord, my fortress of safety; shelter (*sakkōtāh*) my head in the day of arms." Though Cathcart is apparently reading the verb here as an imperative, Freedman (personal communication) sees it as a perfect form. The mantlets were of two kinds: a small, hutlike shelter that could be carried and a larger standing shield rolled on wheels to the top of the siege embankment. Such structures were made of planks or thick wickerwork (Haupt 1907b: 13). They were very heavy and were used exclusively in sieges. These siege towers were also equipped with instruments used to hurl stones and firebrands (see Layard 1849: 281–86). The weapons of the Ninevites are now turned against them. Sweeney (2000: 439, n. 26) argues that the term *hassōkēk* is derived from a root that means "to weave" and notes that the pictures in *ANEP* (368, 372–73) portray bowmen shooting from behind woven shields that apparently serve as the referents for the term "mantlet." Haldar (1947: 51–52) interpreted the word *hassōkēk* in light of Ezekiel 28:14, where it means "the overshadowing one," referring to the deity. He understands the word in Nahum 2:6 to mean "the emblem of the god being raised in connection with the running of the chariots." Cathcart (1973a: 95) calls attention to the repetition in 2:6 [5] of *k*, which appears six times in five out of eight words. Such clusters of consonants may be coincidental but are more likely to have been part of the stylistic repertoire of the author.

2:7 [6]. *The gates of the rivers are opened; and the palace melts away.* Cathcart (1973: 95–96) interprets "the river gates" (*šaʿărê hannəhārôt*) as the Hebrew equivalent to the Akkadian *bāb nāri* ("sluice-gates" on canals and dams controlling the flow of rivers; *AHW*, 95). In light of this observation, some scholars find here graphic confirmation of the classic tradition that Nineveh was destroyed by a flood due to the exceptional rising of the Tigris, along the lines of the prophecy reported by Diodorus (Humbert 1928: 17; W. A. Maier 1959: 253–54; Saggs 1969: 221–22; Robertson 1990: 90; Stronach and Lumsden 1992: 232).

It is good to take a close look at the report of Diodorus, however, and to real-ize that one should not use the writings of the ancient Greek historians to explain the words of Nahum, which are not a historical report as such but a prophetic vision. Diodorus refers to a prophecy that presumably came from the ancestors of the king of Assyria. It is more likely that Didodorus's account was shaped, at least in part, by the content of the book of Nahum, as Kleinert suggests (1910: 524–25). Kleinert points to the fact that Ktesias, the primary source Diodorus used, lived at the royal court of the Achaemenids and that there was a rather high likelihood of contact with Jews there. This may account for the references to darkness (perhaps a solar eclipse) and drunken-ness as part of the larger picture of events associated with the fall of Nineveh. The presumed prophecy Diodorus reported was: "No enemy will ever take Nineveh by storm unless the river shall first become the city's enemy." He then recounted that the final siege lasted no less than three years. His account reads "In the third year, after there had been heavy and continuous rains, it came to pass that the *Euphrates* [emphasis mine], running very full, both inundated a portion of the city and broke down the walls for a distance of twenty stades" (*Bibliotheca Historia*, Book II, 26–27; cf. Spronk 1997: 94–95, from which much of this summary statement is taken).

The Assyrian and Babylonian annals, which were uncovered in the nine-teenth century, do not support the account of Diodorus in matters of detail. In the first place, Nineveh is located on the Tigris, not the Euphrates. Sec-ond, the siege did not last for three years. Third, it is now known that Nineveh fell in the month of August 612 BCE, which is too early for the heavy rains that Diodorus described, as anyone who spends much time in the Middle East knows from personal experience. In short, one must read the ancient Greek his-torians critically. What they said and what happened do not always coincide.

Nineveh had a system of dams and "sluice-gates" to control the waters of the Tebiltu and Khoser Rivers, which flowed through the city (Thompson and Hutchinson 1929: 120–32). The Tebiltu in particular posed a flooding threat that undermined palace structures. Sennacherib changed the course of the Tebiltu within the city. He dammed the Khoser River outside the city to make a reservoir and to regulate the flow of water into the city through a system of double sluice-gates (*ARAB*, 99–100; Reade 1978: 42–72). We know that Sen-nacherib built an aqueduct at Jerwan, northeast of Nineveh, in his efforts to increase the water supplies for the lands and orchards of Nineveh (Jacobsen and Lloyd 1935: 31–43). The Bavian inscription (ca. 690 BCE), which appears on the aqueduct, mentions the **bab nāri**, or "sluice-gate" (Jacobsen and Lloyd 1935: 38). According to Jacobsen and Lloyd (1935: 41), a canal could be a natural river. According to the Babylonian Chronicles (Gadd 1923; Wiseman 1956), Nineveh fell in August, 612 BCE. In classical tradition (Diodorus and

Xenophon), Nineveh was destroyed by a flood through an exceptional rising of the river Tigris. But in the month of August, it is much easier to understand such a "flood" as the result of opening these sluice-gates.

Having said this, however, we must remember that there are serious problems in explaining the fall of Nineveh in this manner, as Luckenbill points out (ARAB, 163–64). Sennacherib built a large platform on which to construct his new palace, expressly to make such an event unlikely. The report by Sennacherib says: "The Tebiltu river, a raging, destructive stream, which, at its high water, had destroyed the mausoleums inside the city and had exposed to the sun their tiers of coffins, and, from the days of old, had come close to the palace and with its floods at high water had worked havoc with its foundations and destroyed its platform." This report concerns the period before the building period of Sennacherib. Ashurbanipal referred to necessary repairs carried out in his reign: "At that time the wall, inside the city of Nineveh, which Sennacherib . . . had built, whose foundation had given way and its turrets fallen, on account of the abundant showers and heavy rains which Adad had yearly sent upon my land" (ARAB, 342, 345; references and quotations taken from Spronk 1997: 95, n. 44).

Spronk (1997: 95) observes: "It is hardly conceivable, however, how attackers opening such sluice-gates could cause a flood strong enough to breach walls and make a palace, as a rule built on high ground, collapse" (cf. ARAB, 163–64). The sluice-gates of the canal system that feed the Tebiltu are too far removed from the city of Nineveh to adequately explain the flooding necessary to damage the palaces. Ewald (1878: 9–10) thought the "river gates" must be those of the Khoser River. Sennacherib built a large reservoir to collect water streaming down from the mountains so as to supply the city of Nineveh by feeding the Khoser River. For a picture of a restored reservoir thirteen kilometers north of Nineveh, see Roaf 1990: 187 (s.v. Nineveh). Rashi (d. 1105) posited sluice-gates along the Tigris as the "water gates" of Nahum 2:7 (as do Rudolph 1975: 172 and van der Woude 1978a), but the waters of the Tigris are too brackish to have been the city's primary water supply.

None of these options adequately explains the flooding required. Moreover, the text in Nahum was written not as a description of what happened after the fact but as a vision of things to come. Up to this point in the book of Nahum, the city of Nineveh itself has not been mentioned explicitly (other than in the title in 1:1b), and nothing specific has been said that could not be said of other large cities in Mesopotamia. Though there are numerous allusions to various Mesopotamian treaty texts, the biblical account includes no specific facts regarding the history of Assyria as such. In short, it is best not to explain the "river gates" of Nahum 2:7 in terms of the Tebiltu, the Khoser, or the Tigris but to recognize here allusions to the primordial floods of Mesopotamian and Canaanite mythology (with Keller 1972: 410–11; Spronk 1997: 96; and others).

The water or flood images here should be compared with the similar images in 1:4, 8. Though the imagery is symbolic in nature, with mythic overtones, it is apropos in light of the physical location of Nineveh on the Tigris River and the actual historical account of how the river was used in the Babylonian assault when the city fell in 612 BCE. According to Greek sources, a succession of excessive rainfalls deluged the area, and the waters of the Khoser River rushed through the overloaded canal system, breaking a hole about two miles wide in the city wall and flooding the city. When the waters receded, the enemy forces stormed into Nineveh and conquered it (Diodorus Siculus, *Bibliotheca Historica*, 2.26–27 [esp. 27: 1–3]; Xenophon, *Anabasis*, 3.4.12). It must be remembered, however, that though archaeological evidence lends some credence to this story, the portrayal of events here is couched in symbolic language with overtones of mythic combat in which the waters of chaos are of primary concern. In the world of mythology the great cosmic waters are destructive powers that were subdued and pushed back in the process of creation itself (cf. Genesis 1:6–9). It is thus possible to see *the rivers* here as the currents of the great cosmic ocean (J. D. W. Watts 1975: 113; cf. Nahum 1:4 and Psalm 93:3).

As Spronk notes, the key to understanding the verse in question is to be found not in the ruins of Küyünjik but within the book of Nahum itself. We have already seen in the earlier discussion of 1:8 that YHWH was to bring an end to the city in a "sweeping torrent" (cf. Kleinert 1910: 523). Keller (1972: 410–11) points to parallel uses of the word *hannəhārôt* ("rivers") in Habakkuk 3:8 and Psalm 93:3 and to the phrase *šaʿar haššāmayim* ("the gate of heaven") in Genesis 28:17. Spronk (1997: 96) calls attention to an Ugaritic text that locates the residence of the supreme god El *mbk nhrm qrb ʾapq thmtm* "at the fountainhead of the two rivers, in the middle of the bedding of the two floods" (*KTU* 1.4.IV.20–21). Watts (1975: 113) also suggests cosmic implications in the reference to floods and rivers here in relation to extrabiblical stories of creation and flood (see also Haldar 1947: 128–29).

The word *nāmôg* literally means "dissolves" or "melts." The form is Niphal perfect, which is used elsewhere in a metaphorical sense of people's "melting away" in fear. It is possible that the poet chose the word in this context to describe how flooding contributed to the destruction of Nineveh. In this context it describes the effect of water inundating the mud-brick palace. See the discussion of the root *mwg* ("to melt") in the earlier section on 1:5. The graphic pictures of the results of the December 26, 2004, earthquake-induced tsunami twenty miles off the coast of Sumatra in Indonesia make it easy to understand how the mud-brick palaces of Nineveh "dissolved." Keil (1949: 24) interpreted the word *nāmôḡ* ("it melts, dissolves") in a figurative sense, as meaning "to vanish through anxiety and alarm," and the word *hêḵāl* ("palace, temple") as referring to the inhabitants of the palace.

2:8 [7]. *And it is determined.* The first three words of v 8 [7] are notoriously difficult to translate. The problem in interpretation is caused by the fact that the MT has four consecutive verbal forms (including the last word in the previous verse), the first two of which are masculine and the other two feminine. Moreover, the word *huṣṣaḇ* is the Hophal perfect of the root *nṣb* ("take one's stand"), which appears nowhere else in the Tanakh. The closest parallel is the Hophal participle *muṣṣāḇ* ("[a ladder] was set up") in Genesis 28:12. Here in Nahum 2:8 the word means that it has been determined by God that Nineveh, the queen, or mistress, of the nations, will be covered with shame (Keil 1949: 24). The verb is used elsewhere in reference to setting up a stone pillar (Genesis 35:14, 20; 2 Samuel 18:18) or the erection of a stone monument (1 Samuel 15:12; 1 Chronicles 18:3), road markers (Jeremiah 31:21), and apparently stelae with royal directives (Longman 1993: 806). In Deuteronomy 32:8 it refers to "fixing the bounds for peoples" (cf. Psalm 74:17). In light of this fact, both the NRSV and the NIV extend the meaning of the verb and translate the Hebrew word *huṣṣaḇ* "it is decreed," with notes calling attention to the fact that the meaning of the word is uncertain. The JPS Tanakh, which takes the word in question as a proper name, reads "And Huzzab is exiled," which continues a long-standing Jewish tradition going back to the Targum.

The traditional translation, "it is determined" (with Hitzig 1881: 254; Strauss 1855; J. Ridderbos 1930: 134; Robertson 1990: 91, and others), remains the most likely interpretation and is followed here (see BDB, 662). This reading, however, has not satisfied many interpreters, because one would expect a feminine form to agree with the subject of the next word, *gullǝṯāh* ("she is exposed, stripped").

W. A. Maier (1959: 259–61) lists twelve different translations, with the persons he identifies who represent that position for the word in question:

1. Huzzab is a proper noun:
   the name of the Assyrian queen: Targum, Rashi (d. 1105), Kimchi (d. 1235).
   a figurative designation of Assyria or Nineveh: Patristic writers; also Keil (1949: 24).
2. Repointed as *ḥazzāḇ* ("lizard"): Hitzig (1881: 254–55) (like the lizard, Nineveh can be brought out of its hole only with great difficulty).
3. Repointed as *ḥazzāḇ* but translated "lady," from the Arabic *zaʿīna*, which means "woman's litter": Davidson (1920: 34–35).

4. Read as *haṣṣəḇî*, "glory," "splendor," "beauty," a name of Nineveh: G. A. Smith (1898: 106).

5. Read as *wəhuṣṣaḇ*, "the palace is dissolved, though firmly established": Henderson (1864: 282).

6. Derived from *nāṣab*, "it is decreed," as in Deuteronomy 32:8; Psalm 74:17: RV and other commentators.

7. Emended to *haśśagāl*, "the queen": Marti (1903: 318).

8. Emended to *hûṣṣəʾāh*, "she is brought forth": Stonehouse (1929: 119).

9. Referring to the goddess Zib: van Hoonacker (1908: 439).

10. Referring to Husur, the small river flowing through Nineveh: Bévenot (1937: 14).

11. Emended to *maṣṣāḇ* or *maṣṣāḇāh*, "foundation": Happel (1902).

12. Emended to *haṣṣəḇî*, "the gazelle": Wellhausen (1898: 162). In the Old Testament the figure of a gazelle is used to picture that which is beautiful and desirable (Song 2:9, 17; 4:5; 7:4; 8:14).

W. A. Maier says that he has listed here only a few examples from "a long line of alterations" by way of emendation proposed by various scholars.

The confusion in interpretation extends back to antiquity and is reflected in the ancient versions as well as in modern translations. Patristic writers and others, including Keil, held that "Huzzab" is a figurative designation of Assyria or perhaps of Nineveh itself (Laetsch 1956: 304). In medieval Jewish tradition, Rashi (d. 1105), Ibn Ezra (d. 1167), and Kimchi (d. 1235) regard Huzzab as the name of the Assyrian queen, a tradition reflected in the Aramaic Targum on the book of Nahum. According to Davidson (1920: 30), some scholars regard Huzzab as a cryptic name for Nineveh, as is Rahab for Egypt and Sheshak for Babylon.

From at least 1527, in Christian circles the term *huṣṣaḇ* has been taken as a proper noun designating the Assyrian queen (see G. A. Smith 1928: 106, n. 6; and also Ewald 1878: 9–10 and others) or, more recently, perhaps as a cult statue of the city goddess Ishtar. In Jewish circles, Rashi (d. 1105) interpreted the word as a reference to the queen in light of Psalm 45:10: "at your right hand stands (*nṣbh*) the queen." Ibn Ezra (d. 1167) and others assumed that the queen's name was "Huzzab," and this remained the prevailing opinion until the twentieth century. The KJV and W. A. Maier (1959: 257) have adopted variations on this position—one that has been ridiculed by G. R. Driver (1964) and Saggs (1969). The Targum has *mlktʾ* ("the queen"). Roberts (1991: 55) emends the text to read *whṣb[h b]glt hʿtlh*: "The princess is made to stand among the captives." Roberts bases this reading on the proposed emendation by Rudolph (1975: 168), who reads *wəhuṣṣəḇāh baggālūṭ hāʿăṯallāh*, "Eingestellt in den Gefangenenzug ist die Hochedle" ["The one of lofty noble birth is made to go into captivity"].

Some scholars argue that the term *huṣṣaḇ* is derived from the root *nṣb* II ("to be weak"; see Saggs 1969: 220–21; Patterson 1990: 69–70), citing Psalm 39:6 and Zechariah 11:16. Taking the word *gullǝṯāh* as the noun "column-base," Saggs (1969: 220–21) translates the passage "Its column-base is dissolved."

Knabenbauer (1886) thought the word means the "splendid" city of Nineveh. In a somewhat different way, others also explain the term as a symbolic name for the city of Nineveh (for example, Theodor of Cyros [d. 457], Cyril [d. 412], Jerome [d. 420], and Calvin [1559]). Hitzig (1881: 254) emended the text to read *ḥazzāḇ* ("lizard") and proposed this as a descriptive designation for Nineveh, which, like the lizard, can be brought out of its hole only with great difficulty. Wellhausen (1898) suggested "the toad," a symbolic designation of Nineveh (see G. A. Smith 1903: 586). Rawlinson (1868: 1110–11) read *huṣṣaḇ* as a geographical term — "the *Zab* country," or the fertile tract of land east of the Tigris, watered by the Upper and Lower Zab Rivers. He noted that Pliny used the term *Zab* to stand for Assyria itself and that the name *Zab* as applied to the rivers is found from as early as the twelfth century BCE in the great inscription of Tiglath-pileser I.

Van der Woude (1978) reads *ḥazzāḇ* ("the wagon"), which is supported by the Greek scroll of the Minor Prophets from Nahal Hever and by the Targum (cf. R. P. Gordon 1974: 425–26; Cathcart and Gordon 1989: 136), and changes the next word from *gullǝṯāh* to *ʿaṯallāh* ("queen") and translates the passage "On a wagon the queen goes into captivity" (cf. also Cheyne 1896; Ruben 1896, 1898: 175; Burney 1926/27: 378; Rudolph 1975: 172).

Richter (1914: 133) suggested that the word in question was used to mock the goddess of Nineveh. Other scholars have found reference to the queen in Nineveh by means of various emendations, such as *haššaḡel* ("the queen"; Budde 1901b: 3262; Marti 1903: 318); *wǝhuṣʾāh ḡālǝṯāh habbaʿălā(ṯā)h* ("[his] mistress is brought out, exiled"; Procksch 1933 in BH³); *hûṣǝʾāh bǝḡālûṯ habaʿălāh* ("the mistress is brought into exile"; Gry 1910; Elliger (1970)). Thus Graham (1927–28: 46) read "*Belit* [the female consort of the god Asshur] is driven forth into captivity." Cheyne (1896) emended *hʿlth* to read *ʿtlyh* and translated the passage "Yahweh is great" or "is lord" (reference from G. A. Smith 1928: 107).

Longman (1993: 806) translates the key word as "Beauty" (from the Hebrew word *ṣǝḇî*) and understands it to be a reference to the cult statue of Ishtar, the city deity of Nineveh. He builds his case on earlier suggestions on the part of Cathcart (1973a: 97) and Delcor (1977: 77). This reading, however, requires an emendation in the addition of the letter *yoḏ*. The same general interpretation can be reached without emendation by reading *huṣṣaḇ* as a verbal form with the meaning "it is determined." It is difficult to believe that the proper name of a particular statue of Ishtar at Nineveh would have been that familiar to the Judean audience the prophet Nahum was addressing, whether we date the book in terms of the historical setting presupposed by the content of the book or those of the historical context of the actual numerical composition of this text within the Book of the Twelve Prophets as we now have it. The city of Nineveh was totally destroyed in 612 BCE.

Cathcart (1973: 96) insists that no satisfactory explanation of the word *huṣṣab* has been given thus far. G. R. Driver (1964: 296) argues for the meaning "(captive) train" for a noun *haṣṣōb*, which he relates to the Arabic *ṣubb^{un}* ("train" of beasts and "columns" of men); cf. the NEB, "the train of captives." But this does not really improve all that much on the suggestion already given by F. Zorell (1957: 678) that *ḥṣb* relates to the Hebrew noun *ṣāb* ("wagon, litter") in Numbers 7:3 and Isaiah 66:20. Cathcart (1973: 97) notes that the Greek text of the Minor Prophets from Naḥal Hever also took *ḥṣb* to mean "the wagon, chariot" (see Barthélemy 1963: 199; van der Woude 1978a), and so does the Targum (see R. P. Gordon 1974: 425–26; Cathcart and Gordon 1989: 136). Reider (1949: 106) saw *ḥṣb* as a contracted form of *hā^ʿăṣēbāh* ("female idol"), an epithet of the Assyrian goddess Ishtar. But such an explanation requires the omission of ʿ for the sake of euphony and also the omission of the final *h* in the biblical text.

More recently, Saggs (1969: 221, 225) analyzed *huṣṣab* as Hophal from the root *nṣb* ("to suck out") in Akkadian; hence he read "It is sucked out, it is dissolved." Roberts (1991: 60) argues that the meaning of *nṣb* in Akkadian as "to suck" or "to lick" does not justify the extension of meaning to "are dissolved." He also rejects Keller's (1971: 122) use of the Arabic root *ṣb* ("to pour out"), which he argues is "very problematic as a cognate for an early Hebrew root." R. L. Smith (1984: 82) derives *wəhuṣṣab* from *nəṣîb* ("pillar"), which he sees as a reference to a statue of the goddess.

Tournay (1962: 304; 1965: 428; with G. A. Smith 1898: 106) persistently emended the text to read *haṣṣəbî* ("The Beauty"), which refers to the statue of Ishtar at Nineveh. He argues that official statues of the gods and goddesses were often carried away by the conquering enemy. In the Lamentation over the Destruction of Sumer and Ur, we read in line 153 "Inanna was carried off from Erech, was brought to enemy territory" (*ANET Sup* 614). Other nouns behind the form in question, which have been discussed, include *haṣṣəbî* ("the gazelle") and *haṣṣāb* ("the lizard"). Both are rejected by Roberts (1991: 60) as "very unconvincing."

An interesting suggestion was made by the medieval Arabic commentator Yéfer ben Ély (reported and accepted by Barthélemy 1992: 807–8) that after the collapse of the palace the enemy turned to the king and the queen; the king trembled in his palace, and the queen sat in a litter. The reference to the king indicates that he is in *ḥṣb*, "he is put down," meaning that he was hanged, knocked down, or pierced through with arrows. Yéfer found in 2:6 [5] a reference to the king's facing the loss of his past glory, but here in 2:8 [7] he faces the loss of his wife's honor. After the collapse of his palace the king was nothing more than a spectator, watching as his queen was exposed and humiliated sexually by victorious soldiers. Spronk (1997: 96) accepts this interpretation and translates the passage "And he is put down, she is exposed, raped." The major difficulty with this reading is that it is based on a presumed parallel in Psalm 39:6, which Spronk (1997: 98) translates "Every man is put down (נִצָּב niph.) . . . 'they are all but a breath.'" But Spronk's translation of the verbal form in question in Psalm 39:6 is doubtful. I agree with Spronk (1997: 97): "Since neither a direct connection with the following words, nor with the preceding verse offers a convincing solution, it seems best to interpret וְהֻצַּב as a short independent phrase."

*She is stripped bare, she is taken away; and her maidens are lamenting, like the sound of doves, beating on their breasts.* The word *gullǝṯāh* is interpreted in two different ways: (1) "she is stripped," which is reflected in the LXX ("she has been exposed"), and (2) "she is taken into exile." The word *gullǝṯāh* ("is stripped"), together with *hōʿălāṯāh* ("she is carried away"), two passive verbal forms from the roots *glh* ("to uncover, remove") and *ʿlh* ("to go up"), describe what happened to Nineveh (or perhaps to the cult statue of Ishtar, the city deity of Nineveh). Keil (1949: 24) argues that the word *gullǝṯāh* means "she is uncovered," after the Piel "to uncover," in reference to shame or nakedness (as in Nahum 3:5; cf. Isaiah 47:2–3; Hosea 2:12). The laying bare and carrying away refer to the complete destruction of Nineveh. Elliger (1970) and *HALOT* (191) suggest repointing the MT as Qal perfect *gālǝṯāh* ("she went into exile"). Patterson (1990: 70) revocalizes the text to read *gôlǝṯāh* ("her exiles/ captives"), a noun with a 3rd pers. f. sg. suffix with a collective meaning. Saggs (1969: 220–25) reads the noun *gullǝṯāh* ("column-base") as in 1 Kings 7:41–42; 2 Chronicles 4:12–13; and translates the passage "Its column-base[s] is/are dissolved."

Spronk (1997: 98). finds in the word *hōʿălāṯāh* an association with *ʿlh*, which denotes the mating of cattle (cf. Genesis 31:10; attested also in Ugaritic and Akkadian; cf. Paul 1982: 492). He interprets the word in reference to "beastly treatment of the queen by victorious soldiers." Such a concrete expression adds interest, but it is not in fact more likely in this context than "she is carried off" or "she is brought up" (to the funeral pyre, as proposed by Ewald 1878: 9–10 and Wellhausen 1898: 162), or even "she is brought up to a safer, higher place" (Siegel 1929–30). Ruben emended *hʿlth* ("is carried away") to read *hʿtlh*, which he translates "The Lady," an analog of the

Assyrian *etellu*, f. *etellitu* ("great, exalted"; see G. A. Smith 1928: 107, n. 1; cf. Cheyne 1896).

The phrase *wəʾamhōṯêhā mənahăḡōṯ* ("her maidens lamenting") describes the reaction to this event. If Nineveh is personified here, some scholars argue that the expression "her maidens" may refer to lesser cities that shared the fate of the capital (Gandell 1901: 642; and so understood much earlier by Theodoret of Cyrus [d. 458], Cyril of Alexandria [d. 444], Jerome [d. 420], and others). Keil (1949: 25) was surely correct to argue that the inhabitants of Nineveh are represented as maids mourning the fate of their mistress. The Piel participle *mənahăḡōṯ* is from the root *nhg* II ("to moan, lament"). An alternate vocalization (represented in some Hebrew Mss, the LXX, Vulgate, and Targum Jonathan) reads the Pual participle *mənōhăḡōṯ* ("forcibly removed"), from the root *nhg* I ("to drive away, lead away"), which appears frequently with reference to conquerors leading away exiles or prisoners of war (Genesis 31:26; Deuteronomy 4:27; 28:37; Isaiah 20:4; Lamentations 3:2). Roberts (1991: 60–61) emends the text to read "[They are] led away" and also adds an additional word—the Qal active participle *hōḡōṯ* from the root *hgh* ("to moan"), which he thinks, as a result of haplography, was lost. It is true that the Vulgate and the Targum appear to reflect an additional word here, but a dittography in the Hebrew text on which these translations are based is also possible. Evidence from the numerical composition of Nahum makes the addition of a word here problematic.

The picture of slave girls moaning like doves (*kəqôl yônîm*) as they are carried away into captivity is reminiscent of scenes from Mesopotamian literature in which cult statues were desecrated ("stripped") and taken away to the victor's temple. Spronk (1997: 98) calls attention to a text in the Mesopotamian myth of Nergal and Erishkigal that speaks of the dead as "moaning like doves all day" (cf. *ANET* 509). The comparison between the groans of despair and the sounds of a dove is also found in Isaiah 38:14 and 59:11. Even today one species of dove is commonly referred to as a mourning dove. On the relation between the sound made by the dove and the Hebrew name of the bird, see Riede (1993: 357). The expression *kəkôl yônîm* ("like the sound of doves") instead of *kayyônîm* ("like the doves") suggests the loudness of the moaning (Keil 1949: 25).

The rare word *məṯōp̄əp̄ōṯ* ("beating [their breasts]") is a Polal participle from the root *tpp* ("to drum"), which is listed in BDB 1074 as a denominative verb derived from the word *tōp̄* ("timbrel, tambourine"). The participle describes a circumstance that accompanies the main action, which is carried out in a continual or repetitive manner (see *IBHS* §37.6.d; J. G. Williams 1976: 221). The noun *lēḇaḇ* ("heart, mind, will, inner person") represents what BDB 523 calls "inner for outer," which might just as well be expressed "outer for inner."

The heart is located inside or beneath the breast and here represents the symbolic core of the existential self. The phrase ʿ*al-libəbēhen* means "upon their breasts." In the culture of the ancient Near East, the action of striking one's breast in such a manner was a sign of mourning expressing intense, desperate sorrow (cf. Luke 18:13; 23:48). There is no reason to emend the text with Hitzig to read *ləbabhen* ("their heart[s]"). The normal form would have been written *libəbêhen*, but the *yod* is frequently omitted as a sign of the plural (Keil 1949: 25).

2:9 [8]. *And Nineveh is like a pool of water; her waters fall; they are draining away*. The city of Nineveh is portrayed as a vast pool of water in circumstances where the "levée" or "dam" (the retaining wall) has burst and the water is pouring out. The water is thus a metaphor for both the strength of the city and its inhabitants.

The word *Nineveh* appears here in Nahum for the first time after the heading in 1:1a. It appears one more time in 3:7 and is concealed in a name acrostic in 3:18. For a work that has Nineveh as its subject, it is surprising how few times the word actually appears in Nahum. Spronk (1997: 99) says: "The poet seems to have waited for the moment that he is about to describe its complete destruction. Instead of the usual association of the name with fame, it is now connected with the description of its eradication. For the same reason the title 'king of Assyria' is only mentioned in 3:18, when there is nothing left of his kingdom." Bliese (1995: 54–55, 70) finds what he believes to be hidden references to the king of Assyria elsewhere in Nahum.

The word *Nineveh* appears nine times in the book of Jonah (1:2; 3:2, 3 [twice], 4, 5, 6, 7; 4:11). The total number of occurrences of the word *Nineveh* in Jonah and Nahum is thus 9 + 3 = 12, with a thirteenth occurrence hidden in the acrostic pattern of Nahum 3:18. The title "king of Nineveh" appears once in the book of Jonah (3:6) but nowhere else in the Tanakh or outside of it.

The city of Nineveh was famous for its many artificial pools of water within the complex of the royal gardens, and also for the wide moats alongside the city walls. Spronk (1997: 99) calls attention to Sennacherib's "famous hydraulic works around Nineveh" (the reservoir, aqueducts, canals, moats, and pools). Moreover, the very name *Nineveh* means "fish-city." That name was occasionally written in the pseudologographic form *Nina*, which is the combination of two Sumerian signs (AYB + KHA) that represent an enclosure with a fish inside (Christensen 1985c: 707; 1996b: 759). Because the rivers Tebiltu and Khoser flowed through the city as well, the simile that presents Nineveh as being like a pool of water is apropos. As Pinker notes (2004b: 402–3), the phrase *kibrēkat-mayim* in 2:9 is described in differing ways: it was surrounded by bodies of water (Targum); it was like a lake (Syriac Peshitta); it was like a fish aquarium (Vulgate); it was calm as the waters of a pool (Rashi [d. 1105]); it

had many riches (Ibn Ezra [d. 1167]); it had many people (Ewald 1840); it
was inundated (Döller 1908), it drained quickly of its waters as a pool (Cathcart 1973a); it was unassailable (Bolle 1990); and so on (references taken from
Pinker 2004b: 402–3). As Spronk observes (1997: 100), the word *bərēkāh*
("pool") is used to denote the pool at the end of the Siloam tunnel in Jerusalem (cf. Isaiah 7:3; 22:9; 36:2). Because these pools were also the sources
of fish, Spronk says: "The poet may have also had in mind here the meaning
of the name Nineveh, namely 'house of fishes' [*sic*]. The token of its strength
is now a simile for its downfall."

As pointed out in the MT, the phrase *mîmê hîʾ* would be translated "from
the days of her" (Laetsch 1956: 302; cf. GKC §130.d., n. 3) or "since the days
that she exists" (Keil 1949: 25). Spronk (1997: 99) has "as long as it existed."
The JPS Tanakh has "from earliest times." The preposition *mem* is used tem-
porally, marking the beginning of a continuous period ("since, from"; see
*HALOT,* 597 [2]; BDB 581 [4.a]). The plural of *yôm* ("day") here denotes
"lifetime" (*HALOT,* 400 [6.c]). As Cathcart (1973a: 101) notes, we have here
an instance of the independent pronoun's functioning as genitive possessive,
or what C. H. Gordon refers to as the *casus obliquus* (*UT,* §6.4; as does Longman 1993: 807). The phrase *mîmê hîʾ* would then mean "from the beginning
of her days," "during her lifetime," or "from of old," as rendered here, or perhaps "from days of yore." But as Pinker (2004b: 402) observes: "Such translations are not comprehensible without extemporaneous interpretive fill-ins."

Because the context suggests a form of the word *mayim* ("water") rather than
the word *yôm* ("day") with the preposition *min* ("from") prefixed, some interpreters emend the text to read *mêmê hîʾ* ("its waters"). For other suggestions, see
Kleinert (1910: 521–22); Richter (1914: 133–34); Weill (1923); Humbert (1927);
and Barthèlemy (1992: 809). The emendation proposed here modifies this conclusion in light of Pinker's arguments (2004b). The MT is modified slightly:

| MT: | *mîmê hîʾ* | *wəhēmmāh nāsîm* |
| Suggested reading: | *mêmệhā <hāwʾû>* | *hēmmāh nāsîm* |

The original consonantal text *mymyh hwʾw hmh* apparently suffered haplography of the letter *heʾ* between the first two words, subsequent confusion of
the letter *wau* and *yod* in the second word, and the attachment of the second
*wau* to the third word, so as to read *mymy hyʾ whmh*. Roberts (1991: 61)
omits the *wau* conjunction on *wəhēmmāh* ("and they") as "an early expansion of the text by a scribe who misdivided it." It is the "waters of Nineveh" that
are "fleeing" in the sense that *they are draining away.* For parallels that show
the verb *nws* ("to flee, run away") with reference to water, see Psalms 104:7;
114:3, 5. As Roberts notes: "This imagery is rooted in the mythological portrayal of Yahweh as the Divine Warrior before whose might even the unruly

waters of chaos are put to flight." In the so-called Zion Tradition, imagery of mighty waters is a frequently used and powerful metaphor to describe the attack of enemy kings (Psalms 46:6–10; 48:4–8 [3–7]; Isaiah 17:12–14). It is difficult to improve on Roberts's concluding words: "Nahum picks up on this older imagery to suggest that the mighty waters of Assyria are no longer a threat to anyone. The tide has turned, Assyria's hosts have fled, and Nineveh is left high and dry." It must also be added, with Spronk (1997: 100), that the image here in 2:9 is that of the inhabitants of Nineveh "rapidly leaving the city, like a big stream of water running from a pool."

The verb *hw²* ("to fall") appears in Job 37:6 — "for he says to the snow, *fall* (*hĕwē²-²ereṣ*) earthward" (see BDB 216–17). Pinker (2004b: 405, n. 23) notes that such a reading of the text here "could serve as a figurative depiction of Josephus' 'water in motion' (*Ant.* 9:239)."

The phrase *mîmê hî²* has been emended in various ways by different scholars. All the ancient versions support the emendation to read *mymyh* ("her waters"), except for the Targum, which has *mymy qdm hy²* ("of the days of old she [is]"). Pinker (2004b: 403) notes that in six out of the sixteen cases elsewhere in the Tanakh in which *mymy* occurs with the meaning "days," it is followed by *qdm* ("of old"). The traditional Jewish commentators (Rashi [d. 1105], Ibn Ezra [d. 1167], Kimchi [d. 1235], Abarbanel [d. 1641]) follow the Targum, but some Hebrew manuscripts support the "watery" version (Gese 1957: 61), and so does Josephus (*Ant.* 9:239), who wrote: "Nineveh shall be a pool of water in motion; so shall all her people be troubled, and tossed, and go away by flight, while they say one to another, 'Stand, stand still'" (references from Pinker).

The following is a list of some of the many different readings of the text and proposed emendations involving the words *mayim mîmê hî²* (see also W. A. Maier 1959: 263–66 and Pinker 2004b: 404):

1. reading *mayim mêmê hî²* — "Nineveh, her waters were like a pool of waters, and they are running away" (Davidson 1896: 35; Cathcart 1973a: 100; Longman 1993: 807; and many others)
2. reading *mēmêhā* in place of *mîmê hî²* — "her waters" (cf. LXX, Syriac, Vulgate; Roberts 1991: 61; cf. Dahood 1970c: 90)
3. omitting the words *mîmê hî²* as a gloss (Nowack 1897: 251; Wellhausen 1898: 162; Happel 1902; G. R. Driver 1906: 33; van Hoonacker 1908: 440; Horst 1938: 160; and others)
4. *mayim hî²* (omitting *mîmê*) — "the water of itself" (Orelli 1893: 231)
5. *mêmê hî²* (omitting *mayim*) — "Nineveh is like a pool of water fleeing away" (G. A. Smith 1898: 322; Junker 1938: 22)
6. *mîmê hî* (omitting *aleph*) — "[the] days of lamentation" (W. A. Maier 1959: 263)

7. "Nineveh is like a pool of waters, whose waters roar as they flee" (Stonehouse 1929)

8. "Nineveh is like a pool of water . . . swelled by an influx from all quarters" (W. H. Green 1877: 202; cf. Jeremiah 51:13)

9. "Nineveh, like a pool of water are her defenders (*ʿammehā*)" (J. M. P. Smith 1911: 322)

10. *mymyh(y)ʾ hmw hnsym* — "Its waters have put fugitives into confusion" (Saggs 1969: 224)

11. *mymy ḥyh hyʾ* — "since the day of disaster" (Pinker 2004b: 404)

12. *mymyh yhmwh* — "the flood overwhelms her" (Pinker 2004b: 404)

13. *mymy hyʾr* — "from the waters of the river" (Pinker 2004b: 404)

14. "Its waters are as a pool, and Nineveh is an isle (*ʾî*)" (Pinker 2004b: 405)

15. *mymyh dʾw* — "Its waters soared" (Pinker 2004b: 405, alternate possibility)

According to W. A. Maier (1959: 264), Martin Luther maintained that previously Nineveh had been populous and glorious; but now it is only a fish pond, the water of which has run off. Maier is surely correct in insisting that Nineveh had the appearance of an inundated area: "It has been flooded (v. 7); its palace sways (and falls); the captured city looks like a pool." As Pinker puts it (2004b: 404): "It seems that it is neither inundating waters nor receding waters that Nahum describes, but standing water, as in a pool."

2:9c–10a [8c–9a]. *"Stop! Stop!" (they cry), but no one turns back. Plunder silver! Plunder gold!* Logoprosodic analysis suggests that the imperatives at the end of 2:9 belong primarily with what follows in 2:10. Repetition of the Qal imperative plural *bōzzû* ("plunder!") indicates direct speech. Presumably the speaker is the prophet Nahum himself. As Longman (1993: 807) suggests: "Nahum becomes so excited about the end of the evil city that he directs its looting in his imagination." It is also possible to see here the introduction of a new speaking voice to enhance the drama, with Spronk (1997: 100; following Alonso Schökel 1988: 154–55; Meier 1992: 34–35). The verbal root *ʿmd*, which normally means "to stand," can be used of both water (Joshua 3:16) and human beings (Jeremiah 4:6) in the sense of "stop, cease doing a thing" (BDB 764, 2.d). Haldar (1947: 56) emended the text to read *ʿmwd ʿmdw*, an inf. abs. followed by a perfect, which he translated "Yea, indeed, they stand," followed by the corroborating statement "There is none who turneth back." The Hiphil participle *mapneh* ("turning back") may be taken in an intransitive sense (Jeremiah 46:5, 21; 47:3; 49:24) or a transitive sense (Judges 15:4; 1 Samuel 10:9; Jeremiah 48:39; see *IBHS* §27.2–3). When applied to a person already fleeing, it means "to turn around" (cf. Jeremiah 46:5).

The booty of war is a common motif, even for the "wars of Yʜᴡʜ" (see Numbers 31:13–24). Assyria gloried in the rich spoils taken from those she conquered (cf. W. A. Maier 1959: 267–70; Johnston 1992: 337). Spronk (1997: 101) cites an informative example in the inscription of Ashurbanipal's conquest of Thebes in Egypt: "That city in its entirety my hands conquered with the help of Ashur and Ishtar. Silver, gold, precious stones, the goods of his palace, all there was, brightly coloured and linen garments, great horses, the people, men and women, two tall obelisks, fashioned of glittering electrum, whose weight was 2500 talents, placed at the gate of the temple, I removed from their positions and took off to Assyria. Booty, heavy and countless, I carried away from Thebes" (Piepkorn 1933: 38–41). The twofold repetition of the imperative verbal form *bōzzû* ("plunder!") reiterates that of *ᶜiməḏû* ("stop!") in the previous verse, heightening the contrast between the conqueror and his victims. The first pair appears as the third element in a triad, the second pair in the initial element of a corresponding triad, which scan $(18 + 8 + 13) \parallel (14 + 12 + 13) = 39 \parallel 39$ morae. Both commands are rhetorical, with no effect in terms of terminating the action in question.

2:10b–c. *And there is no end to the treasure; (and) wealth from all its precious vessels.* The phrase *wəʾên qēṣeh* ("and there is no end") appears again in 3:3 and 3:9 but only twice outside the book of Nahum (both times in Isaiah 2:7). In the middle of the eighth century ʙᴄᴇ, Nineveh was one of wealthiest and most powerful cities in the world. Tribute from the vassal states under her control included all kinds of *treasure* (*təḵûnāh*) and *precious vessels* (*kəlî ḥemdāh*). As Spronk (1997: 101) observes, the poet may have chosen the word *təḵûnāh* ("treasure") rather than the more common word *ʾôṣār* ("treasure") in Isaiah 2:7 because of the relation with the verb *kwn* ("be firm, establish") used in Nahum 2:4, 6 (cf. Delcor 1973: 43 and *HALOT*, 1594). Spronk (1997: 102) calls attention to the assonance with the letter *kaf* in three of the last four words of 2:10 [9].

Greenfield (1985: 84) argues convincingly from evidence in Aramaic texts from Elephantine that we are dealing here with the verbal root *tkn* ("to measure, weigh"). He says: "The poet is simply listing the forms in which the silver and gold were stored in the royal palace of Nineveh: either in the form of *təḵûnāh*—that is gold and silver melted down, weighed, and ready for use—or in the form of precious vessels that originated either in tribute and gifts or in spoils, booty taken from many nations" (cf. Muffs 1969: 60–61, 198). The word *kāḇōḏ*, which is translated "wealth" here, could also be rendered literally as "weight." As argued by Ewald (1878: 10) and Hitzig (1881: 255–56), the preposition *lamed* on the word *lattəḵûnāh* ("to the treasure") continues in force for the word *kāḇōḏ* ("wealth"), which is written defectively, as in Genesis 31:1 (see Keil 1949: 26). Note how Ashurbanipal describes the booty taken from Thebes as being "heavy and countless" (Piepkorn 1933: 40–41). According to Greenfield (1985: 85, n. 16), throughout most of the Persian Empire even coins were valued primarily for their weight. This was certainly the case earlier in the Assyrian and Babylonian Empires (cf. E. S. G. Robinson 1950; Kraay and Moorey 1968). The words *kəlî ḥemdāh* ("precious vessels") refers to gold and silver vessels and jewels, as in Hosea 13:15. According to Movers (1856: 40–41, quoted from Keil 1949: 26, n. 1): "The riches of Nineveh were estimated at an infinitely greater amount than the enormous treasures accumulated in the Persian empire. That the latter is quite in accordance with truth, may be inferred from the fact that the conqueror of Nineveh, the Medes and Chaldeans, of whose immense booty, in the shape of gold, silver, and other treasures, even the prophet Nahum speaks, furnished Ecbatana and Babylon with gold and silver from the booty of Nineveh to an extent unparalleled in all history."

2:11 [10]. *Destruction and desolation and disintegration.* The assonance of the opening three Hebrew words in 2:11 [10]—*bûqāh ûməbûqāh ûməbullāqāh* —is striking and can only be approximated in translation. Note how each word in Hebrew is longer than the preceding one, with the repetition of two and then three consonantal sounds. Spronk (1997: 102) suggests that the poet may have coined new words for the occasion, because all three of these words appear nowhere else in the Tanakh. On the other hand, Coggins (1985: 44) says: "Analogous forms are found in Isaiah 24:1–3, with similar alliterative effect." Machinist (1983: 724) notes that the poet may have been influenced by a common expression in the Assyrian royal inscriptions: "The city I devastated, destroyed" (Akkadian *āla appul aqqar*). Spronk (1997: 102) adds an interesting variant from an inscription of Ashurbanipal: "That city I devastated, I destroyed, demolished with water, annihilated" (Piepkorn 1933: 72–73; cf. Spronk 1997: 102).

The closest approximation in translation is perhaps that of Alonso Schökel (1963: 437) in Spanish, "saqueo, saquería, saqueamiento" (reference taken from Cathcart 1973a: 103). Other attempts to approximate the phenomenon in English include "pillaged, plundered, polluted" and "raid and ravage and ruin" (Jerusalem Bible); "sack, sacking, and ransacking" (Gandell 1901: 643); "waste, bewasted, and devastated" (Davidson 1920: 31); "desert, desolation, and devastation" (Ewald 1878: 10; see G. A. Smith 1903: 586); "devastation, desolation, and destruction" (NRSV; cf. JPS Tanakh; NET Bible); "desolate, dreary, drained" (Moffat 1954: 1016); "dissipation, dispersion, destruction" (Haldar 1947: 58); "Desolation and devastation and dilapidation" (W. A. Maier 1959: 272); and "destruction, devastation, decimation" (Robertson 1990: 92). Some attempts in German include "Leere und Entleerung und Verheerung" (Keil 1888); "Leerung, Ausleerung, Verheerung" (Buber and Rosenzweig 1934); "Wüst, Wüste und Verwüstung" (H. Schmidt 1923: 171;

Rudolph 1975: 166). On the phenomenon of assonance as a means of expressing emphasis, see Rankin (1930) and Saydon (1955). The first two words of the passage, *bûqāh ûməbûqāh*, are both formed from the verbal root *bqq*, which has the sense of "to empty." The word *məbullāqāh* is a Pual participle from the root *blq* ("to lay waste"). The only other occurrence of the root *blq*, apart from the personal name *bālāq* (Numbers 22:2–24:25; Joshua 24:9; Judges 11:25; Micah 6:5), is found in Isaiah 24:1, together with the root *bqq*, just as here in Nahum. And two verses later, in Isaiah 24:3, we find the root *bzz* ("to plunder"), as in Nahum 2:10.

Spronk (1997: 102) calls attention to the fact that the threefold indication of destruction here balances the thrice-repeated *nōqēm yhwh* ("vengeance of Yhwh") in 1:2, which is apropos in light of the principle of inclusion because the verse here marks the structural center of the book of Nahum as a whole. He goes further by way of comparison to find connections between Isaiah 24:1–4 and Nahum (cf. also Cathcart 1973a: 103 and Rankin 1930: 285): Isaiah 24:1 uses the verbs *bqq* ("to empty") and *blq* ("to lay waste"), close to *bzz* ("to plunder") ‖ *bwq* ("to empty") in 24:3 (cf. Nahum 2:10); the verb *pws* ("to disperse, scatter"), also used in Nahum 2:2; the announced destruction of the earth and its inhabitants (cf. Nahum 1:5); and the verbal form *ʾmll* ("to languish") of the earth (cf. Nahum 1:4). Spronk's comment (1997: 103, n. 51) on the repetition of *ʾumlal* in Isaiah 24:4 (cf. Nahum 1:4) supports the conclusion reached in this commentary that this particular change is an authorial decision in the book of Nahum, not a secondary textual alteration.

*And hearts grow faint; and knees give way; and anguish is in all loins, and (on) all their faces. They are gathered as fuel (for burning).* Once again, we find a close parallel in terminology and imagery in the book of Isaiah, where we read in Isaiah 13:7–8 (NASB):

> Therefore all hands will fall limp,
>   and every man's heart will melt.
> And they will be terrified,
>   pains and anguish will take hold of them;
>   they will writhe like a woman in labor.
> They will look at one another in astonishment,
>   their faces aflame.

As Cathcart (1973a: 104) notes, both texts mention the melting of hearts, with less striking parallels as well. Spronk (1997: 103) argues that we have here a common description of anxiety with numerous parallels (cf. Waldman 1975–76: 189–91). Hillers (1965: 86–89) finds an interesting extrabiblical parallel to the description in this verse, which occurs in *UT*, *ʿnt* III:29–32: "Her (Anat's) feet stumble, behind her loins do break; above her face sweats;

the joints of her loins shake; weakened are those of her back" (reference taken from Cathcart 1973a: 105; cf. de Moor 1987: 10). On the expression "melting of the heart," see also Joshua 2:11; 5:1; 7:5; Isaiah 19:1; Ezekiel 21:12; Psalm 22:15). For the most part, it is this passage that has shaped the interpretation of Nahum 2:11 [10]. But it must be noted that the words *qibbəṣû pāʾrûr* ("they gather kindling") are not present here; instead we have a clear reference to faces that are "aflame" and not pale or "perdent leur couleur" (*Bible de Jérusalem*; reference from Cathcart 1973a: 105).

The final two words, *qibbəṣû pāʾrûr*, are commonly a conundrum for translators and interpreters (see Glück 1969). This same expression appears elsewhere only in Joel 2:6, in a context that shows a number of parallels to Nahum (see Spronk 1997: 103; Cathcart 1975: 72–74), which may be translated as follows:

*mippānāyw yāḥîlû ʿammîm //*     Before them the people are strong;
  *kol-pānîm / qibbəṣû pāʾrûr //*     every face is ablaze (in burning anger).

This line scans as a balanced dyad of 14 ‖ 13 morae. Though the verbal root *ḥwl* is usually interpreted to mean "writhe in anguish," as though it were identical with the word *yəḥîlûn* in Isaiah 13:8, it is also possible to translate the root *ḥyl* to mean "be firm, strong," as in Psalm 10:5 and Job 20:21. In Exodus 15:4 the word *ḥayil* means "army," and in Nahum 3:8 the word *ḥêl* means "rampart." The immediate context in Joel 2:5–7, which is military in nature, may be translated as follows:

With a noise as of chariots they leap on the tops of the mountains,
    like the crackling of a flame of fire consuming the stubble,
    like a mighty people arranged for battle.
Before (the enemy) the people are firm/strong,
    all faces are ablaze.
They run like mighty men;
    they climb the wall like soldiers;
And they each march in line,
    nor do they deviate from their paths.

The image of faces that are ablaze seems to reflect that of the glowing red-hot embers of burning fuel.

The most difficult word to translate both in Joel 2:6 and in Nahum 2:11 [10] is *pāʾrûr*. Lehrman (1948: 66) translates the phrase as follows in Nahum: "Their faces have gathered wrinkles." Pinker (personal communication) suggests that we may have here a combined word, with *pāʾrûr = pārʾ + ʾarûr*, which he interprets as a sarcastic expression meaning something like "glory of the doomed." Glück (1969: 21–26) has "Their faces turn grey." Cathcart

(1973a: 103–4) translates the phrase *qibbəṣû pā’rûr* to mean "(the faces of all) gather paleness." Roberts (1991: 62) understands this to mean that all their faces became flushed or that their faces became pale. But these two images are in tension with each other. To be flushed is to be rosy or red, and to be pale is to be colorless. Moreover, the emotional connotation in Joel 2:6 can just as easily be interpreted as that of anger, physical exertion, and military fervor as that of anxious fear. Interpreting the phrase in relation to what precedes it, Spronk (1997: 103) presents a somewhat similar image of faces gathering a glow based on the meaning "to gather redness" (cf. *HALOT*, 860). It is perhaps best to understand this image in terms of gathering the heat from the "redness" (that is, from the glowing embers of the fuel)—in the image of a cooking pot that transfers the "redness" (that is, heat from the fuel) into what is being cooked.

The ancient versions all understood the text in terms of the word *pārûr* ("cooking pot"), with variations on "all their faces were black like a cooking pot." Luther suggested the following: "They are going to be consumed and destroyed the way the chunks of meat thrown into the pot for cooking are generally eaten; like meat in the pot, they are cooked by external evils and persecutions" (citation taken from Spronk 1997: 103).

Calvin (1950: 472) derived the word *p’rwr* from *p’r* and read the passage "All faces withdraw their beauty." Arguing along the same lines, Stonehouse argues that *p’r* means "to be resplendent," which here denotes whiteness. Davidson and J. M. P. Smith, arguing on other grounds, interpret the expression to mean that the faces turned pale. Though Longman (1993a: 808) translates the phrase literally to mean "every face gathered grayness or darkness," he argues that such a translation is not appropriate in English. He says: "A dark face gives the impression of sadness." It is possible to see the initial *pe'*, which is prefixed to *’rr* ("fear"; cf. Akkadian *arāru*), and translate *qbṣw p’rwr* as "convulsed with fear." Görg (1978: 14) makes a somewhat similar argument based on a connection with Egyptian *’rr* ("eine Art Gefäß") together with the article *p3*, which he translates: "Die zunehmend glühende Rotfärbung des Metals." Spronk (1997: 104) suggests another reading in connection with the Hebrew word *tp’rt* ("glory, splendor") in light of the prophecy against Assyria in Isaiah 10 (cf. Peels 1993: 32).

The key to understanding the meaning of the phrase *qibbəṣû pā’rûr* in Nahum 2:11 [10] is found in the logoprosodic analysis of the text. Though the NRSV has "all faces grow pale," it is better to recognize the fact that the two Hebrew words *ûp̄ənê kullām* ("and the faces of all of them") belong with the preceding words in the prosodic structure, which may be rendered quite literally "And anguish is in all (their) loins and the faces of all of them." The scansion in terms of mora count is thus $(19 + 7) + 7 + (19 + 8)$, with the clause "and knees give way" functioning in a pivot pattern, connecting two parallel statements and belonging to both:

| | SAS | | Word count | | |
|---|---|---|---|---|---|
| | Morae | units | | | |
| Destruction and desolation and disintegration— | 19 | 3 | 3 | 3 | 0 |
| and hearts grow faint; | 7 | 1 | 2 | 0 | 2 |
| *and knees give way.* | _7_ | _1_ | 2 | 0 | 2 |
| *And knees give way;* | 7 | 1 | 2 | 0 | 2 |
| and anguish is in all loins and the faces of all of them— | 19 | 3 | 5 | 0 | 5 |
| they are gathered as fuel (for burning). | 8 | 1 | 2 | 0 | 2 |

The verb *qibbəṣû* is a 3rd pers. pl. intensive form of the verbal root *qbṣ* ("gather, collect"), which may be rendered in its normal sense: "They gathered." The problem is the final word, *pāʾrûr*, which is a substantive describing what is gathered. Though the suggestion of paronomasia in terms of *pārûr* ("pot") and *pāʾrûr* has some merit, for the pot gathers the "redness" or heat of the fire in which it is placed. It should be noted that the Hebrew root *pʾr* has produced other terms that add richness to any wordplay. The theophanic hymn in Isaiah 10:33 presents the Divine Warrior as a mighty forester lopping off "boughs" (*pūʾrāh*) of cedar as he destroys the "thickets of the forest" of Lebanon (cf. Nahum 1:4). The denominative verb *təpāʾēr* in Deuteronomy 24:20 is translated in BDB as "thou shalt not go over the boughs (of the olives) after thee (that is, glean)." In Ezekiel 17:6 the *pōʾrōṯ* are the more external parts of the vine that would eventually be pruned and presumably burned.

Because these other terms from the same verbal root suggest something like "boughs or cuttings for burning," a comparable construction in English is the expression "They gathered kindling." Within its larger context, it is best to interpret the phrase in a more general sense, as "they are gathered as fuel (for burning)." The image in Nahum 2:11 [10] appears to be a combination of what appears in Joel 2:6 (*kol-pānîm qibbəṣû pāʾrûr*, "all faces grow pale" [NRSV]) and Isaiah 13:8 (*pənê lĕhāḇîm pĕnêhem*, "their faces will be aflame"). The concept of "redness" being gathered is that of the heat of glowing embers of burning charcoal being gathered by the cooking pot, or perhaps even the image of red-hot metal, within the context of the flames of Yhwh's anger.

Nowell (1990: 260) calls attention to the fact that this verse "looks both ways, pointing out the results of the conquest described in 2:4–10 and leading into the judgment oracle of 2:12–14." She also notes that the three exclamations at the outset are followed "by four phrases describing the physical results of human despair (3 + 4 = 7, i.e., completeness)." Labuschagne (personal communication) notes much the same thing in his independent observation that the total devastation of Nineveh is symbolically emphasized by the *seven* terms or items, three synonyms and four parts of the body: destruction, devastation, destitution and hearts, knees, loins, faces.

## COMMENT

The second and third chapters of Nahum are made up of five cantos (2:1–11 [1:15–2:10]; 2:11–14; 3:1–7; 3:8–13; 3:14–19) dealing with the destruction of Nineveh, which are introduced by a transitional canto (1:11–14) on the more general theme of the defeat of Belial. As we have already seen in the discussion of the first occurrence of the word Belial in 1:11, the term represents a personification of evil used in reference to the power of Assyria as a collective personality or perhaps an epithet for the king of Assyria, who is a *counselor (of) Belial*. The term has mythic overtones and takes on a life of its own in subsequent Jewish literature—particularly in the Pseudepigrapha and Qumran texts—and appears in the Greek New Testament as *Beliar* (2 Corinthians 6:15), a term for the devil. In the Testimony of the Twelve Patriarchs it appears as a proper noun used to designate Satan, and in the Sibylline Oracles it is applied to Nero (see J. M. P. Smith 1911: 308).

### The Destruction of Belial and the Sack of Nineveh

The second occurrence of the word *Belial* in Nahum appears in the opening strophe of the third canto (2:1–11 [1:15–2:10]), which has as its primary focus the visionary account of the sack of Nineveh in vv 4–10 [3–9]. The message of Nineveh's impending doom is at the same time an announcement of "good news" to Judah, which is named explicitly at the outset in 2:1. This "gospel of good news" is summarized in the Hebrew word *šālôm* ("peace"). Once again, the people of Judah will celebrate their pilgrimage festivals in Jerusalem and fulfill their obligations in worship: "For never again shall Belial invade you; he is utterly cut off" (2:1 [1:15]). The good news is the fact that Yhwh himself has come as "scatterer" to destroy the evil Assyrian power once and for all—so as to restore "the pride of Jacob/Israel" (v 3).

The term *Belial* comes close to being a proper noun here (Maag 1980: 226) and is so translated in the Vulgate. According to Spronk (1997: 81), there are no other places in the Tanakh where this is the case, but the situation in 1:11 is closer to the same sense than Spronk realizes, and his argument that the words *lōʾ yôsîp ʿôd laʿăbor-bāk bəlîyaʿal* ("never again will Belial invade you") should be deleted as a gloss is not at all convincing. $BH^3$ proposes the deletion of *kullōh nikrāt* ("he is utterly cut off"), and Seybold removes both *bəlîyaʿal* and *kullōh nikrāt* as glosses (Spronk 1997: 81, n. 23).

Roberts (1991: 47–48) argues that there is no clear evidence for the use
of the term *Belial* as the name of a demon or Satan himself (*HALOT,* 128) in
the Old Testament. The closest approximations to such usage are found in
2 Samuel 22:5 (= Psalm 18:5 [4]) as a designation of the netherworld. Roberts's
argument, however, begs the question. We are concerned here not with a
demon or Satan himself but rather with some sort of personification of evil,
as Haldar argued (1947: 33), which set the stage for what subsequently developed much later in Jewish literature between the testaments and beyond.

The concept of Belial as a personification of evil and the "counselor (of)
Belial" (1:11) calls the reader's attention to the unusual vocabulary used here,
which is lost altogether in translations that interpret the term as a general
statement, such as the NRSV: "Never again shall the wicked invade you."
Whenever the people of God in their land forsake his ways and violate the
terms of God's covenant with them, they face dire consequences, which
include that of invasion and subsequent exile (Deuteronomy 28:49–57).

In this context, the "scatterer" is YHWH himself, who has vanquished the
forces of Belial (the personification of evil in the Assyrian armies) in the battlefield and now turns his attention to the city of Nineveh. For the prophet the
armies engaged against the forces of Belial are the hosts of YHWH, who appear
as chariots of fire running with the force of the storm and the devastation of
an earthquake. The forces of YHWH work within the process of history; however, at the same time, they remain the armies of the great day of judgment,
which will defeat the chaotic power of evil itself. The ambiguity in regard to
the specific identification of the enemy is deliberate. On the one hand, it is
easy to visualize an enemy force addressed as a corporate personality in the
vivid imagery of troops in battle array (cf. 2:4–5 [3–4]). It was common policy
for Assyria to disperse the people they conquered to other regions of their
empire, as they had done with the northern kingdom of Israel a century earlier. The Assyrians themselves now face that same plight; for they, too, will be
scattered.

There is ambiguity here, which appears to be intentional on the author's
part. At first glance, the text seems to be referring to the destruction of Israel
by the Assyrians in times past—that is, to the humiliation of Jacob or Israel
referred to in 2:3 [2]. A close reading, however, has led a number of scholars
to interpret the text in light of the impending destruction of Nineveh referred
to in 2:2 [1] (Happel 1902: 72; Graham 1927/28: 45–46; van der Woude 1978a;
Holland 1986: 30–33; Becking 1995c: 1260; Spronk 1997: 87–88). The main
point of this strophe is that YHWH's actions against Nineveh are at the same
time intended to restore the "pride" of Judah. This provides the poet with the
opportunity to let his words say more than one thing—depending on whether
the hearer or reader relates them to the context of the immediate verse or to

the larger strophe containing that verse. As Israel was plundered in times past by Assyria, now Nineveh is about to be plundered by the Medes and Babylonians.

The editors of the *BHS* indent 2:3 [2], suggesting that it should be considered separate from its immediate context. The NIV sets 2:3 [2] apart as a separate literary unit, with space before and after it, and the NRSV puts the verse in parentheses as a secondary insertion. Logoprosodic analysis, however, indicates that the verse is an integral part of the second strophe (vv 2–3 [1–2]) and constitutes a primary focus of concern within its larger literary context. This verse picks up on the motifs of 1:2–10, with its assurance of deliverance for the people of Israel as the Divine Warrior wreaks his "vengeance" on wicked Assyria. In short, Yhwh has come to destroy Nineveh in order to restore Israel. Vv 2–3 [1–2] constitute a two-part strophe, which scans as follows:

2:2 [1]    $(13 + 9) \parallel (11 + 9) = 22 \parallel 20$ morae
2:3 [2]    $(15 + 8) \parallel (12 + 13) = 23 \parallel 25$ morae

As we have already noted, the "scatterer" of v 2 [1] is Yhwh himself, as the Divine Warrior who has come up against the city of Nineveh to do battle with the Assyrians. The focus, however, is not really on history per se at all, for the battle at hand is cosmic in scope. In the first half of v 3 [2], Yhwh is identified by name as the one who will restore the lost "pride" of his chosen people, who are identified as Jacob or Israel. The question then arises as to the identity of the ones referred to using the 3rd pers. pl. forms in v 2:3b [2b]—in the words *bəqāqûm* ("they have plundered *them*") and *ûzəmōrêhem* ("*their* vine-branches). Those who were plundered and whose grapevines were ruined in times past are the people of Jacob or Israel, but those facing that same plight in this poem are the people of Nineveh. The Divine Warrior has come to restore his chosen people to their proper place as Yhwh's own among the nations. The note of ambiguity here is apparently intentional, with the plural form of the pronoun functioning as a signal to read the poetic dyad in two different ways at the same time—as referring to the past and the present.

The portrayal of the battle scene within the city of Nineveh in vv 4–5 is a curious mixture of what some see as historical detail and others as timeless symbolic description. On the one hand we find detailed descriptions like that of Strauss (1855; reference taken from Keil 1949: 21, n. 1): "The chariots of the Assyrians, as we see them on the monuments, glare with shining things, made either of iron or steel, battle-axes, bows, arrows, and shields, and all kinds of weapons; the horses are also ornamented with crowns and red fringes, and even the poles of the carriages are made resplendent with shining suns and moons: add to these the soldiers in armour riding in the chariots; and it could not but be the case, that when illumined by the rays of the sun above them, they would have all the appearance of flames as they flew hither and thither with great celerity." For an equally plausible description of the Assyrian war chariots, one should compare that of Layard (1849, 2:348).

At the same time, the imagery of the prophet's vision transcends time and space, such that O'Brien (2002a: 59) concludes that it is the army of the Divine Warrior YHWH in battle with Nineveh and not a historical army as such. Others are able to exercise humorous imagination so as to see things the author never intended at all. For instance, take the translation of v 4 in the KJV:

> The chariots shall rage in the streets,
>     they shall jostle one against another in the broad ways:
> They shall seem like torches,
>     they shall run like the lightnings.

With a little imagination, it is not all that difficult to see here a fairly accurate description of automobile traffic in some of our cities today, or perhaps a rather graphic portrayal of a Nascar race. Such is the beauty and power of symbolic poetic language.

As chariots storm the streets and squares in Nineveh, the once invincible Assyrian commanders stumble as they make their way to defend the walls of the city; but it is too late. The mantlet ("covering") is already set up to protect the enemy troops from arrows, spears, and missiles as they assail the city walls. And the "river-gates" are opened (v 7; cf. the gates of the city in 3:13). Much attention has been focused on the literal reading of these words in terms of explaining the role of flooding in the fall of Nineveh. One aspect of that "flood" is certainly that of the attacking force pouring into the city, which is personified in v 8 [7] as a woman led away into exile, with all her maid servants bemoaning her fate. She is stripped bare and taken away as her maidens moan like doves, beating on their breasts. Even if we dismiss the translation of the first word of v 8 [7] as referring to the queen of Assyria by name, or even the suggestion that we find here a reference to some cult statue of Ishtar, it is not easy to dismiss the feminine image itself, which may ultimately find its proper explanation within the world of matrix arithmetic and musical metaphor in relation to the number 15 and the goddess Ishtar (and Inanna before her).

The plundering of Nineveh continues as the city itself drains away like a great pool whose waters are released (vv 9–10). The city that plundered the nations of the world is now plundered—"and there is no end to the treasure." There is an end, however, to the city of Nineveh itself, as summarized in perhaps the most striking verse of the entire book of Nahum. The city that was filled with the world's treasure in booty and tribute has become "emptiness" personified—comparable to the image of *tôhû wāḇōhû* ("formlessness and void") of Genesis 1:2, the primeval chaos present before creation itself. That desolation is presented here in memorable words as a fitting description of the emptiness God wreaked in Nineveh—*bûqāh ûməbûqāh ûməbullāqāh* ("destruction, and devastation, and destitution"). The destruction of Nineveh is total and final. The hearts of all grow faint as anguish moves upward from the knees to the loins and finally to all their faces. They are gathered as fuel for a great conflagration in which all the physical remains of that once great city will go up in smoke.

### Finding Eschatological Meaning in the Destruction of Nineveh

Nahum's gospel to Judah is presented in the familiar image of a military herald running over the mountains, coming from the scene of battle to proclaim "*shalom*"—words of peace, prosperity, and wholeness (cf. Acts 10:36; Romans 10:15). He tells the people of Judah to resume the pilgrimage festivals of times past, for the evil one (Belial) has been cut off and will never invade the land again (2:1 [1:15]). As an act of thanksgiving, God's people are invited to "fulfill your vows" in sacrificial worship.

The sack of Nineveh, as presented here, includes some of the most vivid images of ancient warfare ever written. A "scatterer" has come up against the mighty city of Nineveh (2:2 [1]) in the person of YHWH, who will restore the pride of Jacob or Israel (2:3 [2]). With biting irony, the people of the doomed city are urged to make preparations: "Guard the ramparts, watch the road, gird the loins, marshal strength exceedingly" (2:2 [1]). The "scatterer" has come in the form of the scarlet-clad troops of the Medo-Babylonian coalition (2:4–5 [3–4]; cf. Ezekiel 23:14), against the Assyrians "clothed in blue" (Ezekiel 23:6). But this is no ordinary military conflict, for the scatterer is none other than YHWH himself, working his will through unwitting combatants so as to restore in his zeal (1:2) his covenant people Israel, whom Assyria has devastated (2:3 [2]).

The oracle of the sack of Nineveh begins with repetition of the key word "cut off" in 2:1 [1:15] from 1:13, which serves to tie together Cantos 2 (1:11–14) and 3 (2:1–11 [1:15–2:10]). In 2:1 [1:15] the prophet urges the people of Nineveh to strengthen themselves, but in 2:11 [10] they have become utterly weak. The city that was guarded by her moats and rivers is destroyed as the water gates are opened and the floodwaters dissolve the palace (2:7 [6]); the city itself drains away like a pool of water (2:9 [9]). In 2:3 [2] Judah is devastated, but in 2:11 [10] it is Nineveh that is decimated.

The historical setting of this great moment in Judah focuses on the fall of Nineveh in 612 BCE. The rejoicing at that time, however, was short-lived, for in the year 609 the reformer king Josiah died at the hands of the Egyptians in battle at Megiddo, and in 597 the rod of Assyria passed into the hands of the Neo-Babylonian Empire; ten years later, the Temple in Jerusalem was nothing but smoldering ruins, and the people of Judah were in exile in distant

Babylon. Once again the people could no longer celebrate their pilgrimage festivals. In fact, the Jewish people would never again know freedom from the yoke of foreign domination until the time of the Maccabees in the second century BCE, and then only briefly. So how are we to understand the meaning of the words of Nahum: "Belial has been utterly cut off"?

Ultimate meaning was found when the words of Nahum were lifted out of space and time and interpreted in an eschatological sense by those who put together the Book of the Twelve Prophets as Scripture. Centuries later the words of Nahum were used to portray the "rulers of Kittim" at 4QpNah 3–4 i 3 as a sobriquet of the Romans in Palestine (Doudna 2001: 608; cf. 1 Maccabees 8:1–16). Still later within the context of the Roman Empire, Belial became wickedness incarnate, the Evil One—who indeed would be "cut off" once and for all when a certain woman "gave birth to a son, a male child, who will rule all the nations with an iron scepter" (Revelation 12:5; cf. 19:15). In Messianic Judaism, the crucifixion and resurrection of Yeshua (Jesus) marked the point where sin and death met their end and the words of Nahum's prophecy were fulfilled: Belial was utterly cut off. The faithful live in expectation of the final chapter of that story, when the Messiah will return to establish the Kingdom of God on earth.

# V. DIRGE ON THE LIONS' DEN
## (2:11–14 [10–13])

|  | Morae | SAS units | Word count | | |
|---|---|---|---|---|---|
| **A. The Destruction Is Total: They Are Gathered as Kindling (2:11 [10])** | | | | | **[5.4]** |
| 2:11 [10]Destruction /ᵃ and desolation / and disintegration // | 19 | 3 | 3 | 3 | 0 |
| and hearts grow faint / | 7 | 1 | 2 | 0 | 2 |
| 2:5–11b | 59 | 27 | 32 | | |
| And knees give way / | 7 | 1 | 2 | 0 | 2 |
| 2:9–11c | 29 | 12 | 17 | | |
| And anguish / is in all loins / and (on) all their faces / | 19 | 3 | 5 | 0 | 5 |
| they are gathered as fuel (for burning) // | 8 | 1 | 2 | 0 | 2 |
| 2:1–11 | 128 | 64 | 64 | | |
| **B. Nineveh Is Described Metaphorically as the Lions' Den (2:12 [11])** | | | | | **[4.4]** |
| 2:12 [11]Where / is the den of the lions / | 11 | 2 | 3 | 3 | 0 |
| and the caveᵇ / for the young lions? // | 15 | 2 | 3 | 3 | 0 |
| 2:8–12b | 52 | 21 | 31 | | |
| Where the lion went /ᶜ the lioness was there / | 14 | 2 | 5 | 0 | 5 |
| the lions' cub / and none to frighten (them) away // | 12 | 2 | 4 | 0 | 4 |
| 2:9–12 | 51 | 18 | 33 | | |
| **C. The Lions' Prey Is Consumed in the Lions' Den (2:13 [12])** | | | | | **[4.4]** |
| 2:13 [12]The lionᵈ is tearing / sufficient for ᵉhis cubsᵉ / | 14 | 2 | 4 | 4 | 0 |

| | Morae | SAS units | Word count |
|---|---|---|---|
| and strangled prey / for his lionesses // | 12 | 2 | 2  2  0 |
| 2:10–13b | 46 | 19 | 27 |
| And he fills with torn flesh (m. sg.) /[f] his lairs / | 11 | 2 | 3  0  3 |
| and his dens / with torn flesh (f. sg.) // | 14 | 2 | 2  0  2 |
| 2:12–13 | 26 | 12 | 14 |

### D. Fire and Sword Will Consume Her Chariots and the Young Lions (2:14 [13])    [4.5]

| | Morae | SAS units | Word count |
|---|---|---|---|
| 2:14 [13] "Behold, I am against you" / utterance[g] of YHWH of hosts / | 18 | 2 | 5  5  0 |
| "And I will burn in smoke / her chariots / | 13 | 2 | 3  3  0 |
| 2:12–14c | 34 | 20 | 14 |
| And your young lions / the sword will devour // | 13 | 2 | 3  3  0 |
| 2:13–14d | 22 | 17 | 5 |
| And I will cut (you) off from the land of [h] your prey / | 12 | 1 | 3  0  3 |
| and will be heard no more / the sound of your (military) heralds" //  ס | 18 | 2 | 5  0  5 |
| 2:11–14 | 59 | 26 | 33 |

## Scansion of the Dirge on the Lions' Den in 2:11–14 [10–13])

| | | Morae | SAS units | Word count |
|---|---|---|---|---|
| 2:11 [10] | *bûqắh* /[a] *ûməbûqắh* / *ûməbullāqqắh* ^ | 19 | 3 | 3 = 3 + 0 |
| | *wəlḗḇ nāmḗs* / | 7 | 1 | 2 = 0 + 2 |
| | *ûp̄íq birkáyim* / | 7 | 1 | 2 = 0 + 2 |
| | *wəhaḥālắh* / *bəkol-motnáyim* / | 11 | 2 | 3 = 0 + 3 |
| | *ûp̄ənê kullắm* / | 8 | 1 | 2 = 0 + 2 |
| | *qibbəṣû pāʾrúr* : | 8 | 1 | 2 + 0 + 2 |
| 2:12 [11] | *ʾayyḗh* / *məʿôn ʾărāyốṯ* / | 11 | 2 | 3 = 3 + 0 |
| | *û<məʿārāh hîʾ>*[b] / *lakkəpîrîm* ^ | 15 | 2 | 3 = 3 + 0 |
| | *ʾăšer hālák ʾaryḗh* /[c] *lāḇîʾ šām* / | 14 | 2 | 5 = 0 + 5 |
| | *gûr ʾaryḗh* / *wəʾên maḥărîḏ* : | 12 | 2 | 4 = 0 + 4 |
| 2:13 [12] | *ʾaryḗh*[d] *ṭōrḗp̄* / *bəḏê* [e]*gōr[]áyw*[e] / | 14 | 2 | 4 = 4 + 0 |
| | *ûməhannêq* / *ləlibʾōṯáyw* ^ | 12 | 2 | 2 = 2 + 0 |
| | *wayəmallēʾ-ṭérep̄* /[f] *ḥōráyw* / | 11 | 2 | 3 = 0 + 3 |
| | *ûməʿōnōṯáyw* / *ṭərēp̄áh* : | 14 | 2 | 2 = 0 + 2 |
| 2:14 [13] | *hin(ə)nî ʾēláyiḵ* / *naʾúm* [g] *YHWH ṣəḇāʾốṯ* / | 18 | 2 | 5 = 5 + 0 |

| | SAS | Word |
|---|---|---|
| Morae | units | count |

| | Morae | units | count |
|---|---|---|---|
| *wəhibᶜartî bəᶜāśán / rikḇā́h /* | _13 | 2_ | 3 = 3 + 0 |
| *ûḵəp̄îráyik / tốʾkal ḥā́reḇ ^* | _13 | 2_ | 3 = 3 + 0 |
| *wəhhikrattî mēʾéreṣ* ^h *ṭarpḗk /* | 12 | 1 | 3 = 0 + 3 |
| *wəlốʾ yiššāmáᶜ ᶜôd / qốl malʾāḵḗkēh :* | 18 | 2 | 5 = 0 + 5 |
| 2:11–14 | | | 59 = 26 + 33 |

## NOTES

^a The *mêrəḵâ* on the word *bûqāh* ("desolation") in 2:11a is read as disjunctive.

^b The word *ûmirᶜeh* ("and the feeding place, pasture") is emended to read *ûməᶜārāh* ("and the cave") along with many scholars, which improves the balance in mora count.

^c Reading the sequence of *mûnaḥ* followed by *ʾazlâ* on the word *ʾaryēh* ("lion") in 2:12b as disjunctive.

^d The word ʾaryēh ("lion") at the beginning of 2:13a is in the structural center of this canto (2:11–14), with 29 words on either side.

^e–e Reading *gōrāyw* in 2:13a with 4QpNah in place of *gōrôṯāyw*, which is found nowhere else in *Codex L (BHS).*

^f Reading the *mûnaḥ* on the word *ṭerep̄* ("torn flesh") in 2:13b as disjunctive.

^g Reading the conjunctive accent *ʾazlâ* with Letteris (1880) in place of the disjunctive *paštâ* in L (BHS) on the word *nəʾūm* ("utterance") in 2:14a.

^h Reading the *paštâ* on the word *mēʾereṣ* ("from the land") in 2:14b as conjunctive.

SAS units:

$$[(5 + 4) + (4 + 4)] + [(4 + 4) + (4 + 5)] = 17 + 17 = \mathbf{34} \text{ SAS units}$$

Meaningful center: eight words on either side of the arithmological center:

| | |
|---|---|
| *hālaḵ ʾaryēh lāḇîʾ šām* | The lion went (and) the lioness was there; |
| *gûr ʾaryēh wəʾên mahărîḏ* | (and the) lion cubs with none to disturb. |
| ʾaryēh *ṭōrēp̄ bəḏê ḡōr[]āyw* | The lion has torn sufficient for his cubs, |
| *ûməhanneq ləliḇʾōṯāyw* | and strangled prey for his lionesses; |
| *wayəmallē-ṭerep̄ ḥōrāyw* | and he has filled with prey his lairs. |

Strophic units as shown by the balance in mora count:

| | | | | | | |
|---|---|---|---|---|---|---|
| A | 2:11 | 2 balanced dyads + pivot | [19 + 7] + 7 + [(11 + 8) + 8] | = | 26 + 7 + 27 | morae |
| B | 2:12 | 2 balanced dyads | [11 + 15] + [14 + 12] | = | 26 + 26 | morae |
| C | 2:13 | 2 balanced dyads | [14 + 12] + [11 + 14] | = | 26 + 25 | morae |
| D | 2:14 | 2 balanced dyads + pivot | [(8 + 11) + 13] + 13 + [12 + 18] | = | 32 + 13 + 30 | morae |

Word count:

| 2:8–11 | 46 | (= **23** × 2) words |
| 2:1–11 | 128 | (= **32** × 4) words and **64** words before and after *ʾatnaḥ* |
| 2:4–12 | 96 | (= **32** × 3) words and **52** (= **26** × 2) words after *ʾatnaḥ* |
| 2:12–13 | 26 | words |
| 2:12–14 | 23 | words before *ʾatnaḥ* |
| 1:1–2:14 | 153 | (= **17** × 9) words after *ʾatnaḥ*  [**153** = sum of integers 1 through 17] |

## INTRODUCTION
### Canto 4: Dirge on the Lions' Den (2:11–14 [10–13])

| A | The fuel is gathered, and the conflagration will be total | [5.4] | 2:11 |
| B | Nineveh is described metaphorically as the lions' den | [4.4] | 2:12 |
| B′ | The lions' prey is consumed in the lions' den | [4.4] | 2:13 |
| A′ | Fire and sword will consume her chariots and the young lions | [4.5] | 2:14 |

Bliese (1995) considers 2:4–14 [3–13] as the proper prosodic unit here. When his methodology of metrical chiasm is applied to 2:11–14, based on the distribution of word stresses (that is, counting accents), no such symmetry is found.

## NOTES

**2:11 [Eng. 10].** *Destruction and desolation and disintegration; and hearts grow faint.* This verse plays more than one role in the structure of the book of Nahum. From a prosodic point of view, it constitutes the seventh and concluding strophe in the third canto (2:1–11 [1:15–2:10]). It also plays a role here as the first of four strophes in the transitional fourth canto (2:11–14 [10–13]) to form a structural inclusion with v 14 [13] at the end of the dirge on the lions' den. At the same time, it completes the first half of Nahum by forming a conclusion to the cipher about the total destruction of Nineveh, which is presented in the "bent" acrostic psalm in 1:1–10, with its climax in the image of sopping wet, twisted, matted thorns about to burst into flames to be consumed completely, like dry stubble (cf. 1:10). Notice how the image of burning is picked up again in the first half of v 14 [13] to form an inclusion around the two parallel strophes of the dirge on the lions' den in vv 12–13 [11–12]. The destruction of Nineveh, which is envisioned here, is imminent, and the devastation will be total. Labuschagne (personal communication) notes that this total devastation is symbolically emphasized by the *seven* terms or items used here: three synonyms (destruction, desolation, disintegration) and four parts of the body (hearts, knees, loins, faces) (cf. Nowell 1990: 260).

2:12 [11]. *Where is the den of the lions; and the cave for the young lions?* The lion is a traditional symbol for the king in the Assyrian texts (see W. A. Maier 1959: 277; Johnston 1992: 379–86; cf. Botterweck 1977: 379–80). Spronk (1997: 104–5) calls attention to the parallel text in Isaiah 5:24–30, which announces the judgment of YHWH against the people of Israel in images comparable to those in the book of Nahum in numerous details. In that context, God uses unnamed "nations from afar" (v 26), with specific reference to "a lioness" and to "young lions" (v 29). Spronk sees the book of Nahum as a reversal of this older prophecy and the "young lions" as the nobles mentioned earlier in Nahum 2:6 [5] (cf. also 2:14 [13]).

Doudna (2001: 109) argues that there is no justification for translating the word *maʿôn* as "den" as opposed to any other kind of habitat. Citing Benyus (1992: 95), he argues that lions hide their cubs in bushes when leaving to hunt, but otherwise move from spot to spot within their territory. This observation may be true in a general sense, but it fails to do justice to the poetic imagery here, in which the city of Nineveh itself is presented as the dwelling place of the lions' family. The word *maʿôn* appears in Jeremiah 9:10; 10:22; 49:33; and 51:27 as a desolated city that has become a "lair" for jackals. Moreover, the word *maʿônāh* appears with the meaning "den, lair" of wild beasts in the very next verse in Nahum 2:13 (and elsewhere), along with the synonym *ḥōrāyw* ("his lairs"). The word *maʿôn* also appears as the dwelling place of YHWH in various contexts (Deuteronomy 26:15; Jeremiah 25:30; Psalm 68:6), and the present context implies the contest between YHWH as the "lion of Judah" and Nineveh as the dwelling place of the "lion" of Assyria.

Of the **26** words in the two central strophes (2:12–13 [11–12]) of this transitional canto, 9 portray different epithets for the lion, which include the whole family as it were: the full-grown male lion (*ʾaryēh*); the lioness (*lābîʾ*); the young lion, old enough to go in search of prey (*kəp̄îr*); and the lion cubs, which cannot yet seek prey for themselves (*gûr ʾaryēh* and *gōrāyw*). This leaves **17** words to describe the plight of the lions' prey, which is presented here as torn flesh consumed in the privacy of the lions' den (that is, in the city of Nineveh). The image of the lion also carries overtones of supernatural conflict, for Ishtar (and the mother goddess Inanna before her) was often portrayed mounted on the back of a lion or even as a lioness herself. The same is true of the Canaanite goddess Asherah, who is represented standing on a lion in numerous Egyptian stelae dedicated to her (Puech 1995: 982). The monstrous enemy of God in creation is sometimes depicted as a voracious lion, and in New Testament tradition the devil is described as "a roaring lion" who "prowls around, looking for someone to devour" (1 Peter 5:8).

The emendation of *ûmirʿeh* ("the feeding ground") to read *ûməʿārāh* ("cave") was suggested long ago by Wellhausen (1892: 162) and is followed by

Cathcart (1973a: 105); Machinist (1983: 735, n. 104); Roberts (1991: 62); and many others (including the NRSV). The arguments are based primarily on the context, which appears to call for something in poetic parallelism with *mə'ôn* ("den"), and the word "cave" certainly makes good sense. Freedman et al. (1997: 314) interpret the "cave" as a metaphorical reference to Nineveh, "from which the lion (the Assyrian army) kills its prey for its lioness and cubs."

Though the proposed emendation improves the balance in terms of mora count, it must also be noted, as Roberts observes (1991: 62), that it requires the further change of the masculine pronoun *hw'* to the feminine *hy'*. The letters *yod* and *waw* are easily confused throughout the time period in question, however, so this emendation does not pose a significant problem. The *waw* conjunction may be taken as emphatic.

Following Ehrlich (1912: 295–96), Haldar (1947: 61) chose not to emend the text and interpreted the word *ûmir'eh* to mean "food," translating the passage "Where is the den of lions, and this food for the young lions that the lion went out to fetch." Longman (1993: 810) also rejects the pressure within the academic community to emend the text on the basis of presuppositions about the nature of Hebrew parallelism (as does Spronk 1997: 105). All textual witnesses, including the Wadi Muraba'at scroll, read *mr'h* ("pasturage, meadow"). The word *mir'eh* normally means "pasturage," and the extended meaning here as "feeding ground" is not inappropriate, as Longman observes. Nonetheless, achieving balance in terms of mora count (with seven rather than four morae) tips the balance in favor of accepting the emendation in question. An early copying error in the form of a metathesis appears to have caused the textual difficulty, for as Cathcart (1973a: 106) puts it: "Nahum seems to have *mə'ārāh* rather than *mir'eh* in mind."

*Where the lion went, the lioness was there; the lions' cub, and none to frighten (them) away?* The word *'ăšer* ("which") is to be taken in conjunction with the word *šām* ("there"), at the end of the clause, to mean "in the very place where" (Keil [reprint] 1949: 27). The verb *hlk* ("to go, walk") is sometimes used of animals (1 Samuel 6:12) and could perhaps be rendered "prowled" here in light of the hunting imagery of the context. The word *lābî'* poses difficulties and has been interpreted in different ways. The NIV interprets the word to mean "lioness" (see also BDB 522). Doudna's (2001: 114) argument that the "lioness" translation must be rejected here is not convincing. The Qumran *pesher* (4QpNah), which reads *lby'* ("lioness") in the quotation of the biblical text, interprets the word in terms of the verbal root *bw'* ("to enter"), and so does the LXX, Vulgate, Syriac, and a medieval Hebrew manuscript (Gese 1957: 61). This reading is followed by the NRSV ("where the lion goes"). The Wadi Murabba'at scroll of the Minor Prophets, on the other hand, reads *lby'* ("lioness"). Another possibility is to see the word as a shortened form of the Hiphil inf. const. ("to bring"; cf. Jeremiah 27:7; 39:7; 2 Chronicles 31:10), so as to read "where the lion went to bring [food]." Cathcart (1973a: 106) and Longman (1993: 810) reject the proposed emendation, reading instead the word "lioness." For Cathcart (1973: 106), reading "lioness" here serves "to complete the family!" Spronk (1997: 105) calls attention to the fact that the complete family of the lion, lioness, and cub appears again in the next strophe, with a chiastic structure in the references to the lioness and her cubs (cf. Boadt 1975: 696; Ceresko 1975: 80). Longman (1993: 810) remarks in passing that it is easy to see how these two forms became confused. Roberts (1991: 62), on the other hand, accepts the emendation with a somewhat similar remark: "The corruption is easy to understand, given all the words for lion already mentioned in the passage." The reading in the MT is supported by the text cited in 4QpNah and also by the parallel passage in Isaiah 5:29, which also mentions the *lābî*ʾ ("lioness") next to the *kəpîrîm* ("young lions").

There is a difference in opinion as to exactly whom the metaphor of the lions' family represents. Orelli (1897: 231) thought the image refers to the royal family. Others would include the Assyrian nobles (J. M. P. Smith 1911: 325; Goslinga 1923: 274–75) and other citizens as well (Keil 1888; Rudolph 1975). Spronk (1997: 105–6) sees the young lions as referring to the nobles and the lioness as representing the queen. For him, "The cub is probably the royal prince, mentioned in 1:14 as the one who should keep the royal name alive." For Spronk, the phrase *wəʾên maḥărîḏ* ("there is none to frighten them") is set over against *wəʾên maṣṣîl* ("and none to save") in Micah 5:7; Psalms 7:3 and 50:22. The lion family feels safe in their lair, but those whom they hunt have no security. Attention now shifts to the feeding practice of the lions, with specific emphasis on the word *ṭrp(h)* ("tearing, rending"), which appears three times in 2:13 [12] and again in 2:14 [13].

2:13 [12]. *The lion is tearing sufficient for his cubs, and strangled prey for his lionesses; and he fills his lairs with torn flesh, and his dens with torn prey.* Assyrian kings refer to themselves as lions in their inscriptions, and, as Coggins notes (1985: 44–45): "Isaiah 5:29 pictures the onslaught of the Assyrian army in terms of an attack by lions," which shares much by way of vocabulary and imagery with the text here. The difference between the two passages is the reversal in roles, for the dreaded lion of Assyria is now becoming the prey to the more powerful "lion of Judah." In the MT, the word *gōrāyw* ("his cubs") is read in place of *gōrōṯāyw* in 2:13 [12] to achieve closer balance in terms of mora count. The Dead Sea Scroll 4QpNah reads *gwryw* here, and Cathcart (1973: 107) presents cogent arguments for accepting this as the correct reading. The form *gōrōṯāyw* is found nowhere else. Jeremiah 51:38 has *kəgōrê* (some manuscripts read *kəgûrê*), with the meaning "like the lions' cubs," which is parallel with *kakkəpîrîm* ("like young lions"). This indicates that the absolute form is *gōr*. In both Hebrew and Ugaritic, a masculine noun or a feminine noun without a feminine form in the singular can take the feminine form in the plural (see *UT*, §8.8). If *gōrāyw* is the correct reading, we then have perfect balance in terms of syllable count (as Cathcart observes), and also the necessary balance in terms of mora count for the balanced pair of quatrains in 2:12–13 [11–12], as demonstrated here. Note also the form *gûr,* with the meaning "cub" of the lion, in 2:12 [11].

Dupont-Sommer's suggestion (1963a: 64–65) that *badê* be changed into *baddê* ("limbs"), which is followed by Dahood (1976: 329), is clever but not necessary. The term *badê* is paralleled with the preposition *l* in the next line, and the verb *ṭrp* ("tear, rend") does not always require a direct object (cf. Psalms 17:12; 22:14; and other instances). Though the word *mahannēq* ("strangled prey") seems inappropriate to some commentators, ancient pictorial representations in Assyrian art sometimes present lions killing their prey by placing both paws on the victim's throat. This may be the image the poet is trying to evoke, as Longman suggests (1993: 810). Cathcart (1973a: 107–8) cites pertinent examples, including a well-known Phoenician ivory (ca. 715 BCE) in the British Museum, which shows a lioness standing over a man with its left paw pressing on his neck (see Parrot 1961: figs. 186 and 187). Spronk (1997: 106) adds a further example from the Mesopotamian text Ludlul (at the beginning of the second column of the fourth tablet): "Marduk put a muzzle upon the mouth of the lion about to devour me." He calls attention to the variant reading in another copy of this text, which reads "about to strangle me." Barker and Bailey (1998: 213) argue: "Lions 'strangle' their prey by biting into the throat to cut off the supply of air. This manner of killing is especially effective when the lion attacks a larger animal." The word *hōrāyw* means "his caves" (cf. 1 Samuel 14:11 and Job 30:6). In an attempt to imitate the assonance of the Hebrew, Gandell (1901: 643) translated the second half of this verse "And (he) filled his holes with ravin, and his lairs with rapine."

The verbal form *wayəmallēʾ* is the Piel imperfect with *waw* conversive, which denotes repeated action; the lion is constantly filling his caves with prey. The use of both nouns, *ṭerep* and *ṭərēpāh,* is a poetic device in which masculine forms in the first clause are matched with feminine forms in the second (cf. Watson 1980a: 326–27). The same is true for the masculine form *maʿôn* and the feminine form *maʿônāh* in reference to the dwelling place of the lion. The "torn prey" the poet had in mind stand for the people the Assyrians have "devoured" (cf. Ezekiel 22:25; Hosea 5:14; Micah 5:7; Psalm 7:3). The term *hōrāyw* ("his holes, lairs") applies elsewhere not only to robbers, in which character the Assyrians are exhibited in the figure of the lion, but also to the lions, which carry their prey there (Keil [reprint] 1949: 28).

Lioness mauling an Ethiopian (Kalakh [Nimrun]). Phoenician ivory in the British Museum. From Parrot (1961: 153).

2:14 [13]. *"Behold, I am against you," utterance of* Y̲HWH *of hosts.* Humbert (1933: 101–7) argued that the phrase *hinənî ʾēlayik̲* ("Behold, I am against you") has its origin in the challenge to a duel (Sellin 1930: 370; Haldar 1947: 62). The concluding strophe in the fourth canto is a judgment oracle against Nineveh, picking up the theme of destruction by fire with the burning of Nineveh's chariots. It then returns briefly to the imagery of the "young lions" of Assyria, who will be devoured by the sword.

The word *hinənî* ("behold, I am") marks the beginning of a new strophe that constitutes the climax in the fourth canto (2:11–14 [10–13]). Humbert (1933: 108) argued that the *formula hinənî ʾēlayik̲* always begins a new section, but here it merely begins a new strophe and is also the conclusion of this brief transitional canto (2:12–14 [11–13]). It is presented in the form of direct speech to Nineveh in the 2nd pers. f. sg. Humbert (1933: 101–8) gave the opening phrase, *hinanî ʾēlayik* ("behold, I am against you"), a special title in German that means that Yhwh has summoned his opponent for the deciding battle (cf. Baumgärtel 1961: 279–80). Besides its two occurrences in Nahum (2:14 [13] and 3:5), it occurs only in Jeremiah (21:13; 23:30–32; 50:31; 51:25) and Ezekiel (5:8, 13; 21:8; 26; 28:22; 29:3, 10; 30:22; 34:10; 35:3; 38:3; 39:1). Spronk (1997: 107) finds here further evidence of Nahum's influence on the book of Jeremiah, which he sees as "corroborated by the reference to fire used by Yhwh against his opponents in Jer. 21:13 f.; 50:31 f.; and 51:25." The poet is referring back to the challenge presented in 1:9 ("What do you devise against Yhwh?") with the use of this same preposition *ʾel* ("against"). According to Spronk, the prophet is stating that Yhwh has made the cause of the oppressed his own cause.

The passive participle *nəʾūm* (from the root *nʾm* ["to declare"]) is a formulaic term in the prophetic literature meaning "oracle" (Isaiah 14:22–23; 17:3; 22:25; Jeremiah 8:3; 25:29; 31:38; 49:26; Zechariah 12:2, 7). The use of the epithet *Yhwh ṣəbāʾ ôt* ("Yhwh of hosts") is the language of the "wars of Yhwh" of times past, which adds a cosmic dimension in reference to the heavenly host that comes down to earth to fight for God's people (cf. Judges 5:20; 2 Kings 6:17; cf. 1 Kings 22:19; see Baumgärtel 1961: 279–80). In practical language, the title refers to the enthroned God whose royal decrees carry the day (Isaiah 14:24; Jeremiah 25:27) and who retains exclusive prerogative as deity. Martens (1996: 299) says: "Any competing ideology is idolatry, whether that be the ancient worship of Baal or the modern preoccupation with technique, nationalism, or militarism."

*"And I will burn in smoke her chariots."* The burning of enemy chariots is a common threat in ancient Near Eastern treaty curses (Hillers 1964: 60; Cathcart 1973b: 182), and the singular is frequently used in a collective sense to refer to all the chariots of a nation (Exodus 14:7; Joshua 11:4; 24:6; Judges 4:7, 13; 5:28). In this instance, the term *bəʿāšān* ("in smoke") is an example of metonymy of effect, where smoke represents the fire that produces that smoke (cf. Joshua 8:19–20; Isaiah 65:5; Revelation 14:11). The burning of Nineveh's chariots will not go unnoticed. The smoke will rise as a signal to others (cf. Genesis 19:27; see Spronk 1997: 108).

Pinker (2004e: 45) argues that the Hebrew root *bʿr* ("to burn") is nowhere else linked or even collocated with *ʿāšān* ("smoke"). He notes that medieval Jewish exegetes resolved the difficulty in various ways. Ibn Ezra (d. 1167) interpreted the smoke as Yhwh's anger, which he implied "would be so hot that it will consume the chariots" (reference from Pinker 2004e: 45). Tanhum (d. 1291) said: "The punishment is heavy as the blazing fire which burns with the smoke alone" (Shy 1991: 198; reference from Pinker 2004e: 45). Kimchi (d. 1235) explained the phrase here as "[I will burn its chariots] in a great fire whose smoke is seen at a distance (reference from Pinker 2004e: 46). Abarbanel (n.d.: 269) interpreted the passage to mean that Nineveh's chariots "would be aptly burned till the smoke will rise to heaven" (reference from Pinker 2004e: 45). Finding none of these earlier attempts to explain the passage satisfactory, Pinker emends *wǝhiḇᶜartî ḇeᶜāšān rkbh* ("and I will burn with smoke their chariots") to read *whsᶜrty kᶜšn rkbh* ("and I will twirl [stormtoss] as smoke their chariots") (cf. Hosea 13:3). The emendation is possible, but not persuasive.

Though the text is often emended to read "your chariots" rather than "her chariots," it is better to see the phenomenon of enallage here to announce the approaching prosodic boundary. If one must resort to emendation, a more attractive alternative is to read *rbkh* ("your multitude") with 4QpNah and the LXX in place of *rkbh* ("her chariot[s]") in the MT, with a simple metathesis. Thus Roberts (1991: 64) translates the three words in question "I will burn your abundance with smoke." The *plene* reading of the emended word *riḇḵāh* ("her abundance") then agrees with that of the word *malᵓāḵēḵēh* ("your messengers, envoys") in the next poetic line. But Roberts mistakenly reads all the pronominal suffixes in this verse as 2nd pers. m. sg.—some written defectively (*-kā*) and some with the *mater* (*-kāh*)—and he incorrectly interprets them all as referring back to the lion, the king of Assyria (as does van der Woude 1978a). For Roberts the Hebrew text as it stands in the MT is "garbled" because of "the failure to recognize the use of *-h* as a *mater* to mark the 2nd m. sg. suffix." Machinist (1983: 736, n. 106) emends the text to read *malᵓāḵayiḵ* ("your messengers") in place of what he calls "the strange Masoretic" *malᵓāḵēḵēh*, which may represent a variant of the same form, viz., *malᵓāḵêḵ*, with the final *heᵓ* as dittography of the following *hôy* in 3:1.

G. R. Driver (1938: 271) emended *riḵbāh* to read *rohḇēḵ* and translated it "your pride," a reading that made its way into the NEB (as did Richter 1914: 134). Others have emended the text to read *riḇṣēk* ("your lair") for closer parallelism with the "young lions" in the next line (Marti 1903: 319; J. M. P. Smith 1911: 333); to read *siḇkēḵ* ("your thicket"; Elliger 1970); or to read *brk* ("ton trou" ["breeding hole"]; Keller 1971). Spronk (1997: 108) reads *rkbh* as a feminine form of *rkb* ("chariot"), like *ṭrph* ("torn flesh") in 2:13 [12] (cf. Cathcart 1979: 9). He sees the *mappiq* as a secondary addition so as to match the gender of the parallel nouns *ᶜšn* ǁ *kǝpîrîm* (m.) and *riḵbāh* ǁ *ḥereḇ* (f.) (cf. Watson 1980a: 328).

*And your young lions the sword will devour.* The Assyrians frequently portrayed themselves using lion imagery (D. Marcus 1977: 87). The Assyrian warriors are presented as "young lions" (*kǝpîrîm*) in 2:12 [11], which forms an inclusion with the reference here. Dahood (1959: 161–62) and Miller (1970: 177–86), among others, have shown that animal names were used metaphorically in the Tanakh to denote dignitaries and various classes of people. Schiemann (1967: 367–69) interprets *kəpîrîm* in 2:12–14 to mean "princes." Procksch (1938) suggested emending *kəpîrayik* ("your young lions") to read *gibbôrayik* ("your warriors") but without any textual support.

On the expression *tōʾkal ḥāreb* ("the sword will devour"), compare Deuteronomy 32:42 ("And my sword will devour flesh"); the so-called Song of the Sword in Isaiah 34:5–7; and one of Esarhaddon's vassal treaties (cf. *ANET* 540). Because lions are not normally hunted with swords, Spronk (1997: 108) interprets the statement here as marking a transition from metaphor to reality.

It is best to read the MT as it stands in 2:14 [13], with Longman (1993: 809) and the KJV, ASV, NASB, and JPS Tanakh over against the NRSV and NIV, and to find in this verse a poetic transition to the next "canto" (3:1–7), which is addressed in direct speech (2nd pers. f. sg.) to the city of Nineveh, in which we find (in 3:5) a total repetition of the opening five words in 2:14 [13]: "Behold, I am against you, utterance of YHWH." The focus of the poet's attention shifts in 2:14 [13], first to the city of Nineveh in the 2nd pers. f. sg. (opening line), then to a 3rd pers. f. sg. statement about Nineveh, then back to words directed to Nineveh as a corporate personality using direct speech in 2nd pers. f. sg. forms that set the stage for what follows. In short, we have here in Nahum a normal occurrence of the phenomenon of enallage at a significant prosodic boundary.

*And I will cut (you) off from the land of your prey; and will be heard no more the sound of your (military) heralds.* The traditional translation, "I will cut off your prey from the earth," makes little sense. It is not the victims who will be cut off but the perpetrator of such injustice. Because all of the other references to the Assyrians in this verse concern some kind of action (involving chariots, young lions, messengers), Spronk (1997: 109) translates the noun *ṭarpēk*, which he vocalizes as an infinitive *ṭorpēk,* "your tearing" rather than "prey" or "booty."

In a somewhat similar manner, Freedman et al. (1997: 314) argue: "Just as the young lions devour their prey, so the tables will be turned, and the sword of Yahweh will devour the lions and cut them off from their prey. Yahweh will not destroy the prey, but the lions (i.e., the Assyrian army). The sword of Yahweh both devours and cuts, and the object of these actions is the same in both phrases: the young lions." Freedman et al. read the phrase *mēʾereṣ ṭarpēk* as a construct chain, "(I will cut them off) from the land of your prey." They also argue that 2:14 [13] is related thematically to 3:15, which reads *šām tōʾkəlēk ʾēš takrîtēk tōʾkəlēk kayyāleq,* "There fire will devour you, sword will cut you off; it will devour you like a locust." The object of the verbs here is "you," the

Assyrian army. A further argument advanced by Freedman et al. (1997: 315) focuses on the structure of a thematic chiasm observed in 2:14 [13]. The metaphor appears in the phrases *ûk̲əp̲îrayik̲* . . . *ḥārēb̲* and *wəhik̲rattî* . . . *ṭarpēk̲*. The inside pair focuses on the sword and cutting, whereas the outside pair focuses on the lion tearing or rending his prey. Surrounding this chiastic pairing we find *wəhib̲ʿartî* . . . *rik̲bah* and *wəlōʾ* . . . *malʾāk̲ēk̲ēh*. For Freedman et al., the *rik̲bah* ("chariots") and *malʾāk̲ēk̲ēh* ("messengers") link the metaphor with practical reality, so they conclude: "The metaphor is thus concerned not with the destruction of Assyria in general, but of its military units. Hence the *malʾāk̲ēk̲ēh* represent military heralds who blow their trumpets at the beginning of the battle, thereby initiating various tactical maneuvers."

The form of the suffix on *malʾāk̲ēk̲ēh* ("your heralds") is unusual and thus frequently emended to read *malʾāk̲ayik̲* (Cathcart 1973a: 110; see GKC §911) or *malʾāk̲e(y)k̲āh* (Roberts 1991: 63). Rashi (d. 1105) deleted the final letter as being due to dittography and has been followed by a number of modern scholars, including Friedrich Delitzsch (see Haldar 1947: 63, n. 3). Ben Yahuda (1917: 327) thought that the MT is correct, but proposed translating the word according to an Arabic equivalent, *lâk̲a* ("to grind"). G. R. Driver's (1938: 271) unlikely reading of *maʾăk̲ālēk̲* ("your feeding") appears in the NEB. Laetsch (1956: 302) explained the word as "a fuller form at the end of a section." Van der Woude (1978a) reads *malʾāk̲ek̲āh* ("your messengers") as written defectively with a plural masculine suffix (as does Barthélemy 1992: 813). Krauss (1930: 324) read *mlʾkkm* (with a plural suffix). Haldar (1947: 64, 134) chose to read the MT as given and interpreted the word as a masculine form in which the suffix refers to the Assyrian king.

A more likely explanation of the peculiar lengthening of the word *malʾāk̲ēk̲ēh* ("your envoys") is that it was used to achieve a proper balance in terms of mora count. The MT here scans (18 + 11) + 13 + (12 + 18) = 29 + 13 + 30 morae. The "pivot" in this construction consists of the line "And your young lions the sword will devour," which completes one sentence and begins another, as follows:

|  | Morae | SAS units | Word count |
|---|---|---|---|
| Behold, I am against you, utterance of YHWH; | 18 | 2 | 5 = 5 + 0 |
| and I will burn in smoke her chariots; | 11 | 2 | 3 = 3 + 0 |
| and your young lions the sword will devour. | 13 | 2 | 3 = 3 + 0 |
| And your young lions the sword will devour; | 13 | 2 | 3 = 3 + 0 |
| and I will cut off from the land your prey; | 12 | 1 | 3 = 0 + 3 |
| and the voice of your envoys will be heard no more. | 18 | 2 | 5 = 0 + 5 |

The text as emended by Cathcart (and others) would scan 31 + 13 + 28 morae and thus would no longer be in proper prosodic balance. Such a reading is in line with what Keil ([reprint] 1949: 28–29) suggested long ago when he described the suffix as "a lengthened form, on account of the tone at the end of the section, analogous to ʾōṯāḵāh in Ex. 29:35." Spronk (1997: 109–10) adds the observation that *mlʾkkh,* as a special form of *malʾāḵēḵ,* "would balance the reference to one messenger in 2:1 and emphasize the contrast: the message of peace for Judah coincides with the end of the Assyrian messenger who was certainly associated by the surrounding peoples with bad news."

## COMMENT

The third canto (2:1–11 [1:15–2:10]) opens with reference to the voice of a "messenger" proclaiming *shalom* ("peace") in Judah, a voice that will be readily heard in the land. The fourth canto (2:12–14 [11–13] closes with reference to the "messengers" of Assyria, her envoys who collected tribute from subject nations in times past, whose voices are no longer heard in the land. God, as "scatterer" of nations, is bringing about a complete reversal in Nineveh's fortunes as the beast of prey becomes prey to the lion of Judah.

The opening words of the fourth and concluding strophe are determinative in the book of Nahum: "Behold, I am against you" (2:14 [13]). How we stand before God determines everything. Because of God's grace, Israel was familiar with the words "I am with you" (Exodus 3:12; Joshua 1:5; Jeremiah 1:8, 19; Isaiah 7:14; and so on). As the symbolic new Israel, the followers of Yeshua (Jesus) heard those same words of assurance even as he departed physically from their presence (Matthew 28:20; Acts 8:10). The apostle Paul put these two expressions together when he said: "If God is for us, who is against us?" (Romans 8:31). Nonetheless, as Achtemeier (1986: 22) reminds us: "Faith, like unfaith, needs always ask if it deserves these words that God addressed to Assyria, 'Behold, I am against you.' Then it needs to contemplate the fate of Nineveh and repent (cf. Matt. 12:41)."

### The Center of the Book of Nahum
It is best to interpret 2:11 [10] as a continuation of the cipher in 1:2–10, especially as regards its conclusion in 1:9–10, and to translate it in that context as follows:

What will you devise against YHWH?
It will not arise a second time, namely distress—
    for you will become like entangled thorns;
And though you are like soddened drunkards,
    consumed you will be like dry stubble—completely.

Destruction and devastation and destitution,
  and hearts faint and knees give way—
And anguish is in all loins and (in) all their faces;
  they are gathered as kindling.

This verse, along with the metaphorical images of burning "dry stubble" and "sopping wet, matted thorns" in 1:9–10, suggests that Nahum is a finely crafted literary composition from the outset. This is not the mere memory of once spoken words on the part of a prophet or preacher in ancient Israel.

The evidence points toward a canonical process different from what is often assumed. The text has "undergone an unusually complex process of growth and transformation," as de Vries notes (1966: 476–81), but in quite another manner from what he describes. The text cannot be separated into redactional stages or layers through skillful use of the scholar's scalpel, for in its present form Nahum is a finely crafted numerical and musical composition that is exact in meticulous detail—and the Hebrew text itself is almost perfectly preserved within the Masoretic tradition, at least with regard to the matter of word count.

2:10 [9] constitutes the structural center of Nahum, which has a grand total of **559** (= [**17** + **26**] × 13) words. The arithmological center falls on the Hebrew word *ûlipๅê* ("and the faces of") in 2:11b [10b], with 279 words on either side. A meaningful center is found by adding three words on either side of the arithmological center:

*wǝhalḥālāh bǝkol moṯnayim* ⎹*ûlipๅê*⎸ *kullām qibbǝṣû pāʾrûr*
And anguish is in all loins and (in) the faces of all of them;
  they are gathered as fuel (for burning).

With these seven words in the center, there are **276** (= **23** × 12) words on either side of the "meaningful center" (**559** = **276** + 7 + **276**). The number **276** thus appears to be significant in the composition of the Book of the Twelve Prophets as a whole, for the total word count in the Book of the Twelve is **14,352** = **276** × **26** × 2 = (**26** × **23** × 12) × 2. This coincidence suggests the possibility that the author or composer of Nahum as a numerical composition may have been the same person as the author or composer of the Book of the Twelve Prophets as a whole—with Nahum as perhaps the crowning achievement in that work.

The "meaningful center" here focuses on the totality of Nineveh's punishment in the form of a "riddle in the middle" of the book of Nahum, the content of which is closely tied to 1:8–10 in terms of the immediate context and the earlier cipher. The enigmatic nature of the seven words in question is evident from the difficulty interpreters and translators continue to have with this particular verse, especially the phrase *qibbaṣû pā$^{\jmath}$rûr* ("they are gathered as kindling").

There are 47 verses in Nahum, and the middle verse is 2:10 [9], with **23** verses on either side. Nahum has **559** (= [**17** + **26**] × **13**) words, and the middle word, which is found in 2:11b [10b], is *ûp̄ənê* ("and the faces [of all of them]"), with 279 words on either side of it. There are 2252 letters in Nahum in *Codex L*. If the proposed correction in 3:10b is accepted (see the following commentary), we have **2254** (= **23** × **7** × **7** × **2**) letters in Nahum. The arithmological center in terms of letter count falls between the words *ûp̄ənê* and *ḵullām* in 2:11 [10], with **1127** (= **23** × **7** × **7**) letters on either side of the absolute center. The "meaningful center" consists of 24 letters (12 on each side of the absolute center of Nahum in terms of letter count) and reads as follows:

| | |
|---|---|
| *bkl mtnym wpny klm* | (Anguish is) in all their loins and (in) the faces of them; |
| *qbṣw p$^{\jmath}$rwr* | they are gathered as fuel (for burning). |

Adjustment of optional vowel letters appears to have been a relatively late aspect of the numerical composition of the Hebrew text in the Tanakh. One of its purposes may have been symbolic—to put the divine name YHWH back into the fabric of an already corrupted text without making substantive changes in that same text, which would have violated the canonical injunction of Deuteronomy 4:2 not to add or to subtract anything. Though it was forbidden to restore missing words, it was apparently possible to make adjustments in the letter count so as to achieve numbers that were divisible by the four primary compositional numbers.

From almost every point of view, 2:11 [10] constitutes the center of the book of Nahum—and this verse functions as a pivot connecting the two halves of the book. On the one hand, its content completes the cipher hidden in the acrostic pattern of 1:1–10 and is to be interpreted in light of that cipher. At the same time, in terms of prosodic structure, this verse constitutes both the end of the third "canto" and the beginning of the fourth of seven cantos in the book of Nahum as a whole:

| | | |
|---|---|---|
| 1. | YHWH's wrath—bent acrostic psalm | 1:1–10 |
| 2. | YHWH announces the defeat of Belial (the Wicked One) | 1:11–14 |
| 3. | Vision of the sack of Nineveh | 2:1–11 [1:15–2:10] |
| 4. | Dirge on the lions' den | 2:11–14 [10–13] |
| 5. | Taunt song: "Alas, O city of blood" | 3:1–7 |
| 6. | Taunt song: "Are you better than Thebes?" | 3:8–13 |
| 7. | Locust dirge and concluding question | 3:14–19 |

Though v 11 [10] appears to be the structural center of Nahum from one point of view, it is also possible to see vv 12–13 [11–12] as the center from another perspective because they constitute the two middle verses in the middle canto. In this reading of the concentric literary structure of Nahum, these two middle verses include interesting features in terms of letter count, as follows:

| | | | | |
|---|---|---|---|---|
| 2:12 | 58 | = | 26 + 32 | {letters before and after ʾaṭnaḥ} |
| 2:13 | 49 | = | 26 + 23 | {letters before and after ʾaṭnaḥ} |

In the case of v 13, this letter count assumes the correction of the word *grwtyw* ("his cubs") in BHS to read *gryw* (cf. the reading of *gwryw* in Dead Sea Scroll 4QpNah). In terms of number symbolism, we thus find the divine name Yʜᴡʜ in the letters before *atnah* in both of these verses. And the lion of Judah is a common metaphor for describing the person of Yʜᴡʜ as the "lion king" (cf. Amos 1:2; 3:8). It is thus possible to find more than one lion in the symbolism here. At the same time, the word *Belial*, which appears twice earlier in Nahum (1:11 and 2:1 [1:15]), appears again in 2 Corinthians 6:15 (as *Beliar*) in reference to the devil, who is elsewhere described as a "roaring lion" prowling about "looking for someone to devour" (1 Peter 5:8). The metaphor of the lion is unusually rich in symbolic meaning, and the author of Nahum appears to have been gleefully trashing an icon of the enemy.

### The Lion as Symbol in the Bible and in Ancient Assyria

The lion is a frequently used metaphorical image both in the Bible and in Assyrian culture. In the Assyrian texts, the king is frequently compared with a lion. The refrain here parallels 1:4–6, where the wrathful Yʜᴡʜ appears as Divine Warrior. The "lion of Judah" is a familiar poetic image of Yʜᴡʜ (cf. Amos 3:8 and 1 Kings 13), but lions are also a dominant motif in Assyrian art. Here the den of the mighty Assyrian lion, which has taken so much prey, is destroyed. That "den" is the dwelling place of the lion—namely the city of Nineveh itself, which is the focus of judgment in the book of Nahum. The unit concludes with a prophetic oracle introduced by the familiar words "Declares Yʜᴡʜ of hosts," which makes explicit the divine source of Nineveh's destruction (2:13 [14]).

The word *lbʾt* ("lioness") occurs as a divine name or as a theophoric element in Canaanite personal names. The five inscribed javelin heads found at el-Khadr near Bethlehem and dated c. 1100 ʙᴄᴇ include two references to this deity (Milik and Cross 1954: 5–15). The word also appears in the Ugaritic tablets (*KTU* 4.63), and the place names "Lebaoth" (Joshua 15:32) and "Beth-lebaoth" (Joshua 19:6) suggest the cult of the lioness deity. Puech (1995: 981) identifies the deity with the Canaanite goddesses Asherah, Astarte, and Anat

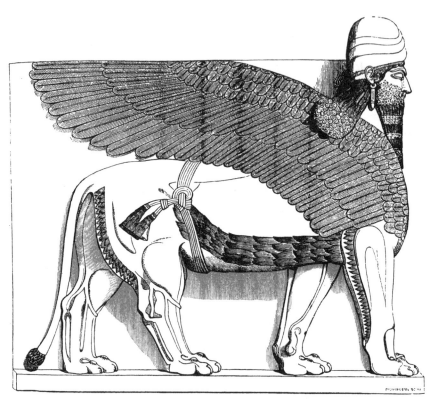

Winged human-headed lion (NW palace, Nimrud). From Layard (1849 1:77).

and notes that in Mesopotamia the association of the goddess Ishtar with a lion(ess) is well documented. In particular, he cites a text from Nineveh that mentions a lioness goddess identified with Ishtar, which symbolizes the military character of the goddess (1995: 983; cf. Thureau-Dangin 1940: 105). It is interesting to note that the goddess Asherah is portrayed in the so-called Qudšu iconography as naked, standing on a lion, and holding snakes in one or both hands (Hendel 1995: 1407). Hendel calls attention to the fact that a goddess epithet from the Proto-Sinaitic inscriptions ḏt bṯn ("The one [f.] of the Snake"), has been plausibly associated with the goddess Asherah. It is not clear how the symbols of the lion and the snake came together in the person of the goddess Asherah and/or other deities in the ancient Middle East.

Spronk (1997: 105) calls attention to numerous parallels between Isaiah 5:24–30, which concerns the Assyrians, and the text of Nahum 2:12 [13] in its larger setting. Note in particular Isaiah 5:29 (and cf. Jeremiah 50:17):

Their roaring is like a lion / like young lions they roar;
They growl and seize their prey / they carry it off and none can rescue.

Other parallels noted by Spronk include these:

| | |
|---|---|
| Isaiah 5:24 | the judgment of God as fire consuming chaff (cf. Nahum 1:10) |
| Isaiah 5:25 | the anger of YHWH (cf. Nahum 1:2) |
| | trembling mountains (cf. Nahum 1:5) |
| | heaps of bodies (cf. Nahum 3:3) |
| Isaiah 5:26 | a rapidly approaching army (cf. Nahum 2:6) |
| Isaiah 5:28 | horses and chariots (cf. Nahum 2:6) |

Isaiah 5:24–30 announces YHWH's judgment against the people of Israel at the hands of the Assyrians. According to Spronk (1997: 105), the book of Nahum may be read as a reversal of this older prophecy, and he thinks the "nobles" mentioned in 2:6 (cf. also 3:18) are the "young lions."

The richness of the symbolic meaning of the lion is explored in different ways in contemporary art forms. C. S. Lewis developed this theme at length in his portrayal of Aslan in *The Chronicles of Narnia*, two of which are now available as Walt Disney films. The musical *The Lion King*, which has also been adapted in a Disney film, picks up the same theme in a very different manner, with a portrayal of the entire lion family and of the conflict of good and evil, both of which are portrayed in the symbol of the lion. The symbolic meaning of the lion in metaphor, as portrayed in the book of Nahum, is timeless and inexhaustible.

## Finding Contemporary Meaning in Nahum 2

The sack of Nineveh is at the same time the defeat of evil itself. This is not just another war in antiquity but rather a war that points beyond itself to the timeless struggle between good and evil. As Craigie (1985: 71) put it: "The practice and perpetuation of human atrocities inevitably invites the opposition of God. And Nahum declares, in his own distinctive way, that the fruits of violence and evil eventually must return to haunt their perpetrators." From a human perspective, the power of evil often appears insurmountable. And from an individual point of view, that may in fact be the case. When we stand up in the face of great evil, we may indeed pay the ultimate price of being destroyed by that evil. But we also know that God's day of vindication will always come in its own time, and those who perpetrate evil will suffer the consequences of their evil deeds.

The splendor of Nineveh before its fall is a reminder of the impermanence of all human symbols of power and wealth. From all outward appearances, the city of Nineveh was invincible. We do well to remember that any fortress can and will succumb to pressures and go the way of Nineveh when its inner strength is sapped by the corruption of violence and unrestrained power. As Rudyard Kipling once put it (reference taken from Craigie 1985: 71):

Lo, all our pomp of yesterday
    is one with Nineveh and Tyre!

Nahum reminds us of the danger in what the ancient Greeks called *hubris*— the frailty of human pride. We do well to seek a city that is more enduring than Nineveh.

The second chapter of Nahum opens with the image of a messenger bringing good tidings to Judah: the times of war are about to end, to be followed by peace, for the enemy is about to be defeated (2:1 [1:15]). The feasts and festivals of Judah will be celebrated once again—in the city of God. As the psalmist put it (in Psalm 48:2–4, 9–14):

Great is YHWH and greatly to be praised,
    in the city of our God is his holy mountain.
It is beautiful in its loftiness, the joy of the earth—
    Mount Zion is like the heights of Zaphon; it is the city of the Great King.
God is in its citadels renowned as a stronghold.
As we have heard so have we seen, in the city of YHWH of hosts,
    in the city of our God, God establishes it forever, Selah.
Walk about Zion and go around it; count the towers thereof.
Mark well its fortresses *and* consider her palaces,
    that you may describe it to the next generation.

The city that endures is the symbolic city of Jerusalem, the city where God is king. And that city is not made with human hands.

For Jews and Christians alike, the city of Jerusalem is ultimately to be understood in metaphorical and eschatological terms. Some Jewish literature envisions a new, restored, earthly Jerusalem in the end times (Tobit 13:9–18; 2 Baruch 32:2–4; Testament of Dan 5:12). Other Jewish and Christian apocalyptic texts portray a new and perfect Jerusalem that will descend from heaven to earth (2 Esdras 7:26; 10:25–54; 13:36; Revelation 3:12, 21:2–22:5). Still other texts describe a perfect Jerusalem in heaven to which the just ascend (2 *Bar.* 4:1–7; 4 *Ezra* 8:52; 4 *Bar.* 5:35; Hebrews 12:22). Speaking allegorically on the two sons of Abraham, Ishmael by the slave woman Hagar and Isaac by the free woman Sarah (Galatians 4:24–26), Paul contrasted the "present Jerusalem" with the "Jerusalem above." For the Christian, God's dwelling place is no longer "the present Jerusalem," nor is "the present Jerusalem" the real mother; rather "the Jerusalem above is free, and she is our mother" (Galatians 4:26).

# VI. First Taunt: Nineveh's Shame Will Be Seen by the Nations (3:1–7)

|  |  | SAS Morae | units | Word count |  |  |
|---|---|---|---|---|---|---|
| **A.** | **"Woe to the City of Bloodshed"—All of It Filled with Deceit and Pillage (3:1)** |  |  |  |  | **[3.4]** |
| 3:1 | Woe / to the city of bloodshed // | 8 | 2 | 3 | 3 | 0 |
|  | all of it / | 3 | 1 | 1 | 0 | 1 |
|  | 2:12–3:1a | 49 |  | 26 |  | 23 |
|  | With deceit *and* pillage / filled / | 9 | 2 | 4 | 0 | 4 |
|  | 2:12–3:1c | 52 |  | 26 |  | 26 |
|  | Never without / prey // | 9 | 2 | 3 | 0 | 3 |
|  | 2:12–3:1 | 55 |  | 26 |  | 29 |
| **B.** | **The Sounds of Battle Are Heard (3:2)** |  |  |  |  | **[3.3]** |
| 3:2 | The sound of a whip / and the sound / of a rattling wheel // | 13 | 3 | 5 | 5 | 0 |
|  | 2:14–3:2a | 34 |  | 19 |  | 15 |
|  | And a horse galloping / | 7 | 1 | 2 | 0 | 2 |
|  | 3:1–2b | 17 |  | 8 |  | 9 |
|  | And a chariot / jolting // | 13 | 2 | 2 | 0 | 2 |
|  | 2:11–3:2 | 78 |  | 34 |  | 44 |
| **C.** | **The Carnage Is Enormous—There Is No End to the Corpses (3:3)** |  |  |  |  | **[4.5]** |
| 3:3 | Horsemen charging / and flash of sword / | 12 | 2 | 4 | 4 | 0 |

|  | SAS Morae | units | Word count |  |  |
|---|---|---|---|---|---|
| and glint of spear / and a multitude of slain / | _14 | 2_ | 4 | 4 | 0 |
| 3:2–3b | 17 |  | 13 |  | 4 |
| And a mass of corpses // | _ 7 | 1_ | 2 | 2 | 0 |
| 2:10–3:3c | 99 |  | 48 |  | 51 |
| And there is no end / to the bodies / | 12 | 2 | 3 | 0 | 3 |
| ᵃand they stumbleᵃ / over their bodies // | 13 | 2 | 2 | 0 | 2 |
| 3:1–3 | 34 |  | 18 |  | 16 |

**D. The End Has Come Because of Nineveh's Harlotry (3:4)**                                                                    [4.4]

| 3:4 |  |  |  |  |  |
|---|---|---|---|---|---|
| Because of the numerous / harlotries of the harlot / | 13 | 2 | 3 | 3 | 0 |
| the pleasing charm / of the mistress of sorceries // | _13 | 2_ | 4 | 4 | 0 |
| 3:3–4b | 22 |  | 17 |  | 5 |
| The one who acquiresᵇ nations / for her harlotry / | 15 | 2 | 3 | 0 | 3 |
| and clans / for her sorceries // | 13 | 2 | 2 | 0 | 2 |
| 3:1–4 | 46 |  | 25 |  | 21 |

**E. YHWH Speaks: "I Will Expose Your Shame to the Nations!" (3:5)**                                                           [5.4]

| 3:5 |  |  |  |  |  |
|---|---|---|---|---|---|
| "Behold, I am against you" (f. sg.) / | 7 | 1 | 2 | 2 | 0 |
| utterance / of YHWH of hosts / | _11 | 2_ | 3 | 3 | 0 |
| 3:4–5b | 17 |  | 12 |  | 5 |
| "And I will lift your (f. sg.) skirt / over your (f. sg.) face // | 16 | 2 | 4 | 4 | 0 |
| 3:1–5c | 55 |  | 34 |  | 21 |
| And I will show nations / your (f. sg.) nakedness / | _13 | 2_ | 3 | 0 | 3 |
| 3:3–5d | 39 |  | 26 |  | 13 |
| And kingdoms / your (f. sg.) shame" // | 12 | 2 | 2 | 0 | 2 |
| 3:4–5 | 26 |  | 16 |  | 10 |

**F. As YHWH's Spectacle of Contempt: "I Will Pelt You with Filth!" (3:6–7a)**                                                 [3.3]

| 3:6 |  |  |  |  |  |
|---|---|---|---|---|---|
| "I will pelt you (f. sg.) / with filth / | 13 | 2 | 3 | 3 | 0 |
| and I will make you (f. sg.) contemptible // | _ 5 | 1_ | 1 | 1 | 0 |
| 3:1–6b | 64 |  | 38 |  | 26 |
| And I will make of you (f. sg.)ᶜ a spectacle // | _ 9 | 1_ | 2 | 0 | 2 |
| 3:4–6 | 32 |  | 20 |  | 12 |
| 3:7 And everyone who sees you (f. sg.) / will flee from you" / | 16 | 2 | 5 | 5 | 0 |
| 3:3–7a | 52 |  | 35 |  | 17 |

| | Morae | SAS units | Word count | | |
|---|---|---|---|---|---|
| **G. Observers Say: "Nineveh Is in Ruins! Who Will Grieve for Her?" (3:7b–d)** | | | [4.3] | | |
| And he will say / "Nineveh is devastated / | 14 | 2 | 3 | 3 | 0 |
| 3:3–7b | | | 55 | 38 | 17 |
| Who / will grieve for her? // | 8 | 2 | 3 | 3 | 0 |
| 3:6–7c | | | 17 | 15 | 2 |
| Where / can I seek comforters / for you (m. sg.)?" // | 15 | 3 | 4 | 0 | 4 |
| 3:1–7 | | | 81 | 49 | 32 |

## Scansion of the Taunt against Nineveh in Nahum 3:1–7

| | Morae | SAS units | Word count |
|---|---|---|---|
| 3:1 *hôy / ʿîr dāmîm* ^ | 8 | 2 | 3 = 3 + 0 |
| *kullāh /* | 3 | 1 | 1 = 1 + 0 |
| *káḥaš péreq / məlēʾāh /* | 9 | 2 | 4 = 0 + 4 |
| *lōʾ yāmîš / ṭārep̄* : | 9 | 2 | 3 = 0 + 3 |
| 3:2 *qôl šôṭ / wəqôl / ráʿaš ʾôp̄ān* ^ | 13 | 3 | 5 = 5 + 0 |
| *wəsûs dōhḗr /* | 7 | 1 | 2 = 0 + 2 |
| *ûmerkāḇāh / məraqqēḏāh* : | 13 | 2 | 2 = 0 + 2 |
| 3:3 *pārāš maʿăleh / wəláhaḇ ḥereb /* | 12 | 2 | 4 = 4 + 0 |
| *ûḇəráq ḥănît / wərōḇ ḥālál /* | 14 | 2 | 4 = 4 + 0 |
| *wəkōḇed pāḡer* ^ | 7 | 2 | 2 = 2 + 0 |
| *wəʾên qḗṣeh / laggəwîyāh /* | 12 | 2 | 3 = 0 + 3 |
| ᵃ*yəkāšəlû*ᵃ */ biḡwîyāṯām* : | 13 | 2 | 2 = 0 + 2 |
| 3:4 *mērōḇ / zənûnê zônāh /* | 13 | 2 | 3 = 3 + 0 |
| *ṭôḇaṯ ḥḗn / baʿălaṯ* ⌐kəšāp̄îm¬ ^ | 13 | 2 | 4 = 4 + 0 |
| *hammukkéreṯ* ᵇ *gôyîm / bizənûnêha /* | 15 | 2 | 3 = 0 + 3 |
| *ûmišpāḥôṯ /bikəšāp̄êha* : | 13 | 2 | 2 = 0 + 2 |
| 3:5 *hin(ə)nî ʾēláyik / nəʾum / YHWH ṣəbāʾôṯ /* | 18 | 3 | 5 = 5 + 0 |
| *wəḡillêṯî šûláyik / ʿal-pānáyik* ^ | 16 | 2 | 4 = 4 + 0 |
| *wəharʾêṯî ḡôyîm / maʿrḗk /* | 12 | 2 | 3 = 0 + 3 |
| *ûmamlākôṯ / qəlônḗk* : | 12 | 2 | 2 = 0 + 2 |
| 3:6 *wəhišlaktî ʿāláyik / šiqqūṣîm / wənibbaltîk* ^ | 18 | 3 | 4 = 4 + 0 |
| *wəśamtîk* ᶜ *kərōʾî* : | 9 | 1 | 2 = 0 + 2 |
| 3:7 *wəhāyāh kol-rōʾayik / yiddôḏ mimmēk /* | 16 | 2 | 5 = 5 + 0 |
| *wəʾāmár / šoddəḏāh nînəwēh /* | 14 | 2 | 1 = 1 + 0 |

|                                              | Morae | SAS units | Word count |
|----------------------------------------------|-------|-----------|------------|
| mî / yānûḏ lāh ^                             | 8     | 2         | 5 = 5 + 0  |
| mēʾayin / ʾăḇaqqēš mǝnaḥămîm / lāḵ :          | 15    | 3         | 4 = 0 + 4  |
| 3:1–7                                         |       |           | 81 = 49 + 32 |

## NOTES

a–a Following the marginal *qere'* reading **wǝkāšǝlû** ("and they stumbled") in 3:3 rather than the *kethiv* **yakāšǝlû** ("they will stumble") in BHS.

b Reading **hammukkeret** ("Who is known [by the nations]") in place of **hammōkeret** ("the one who sells [nations]") in 3:4b, with Dahood (1971: 395–96) and Cathcart (1973a: 129).

c The *ṭiphâ* on **wǝśamtîḵ** ("and I will make of you") in 3:6 is read as conjunctive.

SAS (syntactic accentual-stress) units:

$$\{[3 + 4] + [3 + 3]\} + \{[4 + 5] + [4 + 4] + [5 + 4]\} + \{[3 + 3] + [4 = 3]\} = 52$$
$$(7 + 6) + (9 + 8 + 9) + (6 + 7) = 13 + 26 + 13 = 52 \text{ SAS units}$$

In terms of the 81 words in 3:1–7, the arithmological center falls on the word **kǝśāpîm** ("sorceries") in 3:4a, with 40 words on either side. The meaningful center is found by including three words on either side of the arithmological center:

**ṭôḇaṯ ḥēn baʿălaṯ [kǝśāpîm]**         Graceful is the mistress of [sorceries];
**hammōkeret gôyīm biznûnêhā**         The enslaver of nations by her harlotry,

Strophic units as shown by the balance in mora count:

| A | 3:1   | balanced triad            | [(8 + 3) + 9 + 9]       | = | 11 + 9 + 9    | morae |
| B | 3:2   | balanced dyad + pivot     | [13 + 7 + 13]           | = | 13 + 7 + 13   | morae |
| C | 3:3   | 2 balanced dyads + pivot  | [12 + 14] + 7 + [12 + 13] | = | 26 + 7 + 25 | morae |
| D | 3:4   | 2 balanced dyad           | [13 + 13] + [14 + 13]   | = | 26 + 27       | morae |
| E | 3:5   | balanced dyad             | [(7 + 11) + 16]         | = | 18 + 16       | morae |
|   |       | balanced dyad             | [13 + 12]               | = | 13 + 12       | morae |
| F | 3:6–7a | 2 balanced dyads + pivot | [(13 + 5) + 9 + 16]     | = | 18 + 9 + 16   | morae |
| G | 3:7b–d | balanced dyad + pivot    | [14 + 8 + 15]           | = | 14 + 8 + 15   | morae |

Word count

| | | |
|---|---|---|
| 2:12–3:1 | 26 | words before *ʾaṭnaḥ* |
| 2:11–3:2 | 78 | (= **26** × 3) words and **34** (= **17** × 2) words before *ʾaṭnaḥ* |
| 3:1–3 | 34 | (= **17** × 2) words |
| 3:1–4 | 46 | (= **23** × 2) words |
| 3:1–5 | 34 | (= **17** × 2) words before and **26** words after *ʾaṭnaḥ* |
| 3:4–6 | 32 | words |
| 3:1–7 | 32 | words after *ʾaṭnaḥ* |

## INTRODUCTION

The content of the seven strophes in the fifth canto (3:1–7) may be outlined in a menorah pattern that is determined on prosodic grounds:

**Canto 5: First Taunt: Nineveh's Shame Will Be Seen by the Nations (3:1–7)**

| | | | |
|---|---|---|---|
| A | Alas, O bloody city—all of it filled with deceit and pillage | [3.4] | 3:1 |
| B | The sounds of war resound in the streets | [3.3] | 3:2 |
| C | The carnage is enormous—there is no end to the corpses | [4.5] | 3:3 |
| X | **The end has come because of Nineveh's harlotry** | [4.4] | 3:4 |
| C′ | YHWH speaks: "I will expose your shame to the nations!" | [5.4] | 3:5 |
| B′ | YHWH's spectacle of contempt: "I will pelt you with filth!" | [3.3] | 3:6–7a |
| A′ | Observers say: "Ni]neveh is in ruins! Who will grieve for her?" | [4.3] | 3:7b–d |

In terms of the distribution of SAS units in Nahum 3:1–7, the seven strophes are arranged in perfect symmetry, with the eight SAS units of v 4 in the center:

$$[3 + 4] + [3 + 3] + [4 + 5] + \boxed{4 + 4} + [5 + 4] + [3 + 3] + [4 + 3]$$

Bliese (1995) reaches much the same conclusion on altogether different grounds. Counting word-stress units (that is, the number of accent marks), Bliese arranges the text into what he calls a "metrical chiasmus," which corresponds rather closely to the seven strophes found in the logoprosodic analysis presented here. If his line units are put into the previous strophes rather than his, which he bases on thematic unity, they will come out as follows:

$$(4 + 5) + (5 + 6) + (4 + 4 + 5) + \boxed{5 + 5} + (5 + 4 + 4) + (6 + 5) + (5 + 4)$$

In the center Bliese finds what he calls a "peak," which is indicated here with the box around the ten word-stress units in v 4. To achieve this balanced structure, Bliese makes five changes with regard to the presence or absence of *maqqeph*, whereas the logoprosodic analysis presented here requires only the reading of the accent *ṭip̄ḥâ* as conjunctive in 3:6b. Bliese joins the words *ˤîr-dāmîm* ("bloody city") in v 1, the words *zənûnê-zônāh* ("harlotries of the harlot") and *ṭôḇaṯ-ḥēn* ("pleasing charm") in v 4, and the words *wəharʾêṯî-ḡôyīm* ("and I will show nations") in v 5. And he separates the words *ˤal-pānāyiḵ* ("over your face") in v 5 into two separate word-stress units. He thus finds a 16-line poem with a thematic relationship between the opening word "Woe" in the first line and the words "grieve" and "comfort" in the last three lines. For Bliese (1995: 66), the "Woe" at the beginning and the rhetorical question at the end "give prominence to these lines." Prominence comes from the repetition of other key words as well: *zônāh* or *zənûnîm* ("harlotry") appears three times in v 4, and *kəšāp̄îm* ("sorceries") twice, at the end of each line in that same verse. The double line in the center of the metrical chiasm here points to secondary emphasis at the beginning and end of the poem.

Note the impressive use of symbolic numbers in terms of cumulative word count starting from the beginning of 2:12 [11] in the construction of each of the three briques in the triadic structure (11 ǁ 9 ǁ 9 morae):

2:12 [11]–3:1a     49 = 26 + 23
2:12 [11]–3:1c     52 = 26 + 26

Bliese (personal communication) calls attention to the fact that 2:12 [11] is carefully contrived, with **26** letters before and **32** letters after *aṯnaḥ*, which enhances the significance of the counts starting from that point.

## NOTES

3:1. *Woe to the city of bloodshed!—All of it with deceit (and) pillage filled.* Though *hôy* is the common cry of mourning heard in funeral processions, it no longer represents lamentation for the dead in prophetic usage, particularly in this context. An ominous cry of "woe" (*hôy*), which presents Nineveh as "the city of bloodshed" (*ˤîr dāmîm*), functions at the same time as an ironic announcement of the certain death that Nineveh faces (Zobel 1978: 360–61; cf. Longman 1993: 812). Spronk (1997: 117–18) notes the similarity in language to Isaiah 10:5–11.

The ruthlessness of ancient Assyria is legendary. In ancient states, the capital city was virtually the kingdom; so Nineveh is here described with all the characteristics of the Assyrian monarchy itself. The cruelties perpetrated by that regime are shocking. Captive heads of state were shut up in cages as spectacles for the populace to see, the heads of those already executed were hung around the necks of those still living, and others were flayed alive. Some scholars have concluded that the Assyrians were the most ruthless people of antiquity (see Davidson 1920: 33).

The plural of the word *dām* ("blood") denotes blood that is shed. The term refers to the unnecessary shedding of blood of one's enemy (1 Kings 2:31). As he promised in the covenant agreement with his people, Yhwh will take vengeance on his adversaries (cf. Deuteronomy 32:40–43), and reference to the blood shed by the Assyrians calls for revenge on the part of the "God of vengeance" (1:2; cf. Psalm 79:10). The phrase "city of bloodshed" appears elsewhere in reference to a city that is guilty before God of bloodguilt and about to be judged (Ezekiel 22:2; 24:6).

Many interpreters ignore the Masoretic accentual system and break up the four words of the second clause into two parts: *kullāh kaḥaš*, "all of her a lie," and *pereq mǝlēʾāh*, "of pillage full" (as does Spronk 1997: 117–18; cf. Elliger 1970; Longman 1993: 811; Roberts 1991: 67; and others). It is better to read the text as arranged by the Masoretes and confirmed by logoprosodic analysis. There is a significant caesura after the word *kullāh* ("all of her/it"), and that word is closely connected to the preceding clause, even with the presence of the *ʾatnaḥ* on the previous word, so as to form a balanced triad in terms of mora count (11 + 9 + 9):

> Woe to the city of bloodshed—all of it;
>> with deceit *and* pillage filled;
>>> never without prey.

One of the reasons for this departure from the normal rules, so that the *ʾatnaḥ* does not mark the end of the first segment of this triad, is the simple fact that the poet needed one more word after *ʾatnaḥ* to achieve a specific objective in the numerical composition and to set the stage for another such goal at the end of the second segment of this triad:

| | | |
|---|---|---|
| 2:12–3:1b | 49 = 26 + 23 | word count (before and after *ʾatnaḥ*) |
| 2:12–3:1c | 52 = 26 + 26 | word count (before and after *ʾatnaḥ*) |

The grammatical construction in the second part of this triad is that of hendiadys without a conjunction (see *IBHS* §4.4.1b; cf. the KJV and ASV: "It is all full of lies *and* robbery"). The words *kaḥaš* ("deceit") and *pereq* ("pillage, murder") are examples of asyndeton and are accusatives dependent on the adjective *mǝlēʾāh* ("full"), for "she deceived nations with vain promises of help and protection" (Keil and Delitzsch 1971: 29).

J. Jeremias (1970: 20) finds useful parallel texts using the term *kaḥaš* ("lying, deception") in the book of Hosea (7:3; 10:12–13; 12:1). Spronk (1997: 118) finds what he calls the "best parallel" in Psalm 59: 3, where the psalmist describes enemies as being proud and deceitful and expresses his hope that Yhwh will destroy them. An instructive example of Assyrian deception is found in Isaiah 36:13–20 (= 2 Kings 18:28–35), where the Rabshakeh (an official messenger from Sennacherib) makes promises to Jerusalem that will not be kept while at the same time suggesting that Hezekiah is the one who is deceiving his own people (see Klopfenstein 1964: 297–98). If politics is the art of lying, as some insist, Assyria developed that art to a high degree.

The word *pereq* means "tearing in pieces," an image taken from the lore of the lion, which tears its prey in pieces (Psalm 8:3). The word *yāmîš* is intensive, used intransitively, with the sense of "to depart" (as in Exodus 13:22; Psalm 55:12), and not in a transitive sense of "to cause to depart," for if *ʿîr* ("city") were the subject we would have *tāmîš* (Keil [reprint] 1949: 29).

(*It is*) *never without prey.* The city that is "never without prey" (*lōʾ yāmîš ṭārep*) is about to become prey. The Assyrian kings frequently boasted of the wealth taken from conquered peoples. Ashurbanipal reported: "The whole territory of my land in its entirety they filled to its farthest border (with tribute and booty)" (Piepkorn 1933: 82–83; reference from Spronk 1997: 118).

3:2. *The sound of a whip, and the sound of a rattling wheel, and a horse galloping and a chariot jolting.* The short, staccato effect of two- and three-word phrases is reminiscent of the portrayal of the death of Sisera in the Song of Deborah: "He sank, he fell, he lay still at her feet; at her feet he sank, he fell; where he sank, there he fell dead" (Judges 5:27, NRSV; cf. Nahum 2:5). But here the text is without verbs and without the expected plural forms. The expression "horse galloping" (*sûs dōhēr*) includes the rare word *dōhēr*, which Albright (1936b: 30) translates "chariot driver." The related noun *dhrh* appears in Judges 5:22 with the meaning "dashing, galloping." Spronk (1997: 119) sees the use of this word here, along with the word *lahab* ("flash [of sword]") in the next verse, as a deliberate attempt on the part of the poet to associate the attackers of Nineveh with Yнwн and his heavenly host in the archaic Song of Deborah (cf. Geyer 1987: 176–77 with regard to its "mythological context"). The prophet Joel used similar language (cf. Joel 2:4–5). Haldar (1945: 84, n. 1; 1947: 65, n. 3) related the word *dōhēr* to the roots *dwr* ("to move in a circle") and *drr* ("to run vehemently") and cites other instances in which *medial h* in Hebrew correspond to *medial w* in Akkadian.

The Piel participle *məraqqēḏāh* ("jolting") is from the root *rqd* ("to dance, leap") and is used here as a figurative expression to describe the action of racing war chariots. The words *ûmerkāḇāh məraqqēḏāh* ("chariots jolting") illustrate the use of assonance and alliteration, which is difficult, if not impossible, to render with the same effect in English translation. Spronk (1997: 119) makes a striking observation about the noise of the chariot wheels that merits being quoted in full: "The reference to the frightening noise of the wheels coincides with the fact that in the period of Sennacherib and Ashurbanipal the rims of the large wheels of war chariots were studded with nail-heads" (cf. Nagel 1966: 60 and plates 50 and 51). The sounds of battle are presented here as if the poet were located in the middle of the action itself, with chariots on every side. Haldar (1947: 65) called attention to the parallel in Joel 2:5, where chariots are said to "dance" (*yəraqqēdûn*) on the tops of the mountains, which presents a rather different image. He translated the words "The bounding chariots."

3:3. *Horseman charging, and flash of sword; and glint of spear, and a multitude of (the) slain; and a mass of corpses. And there is no end to the bodies; and they stumble over their bodies.* Spronk (1997: 119–20) reads a tricolon here, followed by two bicola. It is better to see the typical usage of a pair of balanced dyads connected by a pivot that ties the two "versets" in this strophe together, as follows:

| | Morae | | SAS units | | Word count |
|---|---|---|---|---|---|
| Horsemen charging and flash of sword; | 12 | 2 | 4 | 4 | 0 |
|   and glint of spear and a multitude of slain; | 14 | 2 | 4 | 4 | 0 |
|     *and a mass of corpses.* | 7 | 1 | 2 | 2 | 0 |
| And (as for the) mass of corpses; | 7 | 1 | 2 | 2 | 0 |
|   indeed there is no end to the bodies; | 12 | 2 | 3 | 0 | 3 |
|   they stumble over their bodies. | 13 | 2 | 2 | 0 | 2 |

The balance in terms of mora count in v 3 is nearly perfect: $(12 + 14) + 7 + (12 + 13)$. The metaphor itself is mixed, but the two elements are closely connected: the weapons of war achieve their end with the deaths of many. The carnage is presented in graphic detail through forceful repetition.

The word *pārāš* may represent a span, or pair of horses (cf. Cathcart 1973a: 127). Spronk's (1997: 120) argument in favor of interpreting the word as "rider" (or "horseman"), however, is more likely (see also Arnold 1905: 47; Mowinckel 1962: 289–95). The word *maʿăleh* is a Hiphil participle from the root *ʿlh* ("to go up"), which appears in the phrase "bring up (*haʿălû*) horses like bristling locusts" (Jeremiah 51:27; cf. Nahum 3:15). Haldar (1947: 65) interpreted the verb *ʿlh* here to mean the "prancing of horses," so the Hiphil with horsemen as the subject has the sense of "causing to rear" or "to spur on horses so that they rear." Arguing that "there are almost as many interpretations as interpreters," Gandell (1901: 645) listed several other possibilities: "rearing horse (or horseman)," "charging horseman," "mounting horseman," "plundering horseman." The problem is not in the word itself but in how to render the phrase. The literal meaning is "making to go up," and this has been understood by some in reference to the cavalry's leading or heading the rest of the troops and by others in terms of a rider's making his horse bound, rear, or gallop.

A variation of the phrase *ûbəraq ḥănît* (literally, "and lightning of spear") appears in Habakkuk 3:11, which Spronk (1997: 120) thinks is a quotation

from Nahum (note also the parallels he cites between Habakkuk 3:6, 10 and
Nahum 1:5; Habakkuk 3:8–10 and Nahum 1:4; Habakkuk 3:16 and Nahum
1:7). Haldar (1947: 66) read "flaming swords and flashing spears."

On the parallelism of the words *rb* || *kbd* ("number" and "mass") here, see
Kselman (1979: 110–14). The *ḥālāl* are those who are pierced by swords and
spears. The word *pāger* ("corpse") carries the connotation of being left
unburied (see Isaiah 14:19; 34:3). Haldar (1947: 66) argued that the singular
form of *laggawîyāh* ("to the corpse[s]") is used for an indefinite number (cf.
Brockelmann 1941: 225). Stronach and Lumsden (1992: 232) finds a reminder
of the scene presented here in the remains of more than a dozen persons
killed near one of the gates of Nineveh at the time of the final siege.

The marginal variant reading in *BHS* suggests the presence of a textual
problem in the last two words of v 3. Either the imperfect Qal of the *kethiv*
reading *yikšəlû* ("they stumble [over their corpses]") or the Niphal *yikkāšəlû*
("they stumbled") is followed by most interpreters. The perfect Qal of the
*qere'* reading *wəkāšəlû* ("and they stumbled") remains possible, "for the sentence does not express any progress, but simply exhibits the infinite number
of the corpses" (Hitzig, cited by Keil [reprint] 1949: 30). The Assyrians are
stumbling over the bodies of their own soldiers (cf. Nahum 2:6 [5]). Longman
(1993: 813) argues that the 3rd pers. m. pl. suffix on *bigwîyātām* ("over the
corpses") lacks an obvious antecedent and has no literary function. Van der
Woude sees the *mem* here as a gloss of some sort to explain the transition from
corpses to harlotry in the next verse: "They are fallen because of their (sexually heated) bodies" (reference taken from Spronk 1997: 121, n. 10). Five of
the concluding nine words in v 3 refer to corpses. The image presented here
is that of one standing on the battlefield afterward, surrounded by the carnage. Haldar (1947: 66) cited the clause here as "an excellent example of a
climactic parallelism," with the last two words carrying the utmost stress (cf.
Burney 1920: 166–68).

3:4. *Because of the numerous harlotries of the harlot, the pleasing charm of
the mistress of sorceries.* Nineveh is called *zônāh* ("a harlot") because of "the
treacherous friendship and crafty politics with which the coquette in her
search for conquests ensnared the smaller states" (Keil [reprint] 1949: 30, citing Calvin, Michaelis, and others). It was common practice in antiquity for
ruling powers to set up altars of their gods in subject countries. To be sub-
servient to Assyria was thus at the same time to "play the harlot" in terms of
going after foreign gods. Another means of practicing harlotry from a political
point of view was that of offering rewards to foreign rulers who submitted
themselves to the Assyrian king (see Keller 1972: 413–14). But here, unfortunately for those subject peoples, the one who appears at first to be attractive
(*ṭôbat ḥēn,* "good of grace"), bedazzling and ensnaring the nations, proves to

be in fact a "mistress of sorceries" (*baᶜălaṯ kəšāpîm*). It should be remembered that Y<small>HWH</small> himself is described at the outset in Nahum using similar expressions: he is *ṭôḇ*, "good" (1:7), and a *baᶜal*, "lord," of wrath (1:2).

The *mem* in *mērōḇ* ("because of the countless [harlotries]") is causal in function (R. J. Williams 1976: §319), and its use with *rōḇ* ("abundance") and the construction *zənûnê zônāh* ("harlotries of the harlot") intensify the expression. The preposition *mem* at the beginning of the first clause is also interpreted as filling a "double-duty" function that governs the second clause as well (by Longman 1993: 814; cf. Dahood 1971). In the phrase *zənûnê zônāh* ("harlotries of the harlot"), both words come from the same root, *znh* ("commit fornication, be a harlot"), which connotes illicit sexual activity, particularly on the part of a woman—including the matter of prostitution. In this context, the phrase *ṭôḇaṯ ḥēn* (literally, "good or fair of grace") refers to seductive sexual conduct—as suggested in the NRSV translation "gracefully alluring." The term *baᶜal* is used in 1:2 of Y<small>HWH</small> himself in the sense of "possessor or master of." The feminine form *baᶜalaṯ* presents Nineveh as "mistress of sorceries." As Hitzig put it long ago, the term *kəšāpîm* refers to "secret wiles, which, like magical arts, do not come to light in themselves, but only in their effects" (Keil [reprint] 1949: 31, citing Hitzig). In addition to the occurrence of the root *kšp* ("sorcerer") in Akkadian and Ugaritic, Dahood (1983: 59) finds the root in a professional term in the Ebla tablets (in *MEE* 2, 8 rev. II 13).

*The one who acquires nations for her harlotry, and clans for her sorceries.* Pinker (2004c: 5) turns to Rashi (d. 1105) for a plausible solution to the problem as regards the meaning of the word *hammōḵereṯ*, which he explains as the consequence of a מ/נ scribal confusion mitigated by similarity between *mkr* and *nkr*. In his commentary on Hosea 3:2, Rashi interpreted *wā'ekkərehā* as a corruption of *w'mkrh*. He explained *wā'ekkərehā lî* as an expression of merchandise, "a bargain," as in the Midrashic explanation of the words *'ăšer kārîṯî lî* ("which I bought for myself") in Genesis 50:5, and in the cities of the sea they say *kyrh* for *mkyrh*. In Old French, to which Rashi referred, *bargaine* means an agreement to exchange, sell, or buy goods. So Rashi interpreted *w'krh* / *w'mkrh* to mean "I bargained for her." The sense of "bargain" for the root *mkr*, without reference to the outcome of the process, fits well here in Nahum 3:4. Nahum perceived Nineveh as bargaining with other nations using the charms and sorceries of a harlot. Nonetheless, Rashi did not use the same argument to explain the meaning of *mkr*.

Pinker (2004c: 6) suggests: "Perhaps Rashi felt that bargaining with other nations using a harlot's tricks and sorcery was not sufficient cause for a total eradication of the Assyrian." Here in Nahum, Rashi used the phrase "conquer them." Thus Pinker concludes that *mkr* in Nahum 3:4 is a corruption of *nkr*. He notes that Mandelkern (1896: 671) observed that in Aramaic *mkr* also means "purchase a wife" and that the root *mkr* is perhaps close to *nkr*. In Akkadian, *makkûru, namkur(r)u*, and *nakkuru* mean "possession, property," suggesting the possibility of the interchangeability of the *m* and *n*. Pinker also notes that Ibn Ezra (d. 1167) suggested that *w'krh* in Hosea 3:2 is of the same derivation as *hkr n'*, which indicates that he also saw the possibility that the root here is *nkr*.

In his commentary on Hosea 3:2, Ibn Ezra said: "Some say that it means 'I will buy her' as it is said *tkrw m'tm* (Deut 2:6). But it is not correct in sense and grammar. It is of the same derivation as *hkr n'* (Gen 37:2, 38:25) but it should have been *w'kyrh*" (reference taken from Pinker 2004c: 9, n. 36). Gordis (1954: 25) also proposed the derivation of *w'krh* from *nkr* (reference from Pinker). Dahood (1955: 104) mentions that Albright took a similar approach, translating the word "I acquired her in marriage" (reference from Pinker). Nonetheless, Andersen and Freedman (1980: 298–99) do not feel that there is proof that *nkr* means "to purchase." And Ginsberg (1960: 50–69) dismissed such a meaning altogether (reference from Pinker).

Pinker's (2004c: 6) conclusion is more subtle, and also more convincing: "Perhaps, מכר and נכר are close to each other in the sense that each is a bargain, as suggested by Rashi, though the end result of the bargain in each case is different, in the first case it is a "sell" and the second case it is a "buy." Pinker (2004c: 7) argues that in the paleo-Hebrew script the *mem* and *nun* are orthographically similar, so it is not inconceivable that a scribe copied *hmkrt* instead of the original *hnkrt* or that such a scribe even made this correction consciously, believing that he was correcting an error or making the text clearer. Hiebert (1986: 19–20) considers scribal confusion between *mem* and *nun* "common" and uses this confusion to emend the text in Habakkuk 3:4–5 (as do Bolle 1990: 22, n. 11; Zer-Kavod 1990: 35, n. 19b; references from Pinker).

Pinker (2004c: 10, n. 44) lists a long series of cases with *mem/nun* confusion noted by Rabbi A. Haramati: *'yyn* and *'yym* (Ezekiel 26:18); *şdnyn* and *şdnym* (1 Kings 11:33 and 11:5); *rşyn* and *rşym* (2 Kings 11:13 and 11:6); *ḥtyn* and *ḥtym* (Ezekiel 4:9 and 2 Samuel 17:28); *'yyn* and *'yym* (Micah 3:12 and Jeremiah 26:18); *mlkyn* and *mlkym* (Proverbs 31:3 and 25:2, 3); *mlyn* and *mlym* (Job 4:2 and 8:10); *'hryn* and *'hrym* (Job 31:10 and 34:24); *šwmmyn* and *šwmmym* (Lamentations 1:16 and 1:4); *tnyn* and *tnym* (Lamentations 4:3: *kethiv/qere*'); *ymyn* and *ymym* (Daniel 12:13 and 10:14); and others. According to Pinker (2004c: 7), the LXX may have such a change in its reading of *mkr* for *nkr* in 1 Samuel 23:7. Pinker also notes the possibility of interpreting *hnkrt* as "she that alienates," reading the Qal f. sg. participle of *nkr* II with the basic meaning "foreign, strange." The text would then be translated "She that alienates nations with her harlotry and clans with her sorcery."

The basic meaning of the root *mkr* is "to trade" as a merchant, so the NASB translates the passage "Who sells nations by her harlotries / And families by her sorceries." Lipiński and Fabry (1997: 291–92) argue, however, that the verb *mkr* "designates a delivery of goods, generally in return for valuables, with or without the intention of passing ownership. . . . *mkr* signifies a transfer of possession which can, but must not necessarily, amount to a sale." In Joel 4:3 [3:3] and here in Nahum 3:4, the expression *mākar bə* then refers to a kind of barter, which helps to explain why the verb could be used in Esther 7:4 to mean "giving up" to destruction, slaying, and annihilation (Lipiński and Fabry 1997: 293).

In Ugaritic the word *mkr* is tied to the religious sphere (C. H. Gordon 1940: 102). Haldar (1947: 67) thought the meaning is that the city or nation places other nations under her dominion by making them serve her god, for as Nyberg (1941: 33) had shown, *znwnym* has the significance of "belonging to a foreign nation or cult." Sweeney (2000: 443) understands the concept of harlotry in the course of "selling" other nations as a reference to the Assyrian practice of deporting conquered populations from their homelands to foreign territories (see Oded 1979). Spronk (1997: 122) cites a parallel text in Joel 4:3 [3:3]— "(they) traded boys for prostitutes; they sold girls for wine." This interpretation is possible, but as Gandell (1901: 645) argued: "The figurative language of the context makes it probable that *selling* is to be taken metaphorically; treating nations brought under her power simply as articles of merchandize, abandoning them to misery and ruin with utter indifference." Human life itself was of no importance among the Assyrians' subject peoples, for all that mattered to those in power in Assyria was the satisfaction of lustful desire.

Older Jewish exegetes found the expression here in Nahum 3:4b problematic, as noted by Pinker (2004c: 2). Ibn Ezra explained the verse as follows: "It's a metaphor, that she fooled all" (cited by Pinker). Rashi explained the process of deception as that of flattery, arguing that Assyria "knew how to entice the heart of the kings of the land to join it, and then occupied them" (cited by Pinker). Pinker thinks this statement refers to a practice of "diplomatic" persuasion that led initially to alliance and then to subsequent occupation. Kimchi (d. 1235) understood the metaphor of the harlot as implying that Assyria upset the normal order in the region much the same as an infatuation with a harlot upsets the well-being of a family (cited by Pinker). According to Pinker, such infatuation "inevitably leads to loss of independence and complete control by the harlot, so much so that she can sell those infatuated by her as her own possessions." In Pinker's understanding, all of these scholars were struggling with the "buy/sell" problem of Nahum 3:4 in the context of a harlot's activity. The harlot sells her own body, but here in the text Nineveh sells "other" nations, which she would normally want to acquire and keep as her own acquisitions.

English versions of the Bible struggle with this same issue in different ways, sensing that there is something incongruous in the use of the term *hammōḵ-eret* ("the one who sells") in this context. And so the RSV has "betrays," the NRSV "enslaves," the JPS Tanakh "ensnared." For many interpreters it simply does not make sense that Nineveh would *sell* other nations. Moreover, as Pinker notes (2003c: 3), the concept of "selling a nation" in the Hebrew Bible is used exclusively to describe handing over Israel into the hands of others (Deuteronomy 32:30; Isaiah 50:1; 52:3; Psalm 44:13; 1 Samuel 12:9; Judith 2:14; 3:8; 4:2; 10:7; Esther 7:4).

Haupt (1907c: 24) said that the verb *mkr* here means "to cheat, deceive, cozen, beguile, entice" (as did Thomas 1936: 388–89; references from Pinker). Other scholars assign the root *mkr* II the meaning "to cheat, deceive" based on an Arabic cognate *makara* (Hitzig 1881: 258; van Hoonacker 1908: 528; J. M. P. Smith 1911: 338; Goslinga 1923: 292; Thomas 1936: 388–89, 1952: 214; ZLH 435b), but the existence of this meaning for the root in Hebrew remains uncertain (cf. W. A. Maier 1959: 306). Van der Woude (1977a: 111) interprets the meaning to be that Nineveh "sells out" nations, that is, she betrays their trust, but Pinker (2004c: 4) counters with the argument that the verb never means "sell out" or betray" elsewhere in the Hebrew Bible. Haldar (1947: 67) turned to Akkadian and Ugaritic parallels and concluded that the meaning is "that the hostile city throws nations under her dominion through manipulations compared with a cultic act." Pinker (2004c: 4) insists that such meanings as "sell out," "betray," "enslave," "deal deceitfully," and "trade" for the root *mkr* are simply not attested in the Hebrew Bible, where the root always means "sell" or "deliver over to another."

Dahood (1971: 395–96) changes the pointing of *hammōkeret* to read *hammukkeret* (Hophal fem. participle from the root *nkr*, "to know"; cf. 2 Kings 12:6, 8) and reads both occurrences of *beth* here as causal, translating the passage: "the one known by the nations for her harlotries, / and by the clans for her sorceries" (as does Cathcart 1973a: 129). Rudolph (1975: 175) emends *hammōkeret* ("who sold") to read *hakkōmeret* ("who ensnared"). This reading of the verb is accepted by the JPS Tanakh (and others, including Coggins 1985: 49), but this meaning of the Hebrew root is not otherwise attested in biblical Hebrew. Sellin (1930) reads *hamməkatteret* as "who surrounds." Roberts (1991: 70) emends *hammōkeret* to read *hamməšakkeret* ("who made [the nations] drunk"), which he compares with Jeremiah 51:7 and Revelation 17:2. He builds his case on the variant reading of *hmmkrt* in 4QpNah, which he explains as "a corruption of *hmškrt*—in later paleo-Hebrew script *m* and *š* differ only slightly apart from the tail on *m*—and once *š* had been corrupted to *m*, the second *m* would soon be dropped as an obvious dittography, thus producing the present text of the MT" (see also Marti 1903;

G. A. Smith 1928: 109; and others). The argument itself is without flaw but it is not convincing, for the 4QpNah reading could be the result of a simple dittography. If an emendation is required, it is better to go with Dahood's (1971: 395–96) proposed repointing of the word, which makes good sense of a difficult text and yields nearly perfect balance in terms of mora count (15 + 14). Dahood interprets the preposition *b* in both of its occurrences in this verse as "causal *bêt*" (cf. Floyd 2000: 68), though Longman's (1993: 815) "means or instrument" (see R. J. Williams 1976: §243) remains possible. Dahood (1971: 395–96) parses the nouns *gôyīm* and *mišpāḥôt* as genitives of cause (*GHB* §121p; GKC §116 l). In his original doctoral dissertation, Cathcart (1973a: 129, n. 16) explained the prepositions before the two nouns *zənûnehā* ("her harlotries") and *kəšāp̄ehā* ("her sorceries") as partitive, with the meaning "Who sells nations her harlotries, and clans her sorceries."

Two aspects of Nineveh's evil power are singled out: the word "harlotries" (*zənûnîm*) denotes power by seduction in the satisfaction of sensual pleasure, and the word "sorceries" (*kəšāp̄îm*) denotes manipulating others by force. The first concerns the seductive physical attraction of Nineveh as a beautiful city, and the second concerns the belief that Assyria had the greatest gods on their side, enabling them to do as they wished. This combination of harlotry and sorcery in the political sphere is illustrated in the person of Jezebel in 2 Kings 9:22. "Harlotry" indicates that seduction and sorcery represent the forcing of one's will on another.

3.5. *Behold, I am against you, utterance of YHWH of hosts; and I will lift your skirt over your face; and I will show nations your nakedness, and kingdoms your shame.* On the opening clause, see the earlier discussion on 2:14a. The context requires the translation of the term *ʾēlayik* here as "against you," though the normal way of expressing this would be *ʿalayik* (cf. the word *ʿālêhā* ["against her"] in Jonah 1:2, with *ʾēlêhā* ["to her"] in Jonah 3:2, where a great deal rides on the contrast in meaning of these two prepositions). The word *ṣəbāʾôt* ("hosts") comes from the tradition of YHWH's "Holy War" in ancient Israel. The term appears first in 1 Samuel 1:3. In Joshua 5:13–15, we find specific reference to the commander of the army (*ṣəbāʾ*) of YHWH. A dimension of cosmic powers is attached to this word throughout its history.

The word *šûlayik* ("your skirts") is the object of the verb *gillêtî*, from the root *glh*, which means "uncover, expose." It is not the skirt that is uncovered but what is under it, the private parts (cf. the Vulgate, *pudenda tua*). The harlot is stripped not to show her beauty but to shame her. Her clothing is to be lifted so high that her entire body is exposed. A typical punishment for prostitutes in the ancient Near East was to strip them of their clothing in public so as to expose them to public shame and ridicule (Longman 1993: 816). Hillers (1964: 59–60) cites parallel texts in treaty curses concerning the punishment of a prostitute by stripping her. A striking parallel to the threat leveled against Nineveh is found in Isaiah 47:3, with Babylon facing the same ignominy. As Spronk (1997: 123) observes, the LXX translation of *wəgillêtî šûlayik ʿal-pānāyik* as ἀποκαλύψω τὰ ὀπίσω σου ἐπὶ τὸ πρόσωπόν σου, "I shall uncover your buttocks in your presence," is an understatement. Sanderson (1992: 220) notes the appropriateness of Nineveh's punishment. Because Nahum depicts Nineveh's treachery in terms of female prostitution, it is fitting that her punishment is presented in terms of the sexual violence of a man against a woman. Because her former sexual conduct was "shameless," she is now "shamed."

The poet was well aware of the fate women faced in the brutal Assyrian conquests, where such captives were routinely raped (cf. 2:8 [7], and see the later discussion on 3:13). There is nothing in his remarks, however, that can be construed as condoning such violence. He merely states that the violence that has come from Nineveh and is now returning to that city is her just desserts.

According to Eslinger (1995: 154–55), the word *šwl* denotes the genitalia as well as a skirt or robe. Note how the BDB (1907: 788–89) gives two meanings for the word *ʿerwāh* ("nakedness, pudenda"). In reference to the covering of Noah's "nakedness," in Genesis 9:22 we read that Shem and Japheth covered the *ʿerwat ʾăbîhem* ("nakedness of their father"). The same applies to *maʿrēk* ("your nakedness, pudenda") here. A close parallel to v 5 is found in Jeremiah 13:26—*wəgam-ʾănî ḥāśaptî šûlayik ʿal-pānāyik* ("I will pull up your skirt over your face"). For other parallels, see Ezekiel 16:37–38; 23:10, 29; Hosea 2:12; cf. Lamentations 1:8–9). The Hiphil causative verbal form *wəharʾêtî* ("and I will show") has a double direct object ("nations" and "kingdoms") and a double indirect object ("your pudenda" and "your shame"). Nineveh's punishment is the public display of her sin of harlotry.

3:6. *I will pelt you with filth.* Noting that the term *šiqqūṣîm* ("filth") is associated with pagan idolatry (see Deuteronomy 29:17 [16]; 1 Kings 11:5, 7; Hosea 9:10), Longman (1993: 816) argues for a more general meaning, "anything God thinks is detestable"—hence his translation "abominable things." It is possible that the word *šiqqûṣ* in Hebrew carries the connotation of "excrement" (and perhaps of some vulgar expression related to that subject). The word is certainly associated with impurity in the sense of being ceremonially unclean. One of the functions of the Essene Gate in ancient Jerusalem was to enable persons to relieve themselves outside the city walls without bringing impurity to the city itself. In short, it is not sufficient to say, with Spronk (1997: 124): "Now that she is exposed, she is clad with dirt" unless one has in mind the "dirt" that came forth from the bowels of King Eglon in Moab when Ehud thrust that two-edged dagger into his intestines (Judges 3:22).

*And I will make of you a spectacle.* The term *kərōʾî* ("a spectacle") has received much comment in some circles, primarily because Rashi interpreted it to mean "excrement," a proposal accepted by Sellin that appears in the NEB (see Weingreen 1954: 57). Weiss (1963/64: 437) reached the same conclusion in comparing the MT and 4QpNah on this verse. G. R. Driver's (1938: 172–73) proposal to emend the text so as to read *kaddāʾāh*, "as a woman in menstruation," was rejected by Haldar (1947: 68). Lidzbarski (1898: 366) and Cooke (1903: 11) connected the word *rōʾî* with the Moabite *ryt* ("spectacle"), which they derived from *rʾh* (with elision of *ʾ*). Ullendorff (in DOTT, 196) translates lines 11–12 of the Mesha stela "But I fought against the town and took it and I slew all the people of the town, a spectacle [*ryt*] for Chemosh and Moab." Cooke (1903: 11) translated *ryt* in the Moabite stela as "gazingstock" and compared the text to Nahum 3:6, where the KJV translates *rʾy* with the same English word. Albright (1943: 16, n. 55), however, interpreted the word *ryt* in the Moabite stela to mean "satiation" or "intoxication." In support of the traditional rendering of *kərōʾî* from the verb "to see," Spronk (1997: 124) calls attention to how Asshurbanipal treated Elamite nobles "who had spoken in great disrespect against the gods of Assyria." These Elamites were flayed, their flesh was cut off, and they were carried about "to be gazed at by the whole land of Assyria" (Spronk, citing Luckenbill [*ARAB*]).

3:7. *And everyone who sees you will flee from you.* In times past the sight of the Assyrian army approaching was enough to cause people to flee (cf. Isaiah 10:31). Now it is the misery of the city of Nineveh that makes people want to get out of the way (cf. Psalm 31:12 [11]). This is only the third explicit use of the name *Nineveh* in Nahum (cf. 1:1 and 2:9 [8]). Spronk (1997: 125) calls attention to the fact that the name Nineveh appears here in a "purely negative context, indicating that nothing of the former name and fame shall be left." The word *rōʾayik* is linked to the word *rōʾî* ("spectacle") in v 6. The phrase *yiddôd mimmēk* ("he will flee from you") marks the end of the sixth strophe in the fifth canto (3:1–7).

*And he will say: "Nineveh is devastated; who will grieve for her? Where can I seek comforters for you?"* There is no reason to remove the word *wəʾāmar* ("And he said") as a gloss with the *BHS* note. In terms of the prosodic structure of this strophe, we have here a carefully balance dyad in which the two parts are connected by a pivot.

| | Morae | SAS units | Word count | | |
|---|---|---|---|---|---|
| I will pelt you with filth and make you contemptible; | 18 | 3 | 4 | 4 | 0 |
| [*and I will make of you a spectacle*]. | _9 | 1_ | 2 | 0 | 2 |
| And I will make of you a spectacle; | 9 | 1 | 2 | 0 | 2 |
| and everyone who sees you will flee from you. | 16 | 2 | 5 | 5 | 0 |

The word *šāddədāh* ("in ruins, devastated") is a variant form of the Pual perfect *šuddədāh,* from the root *šdd* ("despoil, deal violently with, devastate, ruin";
cf. Jeremiah 48:20). The word *yānûd* ("he will grieve"), which is Qal imperfect from the root *nwd* ("to show grief"), has the sense of shaking the head and
is used for the professional process of mourning an untimely death. Becking
(1995b: 113) observes that the prophetic texts in Nahum 2:4–14 [3–13];
3:1–7, 14–19, which announce the downfall of Nineveh, all conclude with
references to mourning rituals. He argues (1995b: 114) for an allusion to a
curse in the Succession Treaty of Esarhaddon: "May your ghost have nobody
to take care of the pouring of libations to him" (SAA II §47:452). Here the
same idea is phrased in a prohibitive sense rather than as a question. The verb
*nḥm* ("to comfort") appears together with the name *Nineveh* here and in the
heading 1:1, which suggests that we have here a deliberate pun on the name
of the prophet Nahum, "as well as a euphemism for mortuary existence in
the netherworld" (Becking 1995b: 115). As his name suggests, his message
is meant to be a comfort to the peoples who were oppressed by the Assyrians
in times past. Guthe (1923: 70) and others have interpreted the word
*mənaḥămîm* in a technical sense to mean "mourners" or "performers of the
funeral rites" (see also Coggins 1985: 51).

The word *lāk* ("for you") at the end of v 7 is frequently emended to read *lāh*
("for her"), with the LXX, to balance the other occurrence of the word *lāh*
("for her") in the same verse. The Wadi Murabbaʿat scroll has *lk*. Once again
we have here an occurrence of the principle of enallage to mark the approaching prosodic boundary at the end of v 7. Arguing on different grounds, Cathcart (1973a: 132–33) concludes that such a shift in pronouns is common and,
in fact, to be *expected* here. Abrupt change from 3rd to 2nd pers. is common
in Hebrew poetry and prophetic literature (Deuteronomy 32:15; Isaiah 5:8;
Jeremiah 29:19; Job 16:7) and also in Northwest Semitic curses (see Gevirtz
1961: 147, n. 4).

## COMMENT

The woe oracle in vv 1–3 is a commonly occurring prophetic theme that has
its origins in the funeral lament, in which family and friends cried out *hôy,
hôy* ("woe, woe") in the funeral procession. Prophetic woes, however, were
far removed from that context of mourning and grief. Instead they took the
form of invective and were pronounced as curses on those doomed by God
for destruction (cf. Amos 5:18–20; 6:1–7; Isaiah 5:8–24; 10:1–3; Micah
2:1–4). The use of that form here indicates that Nineveh's demise is certain,
as if the city were already dead and on its way to final burial. The literary form
of the woe oracle is normally in two sections: an accusation that states the evil

perpetrated and an announcement of the punishment to be meted out as judgment.

The fifth canto (3:1–7) is directed against Nineveh in its entirety and makes specific use of the word "prey" in v 1 to connect what is said here to the preceding canto (2:11–14 [10–13]), where the same word appears in 2:13 [12] and 14 [13]. The vivid attack depicted in vv 2–3 is an example of Assyrian atrocity in times past, portraying in vivid imagery why that city is justly described as "the city of bloodshed." At the same time, it is part of the prophet's *ḥăzôn* ("vision") of what is in store for Nineveh. The carnage of corpses portrayed here is the direct result of Assyria's policy of deceit and evil trickery, which is presented here with the image of harlotry and sorcery (v 4). The words "Behold, I am against you" (v 5) repeat what appeared earlier in 2:14 [13]. The word *kābōd*, which in 2:10 [9] referred to Assyria's "wealth" (that is, her "mass" of treasure), here becomes *kōbed pāger,* "a mass of corpses" (v 3c).

The opening of this funeral lament over the "city of blood" in v 1 is balanced structurally by a dirge in vv 6–7 that poses the rhetorical question "Nineveh is in ruins—who will mourn for her?" These bracketing verses enclose a graphic vision of bloody carnage (vv 2–3; cf. 2:3–5) that is set over against a prophetic oracle of judgment introduced by the familiar expression "utterance of Yhwh of hosts" (vv 5–6). The imagery here is repulsive, as Nineveh faces vile judgment for her gross harlotry (vv 4–5). Yhwh "will show the nations Nineveh's pudenda . . . and pelt her with filth" (vv 6–7). In the center of this literary unit we find the image of Nineveh as the harlot gracefully alluring, the mistress of sorceries, who has enslaved nations by her prostitution. Her seductive activity will come to an end, for Yhwh himself will lift her skirt and expose her nakedness for all the nations to see (cf. Jeremiah 13:22–26; Isaiah 47:1–3). The first taunt song concludes in v 7 by ridiculing Nineveh with two rhetorical questions: "Who will mourn for her?" and "Where can I find anyone to comfort you?" There will be no compassion but instead great rejoicing at the fall of the wicked city.

The battle scene in vv 2–3 is portrayed in the form of a prophetic vision that is interpreted in v 4. Nineveh will be destroyed because of her "harlotry" in the same manner in which she disposed of her victims in times past. The vivid portrayal of the battle charge and resultant carnage preserves archaic prosodic features:

| | | |
|---|---|---|
| The crack of a whip! | And the rumbling of wheels! | A jolting chariot! |
| Galloping horses! | Cavalry charging! | |
| Flash of swords! | Glistening of spears! | |
| Hosts of slain! | A mass of corpses! | |
| There is no end to the dead bodies; | They stumble over the dead. | |

The use of short couplets (and one triplet) adds emotion and vividness to the battle scene, as does the description of the death of Sisera at the hands of Jael in the Song of Deborah (Judges 5:26–28).

The portrayal of Assyrian power in these few verses is a masterpiece of poetic imagery. Here we find military, political, and economic power combined in all manner of devious corruption. Nineveh is a "bloody city" because of her policy of duplicity—she is filled with lying and plunder (v 1). Here is a nation that "proclaims peace" as it prepares for war, a nation that seals treaties of friendship while plotting the downfall of those very "friends," a nation that denies responsibility for international incidents it covertly perpetrates. Here is a government that takes steps to protect its image in the eyes of its own people as her officials routinely lie about their doings, a government that projects an image of caring in order to hide its rapacious greed and corruption in acts of deceit, neglect, and scorn for those they have victimized.

The poet portrays in staccato beat a blitzkrieg of military conquest that leaves the streets of a hapless city so full of dead bodies that the Assyrian soldiers stumble over the corpses of their own troops (vv 2–3). Assyria's dealings with other nations are pictured as the work of a harlot who is outwardly beautiful and charming as she entices her victims to their doom (v 4).

The patron goddess of Nineveh was Ishtar, the goddess of sex and war. She is even called a harlot in Mesopotamian literature. Stories of her exploits include acts of violence and sensuality. She is a fitting symbol for a brutal empire. As J. D. W. Watts (1975: 116) has put it: "With lustful visions of riches and power Ishtar had *beguiled nations* into war and conquest. Like the Devil of Christian thought, she tempted and demonized all who came within her influence."

Because Assyria lured nations to their death, God pronounces judgment through Nahum in the harshest possible language of metaphor. The nakedness of the harlot is exposed for all to see as she becomes an object of scorn. And in the end the harlot is destroyed—with no one to grieve her death. In pondering the meaning of this text, John Calvin (1846–49, reprint 1950: 480; quotation from Achtemeier 1986: 25) voiced a prayer we would do well to make our own: "Grant, Almighty God, that as we have now heard of punishments so dreadful denounced on all tyrants and plunderers, this warning may keep us within the limits of justice, so that none of us may abuse our power to oppress the innocent, but, on the contrary, strive to benefit one another, and wholly regulate ourselves according to the rule of equity."

# VII. SECOND TAUNT: LIKE THEBES, NINEVEH WILL BE SACKED (3:8–13)

| | Morae | SAS units | Words count | | |
|---|---|---|---|---|---|
| **A. Are You Better Than Thebes in Egypt? (3:8)** | | | | | [4.5] |
| 3:8 Are you (f. sg.) better / than *No-Amon* (Thebes) / | 13 | 2 | 3 | 3 | 0 |
| the one who dwells / on the Nile? / | 12 | 2 | 2 | 2 | 0 |
| 3:4–8b | | | 52 | 36 | 16 |
| Water / is round about her // | 8 | 2 | 3 | 3 | 0 |
| whose rampart is the sea / | 6 | 1 | 3 | 0 | 3 |
| having from the sea / her wall // | 10 | 2 | 2 | 0 | 2 |
| 3:6–8 | | | 34 | 23 | 11 |
| **B. Thebes Had a Strong Ally in Cush, Who "Was Her Strength" (3:9)** | | | | | [3.3] |
| 3:9 Cush was her strength / and Egypt / and that without limit // | 18 | 3 | 5 | 5 | 0 |
| 3:3–9a | | | 80 | 54 | 26 |
| Put and Libya / they were / among your (f. sg.) allies // | 17 | 3 | 4 | 0 | 4 |
| 3:2–9 | | | 93 | 59 | 34 |
| **C. She Went into Exile with Her Infants Dashed to Pieces (3:10a–d)** | | | | | [3.3] |
| 3:10 So it was with her / | 3 | 1 | 2 | 2 | 0 |
| into exile / she went in captivity / | 15 | 2 | 3 | 3 | 0 |
| 3:2–10b | | | 98 | 64 | 34 |

349

| | Morae | SAS units | Words count | | |
|---|---|---|---|---|---|
| Her infants also / were dashed to pieces / | 12 2 | 3 | 3 | 0 | |
| at the head of all the streets // | 8 1 | 3 | 3 | 0 | |
| 3:2–10d | | 104 | 70 | 34 | |

**D. Her Nobles and Dignitaries Were Bound in Fetters (3:10ef)**    [2.2]

| | Morae | SAS units | Words count | | |
|---|---|---|---|---|---|
| And for <all>[a] her nobles / |lots| were cast / | 15 2 | 5 | 0 | 5 | |
| 3:4–10e | | 85 | 55 | 30 | |
| And all her grandees / were bound in fetters // | 16 2 | 4 | 0 | 4 | |
| 3:4–10 | | 89 | 55 | 34 | |

**E. May You Be Inebriated and Seek Refuge from Your Enemy (3:11)**    [3.3]

| | Morae | SAS units | Words count | | |
|---|---|---|---|---|---|
| 3:11 May you (f. sg.) also become drunk / | 6 1 | 3 | 3 | 0 | |
| may you (f. sg.) / pass out (in a drink-induced stupor) // | 9 2 | 2 | 2 | 0 | |
| 3:9–11a | | 34 | 21 | 13 | |
| May you (f. sg.) also / seek refuge / from your enemy // | 16 3 | 5 | 0 | 5 | |
| 3:8–11 | | 52 | 29 | 23 | |

**F. Your Fortresses Will Fall Like First-Ripe Figs (3:12)**    [3.3]

| | Morae | SAS units | Words count | | |
|---|---|---|---|---|---|
| 3:12 All your (f. sg.) fortresses / | 6 1 | 2 | 2 | 0 | |
| are like fig trees / with first-ripe figs // | 11 2 | 3 | 3 | 0 | |
| 3:9–12a | | 44 | 26 | 18 | |
| When shaken / they fall / into the mouth of the eater // | 19 3 | 6 | 0 | 6 | |
| 3:8–12 | | 63 | 34 | 29 | |

**G. Your People and Gates Are Wide Open to Be Violated and Devoured (3:13)**    [5.4]

| | Morae | SAS units | Words count | | |
|---|---|---|---|---|---|
| 3:13 Behold /[b] your (f. sg.) people are women / in your midst / | 14 3 | 4 | 4 | 0 | |
| to your (f. sg.) enemies / | 6 1 | 1 | 1 | 0 | |
| 3:11–13b | | 26 | 15 | 11 | |
| They are wide open / | 9 1 | 2 | 2 | 0 | |
| 3:11–13c | | 28 | 17 | 11 | |
| (Namely) the gates /[c] of your (f. sg.) land // | 7 2 | 2 | 2 | 0 | |
| fire devours / your (f. sg.) gate-bars // | 13 2 | 3 | 0 | 3 | |
| 3:1–13 | | 156 | 92 | 64 | |
| 3:8–13 | | 75 | 43 | 32 | |

## Scansion of the Taunt against Nineveh in Nahum 3:8–13

|  |  | Morae | SAS units | Words count |
|---|---|---|---|---|
| 3:8 | ḥăṯêṭəḇî / minnôʾ ʾāmôn / | 13 | 2 | 3 = 0 + 3 |
|  | hayyōšəḇāh / bayʾōrîm / | 11 | 2 | 2 = 0 + 2 |
|  | máyim / sāḇîḇ lāh ^ | 8 | 2 | 3 = 0 + 3 |
|  | ʾăšer-ḥêl yám / miyyám / ḥômāṯáh : | 15 | 3 | 5 = 0 + 5 |
| 3:9 | kûš ʿāṣəmáh / ûmiṣráyim / wəʾên qêṣeh ^ | 18 | 3 | 5 = 5 + 0 |
|  | pûṭ wəlûḇîm / hāyû / bəʿezrāṯēk : | 17 | 3 | 4 = 0 + 4 |
| 3:10 | gam-hîʾ / | 3 | 1 | 2 = 2 + 0 |
|  | laggōláh / hāləḵáh baššeḇî / | 15 | 2 | 3 = 3 + 0 |
|  | gám ʿōlālêha / yəruṭṭəšû / | 12 | 2 | 2 = 2 + 0 |
|  | bərôʾš kol-ḥûṣôt ^ | 8 | 1 | 4 = 4 + 0 |
|  | wəʿal-<kol>ᵃ-niḵbaddêhā yaddû gôrál / | 15 | 2 | 5 = 0 + 5 |
|  | wəkol-gədôlêha / ruttəqû ḇaziqqîm : | 16 | 2 | 4 = 0 + 4 |
| 3:11 | gam-ʾát tiškərî / təhî / naʿălāmáh ^ | 15 | 3 | 5 = 5 + 0 |
|  | gam-ʾát / təḇaqšî māʿôz / mēʾôyēḇ : | 16 | 3 | 5 = 0 + 5 |
| 3:12 | kol-miḇṣāráyiḵ / təʾēnîm / ʿim-bikkûrîm ^ | 17 | 3 | 5 = 5 + 0 |
|  | ʾim-yinnôʿû / wənāpəlû / ʿal-pî ʾôḵēl : | 19 | 3 | 6 = 0 + 6 |
| 3:13 | hinnêh /ᵇ ʿammêḵ nāšîm / bəqirbêḵ / | 14 | 3 | 4 = 4 + 0 |
|  | ləʾōyəḇáyiḵ / | 6 | 1 | 1 = 1 + 0 |
|  | pāṯôaḥ nipṭəḥû / | 9 | 1 | 2 = 2 + 0 |
|  | šaʿărê /ᶜ ʾarṣēḵ ^ | 7 | 2 | 2 = 2 + 0 |
|  | ʾāḵəláh ʾēš / bərîḥáyiḵ : | 13 | 2 | 3 = 0 + 3 |
| 3:8–13 |  |  |  | 75 = 43 + 32 |

## NOTES

ᵃ Adding the word **kol** ("all") in 3:10b with the LXX. This is the one missing word in L (see the discussion in the introduction under "Logoprosodic Analysis and the Book of Nahum.")

ᵇ Reading the *ʾazlâ* on the word **hinnêh** ("behold") in 3:13a as disjunctive.

ᶜ Reading *mûnaḥ* on the word **šaʿărê** ("gates") in 3:13d, preceded immediately by *gaʿyâ* (= *meṯeḡ*) in Letteris (1880) and Ginsburg (1894), as disjunctive. The BHS omits *gaʿyâ* (= *meṯeḡ*).

SAS (syntactic accentual-stress) units:

$$[(4 + 5) + (6 + 6)] + \boxed{(2 + 2)} + [(6 + 6) + (5 + 4)]$$
$$= (9 + 12) + 4 + (12 + 9) = \mathbf{46} \text{ SAS units}$$

The meaningful center is found by including four words on either side of the arithmological center, which constitutes the whole of the middle strophe (3:10ef):

wəʿal-<kol>-nikbaddệhā                 And for all her nobles
    yaddû  gôrāl                        lots were cast;
wəkol-gədôlệhā ruttəqû bazziqqîm      And all her grandees were bound
                                       in fetters.

Strophic units as shown by the balance in mora count:

| A | 3:8 | 2 balanced dyads | [13 + 11] + [8 + 15] | = | 25 + 24 | morae |
|---|------|------------------|----------------------|---|---------|-------|
| B | 3:9 | balanced dyads | [18 + 17] | = | 18 + 17 | morae |
| C | 3:10a–d | balanced dyad | [18 + 20] | = | 15 + 16 | morae |
| D | 3:10ef | balanced dyad | [15 + 16] | = | 15 + 16 | morae |
| E | 3:11 | balanced dyad | [15 + 16] | = | 15 + 16 | morae |
| F | 3:12 | balanced dyad | [17 + 19] | = | 17 + 19 | morae |
| G | 3:13 | 2 balanced dyads + pivot | [10 + 10] + 9 + [7 + 13] | = | 20 + 9 + 20 | morae |

Word count:

| 3:6–8 | **34** | (= **17** × 2) words and **23** words before ʾatnaḥ |
|-------|--------|----------------------------------------------------|
| 3:3–9 | **34** | (= **17** × 2) words after ʾatnaḥ |
| 3:4–10 | **34** | (= **17** × 2) words after ʾatnaḥ |
| 3:8–11 | **52** | (= **26** × 2) words and **23** words after ʾatnaḥ |
| 3:8–12 | **34** | (= **17** × 2) words before ʾatnaḥ |
| 3:12–13 | **23** | words |
| 3:8–13 | **32** | words after ʾatnaḥ |
| 3:1–13 | **156** | (= **26** × 3 × 2) words, **92** (= **23** × 4) words before ʾatnaḥ and **64** (= **32** × 2) words after ʾatnaḥ |

## INTRODUCTION

The seven strophes in the sixth canto (3:8–13) may be outlined in a menorah pattern, which is determined primarily on prosodic grounds, as follows:

### Canto 6: Second Taunt: Like Thebes, Nineveh Will Be Sacked (3:8–13)

| A | To Nineveh: "Are you (f. sg.) better than Thebes on the Nile?" | [4.4] | 3:8 |
|---|---|---|---|
| B | Thebes had a strong ally in Cush who "was her strength" | [3.3] | 3:9 |
| C | She went into captivity with her infants dashed to pieces | [3.3] | 3:10a–d |
| X | **The leaders of Thebes were carried away in chains** | [2.2] | 3:10ef |
| C′ | Nineveh addressed: You will become drunk and seek refuge | [3.3] | 3:11 |

B′      Your fortresses will fall like first-ripe figs to be eaten      [3.3]   3:12

A′      To Nineveh: "Look at your (f. sg) people—they are
       like women!"      [4.4]   3:13

In the outermost frame of this structure (vv 8 and 13), Nineveh is addressed in the 2nd pers. f. sg. as destined for the same fate she inflicted on Thebes in Egypt. In spite of Egypt's boundless strength, she could not escape—she was taken captive and went into exile. The description of wanton destruction and human suffering is vivid in its graphic detail: her infants were dashed to pieces at the head of every street. The section concludes in 3:13 with an oracle of judgment in which destruction is announced using language reminiscent of ancient Near Eastern treaty curses (see Hillers 1964: 66–68).

In terms of the distribution of SAS units in Nahum 3:8–13, the seven strophes are arranged in perfect symmetry, with v 10ef in the center:

$$[4 + 4] + [3 + 3] + [3 + 3] + \boxed{2 + 2} + [3 + 3] + [3 + 3] + [4 + 4]$$

Bliese (1995) reaches much the same conclusion on altogether different grounds. Counting word-stress units (that is, the number of accent marks), Bliese arranges the text into what he calls a "metrical chiasmus" that corresponds exactly to the seven strophes found in the logoprosodic analysis presented here:

$$(7 + 5) + (4 + 4) + (4 + 4) + \boxed{3 + 3} + (4 + 4) + (4 + 4) + (5 + 7)$$

In the center he finds what he calls a "peak," which is indicated here by the box around the two central numbers (v 10ef). To achieve this balanced structure, Bliese joins the words *minnō²-²āmôn* ("than Thebes") in v 8 and the words *gam-ʿōlālệhā* ("also her young children") in v 10b. He also notes a concentric pattern in the distribution of initial consonants in the fourteen lines:

$$(h \; ² \; k \; p) + (gam \; / \; gam) + \boxed{wə^ʿal \; / \; wə\underline{k}ol} + (gam \; / \; gam) + (k \; ² h \; \; p)$$

Bliese notes that the first words in the central peak lines are three-letter words beginning with **waw** and ending with **lamed**. On either side of this central peak, we find two lines beginning with the word **gam** ("also"). Although the sequence of initial consonants at the ends of this concentric structure (in vv 8–9 and vv 12–13) is not identical, *the* four letters are the same. Moreover, the initial clause *Are you better* in v 8 forms an inclusion with the 2nd pers. *you* in vv 11–13. The parallel occurrences of **gam** ("also") highlight this same transition: *as for her* (Thebes) so *also you* (Nineveh). The double line in the center of the metrical chiasm here points to secondary emphasis at the beginning and end of the poem.

## NOTES

3:8. *Are you better than Thebes; the one who dwells on the Nile?* The root *ṭwb*
("be good, pleasing") is used on two earlier occasions in Nahum. In 1:8,
YHWH is described as *ṭôb* ("good") in the sense of providing a place of refuge
in times of distress. In 3:4, the phrase *ṭôbat ḥēn* ("pleasing charm") refers to
the seductive "beauty" of Nineveh as a harlot and the "mistress of sorceries."
For the sake of euphony, the word *hăṭêṭəbî* ("are you better?") combines elements of the Qal (*tîṭəbî*) and the Hiphil (*têṭibî*) of the related verbal root *yṭb*
("be good, pleasing") with the prefixed *he*-interrogative. Rudolph (1975: 181)
concludes in favor of the Hiphil (as does Spronk 1997: 126), because he
thinks in this context it is not speaking about a developed moral quality ("to
do good") but of an appointed state ("to have been made good"). One could
argue, however, that neither of these concerns expresses exactly what the
author had in mind.

The question is "Are you superior to Thebes?" On one level, the answer is
"Yes," for Assyria defeated Thebes. But the question is better rendered "Will
it go better with you? Shall you have a better fate?" And the implied answer
to that question is "No," for Nineveh will suffer the same fate that she inflicted
on Thebes. One should compare the use of the verbal form *hahêṭēb* ("Do you
do well [to be angry]?") in Jonah 4:4, 9. The Hiphil form of the root *yṭb* ("be
good, well, glad, pleasing") is intensive, similar to the Piel. It does not necessarily place "the moment of comparison in the future" (Spronk's [1997: 126]
understanding of the Hiphil of the verbal root in question). The Qal form, on
the other hand, denotes prosperity in Genesis 12:13 and 40:14 and is applied
here to the prosperous condition of the city, which is strong by virtue of its
physical situation and resources (Keil [reprint] 1949: 32).

The name *No-Amon* is Egyptian (*N⁾lwṯ-⁾imn*) for "the city of (the god)
Amon," that is, Thebes (see Vycichi 1940: 82–88). This full transcription of
the city name is not common, which witnesses again to the wide knowledge
and skill of the author of this poetic work, for the city of Thebes is referred to
here by its Egyptian name *nwt*, which simply means "city." Roberts (1991: 70)
lists examples to show how most foreign transcriptions drop both the name of
the deity and the final *-t* of the word for city.

The identification of *nō⁾ ⁾āmôn* with Thebes was not clear from the time
of the LXX translation (3rd century BCE) until recent times. The LXX appears
to mix three different translations, which are corrected by Aquila (128 CE),
Symmachus (late 2d century CE), and Theodotian (230–240 CE) in differing
ways, all of which make reference to αμ(μ)ων, which Jerome (d. 420) identified with Alexandria (see Spronk 1997: 127). The identification with Alexandria seems to have been made in the Targum and the Midrash Rabba; this

was the common identification for centuries and was still defended by Happel (1902) and van Doorslaer (1949), though already questioned by Luther (see Spronk 1997: 127). Luther translated the term "No, the city of craftsmen" and remarked that the prophet spoke "about some ancient, outstanding, very noble, and very powerful city—either ancient Thebes, which they say had a hundred gates, or about the best fortified city of Ethiopia, which they say was very strong and well-known, located in the delta of the Nile" (see Krause 1962: 157–67; the quotation is from the second version of Luther's commentary, WA 13, 390; reference taken from Spronk 1997: 127, n. 15, who identifies the Ethiopian city Luther mentions with Saba, located in upper Egypt rather than the delta). Luther derived the possible reference to Thebes from Homer's *Iliad* 9, 381–83 (see Burkert 1976: 5–21).

Kalinsky (1748) identified *nō' 'āmôn* with another Egyptian city in the delta and was followed in this respect by Kreenen (1808) and Spiegelberg (1904: 31–36). Cheyne (1903/4) suggested the North Arabic city Rehoboth, and Riessler (1911) proposed Babylon. The discovery of the Assyrian annals, however, enabled scholars to resolve the matter, which was settled by Schneider (1988). With the rise of Memphis in the north, Thebes became primarily a religious center as the city of the god Amon. With the defeat of Memphis by the Assyrians in 663 BCE, the capture of Thebes followed as the symbolic pinnacle of Assyrian expansion (see Grayson 1991: 144). The booty taken from Thebes was enormous, including two huge bronze obelisks.

The plural *yə'ōrîm* ("rivers, streams of the Nile"; cf. Isaiah 7:18; Psalm 78: 44) apparently refers to the Nile and the system of canals in the vicinity of Thebes fed by the Nile (Rudolph 1975: 181). Before the construction of the modern dams at Aswan, the Nile divided into three courses, with five islands in the Nile near Thebes. The word *yām* ("sea") here probably refers to the annual inundation of the land in the flooding of the Nile.

*Water is round about her, whose rampart is the sea, having from the sea her wall.* The words *mîyām ḥômāṯāh* ("from the sea her ramparts") are often emended to read *mayim ḥômāṯāh* ("the waters her wall"). Spronk (1997: 129) calls attention to "a parallel in an Assyrian description of Esarhaddon who speaks of 'kings living in the sea, whose walls are the sea and whose outer wall is the flood'" (cf. Brunner 1952; Berger 1970: 346; Cathcart 1973a: 133–34). The word *yām* ("sea") is used in parallel to *yə'ōrîm* ("the Nile") and probably refers to the regular inundations produced by the flooding of the Nile (G. A. Smith 1903: 587; J. M. P. Smith 1911: 341–42; T. Schneider 1988: 65–68; and others). Great rivers are frequently called *yām* ("sea"), as is the Euphrates in Isaiah 27:1 and Jeremiah 51:36 and the Nile in Isaiah 18:2; 19:5; and Job 41:23. The flooding of the Nile was called *bahr* ("sea") by the Beduins even in modern times because it truly resembled a sea (Keil [reprint] 1949: 33).

Coggins (1985: 52), however, finds here a reference to "Yam, the primordial sea whose power is overthrown by Yahweh." The phrase "from the sea her
ramparts" is a figurative description of the fact that the Nile River functioned
as a fortress wall for the city of Thebes. Rudolph (1975: 181) adds the suffix to
the noun *ḥêl* ("wall") to read *ḥêlāh* ("its wall") with 4QpNah (which has *ḥylh*)
and the various versions. However, as Cathcart (1973a: 134) notes: "The recognition of the suffix of *ḥômātāh* as a double-duty suffix makes the emendation
*ḥêlāh*, proposed in the apparatus of *BH*$^3$ [and *BHS*], quite superfluous." The
word *yām* ("sea") here refers to the Nile, as it does in Isaiah 19:5 (see BDB
411). The relative pronoun *ʾăšer* is used here in a possessive sense, "whose"
(cf. Job 37:17; Psalm 95:5; Isaiah 5:28; 49:23; Jeremiah 31:32).

Van Dijk (1968: 40) emends the MT slightly so as to read *ʾăšer ḥêl yām-m
yām hômātāh* ("her rampart is the Nile, the River her wall"), which is also
possible. Haldar (1947: 69–70) proposed the reading *ʾăšer ḥêlê māyim
hômātāh*, "Whose wall was ramparts of water." The MT reading *mîyām*
("from the sea") is often emended to read *mayim* ("water"; as by G. A. Smith
1928: 110; Cathcart 1973a: 133; Roberts 1991: 71; Longman 1993: 819), but
this is not necessary. The proposed emendation shortens the line by two
morae, producing an unbalanced line from a prosodic point of view. The MT
as it stands scans [13 + 12] ‖ [8 + (6 + 10)] = 25 ‖ 24 morae.

The poet apparently chose to lengthen the line by using the unusual reading preserved in the MT. The reading of the various versions is relatively easy
to explain, because the translators were working from unpointed Hebrew
texts. And the principle of *lectio difficilior* suggests which of these two readings
is more likely to be original—namely, the MT as it stands. It is better to retain
the reading that is more difficult to explain as the one more likely to be in fact
the original text, especially when the meaning itself is essentially the same
with either text. The two-part reference to the walls in relation to the city
reflects the fact that the ramparts of city walls were often protected by an
outer wall built some distance from the rampart. According to Cathcart (1973a:
134), this outer wall is the *ḥêl* in relation to the *ḥômāh*, the "inner wall" or
"rampart" (cf. Isaiah 26:1; Lamentations 2:8; de Vaux 1961: 232–33; Cathcart
1973a: 134).

3:9. *Cush (Ethiopia) was her strength, Egypt too, and that without limit;
Put, that is the Libyans, they were among your allies.* Cathcart (1973a: 135),
Roberts (1991: 71), and Longman (1993: 819) restore the *mappiq* to mark the
3rd pers. f. sg. suffix so as to read "her strength," with the LXX, Syriac, Targum
and some texts of the Vulgate. Spronk (1997: 130) argues, however, that the
*mappiq* is not necessary because the ending in *ʿāṣəmāh* ("her strength") can
be interpreted as a rare form of the 3rd pers. f. sg. suffix (see Joüon and Muraoka

1993: §94h). It is also possible to leave the Hebrew text as is and to supply the "missing" suffix from the context, as did Keil ([reprint] 1949: 33).

In this translation, Cush and Egypt are treated as a hendiadys of the predicate within a single clause, which may be rendered "Cush is her strength, *and* Egypt too, and that without limit." The meaning is that there was no end to the strength Egypt could muster, together with her allies. The identification of Cush as Ethiopia poses problems, because ancient Ethiopia is not the same region as modern Ethiopia (that is, Abyssinia). The region now called Sudan, which from the Roman period was known as Nubia, is what is in view here. This was the home of the so-called Cushite Dynasty 25 in ancient Egypt, which controlled Thebes during the late eighth and early seventh centuries BCE.

The reading of *bəᶜezrātēk* to mean "among your allies" is based on the interpretation of *ᶜezrāh* ("help") in the concrete sense of "helper" or "ally" (BDB 741). The preposition *b* here is the *bêt* of identity rather than being used in a locative sense (*DCH* 2:84 [7]). Spronk (1997: 130) changes the pronominal suffix on *bəᶜezrātēk* ("among your allies") from 2nd pers. f. sg. to 3rd pers. f. sg. *bəᶜezrātāh* ("among her allies") with the LXX, Syriac, and most commentators, arguing that Put and the Libyans were political allies of Egypt rather than Assyria (cf. van Doorslaer 1949: 286). It is better to read the MT as it stands and to see here another example of enallage, which also reflects the peculiar historical circumstances in which Assyria enlisted the aid of whatever allies she could find in the region, as was often the case elsewhere in the period of Assyrian expansion in the Levant.

Baker (1980; 1992: 560) finds a *waw explicativum* here and translates the text "Put, that is Libya" (as did Simons 1954: 180–83), which is followed here. Miller (1970: 168) posits a connection with the Ugaritic *ġzr* and translates the text "as your might," but the traditional translation presents a better description of the role of the Libyans as allies of Assyria in this particular instance. Cathcart (1979: 11) calls attention to the Canaanite *izirtu* ("military help"), which appears several times in the El-Amarna tablets: "Let him give you soldiers and chariots as help for you so that they may protect the city" (*EA* 87:13) and "I have provided help for Tyre" (*EA* 89:18).

The poetic line in 3:9 of the MT has a two-part structure, with the two nations Cush and Egypt appearing in separate SAS units. Put and Libya, on the other hand, appear within a single SAS unit in the second half of v 9. Like Ethiopia to the south, Libya to the west was often in conflict with Egypt in the Third Intermediate Period (ca. 1100–650 BCE) in Egyptian history, such that the strength of this political alliance was apparently tenuous at best. In fact, it is possible to interpret the pronoun "your" in this context to indicate that Assyria made use of this fickle relationship among former allies to achieve her own ends in the conquest of Egypt under Ashurbanipal. Just as *Ethiopia* and *Egypt* refer to the same people in the period of the Cushite Dynasty 25 (ca. 716–664 BCE), the same appears to be true of *Put* and *Libya*.

3:10. *So it was with her—into exile she went in captivity.* According to Labuschagne (1966: 201), the repeated particle *gam* has here the force of "nevertheless" (as thinks Spronk 1997: 131). Longman (1993: 820) argues that the word *gam* ("also") at the beginning of v 10 "introduces a clause that implies a logical contradiction: Thebes possessed great power in the arena of nations; yet Thebes went into exile." This construction requires the sense of "yet" in this context, as in the NIV. The logoprosodic analysis, however, suggests a somewhat different use of the particle **gam** in this context, for the words **gam-hîʾ**, which are connected by **maqqēp̄**, may be read as a rhythmic "bridge," or pivot, that connects vv 9 and 10, as follows:

| | Morae | SAS units | Word count | | |
|---|---|---|---|---|---|
| <sup>3:9</sup> Cush was her strength; Egypt too, | 12 | 1 | 2 | 2 | 0 |
| and that without limit; | 6 | 1 | 2 | 2 | 0 |
| Put and the Libyans, they were your help— | 17 | 3 | 4 | 0 | 4 |
| [so it was with her (that is, Thebes)]. | _3 | 1_ | 2 | 2 | 0] |
| <sup>3:10</sup> So it was with her (that is, Thebes)— | 3 | 1 | 2 | 2 | 0 |
| into exile she went in captivity; | 15 | 2 | 3 | 3 | 0 |
| Her infants also were dashed to pieces | 12 | 2 | 3 | 3 | 0 |
| at the head of all the streets. | 8 | 1 | 3 | 3 | 0 |

In terms of mora count, these two verses may be scanned 35 + 3 + 35 morae, with the two-word statement functioning as a pivot between two poetic triads of identical length on either side of this particular usage of the particle **gam**. The phrase **gam hîʾ** ("so it was with her [that is, Thebes]") is the first of four occurrences of the particle **gam** in Nahum—two in v 10 in reference to Thebes and two in v 11 in reference to Nineveh (in 2nd pers. direct address—"you also"). In between we find the center of the sixth canto (3:8–13), which is a single dyad (v 10ef).

| | Morae | SAS units | Word count | | |
|---|---|---|---|---|---|
| And for <all> her nobles / lots were cast / | 15 | 2 | 5 | 0 | 5 |
| and all her grandees / were bound in fetters // | 16 | 2 | 4 | 0 | 4 |

This dyad of nine words in the Hebrew text constitutes the "peak" in Bliese's (1995) analysis of Nahum 3:1–7 as a "metrical chiasm."

Like many others, Longman (1993: 820) has difficulty reconstructing the poetic form of the first half of v 10 and posits a "pivot" of a different sort: "The verb as a pivot to be read with both the first and second colons [*sic*]." The second *gam,* in the first half of v 10, does not introduce a contrasting statement, nor is it connected by *maqqēp̄* to what follows, so Longman (and also the NIV) leaves it untranslated. In this instance we find the more common emphasizing function in the particle *gam* (see Labuschagne 1966; Muraoka 1969, 1985), which is translated "even" in the NRSV.

Dahood (1969a: 271) interprets the *l* in *laggōlāh* as an emphatic lamed with the feminine participle *gōlāh* and renders the text "Yet she was an exile herself." Cathcart (1973a: 136) interprets the *l* here as a preposition, with *laggōlāh* a stylistic variant of the normal *baggōlāh*, balanced by *baššeḇî* ("into captivity"), in the next SAS unit. The meaning of *laggōlāh* ("emigration") is strengthened by the word *baššeḇî* ("into captivity") and the perfect form of the verb *hālaḵāh* ("she went"). The prophet holds up before Nineveh a momentous event of the past as a mirror to show the fate awaiting her in the present.

The threat of exile appears in curses of the texts of treaties, such as that of Esarhaddon with King Baal of Tyre: "May Melqart and Eshmun deliver your land to destruction, your people to be deported" (*ANET* 534; reference from Spronk 1997: 131). A good example of such treatment is that of Shalmaneser after the sack of Samaria (2 Kings 17:6).

The brutal treatment of children was apparently not exceptional (cf. 2 Kings 8:12; Isaiah 13:16; Hosea 10:14; 14:1; Psalm 137). Children were taken up by the body or legs, and their heads were dashed against a wall (see Davidson 1920: 37). On the "head of all the streets" as a place of such misery, see Isaiah 51:20 and Lamentations 2:19 and 4:1. Such calculated acts of terror were intended to cow vanquished enemies so as to deter subsequent revolt against Assyria. The term *yəruṭṭəšû* ("[they] were dashed to pieces") appears to have been a technical term used for this practice (2 Kings 8:12; Isaiah 13:16; Hosea 14:1 [13:16]). A similar practice was to rip open pregnant women (Amos 1:13; Hosea 13:16).

The verbal form used here is a preterit describing past action rather than an imperfect describing future action ("they will be dashed to pieces"), so there is no need to emend the text to read a Pual perfect *ruṭṭəšû* ("they were dashed in pieces"), as suggested in the *BHS* note. The imperfect verbal form between two perfect forms was used to denote actions taking place at the same time (see Spronk 1997: 131; cf. *HALOT* 1141). The MT reading is supported by the Dead Sea Scrolls (4QpNah 3:10), as well as the Syriac and Vulgate.

*And for <all> her nobles lots were cast; and all her grandees were bound in fetters.* Research on the Book of the Twelve Prophets in the BIBAL Forum (see

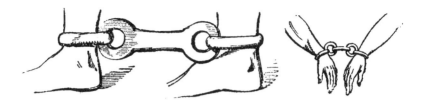

Left: Manacles for the feet (Khorsabad). Right: Manacles for the hands (Kouyun-jik). From Layard (1856: 325).

www.bibal.net) indicates that one word has dropped out of the text of Nahum in *Codex L* and that the word missing is after *ʾatnaḥ*. That lost word appears to be *kol* ("all"), which is restored here in 3:10b along with the LXX. Within the poetic structure of 3:8–13, the poetic dyad in v 10b constitutes a separate strophic unit that is the shortest strophic unit found anywhere in Nahum and also the structural center of this canto (see the "Comment" section later). Moreover, this is one of five places in the book of Nahum where a strophic boundary falls within a given verse (others are found in 1:12; 2:5 [4]; 3:7; and 3:19). On the meaning of **nikbaddêhā** as "her nobles," cf. Isaiah 3; 23:8, where the merchants of Tyre are referred to as **nikbaddê ʾāreṣ** (cf. BDB 457b and Genesis 34:19, Numbers 22:15). The most striking parallel text is found in Psalm 149:8, which reads "to bind their kings with fetters / and their nobles with chains of iron."

On the casting of lots in the Old Testament, see Lindblom (1962b) and Renner (1958). Casting lots suggests the distribution of the prisoners as slaves among the victorious troops (cf. Joel 4:3 and Obadiah 11). Spronk (1997: 131) suggests that the rare verbal root **rtq** ("to bind") was probably chosen for purposes of assonance with the noun **bazziqqîm** ("with chains").

3:11. *May you yourself also become drunk.* The particle **gam** appears twice in v 11 in parallel lines, both times with its common emphasizing function, which is translated here as "also." Keil (1949: 36) argued that **gam hîʾ** in v 10 corresponds to **gam ʾat** here—"as she, so also you." The four occurrences of the intensifying particle **gam** in vv 10–11 produce a dramatic sense of mounting intensity in the evils that threaten the city of Nineveh. The appearance of the independent personal pronoun before the verb, which is repeated in the second line of this verse, is also emphatic in nature—hence the translation "you yourself."

The verb here **tiškərî** ("may you become drunk"), which many interpret as Qal imperfect 2nd pers. f. pl., is better read as jussive (that is, an indirect imperative), which is clearly the case with the corresponding verb **təhî** ("may it become") in the second part of this poetic line. Roberts (1991: 71) recognizes the jussive form in the latter instance, but he chooses to emend the text so as to get rid of it, arguing: "There is no reason for the jussive form" (see also J. M. P. Smith 1911: 357). The same is true of the verbal form *təḇaqšî* ("may you seek"), which is in poetic parallelism with *tiškərî*. The statement "May you yourself also become drunk," which is often explained as common imagery for defeat in battle, is an allusion to the literary motif of the cup of Yʜwʜ's wrath (see Jeremiah 25:15–29; 49:12–13; 51:7; Job 21:20; Psalms 60:5; 75:9; Habakkuk 2:15–16; Lamentations 4:21; Ezekiel 31–34; Isaiah 51:17–23; Obadiah 16; Zechariah 12:2). Drunkenness in this context is a figure for the stupefaction caused by calamity.

Spronk (1997: 132) explains the reference to becoming drunk here quite independent of the "cup of wrath" motif, which he sees as a later development. He sees 3:11 as a tricolon and notes that the three verbs here appear to have their counterparts in 1:7, 8, and 10 in reverse order. This is in keeping with the interpretation of drunkenness as a motif in 1:10 with its reference to "beer drinkers" (see the discussion on that verse). The expression "seeking shelter from the enemy" corresponds to the confession in 1:7 that Yʜwʜ is "a shelter in the day of distress."

Elliger (1970) suggested emending the text from *tiškərî* ("may you become drunk") to read *tiššāḇərî* ("you [too] will be broken, crushed"), but there is no external support for this change, and the imagery of drunkenness is a common figure for defeat in battle (Isaiah 49:26; Jeremiah 25:27; 51:21). Drunkards often pass out and drool wine from their mouths, while blood flows out of the mouths of slain warriors on the battlefield.

*May you pass out (in a drink-induced stupor).* Except for the 2nd pers. f. sg. suffix at the end of v 9, the text about Thebes in 3:9–10 is in the 3rd person. But in 3:11 the author shifts to direct address in three 2nd pers. f. pl. verbal forms, all with jussive force, which mark the beginning of a new strophe (3:11–12). The words *təhî naʿălāmāh* in v 11 cause difficulty among some translators and interpreters because of their failure to observe that the verbal form is jussive, or indirect imperative, from the root *hyh* ("to be") together with the Niphal f. sg. participle of the root *ʿlm* ("to conceal, hide"), with the meaning "May you become obscured (as to the senses; fig. for swoon)" (BDB 761), that is, may you pass out in a drunken stupor. J. M. P. Smith (1911: 357) dismisses this "inexplicable jussive" with the remark that "there is scarcely any basis for the rendering 'mayest thou be'" suggested in BDB (cf. Roberts 1991: 71).

On the use of the imperfect plus the participle to express continuing condition, J. M. P. Smith (1911: 357) cites what he calls an "exact parallel of this idiom" as given by Haupt. This example, however, comes from Arabic *gušiya ʿalayhi* ("a cover was put upon him") and does not prove his point. It is more likely that the verb here is to be interpreted as jussive. W. A. Maier

(1959: 331) mistakenly explains the form here as an imperfect indicative on the basis of GKC §145p and calls attention to the use of the verb with the participle as discussed in GKC §116r. The parallel passage cited by Gesenius in Genesis 1:6 is instructive for our purposes, with the jussive *yəhî* ("let there be") followed by the imperfect consecutive form with a participle *wîhî mabdîl* ("and let it separate"). In both instances the sense of the verbal form in Genesis 1:6 is jussive, as is apparently the case here in Nahum 3:11 as well.

Many translators focus their attention on the primary meaning of the root *ꜥlm* and thus come up with translations like the following: "Thou shalt be hid" (KJV), "You will go into hiding" (NRSV and NIV), "You will be hidden" (NASB), and so on. The JPS Tanakh renders it "(You will be) utterly overcome," but Longman (1993: 821–22) prefers "you will pass out." Rudolph (1975: 182) has shown that the root *ꜥlm* can have a reflexive sense in the Niphal—in the sense of "to be hidden in oneself, to be unconscious, to pass out." The image is that of someone slipping into an unconscious stupor from heavy drinking, hence the translation "May you become unconscious" or "May you collapse in unconsciousness"—that is, pass out in a drink-induced stupor. Haupt (1907c: 32) interpreted the participle *naꜥălāmāh* to mean "overcome = fainting, falling into a swoon." Locher (2001: 150–51) explains the word *naꜥălāmāh* as referring to "a lower level of consciousness" that manifests itself as helplessness in the face of the enemy. He translates *təhî naꜥălāmāh* as "You also [like Thebes in vv 8–10] will be drunken and out of your senses."

Dahood (1955: 104) read the phrase *təhî naꜥălāmāh* as "you will be made young again," which Cathcart (1973a: 138) accepts. G. R. Driver (1938: 271) suggests emending the text to read *nꜥlph,* from the root *ꜥlp* ("to cover, faint, swoon away"). Michaelis explained the word *naꜥălāmāh* as a privative denominative of *ꜥlmh,* meaning "deflowered, devirginated" (see Haupt 1907c: 32). Gaster (1937a: 164) emends the text to read *ləꜥalmāh* "(you will become) a serving-maid." Elliger (1970) suggests the reading *neꜥēlāp̄āh* ("be destroyed"; cf. Targum). Spronk (1997: 132) interprets the verbal root *ꜥlm* here to mean "to darken" (as did HALOT 789; Hitzig 1881: 260; Balaban 1962: 237) and translates the clause *təhî naꜥălāmāh* "You will be darkened," which he compares with 1:8 and the statement there that Yhwh pursues his enemies into darkness. Keil ([reprint] 1949: 36) points out that the word *neꜥēlām* always means "hidden," so for him Calvin's interpretation remains the correct one: "Thou wilt vanish away as if thou hadst never been; the Hebrews frequently using the expression being hidden for being reduced to nothing."

Gaster (1937: 164), G. R. Driver (1938: 271), Dahood (1955: 104), and Cathcart (1973a: 137; so also the NEB) have emended the text from *tiškərî* ("you will become drunk") to read *tiśśākərî* as "you will hire yourself out." Haldar (1947: 72) suggested reading *tskry* ("you shall be shut up," that is, surrendered), which he compared to Isaiah 19:4. Duhm (1911: 106; cf. *BHS* note) suggested reading *tiśśābərî* ("your will be shattered"). It is better to read the MT without emendation, with Roberts (1991: 68), Longman (1993: 821), and most English translations, but to interpret all three verbal forms in this verse in a jussive sense, as I have already argued.

*May you also seek refuge from your enemy.* In short, the poet said, may the tables be turned on wicked Assyria. As others have sought refuge from Assyria as their enemy, may Assyria, too, seek refuge from a more powerful adversary. Let the one who has oppressed other peoples be oppressed in like manner, for indeed the cup of Yhwh's wrath is now extended to the city of Nineveh, which must consume that cup of wrath to its very dregs.

Florit (1932) suggests reading "You will seek shelter *with* the enemy," as a reference to the Assyrians' accepting help from Egypt against the Babylonians and Medes after the fall of Nineveh.

3:12. *All your fortresses are like fig trees, with first-ripe figs.* The image of the early ripe figs, which are easily obtained and swiftly eaten, appears also in Isaiah 28:4, where it symbolizes the imminent destruction of Samaria. Parrot (1955: 79) interprets *mibṣārayik* ("your fortresses") as a reference to Ashur and Tarbiṣu, the latter a town located in the vicinity of Nineveh. The Babylonian Chronicle reads "They captured the town of Tarbiṣu, a city in the province of Nineveh. . . . He pursued [down the bank of the river] Tigris and encamped against Assur. He made an attack upon the town" (Wiseman 1956: 56–57, lines 25–26 of BM 21901). Spronk (1997: 133), however, notes that the term *mibṣārāyik* ("your fortresses") appears again in 3:14, which "makes it more likely that the poet meant the fortresses protecting the wall and especially the gates of Nineveh" (the text has been read this way by Wellhausen 1898: 164; Marti 1903: 322; and van der Woude 1978a).

Along with other scholars before and after him (see G. A. Smith 1928: 111; Coggins 1985: 54–55; and others), Cathcart (1973a: 139) emends the text to read *ᶜam* ("[your] troops") in place of the preposition *ᶜim* ("with"), with a double-duty suffix on *mibṣārayik* ("your fortifications"). In so doing he ignores the *maqqēp* that connects this word with *bikkûrîm* ("early figs"). The result is what appears to be a balanced dyad: "All your fortifications are fig-trees; your troops are early figs." Cathcart rejects the emendation to *ᶜammēk* ("your defenders") proposed by J. M. P. Smith (1911: 346), Nowack (1897: 255), Marti (1903: 322), and others because the addition "would spoil the syllable count of a finely structured verse: the syllable count is 8/4/8/4 and the stress-unit count 3/2/3/2." We would add the balance in terms of mor-count and note that the proper break in the second line is after *yinnô'û* ("they are shaken") with its disjunctive accent (*zāqēp gādôl*); thus the mora count is 12/6/6/13, the syllable count 8/4/4/8, and the word-stress count 3/2/2/3.

There is irony in 3:12, for Sennacherib planted fig trees along the major streets in Nineveh to help beautify the city and encouraged the citizens to eat the fruit of these trees (see *ARAB*, 368). The extended simile here compares the siege of Nineveh with reapers shaking fig trees in order to harvest their fruit. The first ripe fruits appear early in the season and drop from the trees more easily than the later crop (cf. Isaiah 28:4). Workers climbed the trees in order to harvest the later crop, which they picked by hand. The first fruits, however, were gathered quickly by simply shaking the trees (Dalman 1964: 378–80). The point is clear: Nineveh will fall quickly and easily to enemy forces. Again there is a deliberate note of irony here, for the Assyrian kings encouraged their troops to consume the fruit of the conquered city's fruit trees (*ARAB*, 32, 261–62).

*If they are shaken, then they will fall into the mouth of the eater.* This line opens with the conditional particle *'im* ("if"), with a verb in the imperfect *yinnô'û* ("they are shaken") in the protasis: "If they are shaken" (GKC §159q). The *waw* conjunction introduces the result of the action that the protasis expresses and carries the meaning "then." In such cases, the apodosis takes the perfect and carries the force of "Then it will follow from this."

The MT is read as it stands without emendation, along with the ancient versions, W. A. Maier (1959: 8), Roberts (1991: 71), Longman (1993: 821), Spronk (1997: 134), and others (including the NRSV, NIV, and JPS Tanakh). Longman (1993: 822) rejects Cathcart's proposed emendation as "totally unnecessary and motivated by incorrect assumptions concerning the workings of Hebrew poetry" (as does Roberts 1991: 71). It should be noted, however, that Cathcart (1973a: 139) seems to be aware of the problem, at least in part, for he adds a comment that questions the validity of his own work: "Although we have followed the majority of scholars, taking *'m* as parallel to *mibṣārayik*, we are not absolutely convinced that parallelism must be established in this verse."

Spronk (1997: 134) calls attention to an interesting parallel passage in an Assyrian oracle where Ishtar promises to support Esarhaddon: "Your enemies shall roll like (ripe) apples before your feet" (cf. Weippert 1983: 285; *ANET* 605).

*3:13. Behold your people are women in your midst—to your enemies they are wide open.* The prosodic structure presents two balanced dyads joined by a pivot consisting of two words, "they are wide open," and belongs to both dyads in this verse, completing one verset and starting the other:

|  | SAS<br>Morae | units | Word<br>count |
|---|---|---|---|
| Behold your people are women in your midst | 14 3 | 4 | 4 0 |
| to your enemies *they are wide open.* | 15 2_ | 3 | 3 0 |
| *They are wide open*—(namely) the gates of your land; | 16 3 | 4 | 4 0 |
| fire devours your gate-bars. | 13 2 | 3 | 0 3 |

In the first verset, the connotation is that the women are open to sexual exploitation (cf. Nogalski 1993b: 119–20). In the second verset, it is the gates of the city that are wide open, because fire devours the gate-bars. In this instance, the two pairs of dyads with the pivot scan $(14 + 6) + 9 + (7 + 13) = 20 + 9 + 20$ morae.

Though allusion to common imagery from the language of treaty curses is present in Nahum 3:13, the prosodic structure suggests a more complex use of the image of feminine vulnerability in times of war. One of the human tragedies of war, past and present, is the fate of innocent women, who are indeed seen to be "wide open" to callous soldiers who rape them. Here "the women in your midst" become a symbol for the people of Nineveh as a whole in the prophet's vision, for the city of Nineveh faces the same plight she inflicted on so many others in times past. In the words *pātôaḥ niptaḥû* ("they are wide open") we have the relatively rare combination of a Qal inf. const. with a Niphal perfect verb of the same root, which emphasizes the passive role played by women in such circumstances and intensifies the meaning of the verb itself, adding depth of meaning to the pivot pattern in this context. For a similar interpretation of what he calls "sexual connotations," see Nogalski (1993b: 119–20; cf. Genesis 29:31; 30:22; Song of Solomon 5:5).

It should be noted that the pivot pattern is frequently found in Hebrew poetry and is sometimes difficult to render in English translation. Floyd (2000: 74) reaches a similar conclusion about the translation of the word *ʿammēḵ* as "your people," but he interprets the meaning differently—"as a description of the extent to which the men of the city have been killed off (cf. 3:3), leaving a population that consists largely of noncombatant females (cf. Isa 3:25–4:1)." The NRSV, NIV, and JPS Tanakh all translate the word *ʿammēḵ* as "your troops," which is a correct interpretation in one sense. The word *ʿam* is used in that sense elsewhere (1 Samuel 11:11; 1 Kings 20:10), but generally such usage is in conjunction with other military terminology such as *ʿam haṣṣābāʾ* ("men of war") in Numbers 31:32 and *ʿam hammilḥāmāh* (also translated "men of war") in Joshua 8:1, 3, 11 and elsewhere). It is better, however, to retain the more general meaning of the word *ʿam* as "people" here and to realize that the prophet had in view the plight of the entire city of Nineveh—including the military personnel that made up the Assyrian army.

Hillers (1964: 66–68) notes that the use of language that calls the Assyrian military troops "women" has parallels as a treaty curse in the ancient Near East. In the Hittite Soldier's Oath (*ANET* 354) we read "Let them change his troops into women"; "may his warriors become women." An Assyrian treaty (*ANET* 533) uses similar language. The same sentiment appears elsewhere in the Bible in reference to the Egyptians (Isaiah 19:16) and to the Babylonians (Jeremiah 50:37; 51:30).

Presuppositions about the nature of Hebrew poetry cause some to emend the text unnecessarily. Thus some delete ʿammēk as a "misplaced correction" of ʿam in 3:12 (Marti 1903: 322; J. M. P. Smith 1911: 346–47; G. R. Driver 1938: 271). Elliger (1970) suggests removing the concluding three-word clause, "Fire devours your gate-bars," as a gloss. G. R. Driver's translation, "The women in thy midst are fallen to thine enemies," ignores the Masoretic accentual system.

*Wide open are the gates of your land; (for) fire has devoured your gate-bars.* In the second half of v 13, the words pāṯôaḥ nip̄tǝḥû ("They are wide open") introduce the more obvious concept of the gates of the land being open to the enemy because the wooden bars that seal the gates of the city from within (habbǝrîḥîm) have been destroyed by fire—presumably along with the city itself, within the context of the prophet's vision.

J. M. P. Smith (1911: 347) may be correct in interpreting šaʿărê ʾarṣēk ("the gates of your land") as referring to forts protecting the country's borders or to the outer defenses of Nineveh. Cathcart (1968: 513), however, prefers to interpret the phrase šaʿărê ʾarṣēk to mean "gates of your city," citing his own earlier study and the work of Dahood (1963: 297–98), van Dijk (1968: 53), and Tromp (1969: 31–33) and various comments on the part of Jerome to support his case that ʾereṣ can mean "city, metropolis." As Coggins notes (1985: 55): "It is possible to visualize something of the importance of the gates from the elaborate modern reconstructions of the Assyrian gates in the British Museum in London."

## COMMENT

The prophetic judgment of 3:8–13 makes it clear that Nineveh will experience the same fate meted out to Thebes, which is located on the Nile River 440 miles south of Memphis and 150 miles north of the first cataract at Aswan.

### Nahum and the Fall of Thebes

The destruction of Thebes (nō² ²āmôn) at the hands of Asshurbanipal in 663 BCE marked the zenith of Assyrian expansion and a high point in Assyrian brutality. After the defeat of the Egyptian army at Memphis in the delta of northern Egypt, the taking of Thebes itself was primarily a symbolic act marking "the pinnacle of Assyrian achievement in Egypt" (Grayson 1991: 144). The sack of Thebes cost Judah much as well; in his commemoration of this event, Ashurbanipal listed Manasseh ("king of Iaudi") among the twenty-two kings who had "brought their rich gifts before me and kissed my feet." Manasseh also contributed soldiers to the Assyrian forces (*ARAB*, 340–41).

Thebes, which was the illustrious capital of Egypt during much of her history, is situated on a large bend of the Nile where the river opens into a broad and fruitful valley. Some describe it as the world's first great monumental city. Achtemeier (1986: 25) says that Thebes was "the first great city of the Orient, and it remained one of the world's leading cities for over fourteen hundred years." Even today tour groups that include a visit to Luxor and Karnak and the ruins of ancient Thebes often find this the highlight of their entire journey. The vastness of the temple of Karnak, once experienced, is not forgotten. The greatness of this city was legendary in Nahum's time, as was her fall to Assyria. The point is clear. Even the greatest of kingdoms cannot survive in defiance of YHWH.

Ethiopia controlled Egypt at this time, in the Cushite Dynasty 25 (717–663 BCE), with its capital at Thebes. Though the Ethiopian ruler Piye conquered Tefnakht, the only official pharaoh in the ephemeral Saite Dynasty 24 (ca. 724–717 BCE), the descendants of Tefnakht in Sais (Memphis) established Dynasty 26 (ca. 663–525) in Egypt under Psammeticus I. It was Pharaoh Neco (who ruled 609–595 BCE), the son of Psammeticus I, who slew Josiah at Megiddo and installed Jeohiakim in place of Jehoahaz in Jerusalem (2 Kings 23:29–35). As I have shown elsewhere (Christensen 1989b: 147): "The 24th Dynasty in Egypt is like the reign of Odo, son of Robert the Strong, who delivered Paris from the Vikings and consequently became the first 'Capetian' king of France long before his brother's grandson, Hugh Capet, established France's illustrious dynasty that replaced the Carolingian line for good."

### The Menorah Pattern of the Two-Part Taunt Song against Nineveh in Nahum 3:1–13

Another way of exploring the concentric structure of 3:8–13 is to place it in a larger literary context, which combines the two taunt songs in a single menorah pattern as follows:

A    The sounds of war resound in the "bloody city" of Nineveh    3:1–2

B      There are hosts of slain—they stumble over their corpses    3:3

C        Because of her harlotries, YHWH will show nations her nakedness    3:4–5

X          **YHWH will make Nineveh a spectacle—with no comforters**    3:6–7

C′        Nineveh will be destroyed the same as Thebes in Egypt    3:8–9

B′    The people will be taken captive with carnage in the streets         3:10–11
A′    Nineveh's fortresses will fall as the gates of the land are opened wide   3:12–13

In terms of the 155 words in 3:1–13, the arithmological center falls on the word *mēʾayin* ("from whence") in 3:7b, with 77 words on either side.

The meaningful center is found by including 11 words on either side of the arithmological center:

| | |
|---|---|
| *wəhāyāh ḵol-rōʾayiḵ yiddôḏ mimmēḵ* | And everyone who sees you will flee from you |
| *wəʾāmar šāddəḏāh nînəwēh* | And he will say: "Nineveh is devastated; |
| *mî yānûḏ lāh* | Who will grieve for her?" |
| *mēʾayin ʾăḇaqqēš mənaḥămîm lāḵ* | Where can I seek comforters for you? |
| *hăṯêṭəḇî minnōʾ ʾāmôn* | Are you better than *No-Amon* (Thebes), |
| *hayyōšəḇāh bayʾōrîm* | The one who dwells on the Nile? |
| *mayim sāḇîḇ lāh* | Water is round about her. |

In this instance the content of the meaningful center focuses on the certainty of Nineveh's imminent demise. The Divine Warrior will make a spectacle of Nineveh for all to see, and there will be none to show compassion on that wicked city in the day of its destruction, says the man whose very name is "compassionated," for the term in all likelihood is a passive formation. Note the apparent pun on the prophet's name, *Nahum*, in the word of judgment he declares on Nineveh that there will be none to mourn—*mənaḥămîm*.

As numerous commentators have shown, Nahum was a master of metaphor. We have already examined his portrayal of Nineveh as a lion in its den deprived of its prey (2:11–14) and as a harlot shamed and exposed for all to see (3:1–7). Here in the third of four successive taunt songs and/or funeral dirges in Nahum we see Nineveh as dazed and passing out in a drink-induced stupor (v 11). That sorry image stands in stark contrast to the "daring comparison" to Thebes, the magnificent capital of Ethiopia and Egypt (Achtemeier 1986: 25). Even Thebes, in all her glory, went into captivity (v 10), so the prophet poses his telling rhetorical question: "Are you better than Thebes?" (v 8).

In one sense, the question itself is a bit ridiculous. An honest response on Assyria's part would be a resounding "Yes, of course we are!" After all, Assyria had conquered Thebes. But the point of the prophet's question was not to compare the relative strength of these two world powers but rather to announce the simple fact that political power means nothing at all in relation to the power of Yhwh (cf. 1:6). The taunt song about Nineveh and Thebes is an argument against trusting in false security. And that argument applies to any great nation, in the present as well as in the distant past.

The city of Nineveh placed her trust in her fortifications and in her defense system of moats and rivers, much the same as Thebes did in a comparable setting: "Water is round about her; whose outer-wall is the sea, having from the sea her ramparts" (v 8). These words were written to describe Thebes with her moats and canals and the Nile River, but they applied just as well to the systems of defense in Nineveh beside the Tigris River in what is today the country of Iraq.

Nineveh put her trust in a system of outlying fortifications, but these fortresses were described by the prophet as "first-ripe figs" ready to "fall into the mouth of the eater" as soon as the fig tree itself was shaken (v 12). And so it was as the destruction of Nineveh itself unfolded before the combined forces of the Medes and the Babylonians. In time of war, Nineveh's mighty warriors became like weak women, vulnerable to violation by wanton soldiers and to ultimate destruction (v 13).

### Nahum and the Cup of YHWH's Wrath

The image of Nineveh as inebriated and passing out in a drink-induced stupor (v 11) suggests a familiar image in the prophetic literature of ancient Israel, namely the figure of the cup of YHWH's wrath. Though the prophet Jeremiah subsequently expanded this image at length in reference to Babylon (see Jeremiah 25), the image itself apparently had its origin in reference to Nineveh. As Hay put it (1960: 75): "The drinking of the cup symbolizes the judgment of the nations, a judgment that is articulated in the oracles (against foreign nations)," of which Nahum is a prime example.

Cross (personal communication) suggests that the cup of wrath motif may ultimately be traced back to some ancient rite in which the cup contained blood rather than wine (see Christensen 1975a: 199). He finds a possible reflex of this rite in the Ugaritic literature where the warrior goddess ʿAnat drinks blood without a cup in a gory battle scene (cf. *UT*, ʿnt:II:6–35). The obvious parallel to the cup of wine or blood in the Eucharist of Christian tradition is suggestive. Within the context of YHWH's "Holy War" the cup of wine or blood was apparently a victory cup used in celebration. Its original cultic-ideological connection appears to be preserved in Psalm 116:13, which reads:

I will lift up the cup of salvation and call on the name of YHWH;
I will pay my vows to YHWH in the presence of all his people.

In a typical reversal of imagery, the cup of victory becomes a cup of wrath or poison that the nations are forced to drink to their destruction.

The cup of YHWH's wrath, as subsequently used by Jeremiah (cf. 49:12–13; 51:7), appears to be secondary to the more basic image of the "sword of YHWH's wrath" (see Christensen 1975a: 201). In Jeremiah 25:16 it is said that the nations will "stagger and be crazed," not because of the cup of wine but "because of the sword," which Yhwh is sending among them. The most important text for reconstructing the history of the motif of the cup of Yhwh's wrath is found in Isaiah 51:17–23. Cross (1966: 28–30; 1969: 157–65) discusses the larger context of this poem, which combines notions of cosmic warfare with the theme of ritual conquest and a royal processional to Zion within the protoapocalyptic thought of Second Isaiah.

Here in Nahum we find a precursor to the motif of the cup of Yhwh's wrath proffered to the nations, and to Babylon in particular. The prophet-poet envisions Nineveh as someone in a drunken state in 1:10, where we find a mixed metaphor that combines the image of judgment by fire with that of inebriation. Here in 3:11 that image appears once again in the context of judgment by fire (3:13) and that of judgment by fire and sword (3:15). In her drunken state Nineveh will be destroyed. The gates of the city will be flung wide open to her enemies (3:13; cf. 2:6 [5]).

Nineveh will stagger about as one who is drunk, for as the prophet Jeremiah put it on another occasion (Jeremiah 25:17, 27–29, as preserved in the LXX):

> So I took the cup from Yhwh's hand
>     and I made all the nations to whom Yhwh sent me drink it.
> "Drink, be drunk and vomit! Fall and rise no more!
>     because of the sword which I am sending among you."
> And if they refuse to take the cup from your hand to drink,
>     then you shall say—thus spoke Yhwh: "You must drink!
> For look! I begin to work evil at the city which is called by my own name;
>     and shall you go unpunished?
> You shall not go unpunished,
>     for I am sending a sword against the inhabitants of the earth."

It should be noted that no specific nations are mentioned here. The agent of Yhwh's wrath is "a sword" (vv 16, 29), which Yhwh has summoned. The imagery is that of Yhwh's "Holy War," and the agent of Yhwh's destruction is unimportant to the prophet; for this is Yhwh's battle.

There is no place to hide, for there is no escape from the cup of Yhwh's wrath—unless he transforms that cup into the cup of blessing so as to become a cup of joy. This is the "new wine" of the Gospels (cf. John 2:1–11; Mark 2:22). Nahum has already made it clear that Yhwh will by no means acquit those who are guilty (1:3). But Nahum has also already called attention to the fact that this "avenging God" is at the same time "slow to anger" (1:3) and "a stronghold in the day of distress" (1:7). And he himself gives this cup of wrath to his Son in our place (Mark 10:38; 14:36; and elsewhere) and offers to us his "cup of blessing" (1 Corinthians 11:25), which is the cup of the renewed covenant, by which that very cup is once again filled with "blood" as a symbol of divine victory in Yhwh's "Holy War" (cf. Mark 14:24). As Achtemeier (1986: 27) puts it with keen insight: "Surely the message of Nahum helps us see anew the mercy in that cup."

**Nahum and the Particle *Gam***

The particle *gam* appears four times in Nahum as a structural frame around the center of the sixth canto (3:8–13), which has its focus on the nobles and grandees of Nineveh going into exile and her children being dashed to pieces in the streets of the city, as had also been the case earlier in Thebes. The emphasizing particle *gam* appears twice in v 10 in reference to Thebes and twice again in v 11 in reference to Nineveh.

The word *gam* has been the focus of scholarly attention through the years. Jacob (1912: 281) thought the particle *gam* emphasizes constructions that are already emphatic (see van der Merwe 1990: 9). Labuschagne (1966) also focused attention on the interpretation of *gam* as an emphasizing particle. Muraoka (1969, 1985) subsequently argued that a number of Labuschagne's examples also include an additive function. Van der Merwe (1990: 184) sees *gam* as a connector with a "focusing" function whereby "different types of connections are possible." He reaches this conclusion: "If the different functions are compared, it becomes clear that with regard to the sentence in which it occurs, *gam primarily marks for focus the referent of the element(s) that are within its syntactic domain. In other words, gam may be construed as an inducer of bound focus*" (1990: 185; emphasis his). So *gam* appears only where the element to be marked for focus is connected with some other element in the specific context.

In 3:10 we find with regard to Thebes a reference to the destruction of her young children, then a casting of lots. In 3:11 we find with regard to Nineveh a reference to passing out (in a drink-induced stupor) and to seeking refuge from an enemy, followed by a shaking of figs (v 12). It may be that the aleatory shaking of a two-sided counter (casting lots) in v 10 corresponds in some way to the shaking of figs in v 12.

According to the Talmud (B. Sanhedrin 108b–109a; Y. Peah 8: 9, 21b; B. Hagigah 5b), one of Rabbi Akiba's teachers was a sage by the name of Nahum Ish Gamzo. One wonders if there is a direct connection between this man's given name and the curious fourfold usage of the word *gam* in Nahum 3:10–11. In the Talmudic story, the name *Nahum* is related to the idea of divine comfort (*neḥāmāh*). The reason he is called *Ish Gamzo* is that he is the man (*ish*) who always says: "This, too (*gam zo*), is for the good," taking a positive attitude about misfortune. In the book of Nahum we move from a

reference to **gam hî** ("so it was with her" [Thebes]) to a reference to **gam ʾat**
("so also you" [Nineveh]). The reference in both instances is to unspeakable
human suffering in time of war, which was understood at the same time to be
a message of comfort to Judah (cf. Nahum 2:2–3 [1–2]). In the Talmudic
story, the expression **gam zô ləṭôbāh** ("This too is for the good") becomes a
moral lesson that has attracted and repelled readers through the centuries.
The exaggerated suffering on the part of both Nahum Ish Gamzo and Rabbi
Akiba suggests that exceptional individuals are able to bear more suffering
than the rest of us.

Rabbi Robert Scheinberg explains why he never liked these stories—until
he learned a powerful lesson that gave him a new way to understand Nahum's
words (see his Yom Kippur message at http://hobokensynagogue.org/YK-1999
.pdf). He tells a story worth reflection, one from the work of Dr. Rachel
Remen, a physician who has written extensively on the experiences of people
facing life-threatening illnesses. According to Scheinberg she said:

I once worked with a young man with osteogenic sarcoma of the right leg.
He had been a high school and college athlete until the time of his diagnosis and his life had been good. Beautiful women, fast cars, personal
recognition. Two weeks after his diagnosis, they had removed his right leg
above the knee. This surgery, which saved his life, also ended his life. Playing football was a thing of the past.

He refused to return to school, he began to drink heavily, to use drugs,
and to have one automobile accident after another. He was a powerfully built
and handsome young man, profoundly self-oriented and isolated, filled
with a sense of injustice and self-pity. In our second meeting, I gave him a
drawing pad and asked him to draw a picture of his body. He drew a crude
sketch of a vase, just an outline. Running through the center of it he drew
a deep crack. He went over and over the crack with a black crayon, gritting
his teeth and ripping the paper, tears of rage in his eyes. After he left, I
folded the picture up and saved it. It seemed too important to throw away.

Over the next months, he would bring in clippings from our local news-
paper about young people who had survived accidents or who had severe
medical difficulties: his reactions were always the same—a harsh judgment
of the well-meaning efforts of doctors and parents. He was still enraged, but
underneath this anger a concern for others was growing. Later, he asked me
if I thought he could visit young people in the surgical wards of a local hospital. He came back from these visits full of stories, delighted to find that he
could reach young people. He was often able to be of help when no one
else could.

Once he visited a young woman with breast cancer, at age 21, who had
just had both of her breasts removed surgically. He visited her on a hot mid-

summer day, wearing shorts, his artificial leg in full view. Deeply depressed, she lay in bed with her eyes closed, refusing to look at him. He tried everything he knew to reach her, but without success. He said things to her that only another person with an altered body would dare to say. He made jokes. He even got angry. She did not respond. All the while, a radio was softly playing rock music.

Frustrated, he finally stood, and in a last effort to get her attention, he unstrapped the harness of his artificial leg and let it drop to the floor with a loud thump. Startled, she opened her eyes and saw him for the first time. Encouraged, he began to hop around the room snapping his fingers in time to the music and laughing out loud.

After a moment, she burst out laughing: "Well, if you can dance, maybe I can sing!"

This young woman became his friend and began to visit people in the hospital with him. She encouraged him to return to college to study psychology. Eventually she became his wife, a very different sort of person from the models and cheerleaders he had dated in the past.

But long before this, we ended our sessions together. In our final meeting, I opened his chart and found the picture of the broken vase he had drawn two years before. Unfolding it, I asked him if he remembered the drawing he had made of his body. He took it in his hands and looked at it for some time. "You know," he said, "it's really not finished." Taking a yellow crayon, he began to draw thick, yellow lines radiating from the crack in the vase to the very edge of the paper. I watched, puzzled. He was smiling.

Finally, he put his finger on the crack, looked at me, and said softly: "This is where the light comes through."

*Gam zô lǝṭôḇāh* ("This too is for the good")!

# VIII. THE LOCUST DIRGE: AN IMAGE OF IMMINENT RUIN (3:14–19)

| | Morae | SAS units | Words count | | |
|---|---|---|---|---|---|
| **A. Prepare for the Siege—Strengthen Your Defenses (3:14)** | | | | | [4.4] |
| [3:14] Water for the siege / draw for yourselves / | 12 | 2 | 4 | 4 | 0 |
| strengthen / your defenses // | 10 | 2 | 2 | 2 | 0 |
| 3:11–14b | | | 40 | 26 | 14 |
| Go into the mud / and tread the clay / | 15 | 2 | 4 | 0 | 4 |
| make strong /[a] the brick-mold // | 9 | 2 | 2 | 0 | 2 |
| 3:11–14 | | | 46 | 26 | 20 |
| **B. Fire and Sword Will Devour You Like the Locust (3:15a–c)** | | | | | [2.2] |
| [3:15] There[b] the fire will devour you / | 9 | 1 | 3 | 3 | 0 |
| 3:12–15a | | | 38 | 23 | 15 |
| The sword will cut you off / | 7 | 1 | 2 | 2 | 0 |
| 3:14–15b | | | 17 | 11 | 6 |
| It will devour you / like the young locust // | 9 | 2 | 2 | 2 | 0 |
| 3:11–15c | | | 52 | 32 | 20 |
| **C. Your Merchants Have Multiplied Like Locusts That Fly Away (3:15d–16)** | | | | | [4.4] |
| Become heavier (m. sg.) like the young locust / | 7 | 1 | 2 | 0 | 2 |
| become heavier (f. sg.)[c] like the winged-locust // | 9 | 1 | 2 | 0 | 2 |
| 3:14–15 | | | 23 | 13 | 10 |

| | Morae | SAS units | Words count | | |
|---|---|---|---|---|---|
| 3:16 You have increased / your merchants / | 8  2 | 2 | 2 | 2 | 0 |
| *3:11–16a* | 58 | 34 | 24 | | |
| (They are) more than the stars / of the heavens // | 12  2 | 2 | 2 | 2 | 0 |
| a young locust sheds its outer skin / and flies away // | 10  2 | 3 | 0 | 3 | |
| *3:14–16b* | 30 | 17 | 13 | | |

**D. Your Palace Officials Are Like Locusts That Fly Away in the Heat (3:17)**   [4.2.4]

| | Morae | SAS units | Words count | | |
|---|---|---|---|---|---|
| 3:17 Your magicians / are like winged locusts / | 10  2 | 2 | 2 | 2 | 0 |
| your astrologers / are like swarming locusts // | 12  2 | 3 | 3 | 0 | |
| *3:15–17b* | 23 | 16 | 7 | | |
| They settle in the walls / on a cold day / | 18  2 | 4 | 0 | 4 | |
| *3:14–17c* | 39 | 22 | 17 | | |
| The sun shines forth / and they fly away / | 11  2 | 3 | 0 | 3 | |
| and their place is not known / where are they? // | 13  2 | 4 | 0 | 4 | |
| *3:16–17* | 23 | 9 | 14 | | |

**E. Your Shepherds Are Asleep and Your People Scattered (3:18)**   [4.4]

| | Morae | SAS units | Words count | | |
|---|---|---|---|---|---|
| 3:18 [d]Your shepherds are asleep / O king of Assyria / | 14  2 | 4 | 4 | 0 | |
| *3:14–18b* | 50 | 26 | 24 | | |
| [d]Your nobles / slumber // | 10  2 | 2 | 2 | 0 | |
| *3:14–18b* | 52 | 28 | 24 | | |
| [d]Your people are scattered / upon the mountains / | 16  2 | 4 | 0 | 4 | |
| *3:17–18c* | 26 | 11 | 15 | | |
| [d]And there is none /[e] to gather them // | 7  2 | 2 | 0 | 2 | |
| *3:17–18* | 28 | 11 | 17 | | |

**F. There Is No Healing to Your Wound (3:19ab)**   [2.2]

| | Morae | SAS units | Words count | | |
|---|---|---|---|---|---|
| 3:19 There is no assuaging /[f] your hurt / | 10  2 | 3 | 3 | 0 | |
| | 31 | 14 | 17 | | |
| It is grievous / your wound // | 8  2 | 2 | 2 | 0 | |
| *3:18–19a* | 17 | 11 | 6 | | |

**G. Your Demise Brings Joy, for Who Has Not Experienced Your Evil? (3:19c–f)**   [4.4]

| | Morae | SAS units | Words count | | |
|---|---|---|---|---|---|
| All / who hear the news of you / | 10  2 | 3 | 0 | 3 | |
| they clap their hands / over you / | 11  2 | 3 | 0 | 3 | |
| *3:18–19d* | 23 | 11 | 12 | | |

|  | Morae | SAS units | Words count |  |  |
|---|---|---|---|---|---|
| For / upon whom / | 5 | 2 | 3 | 0 | 3 |
| has not come your evil / unceasingly? // | 16 | 2 | 4 | 0 | 4 |
| 3:14–19 |  |  | 76 | 33 | 43 |
| 1:1–3:19 | 559 |  | 299 | 260 |  |

## Scansion of the Locust Dirge in 3:14–19

|  | Morae | SAS units | Words count |
|---|---|---|---|
| 3:14 *mî māṣôr / šaʾăbî-lā́k /* | 12 | 2 | 4 = 4 + 0 |
| *ḥazzəqî / mibṣāráyik ^* | 10 | 2 | 2 = 2 + 0 |
| *bóʾî baṭṭîṭ / wərimsî bahómer /* | 15 | 2 | 4 = 0 + 4 |
| *hahăzîqî /ᵃ malbén :* | 9 | 2 | 2 = 0 + 2 |
| 3:15 *šămᵇ tōʾkəlḗk ʾḗš /* | 9 | 1 | 3 = 3 + 0 |
| *takrîtḗk ḥéreb /* | 7 | 1 | 2 = 2 + 0 |
| *tōʾkəlḗk / kayyáleq ^* | 9 | 2 | 2 = 2 + 0 |
| *hitkabbēd kayéleq /* | 7 | 1 | 2 = 0 + 2 |
| *hitkabbədîᶜ kāʾarbéh :* | 9 | 1 | 2 = 0 + 2 |
| 3:16 *hirbêt / rōkəláyik /* | 8 | 2 | 2 = 2 + 0 |
| *mikkôkəbê ḷ haššāmáyim ^* | 12 | 2 | 2 = 2 + 0 |
| *yéleq pāšaṭ / wayyāᶜṓp :* | 10 | 2 | 3 = 0 + 3 |
| 3:17 *minnəzāráyik / kāʾarbéh /* | 10 | 2 | 2 = 2 + 0 |
| *wəṭapsəráyik / kəḡôb gōbáy ^* | 12 | 2 | 3 = 3 + 0 |
| *hahônîm baggədērôt / bəyôm qārā́h /* | 18 | 2 | 4 = 0 + 4 |
| *šemeš zārəhā́h / wənôdád /* | 11 | 2 | 3 = 0 + 3 |
| *wəlōʾ-nôdáᶜ məqômô / ʾayyā́m :* | 13 | 2 | 4 = 0 + 4 |
| 3:18 *nāmû rōᶜêka / mélek ʾaššûr /* | 13 | 2 | 4 = 4 + 0 |
| *yiškənû / ʾaddîrêka ^* | 10 | 2 | 2 = 2 + 0 |
| *nāpšû ᶜamməká /ᶜal-hehārîm /* | 16 | 2 | 4 = 0 + 4 |
| *wəʾên /ᶜ məkabbḗs :* | 7 | 2 | 2 = 0 + 2 |
| 3:19 *ʾên-kēhâh /ᶠ ləšibréka /* | 10 | 2 | 3 = 3 + 0 |
| *naḥlâh / makkātéka ^* | 8 | 2 | 2 = 2 + 0 |
| *kṓl / šōmə́ᶜê šimᶜăká /* | 10 | 2 | 3 = 0 + 3 |
| *tāqəᶜû kắp / ᶜālệka /* | 11 | 2 | 3 = 0 + 3 |
| *kî / ᶜal-mî /* | 5 | 2 | 3 = 0 + 3 |
| *lōʾ-ᶜābərā́h rāᶜātəká / tāmî́d :* | 15 | 2 | 4 = 0 + 4 |
| 3:14–19 |  |  | 76 = 33 + 43 |

## NOTES

<sup>a</sup> Reading *mêrəkâ* on the word *hahăzîqî* ("strengthen") in 3:14d, preceded immediately by *ga'yâ* (= *meteḡ*) in Letteris (1880) and Ginsburg (1894), as disjunctive. The BHS omits *ga'yâ* (= *meteḡ*).

<sup>b</sup> Reading the *yəṭîḇ* on the word *šām* ("there") in 3:15a as conjunctive.

<sup>c</sup> Reading the *ṭip̄ḥâ* on the word *hiṯkabbəḏî* ("multiply") in 3:15b as conjunctive.

<sup>d</sup> These letters indicate that the word *Nineveh* is spelled out with the initial Hebrew letters of four successive half-lines.

<sup>e</sup> Reading the *mêrəkâ* on the word *wə'ên* ("and there is none") in 3:18b as disjunctive.

<sup>f</sup> Reading the *mûnaḥ* on the word *kēhāh* ("[there is no] assuaging") in 3:19a as disjunctive.

SAS units:

$$(4 + 4) + (2 + 2) + (4 + 4) + \boxed{4 + 2 + 4} + (4 + 4) + (2 + 2) + (4 + 4)$$
$$(8 + 4 + 8) + \boxed{10} + (8 + 4 + 8)$$
$$= 20 + 10 + 20 = 50 \text{ SAS units}$$

Meaningful center: eight words on either side of the arithmological center:

| | |
|---|---|
| *minnəzārayiḵ kā'arbeh* | Your magicians are like grasshoppers; |
| *wəṭap̄sərayiḵ kəḡôḇ gôḇāy* | Your astrologers are like locusts upon locusts, |
| *hahônîm baggəḏērôt* \boxed{*bəyôm qārāh*} | That settle in the walls \boxed{on a cold day}. |
| *šemeš zārəḥāh wənôḏaḏ* | The sun shines forth and they fly away; |
| *wəlō' nôḏa' məqômô 'ayyām* | And their place is not known, where are they? |

Strophic units in 3:14–19 as shown by the balance in mora count:

| | | | | | | |
|---|---|---|---|---|---|---|
| A | 3:14 | 2 balanced dyads | [12 + 10] + [15 + 9] | = | 22 + 24 | morae |
| B | 3:15a–c | balanced triad | [9 + 7 + 9] | = | 9 + 7 + 9 | morae |
| C | 3:15d–16 | 2 balanced dyads | [8 + 10] + [8 + 12] | = | 18 + 20 | morae |
| D | 3:17 | 2 balanced dyads | [10 + 10] + 10 | = | 20 + 10 | morae |
| | | + pivot | + [11 + 7] | | + 18 | |
| | | balanced dyad | [11 + 13] | = | 11 + 13 | morae |
| E | 3:18 | 2 balanced dyads | [14 + 10] + [16 + 7] | = | 24 + 23 | morae |
| F | 3:19ab | balanced dyad | [10 + 8] | = | 10 + 8 | morae |
| G | 3:19c–f | 2 balanced dyads | [10 + 11] + [5 + 15] | = | 21 + 20 | morae |

Word count:

| | | |
|---|---|---|
| 3:11–14 | **46** | (= **23** × 2) words and **26** words before *'aṯnaḥ* |
| 3:14–15 | **23** | words |

| 3:14–16 | 17 | words before ʾaṭnaḥ |
|---|---|---|
| 3:16–17 | 23 | words |
| 3:17–18 | 17 | words after ʾaṭnaḥ |
| 3:18–19b | 17 | words |
| 3:17–19 | 46 | (= 23 × 2) words |

## INTRODUCTION

The seven strophes in the seventh canto (3:14–19) may be outlined in a menorah pattern that is determined primarily on prosodic grounds, as follows:

### Canto 7: The Locust Dirge: An Image of Imminent Ruin (3:14–19)

| A | Prepare for the siege—strengthen your defenses! | [4.4] | 3:14 |
|---|---|---|---|
| B | Fire will devour you and the sword will cut you off | [2.2] | 3:15a–c |
| C | It will devour you like a plague of locusts | [4.4] | 3:15d–16 |
| X | **Your palace officials fly away in the heat like locusts** | [4.2.4] | 3:17 |
| C′ | Your shepherds are asleep and the people scattered | [4.4] | 3:18 |
| B′ | Your wound is incurable | [2.2] | 3:19ab |
| A′ | All rejoice at your fall; for on whom has not come your evil? | [4.4] | 3:19c–f |

In terms of the distribution of SAS units in 3:14–19, the seven strophes are arranged in perfect symmetry with vv 16c–17 in the center:

$$[4 + 4] + [2 + 2] + [4 + 4] + \boxed{4 + 2 + 4} + [4 + 4] + [2 + 2] + [4 + 4]$$

Bliese (1995: 68–71) divides 3:14–19 into two parts: a ten-line "metrical chiasm" in 3:14–17 and a "homogeneous poem" with the "final five pentameters" in vv 18–19. When this methodology is applied to 3:14–19 as a whole, based on the distribution of word stresses (that is, counting accents), no such symmetry is found. Instead we have the following:

$$\underset{11}{[5 + 6]} + \underset{15}{[(3 + 2 + 2) + (4 + 4)]} + \underset{18}{\boxed{3 + 5 + 4 + 6}} + \underset{15}{[(6 + 5) + (2 + 2)]} + \underset{11}{[6 + 5]}$$

## NOTES

3:14. *Water for the siege draw for yourselves; strengthen your defenses.* Though Nineveh's fate is sealed, she is ironically bidden to make every preparation possible for a long siege. *Water for the siege* refers to drinking water, which was the primary necessity for survival in siege warfare (Schmoldt 2004b: 230). Lambdin (1953: 368) studied the root *šʾb* in conjunction with its appearance in the Amarna letters in the term *šu-i-ib-da*, which represents the Egyptian *šwbty*. He saw the word as originally Canaanite (as had Albright 1936a: 30, n. 49).

*Go into the mud and tread the clay; make strong the brick-mold.* The act of going to the "mud" implies treading it into clay. The word *ṭîṭ* ("mud") also appears in Isaiah 41:25, where it refers to potter's clay. Some scholars emend the text to read *bûs* ("trample underfoot") in place of *bôʾ* ("go"), as in Zechariah 10:5. While this change provides closer parallelism to the verbal root *rms* ("to tread [the clay]"), the parallel text in Isaiah 41:25 provides a clear example of the verbal roots *bwʾ* ("to go") and *rms* ("to tread") in poetic parallelism. The exact meaning of the word *malbēn* remains uncertain, though there is consensus that it has something to do with making bricks. It seems best at this point to translate it "brick mold," along with Longman (1993: 821) and Spronk (1997: 135). Longman argues that the *mem* prefix denotes place and points to Jeremiah 43:9, which includes a useful parallel statement that he translates as "strengthen the brick terrace" (1993: 823). For an example of the sort of brick-making envisioned in Nahum 3:14, see the Egyptian representation in *ANEP*, plate 115.

3:15. *There the fire will devour you; the sword will cut you off.* The word *šām* ("there") connects this verse with the portrayal of the siege of Nineveh in the previous verse—that is, the place that was fortified with such care. As a locative adverb, it refers to either the clay pit or the fortifications of the city on which the people were working. The word *šām* ("there") also appears in 2:12 [11], where it denotes the lions' den, which the sword "devours" in 2:14 [13]. Cathcart (1973a: 143) interprets *šām* to mean "behold," seeing it as equivalent to El Amarna *šumma*, "behold" (see Moran 1953: 78–80; Dahood 1957: 306–9; cf. Psalm 139:8). W. A. Maier (1959: 344) interpreted *šām* as an adverb of time, "then." The verb *tōʾkəlēk* ("it will devour you"), which appears twice in the first half of v 15, includes both fire and sword as subject. The sword is personified elsewhere and portrayed as consuming or devouring a defeated enemy (Deuteronomy 32:42; 2 Samuel 2:26; 11:25; 18:8; Hosea 11:6; Jeremiah 2:30; 12:12). This key word was introduced in Nahum 1:10, where it lacks a clear subject. It appears again in 2:14 [13] in the image of the "devouring sword." Here in 3:15 that sword cuts off the enemy, devouring them like the locust—"completely," as indicated in the acrostic of 1:9–10. The subject is neither the sword nor fire, as such, but the combination of the two.

*It will devour you like the young locust.* The word *kayyāleq* ("like the locust") is the nominative, not the accusative as some have taken it (Calvin 1559; Ewald 1878: 13; and Hitzig 1881: 262). The locusts are not devoured by the fire or the sword; it is they that devour like the sword and the fire. Keil (1949: 38) described the curious shift here in reference to the locusts as follows: "Fire and sword will devour Nineveh and its inhabitants like the all-consuming locusts, even though the city itself, with its mass of houses and people, should resemble an enormous swarm of locusts." The locust imagery is well known from Amos 7:1–3 and Joel 1–2, both of which present the image of locusts devouring the land of Israel. The locust plague is also the eighth of the ten plagues visited on Egypt in the story of the Exodus. Riedel emended *kyylq* to read *kylph* "battleaxe" (see G. A. Smith 1928: 111).

The different names for the locust in the Tanakh correspond to the different stages of its development from the larva to the mature insect (Joel 2:25; see Feliks 1962: 115; reference from Pinker 2003b: 560–61). According to Pinker (2003b: 561), the female locust deposits eggs in a hole dug in the earth, from which a dark wingless larva emerges and "licks up" the vegetation. Pinker is interpreting the verbal root *yālaq* to mean "he/it licks." The *yeleq* casts off its skin and becomes a *ḥāsîl* ("devourer") that grows very fast, ravaging vegetation. After casting off its skin a second time, it becomes a *nzm* ("lop off") with rudimentary wings but is not yet able to fly. At this stage, the insect gnaws at small tree branches, "lopping them off." The insect casts off its skin two more times as it becomes a full-grown and winged locust (*Schistocerca gregaria*), which is called *ʾarbeh* ("multitudinous"). Nahum calls the "swarms of locusts" *gōbāy* (see 3:17).

Nahum 3:15 functions as a summary describing the coming fate of Nineveh," as Spronk (1997: 136) argues; but his decision to ignore the *ʾatnaḥ*, which he mistakenly refers to as *revia*, is misinformed. The verse is a strophic unit as it stands in the MT, which may also be scanned in a pivot pattern:

| | | |
|---|---|---|
| There the fire will devour you; | 9 | morae |
| the sword will cut you off. | 7 | morae |
| *It will devour you like the young locust!* | 9 | morae |
| *It will devour you like the young locust!* | 9 | morae |
| Increase in substance (m. sg.) like the young locust! | 7 | morae |
| Increase in substance (f. sg.) like the swarming locust! | 9 | morae |

This curious combination of two short strophes, which may also be scanned as a single prosodic unit—[(9 + 7) + 9 + ( 7 + 9)] = 16 + 9 + 16 morae— brings us back to the opening canto in 1:1–10, where the "fire" of Yhwh's wrath is introduced in 1:6 and spelled out in detail in the "bent" acrostic cipher and finds its conclusion in 2:11 [10]. Yhwh's "fire" will devour Nineveh "completely" (*mālēʾ*), no matter how noncombustible she appears to be (cf. 1:10). The boughs are being gathered as fuel for burning (2:11 [10]), and the conflagration will mean total destruction, as emphasized in the acrostic on the word *mālēʾ* ("completely") in 1:9–10. What better image to choose to emphasize this point than that of a locust plague? As Spronk (1997: 137) puts it, the point is "that the burning fire resembles swarms of locusts completely ruining the crops." The example he cites from one of the curses of Esarhaddon's vassal treaties is apropos: "May the gods let locusts, lice, caterpillars, and 'devourers' eat up your cities, your land, and your districts" (*ANET* 540; reference and translation those of Spronk).

*Become heavier* (m. sg.) *like the young locust; become heavier* (f. sg) *like the swarming locust.* The word *hiṯkabbēḏ* was read as imperative by Keil (1949: 38; cf. also Cathcart 1973a:144), who explained the 2nd pers. m. sg. form *hiṯkabbēḏ* ("show yourself heavy by virtue of the multitude") as referring to the people of Nineveh, whereas in the 2nd pers. f. sg. form, *hiṯkabbəḏî*, the prophet was thinking of the city as such. It is also possible to read the word *hiṯkabbēḏ* as an inf. abs. used as a noun: "becoming heavier as locusts (in the larval stage)." It would then function here as an adverbial accusative (GKC §118n; cf. §113y, bb; §145o). The *yod* at the end of the word *hiṯkabbəḏî* could also be explained as *yod-compaginis* (GKC §90l). Compare the Ugaritic enclitic particle *-y*, which can also be used with verbal forms and is often used to give emphasis (see Tropper 1994: 473–82; Spronk 1997: 137). This explanation makes it possible to retain the MT without emendation by regarding "the second form as a deliberate variation of the same word in the parallel line" for purposes of emphasis (reference and quotation taken from Spronk 1997: 137). Tanhum thought the intended meaning was "Become stronger as the locust (i.e., 'increase your army')" (see Hirshler 1930: 69; reference from Pinker 2003b: 561; on Tanhum see Shy 1991).

Kselman (1979: 110–14) argues that the words *rb* ‖ *kbd* in Hebrew, and their Akkadian equivalents *kabtu* ‖ *rabû*, form a word pair. As Pinker notes (2003b: 561), it is possible that this association was at play in understanding *hiṯkabbēḏ* as "multiply" (cf. Jeremiah 30:19; Nahum 3:3, 15–16; Habakkuk 2:6). Though many scholars interpret *htkbd* to mean "multiply, grow in number," this is not likely if the *yeleq* represents the locusts at the larval stage in their life cycle, when they cannot multiply by reproducing. The MT has several words for "locusts" or "grasshoppers" (here *yeleq* and *ʾarbeh*), referring to the different stages of growth. According to Sellers (1935–36: 82–83), the word *yeleq* ("young locust") is the general term for locusts (cf. J. A. Thompson 1974: 405–11; Riede 1993: 353–56; see also Allen 1976: 49). The comparison of Nineveh with a swarm of locusts is carried further in the imagery of the next two verses.

According to Pinker (2003b: 559), Rashi (d. 1105) and Kimchi (d. 1235) understood the meaning as "sweep (as with a broom)," but he notes that such a "clean-up" meaning in reference to the destructive activity of locusts is rather late (see Tractate Niddah 56ᵃ). J. Hirshler (1930: 69) translated *htkbd* as "gather"

Difficulty in interpreting v 15 has led to a number of proposed emendations. Many scholars delete the words *tōʾḵəlēḵ kayyāleq* ("it will devour you like grasshoppers") as a gloss (cf. *BHS* note; Wellhausen 1898: 164; Ruben

1899: 459; J. M. P. Smith 1911: 358; Nogalski 1993b: 124–25). At one point, Spronk (1993b: 185) advocated the deletion of the last four words in 3:15. Pinker (2003b: 559) removes the words *kayyeleq hitkabbədî* as a gloss, which is not necessary. Others change the first occurrence of *kayyāleq* to read *kêla-pāh*, "battle-ax" (cf. Psalm 74:6; Nowack 1922; Bévenot 1937). Richter (1914: 136–37) deleted the first occurrence of *kayyāleq* and read the second occurrence of *tōʾkəlēk* as *tēlēk*, "you will disappear," which he relocates.

3:16. *You have increased your merchants; (they are) more than the stars of the heavens.* There is no compelling reason to emend *hirbêt* ("you have increased") to read the imperative form *harbî* with G. R. Driver (1938: 271) and Elliger (1970). Cathcart (1973: 145) parses *hirbêt* as a precative perfect so as to interpret the text in an imperative sense without emendation. It is just as easy to read the text as it stands in the MT and not to interpret the text in an imperative sense at all, with Roberts (1991: 69) and Longman (1993: 824; as do the NRSV, NIV, and JPS Tanakh). Kselman's (1979: 111) attempt to connect vv 15b and 16a on the basis of a parallel word pair *rb* || *kbd* is dismissed by Spronk (1997: 138) because the argument is based on the parallel text in Jeremiah 30:19, where *kbd* has the meaning "to honor" rather than referring to an increase in number. Merchants were an important part of Assyrian culture, and their activity was often closely connected with military expansion, as shown in the following text by Sargon II: "I made the fearful lustre of Asshur, my lord, fell down [*sic*] the inhabitants of Egypt and Arabia. The mentioning of my name made their hearts pound and weakened their arms. I opened the sealed borders of Egypt, mixed the inhabitants of Assyria and Egypt and made them trade" (*TUAT*, I/4, 382; reference taken from Spronk 1997: 138). Usually vast numbers are compared to "the stars of heaven," but here they are spoken of as exceeding them.

*A young locust sheds its outer skin and flies away.* The NIV translation in v 16, "like locusts they strip the land," is rejected by Longman (1993: 824–25), who translates the verb *pāšaṭ* ("emerges, strips off") as "the locust emerges [from the cocoon] and flies away." The concept of a cocoon, however, is not appropriate. What is being stripped away is the outer layer of the locust itself in its larval stage. The verb *pāšaṭ* means "to take off (clothes from oneself)." This is the only place where the word is used of locusts. The meaning of the text itself is clear: when danger threatens the Assyrians, the military leaders are the first to take flight.

Keil (1949: 39) argued that the word *pāšaṭ* "never means anything else than to plunder, or to invade with plundering . . . and the meaning forced upon it by Credner, of the shedding of the wing-sheaths by locusts, is perfectly visionary, and has merely been invented by him for the purpose of establishing his false interpretation of the different names given to the locusts in Joel i.4." Keil concludes: "The *yeleq* is rather the innumerable army of the enemy, which plunders everything, and hurries away with its booty." Spronk (1997: 139) regards all twelve words in the lines relating to what he calls "the deviating locust imagery" in vv 16b–17a to be secondary additions to the text—"probably interpretative remarks originally written in the margin . . . (and) part of a first reinterpretation of the prophecy relating it to Babylon." His reasoning seems to be based primarily on prosodic grounds in that he finds here an unusually long strophe in which he is unable "to find a plausible arrangement in verses." There is no textual evidence whatsoever for his conclusion that these lines constitute a secondary gloss.

Logoprosodic analysis indicates that vv 15–17 constitute three strophes that deal with the image of the locust in differing ways. In v 15a–c the destruction caused by fire and sword is likened to the devastation of a locust plague. In vv 15d–16 the metaphor shifts to the vast number of insects in such a plague and the fact that they have the power of flight—the young locust sheds its outer skin and flies away. In the third strophe (v 17), which constitutes the center of the seventh canto, the metaphor shifts to another aspect of the life of the locust. On a cold day, these insects are in a suspended state of physical activity, but when the heat of the sun appears, they fly away. So, like them, the court officials are the first to forsake their king and to flee from the doomed city of Nineveh.

3:17. *Your palace magicians are like winged locusts; your astrologers are like the swarming locusts that settle in the walls on a cold day.* The exact meaning of the terms *minnəzārayik* and *ṭapsərayik,* translated here as "your magicians" and "your astrologers," is difficult to determine. Albright (1953: 4) related the term *minnəzārayik* to the verbal root *nzr* ("to vow") and translated it "religious votaries." Torczyner (1936: 7) rejected the association of *mnzryk* with the Akkadian *mansāru* or *maṣṣāru* ("guard") and emended the word *minnəzārayik* to read *manzāzayik,* which he interpreted as a cognate of the Akkadian *manzāzu,* "garrison, guardsman." Though some would connect the first of these two words with the word *maṣṣaru* ("guard") in Akkadian, Longman (1993: 825) also argues for its derivation from the Akkadian word *manzāzu* ("courtier"). Roberts (1991: 71) advances the same argument. The term *ṭipsār* ("officials") is also apparently derived from the Akkadian cognate *ṭupšarru* ("scribe"; Sumerian DUB.SAR), which specifies a class of Assyrian officials. According to de Vaux (1961: 251), the *ṭipsār* is the person in charge of conscription, a "recruiting officer." According to Machinist (1983: 736), the term designates military officials who recorded the names of recruits and the military activities of Assyrian kings. Because the term appears here in a military context, Cathcart (1973a: 147) accepts de Vaux's position, but this does not seem to fit the only other occurrence of this word in the Bible, in

A locust as part of a Hebrew seal inscription. From
Staples (1931: 50).

Jeremiah 51:27, according to Longman (1993: 826). More recently, Cathcart
(1992: 998) has adopted the interpretation of Parpola (1970–71, I:2), who
shows that the terms *manzāzayiḵ* and *ṭipsārayiḵ* appear together in Neo-
Assyrian sources, with the meaning "astrologer" for *ṭipsārayiḵ* and something
like "augurs, magicians, etc." for *manzāzayiḵ*. These positions represent palace
officials.

Spronk (1997: 140) calls attention to the fact that the Targum translates the
first clause in v 17 with "behold your plates gleam like the locust" (cf. Gordon
1983), which he interprets as referring to the "the scaled armour of the
Assyrian warriors." He finds the same idea in Revelation 9:7–10 in reference
to demonic locusts with "scales like iron breastplates."

Repetition in the words *kəgôḇ gōḇāy* ("like swarming locusts") suggested a
large number to Keil (1949: 40; cf. Amos 7:1); Haldar (1947: 75); and W. A.
Maier (1959: 355; cf. GKC §133i, l). This conclusion is certainly preferable
to the removal of one of the words as dittography, as has frequently been
done. The reduplicated form is present in the Dead Sea Scrolls manuscript

from Wadi Murabbaᶜat. A Hebrew seal inscription from the sixth or seventh century BCE published by Avigad (1966: 50–52) reads *lᶜzry w hgbh,* and underneath the inscription is a figure of a locust. Avigad offers two explanations for the form *hgbh* ("the locust"). Either it is an unknown variant of the biblical *gōbay,* with the last syllable contracted from the diphthong (*gōbeh* from *gōbay,* like *śādeh* from *śāday*) or it is the singular of the plural *gēbîm,* "locusts," found in Isaiah 33:4.

The word *hahônîm* is a Qal m. pl. participle from the root *ḥnh* ("to encamp, settle at"). Locusts symbolize the horde of Assyrian merchants and officials as they stay for a night, then are off and away when the sun comes forth. To find a safe place for the night, they "encamp" by the walls (Helfmeyer 1986: 18). The Ugaritic word *gdrt* ("fence, hedge") may be a cognate of Hebrew *gədērāh* ("wall"), with the plural *gədērôt.* If so, the term *baggədērôt* here may have the same meaning (see Pritchard 1959: 9–10 and the review of Pritchard's work by Michaud 1960: 103).

*On a cold day, the sun shines forth and they fly away; and their place is not known. Where are they?* Locusts are known to settle in clusters. Here they are benumbed by cold and seek shelter from it in walls made of loose stones and earth. The warm rays of the sun revive the torpid insects, which then fly away, leaving no trace of their presence. The phrase *bəyôm qārāh* ("on a cold day") also appears in Proverb 25:20. Because he has removed the immediate context as a scribal gloss, Spronk (1997: 140) finds here the image of "stars disappearing at dawn." The assonance between the words *nôdad* ("flee") and *nôdaᶜ* ("know") in the last poetic line of v 17 is not possible to render in translation.

Elliger (1970) proposes moving the *waw* from the beginning of the word *wəlōʾ* ("and not") so as to read the plural verbal form *wənôdədû* ("and they flee"), but the LXX supports the singular MT reading, and the subject is *gôb* ("swarm"), not individual locusts. Cathcart (1973a: 148) finds the 3rd pers. m. sg. suffix on *məqômô* ("its place") "mysterious" and suggests that perhaps it refers back to *gôb,* "swarm." W. A. Maier (1959: 356) noted that many scholars arbitrarily emend the text to read a plural suffix form *məqômām,* including: Nowack (1897: 257), Happel (1902), Guthe (1923: 71), Sellin (1930: 375), Horst (1938: 164), Ehrlich (1905: 298), and others. Roberts (1991: 72, n. 24), on the other hand, maintains: "The singular verb form *nôdad* and the singular suffix on *məqômô,* 'its place,' are both acceptable, since *gôb gōbāy,* 'a swarm of locusts,' is a collective." Haldar (1947: 75) interpreted the *-ô* as an example of a modified form of the archaic nominative ending *u.*

Many scholars have problems with the final word in v 17—*ʾayyām* ("Where are they? cf. Isaiah 19:12; GCK §100.o; DCH 1:202). Longman (1993: 826), along with others, attaches the word to v 18. Roberts (1991: 72) correctly reads the word at the end of 1:17 and argues: "The use of the interrogative particle here prevents one from interpreting 'its place' as a reference to the former place of the locust swarm; the particle is in no way redundant." The KJV, NRSV, NIV, NASB, and JPS Tanakh read the text as it stands at the end of v 17 in the MT, but with divergence of opinion on its meaning. Logoprosodic analysis supports the verse division of the MT as it stands and rules out division into two words—*ʾôy māh* (with the *BHS* note) or perhaps *ʾîyēh hēm* ("where are they?"). Longman (1993: 826) interprets the *ʾayyām* as a combination of the word *ʾê* ("where") with the enclitic particle *mem*. The best reading, however, remains that of a combination of the interrogative *ʾê* ("where") with a 3rd pers. m. pl. pronominal suffix. Keil (1949: 41) wrote: "These words depict in the most striking manner the complete annihilation of the army on which Nineveh relied." Attempts to emend the text so as to read *ʾêkāh* ("where?") or *ʾôy māh* ("woe, why . . .") are not convincing. Nogalski (1993b: 44) changes the text to read the adjective *ʾāyōm* ("dreadful") modifying *maqômô* ("its place"), but this represents a conjecture on his part.

3:18. *Your shepherds are asleep, O king of Assyria; your nobles slumber.* The shift from a 2nd pers. f. sg. to a 2nd pers. m. sg. suffix form is another instance of the phenomenon of enallage, which marks many of the strophic boundaries in the book of Nahum. The referent is now *melek ʾaššûr* ("the king of Assyria"), who is addressed directly here. The king is often called a shepherd in the literature of the ancient Near East (cf. Seibert 1969: 7–10; de Moor 1982: 36–45). Though the title as such is never given to the king in ancient Israel, the suggestion is present in the familiar story of David as both shepherd and king (cf. also 2 Samuel 5:2; 7:7; Psalm 78:71–72). Note that Cyrus is called the shepherd of YHWH in Isaiah 44:28. The "shepherds" here are the officers under the authority of the "king of Assyria," and the term *rōʿêkā* ("your shepherds") is in poetic parallelism with *ʾaddîrêkā* ("your nobles") and *ʿammakā* ("your people") (R. L. Smith 1984: 90).

The word *nāmû* ("they are asleep"), from the root *nwm* ("to slumber"), denotes here "the sleep of death" (Keil 1949: 41; see Theodor of Cyros [d. 457]; Strauss 1853; Goslinga 1923: 342; cf. *HALOT* 643; cf. also Psalm 13:4; Jeremiah 51:39, 57). Others understand it more literally in the sense that the shepherds fail in their duties by falling asleep (Rashi [d. 1105]; Kreenen 1808; Wellhausen 1898: 165; van Hoonacker 1908; Schmidt 1923: 174–75). Van der Woude (1978a) proposes emending *nmw* to read *nmy*, a word borrowed from Akkadian *namu/nawu* ("pasturage, residence") and translates the passage "Where are they, the residences of your shepherd?" Kraeling (1966: 241) labels the expression *melek ʾaššûr*, "O King of Assyria," as "metrically superfluous" and "glossatory." Cathcart (1973a: 148–49) counters with a prosodic analysis in which he finds "a vocative suspended between two cola" that scan 7/4/7 in syllable count and 3/2/3 in stress count. The prosodic situation, however, is more complex than Cathcart observes.

Cathcart (1973a: 149) emends *yiškənû* ("they will camp") so as to read *yāšənû* ("they are at rest"), along with others including Roberts (1991: 76), who argues that the Hebrew text behind the LXX apparently read *yāšənû* ("they will sleep") as well (as does Rudolph 1975: 183). Others propose emending the text to read *yiškəbû* ("they are lying down"; see Happel 1902 and Alonso Schökel 1980; reference from Spronk 1997: 142). Keil (1949: 41) found here a parallel reference to "the rest of death." Roberts's remark that the root *škn* is never used absolutely to refer to the slumber of death (contra W. A. Maier 1959: 360) cannot be sustained. Cathcart (1973: 149) points to Isaiah 26:19 and Psalm 94:17 to show that "*šākan* can have the notion of '(the body) reposing in death,' or even of 'being entombed.'" He says that in Isaiah 22:16 and Psalm 49:12, the word *miškan* refers to a resting-place of the dead, namely the "tomb" (see Dahood 1966 a: 298–99; 1968: 138; Tromp 1969: 32). In light of this, Longman (1993: 827) correctly rejects the proposed emendation (as do the KJV, NIV, ASV, and NASB). Spronk (1997: 142–43) suggests that the use of the root *škn* ("to stay") may be explained in light of Judges 5:17, where Asher is reproached for not taking part in the battle against Sisera: "Asher sat still at the coast of the sea, settling down (*yškwn*) by his landings" (cf. also Jeremiah 51:30 with regard to the officers of Babylon). In this sense, Assyria's nobles remain inactive (Barthélemy 1992: 822). Machinist (2000: 667) calls attention to the fact that the language used here in "the sleep of death" is a reversal of the language Isaiah applied earlier to the aggressive campaigning of the Assyrian army, without sleep or slumber (Isaiah 5:27; cf. Psalm 121:4).

Spronk (1997: 141–43) calls attention to the acrostic pattern in the initial letters of four successive lines in v 18, which spell out the word *nynw* ("Nineveh"). This is in keeping with the name acrostic that spells out the word *ʾšwr* ("Assyria") in 1:12 in the initial consonants of four successive words. At the same time, it functions as an inclusion with the telestic that spells out the name YHWH at the end of four successive poetic lines in 1:1–3 (and the acrostic there reads "I am YHWH"). Each of the three words handled in this manner has four consonants, and the acrostic or telestic pattern is thus used with successive words ("Assyria," in 1:12), successive SAS units ("Nineveh," in 3:18), and successive poetic lines ("YHWH," in 1:1–3).

The four-line acrostic in v 18, which spells out the word *Nînəwē(h)* ("Nineveh"), may be translated as follows:

נ  Your shepherds are asleep, O king of Assyria;
י  Your nobles slumber.

בּ      Your people are scattered upon the mountains;
וֹ      And there is none to gather them.

As a pair of dyads, these four half-lines scan $(13 + 10) \parallel (16 + 7) = 23 \parallel 23$ in mora count; $(9 + 7) \parallel (10 + 5) = 16 \parallel 15$ in syllable count; $(4 + 2) \parallel (4 + 2) = 6 \parallel 6$ in word-stress units; and $3 \parallel 3$ in SAS units. From a prosodic point of view, there is perfect balance between these two poetic dyads.

In light of this acrostic in v 18, it is better not to describe the structure here in a manner that disturbs the acrostic pattern in the way Cathcart (1973: 123) proposes. Nonetheless, it is possible to read a pivot pattern here, but one that is quite different from what Cathcart describes. His "vocative suspended between two cola" is still evident—and it scans 9/5/10 in mora count. But the primary pivot here, from a prosodic point of view, consists of four words that complete one sentence, begin another, and belong to both (what some might call "Janus parallelism"):

|  | Morae | SAS units | Word count |  |  |
| --- | --- | --- | --- | --- | --- |
| Your shepherds are asleep, O king of Assyria; | 14 | 2 | 4 | 4 | 0 |
| your nobles slumber; | 10 | 2 | 2 | 2 | 0 |
| *your people are scattered upon the mountains.* | _16 | 2_ | 4 | 0 | 4 |
| *Your people are scattered upon the mountains;* | 16 | 2 | 4 | 0 | 4 |
| and there is none to gather them; | 7 | 1 | 2 | 0 | 2 |
| there is no assuaging your hurt, your wound is grievous. | _18 | 4_ | _5_ | _5_ | _0_ |

When the pivot is counted as part of each "half" in this structure, the balance in terms of mora count becomes $(24 + 16) \parallel (16 + 25) = 40 \parallel 41$ morae.

A difference of two or fewer morae in respective prosodic units constitutes "perfect" balance in the system of logoprosodic analysis, which is an attempt to describe the musical phrasing of the text as revealed by careful study of the *te'amim* (accent marks) in the Masoretic accentual system. See the section headed "Logoprosodic Analysis and the Text of Nahum" in the introduction to this commentary. Note that vv 18–19b can also be scanned in two parts, as in the translation presented in this commentary, with v 18 as a balanced pair of dyads—$(14 + 10) \parallel (16 + 7) = 24 \parallel 23$ morae—and v 19ab as a balanced dyad—$10 \parallel 8$ morae.

*Your people are scattered upon the mountains; and there is none to gather (them).* The verb *nāpōšû* ("they are scattered") is traditionally interpreted as a Niphal perfect from the root *pwš* II ("to be scattered"). Being scattered upon the mountains reflects the imagery of the flock (cf. Numbers 27:17; 1 Kings 22:17; Zechariah 13:7). Roberts (1991: 76) argues that the primary meaning of the root *pwš* is "to leap about," and thus we must assume a by-form of *pwṣ* ("to scatter, disperse") or correct the text to read *nāpōṣû* (BDB 807). Rudolph (1975: 183) also sees a *Nebenform* [by-form] of the root *pwṣ* ("to scatter"), which is how the text is interpreted here in this commentary. Rashi noted that an interchange between *ṣ* and *š* may occur (see Englander 1942/43: 478; cf. 1 Kings 22:17). Haldar (1947: 77) expressed no doubt "that the same verb [*nāpōṣû*] is to be assumed here." Following Dahood (1966a: 61), Cathcart (1973a: 149) argues for a form of the verb that is related to the noun *nepeš* ("soul, living-being, life, person") and repoints the MT to read *nippašû* ("they expire") in place of *nāpōšû* ("they are scattered"), from the verbal root *pwš* II, "to be scattered." In particular, Cathcart finds here a Piel form with privative sense, "to expire." Longman (1993: 828) agrees with Cathcart in principle but posits the Niphal form *nippašû*, with the sense "to catch the breath."

Longman (1993: 828) interprets the word ʿ*amməkā* ("your people") to mean "troops" and concludes that "the army is exhausted and disorganized and will provide no further resistance to attack." It is better to retain the more common reading of ʿ*am* as "people" in general and to see the entire populace of Nineveh in flight as the city is destroyed.

Cathcart (1973a: 149) interprets the phrase *wəʾēn məqabbēṣ*, "with none to gather them up," to mean "gather them up for burial." Though this is conjecture on Cathcart's part, some support is found in the parallel usage of the verbal root *qbṣ* ("to gather") in 2:11 [10], at the structural center of Nahum, in the image of boughs gathered as fuel for burning. Cathcart (1973a: 149) turns to ancient treaty texts to find presumed parallels in the form of ancient curses and the fact that "the curse of no burial is frequent in ancient Near Eastern texts as Hillers has shown" (see Hillers 1964: 68–69). The picture presented here, however, is not that of military troops with an exhausted and disorganized army that can provide no further resistance, as Longman concludes (1993: 828). W. A. Maier (1959: 358) described the picture more accurately in the image of "dispersed, unguided flocks with dead shepherds." He gave us an apt summary statement: "This scattering is final, for the prophet warns, 'There is no one to gather [them].' Nineveh is wiped out forever; and when the people of the Assyrian Empire are finally scattered, the complete end of that nation has come. A day of rebuilding and restitution will never dawn. How exactly was this prediction, spoken in the apex of Assyrian power, fulfilled! Not only the capital, but subsequently the whole empire collapses and passes out of existence almost overnight, its fugitive people never to be reunited."

3:19. *There is no healing for your injury; your wound is incurable.* The wrath of the Divine Warrior against the evil city of Nineveh occasions the concluding funeral dirge in 3:14–19. Many translators, past and present, have interpreted the word *kēhāh* to mean the same as the *hapax legomenon* *gēhāh* ("healing") in Proverb 17:22, with the LXX (G. A. Smith 1928: 113). But this is interpreting one *hapax legomenon* by another. Keil (1949: 41) called attention to "the extinction of the wound" in Leviticus 13:6, that is, to "the softening or anointing of it." Roberts (1991: 76 n. 3) translates *kēhāh* as "a dimming, lessening, alleviation" of an injury, from the root *khh*, "to grow dim, faint." W. A. Maier (1959: 363) interpreted the words *kēhāh* and *gēhāh* ("healing") as essentially the same word and called attention to other examples where the letters g and k appear to have been interchanged: *knn* and *gnn*, *sgr* and *skr*, *rgl* and *rkl*. This observation is suggestive, if not demonstrable. The word *šibrekā* ("your injury") means literally "your fracture," as of a bone (cf. Leviticus 21:19; 24:20), and so refers to disaster and ruin generally (Gandell 1901: 649). The fracturing of a limb is sometimes applied to the collapse or destruction of a state or kingdom (cf. Psalm 60:4; Lamentations 2:11). The root *šbr* ("to break, fracture") appears in Ezekiel 21:11 [6], where Cathcart (1973: 150) translates *šibrôn motnayim* as "breaking of the loins." He also cites Ginsberg in the *ANET* for parallel use of the root *tbr* ("to fracture") in the *UT*, *ʿnt*:III:30; *bʿdn ksl t tbr* ("behind her, her loins do break"); and elsewhere in the Ugaritic texts. The more general term "injury" is used in the translation presented here, though the nature of that injury is the "breaking apart" (or "fracture") of the Assyrian Empire itself, which is triggered by the sack of Nineveh. The word *naḥlāh* is a Niphal participle from the root *ḥlh* ("to be sick, ill, weak"). Longman (1993: 828) leans on the LXX translation of the term in question as ἴασις ("healing") to determine the meaning here. In the translation of *lašibrekā* as "for your injury (or 'fracture')" I am following Cathcart (1973a: 150), along with Roberts (1991: 76) and Longman (1993: 827). The word *makkātekā* ("your wound") is used elsewhere of plagues sent by God (Leviticus 26:21; Deuteronomy 28:59, 61; 29:21).

Hillers (1964: 64–66) finds a series of significant parallels in the expression of the "incurable wound" in treaty texts. In particular, the threat with an incurable wound appears in the curses of the vassal treaties of Esarhaddon: "May Gula, the great Physician, put sickness and weariness in your hearts, an unhealing wound in your body. Bathe in your blood as in water." As Spronk (1997: 143–44) notes, the text in 3:19 can also be compared to the curses at the end of the Code of Hammurabi (both references here are taken from Spronk):

> May Ninkarrak, the daughter of Anum, my advocate in Ekur,
> inflict upon him in his body a grievous malady,
> an evil disease, a serious injury which never heals,
> whose nature no physician knows,
> which he cannot allay with bandages,

which like a deadly bite cannot be rooted out,
and may he continue to lament (the loss of) his vigor
until his life comes to an end! (*ANET* 180)

*All who hear the news of you clap their hands over you; for upon whom has not come your evil unceasingly?* The only note of joy in Nineveh's dirge is that which expresses the gladness of oppressed peoples at her fall. The concluding dyad here is "tacked on" so as to end the book of Nahum with a question—as is also the case in Jonah 4:11 (see Glasson 1969/70: 54–55). Cathcart (1973a: 150) calls attention to the fact that "names of parts of the body do not require a suffix" (cf. Astour 1963: 6, n. 4; Dahood 1966a: 89; 1970a: 52). The clapping of hands appears to have diverse implications and can express both positive and negative feelings. In this instance, however, there is little doubt that the term *tāqəʿû kap̄* ("they clap their hands") denotes "a gesture of triumph or approval" (Fox 1995: 54).

The final question in Nahum picks up parallel words and expressions from 1:9; 2:12; 3:7–8, 17. Moreover, Nahum and Jonah are the only two books in the Bible to end with rhetorical questions. Glasson (1969/70: 54) regards the book of Jonah as a reaction to the prophecy of Nahum, "designed to rebuke the cruel temper of the earlier prophecy." Spronk (1997: 144) considers this concluding question "an early gloss" that "was added by one of the first commentators of the text." Logoprosodic analysis suggests a different picture, with the numerical composition of Nahum taking place at the time that the Book of the Twelve Prophets was put together. The "first commentator" Spronk is referring to is apparently the author or composer of the book itself, for this so-called addition is not a scribal "gloss" at all. The two lines are carefully contrived in terms of the prosodic structure and the total word count (and letter count) for the book of Nahum as a whole, and they provide a balanced couplet on their own. In terms of balance, we find:

| | |
|---|---|
| mora count: | $(10 + 11) \parallel (5 + 15) = 21 \parallel 20$ |
| syllable count: | $(7 + 7) \parallel (3 + 10) = 14 \parallel 13$ |
| word-stress units: | $(3 + 3) \parallel (3 + 3) = 6 \parallel 6$ |
| SAS units: | $4 \parallel 4$ in. |

In short, there is perfect balance on all counts and no need for the notes in the *BHS* (and the $BH^3$) that say "add?" with regard to two out of the nine words in this concluding dyad. Nor is there any reason to change the pronominal suffix, as suggested in the *BHS* (and the $BH^3$), from the 2nd pers. m. sg. *ʿālêkā* ("over you") to the feminine form *ʿālayik* ("over you") on the words *rōʿêkā* ("your shepherds") and *ʾaddîrêkā* ("your nobles") here and earlier in v 18; for here we have the concluding example in the book of Nahum of the phenomenon of enallage, which marks most of the prosodic boundaries in this book that is a tour de force in the classical art of Hebrew poetry as a numerical and musical composition.

In times past, numerous scholars expressed concern about the prosody of v 19, though few went as far as J. M. P. Smith (1911), who commented on the word ʿālêḵā ("over you") as follows: "This is unnecessary to the sense and constitutes a blemish upon the otherwise perfect elegiac rhythm. It is probably the work of a glossator." It is easy to understand J. M. P. Smith's consternation because of the faulty premise on which his work was based due to his understanding of Hebrew prosody. This verse is one of five places in Nahum where a strophic boundary falls within a verse (see also 1:12; 3:7, 10, and 15). The concluding dyad here is set over against a quatrain in v 14, of essentially the same length in terms of mora count, within the concentric rhythmic structure of the seventh and concluding "canto" (3:14–19), with both parts scanning SAS units as follows: $(2 + 2) \parallel (2 + 2) = 4 \parallel 4$.

With the full turn of events, the oppressor now suffers and justice is achieved. At this point, as Sweeney (2000: 446) observes: "The book of Nahum comes full circle by returning to the motif with which the book began in the first statements of its semi-acrostic introduction."

## COMMENT

On four separate occasions the book of Jonah describes Nineveh as a "great city" (1:2; 3:2; 3:3; 4:11), and these four statements form an *inclusio* around each half of that book (Christensen 1985d: 133–40, esp. 139–40).

| | |
|---|---|
| 1:2 | **Great city** |
| 1:4 | Great wind |
| 1:4–9 | Great storm—great fear |
| 1:12–16 | Great storm—great fear |
| 2:1 | Great fish |
| 3:2 | **Great city** |
| 3:3 | **Great city** |
| 4:1 | Great evil (Jonah's anger) |
| 4:6 | Great joy (over the qîqāyôn plant) |
| 4:11 | **Great city** |

The Tigris becomes navigable at Nineveh, which makes the site a significant crossroad in widely extended trade. According to Strauss (1855: 19): "The point at which Nineveh was situated was certainly the culminating point of the three quarters of the globe—Europe, Asia, and Africa; and from the earliest times it was just at the crossing of the Tigris by Nineveh that the great military and commercial roads met, which led into the heart of all the leading known lands."

### The Mixed Metaphor of a Locust Plague in Nahum

The book of Nahum ends with a remarkable funeral lament over the "great city" of Nineveh, which forms an inclusion with the introductory psalm of Nahum (1:1–10). That opening hymn of theophany declared that no evil could stand in the presence of Yhwh's avenging wrath. The concluding oracle confirms the message that Yhwh will by no means acquit the guilty (1:3) with the portrayal of evil removed as the wicked city is destroyed. The concluding lament moves from a taunt song (vv 14–17), much like the two taunt songs that precede it in vv 1–13, to a brief funeral dirge (vv 18–19).

Using bitter irony, the author urged the people to prepare for a siege by strengthening their fortifications—"Draw water for the siege, strengthen your defenses!" (vv 14–15). But all this is in vain, as the vision of vv 16–18a makes clear. Like locusts, the leaders of Nineveh fly away, no one knows where, leaving the hapless king to his fate. His injury is fatal, and everyone who hears the report claps his hands (v 19b). The dirge concludes with a rhetorical question: for who has not felt your endless cruelty?

The locust dirge (3:14–19) has seven strophes with twelve versets. The first strophe (v 14) has two versets (two balanced dyads) that focus on two aspects of the preparation of a city in antiquity to withstand a military siege. The most important necessity was an adequate water supply; so the prophet urged the inhabitants to draw water for the siege. The second most important act by way of preparation was to strengthen the defenses of the city; so the people were told to prepare bricks to reinforce the city walls. Excavations at Nineveh show evidence that suggests hurried repair of the normally high quality masonry of the city walls with rough stones in some sections (cf. Stronach and Lumsden 1992: 231). Spronk (1997: 135) correctly cautions, however, against any direct connection between this observation and the book of Nahum as such.

The second strophe (v 15a–c) is a single verset in the form of a balanced triad that picks up motifs of destruction by fire and sword from earlier in the book of Nahum and combines this with the image of the destructive power of a plague of locusts. The destruction of Nineveh by fire was related by ancient writers (Herodotus 1921: i.106, 185; Diodorus Siculus 1950: ii.25–28; Athenaeus 1967–1980: xii.529) and is also confirmed by archaeological excavations.

There are few natural events that can match the destructive power of a locust plague in the Middle East. John D. Whiting described the locust plague of 1915 in these words: "In passing the Jordan Valley these fliers of recent date came in clouds sufficiently dense to darken the sun and cleared this Jericho oasis of its vegetable gardens and the leaves from the fruit trees, rendering it for a while as barren as the parched wilderness encircling it. The entire devastation was wrought by two visits lasting but a day or so each, after which diligent search could not produce a single locust" (*National Geographic*,

December 1915, p. 544, col. B; reference from Laetsch 1956: 311). Adding to this image of destruction, the poet picked up on words used earlier for the "heaps" (*kābōd*) of wealth in 2:10 [9] and the "heaps" (*kabōd*) of corpses in 3:3. This time he uses parallel imperative forms of this same verbal root (*hitkabbēd* and *hitkabbēdî*) so as to say: "Heap up your defenders so that they can become a heap of corpses." The great mass of wealth plundered from the nations is not sufficient to save the wicked city. Nahum expands on the image of Nineveh's immense wealth. All such power and pelf, though it multiply like locusts, is useless. It is as fleeting as grasshoppers that consume everything in sight and quickly move on; for no one can stand before the awesome wrath of God.

In the third strophe (vv 15d–16) the metaphor of the locusts focuses on the vast multitude of these insects. Nineveh's officials in both government and economic life are likened to locusts in reference to their vast numbers; for her merchants have increased more than the stars of the heavens (v 16a). But having made that observation, the poet quickly shifted his attention to another aspect of the metaphor in a reflection on a specific aspect of the life cycle of this insect—the metamorphosis of the locust in the early stages of its development, as envisioned by the prophet Nahum: "A locust sheds (its outer skin) and flies away" (v 16c). A similar phenomenon was explored by Tennyson in relation to the dragonfly in these words (taken from Davidson 1920: 39):

Today I saw the dragonfly
Come from the wells where he did lie.
An inner impulse rent the veil
Of his old husk; from head to tail
Came out clear plates of sapphire mail.
He dried his wings: like gauze they grew;
Through crofts and pastures wet with dew,
A living flash of light he flew.

The focus is on the mysterious nature of flight as the insect "takes off its clothes," as it were, and flies away.

In the fourth strophe (v 17), the poet shifted his attention to yet another aspect of the life experience of locusts, which become torpid with the cold but under the warmth of the sun revive and take flight. Nahum uses this image to describe the response on the part of the court officials in the palaces of Nineveh. In his *ḥăzôn* ("vision") the locusts seek refuge in the stone walls *on a cold day*, but with the warmth of the sun they soon take flight and move on. Such is the case of the officials who are the first to abandon the king in their flight to greener and safer pastures beyond. The dyad at the center of this middle strophe (vv 16–17) likens these court officials to grasshoppers and

locusts with respect to both their numbers and their perfidy in taking flight
as things begin to heat up in the doomed city of Nineveh.

## The Concluding Funeral Dirge in Context

The word *Nineveh* appears explicitly three times in Nahum—in 1:1 (first
fanto), 2:9 [2:10] (third canto), and 3:7 (fifth canto). Because the poet included a fourth instance in the form of an acrostic on the word *nynw(h)*
("Nineveh") in four successive half-lines in 3:18 in the seventh canto (3:14–19),
the word appears in the first, third, fifth, and seventh cantos of Nahum. The
fifth strophe (v 18) in the locust dirge consists of two dyads with another name
acrostic; the name of the city of Nineveh is spelled out in the initial letters of
four consecutive half-lines. The content of this verse turns to the image of the
"shepherds" and "nobles" of Assyria in words that are addressed directly to the
king of Assyria. In the prophet's vision, the people of Assyria are scattered on
the mountains with no one to gather them. The sixth strophe (v 19ab), which
is a single dyad like the second strophe (v 15ab), makes clear that the wound
to be inflicted on Nineveh is grievous: "There is no assuaging your hurt."

Nahum is organized in seven cantos, each of which has a *meaningful center* determined with meticulous precision on the basis of word count. These
seven meaningful centers of the major prosodic units in that seven-part outline may be strung together to form a précis of the book itself in the form of a
play of ideas around successive centers that is reminiscent of the structure of
music itself in our own time. This is what Ernest McClain (personal communication) describes as "a legitimate parallelism between two related 'time arts'
for they require time to register their effects and variation to hold attention,
and words (like tones) carry an aura of their own." These seven meaningful
centers are as follows:

A    Mountains quake before him and the hills melt away,
         and the earth crashes in ruins before him,
     Yea, the world and all who dwell (in it)—
         in the presence of his fury who can stand;           [1:5–6a]

B    I have afflicted you and I will afflict you no more;
         and now I will break (Assyria's) rod from upon you.   [1:12b–13a]

C    (Chariots) rush to and fro in the squares (in Nineveh).   [2:5b]

X    The lion went and the lioness was there;
         and the lion cubs with none to disturb.
     The lion has torn sufficient for his cubs,
         and strangled prey for his lionesses,
         and he has filled with prey his lairs.                [2:12c–13c
                                                               [13c–14c])

C′   Harlotry of the harlot;
        graceful is the mistress of sorceries—
     The enslaver of nations by her harlotry,
        and clans by her witchcraft.                    [3:4]

B′   And for all her nobles lots were cast
        and all her grandees were bound in fetters.     [3:10ef]

A′   Your magicians are like grasshoppers;
        your astrologers are like locusts upon locusts
        that settle in the walls on a cold day.
     The sun shines forth and they fly away;
        and their place is not known. "Where are they?"   [3:17]

It is easy to see the content of Nahum as a whole by careful perusal of these seven statements. The Divine Warrior has appeared, and the cosmos itself reels in the presence of his wrath. Though Yʜᴡʜ has afflicted his people, he has now turned his anger on Assyria so as to deliver his people. The chariots of warfare storm the streets and squares of Nineveh, the city where the "lion" of Assyria devours its prey. Though Assyria has enslaved nations, her officials now face the same plight, so they take flight like locusts, inactive for the moment "on a cold day." But as the heat comes, "they will fly away." Yʜᴡʜ is breaking the rod from upon his people so as to restore Israel's glory.

The lion imagery in 2:12–13 has a twofold meaning. On the one hand, wicked Assyria is portrayed as a lion that has mangled the nations to provide for its own nepotistic desires. On the other hand, the lion of Judah is about to seize from this very nation "sufficient for his own cubs" in Jerusalem. And those on the sidelines who observe the coming carnage will proclaim what Yʜᴡʜ has done: "Nineveh is in ruins; who will mourn for her?"

The concluding strophe in the locust dirge, and the book of Nahum as a whole, gives the response that the prophet envisions to the calamity that is about to unfold in the city of Nineveh: "All who hear the news of you will clap their hands over you!" The destruction of this wicked city is welcome news to her many victims. The prophet envisions the sound of people everywhere clapping their hands—some in derision and mockery, others in great joy. Borrowing the words of the late Martin Luther King Jr., Achtemeier (1986: 28) says: "The whole earth breathes a great sigh, 'Free at last! Free at last! Thank God Almighty! Free at last!'" She compares this celebration to that of the Israelites on their deliverance from slavery in Egypt (Exodus 15) and to that of the Allies when Nazi Germany fell in World War II. It is right to be glad when tyrants fall and people are delivered from the abuse of human power.

We do well to remember that the book of Nahum is concerned with God's action and not our own. Vengeance must be left in the hands of God for him to mete out in his own time. Human hatred accomplishes nothing of lasting worth. It is right to resist evil, but we must not become evil in the process of dealing with it. A line must be carefully drawn, however difficult that may prove to be, between the call to suffer the consequences of evil and the desire to remove what appear to be the sources of evil through acts of violence. Well-intended actions taken to destroy evil sometimes abet the very forces we oppose in unexpected ways. A war against terror may be justified, and even necessary, but it poses deep problems. Violence inevitably breeds violence, and sometimes legitimate acts to eliminate violence further the evil intent we would eliminate by brute force. The way of the suffering servant, who submits in the assurance that God will act in due course in ways beyond our immediate understanding, often remains the path of wisdom when wedded to actions on our part, both as individuals and as nations, that exclude violence.

At first glance, the final dyad appears to be somewhat unrelated to what has been said before it as the poet poses a rhetorical question: "For upon whom has not come your evil unceasingly?" The logoprosodic analysis, however, indicates that we have here the other half of a quatrain (two versets) with two poetic dyads in perfect balance: $(10 + 11) \parallel (5 + 16) = 21 \parallel 21$ morae. This is no unrelated afterthought any more than the opening heading at the beginning of the book of Nahum is unrelated to all that follows.

# Index of Authors

Abarbanel, Isaac, 19, 161, 178, 241, 262, 274, 295, 319
Abou-Assaf, A., 246
Achtemeier, Elizabeth R., 42, 209, 222–24, 233–34, 249–50, 322, 348, 367, 397
Aharoni, Y., 159, 247
Albright, W. F., 190, 194, 199, 204, 220–21, 247, 340, 345, 379, 384
Allen, Leslie C., 382
Allis, O. T., 23, 161, 177
Alonso Schökel, Luis, 175–77, 296, 298, 388
Alter, Robert, 277
Alting, Jacob, 5
Altshuler, Yehiel Hillel, 19, 153
Andersen, Francis I., 153, 162, 164, 186, 340
Aquila, 204, 354
Armerding, C. E., 24, 281
Arnold, W. R., 21, 174, 176, 185, 259
Assemanius, J. S., 160
Astour, Michael C., 392
Athenaeus of Naucratis, 394
Avigad, Nahman, 159, 386

Baker, David W., 357
Bailey, Waylon, 245, 259–60, 316
Balaban, M., 362
Barker, Kenneth L., 245, 259–60, 316
Barth, C., 193, 268
Barthélemy, D., 193, 203, 290, 294, 321, 388
Baumann, A., 187
Baumgärtel, F., 318
Becking, Bob, 24 40, 179, 194, 201, 220, 231, 232, 263, 267–68, 304, 346
Ben Yahuda, E., 321
Benyus, J. M., 313
Ben Zvi, E., 51

Bellermann, J., 6
Berger, P. R., 355
Bergman, Jan, 180, 195
Berlin, Adele, 7, 41, 277
Berlin, M., 175
Berlinerblau, J., 260
Bévenot, Hugh, 280, 288, 383
Bibliander, Th., 166
Bickell, Gustav, 5, 20–22, 193, 197, 239
Billerbeck, A., 20, 53, 160, 276
Black, Jeremy A., 244
Bliese, Loren, 5, 23, 155, 172, 191, 201–02, 228, 259, 263, 267, 269–70, 293, 333–34, 353, 379
Boadt, Lawrence, 315
Boer, P. A. H. de, 153
Bolle, M., 153, 294, 340
Botta, Emille, 53
Botterweck, G. J., xvi, 195, 313
Breiteneicher, Michael, 20, 189
Bremer, John, 25
Brenner, A., 271
Bright, John, 154
Brockelmann, C., 338
Brockington, L. H., 176, 264
Brongers, H. A., 241
Brunner, H., 355
Budde, Karl, 21, 55, 152, 161, 289
Buhl, F., 185, 199
Bullinger, E. W., 241
Burkert, Walter, 355
Burney, C. F., 235, 289, 338

Calvin, John, 19, 154, 223, 250, 262–63, 289, 301, 338, 348, 362, 380
Cannon, W. W., 176

399

# Index of Subjects

Abdi-Ashirta, 195
Achish of Gath, 277
acrostic, 4–5, 20–24, 39, 65, 160, 171, 173–76, 180, 185, 190, 193, 196, 198, 209–13, 219, 388
Adad, 183, 189, 285
Amenophis III, 195
Anat, 235, 299, 369
Anu/An, 244
Apollo's number, 9
archaeomusicology, 25–39
Asherah, 245, 313, 325, 326
Ashurbanipal, 53–55, 57–60, 156, 165, 217, 232, 243–45, 276, 282–83, 285, 297, 336, 358, 367
Asshuretililani, 59–60
Assyrian treaty texts, 24
Astarte, 325
Atrahasis, 182
attribute formula (Exodus 34:6–7), 17

Baal, 177, 178–79, 182–83, 212, 216, 318
Babylon, 25, 56–64, 217–18, 231, 273, 298, 355, 369–70, 388
Babylonian Chronicles, 284
Balaam, son of Beor, 158
Bashan, 183, 184, 185, 186
Bavian inscription, 284
Bel/Enlil, 244
Belial, 47, 225–26, 228–30, 232–36, 242, 248–49, 251, 253, 261, 303–4, 307–8, 325
Belshazzar, 218
*beth essentiae*, 273

Book of the Twelve Prophets, 2, 4, 8–11, 23–24, 39, 44–46, 50–52, 56–57, 221, 248, 290, 308, 323, 359, 392

canonical process, 23, 151
Carmel, 183–86, 212
*casus obliquus*, 294
*casus pendens*, 181
"compositional numbers," xix
corporate personality, 243, 264, 304
covenant-love, 180
*Curse of Agade*, 41
Cyaxares, 263
Cyrus, 262, 387

Darius the Mede, 218
David, 32, 36, 61, 277, 387
Davidic musicology, 30
Day of Nikanor, 21–22, 40, 56
Day of Yhwh, 22, 46
Divine Warrior, 28, 42–44, 54, 181–82, 187, 191, 193, 198, 213, 217–18, 262, 269, 278, 294, 302, 305–06, 325, 368, 390, 397

Ea/Enki, 244
El, 177, 179, 183, 212, 216, 286
Elijah, 212
Elisha, 265
Ellil/Enlil, 32, 35, 244
El Shaddai (the "mountain God"), 26–27, 29–30
emphatic lamed, 181, 194
enallage, 230, 232–33, 241–42, 246, 357
enclitic mem, 187, 206, 208, 243

# Index of Biblical
# and Other Ancient Sources

Page numbers are in italics.

# Index of Languages